Matlab - Modelling, Programming and Simulations

edited by
Emilson Pereira Leite

Matlab - Modelling, Programming and Simulations

Edited by Emilson Pereira Leite

Republished by InTech

Janeza Trdine 9, 51000 Rijeka, Croatia

Publishing Process Manager Iva Lipovic

Technical Editor Goran Bajac

Cover Designer Martina Sirotic

Additional hard copies can be obtained from orders@intechopen.com

Matlab - Modelling, Programming and Simulations, Edited by Emilson Pereira Leite
p. cm.
ISBN 978-953-307-125-1

For EU product safety concerns:
IN TECH d.o.o., Prolaz Marije Krucifikse Kozulić 3, 51000 Rijeka, Croatia,
info@intechopen.com or visit our website at intechopen.com.

Meet the editor

Emilson Pereira Leite is a Professor at the Institute of Geosciences, University of Campinas, Brazil. He received his PhD in Geophysics from University of São Paulo in 2005. He has published around 20 articles in peer-reviewed journals, conferences and popular science magazines. He has been working with MATLAB® for the last decade and is the Editor of the book entitled "Matlab - Modelling, Programming and Simulations", published by Sciyo in 2010.

Contents

Preface

During the last decade the use of MATLAB® has been consistently increasing in scientific academic institutions as well as in several branches of industry that deal with topics ranging from economics to spacecraft orbit simulations. This software package has been proved to be very efficient and robust for numerical data analysis, modelling, programming, simulation and computer graphic visualization.

This book is a collection of 20 excellent works presenting different applications of several MATLAB® tools that can be used for educational, scientific and engineering purposes. Most of the authors have been working with MATLAB® for several years and are recognized experts in their fields.

Chapters include tips and tricks for programming and developing Graphical User Interfaces (GUIs), power system analysis, control systems design, system modelling and simulations, parallel processing, optimization, signal and image processing, finite different solutions, geosciences and portfolio insurance. Thus, readers from a range of professional fields can benefit from the content of this book.

I would like to thank the authors for spending a significant part of their time and efforts to complete each chapter, providing high-quality information for world-wide readers. Also, I must say that the very well organized Sciyo on-line system had significantly facilitated making chapter revisions and organizing them, as well as keeping track of deadlines, in order to have this book developed in the most timely and efficient way. Therefore, I thank the Sciyo team, including the Editorial board, for their support and for accelerating the whole process of writing of this book.

Editor

Emilson Pereira Leite
Institute of Geosciences – University of Campinas
Brazil

1

Tips and tricks for programming in Matlab

Karel Perutka
Tomas Bata University in Zlin, Faculty of Applied Informatics
Czech Republic, European Union

1. Introduction

Matlab is the software developed by the MathWorks, Inc., Natick, USA. In 1984, the first version appeared. Software was primarily used only for the mathematical computation enabling the computation of complicated matrix equations and their systems. All major functions can directly use the matrix as the input. From that year, the software is still under development enlarging the area of the users every year. Matlab became the standard in the area of simulation and modelling and it is used by the researchers and students at universities mainly in the areas of Control Engineering, Power Plant Systems, Aerospace, Bioinformatics, Economics and Statistics. In comparison to other software such as Mathematica or Maple, Matlab has several advantages. Let us mention some. Its open architecture enables sharing all source code among the user community and several different areas are solved and the solution appears usually as a new toolbox. Simulink is the important Matlab enlargement which simplifies the computation very much. You just drag and drop the blocks to the new window from the block libraries and connect them and run the model. Matlab is used not only at universities but also in practice, for instance by NASA or General Motors. Most Matlab users are from the major world countries, such as USA, Japan, China, and India. Nice book was written by Hanselman and Littlefield (Hanselman and Littlefield, 2005). And interesting paper about teaching using Matlab was written by Perutka and Heczko (Perutka & Heczko, 2007). This chapter provides some chosen tips and tricks to the beginners in Matlab programming and should ease the first steps in programming. These tips and tricks are based on the experience of chapter author with teaching Matlab programming in the undergraduate curriculum for several years. The author mostly worked in MATLAB version 6.5, for which tips are. They are unsorted and each chapter provides one tip or trick only.

2. Placing picture as dialog background

Being bored from standard look of GUI created in Matlab? If you create dialog in Matlab using GUIDE or set of functions `figure`, `uimenu`, `uicontrol` and `axes`, the dialog background is usually based on the settings of the system, for example in older Microsoft Windows it was grey - Windows Classic Theme. However, if you need to have your picture as the figure background, there is possible to use the following solution. Such example is

shown in figure 1. The dialog in this figure contains only 3 grey pushbuttons (`online ident.`, `Gr`, `>>`) and background picture.
What to do first? You have to draw the picture in the extern software, for example in Corel DRAW! and save it in one of the formats that Matlab supports, for instance as JPG or BMP. You can get the list of supported formats from the Matlab Help Dialog. Don't forget to write down the width and height of the picture or their ratio. Create new dialog using the command `figure` or by GUI. Set the size of the new window in accordance with the picture width and height or their ratio. How? If you working with GUIDE, double-click the window in GUIDE and Property Inspector should appear. Change the *Units* property on *Pixels* and after that change in the *Position* property the third and fourth value to the width and height of the figure or keep these values in the ratio of the picture you would like to show. If you created the dialog using `figure` function in M-file, include in the list of properties *Units* and *Position* and set them in similar way as was described for the GUI created by GUIDE. Now you need to load the figure in the Matlab Workspace, create axes and put the figure inside them. This tip is based on work of Perutka (Perutka, 2007). Inspire yourself by the following code which will be commented

```
STCssu=imread('STCssu.jpg','jpg');
axes('Position',[0 0 1 1]);
image(STCssu);
axis off;
clear STCssu
```

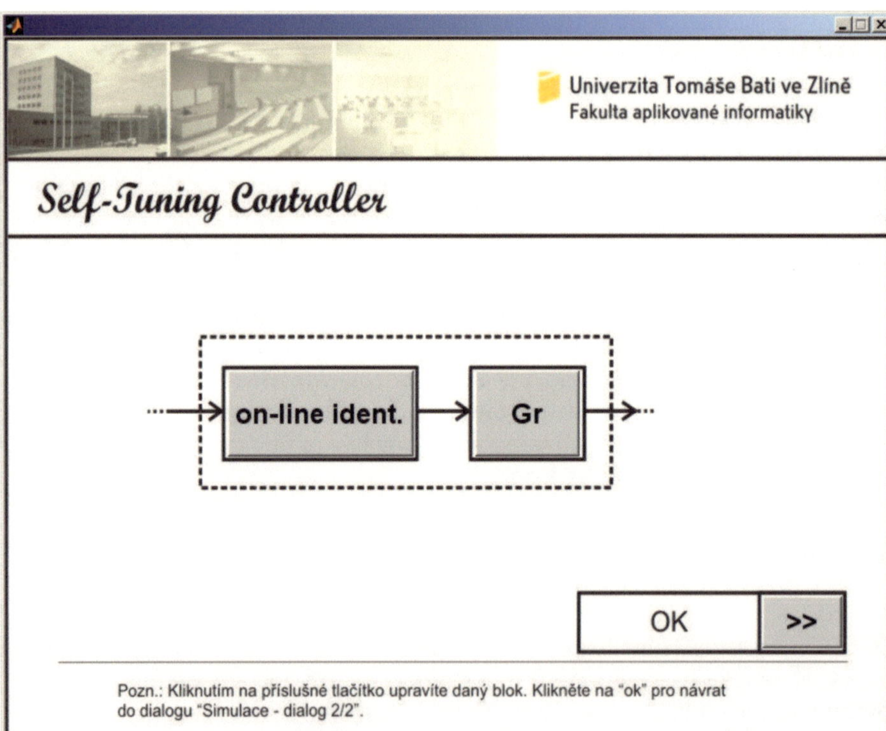

Fig. 1. Dialog with picture as its background

This code should be placed in the file where the figure is defined. The line 1 of the code is responsible of loading the picture in the Matlab Workspace using the function `image`. In this case, *STCssu.jpg* is the name of picture file and the picture is loaded to the *STCssu* variable. Line 2 creates the axes with their range just for all dialog area. Command in line 3 draws the image from the *STCssu* variable to the axes created by line 2. The axes description is hidden by the command on line 4. If you don't re-draw the dialog, you can delete the variable from the Matlab Workspace, as it is shown in line 5. But if you re-call the dialog, don't use line 5. For the dialog re-calling, lines 2 to 4 are enough.

3. Short online help for every object in dialog

Imagine the situation depicted in figure 2. There is a short text "If you click this button, you will open the dialog of setting the controller parameters." in the box. This text is shown if you keep the cursor on the button *Gr* for a while. This might be useful especially in the case of two sorts of objects in dialog (button or edit text) to provide necessary short information what should be written as the text (edit text) or what will happen when the button is pressed. But short information can be displayed over every object in dialog which has the property *TooltipString*.
If you created your dialog by GUIDE, open it in GUIDE again and double click the object for which you would like to create the short help.

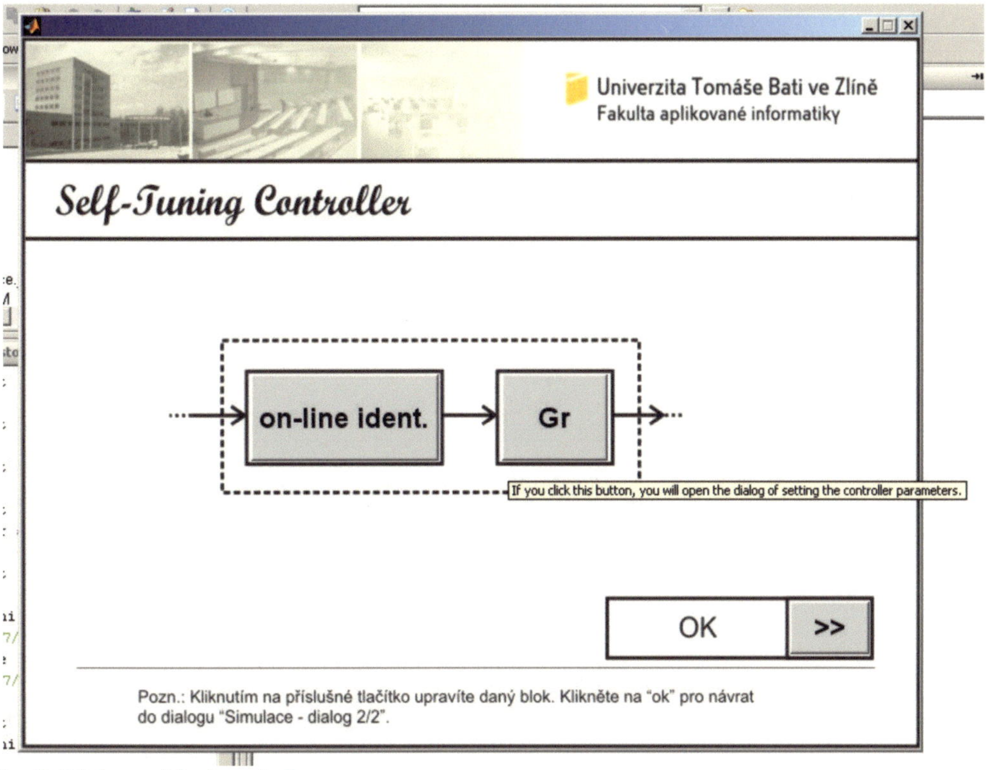

Fig. 2. Dialog with short help

The Property Inspector dialog should appear, find the property denoted as *TooltipString* and write some string as the input. The string you write will appear as the short help for the object after calling the dialog again.
If you created the object by the *uicontrol* function, just read the sample code below

```
6 hButtonClose = uicontrol('Style', 'pushbutton',...
7                'String', 'Close',...
8                'Parent', hFigure,...
9                'Tag', 'tButtonClose',...
10               'Units', 'pixels',...
11               'Position', [560 75 100 30],...
12               'TooltipString', 'Press the button for exit.',...
13               'Callback', 'closeIt');
```

The code in lines 6 to 13 presents the definition of pushbutton object in the dialog created by commands in M-file. The *TooltipString* property of *uicontrol* is defined in line 12, the text "Press the button for exit." is shown as a short help when the cursor will be on the button "Close".

4. More pictures in one dialog and their control

It is sometime necessary to place more than one picture in the dialog, have a look at figure 3. The dialog in figure 3 includes 9 JPG pictures. The digital clock consists of 8 pictures, 6 pictures are the digits of the clock. The background of analogue clock is the remaining picture. These pictures are shown similarly as is described in "Placing picture as dialog background", it means the pictures are drawn using `image` function to pre-defined axes. The dialog in figure 3 was created as a set of commands in M-file and it is defined by lines 14 to 24, the *Render* and *DoubleBuffer* properties should be set according to lines 23 and 24.

```
14 hFigure = figure('Units', 'pixels',...
15                 'Position', [100 50 770 690],...
16                 'MenuBar','None',...
17                 'Name', 'Hodiny',...
18                 'Tag', 'tWindow',...
19                 'NumberTitle', 'off',...
20                 'Resize', 'off',...
21                 'Visible', 'off',...
22                 'BackingStore', 'off',...
23                 'Renderer', 'painters',...
24                 'DoubleBuffer', 'on');
```

When figure is defined, all `axes` objects are created, example for one `axes` object is shown in lines 25 to 33

```
25 hAnalog = axes('Units', 'pixels',...
26        'Position', [30 210 460 460],...
27        'Visible', 'on',...
28        'Parent', hFigure,...
29      'Tag', 'tAnalog',...
30      'XTickLabelMode', 'manual', 'YTickLabelMode', 'manual',...
```

```
31      'XColor', 'k', 'YColor', 'k',...
32      'DrawMode', 'fast',...
33      'Color', 'k');
```

This step is followed by step in which all images are read into Matlab Workspace using the `image` function, the image file are in the same directory as the source code, for one image the code will be

```
34      File_Analog = imread('clock.jpg');
```

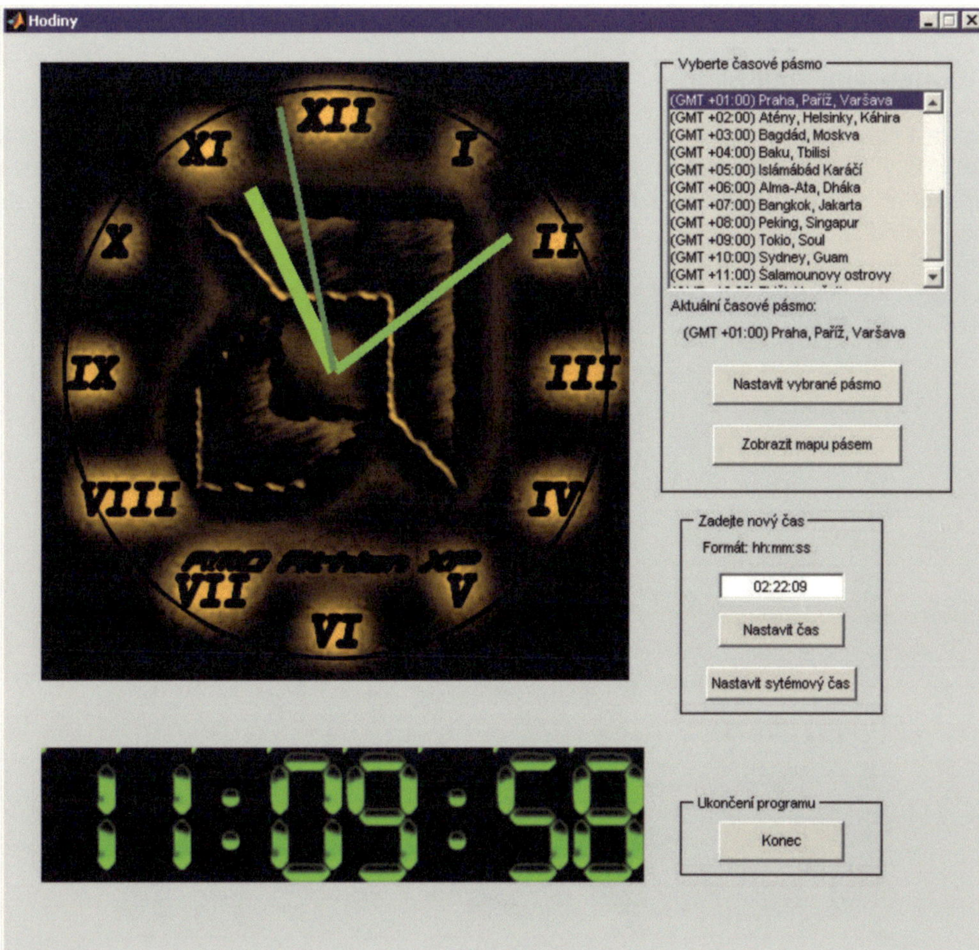

Fig. 3. Dialog with more pictures

Now have a careful look at the following source code, lines 35 - 39

```
35      set(0, 'CurrentFigure', hFigure);
36      set(hFigure, 'CurrentAxes', hAnalog);
37      image(File_Analog);
```

```
38     axis image;
39     axis off;
```

The source code on lines 35 - 39 shows how to switch among several axes in one dialog. Line 35 gives us an example where the dialog identified by `hFigure`, line 14, is set as the active one. And line 36 shows us the example of setting one of the axes as the active one. The axes are in the dialog, which is identified by `hFigure`, line 14, and the axes are identified by `hAnalog`, line 25. Now you show the chosen picture, line 37, which was read by line 34. Finally, you place the axis just to the borders of the image, line 38, and you hide the ticks, line 39. This tip is based on the example provided by Perutka (Perutka, 2005).

5. Button with your picture

Figure 4 shows the green dialog with two options to be chosen, they are both yellow and black. If you click "Stromek" or "Kytka", new dialog appears. The dialog in figure 4 consists of 3 `axes` objects to which the pictures are drawn, one `axes` object shows the background and 2 `axes` objects show pictures as "buttons".

Fig. 4. Dialog with "2 buttons" with our picture.

Now let us look at the source code, lines 40 - 64. These lines provide the full source code for figure 4. See line 59 or 63. There is another syntax of `image` function in comparison to line 3. The `ButtonDownFcn` property is used, its value is set on the name of function or file, which should be called if the picture or axes are clicked. For example if you click on "Kytka", there will be called the file *kytka.m* according to line 63.

```
hFigure = figure('Units','pixels',...
            'Position',[160 160 470 350],...
            'MenuBar','None',...
            'Name','Volba',...
            'Tag','tOkno',...
            'NumberTitle','off',...
            'Resize','off',...
            'Visible','on',...
            'BackingStore','off',...
            'Renderer','painters',...
            'DoubleBuffer','on');
    hlavniObr=imread('vyberte.jpg');
    prvniObr=imread('stromek.jpg');
    druhyObr=imread('kytka.jpg');
    hlavniAxes=axes('Position',[0 0 1 1]);
    image(hlavniObr);
    axis off
    prvniAxes=axes('Units','pixels',...
        'Position',[200 152 230 35]);
    image(prvniObr,'ButtonDownFcn','stromek');
    axis off
    druhyAxes=axes('Units','pixels',...
        'Position',[200 65 230 35]);
    image(druhyObr,'ButtonDownFcn','kytka');
    axis off
```

6. New picture on button click

This task is connected with the previous example, see similar figure 5 and lines 65 to 71. If you click "the button", the button changes the color for a while, i.e. for 0.5 s, line 69. Actually, you set the axes, which will be "the button", as active, line 65. You read the image to the Matlab Workspace variable, line 66, and draw it in the selected axes, line 67, and hide the description of axes, line 68. To keep the illusion of the button, you draw the previous picture back, line 70, together with the option to be clicked again, i.e. there is `ButtonDownFcn` property included, line 70, there will be called the file *kytka.m* if you click "the button".

```
65      set(hFigure,'CurrentAxes',druhyAxes);
66      cervKytka=imread('kytka1.jpg');
67      image(cervKytka);
68      axis off
69      pause(0.5);
70      image(druhyObr,'ButtonDownFcn','kytka');
71      axis off
```

Fig. 5. New picture on "button" click.

7. Set of buttons with your pictures in dialog, each button is pressed on given key

Typical task for simple menu controlled by keyboard is the following one. You have a list of menu items such as in figure 6. The list is controlled by 3 keys. First key is used for moving up. One press means one item up. Second key is used for moving down and the last key selects the menu item. Menu in figure 6 has five items namely *New game, Load game, Game help, Options, Exit*. Function for menu control is shown as the source code in lines 72 to 173. Each menu item is represented by its own `axes` object. There are two pictures for each menu item, black for inactive state and grey for active item. The grey picture is shown when the item is selected or chosen. Moving up is realized by "w" key - line 75, down by "s" key - line 79 and selection by "l" key - line 83. You should be familiar with the basics of programming in Matlab to fully understand it. Let us describe the function in brief. All necessary variables are loaded before the function body using the line 73, file *defineglobal.m* Lines 74 to 105 show the menu control and selection. Line 74 shows how to load the key pressed - there is `CurrentCharacter` property for `get` function, and `dMenu` is the dialog identifier, lines 75 - 82 show moving up ad down. Lines 106 – 172 show the way of changing the pictures during move or selection. For one change of menu item all pictures are redrawn. This tip is based on the work of Hrubos consulted by me (Hrubos, 2009).

```
function keyboardmenu
defineglobal
switch lower(get(dMenu,'CurrentCharacter'))
    case 'w'  % up
      if kPosition <= 5 && kPosition > 1
            kPosition = kPosition - 1;
      end
    case 's'  % down
      if kPosition < 5 && kPosition >= 1
            kPosition = kPosition + 1;
      end
    case 'l'
      if kPosition == 1
            set(dMenu,'Visible','off');
            levelA
      end
      if kPosition == 2
            loadgame
            set(dLoad,'Visible','on');
      end
      if kPosition == 3
            gamehelp
      end
      if kPosition == 4
            set(dOptions,'Visible','on');
      end
      if kPosition == 5
            set(dMenu,'Visible','off');
            clear all
            exitmenu = 1;
      end
    otherwise
      wavplay(zMenu,zMenuF)
end
if exitmenu == 1
      clear all
      return
else
    set(dMenu, 'Units', 'pixels');
    if kPosition == 1
      set(0,'CurrentFigure',dMenu);
      set(dMenu,'CurrentAxes',dMenuNewGameAxes);
      image(oNewGame1); axis off;
      set(dMenu,'CurrentAxes',dMenuLoadGameAxes);
      image(oLoadGame0); axis off;
      set(dMenu,'CurrentAxes',dMenuGameHelpAxes);
      image(oGameHelp0); axis off;
      set(dMenu,'CurrentAxes',dMenuOptionsAxes);
      image(oOptions0); axis off;
      set(dMenu,'CurrentAxes',dMenuExitAxes);
      image(oExit0); axis off;
```

```
        elseif kPosition == 2
          set(0,'CurrentFigure',dMenu);
          set(dMenu,'CurrentAxes',dMenuNewGameAxes);
          image(oNewGame0);axis off;
          set(dMenu,'CurrentAxes',dMenuLoadGameAxes);
          image(oLoadGame1);axis off;
          set(dMenu,'CurrentAxes',dMenuGameHelpAxes);
          image(oGameHelp0); axis off;
          set(dMenu,'CurrentAxes',dMenuOptionsAxes);
          image(oOptions0); axis off;
          set(dMenu,'CurrentAxes',dMenuExitAxes);
          image(oExit0); axis off;
        elseif kPosition == 3
          set(0,'CurrentFigure',dMenu);
          set(dMenu,'CurrentAxes',dMenuNewGameAxes);
          image(oNewGame0); axis off;
          set(dMenu,'CurrentAxes',dMenuLoadGameAxes);
          image(oLoadGame0); axis off;
          set(dMenu,'CurrentAxes',dMenuGameHelpAxes);
          image(oGameHelp1); axis off;
          set(dMenu,'CurrentAxes',dMenuOptionsAxes);
          image(oOptions0); axis off;
          set(dMenu,'CurrentAxes',dMenuExitAxes);
          image(oExit0); axis off;
        elseif kPosition == 4
          set(0,'CurrentFigure',dMenu);
          set(dMenu,'CurrentAxes',dMenuNewGameAxes);
          image(oNewGame0); axis off;
          set(dMenu,'CurrentAxes',dMenuLoadGameAxes);
          image(oLoadGame0); axis off;
          set(dMenu,'CurrentAxes',dMenuGameHelpAxes);
          image(oGameHelp0); axis off;
          set(dMenu,'CurrentAxes',dMenuOptionsAxes);
          image(oOptions1); axis off;
          set(dMenu,'CurrentAxes',dMenuExitAxes);
          image(oExit0); axis off;
        elseif kPosition == 5
          set(0,'CurrentFigure',dMenu);
          set(dMenu,'CurrentAxes',dMenuNewGameAxes);
          image(oNewGame0); axis off;
          set(dMenu,'CurrentAxes',dMenuLoadGameAxes);
          image(oLoadGame0); axis off;
          set(dMenu,'CurrentAxes',dMenuGameHelpAxes);
          image(oGameHelp0); axis off;
          set(dMenu,'CurrentAxes',dMenuOptionsAxes);
          image(oOptions0); axis off;
          set(dMenu,'CurrentAxes',dMenuExitAxes);
          image(oExit1); axis off;
        else
        end
    end
```

Fig. 6. Part of dialog with set of "buttons" as pictures

8. Showing the vectors in dialogs

This part shows an example how to show vectors in dialog. There are several possibilities but this example seems to me as the simplest one. The realisation is provided in lines 174 to 251, and sample output is shown in figure 7. It is based on the following. The vectors of same length with numeric values change their data type using `num2str` function and they are added into one `listbox` in dialogue, each column for one data vector. And now the short description of provided source code is going to be outlined. Lines 174 and 175 predefine the name of colors to be used in the dialog, lines 176 - 180 defines new dialog, and lines 181 - 189 new menu and its items. The background of the dialog was created in Adobe Photoshop and the code for showing it in the dialog is in lines 190 - 192. There are several objects in the dialog. They are given by the code in lines 196 - 241. The position of objects depends on the screen resolution and therefore the `k_y` variable is used. The most important code for this example is in lines 242 - 251. The data are given via the `String` property, lines 250 and 251 have to be one line actually! The data type change is realized for the matrix, because each input in lines 250 and 251 is actually the vector.

```
174  cerna=[0 0 0];
175  cervena=[1 0 0];
176  hf6=figure('Color',cerna,...
177          'Name','Tabulka t, u1, y1, w1',...
178          'MenuBar','None',...
179          'Resize','off',...
```

```
        'NumberTitle','off');
hmenu4=uimenu('label','Zobrazit tabulku :');
hmenu42=uimenu(hmenu4,'label','t,u2,y2,w2',...
                 'CallBack','tu2y2w2');
hmenu43=uimenu(hmenu4,'label','t,e1,e2',...
   'CallBack','te1e2');
hmenu44=uimenu(hmenu4,'label','t,T11,T21,K1',...
   'CallBack','tT11T21K1');
hmenu45=uimenu(hmenu4,'label','t,T12,T22,K2',...
   'CallBack','tT12T22K2');
  axes('Position',[0 0 1 1]);
  image(vysledky);
  axis off;
  close(hf10);
  dial7;
  pause(1);
  text17 = uicontrol(hf6,...
     'HorizontalAlignment','center',...
     'BackgroundColor',cerna, ...
     'ForegroundColor',cervena, ...
     'Units','points', ...
    'Position',[134 k_y*213.25 29.75 13.5], ...
    'Style','text', ...
    'String','t(s)');
  text18 = uicontrol(hf6,...
     'HorizontalAlignment','center',...
     'BackgroundColor',cerna, ...
     'ForegroundColor',cervena, ...
     'Units','points', ...
    'Position',[174 k_y*213.25 29.75 13.5], ...
    'Style','text', ...
    'String','u1');
  text19 = uicontrol(hf6,...
     'HorizontalAlignment','center',...
     'BackgroundColor',cerna, ...
     'ForegroundColor',cervena, ...
     'Units','points', ...
    'Position',[219 k_y*213.25 29.75 13.5], ...
    'Style','text', ...
    'String','y1');
  text20 = uicontrol(hf6,...
     'HorizontalAlignment','center',...
     'BackgroundColor',cerna, ...
     'ForegroundColor',cervena, ...
     'Units','points', ...
    'Position',[259 k_y*213.25 29.75 13.5], ...
    'Style','text', ...
    'String','w1');
  text24 = uicontrol(hf6,...
     'HorizontalAlignment','right',...
     'BackgroundColor',cerna, ...
```

```
    'ForegroundColor',cervena, ...
    'Units','points', ...
   'Position',[130 k_y*109.25 264.75 k_y*121.5], ...
   'Style','frame');
 text24 = uicontrol(hf6,...
    'HorizontalAlignment','right',...
    'BackgroundColor',cerna, ...
    'ForegroundColor',cervena, ...
    'Units','points', ...
   'Position',[130 k_y*109.25 264.75 k_y*101.5], ...
     'Style','frame');
ddd=size(param1); d1=ddd(1,2);
text24 = uicontrol(hf6,...
      'HorizontalAlignment','right',...
      'BackgroundColor',cerna, ...
      'ForegroundColor',cervena, ...
      'Units','points', ...
     'Position',[134 k_y*113.25 256.75 k_y*93.5], ...
     'Style','listbox', ...
     'String',num2str([param1(:,d1) real(simout1(:,1))
 real(simout1(:,2)) real(simout1(:,3))]));
```

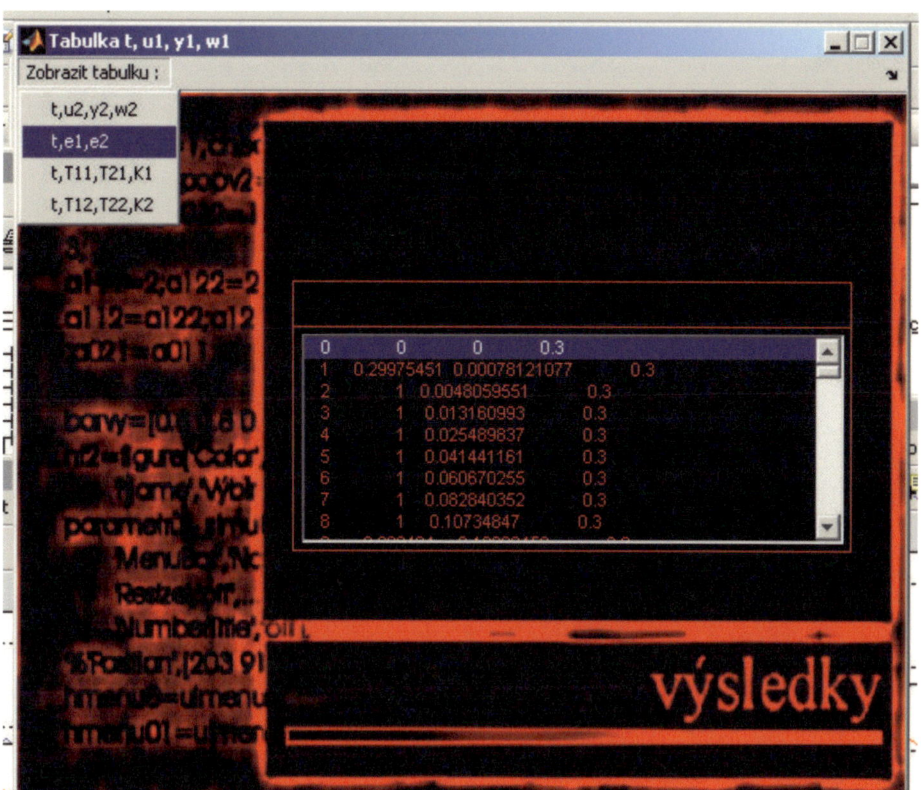

Fig. 7. Dialog with vectors, data, shown in table

9. Nicely drawn results from Simulink

Simulink provides `Scope` block for drawing the results of simulation. It is a fast solution. If you want to manage the look of the graph, saving the data to Matlab Workspace and drawing them by the chosen plotting function is the easiest way. The following example shows it, lines 252 to 266 and figures 8 to 10.

```
252    close all
253    clear all
254    clc
255    a=0.1; b=0.01; c=0.5;
256    sim('untitled1',[0 10])
257    t=v(:,1);
258    x=v(:,2);
259    Dx=v(:,3);
260    plot(t,x,'r')
261    hold on
262    plot(t,Dx,'k')
263    title('x and its derivation')
264    xlabel('time [t]')
265    ylabel('x(t), Dx(t)')
266    legend('x(t)', 'Dx(t)')
```

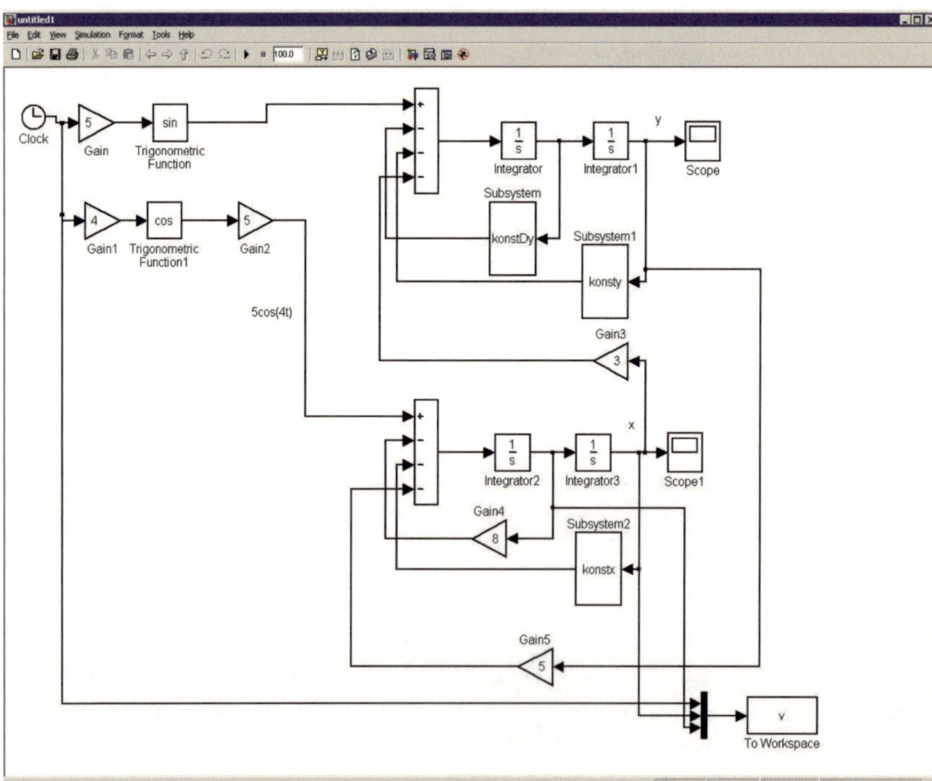

Fig. 8. Simulink model with `Scope` and `To Workspace` blocks

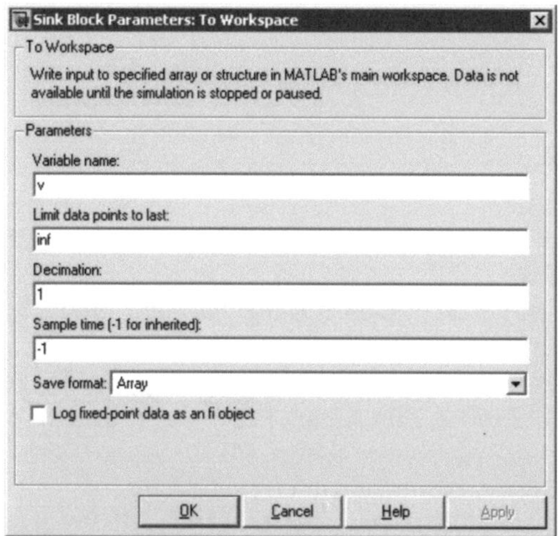

Fig. 9. Setting the parameters of `Scope` block

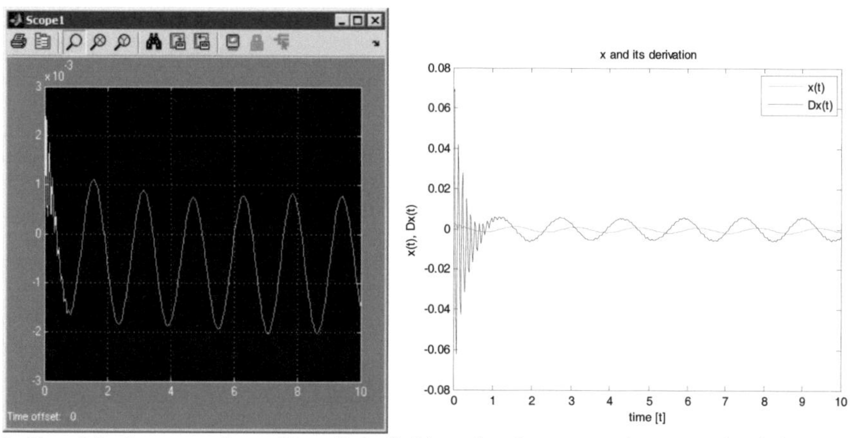

Fig. 10. Graphical output from Simulink (left) and using `plot` function (right)

Firstly, the Simulink model named as *untitled1.mdl* is created according to figure 8. `To Workspace` block saves the data into `v` variable as an array, see the settings in figure 9. Time is the first input to the `To Workspace` block. Simulation of the model is called by `sim` function, line 256. You can view the simulation results by clicking the blocks `Scope` and `Scope1` in the model, see figure 10 - left part. Lines 257 - 266 are responsible for nice and easy-to-edit graphical output, right part of figure 10. The data are sent to variables in lines 257 - 259.

10. Conclusion

This chapter presented some tips and tricks for programming in Matlab which appeared to be useful during the classes and it might be useful mostly for students and beginners. Almost all of them are oriented on working with GUI, only one tip is used with Simulink, the most common Matlab enlargement. The reader should be familiar with the basics of Matlab programming.

11. Acknowledgement

This chapter was supported by the grant MSM 7088352102.

12. References

Hanselman, D.C. & Littlefield, B. (2005). *Mastering MATLAB 7*, Prentice Hall, ISBN 0-13-143018-1, USA.

Hrubos, P. (2009). *Software aid for Matlab teaching*, bachelor thesis, Tomas Bata University in Zlin, Zlin, Czech Republic (in Czech)

Perutka, K. (2005). *Matlab – Bases for students of automation and IT*, Tomas Bata University in Zlin, ISBN 80-7318-355-2, Zlin, Czech Republic (in Czech)

Perutka, K. (2007). *Decentralized adaptive control*, Ph.D. thesis, Tomas Bata University in Zlin, Zlin, Czech Republic, European Union (in Czech)

Perutka, K. & Heczko, M. (2007). Teaching of MATLAB Programming Using Complex Game. In: *FIE2007, 37th IEEE/ASEE Frontiers in Education Conference*, S1H 13-18, IEEE, ISBN 1-4244-1084-3, Milwaukee, WI, USA.

2

Using MATLAB to develop standalone graphical user interface (GUI) software packages for educational purposes

A. B. M. Nasiruzzaman
Department of Electrical & Electronic Engineering,
Rajshahi University of Engineering & Technology
Bangladesh

1. Introduction

In the institutes where laboratory facilities are not that much available, and industries are located in remote areas, Personal Computer (PC) can be used to facilitate science and engineering education. Programming and simulation tools can be used widely for preparing such a PC based setting for students. But to develop a software, toolbox or standalone applications one had to rely on C++, Visual basic, or Java. For a computer science or information technology student it is easy to program in these environments but for other science and engineering students this pose a problem since they are not familiar with these programs and require excellent programming expertise. MATLAB (MathWorks, 2009), flagship software in scientific computing, is extensively used all over the world. Particular factors that support the selection of MATLAB are:

- A flexible software structure of MATLAB comprising libraries, models, and programs enables one to integrate different model components in one package conveniently.

- Fast development with MATLAB using powerful calculation and visualization means of the package enables one to expand the software quickly and efficiently without developing any extra programming tools.

- A wide selection of TOOLBOXes, comprehensive collections of predefined functions for solving application-specific problems, is already available with MATLAB and is likely to grow even faster in the future.

The use of MATLAB (short for MATrix LABoratory) is increasing day by day (McMohan, 2007; Littlefield & Hanselman, 2004). Science and engineering students use this software broadly for educational purposes (Chapman, 2007). Graphical User Interface (GUI) is an environment available with renowned software that gives the option to the user developing software packages for personal and problem specific uses. It is a way of arranging information on a computer screen that is easy to understand and use because it uses icons, menus and a mouse rather than only text and programs written in high level language which is often not much handy for others except for programmers. The rapidly developing software MATLAB for technical computation is giving two releases per annum with extended capabilities which enhances user performance and boosts customer satisfaction. Collaterally, its size is increasing. With every release MATLAB takes a new look with new features and changes. Each version is accompanied by major bug fixes, enhanced help menus, removal of undocumented deprecated functions, and development of alternative functions. In case of GUI this change is more rapid, functions are being obsolete and new efficient functions are generated. Due to this reason a GUI developed in one version may not be used in other version (Marchand, 2002; Smith, 2006). So other ways must be taken into deliberation to solve this setback. This chapter presents a guide to develop standalone software tools and/or packages using the enormous competence of MATLAB GUI which can be used in educational and training institutes for learning purposes of freshman or sophomore students.

But another problem arises simultaneously, the huge size and memory requirements of these new releases of MATLAB prevents its uses on the PCs having low memory. Sometimes the programs developed by the recent versions of MATLAB cannot be used by the previous ones due to lack of version compatibility option. So, although instructors can develop interactive tutorial packages for students using the recent versions of MATLAB which they can afford easily, the developed software cannot be used in the laboratories having older facilities. Students also cannot take the advantage of using the new software since he does not have the financial capacity of purchasing newer versions or upgrading MATLAB and high performance PC. To solve this hindrance MATLAB standalone project development tools can be used.

This chapter describes the development of an interactive computer based GUI for MATLAB which can be used in any Pentium III graded PC. It has been prepared for anyone who has little or no exposure to MATLAB. Readers are guided through new concepts to build easy-to-use GUI, acting as a 'wrapper' for experimental simulation codes written by the educator. Even though the chapter is written based on the recent release of MATLAB 2009a, this can be used as a guide for other versions starting from MATLAB 6. It is designed to relieve the coder from most of the programming burden, and to provide with a friendly, consistent approach to the development of standalone MATLAB programs.

2. Getting Started

MATLAB GUI can be built in two ways.

(a) Using GUIDE (GUI Development Environment)
(b) Coding from MATLAB editor

The first approach of building GUI is straightforward and will be discussed in this chapter. Once completed several examples of building GUI, anyone can learn how to code from MATLAB editor.

To initiate GUIDE let's write *guide* in the MATLAB command window and press ***Enter*** key. This will open the GUIDE Quick Start window as shown in Fig. 1, where there are two tabs (Create NEW GUI and Open Existing GUI). Under the Create New GUI tab four GUI templates are available. Selecting the Blank GUI (Default) template and pressing Ok at the bottom of the window opens the design window as shown in Fig. 2.

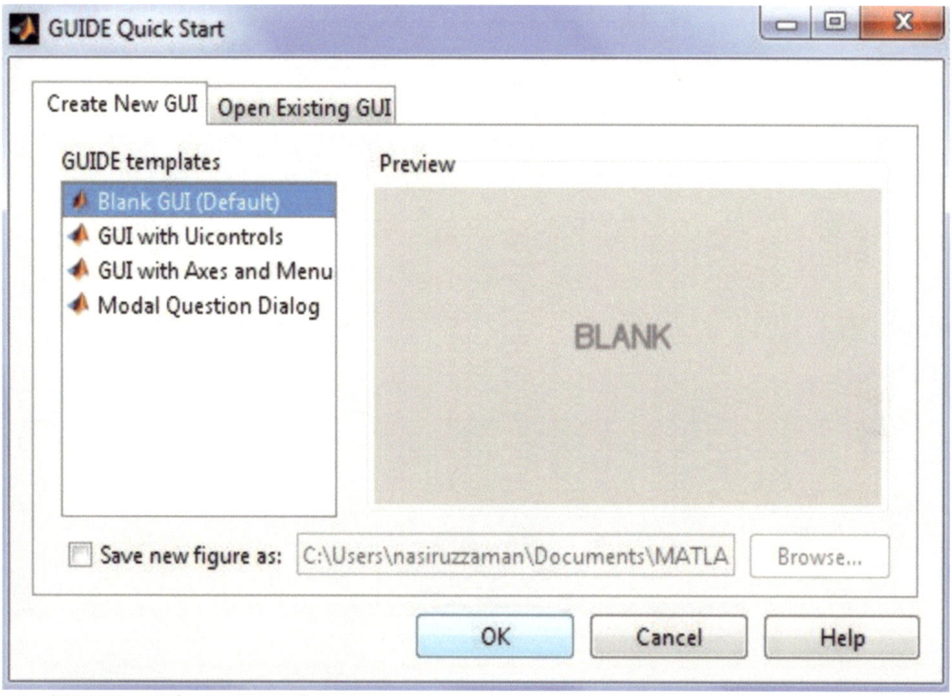

Fig. 1. GUIDE quick start window

The GUI is not yet saved, so at the top of the window it is shown *untitled.fig*. Once the work is saved the title of the GUI will be reflected here. *.fig is the extension of GUI figure files. Generally, a GUI requires two files the figure (*.fig) files where various components are aligned and the code (*.m) files where the coding is done. There is also provision to run the GUI using the single *.m file. At the top of the window Menu and Shortcuts can be found. To the right there are some GUI controls which are very important to learn for building GUI. The blank portion is used for the design purpose of the GUI.

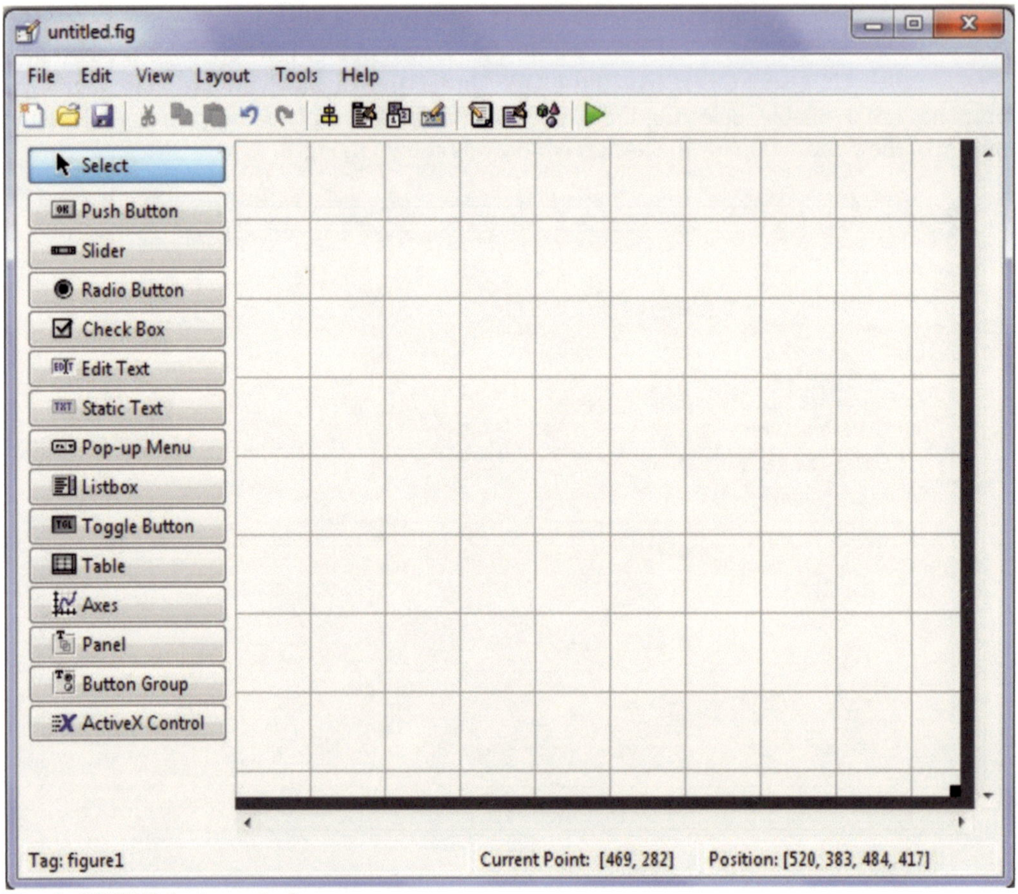

Fig. 2. GUIDE design window

3. GUI Components

Some basic GUI components are

(a) Push Button
(b) Slider
(c) Radio Button
(d) Check Box
(e) Edit Text
(f) Static Text
(g) Pop-up Menu
(h) Listbox
(i) Toggle Button
(j) Table
(k) Axes
(l) Panel
(m) Button Group
(n) ActiveX Control

These components may vary depending on the version of MATLAB. These examples are taken from MATLAB 2009a version.

4. A Simple Calculator

The target of this chapter is to give the reader a quick look at GUI of MATLAB rather than discussing each and every item. Readers will be able to learn with examples. The first example here will be considered to build a simple calculator. Two numbers provided by user will be added, subtracted, multiplied, and divided. The result will be displayed in a box. The first step of building a GUI is to have a rough sketch of the GUI. To build a simple calculator some basic components are needed:

(a) Two input boxes (Edit text)
(b) One output box (Static text)
(c) Four options for addition, subtraction, multiplication, and division (this can be accomplished in many ways. Here let's take four Radio Buttons)
(d) One Calculate button (Push Button)

To enhance the GUI one also can add some static texts to show various signs. In this example two more static texts are used. One is for the sign of calculation (+,-,x,/) and the other is to show (=) sign. The GUI will look like Fig. 3.

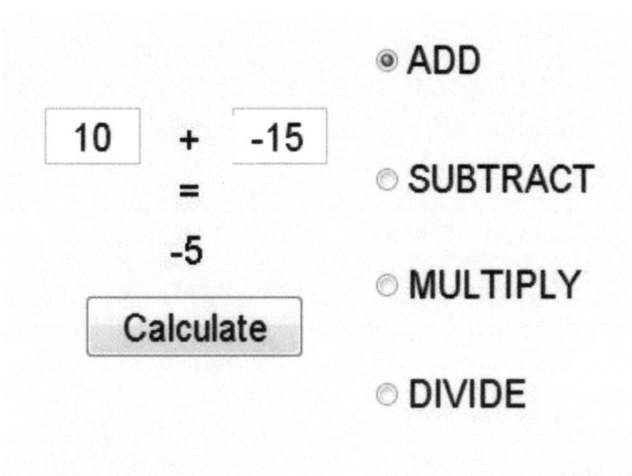

Fig. 3. A simple calculator

5. Adding Components

Now since the concept of the GUI has been built, the next step is to add all components required for building the calculators. Adding components to the *.fig file is very easy. Just click the item on the left, drag and drop to the blank space and the component is added. First consider adding the two static text components for entering two numbers. Select ***Edit Text*** and drag and drop to the blank space of the figure two times. Now the GUI will somewhat look like Fig. 4.

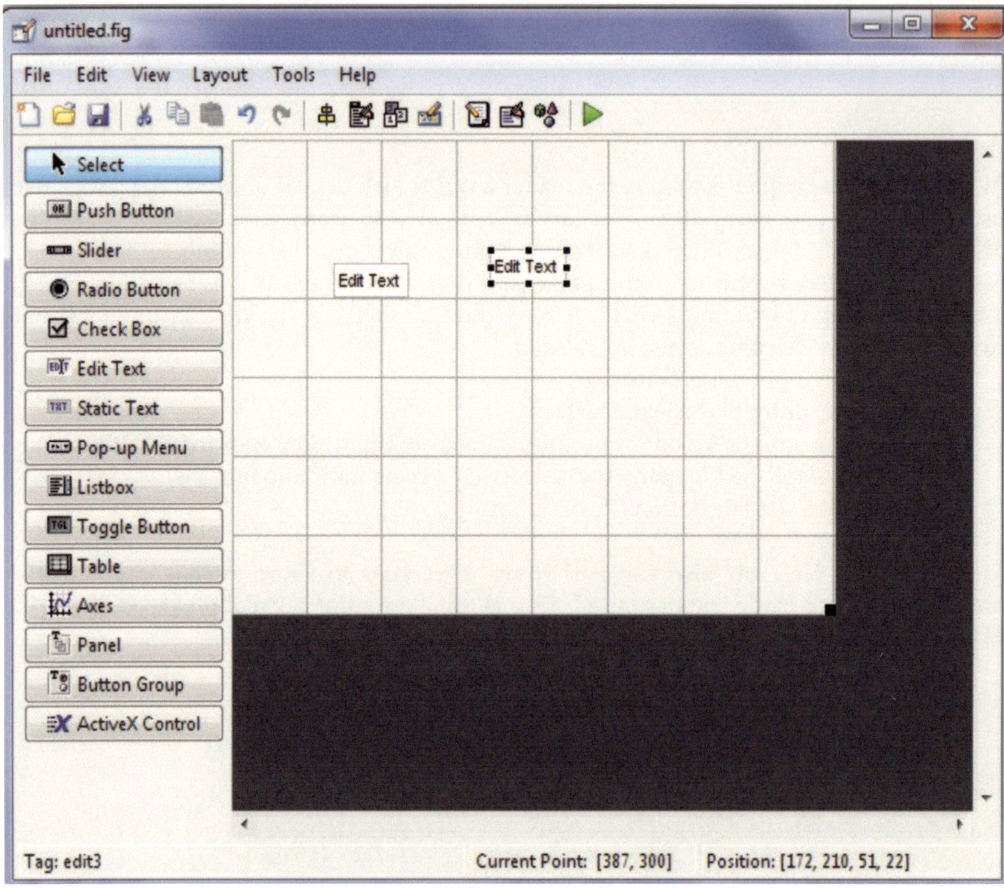

Fig. 4. Adding edit text controls to the GUI

Now the newly added editable text boxes must be modified as per the need of the GUI. Here two numbers are added; hence it is a good idea to give two numbers as input from the very first so the inexperienced user will understand the purpose of the GUI. This task can be performed using Property Inspector.

6. Property Inspector

Now right clicking on the component and selecting the Property Inspector will open the window as in Fig. 5. The left column gives the property name and the right column shows property values. String and Tag properties worth emphasizing since it is essential for programming a GUI. The String property has value Edit Text. Anything can be written here. Lets write *10* here and change the Tag to *number1*. Now the property inspector should look like Fig. 6. Similarly, change the property of the second Edit text. It is changed as: String *-15* and Tag *number2*.

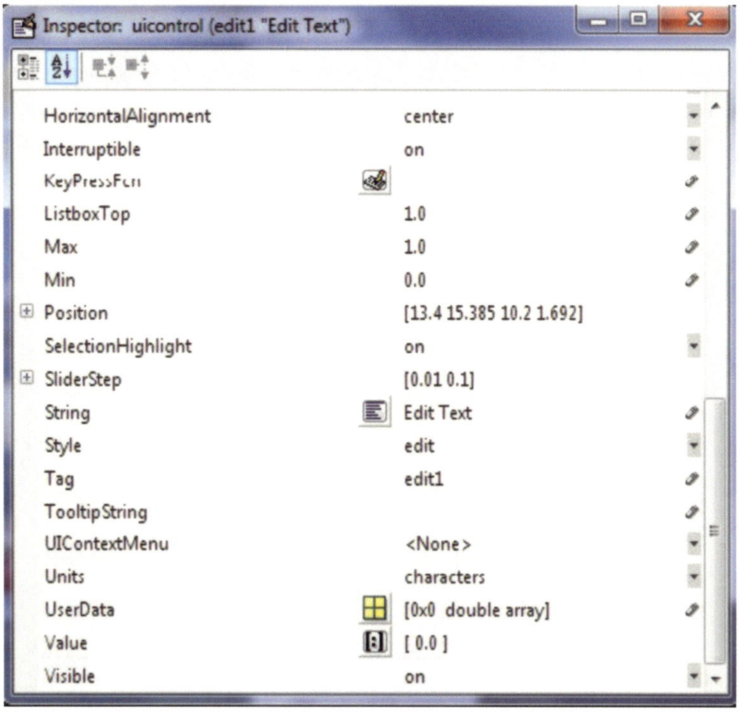

Fig. 5. Property inspector

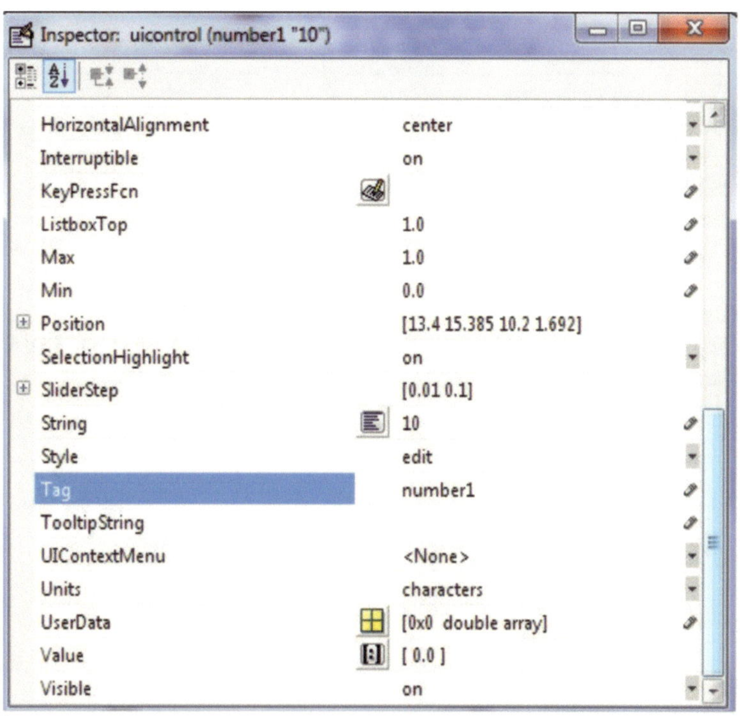

Fig. 6. Edited property inspector

7. Aligning Objects

One can align objects in the GUI to make the outlook of the GUI better. It can be done by clicking Tools menu and then selecting Align Objects. Then using the controls there objects can be aligned as in Fig. 7.

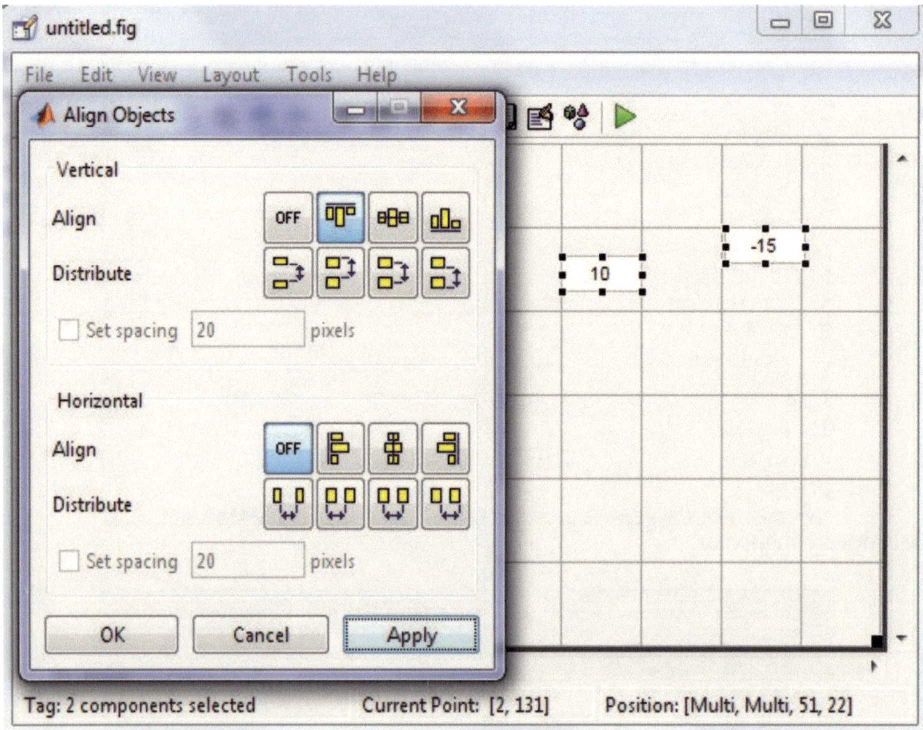

Fig. 7. Aligning objects

8. Adding More Components

More components can be added to the GUI. In Fig. 8 some Static Text controls are added and Fig. 9 shows the complete GUI with all components, Radio and Push Buttons are added here. The property modified for these components are given in Table 1.

Component	FontSize	String	Tag
Edit Text1	15	10	edit1
Edit Text1	15	-15	edit2
Static Text1	15	+	text1
Static Text2	15	=	text2
Static Text3	15	-5	text3
Push Button	15	Calculate	pushbutton1
Radio Button1	15	ADD	radiobutton1
Radio Button2	15	SUBTRACT	radiobutton2
Radio Button3	15	MULTIPLY	radiobutton3
Radio Button4	15	DIVIDE	radiobutton4

Table 1. Properties of various controls used in this chapter

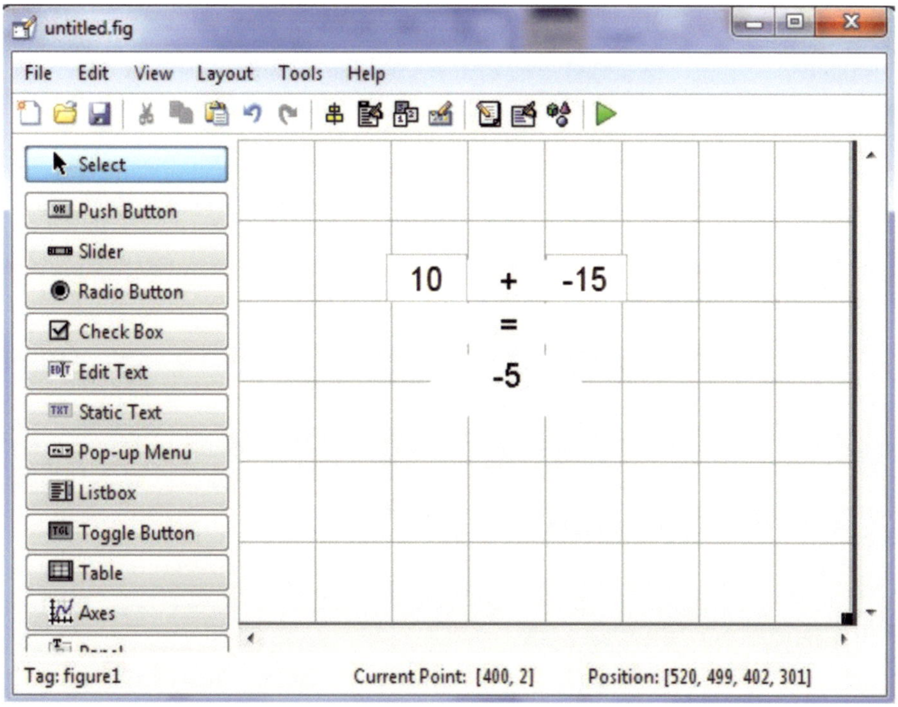

Fig. 8. Adding static text to GUI

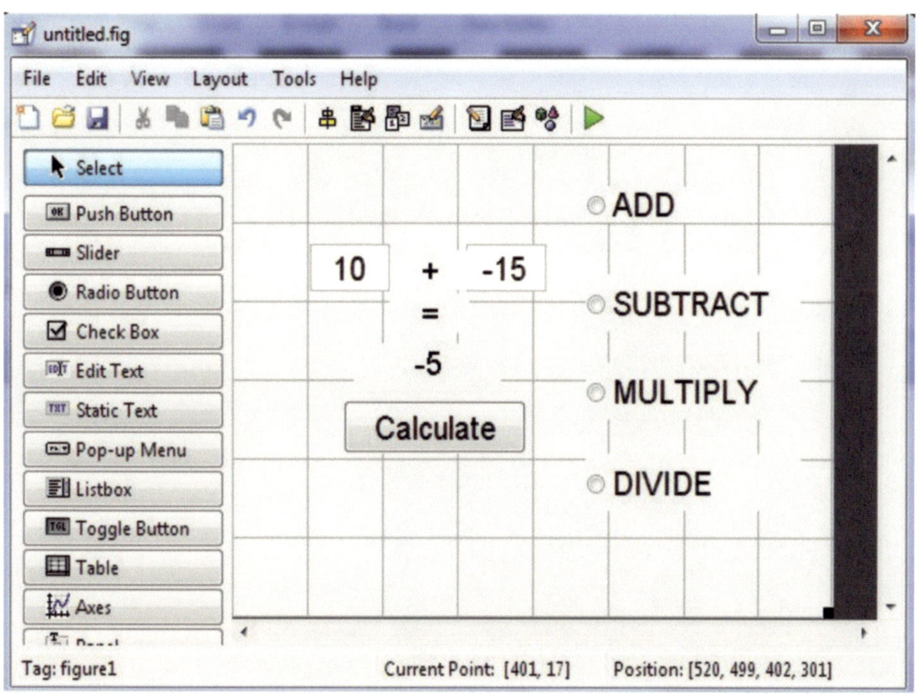

Fig. 9. Complete figure of a simple calculator

9. Programming the GUI

Now all the components are added. The GUI is saved in the name *test1.fig*. The rest task is coding the M-file. It can be accessed by clicking M-file Editor from View menu. When the m-file opens it somewhat looks like Fig. 10. This is a multi-function m-file. Codes are written under various functions. Functions are generated automatically. The opening function and callback functions are most important. Functions can be accessed as shown in Fig. 11.

When the GUI is first open the default action will be to work as adder. For this purpose let's modify the opening function of the GUI as in Fig. 12.

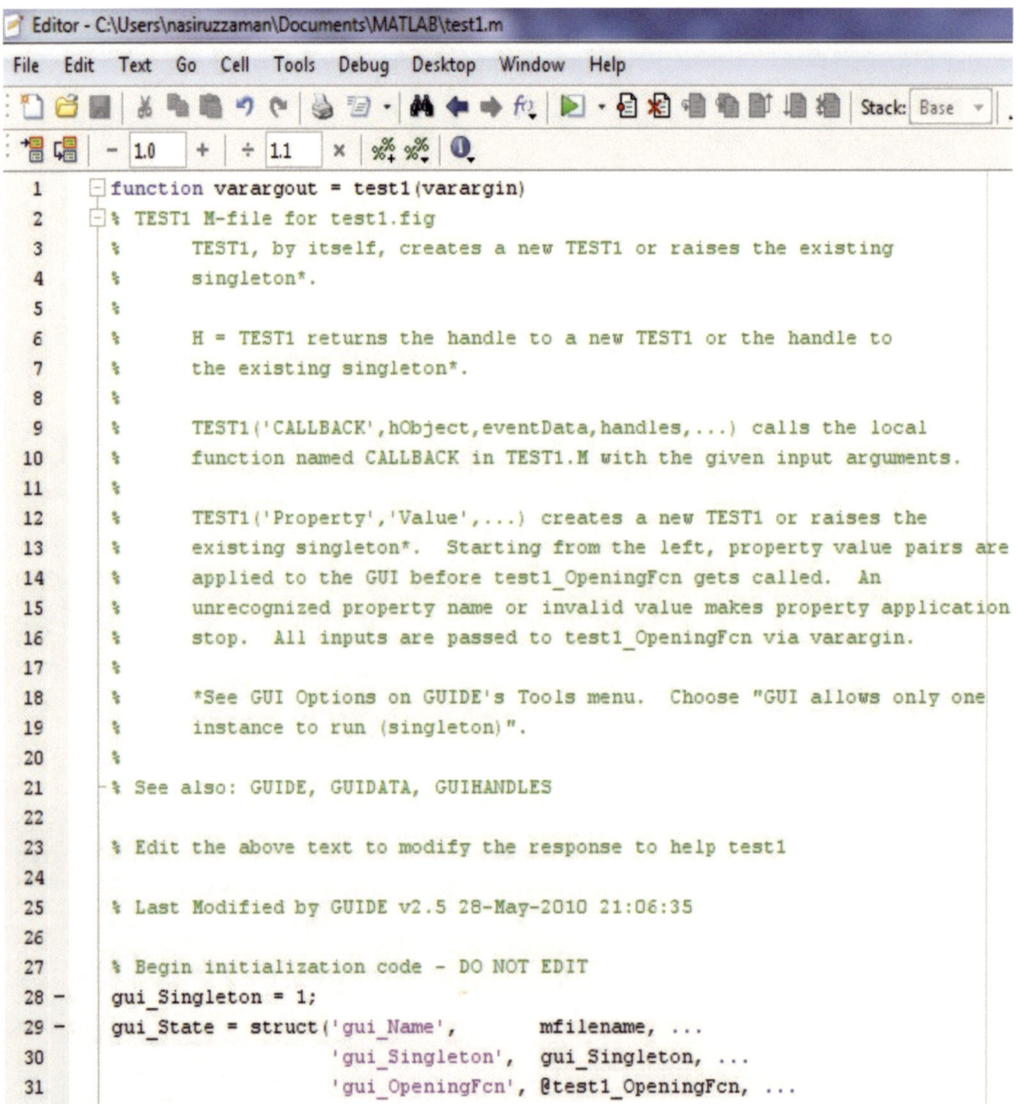

Fig. 10. M-file for simple calculator

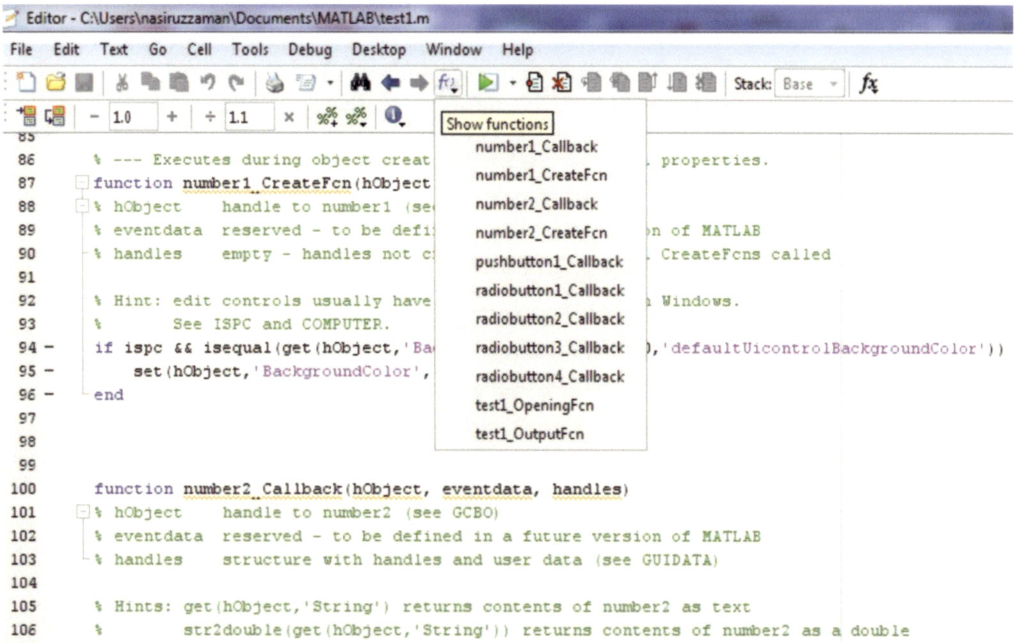

Fig. 11. Accessing functions in *.m file

```
% --- Executes just before test1 is made visible.
function test1_OpeningFcn(hObject, eventdata, handles, varargin)
% This function has no output args, see OutputFcn.
% hObject    handle to figure
% eventdata  reserved - to be defined in a future version of MATLAB
% handles    structure with handles and user data (see GUIDATA)
% varargin   command line arguments to test1 (see VARARGIN)

% Choose default command line output for test1
handles.output = hObject;

% Update handles structure
guidata(hObject, handles);

% UIWAIT makes test1 wait for user response (see UIRESUME)
% uiwait(handles.figure1);

clc
movegui('center')
set(handles.radiobutton1, 'Value', 1);
set(handles.radiobutton2, 'Value', 0);
set(handles.radiobutton3, 'Value', 0);
set(handles.radiobutton4, 'Value', 0);
```

Fig. 12. Opening function of simple calculator

10. Programming Radio and Push Button

The radiobuttons should be mutually exclusive and when a radiobutton is selected corresponding operating notation should be reflected in the symbol text box. This job is done in the radiobutton callback function. One example (multiply radio button) is given in Fig. 13. The Calculate (Push) button is also programmed as in Fig. 14.

```
% --- Executes on button press in radiobutton3.
function radiobutton3_Callback(hObject, eventdata, handles)
% hObject    handle to radiobutton3 (see GCBO)
% eventdata  reserved - to be defined in a future version of MATLAB
% handles    structure with handles and user data (see GUIDATA)

% Hint: get(hObject,'Value') returns toggle state of radiobutton3
set(handles.radiobutton1, 'Value', 0);
set(handles.radiobutton2, 'Value', 0);
set(handles.radiobutton3, 'Value', 1);
set(handles.radiobutton4, 'Value', 0);
set(handles.text1, 'String', 'x');
```

Fig. 13. Radio Button callback

```
% --- Executes on button press in pushbutton1.
function pushbutton1_Callback(hObject, eventdata, handles)
% hObject    handle to pushbutton1 (see GCBO)
% eventdata  reserved - to be defined in a future version of MATLAB
% handles    structure with handles and user data (see GUIDATA)
a = str2double(get(handles.number1, 'String'));
b=  str2double(get(handles.number2, 'String'));
index1 = get(handles.radiobutton1, 'Value');
index2 = get(handles.radiobutton2, 'Value');
index3 = get(handles.radiobutton3, 'Value');
index4 = get(handles.radiobutton4, 'Value');
if index1==1
    c=a+b;
else if index2==1
        c=a-b;
    else if index3==1
            c=a*b;
        else if index4==1
                c=a/b;
            end
        end
    end
end
set(handles.text3, 'String',c);
```

Fig. 14. Push Button callback

11. Running the GUI

If the GUI is completed programming and run (whole code is given later) the window should look somewhat like Fig. 15 and if someone wants to multiply, the window will be like Fig. 16.

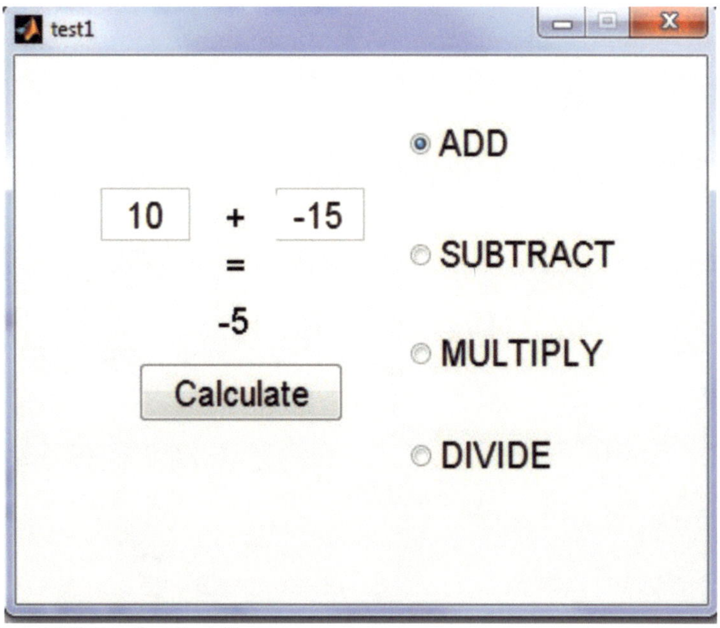

Fig. 15. Running GUI for the first time

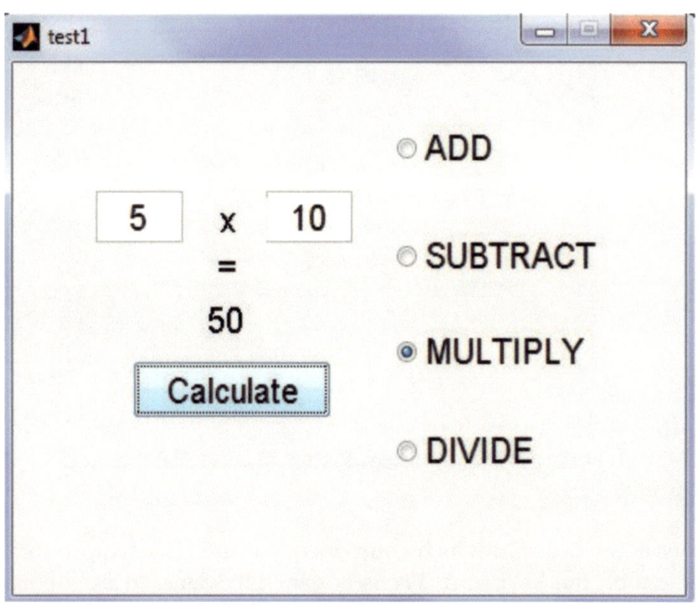

Fig. 16. Modifying and running GUI for multiplication

12. Some Additional Tools

There are also some additional options to make the GUI more attractive. Two examples are Object browser and Tab editor which are given in Fig. 17 and 18 respectively. The Object Browser displays a hierarchical list of the objects in the figure. It can be opened from View > Object Browser or by click the Object Browser icon on the GUIDE toolbar.

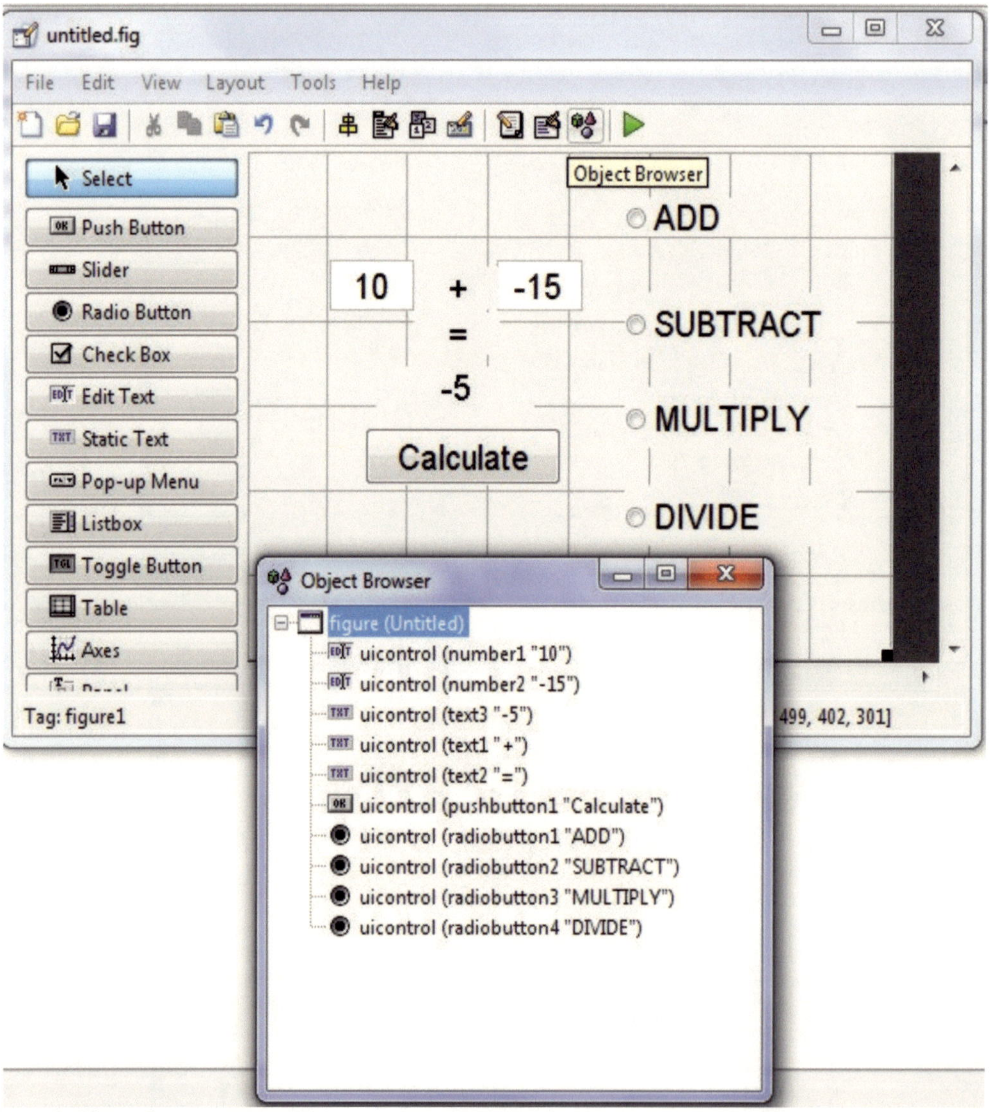

Fig. 17. Object browser

A GUI's tab order is the order in which components of the GUI acquire focus when a user presses the Tab key on the keyboard. Focus is generally denoted by a border or a dotted border. To examine and change the tab order of the panel components, click the panel background to select it, then select Tab Order Editor in the Tools menu of the Layout Editor.

The Tab Order Editor displays the panel's components in their current tab order. To change the tab order, select a component and press the up or down arrow to move the component up or down in the list.

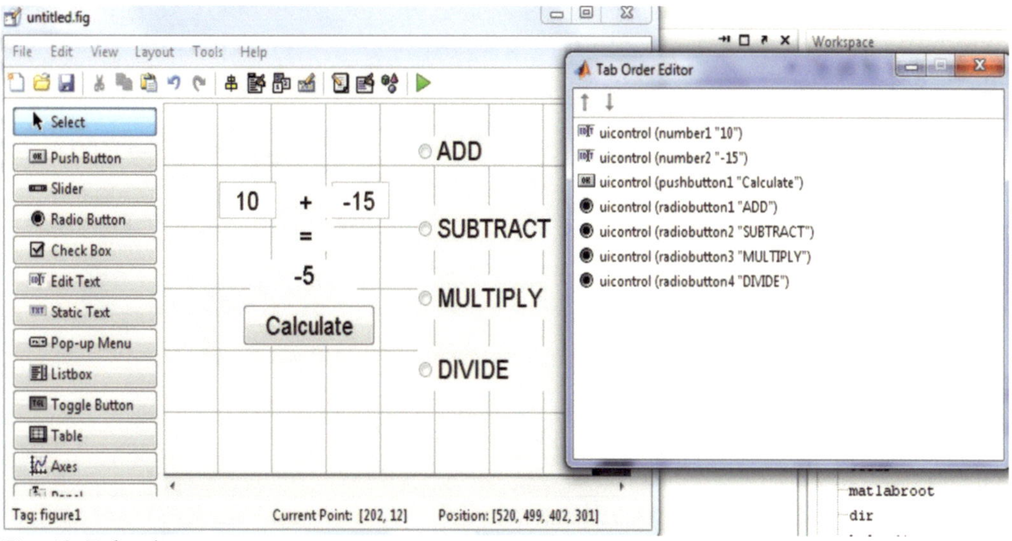

Fig. 18. Tab editor

13. Running GUI from a Single *.m File

Up to this point to run a GUI, both *.fig and *.m files are required. A GUI can also run from a single *.m file which will be demonstrated here. At first go to the test1.fig file in the GUIDE and select Export from the File menu as depicted in Fig. 19. Let's save the GUI in the name *test_standard.m.*

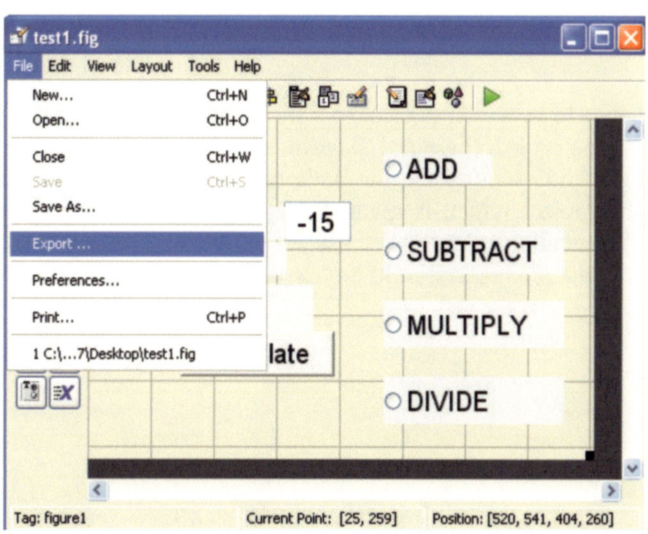

Fig. 19. Running GUI from a single *.m file

14. Standalone Application Project

In this final step, the standalone project will be developed. Enter deploytool in the MATLAB command window (It may be needed to setup the MATLAB compiler by entering mbuild -setup and following steps in the command window). The MATLAB development project window appears as in Fig. 20. Clicking the new deployment project icon as shown in Fig. 20 opens a window as in Fig. 21.

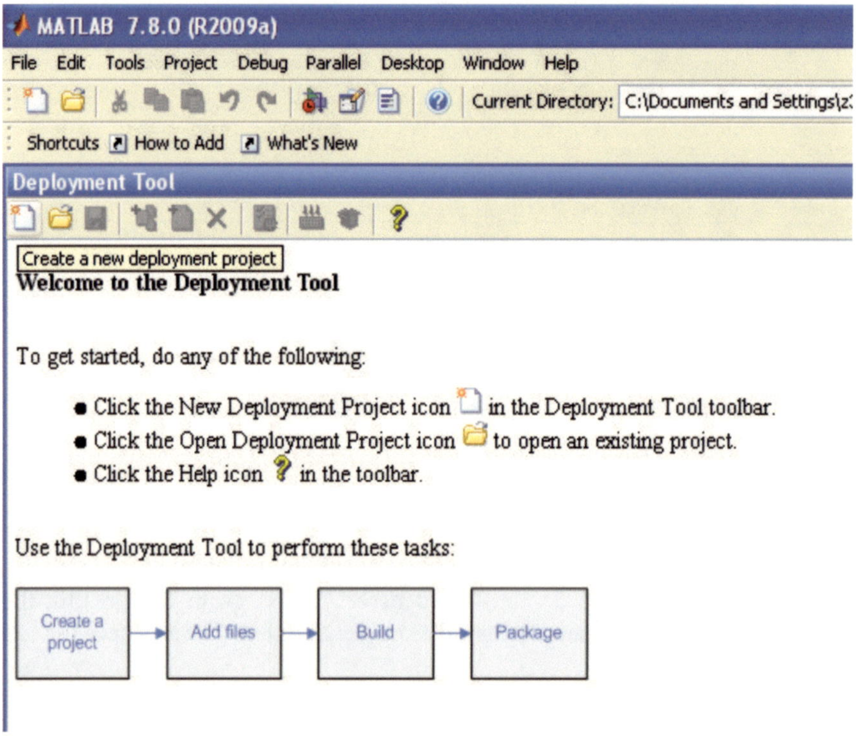

Fig. 20. Deployment tool

Here the project needs to be saved (let's save it by the name *test_project.prj*). After that, files should be added to the project (here *test_standard.m)* which is given in Fig. 22. The state of the deployment tool window after the file have been added is shown in Fig. 23. The next step is to build the project which is given in Fig. 24. After the compilation process the executable file will be available. The file can be found in the specified location in the ***distrib*** folder. In this project the file name should be *test_project.exe*. If the file is clicked in any PC it will run as in Fig. 25.

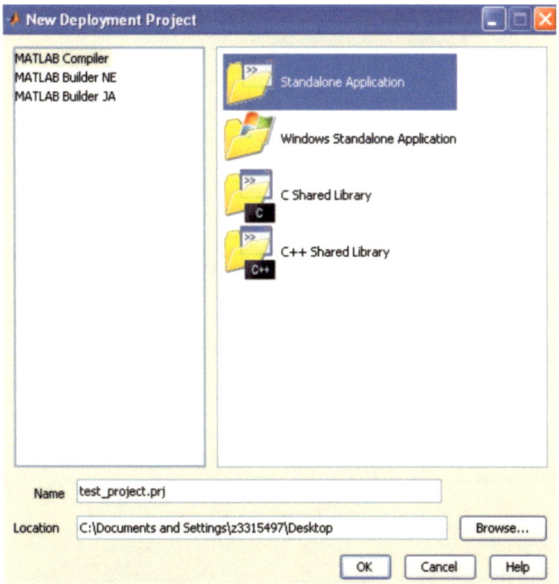

Fig. 21. New deployment project window

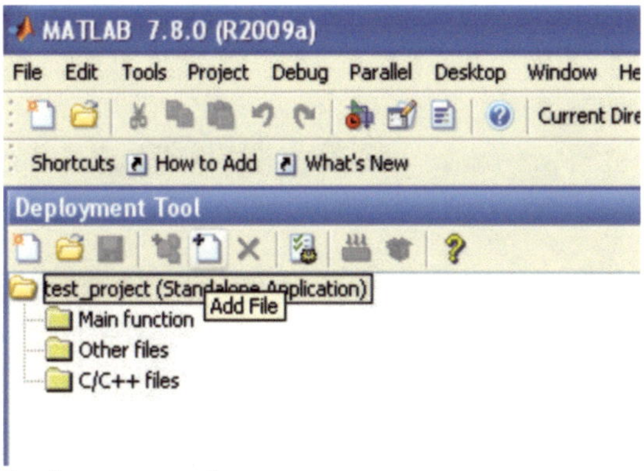

Fig. 22. Adding file to deployment tool

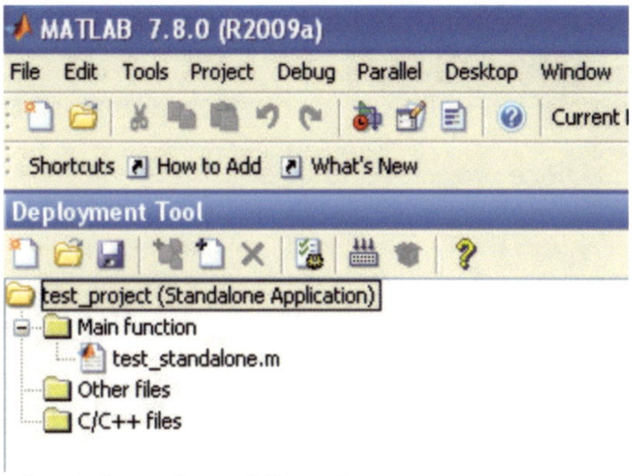

Fig. 23. Deployment tool window after adding file

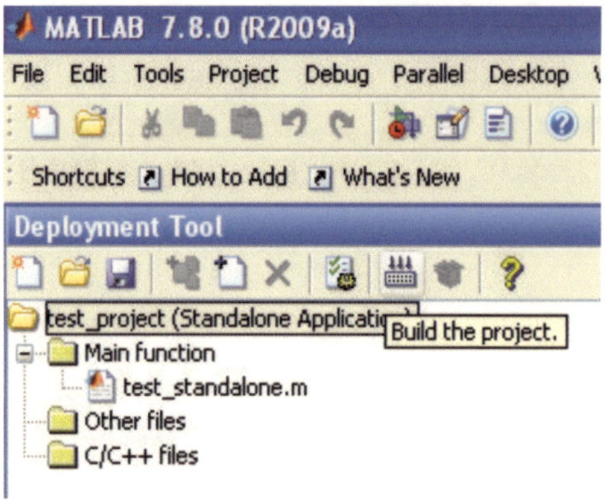

Fig. 24. Build Project

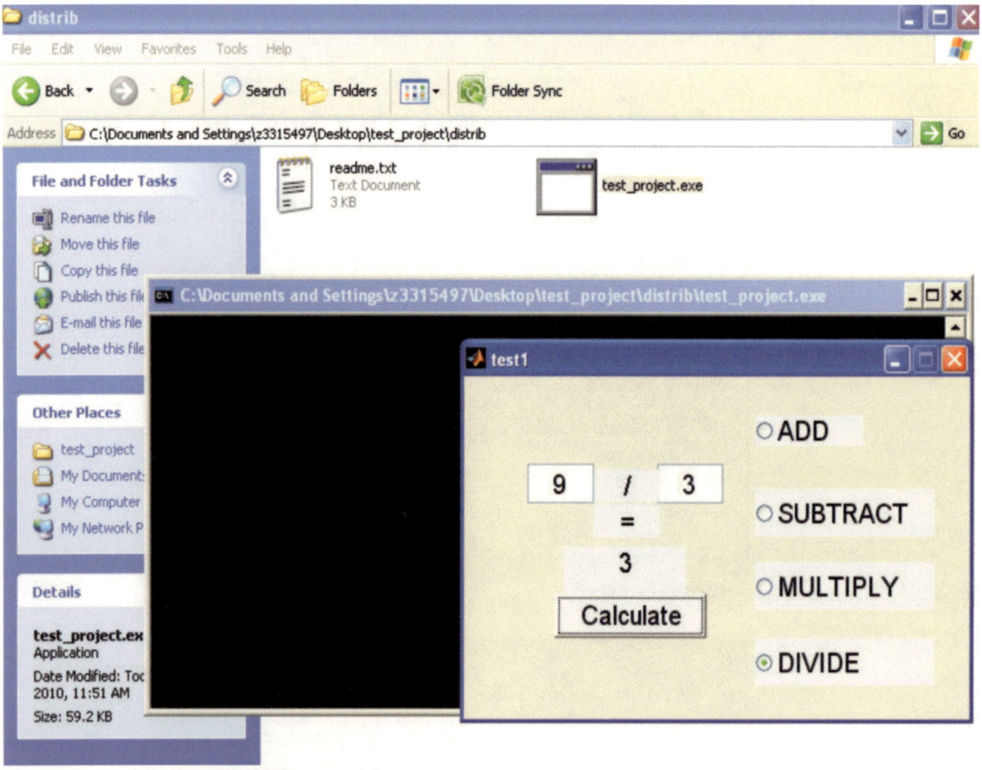

Fig. 25. Running the standalone project

15. Conclusion

A standalone MATLAB project is discussed here which will be very useful for educational purposes. Students can develop their projects in home and demonstrate in the class. Teachers can build excellent software packages in powerful computers and without can run it the classroom PCs with limited resource. There is no need of version compatibility, no need of huge memory requirement. After completing the project in this chapter it will open a new horizon for MATLAB users. For first time users codes are given in the next article. In case of any question regarding this issue the author can be contacted at nasiruzzaman@ieee.org.

16. MATLAB Code

```
function varargout = test1(varargin)
% TEST1 M-file for test1.fig
%      TEST1, by itself, creates a new TEST1 or raises the existing
%      singleton*.
%
%      H = TEST1 returns the handle to a new TEST1 or the handle to
%      the existing singleton*.
%
%      TEST1('CALLBACK',hObject,eventData,handles,...) calls the local
%      function named CALLBACK in TEST1.M with the given input arguments.
%
%      TEST1('Property','Value',...) creates a new TEST1 or raises the
%      existing singleton*.  Starting from the left, property value pairs are
%      applied to the GUI before test1_OpeningFcn gets called.  An
%      unrecognized property name or invalid value makes property application
%      stop.  All inputs are passed to test1_OpeningFcn via varargin.
%
%      *See GUI Options on GUIDE's Tools menu.  Choose "GUI allows only one
%      instance to run (singleton)".
%
% See also: GUIDE, GUIDATA, GUIHANDLES

% Edit the above text to modify the response to help test1

% Last Modified by GUIDE v2.5 28-May-2010 22:04:08

% Begin initialization code - DO NOT EDIT
gui_Singleton = 1;
gui_State = struct('gui_Name',       mfilename, ...
                   'gui_Singleton',  gui_Singleton, ...
                   'gui_OpeningFcn', @test1_OpeningFcn, ...
                   'gui_OutputFcn',  @test1_OutputFcn, ...
                   'gui_LayoutFcn',  [] , ...
                   'gui_Callback',   []);
if nargin && ischar(varargin{1})
    gui_State.gui_Callback = str2func(varargin{1});
end

if nargout
    [varargout{1:nargout}] = gui_mainfcn(gui_State, varargin{:});
```

```
else
   gui_mainfcn(gui_State, varargin{:});
end
% End initialization code - DO NOT EDIT


% --- Executes just before test1 is made visible.
function test1_OpeningFcn(hObject, eventdata, handles, varargin)
% This function has no output args, see OutputFcn.
% hObject    handle to figure
% eventdata  reserved - to be defined in a future version of MATLAB
% handles    structure with handles and user data (see GUIDATA)
% varargin   command line arguments to test1 (see VARARGIN)

% Choose default command line output for test1
handles.output = hObject;

% Update handles structure
guidata(hObject, handles);

% UIWAIT makes test1 wait for user response (see UIRESUME)
% uiwait(handles.figure1);

clc
movegui('center')
set(handles.radiobutton1, 'Value', 1);
set(handles.radiobutton2, 'Value', 0);
set(handles.radiobutton3, 'Value', 0);
set(handles.radiobutton4, 'Value', 0);


% --- Outputs from this function are returned to the command line.
function varargout = test1_OutputFcn(hObject, eventdata, handles)
% varargout  cell array for returning output args (see VARARGOUT);
% hObject    handle to figure
% eventdata  reserved - to be defined in a future version of MATLAB
% handles    structure with handles and user data (see GUIDATA)

% Get default command line output from handles structure
varargout{1} = handles.output;



function number1_Callback(hObject, eventdata, handles)
% hObject    handle to number1 (see GCBO)
% eventdata  reserved - to be defined in a future version of MATLAB
```

```
% handles    structure with handles and user data (see GUIDATA)

% Hints: get(hObject,'String') returns contents of number1 as text
%        str2double(get(hObject,'String')) returns contents of number1 as a double


% --- Executes during object creation, after setting all properties.
function number1_CreateFcn(hObject, eventdata, handles)
% hObject    handle to number1 (see GCBO)
% eventdata  reserved - to be defined in a future version of MATLAB
% handles    empty - handles not created until after all CreateFcns called

% Hint: edit controls usually have a white background on Windows.
%       See ISPC and COMPUTER.
if ispc && isequal(get(hObject,'BackgroundColor'),
get(0,'defaultUicontrolBackgroundColor'))
   set(hObject,'BackgroundColor','white');
end



function number2_Callback(hObject, eventdata, handles)
% hObject    handle to number2 (see GCBO)
% eventdata  reserved - to be defined in a future version of MATLAB
% handles    structure with handles and user data (see GUIDATA)

% Hints: get(hObject,'String') returns contents of number2 as text
%        str2double(get(hObject,'String')) returns contents of number2 as a double


% --- Executes during object creation, after setting all properties.
function number2_CreateFcn(hObject, eventdata, handles)
% hObject    handle to number2 (see GCBO)
% eventdata  reserved - to be defined in a future version of MATLAB
% handles    empty - handles not created until after all CreateFcns called

% Hint: edit controls usually have a white background on Windows.
%       See ISPC and COMPUTER.
if ispc && isequal(get(hObject,'BackgroundColor'),
get(0,'defaultUicontrolBackgroundColor'))
   set(hObject,'BackgroundColor','white');
end


% --- Executes on button press in pushbutton1.
function pushbutton1_Callback(hObject, eventdata, handles)
```

```
% hObject    handle to pushbutton1 (see GCBO)
% eventdata  reserved - to be defined in a future version of MATLAB
% handles    structure with handles and user data (see GUIDATA)
a = str2double(get(handles.number1, 'String'));
b=  str2double(get(handles.number2, 'String'));
index1 = get(handles.radiobutton1, 'Value');
index2 = get(handles.radiobutton2, 'Value');
index3 = get(handles.radiobutton3, 'Value');
index4 = get(handles.radiobutton4, 'Value');
if index1==1
   c=a+b;
else if index2==1
      c=a-b;
   else if index3==1
         c=a*b;
      else if index4==1
            c=a/b;
         end
      end
   end
end
set(handles.text3, 'String',c);



% --- Executes on button press in radiobutton1.
function radiobutton1_Callback(hObject, eventdata, handles)
% hObject    handle to radiobutton1 (see GCBO)
% eventdata  reserved - to be defined in a future version of MATLAB
% handles    structure with handles and user data (see GUIDATA)

% Hint: get(hObject,'Value') returns toggle state of radiobutton1
set(handles.radiobutton1, 'Value', 1);
set(handles.radiobutton2, 'Value', 0);
set(handles.radiobutton3, 'Value', 0);
set(handles.radiobutton4, 'Value', 0);
set(handles.text1, 'String', '+');

% --- Executes on button press in radiobutton2.
function radiobutton2_Callback(hObject, eventdata, handles)
% hObject    handle to radiobutton2 (see GCBO)
% eventdata  reserved - to be defined in a future version of MATLAB
% handles    structure with handles and user data (see GUIDATA)

% Hint: get(hObject,'Value') returns toggle state of radiobutton2
set(handles.radiobutton1, 'Value', 0);
```

```
set(handles.radiobutton2, 'Value', 1);
set(handles.radiobutton3, 'Value', 0);
set(handles.radiobutton4, 'Value', 0);
set(handles.text1, 'String', '-');


% --- Executes on button press in radiobutton3.
function radiobutton3_Callback(hObject, eventdata, handles)
% hObject    handle to radiobutton3 (see GCBO)
% eventdata  reserved - to be defined in a future version of MATLAB
% handles    structure with handles and user data (see GUIDATA)

% Hint: get(hObject,'Value') returns toggle state of radiobutton3
set(handles.radiobutton1, 'Value', 0);
set(handles.radiobutton2, 'Value', 0);
set(handles.radiobutton3, 'Value', 1);
set(handles.radiobutton4, 'Value', 0);
set(handles.text1, 'String', 'x');


% --- Executes on button press in radiobutton4.
function radiobutton4_Callback(hObject, eventdata, handles)
% hObject    handle to radiobutton4 (see GCBO)
% eventdata  reserved - to be defined in a future version of MATLAB
% handles    structure with handles and user data (see GUIDATA)

% Hint: get(hObject,'Value') returns toggle state of radiobutton4
set(handles.radiobutton1, 'Value', 0);
set(handles.radiobutton2, 'Value', 0);
set(handles.radiobutton3, 'Value', 0);
set(handles.radiobutton4, 'Value', 1);
set(handles.text1, 'String', '/');


% --- Executes on slider movement.
function slider1_Callback(hObject, eventdata, handles)
% hObject    handle to slider1 (see GCBO)
% eventdata  reserved - to be defined in a future version of MATLAB
% handles    structure with handles and user data (see GUIDATA)

% Hints: get(hObject,'Value') returns position of slider
%        get(hObject,'Min') and get(hObject,'Max') to determine range of slider


% --- Executes during object creation, after setting all properties.
function slider1_CreateFcn(hObject, eventdata, handles)
```

```
% hObject    handle to slider1 (see GCBO)
% eventdata  reserved - to be defined in a future version of MATLAB
% handles    empty - handles not created until after all CreateFcns called

% Hint: slider controls usually have a light gray background.
if isequal(get(hObject,'BackgroundColor'), get(0,'defaultUicontrolBackgroundColor'))
   set(hObject,'BackgroundColor',[.9 .9 .9]);
end
```

17. References

Chapman, S. J. (2007). *MATLAB Programming for Engineers,* (4th), Thomson Learning, 049524449X

Littlefield, B. L. & Hanselman, D, C. (2004). *Mastering MATLAB 7,* (1st), Prentice Hall, 0131430181

Marchand, P. (2002). *Graphics and GUIs with MATLAB,* (3rd), Chapman & Hall, 1584883200

MathWorks, Inc. (2009). *MATLAB® Creating Graphical User Interfaces,* The MathWorks, Inc, Natick, MA 01760-2098, USA

McMahon, D. (2007). *MATLAB Demystified,* (1st), McGraw-Hill Publishing, 0071485511

Smith, S. T. (2006). *MATLAB Advanced GUI Development,* (1st), Dog Ear Publishing, 1598581813

3

Teaching practical engineering for freshman students using the RWTH – Mindstorms NXT toolbox for MATLAB

Alexander Behrens, Linus Atorf and Til Aach
Institute of Imaging & Computer Vision, RWTH Aachen University, 52056 Aachen Germany

1. Introduction

As a powerful programming and simulation tool, MATLAB®(The MathWorks, 1994) becomes more and more important in today's curricula of electrical engineering. Its intuitive way to map matrices and vector algebra from mathematical formulas to program algorithms allows an easy and fast introduction to programming basics, especially for beginners. Furthermore, the manifold functionalities of MATLAB enable the user to abstract and solve complex engineering tasks and mathematical problems, which become important when teaching core electrical engineering and computing concepts. Thus, MATLAB is often used as a valuable tool to develop demo applications and address real–world problems in freshman courses (Devens, 1999; Director et al., 1995). Many examples are given in the literature, such as introduction courses to digital signal processing (DSP) (Anderson et al., 1996; McClellan & Rosenthal, 2002; McClellan et al., 1997; 2002; Saint-Nom & Jacoby, 2005; Sturm & Gibson, 2005; Vicente et al., 2007), applied automatic controls (Narayanan, 2005), computer programming (Azemi & Pauley, 2008) as well as to graphical user interface (GUI) design (Lee et al., 2005). Since MATLAB is also widely used in industry for algorithm and simulation development, the acquisition of advanced programming skills in MATLAB becomes important in engineering education.

Besides the establishment of project–based laboratories using interactive software tools, many practical projects showed that robotics can be used in an efficient way to teach and motivate students (Azlan et al., 2007; Christensen et al., 2004; Cliburn, 2006; Dagdilelis et al., 2005; Klassner & Anderson, 2003; Lau et al., 2001; Maher et al., 2005; Michaud, 2007; Mota, 2007; Neilsen, 2006; Patterson-McNeill & Binkerd, 2001; Pomalaza-Raez & Groff, 2003; Sharad, 2007; Vallim et al., 2006; Williams, 2003; Ye et al., 2007). Thus, they overcome the problem of dropping motivation during traditional and more theoretical lectures of core electrical engineering and computing concepts. Studies showed that a pedagogical approach that places students in situations where they "feel like engineers" is likely to enhance student motivation best (Vallim et al., 2006).

Driven by both above teaching aspects, the combination of MATLAB and robots is used for a new first–semester learning module, established in 2007–2008 in the curriculum in Electrical Engineering and Information Technology at RWTH Aachen University, Aachen, Germany (Behrens & Aach, 2008; Behrens et al., 2008; 2010). In this laboratory for freshman students, termed "MATLAB meets LEGO Mindstorms", digital signal processing is combined with computer programming and problem–oriented engineering. It gives the students their first insights into practical methods and basic engineering concepts and helps them to apply their knowledge to other challenges later on in their studies. After only two months of lectures and seminars, the students participate in this mandatory full–time eight–day project. Working together in teams, the students enhance their first MATLAB programming skills and apply mathematical foundations, which are taught in the affiliated lecture "Mathematical Methods of Electrical Engineering". To avoid an exclusive focus on programming, real–world problems and practical tasks are emulated by using LEGO®Mindstorms®NXT robots (The LEGO Group, 2006c). Besides six mandatory exercises, the students are given time to create their own applications and to define creative robot tasks. The students collaborate in teams of two and four, and are involved in discussions and presentations. For a high student motivation and an increased learning effort during the project, good supervision and a simple and intuitive interface between MATLAB and the Mindstorms robots are essential to ensure fast prototyping and program development. Based on the objective to teach MATLAB fundamentals to beginners and to realize innovative robot applications in a short period of time, the MATLAB $\leftrightarrow$ robot interface must also provide high usability and a well structured documentation. Therefore the new "RWTH – Mindstorms NXT Toolbox" for MATLAB has been created and applied in the laboratory. Furthermore it is published as free and open source software (RWTH Aachen University, Germany, 2008), and accessible for third party projects.

1.1 Previous Work

In previous work, G. Gutt (2006) provided a first remote control MATLAB $\leftrightarrow$ Mindstorms interface, which uses additional communication software to establish a Bluetooth connection between MATLAB and Mindstorms NXT robots. Since the received Bluetooth packets are always buffered in files, this implementation does not provide a direct and intuitive computer–robot communication suitable for first–semester projects. Another implementation using Simulink®, complex simulation models, and advanced control engineering concepts was developed by T. Chikamasa (2006). This toolbox provides a simulation mode and produces embedded code, which does not allow the program code to be debugged step–wise. Also, it focuses on advanced control theory and requires an initial familiarity with Simulink, which can hardly be expected of freshman students.

Thus, no satisfying software interface between MATLAB and LEGO Mindstorms NXT fulfilling the requirements of a direct and powerful interface was available. Therefore the new RWTH – Mindstorms NXT Toolbox, which is fully integrated into the MATLAB environment and maps the complete functionality of the Mindstorms hardware to the user, was developed. After a period of only four months development time, the first toolbox release and the practical exercises used in the first semester term of the project "MATLAB meets LEGO Mindstorms" were finalized by a core team of eight supervisors in 2007. Since then the toolbox has been consequently improved and extended.

2. LEGO Mindstorms NXT

LEGO Mindstorms NXT is a low–cost and widely used toy robot kit. It is available as a commercial hardware package for private use, as well as an education set (The LEGO Group, 2007). The NXT education set includes a programmable NXT intelligent brick with an integrated USB and Bluetooth communication interface, four different types of sensors (touch, sound, light, and ultrasonic distance sensor), and three servo motors, as illustrated in Fig. 1.

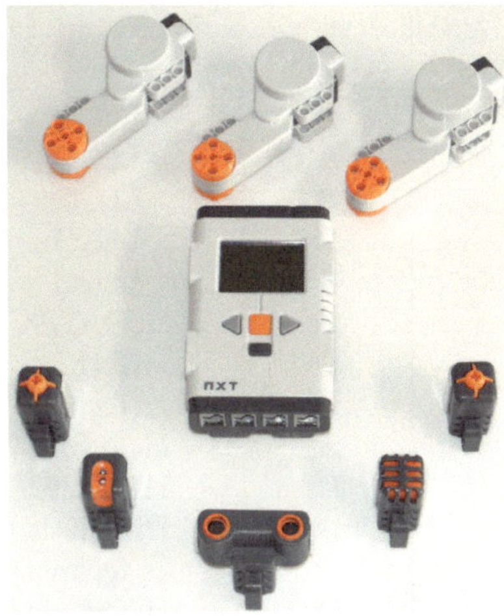

Fig. 1. LEGO Mindstorms NXT hardware of the standard education kit: Five sensors (light, sound, ultrasonic, and two touch sensors), three servo motors, and the programmable NXT intelligent brick.

Furthermore several different plastic LEGO bricks are provided for construction. The NXT brick contains an Atmel®32–bit ARM processor running at 48 MHz, 256 KB flash and 64 KB RAM memory. Its monochrome graphical LCD display has a resolution of 100×64 pixels. In total four sensor input ports supporting both a digital and analog interface, as well as three output ports for motors or lamps are available.

In addition to the sensors included in the standard Mindstorms kit, many other sensors are provided by third party vendors. HiTechnic (2001) offers a wide range of additional analog and digital NXT sensors, like e.g. compass, acceleration and infrared sensors. Supported by LEGO, the sensors are integrated in the common plastic shells and designed like the standard NXT sensors. Furthermore CODATEX (2007) distributes an RFID sensor and individual ID–tag transponders. Mindsensors.com (2005) offers advanced sensor kits and controller interfaces for Mindstorms, which are not encapsulated as HiTechnic sensors. In Table 1 a short overview of the most common NXT sensors is given.

Beyond the variety of commercially available sensors, LEGO provides a hardware developer kit specification (The LEGO Group, 2006b, Hardware Developer Kit) which can be used for individual sensor development. Examples of customized sensors are given by Gasperi et al. (2007).

2.1 NXT Programming Languages

To control LEGO Mindstorms NXT robots, a wide range of programming interfaces is available in the literature. These include compiler–based programming languages (C, C++, Java, .NET), interpreted languages (MATLAB, Python, Perl), as well as graphically oriented tools and simulation software (LabVIEW, RoboLab, Simulink). Despite the high variety of available packages, all programming concepts can mainly be categorized by two properties. The first one is determined by the type of program execution.

Embedded code: In this scenario, programs are usually developed on a computer using a programming development software first, e.g. NXT–G (National Instruments Corporation,

Sensor	Analog/ Digital	Vendor	Toolbox support (v4.03)
Touch	A	LEGO	yes
Light	A	LEGO	yes
Sound	A	LEGO	yes
Ultrasonic	D	LEGO	yes
Color	A	LEGO	no
RFID	D	CODATEX	yes
Compass	D	HiTechnic	yes
Accelerometer	D	HiTechnic	yes
Gyro	A	HiTechnic	yes
Color	D	HiTechnic	yes
Color V2	D	HiTechnic	no
IRSeeker	D	HiTechnic	yes
IRSeeker V2	D	HiTechnic	no
EOPD	D	HiTechnic	no
IRLink	D	HiTechnic	no
IRReceiver	D	HiTechnic	no
NXTCam	D	mindsensors.com	no
Sony PlayStation Controller	D	mindsensors.com	no

Table 1. Overview of most common LEGO Mindstorms NXT sensors.

2006), NXC (Hanson, 2006), ROBOTC (Robotics Academy, 2006), leJOS (Solorzano, 2007), and then translated into NXT bytecode. After downloading the code onto the NXT, no external computer is required anymore. The program code is always executed on the NXT hardware platform.

The NXT's firmware usually provides a virtual machine and executes bytecode while taking care of low–level hardware functionality. In some cases, the embedded program code can also be plain text and is executed by an interpreter, e.g. pbLua (Hempel, 2007). Due to direct hardware access to sensors and motors with minimal latency, real–time applications are possible. On the other hand, the program complexity is restricted by the limited resources of the NXT, such as memory, CPU speed, and display resolution.

Remote control: Programs using a remote control concept typically run on a computer or other host devices, e.g. a mobile phone. Commands specified in the LEGO Mindstorms NXT communication protocol (The LEGO Group, 2006a, Bluetooth Developer Kit) are sent to the NXT via Bluetooth or USB connections. These commands are then interpreted and executed by the firmware. In a similar way sensor and motor data can be retrieved. Since the actual robot control programs do not run on the NXT platform, they can utilize all resources, devices and technologies of their host systems. However, they are limited by the set of available remote commands and by the transfer time delay, which often impedes the realization of true real–time applications.

The second way to categorize Mindstorms interfaces is specified by the required NXT firmware. While some implementations are adapted to the original LEGO NXT firmware, other programming languages need a specific or customized firmware on the NXT for program execution.

NXT firmware: The standard configuration of the NXT includes the LEGO Mindstorms NXT firmware, maintained as open source code by LEGO. Its main purpose is to execute bytecode generated by LEGO's standard programming language, NXT–G. This firmware also supports the NXT communication protocol to execute so–called direct commands, remotely sent by other devices or computers.

Besides the official LEGO release, some firmware modifications are available, keeping full compatibility to compiled NXT–G binaries and to direct commands. The most prominent example is John Hansen's enhanced firmware, which fixes known bugs and adds advanced functionality. It comes with the Bricx Command Center (Hanson, 2002) development environment for the programming language NXC (Hanson, 2006).

Custom firmware: In the literature a variety of custom firmware versions is available. Some are based on the original release by LEGO, whereas others provide alternative firmware implementations. The custom firmware usually provides a virtual machine that can execute bytecode or plain text for a certain programming language. Prominent examples are leJOS (Solorzano, 2007) for Java programs, the Lua interpreter pbLua (Hempel, 2007), NXTalk (HPI Software Architecture Group, 2006) as a Smalltalk implementation, and ECRobot (Embedded Coder Robot) for Simulink (Chikamasa, 2006).

Another purpose of custom firmware is the execution of machine code directly on the ARM CPU, or the integration of specialized programs straight into the firmware. One implementation providing such capabilities is given by nxtOSEK (Chikamasa, 2007). Other efforts provide toolchains or compilers for custom firmware development, such as NXTGCC (Pedersen, 2006) or the IAR Embedded Workbench (IAR SYSTEMS, 2009) for LEGO Mindstorms NXT.

The most common interfaces are listed in Table 2. Note that the list is not exhaustive at all.

Name	Language Type	Standard Firmware	Embedded/ Remote
leJOS NXJ	Java	no	embedded
iCommand	Java	no	remote
NXC	C–like	yes	embedded
ROBOTC	C–like	no	embedded
NXT++	C++	yes	remote
Mindsqualls	.NET	yes	remote
MS Robotics Studio	.NET	yes	remote
NXT_Python	Python	yes	remote
LEGO::NXT	Perl	yes	remote
NXT-G	LabVIEW–like	yes	embedded
RoboLab	LabVIEW–like	no	embedded
ECRobot	Simulink	no	embedded
RWTH – Mindstorms NXT Toolbox	MATLAB	yes	remote

Table 2. Most common programming languages for LEGO Mindstorms NXT.

3. RWTH – Mindstorms NXT Toolbox for MATLAB

Since the target audience of the RWTH – Mindstorms NXT Toolbox for MATLAB are freshman students without any or only basic programming skills, the main objective of the toolbox is a direct and intuitive usability of the control interface. Beginners must be enabled to start with simple high–level commands to obtain results rapidly, while intermediate users can use more advanced functions. Using MATLAB as development tool, essential key features such as easy visual debugging by step–by–step execution, 2D and 3D plotting capabilities, a GUI designer, and additional toolboxes are directly provided. Furthermore advanced algorithms and technologies, as well as external hardware such as webcams can easily be integrated into individual robotic projects. However, an intuitive and consistent development environment will only be preserved, if the algorithms are entirely developed in MATLAB code. Thus, the usage of additional third–party software is avoided. As an exception, external USB and Bluetooth hardware drivers are used.

In addition to good usability, a well–written documentation is essential, especially for beginners. Apart from a list of functions and appropriate descriptions, genuine algorithmic examples are provided. Tutorials and step–by–step guides integrated in the toolbox help students to get started and extend their knowledge. Since software which is compatible to different operation systems can easily be distributed in bigger education projects, the framework is designed in MATLAB to run on Windows, Mac OS, and on Linux platforms. Furthermore low–level implementation details for hardware interaction (such as certain drivers or external libraries) are masked by a universal abstraction layer. Thus, the users are able to utilize both Bluetooth and USB connections to the NXT promptly without making any modifications to their program code.

Using the original LEGO NXT firmware the toolbox functionality is mainly limited to the MATLAB $\leftrightarrow$ NXT communication specified by the Mindstorms communication protocol. However, the usage of the original firmware allows a lower toolbox development effort, and a less complex initialization procedure, since the NXT does not have to be flashed again with a custom firmware.

3.1 Software Design

The RWTH – Mindstorms NXT Toolbox is a framework to control NXT robots remotely. Since MATLAB is an interpreted language, the use of embedded code is omitted. This is obvious, because the development of a full MATLAB runtime and a virtual machine or interpreter for the NXT platform with only 256 KB of available flash memory and 64 KB RAM is unfeasible. Thus, the user program is executed by the host computer, which highly outperforms the NXT's computational resources, especially regarding CPU speed. However, the characteristics of the established communication channel between NXT and computer, i.e. limited bandwidth and time delay, impede real–time control loops for wireless robots. Also, the complete functionality of the NXT is not immediately available via the specified remote commands. But aside from this technical point of view, the remote concept still combines a powerful programming environment with an adequate way for beginners to control robots, analyze data, and get results very quickly.

Based on this concept 117 MATLAB functions are provided by the toolbox (version 4.03), organized in a multi–layer software architecture. A global overview of these command layers and the hardware interaction is shown in Fig. 2.

Using individual motor and sensor settings, high–level functions and control loops are available within the third and fourth command layer. Relying on low–level functions, direct com-

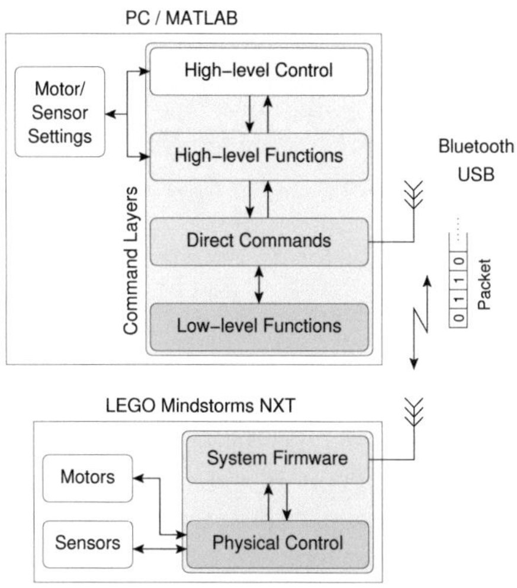

Fig. 2. Overview of the communication between MATLAB and NXT hardware using a multi–layer architecture.

Length, LSB	Length, MSB	Command Type	Command	Byte 5	Byte 6	...

Fig. 3. Structure of a valid Bluetooth packet, defined by LEGO's NXT Bluetooth communication protocol. For a USB communication the first two bytes describing the length of the data packet are omitted.

mands are transmitted via the USB and the wireless Bluetooth communication channel. Each of these commands is specified in the packet–based NXT communication protocol and consists of exactly one data packet. Optional reply packets can be requested for each command. The packet structure is illustrated in Fig. 3.

In the case of transmission via Bluetooth the first two bytes determine the total length of the packet. The command type specifies which category the command is from and whether the NXT should send a reply packet or not. The next byte defines the individual command. What follows is payload and depends on the command. When a command packet is received by the NXT brick, the firmware interprets the content and acts accordingly, e.g. by controlling motors or sensors.

From the technical point of view, the interface of the PC Bluetooth hardware (e.g. a Bluetooth USB stick) is based on the serial port profile (SPP), which uses the radio frequency communication (RFCOMM) protocol and emulates serial ports. Hence, the whole Bluetooth communication is carried out via virtual serial ports. Those are called COM ports in Windows, or can found in the device folders /dev/rfcomm on Linux and /dev/tty on Mac OS, respectively. For data exchange via USB, no additional computer hardware is required, except a USB cable and a free USB port. When the NXT is connected to a Windows or Mac OS machine, the direct commands exchange data with the NXT USB driver "Fantom" (DLL–library and system driver). Since LEGO does not offer any specific NXT USB driver for Linux, the open source library "libusb" (Erdfelt, 2008) is then loaded by the toolbox to handle the USB communication. Via USB connections, direct commands are typically executed within 3 ms (depending on host system specifications), including the time to receive a reply–package if requested. Using Bluetooth, a larger latency of about 30 ms is experienced every time the NXT has to switch from transmission to receive–mode and vice versa. Although a lag in the order of some seconds can be observed infrequently (depending on Bluetooth link quality and surrounding interference), the overall communication protocol can be considered reliable.

3.1.1 Command Layers

Table 3 shows a complete overview of the toolbox functions, categorized in different command layers.

Low–level Functions: The lowest layer consists mostly of private functions, which are not directly accessible by the user (i.e. most of them reside in the "private" directory of the toolbox directory structure). These functions include debug procedures, named constants, look–up operations, so–called MATLAB "prototype files" handling external libraries and drivers, as well as functions for binary packet management. Since many low–level functions are called frequently, optimization techniques like look–up tables and mex–files are used for maximal performance.

Direct NXT Commands: This layer provides the first usable front–end of the toolbox. According to the NXT communication protocol, packet–based commands are defined, which can be sent to the NXT via a USB or Bluetooth connection. The interface of these direct commands is implemented as close as possible to the protocol specifications to make it easy for other developers to extend or adapt the open source code. Abstract functions to handle the communication between NXT and computer — independent from the connection type and operating system — are integrated. In relation to the OSI reference model (Day & Zimmermann, 1983), these functions represent the presentation and application layers of the protocol stack.

High–Level Functions: To provide a more user–friendly interface than the direct NXT commands, high–level functions are established. Going far beyond the implementation of the communication protocol, certain feature and parameter combinations are hidden from the user to focus more on essential and robot–related problems. For example, instead of requiring knowledge about specific sensor settings, operation modes, and timeout periods in order to operate the NXT sensors, straightforward instructions are provided for simple actions such as "open sensor, retrieve data". Also complex I^2C command sequences, which are used with digital sensors, are combined into single functions. Possible exceptions are caught wherever possible, and if program execution cannot resume, meaningful error messages are generated. Furthermore main functions to establish and control the NXT $\leftrightarrow$ PC connection via Bluetooth or USB are provided. Some advanced functions are given to read or write complete sets of firmware registers (so-called I/O maps) at once.

High–Level Control and Utilities: Layer four mainly features an object–oriented interface to the NXT actors. The many variable motor options and complex parameter combinations are mapped to properties of the motor class in MATLAB. Functions with integrated control capability handle conditional tasks while interacting with the motors, e.g. pausing further program execution until the servo motor has rotated to a certain position, or helping a motor to reach a specific encoder target. To overcome limitations of the direct commands provided by the NXT firmware, optionally a customized and advanced motor control program with a higher precision control can be used, which runs embedded on the NXT.

Layer	*Description*	*Output/Motors*	*Input/Sensors*	*General*	*Bluetooth/USB*
4	**High-Level Control and Utilities**	**NXTMotor** .ReadFromNXT .SendToNXT .Stop .WaitFor .ResetPosition **NXC_MotorControl**		**OptimizeToolboxPerformance** **GUI_WatchMotorState** **GUI_WatchSensor** **ToolboxTest** **ToolboxBenchmark** **ToolboxUpdate**	**COM_MakeBTConfigFile**
3	**High-Level Functions**	**DirectMotor Command** **StopMotor** **SwitchLamp** NXC_ResetErrorCorrection	**OpenLight** **GetLight** **OpenSound** **GetSound** **OpenSwitch** **GetSwitch** **OpenUltrasonic** **GetUltrasonic** **USMakeSnapshot** **USGetSnapshotResults** **OpenAccelerator** **GetAccelerator** **OpenColor** **CalibrateColor** **GetColor** **OpenCompass** **CalibrateCompass** **GetCompass** **OpenGyro** **CalibrateGyro** **GetGyro** **OpenInfrared** **GetInfrared** **OpenRFID** **GetRFID** **CloseSensor**	**readFromIniFile** MAP_GetCommModule MAP_GetInputModule MAP_GetOutputModule MAP_GetSoundModule MAP_GetUIModule MAP_SetOutputModule NXC_GetSensorMotorData	**COM_OpenNXT** **COM_OpenNXTEx** **COM_CloseNXT** COM_ReadI2C **COM_SetDefaultNXT** **COM_GetDefaultNXT**
2	**Direct NXT Commands**	**NXT_SetOutputState** **NXT_GetOutputState** **NXT_ResetMotorPosition**	**NXT_SetInputMode** **NXT_GetInputValues** NXT_ResetInputScaledValues NXT_LSRead NXT_LSWrite NXT_LSGetStatus	**NXT_PlayTone** NXT_PlaySoundFile NXT_StopSoundPlayback NXT_StartProgram NXT_GetCurrentProgramName NXT_StopProgram NXT_SendKeepAlive NXT_GetBatteryLevel NXT_GetFirmwareVersion NXT_SetBrickName NXT_ReadIOMap NXT_WriteIOMap NXT_MessageWrite NXT_MessageRead	COM_CreatePacket COM_SendPacket COM_CollectPacket
1	**Low-Level Functions**	**MOTOR_A** **MOTOR_B** **MOTOR_C** *byte2outputmode* *byte2regmode* *byte2runstate* *outputmode2byte* *regmode2byte* *runstate2byte*	**SENSOR_1** **SENSOR_2** **SENSOR_3** **SENSOR_4** *byte2sensortype* *byte2sensormode* *sensortype2byte* *sensormode2byte* *waitUntilI2CReady*	**DebugMode** *isdebug* textOut *dec2wordbytes* *name2commandbyte* *commandbyte2name* *wordbytes2dec*	checkStatusByte *createHandleStruct* *checkHandleStruct* *getLibusbErrorString* *getVISAErrorString* *getReplyLengthFromCmdByte* *fantom_proto* *libusb_proto*

Table 3. Overview of the toolbox functions categorized in different command layers.
(NXT_* = NXT direct commands, COM_* = Functions related to the NXT communication, MAP_* Functions related to the NXT I/O maps, NXC_* = Functions which interact with the NXC program "MotorControl", **bold** = Main functions, *italic* = private functions)

In addition to the comfortable motor interface, several tools are offered in this layer: Utilities to monitor the current motor and sensor state, an assistant to create a Bluetooth configuration file, an update notifier, as well as various tools for benchmarking and integrity testing the toolbox.

3.1.2 Advanced Motor Control

When trying to control motors via direct commands (i.e. "NXT_SetOutputState"), two problems become apparent. First, the motors cannot be turned to a precise position, since they often overshoot (i.e. turn too far). This characteristic is caused by the motor control of the LEGO firmware. It only turns off the power to the motor when the desired encoder target (property "TachoLimit") is reached, leaving the motor spinning freely in coast mode. An automatic "braking" mode is not available. Instead, the LEGO firmware provides an automatic error correction mechanism to compensate cumulative error displacements. Unfortunately, due to large overshootings, this displacement correction can lead to unexpected results, which causes another difficulty. For example, the next direct motor command will be ignored by the firmware, if the current absolute motor position already exceeds the next target position. Both characteristics clearly impede an intuitive motor control.

Even though the internal error correction of the firmware can be deactivated by overwriting specific bytes in the firmware register using complex input/output map commands, a precise motor control which automatically turns the motor to a specific position is still not available. To overcome this problem, the advanced program "MotorControl" was developed. The program runs directly on the NXT to control the motors in real–time, without being slowed down by Bluetooth or USB latencies. It is programmed in NXC (Pedersen, 2006) and is downloaded on the NXT as a binary 32 KB large RXE file. During execution of MATLAB programs, "MotorControl" keeps running on the NXT as background process, and controls the motor movement in a control loop. The control parameters are specified via the motor class in MATLAB (toolbox function layer four), and then transmitted to the NXC program using a specified message-based communication protocol. Besides a motor position accuracy of ± 1 degree in most cases, smooth braking and acceleration modes, synchronized motor movements, monitored motor information, and a manual emergency stop (by pressing a button on the NXT brick) are supported. Further information about "MotorControl", its features and its communication protocol are given at `http://www.mindstorms.rwth-aachen.de/trac/wiki/MotorControl`. Since it is designed independently from the MATLAB environment, also other Mindstorms NXT remote control interfaces can adapt the concept and utilize "MotorControl" for their own projects.

3.2 Documentation and Toolbox Help

Besides an adequate program interface, a complete and easily accessible documentation of the toolbox functions and their features is very important for a high level of usability. Thus, the documentation of the RWTH – Mindstorms NXT Toolbox is fully integrated into the common MATLAB help browser, just like any other commercial MATLAB toolbox, as shown in Fig. 4. This is achieved by providing specially formatted XML help and content files.

From each m–file a HTML–formatted MATLAB help file is published using the *wg_publish* script (Garn, 2006). Since every major function is located in a separate m–file, the relevant information is extracted from the customized header format. The layout of the HTML pages is designed like the standard MATLAB text layout, using single cascading style sheets (CSS). Besides interface descriptions, the help content includes example code and see–also links.

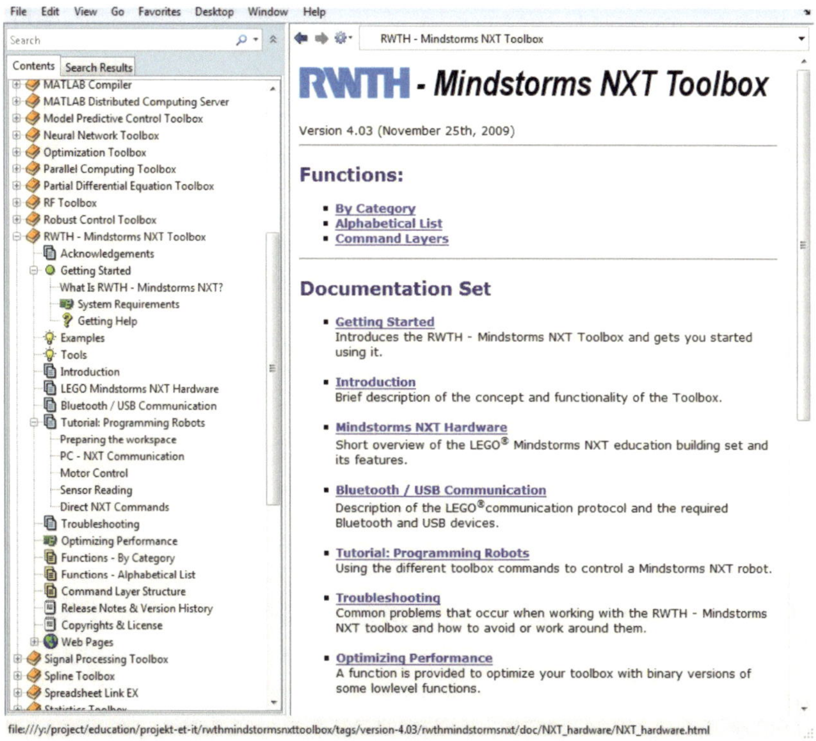

Fig. 4. Documentations and help text of the toolbox integrated in the MATLAB help browser.

Furthermore comprehensive tutorials, first–step demo programs and help pages for beginners are provided. In addition to the help browser support, the common MATLAB help command `help <function>` displays the function's help text in the command window.
Since the toolbox is published as an open source project, the complete source code is well and comprehensively commented so that other developers are able to extend and adapt the toolbox easily. The toolbox (v4.03) consists of more than 14.000 source lines in total. One third are comments, one third are help text, and the remaining third comprises executable code.

3.3 Version History

The first stable toolbox release 1.0 had been completed in December 2007 before the first "MATLAB meets LEGO Mindstorms" lab course started. It featured Bluetooth connections only and provided a basic motor control support via direct commands. Nevertheless the presented robot creations by students were truly impressive (Behrens et al., 2008; 2010).
The toolbox website was created in February 2008, and version 1.0 was made publicly available for download under the GNU General Public Licence (Free Software Foundation, 2007).
During summer 2008, USB connections and an improved communication layer were introduced with version 2.0. It enabled the construction of stationary robots with very fast response times. Also the possibility to connect to multiple NXT devices at the same time was another new feature.
Later in 2008, the first embedded NXC program was developed to offer precise motor rotations. Although the control mechanism often led to abrupt motor movements, the position

accuracy was highly improved. The interface to these new motor functions used the object–oriented paradigm for the first time. Additionally, more external sensors were supported. The resulting stable toolbox 2.03 was used during the student project in 2008.
In 2009, the focus was put on higher precision of the embedded motor control program. Smooth braking was achieved by introducing a custom control algorithm. Other improvements include further documentation, stability and performance issues. The version number has finally arrived at 4.03, which is the latest stable version recommended to be used as of May 2010.

3.4 System Requirements

In summary the RWTH – Mindstorms NXT Toolbox for MATLAB can be used on standard PC and NXT hardware. The system requirements of the current release version 4.03 are listed in Table. 4.

- Operating system: Windows, Linux, or Mac OS
- MATLAB Version 7.7 (R2008b) or higher
- LEGO Mindstorms NXT building kit (compatible with NXT 1.0 retail, NXT 2.0 retail, and NXT Education)
- LEGO Mindstorms NXT firmware v1.26 or higher, or compatible
- For Bluetooth connections: Bluetooth 2.0 adapter recommended model by LEGOő (e.g. AVM BlueFRITZ! USB) supporting the serial port profile (SPP)
- For USB connections: Official Mindstorms NXT Driver "Fantom", v1.02 or higher (Windows, Mac OS), "libusb" (Linux), 32–bit version of MATLAB

Table 4. System requirements of the RWTH – Mindstorms NXT Toolbox v4.03.

In the case of using an older MATLAB version such as 7.3 (R2006b), the NXT motors can be alternatively controlled via the classic motor control functions offered until toolbox release 2.04. For more information using individual system configurations, a version guide and changelogs are provided on the toolbox web page.

3.5 Example Code

A basic example program using high–level functions and direct commands is shown in Listing 1. The program first establishes a Bluetooth connection to the NXT, then plays a tone, gets the current battery level, and finally closes the connection again.

```
handle = COM_OpenNXT('bluetooth.ini'); % open a Bluetooth connection using
COM_SetDefaultNXT(handle);             % parameters from configuration file

NXT_PlayTone(800,500);                 % play tone with 800Hz for 500ms

voltage = NXT_GetBatteryLevel;         % get current battery level

COM_CloseNXT(handle);                  % close Bluetooth connection
```

Listing 1. Basic program example.

A comparison between high–level functions and direct commands for sensor reading is given in the next Listings 2 and 3. Both programs request the current raw 10–bit value of the NXT light sensor. In the case of using direct NXT commands (command layer two), data packets have to be requested and verified by the user program code until a valid packet is received from the sensor. This control mechanism is necessary, since the light sensor can still be busy in its initialization step. A control loop, which requests packets every 300 ms in the case of an invalid data is shown in Listing 2.

```
% initialize the sensor
NXT_SetInputMode(SENSOR_1, 'LIGHT_ACTIVE', 'RAWMODE', 'dontreply');

data = NXT_GetInputValues(SENSOR_1); % get light sensor value

if ~data.Valid              % check valid flag, re-request data if necessary
    startTime = clock();    % initialize timeout counter
    timeout   = 0.3;        % set time out to 300 ms

    while (~data.Valid) && (etime(clock, startTime) < timeout)
        data = NXT_GetInputValues(SENSOR_1); % re-request until valid/timeout
    end
end

light = double(data.NormalizedADVal); % use normalized light value (10 bit)
```

Listing 2. Program reads the current value of the light sensor using direct NXT commands.

Using high–level functions from command layer three, the control loop in Listing 2 is hidden from the user to provide a better usability for sensor reading. Thus, the whole program simplifies to only two commands, as shown in Listing 3.

```
OpenLight(SENSOR_1, 'active'); % initialize light sensor

light = GetLight(SENSOR_1);    % get light sensor value
```

Listing 3. Reprogramming of the program code in Listing 2 using high–level functions.

In addition to the high–level features, the RWTH – Mindstorms NXT Toolbox provides applications for motor and sensor data monitoring. Since e.g. the initialization of parameter settings, sensor tests, or calibration processes are often necessary for the development of individual control algorithms, the users are able to test and measure sensor characteristics, as illustrated in Fig. 5.
An example of using objects of the NXTMotor class (command layer four) to control the NXT servo motors in MATLAB is shown in the next two listings. First, several motor objects for

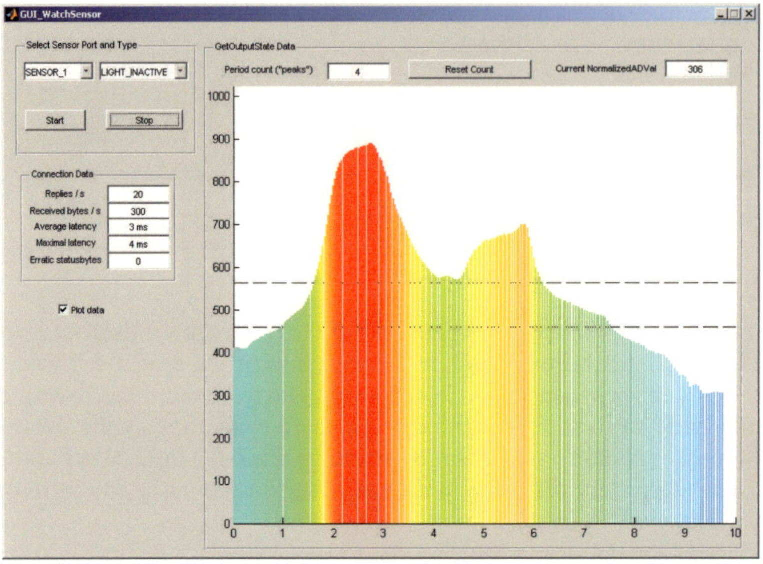

Fig. 5. The "Watch Sensor GUI" provides a comfortabke data monitoring tool for several NXT sensors.

different robot movements are created in Listing 4. Based on these objects, an algorithm of an explorer robot which drives an eight–shaped loop on the floor becomes structured and very simplified, as shown in Listing 5.

```
leftWheel     = MOTOR_B; % set parameters
rightWheel    = MOTOR_C;
bothWheels    = [leftWheel; rightWheel];
drivingPower = 60;       % in percent
turningPower = 40;       % in percent
drivingDist  = 1500;     % in degrees
turningDist  = 220;      % in degrees

% create objects for drive forward:
mForward = NXTMotor(bothWheels, 'Power', drivingPower, 'TachoLimit',
    drivingDist);

% create object for turning the bot left:
mTurnLeft1 = NXTMotor(leftWheel,  'Power', -turningPower, 'TachoLimit',
    turningDist);
mTurnLeft2 = NXTMotor(rightWheel, 'Power',  turningPower, 'TachoLimit',
    turningDist);

% create object for turning the bot right:
mTurnRight1      = mTurnLeft1;            % copy objects
mTurnRight2      = mTurnLeft2;
mTurnRight1.Port = rightWheel;            % swap wheels
mTurnRight2.Port = leftWheel;
```

Listing 4. Initialization of motor objects for different robot movements.

```
for n=1:1:8
  mForward.SendToNXT();                     % drive forward
  mForward.WaitFor();

  if (n < 4) || (n == 8)
    mTurnLeft1.SendToNXT();                 % make left-turn
    mTurnLeft1.WaitFor();
    mTurnLeft2.SendToNXT();
    mTurnLeft2.WaitFor();
  else
    mTurnRight1.SendToNXT();                % make right-turn
    mTurnRight1.WaitFor();
    mTurnRight2.SendToNXT();
    mTurnRight2.WaitFor();                  % resulting route    _
  end                                       % of the robot:     |_|
end                                         %                   |_|
```

Listing 5. Program code of an explorer robot driving an eight–shaped loop.

4. Software Project Management

To maintain the current and previous versions of the RWTH – Mindstorms NXT Toolbox, the revision control system Subversion® (The Apache Software Foundation, 2000) is used. Thus, changes and developments of each single file of the toolbox can be easily controlled. Furthermore merging of new program code contributed by different programmers becomes structured and traceable. In addition to the revision control of source code, the toolbox is administrated using the web–based project management tool Trac (Edgewall Software, 2003). It provides a wiki, an issue tracking system for bug reports, a user administration, and a road map schedule for project management.
Using an individual layout the RWTH – Mindstorms NXT Toolbox is published as an open source software on the web page `http://www.mindstorms.rwth-aachen.de` (see Fig. 6).

5. Educational Projects, Evaluations and Results

5.1 Freshmen Project "MATLAB meets LEGO Mindstorms"

The development of the RWTH – Mindstorms NXT Toolbox for MATLAB was motivated by the establishment of a new laboratory "MATLAB meets LEGO Mindstorms" for freshman students at the RWTH Aachen University, Aachen, Germany. Started in winter term 2007, the project has become an annual mandatory project for each first–semester Bachelor student of electrical engineering. Within this eight–day full–time course three objectives are addressed. First, mathematical foundations are mapped to MATLAB program code. Based on this, more complex tasks and algorithms are then described within the MATLAB environment. Going beyond simulations, real applications are performed by LEGO Mindstorms NXT robots, which are designed and constructed by the students themselves.
While many other robotic education projects are designed for senior students, this project is intentionally established for freshman students. Each winter term almost 400 students participate in the laboratory and are guided by more then 80 supervisors simultaneously. Using about 200 robot kits, students grouped into teams of two are distributed over 23 institutes of the Electrical Engineering Department. The project tasks are separated into three working

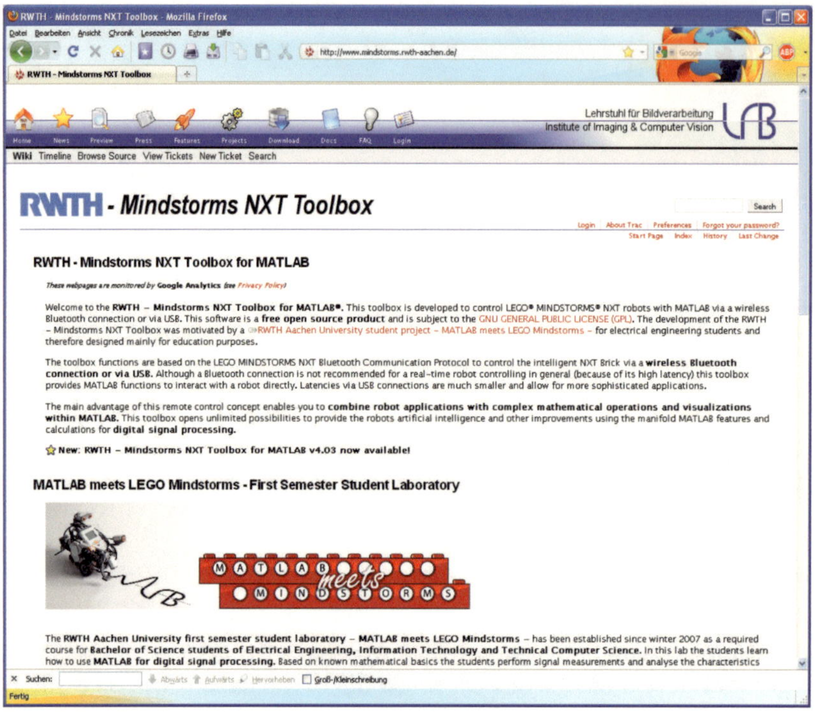

Fig. 6. Web page of the RWTH – Mindstorms NXT Toolbox.

steps. First, each student team has to work on basic exercises to get familiar with the Mindstorms NXT hardware and to foster their MATLAB skills. In the second part, two student teams work together on individual tasks and develop a own robot. At the end the students present their work in a 15 minute presentation.

Basic Exercises: During the first five project days the students perform six mandatory exercises which address basic MATLAB functions like loops, if–conditions, GUIs, timer objects, the RWTH – Mindstorms NXT Toolbox functionality and its interaction with the NXT hardware, as well as the characteristics of the different Mindstorms sensors (touch, sound, light, ultrasonic) and the NXT motors. Furthermore, MATLAB features and programming principles combined with mathematical fundamentals are introduced in a practical and demonstrative way.

For example, one exercise focuses on programming structures like loops, if–conditions and arrays. Here the students implement a traffic light control system using LEGO lamps and the NXT sound sensor. Depending on the number of detected handclaps, the lamps are switched on and off. The values of the sound sensor are continuously read and filtered by applying a moving window to the data stream. This provides a value of how many claps occurred during the last 15 samples for each time instance. The different states of the traffic lights can then be determined by thresholding the filtered data stream. An abstract of the program code is given in Listing 6.

```
function detectClaps()
  h = COM_OpenNXT();                  % open connection to NXT
  COM_SetDefaultNXT(h);

  OpenSound(SENSOR_1, 'DB');          % initialize sound sensor
  SwitchLamp(MOTOR_A, 'off');         % turn off lamp

  values = zeros(15, 1);              % initialize slinding window

  for n = 1:1:500
    s = GetSound(SENSOR_1);           % get current sound value
    values = [values(2:end); s];      % fill sliding data vector
    pause(0.01);                      % delay reading to be able to detect
  end                                 % hand claps within 15 data samples

  % ... analyze data samples ...

  COM_CloseNXT(h);                    % close connection to NXT
end
```

Listing 6. Abstract of the `detectClaps` function to control lamps based on a handclap detection.

Individual Tasks: In the second part of the project the students are given room to become more creative and are free to develop their own ideas and innovative robot applications. In the case of a lack of creativity, the students can start from three optional pre–documented tasks. However, in winter term 2010 81% of the students created their own robots. One of these inventions is given by a stationary crane with two degrees of freedom and a grabber mounted to the end of its arm, as shown in Fig. 7.

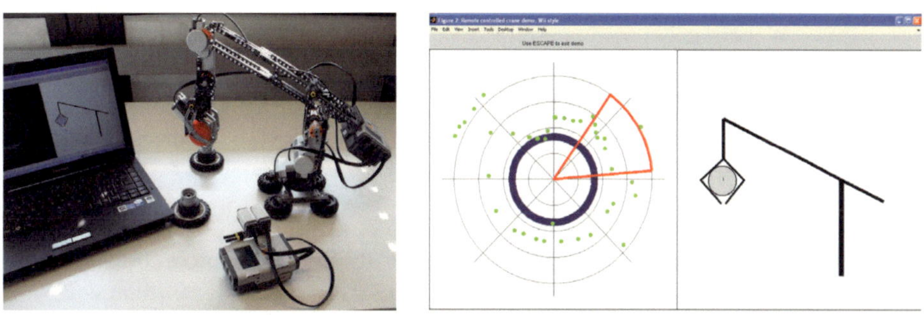

Fig. 7. Left: Robotic crane grabs balls. Based on acceleration measurements it is remotely controlled by tilting a second NXT interface. Right: GUI shows distances (green dots) between robot and single objects on the table using an ultrasonic sensor. Its field of view is highlighted in red. The distances are plotted in a 360° compass diagram (left). Side view of the current arm position (right).

It utilizes a light sensor to detect whether an object was picked up (and to distinguish between different colors) as well as an ultrasonic sensor to locate objects in its vicinity. The crane is controlled wirelessly via Bluetooth. A second NXT brick, connected via a USB cable, is used as a remote control. It contains a touch sensor to detect pressed keys and an acceleration sensor which is used to detect roll and pitch motions by exploiting gravity. Thus the user can tilt the remote to adjust the crane's position. The touch sensor is used to open and close the grabber. A MATLAB GUI displays the robot's current orientation and status on the computer monitor.

In the following listings an abstract of the program code is presented. At first the program connects the PC to the NXT devices, as described in Listing 7.

```
% connect 1. NXT (robo crane) via Bluetooth / 2. NXT (remote control) via USB
hCrane  = COM_OpenNXTEx('Bluetooth', '', 'bluetooth.ini');
hRemote = COM_OpenNXTEx('USB', '');
```

Listing 7. Establishment of the PC ↔ NXT connections.

Then the NXT sensors are initialized and the motor objects for the basic movements are created (Listing 8).

```
portLight  = SENSOR_1;          % set up ports (crane)
portUS     = SENSOR_4;
portSwitch = SENSOR_1;          % set up ports (remote control)
portAccel  = SENSOR_4;

OpenLight(portLight, 'active', hCrane);    % initialize sensors
OpenUltrasonic(portUS,         hCrane);
OpenSwitch(portSwitch,      hRemote);
OpenAccelerator(portAccel, hRemote);

% set up motor objects for basic crane movement
mTurn = NXTMotor('A', 'TachoLimit', 0, 'SpeedRegulation', false);
mLift = NXTMotor('B', 'TachoLimit', 0, 'SpeedRegulation', false);

% set up motor objects for grabber control
mOpenGrabber  = NXTMotor('C', 'Power',  GRABBER_POWER, 'TachoLimit',
    GRABBER_ANGLE);
mCloseGrabber = NXTMotor('C', 'Power', -GRABBER_POWER, 'TachoLimit',
    GRABBER_ANGLE);
mCloseGrabber.SpeedRegulation = false;
```

Listing 8. Initialization of the NXT sensors and creation of the NXT motor objects for basic movements.

In a further calibration process, the crane moves to its default start position. Then the main control loop is executed. Sensor data is read continuously from the remote control, and motor commands are sent to the crane to update and control its movement. Simultaneously, information about the ultrasonic sensor and the motors are retrieved from the crane and displayed in the MATLAB GUI for monitoring. Listing 9 shows the code abstract of the main control loop.

```
acce          = GetAccelerator(portAccel, hRemote); % acce is a 1x3-vector
buttonPressed = GetSwitch(portSwitch, hRemote);

if buttonPressed                    % handle touch sensor interaction
  if grabberIsOpen
    mCloseGrabber.SendToNXT(hCrane);
  else
    mOpenGrabber.SendToNXT(hCrane);
  end
  grabberIsOpen = ~grabberIsOpen;
end

yAbs = abs(acce(2));                % determine displacement in y-direction
if yAbs >= minAccelVal              % consider minimal tilt of remote control
  yAbs = min(yAbs, maxAccelVal);    % clip too high values

  mTurn.Power = ((yAbs-minAccelVal) / maxAccelVal) * 100 * (sign(acce(2)));
  mTurn.SendToNXT(hCrane);          % calc new power (linear interpolation)
else                                % for horizontal movement
  mTurn.Stop('off');
end

% ... similar code for vertical movement ...

tmp = mTurn.ReadFromNXT(hCrane); % read current motor rotation angle
curPos = rem(-tmp.Position / gearFactor + 90, 360); % calc crane position
phi = curPos * pi / 180;            % calc rotation angle of crane in radians

distUS = GetUltrasonic(portUS, hCrane);   % read ultrasonic sensor
if distUS < 1                             % if vision is free
    distUS = 255;                         % assume max. distance in cm
end

[u, v] = pol2cart(phi, distUS);    % update graphics
compass(u, v);
drawnow;
```

Listing 9. Code abstract of the crane's main control loop.

The example shows that complex tasks and even advanced multi–NXT applications can easily be structured and designed by the students using the RWTH – Mindstorms NXT Toolbox.

Presentation: On the last project day, the students present results and demonstrate their individual applications during a 15–minute presentations. Furthermore many descriptions, pictures, and videos of the robots and their characteristics are presented as blogs on the project web page `http://www.lfb.rwth-aachen.de/mindstorms`, and the video portal `www.youtube.com`.

After the student laboratory, an anonymous and voluntary online evaluation is carried out. Up to 38 questions about the general project concepts, specific exercises, and personally achieved improvements are answered. The summarized evaluation results of the last three semester terms are shown in Fig. 9. From the students' point of view, the results show that the course and the established toolbox have achieved the goal of introducing MATLAB as a software to solve real–world problems. Every year, on average 49% of the students rate their improvement in MATLAB programming skills as "excellent" and 42% as "good" after the project.

Fig. 8. Robot descriptions on the project web page (left). Videos of the student projects (right).

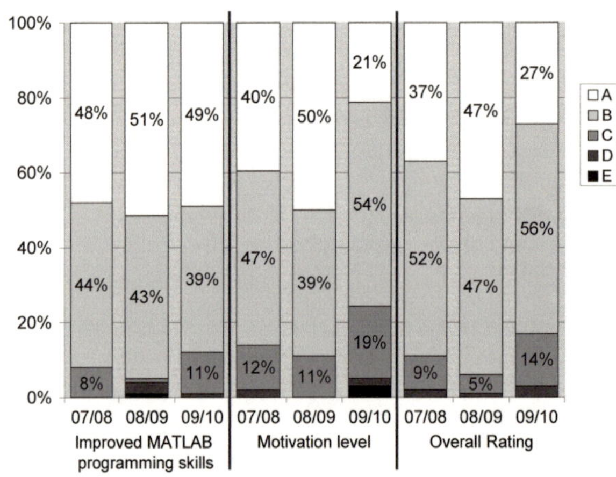

Fig. 9. Evaluation results of the last three project terms based on an anonymous student online evaluation (A: excellent, B: good, C: average,D: below average, E: inadequate).

Even though these results are based on the students' own subjective self–assessment, they agree well with the skills objectively required to pass the project, such as the ability to develop and program one's own individual robot, based on MATLAB programs using the RWTH – Mindstorms NXT Toolbox. Also the motivation level and overall ratings show that the project augments student motivation and helps the students to develop their programming skills. Furthermore, each year about 47% of the students say they would use MATLAB for future programming tasks. More evaluation results and further descriptions of the project and its educational objectives can be found in Behrens et al. (2010).

5.2 Other Education Projects

Besides the "MATLAB meets LEGO Mindstorms" course, other universities and schools are encouraged to introduce the toolbox into their own practical robotics courses.

One example is given by the "Fundamentals of Engineering Design Course" for Biomedical Engineers at the New Jersey Institute of Technology, Newark, USA (Parameswaran et al., 2009). In this three–hour semester long project about 60 students solve robotic surgery tasks

with the RWTH – Mindstorms NXT Toolbox for MATLAB and a modeling software. Various MATLAB projects, like a basketball and football shooting robot, or a gymnast robot are developed by students in the biomechanics project at the Locomotion laboratory at Friedrich Schiller University of Jena, Germany (Seyfarth, 2009). Inspired by the objectives and structure of the "MATLAB meets LEGO Mindstorms" project, a similar student laboratory called "Robotics with MATLAB and LEGO NXT" is established at the Villanova University, Villanova, USA (Konyk & Nersesov, 2010). At the Department of Automatic Control, Lund Institute of Technology, Lund, Sweden a student project in automatic control is given during the second study period (Akesson, 2009). Addressing a control engineering topic, the RWTH – Mindstorms NXT Toolbox is introduced in a control systems course at School of Information Technology and Engineering, University of Ottawa, Ottawa, Canada (Habash, 2008). Another first semester project is conducted by freshman students of the cybernetic engineering course at the Otto-von-Guericke University Magdeburg, Magdeburg, Germany. Currently, also the University of Cambridge, Cambridge, United Kingdom, is establishing a new student lab for engineering undergraduates (Gee, 2010), using the toolbox and about 130 NXT robotic kits.
Besides student courses and laboratories, the RWTH – Mindstorms NXT Toolbox is also used in final projects and theses. Examples are given by the gesture controlled robot at the Department of Electrical and Computer Engineering, University of Illinois, Chicago, USA (Mahajan, 2009), and the "Technical Lego Robot Entertainment Device" developed at the Faculty of Engineering and Computing, Coventry University, Coventry, United Kingdom (Ischebeck, 2008).
Since this list of examples is not exhaustive, many more are given on the toolbox web page `http://www.mindstorms.rwth-aachen.de`.

5.3 The MathWorks Support

After the first release of the RWTH – Mindstorms NXT Toolbox was official published in 2008, The MathWorks also offered free code to control LEGO Mindstorms NXT robots remotely via Bluetooth. In a similar way the NXT interface was designed using sensor and motor objects. However, only the direct commands of the NXT communication protocol were implemented. Because of less functionality than the RWTH – Mindstorms NXT Toolbox, which is also freely available at MATLAB Central File Exchange (The MathWorks, 2008b), The MathWorks decided in 2010 to withdraw their code and officially feature and promote the RWTH – Mindstorms NXT Toolbox on their Academia web pages (The MathWorks, 2008a). Furthermore The MathWorks promotes the toolbox and the "MATLAB meets LEGO Mindstorms" freshman course in their MATLAB Digest Academic Journal (Behrens & Aach, 2008), and awards the best student group of the project with the "MATLAB Team Award" since 2009.

6. Conclusion

The development of the RWTH – Mindstorms NXT Toolbox showed that the MATLAB environment is feasible to design complex libraries and educational applications from scratch, and generate exhaustive and professional documentation in a very short development time. Providing an intuitive interface to external devices such as LEGO Mindstorms NXT robots, even total MATLAB beginners become quickly familiar in programming and are able to develop their own complex programs in relatively short practical courses.
The command layer design of the RWTH – Mindstorms NXT Toolbox with its high–level control functions enables the user to control NXT robotics easily and focus on the main course objectives, like efficient MATLAB programming, digital signal processing, control engineering,

biomechanics, or software design. Besides the evaluation results of the related student laboratory "MATLAB meets LEGO Mindstorms" at RWTH Aachen University, Aachen, Germany, many other educational projects for undergraduate students showed an easy and effective integration of the RWTH – Mindstorms NXT Toolbox in their MATLAB courses. Additionally, the implementation of the MATLAB toolbox published as free open source software at `http://www.mindstorms.rwth-aachen.de` provides a transparent and adapable computer–robot communication framework for MATLAB.

7. Acknowledgement

We would like to thank Robert Schwann, Bernd Neumann, Rainer Schitzler, Johannes Ballé, Thomas Herold, Aulis Telle, and Axel Cordes for the collaboration of designing the practical exercises of the "MATLAB meets LEGO Mindstorms" project, and the feedback and proposals for the toolbox development. Additionally we would like to thank Tobias G. Noll and Kay Hameyer for their fruitful input to this project.

8. References

Akesson, J. (2009). FRT090 Projects in Automatic Control, *Institute of Technology, Lund University, Lund, Sweden* .
URL: *http://www.control.lth.se/course/FRT090/*

Anderson, D., McClellan, J., Schafer, R., Schodorf, J. & Yoder, M. (1996). DSP First - A First Course in ECE, *Proc. 13th Asilomar Conference on Signals, Systems and Computers*, Vol. 1, pp. 226–230.

Azemi, A. & Pauley, L. (2008). Teaching the Introductory Computer Programming Course for Engineers Using Matlab, *38th Annual Frontiers in Education Conference (FIE)*, pp. T3B–1 –T3B–23.

Azlan, N., Zainudin, F., Yusuf, H., Toha, S., Yusoff, S. & Osman, N. (2007). Fuzzy Logic Controlled Miniature LEGO Robot for Undergraduate Training System, *Proc. 2nd IEEE Conf. on Industrial Electronics and Applications (ICIEA)*, pp. 2184–2188.

Behrens, A. & Aach, T. (2008). Freshman Engineers Build MATLAB Powered LEGO Robots, *MATLAB Digest | Academic Edition, The MathWorks* **2**(3): 1–4.

Behrens, A., Atorf, L., Schwann, R., Ballé, J., Herold, T. & Telle, A. (2008). First Steps into Practical Engineering for Freshman Students Using MATLAB and LEGO Mindstorms Robots, *Acta Polytechnica Journal of Advanced Engineering* **48**(3): 44–49.

Behrens, A., Atorf, L., Schwann, R., Neumann, B., Schnitzler, R., Balle, J., Herold, T., Telle, A., Noll, T. G., Hameyer, K. & Aach, T. (2010). MATLAB Meets LEGO Mindstorms – A Freshman Introduction Course Into Practical Engineering, *IEEE Transactions on Education* **53**(2): 306–317.

Chikamasa, T. (2006). Embedded Coder Robot NXT Demo.
URL: *http://www.mathworks.com/matlabcentral/fileexchange/*

Chikamasa, T. (2007). nxtOSEK.
URL: *http://lejos-osek.sourceforge.net/*

Christensen, M., Douglas, S., Wood, S., Kitts, C. & Mahler, T. (2004). The Infinity Project brings DSP brains to robots in the classroom, *Proc. 3rd IEEE Signal Process. Edu. Workshop*, pp. 88–91.

Cliburn, D. (2006). Experiences with the LEGO Mindstorms throughout the Undergraduate Computer Science Curriculum, *36th Annual Frontiers in Education Conference (FIE)*, pp. 1–6.

CODATEX (2007). CODATEX Hainzlmaier GmbH & Co.KG.
URL: *http://www.codatex.com*

Dagdilelis, V., Sartatzemi, M. & Kagani, K. (2005). Teaching (with) Robots in Secondary Schools: some new and not-so-new Pedagogical problems, *Proc. 5th IEEE Int. Conf. on Advanced Learning Technologies (ICALT)*, pp. 757–761.

Day, J. D. & Zimmermann, H. (1983). OSI Reference Model, *Proceedings of the IEEE* **71**(12): 1334–1340.

Devens, P. (1999). MATLAB & Freshman Engineering, *Proc. American Society for Engineering Education (ASEE), Annual Conference*.

Director, S., Khosla, P., Rohrer, R. & Rutenbar, R. (1995). Reengineering the Curriculum: Design and Analysis of a New Undergraduate Electrical and Computer Engineering Degree at Carnegie Mellon University, *Proceedings of the IEEE* **83**(9): 1246–1269.

Edgewall Software (2003). Trac - Integrated SCM & Project Managment.
URL: *http://trac.edgewall.org/*

Erdfelt, J. (2008). libusb.
URL: *http://www.libusb.org*

Free Software Foundation (2007). GNU General Public License.
URL: *http://www.gnu.org/licenses/licenses.html*

Garn, W. (2006). Generate help files from m-files.
URL: *http://www.mathworks.com/matlabcentral/fileexchange/9687-generate-help-files-from-m-files*

Gasperi, M., Hurbain, P. & Hurbain, I. (2007). *Extreme NXT - Extending the LEGO MINDSTORMS NXT to the Next Level*, Technology in Action Press.

Gee, A. (2010). Preparing for the Week 1 Lego Mindstorms Exercise, *University of Cambridge, Cambridge, United Kingdom* .
URL: *http://mi.eng.cam.ac.uk/~ahg/pre_lego/*

Gutt, G. (2006). Controlling NXT from MathWorks MATLAB.
URL: *http://nxtasy.org/2006/11/28/controlling-nxt-from-mathworks-matlab/*

Habash, R. (2008). ELG3150: Project (Matlab and Lego Mindstorms), *School of Information Technology and Engineering, University of Ottawa, Ottawa, Canada* .
URL: *http://www.site.uottawa.ca/ rhabash/ELG3150Project.htm*

Hanson, J. (2002). Bricx Command Center.
URL: *http://bricxcc.sourceforge.net*

Hanson, J. (2006). Not eXactly C.
URL: *http://bricxcc.sourceforge.net/nbc/*

Hempel, R. (2007). pbLua.
URL: *http://www.hempeldesigngroup.com/lego/pblua/*

HiTechnic (2001). HiTechnic Division Dataport Systems, Inc.
URL: *http://www.hitechnic.com*

HPI Software Architecture Group (2006). NXTalk.
URL: *http://www.hpi.uni-potsdam.de/hirschfeld/projects/nxtalk/index.html*

IAR SYSTEMS (2009). IAR Embedded Workbench.
URL: *http://www.iar.com/website1/1.0.1.0/1483/1/*

Ischebeck, C. (2008). Technical Lego Robot Entertainment Device, *Faculty of Engineering and Computing, Coventry University, United Kingdom* .

Klassner, F. & Anderson, S. (2003). LEGO MindStorms: Not Just for K-12 Anymore, *IEEE Robot. Automat. Mag.* **10**(2): 12–18.

Konyk, S. & Nersesov, S. (2010). Robotics with MATLAB and LEGO NXT, *Villanova University, Villanova, USA* .

Lau, P., McNamara, S., Rogers, C. & Portsmore, M. (2001). LEGO Robotics in Engineering, *Proc. American Society of Engineering Education (ASEE), Annual Conference.*

Lee, S.-H., Li, Y.-F. & Kapila, V. (2005). Development of a Matlab-Based Graphical User Interface Environment for PIC Microcontroller Projects, *Computers in Education Journal* **15**(3): 41–56.

Mahajan, R. (2009). Gesture controlled robot, *Department of Electrical and Computer Engineering, University of Illinois, Chicago, USA* .

Maher, R., Becker, J., Sharpe, T., Peterson, J. & Towle, B. (2005). Development and Implementation of a Robot-based Freshman Engineering Course, *Proc. American Society for Engineering Education (ASEE), Annual Conference.*

McClellan, J. & Rosenthal, J. (2002). Animating Theoretical Concepts for Signal Processing Courses, *Proc. American Society for Engineering Education (ASEE), Annual Conference.*

McClellan, J., Schafer, R. & Yoder, M. (1997). Experiences in Teaching DSP First in the ECE Curriculum, *Proc. 27th Frontiers in Education Conference (FIE)*, Vol. 2, pp. 891–895.

McClellan, J., Schafer, R. & Yoder, M. (2002). *Signal Processing First*, Prentice-Hall.

Michaud, F. (2007). Engineering Education and the Design of Intelligent Mobile Robots for Real Use, *Int. Journal of Intelligent Automation and Soft Computing* **13**(1): 19–28.

Mindsensors.com (2005).
URL: *http://www.mindsensors.com*

Mota, M. I. G. (2007). Work In Progress - Using Lego Mindstorms and Robolab as A Mean To Lowering Dropout and Failure Rate In Programming Course, *Proc. 37th Frontiers in Education Conference (FIE)*, pp. F4A1–2.

Narayanan, G. (2005). Select MATLAB commands used in Teaching Applied Automatic Controls, *American Society for Engineering Education (ASEE), Annual Conference.*

National Instruments Corporation (2006). NXT-G.
URL: *http://www.ni.com/academic/mindstorms/*

Neilsen, M. (2006). Research Experiences in Robotics, *Proc. Int. Conf. Society for Information Technology and Teacher Education*, Vol. 1, pp. 3914–3919.

Parameswaran, A., Khatri, A., Mantialla, B. & Redling, J. (2009). Fundamentals of Engineering Design Course for Biomedical Engineers, *New Jersey's Science & Technology University, Newark, USA* .
URL: *http://catalog.njit.edu/courses/#fed.phpfed101*

Patterson-McNeill, H. & Binkerd, C. L. (2001). Resources for Using LEGO Mindstorms, *J. of Computing Sci. in Colleges* **16**(3): 48–55.

Pedersen, R. U. (2006). NXTGCC.
URL: *http://nxtgcc.sourceforge.net/*

Pomalaza-Raez, C. & Groff, B. H. (2003). Retention 101: Where Robots Go... Students Follow, *Journal of Engineering Education* **92**(1).

Robotics Academy (2006). ROBOTC.
URL: *http://www.robotc.net/*

RWTH Aachen University, Germany (2008). RWTH - Mindstorms NXT Toolbox.
URL: *http://www.mindstorms.rwth-aachen.de*

Saint-Nom, R. & Jacoby, D. (2005). Building the first steps into SP Research, *Proc. IEEE Int. Conf. on Acoustics, Speech, and Signal Processing (ICASSP)*, Vol. 5, pp. 545–548.

Seyfarth, A. (2009). Locomotion Laboratory.
URL: *http://www.lauflabor.uni-jena.de/wiki/index.php/Matlab-Seite*

Sharad, S. (2007). Introducing Embedded Design Concepts to Freshmen and Sophomore Engineering Students with LEGO MINDSTORMS NXT, *IEEE Int. Conf. on Microelectronic Systems Education*, pp. 119–120.

Solorzano, J. (2007). leJOS.
URL: *http://lejos.sourceforge.net*

Sturm, B. L. & Gibson, J. (2005). Signals and Systems Using MATLAB: An Integrated Suite of Applications for Exploring and Teaching Media Signal Processing, *Proc. 35th IEEE Frontiers in Education Conference (FIE)*.

The Apache Software Foundation (2000). Subversion.
URL: *http://subversion.apache.org/*

The LEGO Group (2006a). Bluetooth Developer Kit.
URL: *http://mindstorms.lego.com/en-us/support/files/default.aspx*

The LEGO Group (2006b). Hardware Developer Kit.
URL: *http://mindstorms.lego.com/en-us/support/files/default.aspx*

The LEGO Group (2006c). MINDSTORMS.
URL: *http://www.mindstorms.com*

The LEGO Group (2007). LEGO Education.
URL: *http://www.legoeducation.com*

The MathWorks (1994). MATLAB.
URL: *http://www.mathworks.com*

The MathWorks (2008a). LEGO Mindstorms NXT Software for MATLAB and Simulink.
URL: *http://www.mathworks.com/programs/lego/*

The MathWorks (2008b). MATLAB Central File Exchange.
URL: *http://www.mathworks.com/matlabcentral/fileexchange/*

Vallim, M., Farines, J.-M. & Cury, J. (2006). Practicing Engineering in a Freshman Introductory Course, *IEEE Transactions on Education* **49**(1): 74–79.

Vicente, J., Garcia, B., Mendez, A., Ruiz, I. & Lage, O. (2007). EasySP: The Easiest Form to Learn Signal Processing Interactively, *Proc. IEEE Int. Conf. on Acoustics, Speech, and Signal Processing (ICASSP)*, Vol. 3, pp. 713–716.

Williams, A. (2003). The Qualitative Impact of Using LEGO MINDSTORMS Robots to Teach Computer Engineering, *IEEE Trans. Edu.* **46**(1): 206.

Ye, D., Brutman, I., Georgi, G. & Folan, L. (2007). Freshman Project: Autonomous Underwater Vehicle (AUV), *Proc. American Society for Engineering Education (ASEE), Annual Conference*.

4

A student friendly toolbox for power system analysis using MATLAB

A. B. M. Nasiruzzaman
Department of Electrical & Electronic Engineering,
Rajshahi University of Engineering & Technology
Bangladesh

1. Introduction

There are various premier software packages available in the market, either for free use or found at a high price, to analyse the century old electrical power system. Universities in the developed countries expend thousands of dollars per year to bring these commercial applications to the desktops of students, teachers and researchers. For teachers and researchers this is regarded as a good long-term investment. As well, for the postgraduate students these packages are very important to validate the model developed during course of study. For simulating different test cases and/or standard systems, which are readily available with these widely used commercial software packages, such enriched software plays an important role. But in case of underdeveloped and developing countries the high amount of money needed to be expended per year to purchase commercial software is a far-fetched idea. In addition, undergraduate students who are learning power system for the very first time find these packages incongruous for them since they are not familiar with the detailed input required to run the program. Even if it is a simple load flow program to find the steady-state behaviour of the system, or an elementary symmetrical fault analysis test case these packages require numerous inputs since they mimic a practical power system rather than considering simple test cases. In effect, undergraduate students tend to stay away from these packages. So rather than aiding the study in power system, these create a bad impression on students' mind about the very much interesting course.

Many researchers have tried a lot to solve this overarching problem. With the advent of personal computers (PCs) the solution to this issue has been very easy. Then came MATLAB, a flagship software for scientific and engineering computation. A revolution occurred in the field of science. Teaching and learning became very much easier than ever with the powerful graphical tools of MATLAB. Many researchers have developed various attractive software packages to aid to the power system analysis and design. A few have focused on the power engineering education field. This chapter discusses an excellent software package based on MATLAB developed mainly to aid in power system study. Although the program is developed using MATLAB, it is compiled such that it can be used outside MATLAB environment.

2. Overview of Software Packages for Power Engineering

To facilitate power engineering analysis and design various companies have developed diverse software. Among them some are used widely and some are built to meet specific purpose of a company. There are PSS®E, ETAP, NEPLAN and much more commercial programs. PSAT, Power World Simulator, and POWERHU basically developed to facilitate power engineering education and sometimes available with textbooks. Among these programs some are code based and some are model based. Some written in C, and Java, others depend on MATLAB.

PSS®E (Siemens, 2009) developed by Siemens Power Technologies International (Siemens PTI) has various modules like power flow, short circuit, dynamic simulation, contingency analysis, optimal power flow, linear network, reliability assessment, and small signal analysis. These modules requires a solid idea about the whole generation, transmission, and distribution system, various control devices used at different points to improve power system quality. This software is a benchmark against which other newly developed software is tested.

ETAP (Operation Technology, 2009) offers a group of fully integrated power engineering software solutions including arc flash, load flow, short circuit, transient stability, relay coordination, optimal power flow, and more. Its modular functionality can be customized to fit the needs of any company, from small to large power systems. ETAP is a comprehensive analysis platform for the design, simulation, operation, and automation of generation, distribution, and industrial power systems. As a fully integrated enterprise solution, ETAP extends to a real-time intelligent power management system to monitor, control, automate, simulate, and optimize the operation of power systems.

BCP (i.e., Busarello + Cott + Partner AG) was founded 1988 in Zurich, Switzerland and is specialized in the field of power systems engineering. BCP is the developer and owner of the power system analysis tool NEPLAN (BCP, 2010). Small and large utilities, industrial organizations, engineering companies and universities in more than 80 countries around the world use this product. NEPLAN is the planning, optimization and simulation tool for transmission, distribution, generation and industrial networks. It covers all aspects of modern power system planning and analysis. NEPLAN offers several starter packages. These starter packages are extendable with many useful modules. All these modules may be added to a starter package at any time. It is available in 9 languages.

The Power System Analysis Toolbox (PSAT) is a MATLAB toolbox for electric power system analysis and simulation (Milano, 2005). All operations can be assessed by means of graphical user interfaces (GUIs) and a SIMULINK based library provides a tool for network design. The main features of PSAT are: power flow, optimal power flow, small signal stability analysis, time domain simulation, FACTS models, wind turbine models, conversion of data files from several formats; Export results to MS Excel and LaTeX files.

PowerWorld Simulator (PowerWorld Corporation, 2009) is an interactive power systems simulation package designed to simulate high voltage power systems operation on a time frame ranging from several minutes to several days. The software contains a highly effective power flow analysis package capable of efficiently solving systems with up to 100,000 buses.

PowerWorld Simulator is ideally suited for teaching power systems operations and analysis and for performing research. In fact, the original version of the simulator software was built as a tool for teaching power systems and presenting power systems analysis results to technical and non-technical audiences alike. Since that time, simulator has evolved into the highly powerful power systems analysis and visualization platform that it is today. Simulator has been, and continues to be, used effectively in undergraduate and graduate level classes in power systems operation, control, and analysis. Concepts are presented simply, yet the software has sufficient detail to challenge advanced engineering students.

MATLAB 4.0 was used to develop a software package named POWERHU (Songur & Ercan, 1997) keeping in mind power engineering students. It has the excellent feature of solving problems in a way that most widely used power system analysis textbooks use. It is capable of performing load flow study, impedance calculation, fault calculation, and transient stability analysis.

PSS®E, ETAP, and NEPLAN are mainly used in industries and for research purposes. They are not suitable for first time learners of power system. PSAT and PowerWorld Simulators are excellent tools that can be used to teach and learn power system. But the problem here is that these packages are mainly model based and does not give the chance to see the inner structure of the program. It just takes inputs and provides outputs after some processing. The students may not see the inner structure of the program which is required very much to develop insight into the behaviour of various components of power system. POWERHU takes into account the problems of PSAT and PowerWorld Simulator. It provides a step by step solution so that the confidence can be built up towards solving more complex problems. But this program is not MATLAB independent. One has to start MATLAB first to run this program, and the size and cost of MATLAB license is increasing day by day. This is why; it may not be possible for students in some developing countries to use this program in the laboratories since they may not have the high performance computers. Also, the program may not run in the recent versions of MATLAB since many old commands of MATLAB have been obsolete. The POWERHU is neither standalone nor it is made version independent. It was developed and tested in MATLAB 4.0 and no improvement was reported after that.

3. Structure of Student Friendly Power System Analysis Toolbox

Power system analysis courses taught in undergraduate levels cover mainly basic concepts of power system like single-line diagram, per unit system, modelling of generators, transformers, transmission lines and loads, load flow analysis, fault analysis, stability studies etc. The purpose of such courses is to develop a fundamental idea about the power system among the undergrads so that they can develop their own skills and aptitudes for solving real world power engineering problems. The huge computations required for these courses are handled by computers and now-a-days MATLAB is used extensively for scientific and engineering computation. In this chapter, a student friendly toolbox developed to assist students during their course of study in basic power system courses is presented. The toolbox takes into account the fresh students having no idea about the course and can alone be used as a textbook. The help menu in the toolbox provides details of problems solved with sufficient background materials so that each and every module can be grasped and mastered with ease. One can easily see the inner structure of the program to understand how to code a power engineering problem. The main advantage of the toolbox is that apart from using the software within MATLAB it is made version compatible and can be used without MATLAB. So it can be regarded as a standalone software package for power system analysis. The software was developed in MATLAB 6.5 and now successfully tested in the recent version of MATLAB 2010a. The toolbox is divided into different modules to focus different areas of power system as follows:

a) Fault analysis of a motor-generator set
b) Demonstration of symmetrical components
c) Fault analysis of unloaded alternator
d) Synchronous machine transients (balanced)
e) Synchronous machine transients (unbalanced)
f) Fault analysis of interconnected buses
g) Single machine stability analysis (classical)
h) Single machine stability analysis (modern)
i) Load flow

When the program is run the main window appears as in Fig. 1.

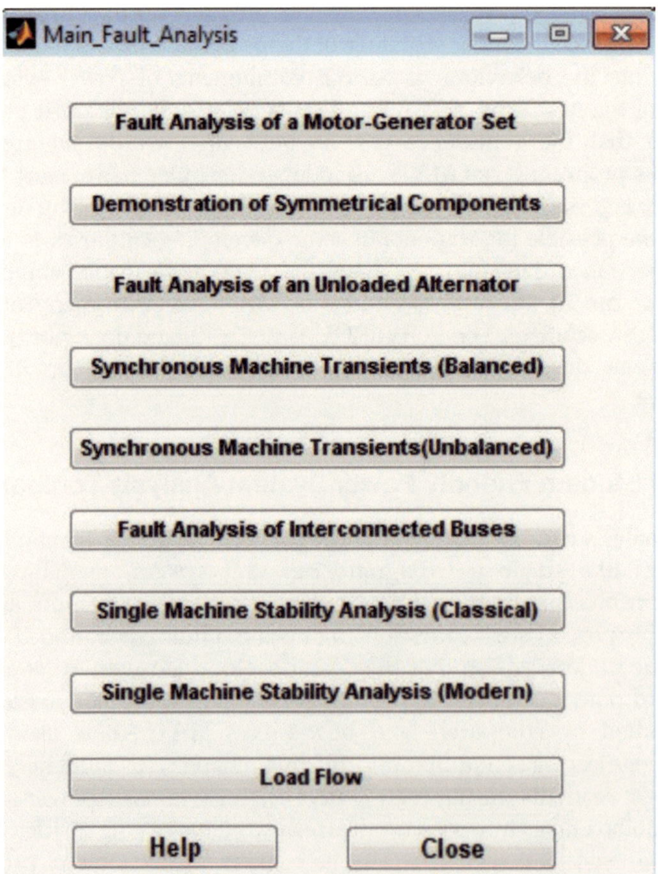

Fig. 1. Main window of student friendly power system analysis toolbox

4. Fault Analysis of a Motor-Generator Set

This toolbox can be used to study various types of faults encountered in power system and was reported on (Rabbani et al., 2006) which is again presented here in a slight different format.

The effect of a fault in the line connected in between the motor and generator can be visualised using this module which is shown in Fig. 2. The effect of change of various parameters is visualised using this module. This example is taken from a classical textbook of power system (Stevenson, 1982).

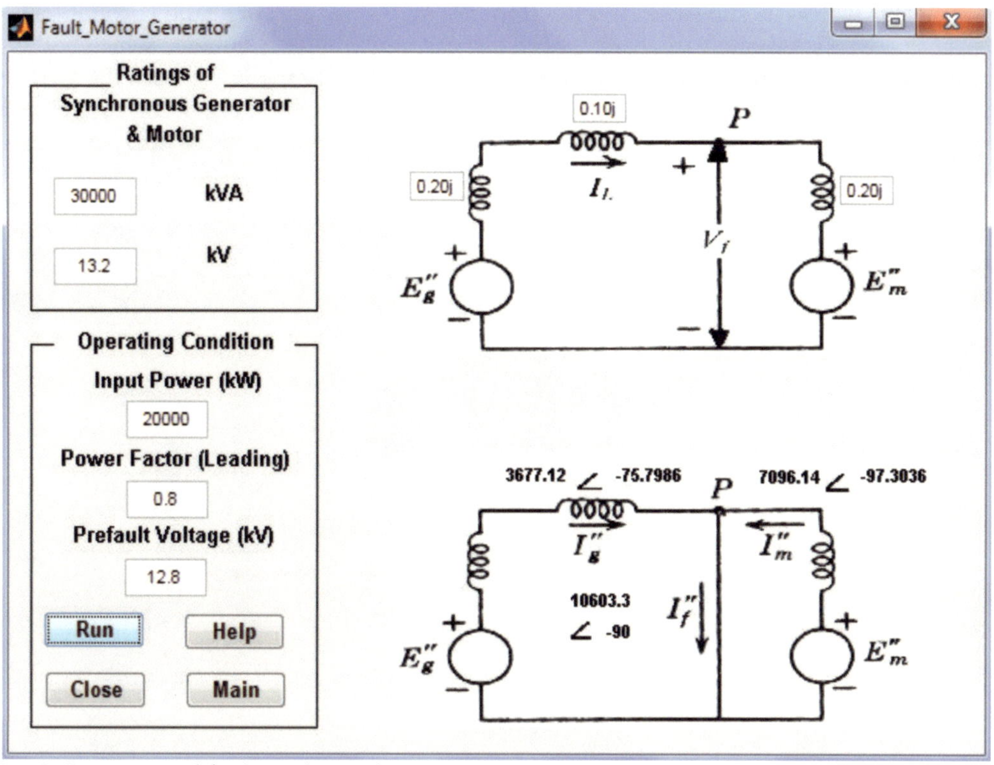

Fig. 2. Symmetrical fault analysis of a motor-generator set

The idea behind the example is to consider a case when a symmetrical three phase fault occurs in the connecting line of a motor-generator set when the system was running full load. The fault current is the contribution from both generator and motor. The magnitude and angle of the fault, generator and motor currents are found by simulating the program. The effect of the pre-fault operating conditions like input power, power factor, and pre-fault voltages on the fault currents can be observed. The impedances of motor, generator, and transmission lines can be changes individually and their impact on fault current can be noticed. The power and voltage ratings of the motor and generator can be modified to see its influence on fault currents. This problem is analysed here with a very attractive user friendly Graphical User Interface (GUI) (MathWorks, 2009) developed using MATLAB GUIDE (GUI Design Environment).

One need not go to the main program each time, save this and run again and need not be worried about unintentionally changing the program and generate an unexpected error. It also provides a help menu for an easy understanding of the problem for the first time user and a step by step procedure of developing program to solve the problem using PC. It provides a complete formulation and solution of the problem. A glimpse of the help file for this module is given in Fig. 3. The help file first describes the problem then the inputs required for running the program are clarified. The next step is to provide a step by step solution procedure for the problem which is given in the textbooks. The last step describes a complete methodology to develop MATLAB program for solving the problem.

After analysing this module a student develops the very basic idea of a fault encountered in power system. By varying various parameters he can verify hand calculation which builds a confidence within him. This hands-on, user friendly interactive module excites the learners to pursue their study of power system. The preliminary objective of providing such a basic problem first is to reinforce students' decision to take power system analysis course, immediately upon starting the course, and help them feel included.

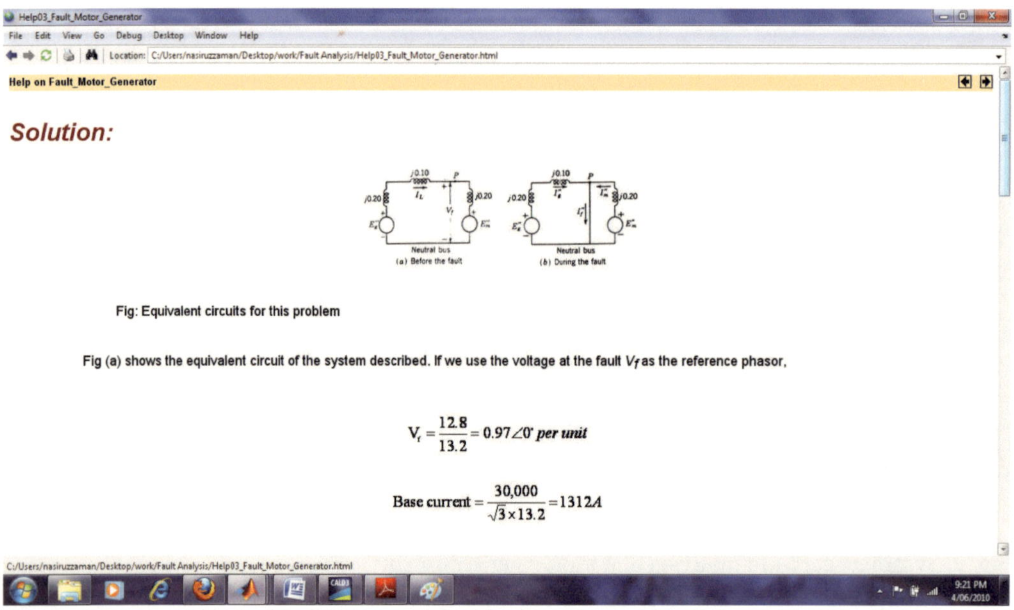

Fig. 3. A portion of help file for symmetrical fault analysis of a motor-generator set

5. Demonstration of Symmetrical Components

Symmetrical components allow unbalanced phase quantities such as currents and voltages to be replaced by three separate balanced symmetrical components. The concept of symmetrical components is an indispensible tool for investigating unbalanced systems. The idea of symmetrical components is found in the paper (Fortescue, 1918). According to Fortescue's theorem, three balanced system of phasors can be constructed from three unbalanced phasor quantities. The balanced components of phasors have the following properties:

a) The *positive sequence components* have three phasors equal in magnitude. Each are displaced 120^0 with each other in phase. It has the phase sequence of the original phasor.
b) The *negative sequence components* also have three phasors equal in magnitude, displaced 120^0 with each other in phase. The difference with the positive sequence component is that the negative sequence components have the opposite phase sequence than that of the positive one.
c) The *zero sequence components* are equal in magnitude and zero phase difference from each other.

In this module as shown in Fig. 4 unbalanced phasors are converted to balanced set of positive, negative, and zero sequence components.

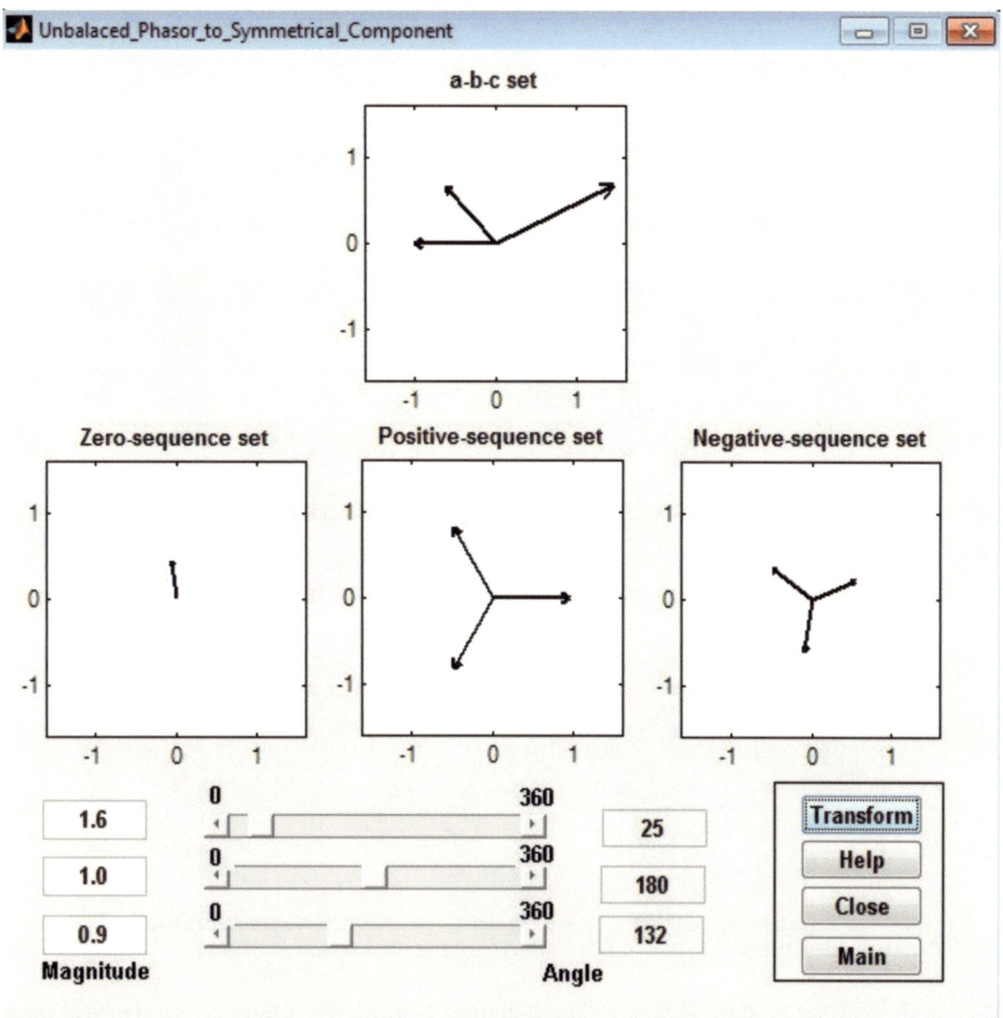

Fig. 4. Conversion of unbalanced phasor to symmetrical components

The a-b-c set in the figure is the unbalanced set of phasors which can be entered in the system using the editable text boxes named as ***Magnitude*** and ***Angle***. In this particular example the magnitudes of three phasors are 1.6, 1.0, and 0.9, while the angles are 25^0, 180^0, and 132^0 respectively. The GUI also has the provision to change the angles using the slider whose range varies from 0 to 360 degrees. After setting all these parameters the user needs to press the ***Transform*** button and the results are displayed in the three figures titled ***Zero, Positive, and Negative-sequence set***. Like other modules of this toolbox the ***Help*** button provides a detail description of the symmetrical components and some worked out examples to facilitate plumbing the concept. ***Close*** button terminates the program. By pressing the pushbutton ***Main*** the main window of the toolbox as in Fig. 1 is returned.

6. Fault Analysis of an Unloaded Alternator

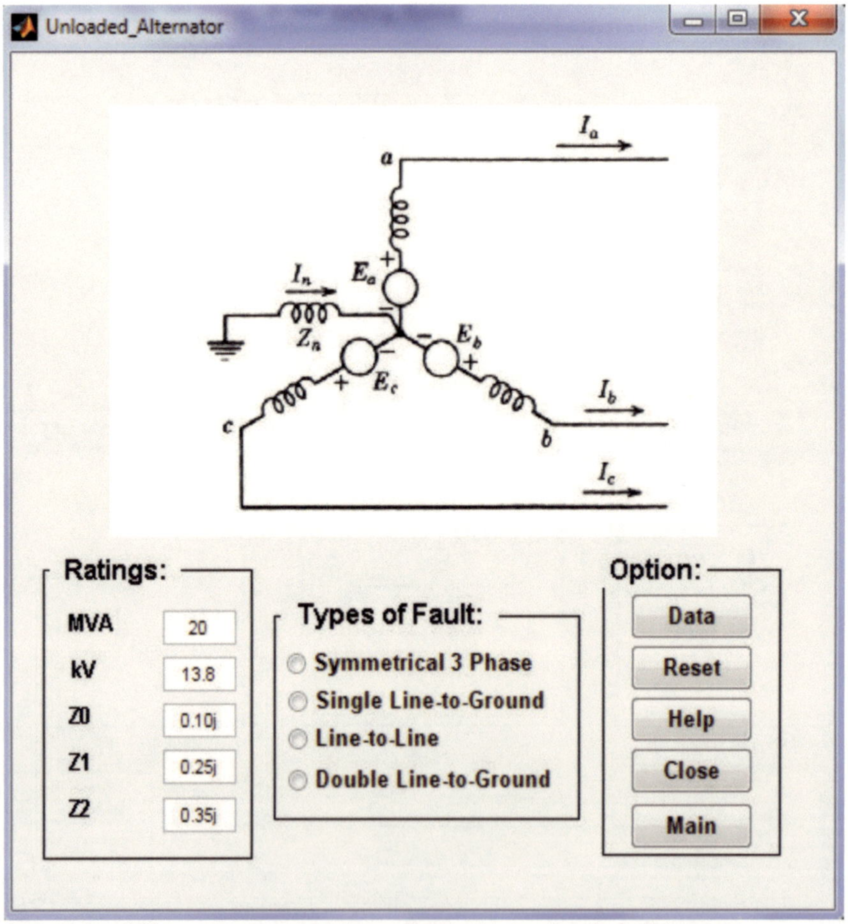

Fig. 5. Module for different types of fault analysis of an unloaded alternator

This module of the toolbox shown in Fig. 5 is used to study the effect of symmetrical three phase, single line-to-ground, line-to-line, and double line-to-ground faults at the terminal of a previously unloaded alternator which has a rating 20MVA and 13.8kV in this default example taken from (Stevenson, 1982). The ratings of the alternator (***MVA*** and ***kV***) can be changed as well as the sequence reactance (***Z0, Z1,*** and ***Z2***) of the machine can be modified to see the effect of various types of faults on fault currents and voltages. If ***Data*** button is pressed fault currents and voltages are displayed in a separate window. Initially there is no fault selected as reflected by Fig. 5. If ***Line-to-Line*** fault is selected then GUI is modified as in Fig. 6 and the result on the analysis is presented in Fig. 7 respectively.

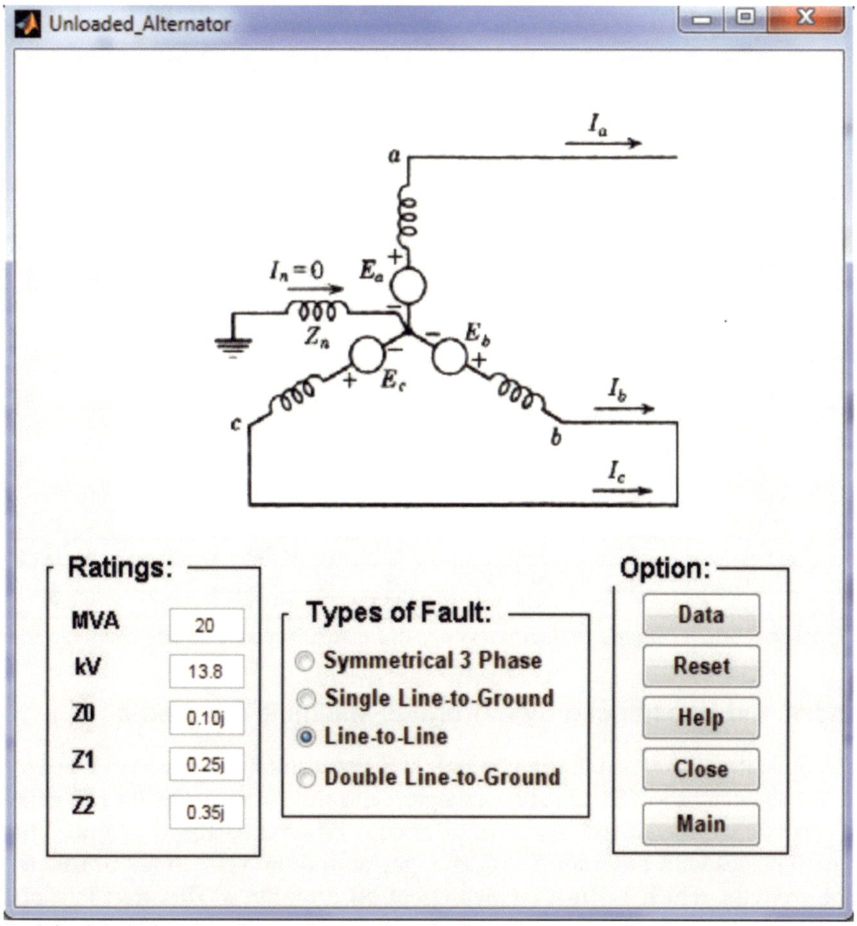

Fig. 6. Modified GUI for simulating line-to-line fault at the terminal of an unloaded alternator

The voltage and current data as shown in Fig. 7 validates some general concept of power system. The first one is the phase a current is zero since the machine was previously unloaded and the line-to-line fault is simulated in phases b and c. Also the voltage difference between phases b and c is zero since these two phases are short-circuited together. The b and c phase currents are same in magnitude but are of opposite phases since they are directly opposing each other as viewed in Fig. 6. This statement is also valid for V_{ab} and V_{ca}. The ***Help, Close,*** and ***Main*** buttons perform functions as described earlier and the ***Reset*** button initializes the module. Table 1 provides voltage and current data by running the program using the ratings as it is shown in Fig. 5 for different types of faults.

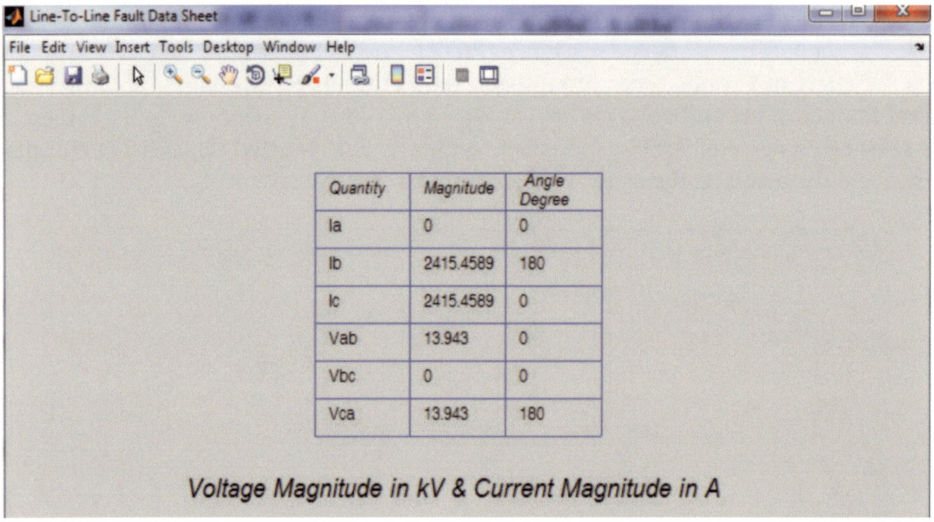

Quantity	Magnitude	Angle Degree
Ia	0	0
Ib	2415.4589	180
Ic	2415.4589	0
Vab	13.943	0
Vbc	0	0
Vca	13.943	180

Fig. 7. Voltages and currents after fault

Fault	Symmetrical 3 Phase		Single Line-to-Ground		Line-to-Line		Double-Line-to-Ground	
Quantity	*Magnitude*	*Angle degree*	*Magnitude*	*Angle degree*	*Magnitude*	*Angle degree*	*Magnitude*	*Angle degree*
I_a	3346.9981	-90	3586.0265	-90	0	0	0	0
I_b	3346.9981	30	0	0	2415.4589	180	4021.2983	132.2
I_c	3346.9981	150	0	0	2415.4589	0	4021.2983	47.78
V_{ab}	0	0	8.0684	77.78	13.943	0	5.6717	0
V_{bc}	0	0	15.7714	-90	0	0	0	0
V_{ca}	0	0	8.0684	102.2	13.943	180	5.6717	180

Table 1. Currents and Voltages of various types of faults after simulating the system in Fig. 5

7. Balanced and Unbalanced Synchronous Machine Transients

Under steady state condition the rotor m.m.f. and the resultant stator m.m.f. are stationary with respect to each other. So the flux linkages with the rotor circuit do not change with time and no voltage is induced in the rotor circuit. When a balanced or unbalanced fault occurs flux linkages with the rotor circuit changes with time. This causes transient currents in the rotor circuit which in turn creates effect on armatures. This transient analysis is visualised in this module as depicted in Fig. 8 for balanced 3 phase short circuit and in Fig. 9 for unbalanced fault (line-to-line) at the terminal of an alternator.

The field voltage, self and mutual inductances, resistances, frequency, initial torque angle, and time span are the inputs for the module. Two standard frequencies (50 and 60Hz) can be chosen from the drop-down menu in the GUI. The time span can be varied according to the region of interest of the simulation. In case of unbalanced fault analysis there is an extra provision to select between line-to-line and line-to-ground fault. These two modules can be switched using the ***Unbalanced*** and ***Balanced*** buttons in the balanced and unbalanced modules respectively. By pressing the ***Simulate*** button the transient curves can be obtained which takes some time depending upon the time span since it is required to solve differential equations.

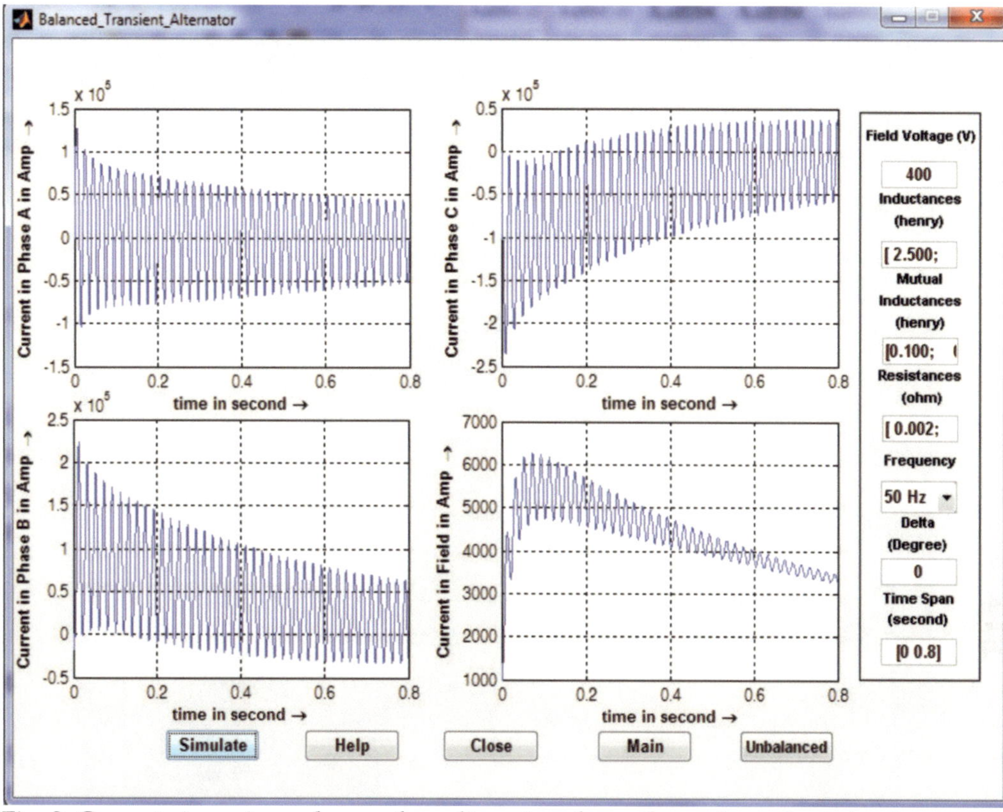

Fig. 8. Currents in various phases of an alternator after a three phase short circuit occurs at its terminal

8. Fault Analysis of Interconnected Buses

In this module a very much challenging problem of power system analysis course is described. The generalised case of finding voltages and currents after the occurrence of symmetrical three phase fault at any bus of a power system is either solidly grounded or shorted with some impedance is the most interesting problem in this toolbox. For example, a simple 11 bus test case is considered as shown in Fig. 10. The pre-fault voltages at various buses can be found by load flow study. Generally, if such accuracy is not important the pre-fault bus voltages are assumed to be unity. The transient impedance of the generators are on a 100MVA base are given in Table 2.

Generator	Ra	X'_d
1	0	0.20
10	0	0.15
11	0	0.25

Table 2. Generator resistance and reactance for simple 11 bus system in Fig. 10

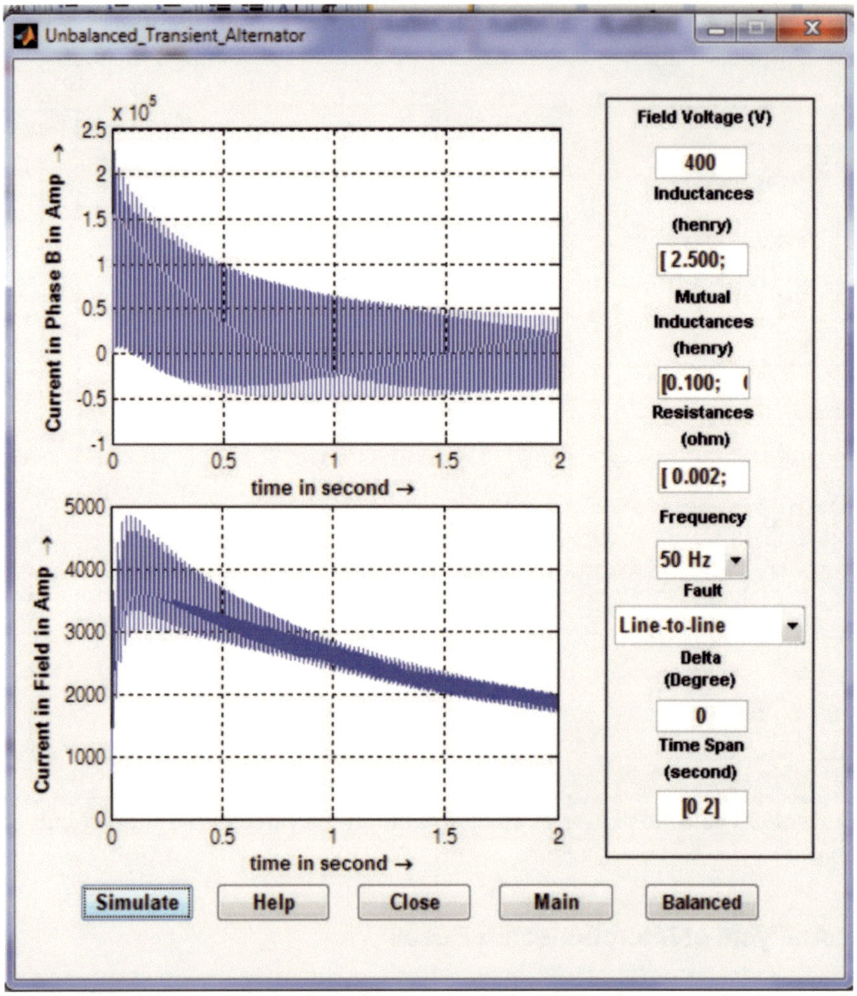

Fig. 9. Simulation of line-to-line fault at the terminal of a 50Hz alternator for 2 seconds

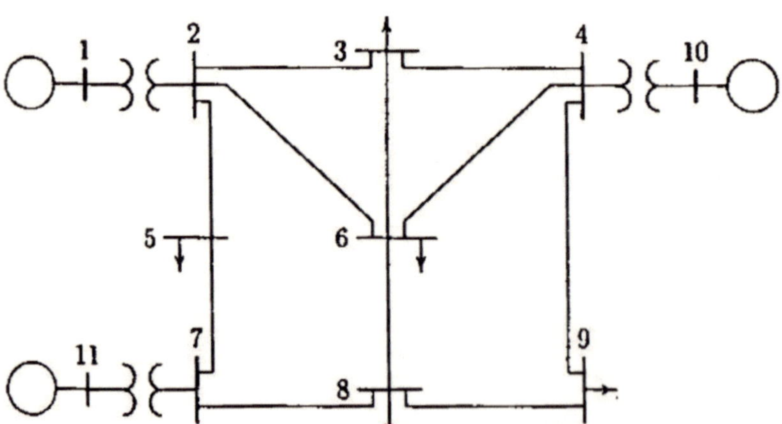

Fig. 10. Simple 11-bus power system for fault studies (Saadat, 2009)

The line and transformer data along with the half of susceptance value is given in Table 3 in per unit. These data are incorporated in the program and the pre-fault bus voltages are assumed to be 1 and a solid 3 phase symmetrical fault is simulated at bus 8. The resulting GUI looks like Fig. 11. The ***Voltage Data*** corresponds to the various bus voltages after the fault and the ***Current Data*** represents various currents flowing in various lines in the system after the fault has occurred. The voltage and current data after the fault are given in Fig. 12 and Fig. 13 respectively. If any bus was faulted with some impedance this can be done by entering ***Fault Impedance*** as r+jx format.

From Bus	To Bus	R pu	X pu	½ B pu
1	2	0.00	0.06	0.0000
2	3	0.08	0.30	0.0004
2	5	0.04	0.15	0.0002
2	6	0.12	0.45	0.0005
3	4	0.10	0.40	0.0005
3	6	0.04	0.40	0.0005
4	6	0.15	0.60	0.0008
4	9	0.18	0.70	0.0009
4	10	0.00	0.08	0.0000
5	7	0.05	0.43	0.0003
6	8	0.06	0.48	0.0000
7	8	0.06	0.35	0.0004
7	11	0.00	0.10	0.0000
8	9	0.052	0.48	0.0000

Table 3. Line and transformer data for simple 11 bus system in Fig. 10

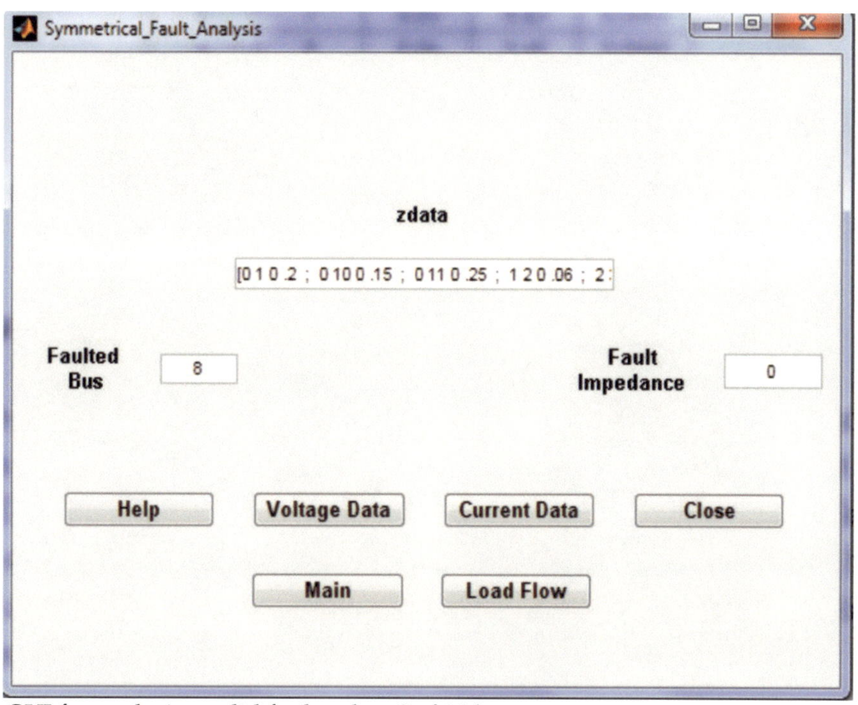

Fig. 11. GUI for analysing solid fault at bus 8 of 11 bus system

Bus No.	Voltage Magnitude	Angle Degree
1	0.80817	-1.818
2	0.75083	-2.5443
3	0.68819	-1.5987
4	0.74914	-2.4902
5	0.70073	-2.3762
6	0.54537	-1.0194
7	0.56179	-3.8128
8	0	0
9	0.30076	2.4499
10	0.83621	-1.4547
11	0.68663	-2.2272

Fig. 12. Voltage at various buses after a 3 phase symmetrical fault at bus 8 of Fig. 10

From Bus	To Bus	Current Magnitude	Angle Degree
0	1	0.96972	-82.4034
0	10	1.1029	-82.6275
0	11	1.2601	-85.141
1	2	0.96972	-82.4034
2	3	0.20532	-87.8751
2	5	0.323	-79.9626
2	6	0.44267	-81.6497
4	3	0.1503	-88.4042
3	6	0.35561	-88.0987
4	6	0.33055	-82.3804
4	9	0.62294	-81.3672
10	4	1.1029	-82.6275
5	7	0.323	-79.9626
6	8	1.1274	-83.8944
7	8	1.582	-84.0852
11	7	1.2601	-85.141
9	8	0.62294	-81.3672
8	8	3.3319	-83.5126

Fig. 13. Currents at various lines after a 3 phase symmetrical fault at bus 8 of Fig. 10

9. Stability Analysis

Power system stability is defined as 'Power system stability is the ability of an electric power system, for a given initial operating condition, to regain a state of operating equilibrium after being subject to a physical disturbance, with most system variables bounded so that practically the entire system remains intact by (Kundur et. Al., 2004). Broadly, the power system stability is classified as:

a) Rotor angle stability
b) Voltage stability
c) Frequency stability

In this module mainly the rotor angle stability is considered. When a 3 phase short circuit occurs in a line very close to a generator bus of an interconnected power system, the voltage of the bus essentially becomes zero. So the electrical output power also becomes zero. But the mechanical power input to the turbine-generator system remains constant. Hence the generator accelerates. This acceleration means that the rotor angle of the generator will keep increasing. Now, in order to clear the fault the circuit breakers are tripped to remove the faulted line out of the system. Depending upon the time of tripping the rotor angle of the generator of the faulted bus will then wither settle down to a new equilibrium, or keep on increasing resulting in instability. This is an example of rotor angle stability which occurs mainly due to the mismatch of electrical output and mechanical input power of the alternator. Rotor angle stability can be analysed for either for small or large disturbances and generally this type of stability analysis if performed for 2 to 10 seconds i.e., this is an example of short term stability.

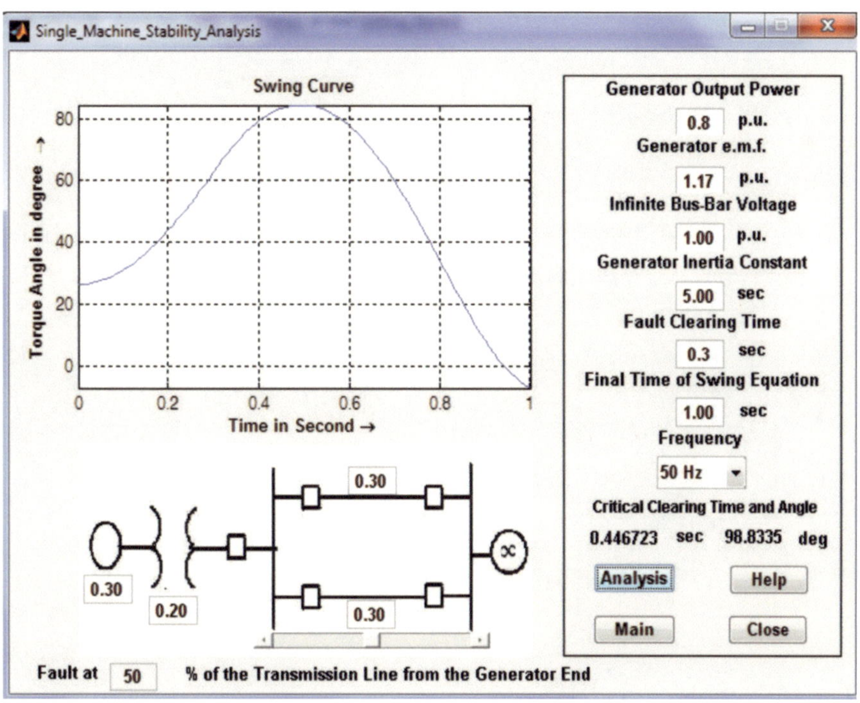

Fig. 14. Stability analysis module

The example that have considered here is a single machine system connected to an infinite bus via two parallel transmission lines as demonstrated in Fig. 14. In this case the stability of the single machine is considered subjected to a symmetrical 3 phase fault in one of the two parallel lines. The position of the fault along the line can be changed and its effect on stability can be visualised. The example shown in Fig. 14 simulates a fault at the middle (50%) of the transmission line. The fault location can be varied either by using the slider control of the GUI or by entering the fault position as a percentage (0% for a fault at the transformer terminal and 100% for the fault at the infinite bus). The generator, transformer, and transmission line reactances can be varied. Various ratings can be changed such as ***Generator output power, Generator e.m.f., Infinite bus-bar voltage, Generator inertia constant***. ***Fault clearing time*** is very essential for this type of stability and system may become stable or unstable for a same fault with different fault clearing time. The final time that needs to be visualised the rotor angle change due to the application of the fault is entered in the textbox ***Final time of swing equation***. The frequency of the system can be set to either 50Hz or 60Hz. The program plots angular swing of the generator with respect to time and gives the ***critical clearing time*** and ***critical clearing angle*** of fault which is very important in stability studies.

10. Load Flow Analysis

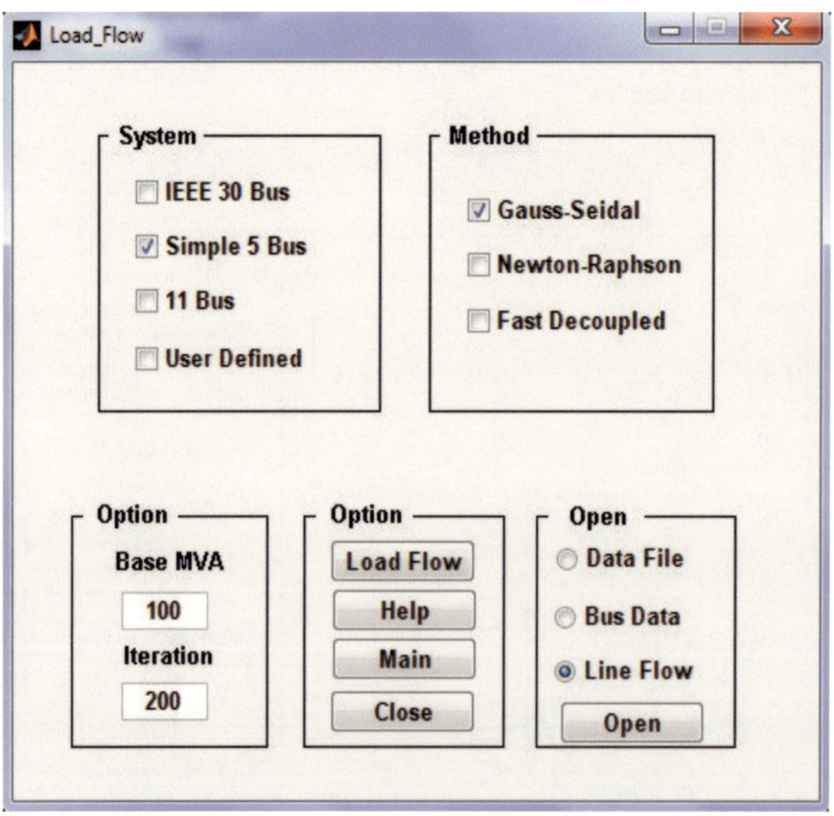

Fig. 15. Load flow analysis module

Load flow or power flow analysis is performed in a power system analysis course to determine voltage magnitudes and angles of various bus bars as well as real and reactive power flow in a power system. It is basically a problem of solving a system of nonlinear equations and various methods have been proposed in the literatures for solving load flow problems efficiently. Gauss-Seidel, Newton-Raphson, Decoupled Newton-Raphson methods are very much common for undergraduate studies and these are considered in building the toolbox. The module is shown in Fig. 15. There are various test systems like IEEE-30 bus system, 11 bus system as in Fig. 10 and simple 5 bus system as in Fig 15 (Stevenson, 1982) are made available with this toolbox. User can build own system also. After running the load flow program the ***Bus Data*** and ***Line Flows*** are available.

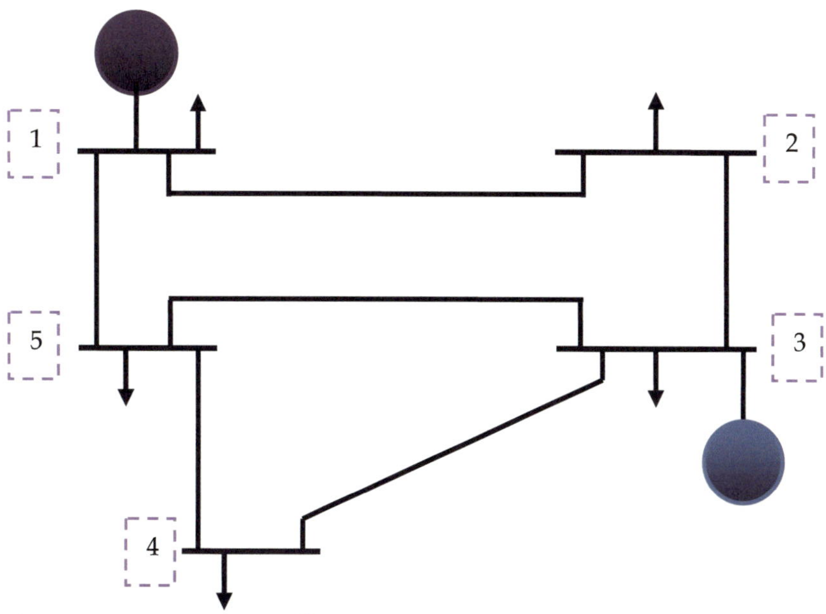

Fig. 16. Simple 5-bus power system for load flow analysis

The input required to conduct load flow of a simple 5 bus system is given in Fig. 16 whereas Fig. 17 and 18 gives the output of the load flow study using Gauss-Seidel method.

```
%         Bus Bus  Voltage Angle   ---Load---- -------Generator----- Static Mvar
%         No  code Mag.    Degree  MW    Mvar  MW  Mvar Qmin Qmax    +Qc/-Ql
busdata=[1   1    1.04    0.0     65    30    0   0     0    0       0
         2   0    1.00    0.0     115   60    0   0     0    0       0
         3   2    1.02    0.0     70    40    180 0     0    0       0
         4   0    1.00    0.0     70    30    0   0     0    0       0
         5   0    1.00    0.0     85    40    0   0     0    0       0];

%
%          Bus   bus    R        X        1/2 B        1 for Line code or
%          nl    nr     p.u.     p.u.       p.u.       tap setting value
%          Bus   bus    R        X       1/2 B     1 for Line code or
%          nl    nr     p.u.     p.u.    p.u.       tap setting value
linedata=[1      2     0.042    0.168   0.041/2            1
          1      5     0.031    0.126   0.031/2            1
          2      3     0.031    0.126   0.031/2            1
          3      4     0.084    0.336   0.082/2            1
          3      5     0.053    0.21    0.051/2            1
          4      5     0.063    0.252   0.061/2            1];
```

Fig. 17. Input for load flow analysis of system in Fig. 16

```
                     Power Flow Solution by Gauss-Seidel Method
                       Maximum Power Mismatch = 0.000855708
                              No. of Iterations = 79

 Bus  Voltage  Angle    ------Load------    ---Generation---    Injected
 No.  Mag.     Degree     MW       Mvar       MW       Mvar       Mvar
  1   1.040    0.000    65.000    30.000   234.588   100.157     0.000
  2   0.961   -6.324   115.000    60.000     0.000     0.000     0.000
  3   1.020   -3.717    70.000    40.000   180.000   110.249     0.000
  4   0.920  -10.878    70.000    30.000     0.000     0.000     0.000
  5   0.968   -6.163    85.000    40.000     0.000     0.000     0.000

 Total                 405.000   200.000   414.588   210.406     0.000
```

Fig. 18. Bus data after load flow for the system in Fig. 16

11. Conclusion

Programs developed in this software package cover all the topics of basic power system analysis course. Examples from various widely available textbooks (Bergen & Vittal, 1999; Elgerd, 1983; Glover, 2007; Grainger & Stevenson, 1994; Saadat, 2009; Stevenson, 1982; Wood & Wollenberg, 1996) are taken as examples. These textbooks are used all over the world. So, students running the software find a familiar environment around. Apart from this, other examples can be tested using this toolbox since the programs are written in a generalised way. Although codes are written in MATLAB, the software is compiled so that it can run without MATLAB. This feature is very much useful for computers having low memory, which increases the versatility of the toolbox. Extended help files are available with step by step solution procedure. So the toolbox can be used as alternative to textbook, albeit this is not recommended. Anyone can see the inner structure of the program and learn to code power engineering problems.

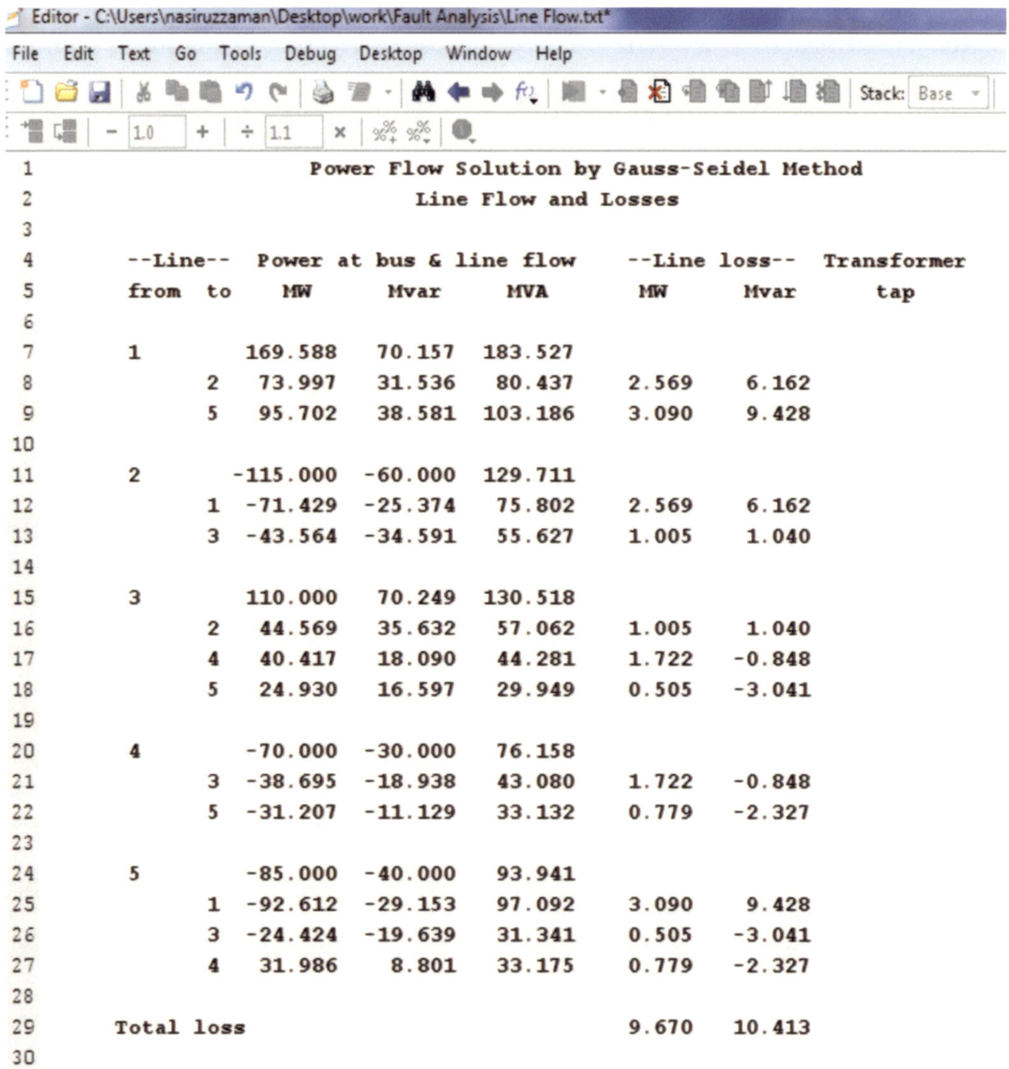
Editor - C:\Users\nasiruzzaman\Desktop\work\Fault Analysis\Line Flow.txt*

Power Flow Solution by Gauss-Seidel Method
Line Flow and Losses

--Line-- from	to	Power at bus & line flow MW	Mvar	MVA	--Line loss-- MW	Mvar	Transformer tap
1		169.588	70.157	183.527			
	2	73.997	31.536	80.437	2.569	6.162	
	5	95.702	38.581	103.186	3.090	9.428	
2		-115.000	-60.000	129.711			
	1	-71.429	-25.374	75.802	2.569	6.162	
	3	-43.564	-34.591	55.627	1.005	1.040	
3		110.000	70.249	130.518			
	2	44.569	35.632	57.062	1.005	1.040	
	4	40.417	18.090	44.281	1.722	-0.848	
	5	24.930	16.597	29.949	0.505	-3.041	
4		-70.000	-30.000	76.158			
	3	-38.695	-18.938	43.080	1.722	-0.848	
	5	-31.207	-11.129	33.132	0.779	-2.327	
5		-85.000	-40.000	93.941			
	1	-92.612	-29.153	97.092	3.090	9.428	
	3	-24.424	-19.639	31.341	0.505	-3.041	
	4	31.986	8.801	33.175	0.779	-2.327	
Total loss					9.670	10.413	

Fig. 19. Line flows and losses for the system in Fig. 16

The toolbox is currently used as a supplement to Power System Analysis (EEE 461) course in the Department of Electrical & Electronic Engineering, Rajshahi University of Engineering & Technology, Kazla, Rajshahi-6204, Bangladesh (*www.ruet.ac.bd*). The author can be contacted at *nasiruzzaman@ieee.org* in case of any enquiry about the software.

12. References

BCP, Inc. (2010). http://www.neplan.ch/html/e/e_home.htm

Bergen, A. R. & Vittal, V. (1999). *Power System Analysis*, (2nd), Prentice Hall, 0136919901

Elgerd, O. I. (1983). *Electric Energy Systems Theory: An Introduction*, (2nd), McGraw-Hill Higher Education, 0070192316

Fortescue, C. L. (1918). Method of Symmetrical Co-Ordinates Applied to the Solution of Polyphase Networks. *AIEE Transactions*, Vol. 37, No. 2, (Jul 1918)

Glover, J. D., Sarma, M. S. & Overbye, T. (2007). *Power System Analysis and Design*, (4th), CL Engineering, 0534548849

Grainger, J. J. & Stevenson Jr, W. D. (1994). *Power System Analysis*, (1st), McGraw-Hill Higher Education, 0071133380

Kundur, P., Paserba, J., Ajjarapu, V., Andersson, G., Bose, A., Canizares, C., Hatziargyriou, N., Hill, D., Stankovic, A., Taylor, C., Van Cutsem, T. & Vittal, V. (2004). Definition and classification of power system stability IEEE/CIGRE joint task force on stability terms and definitions. *IEEE Transactions on Power Systems*, 19, 3, (Aug 2004) (1387 - 1401), 08858950

MathWorks, Inc. (2009). *MATLAB® Creating Graphical User Interfaces*, The MathWorks, Inc, Natick, MA 01760-2098, USA

Milano, F. (2005). An Open Source Power System Analysis Toolbox. *IEEE Transactions on Power Systems*, Vol. 20, No. 3, (Aug 2005), 08858950

Operation Technology, Inc. (2009). http://etap.com

PowerWorld Corporation (2009). http://www.powerworld.com

Rabbani, M. G., Nasiruzzaman, A. B. M., Sheikh, R. I. & Anower, S. (1996). MATLAB Based Fault Analysis Toolbox for Electrical Power System, *Proceedings of International Conference on Electrical and Computer Engineering, 2006. ICECE '06.*, pp. 116-119, 98432-3814-1, Dhaka, Dec 2006, IEEE Bangladesh Section, Dhaka

Saadat, H. (2009). *Power System Analysis*, (2nd), McGraw-Hill Higher Education, 0071281843

Siemens, PTI. (2009). http://www.energy.siemens.com/us/en/services/power-transmission-distribution/power-technologies-international/software-solutions/pss-e.htm

Songur, M. & Ercan, B. (1997). POWERHU-a PC-based electric power system analysis software package for electric power system courses. *IEEE Transactions on Education*, Vol. 40, No. 4, (Nov 1997), 00189359

Stevenson Jr, W. D. (1982). *Elements of Power System Analysis*, (4th), McGraw-Hill Higher Education, 0070665842

Wood, A. J. & Wollenberg, B. F. (1996). *Power Generation, Operation, and Control*, (2nd), Wiley Interscience, 0471586994

5

A Matlab® interactive tool for computer aided control systems design in frequency domain: FRTool

Robin De Keyser and Clara Ionescu
Ghent University, Electrical energy, Systems and Automation, Technologiepark 913, B9052 Gent, Belgium

1. Introduction

Looking back at the history of control engineering, one finds that technology and ideas combine themselves until they reach a successful result, over the timeline of several decades (Bernstein, 2002). Simple dynamical compensators (such as PID, Phase-Lead, Phase-Lag, etc) have done in the past a remarkably good and efficient job in real-life control applications. Theoretical insight in the closed-loop behavior is provided by powerful and well-developed theories - which are considered as basic knowledge for every control engineer - such as the Root Locus and the Frequency Response techniques. In the past, these theories have been extensively used as *analysis tools* - e.g. the stability analysis of a given control system based on closed loop poles (Root Locus - RL) or Nyquist criterion (Frequency Response - FR). However, analysis implies *that a controller is already available*, irrespective of its design method.

Nowadays, thanks to the computational and graphical power of modern computers, many of these theories can be implemented as interactive graphical design tools. In this way, control engineering moves away from being an abstract and mathematical-oriented discipline and it evolves gradually towards a mature engineering discipline. An extensive reflection upon the role of information science in control engineering has been given in (Dormido, 2004). This new way of interactive control education provides practical insights into control systems fundamentals (Wittenmark *et al*, 1998; Dormido *et al*, 2002). Such combinations of interactive environment and animation bring visualization to a new level and aid learning and active participation by control engineering students (Kheir *et al*, 1996; Johansson *et al*, 1998).

Recently, a Root Locus RL toolbox has been introduced in Matlab - in this chapter, a Frequency Response toolbox (FRtool) will be presented. Although some other computer aided design (CAD) tools based on frequency response have been developed in the past (Balakrihsnan & Boyd, 1994; Satoh *et al*, 1994; Piguet & Gillet, 1997; Pouliz & Pouliezos, 1997; Piguet *et al*, 1999), the one presented in this contribution is highly interactive, graphical, easy-to-use and posing an elegant simplicity (especially for non-experts, as limited control engineering insight is required). The Matlab® controller design tool based on the root locus method (*rltool*) cannot handle systems with time-delay without approximating the dead-time by a rational transfer function. To tackle this problem, the FRtool operates with frequency diagrams (Nichols charts) - and in this way, the dead-time can be treated without any approximation.

The paper is structured as follows: the FRtool graphical interface is depicted in the next section, followed in the 3rd section by a description of the underlying frequency response concepts. In the 4th section, four examples are given:

i) a time-delayed and integrating transfer function of a (chemical) process;

ii) a second order system (velocity control);

iii) a mass spring damper system, defined by a 4th order transfer function with poor damping factors and

iv) a high order system (6th order)

A final section concludes this contribution.

2. FRTool Graphical Interface

Probably the most important feature of the FRtool is the user-friendly graphical interface (drag & drop and zoom included). It also has the possibility to display design specifications as graphical restrictions on the Nichols plot - including a real-time update while dragging controller's poles and zeros. It can also import/export process and controller from or to the Matlab workspace and has options to print Nichols, Nyquist or Bode curves and closed-loop responses, as depicted in figure 1.

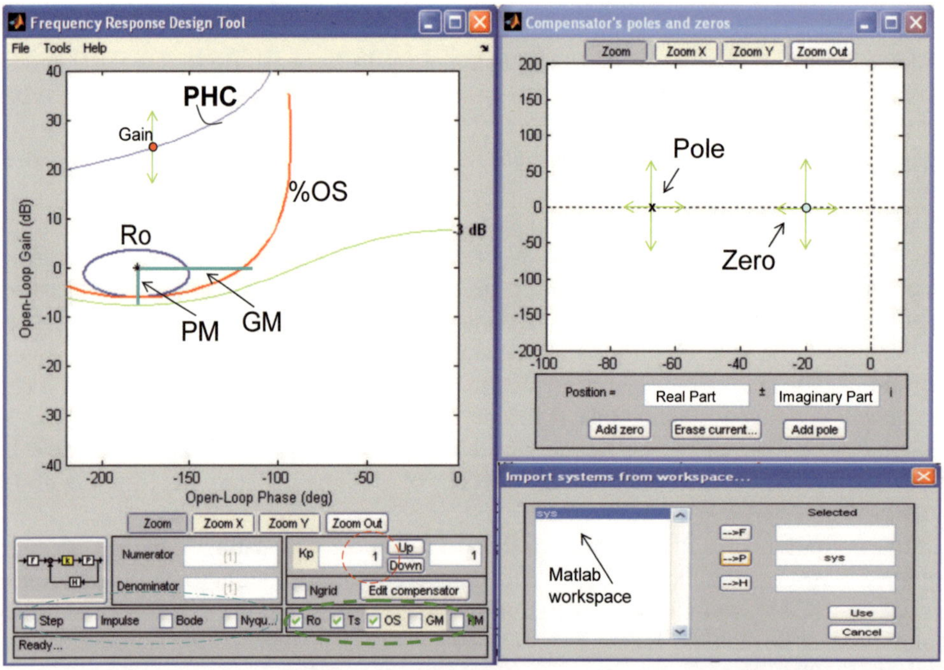

Fig. 1. Graphical interface of FRtool. After the system has been imported from Matlab workspace (see window in the lower right part), it appears as a curve in the Nichols chart corresponding to the loop frequency response (PHC).

The design specifications can be introduced using the options denoted in the bolded dashed green line; e.g. the overshoot ($\%OS$) and the robustness (Ro) specifications are visible in the chart. Closed-loop performance can be evaluated with the options in the dashed-dotted blue line. The upper right window in figure 1 is used to design the compensator by dragging compensator's poles and zeros with the mouse. Additionally, pre-filter $F(s)$ or feedback $H(s)$ transfer functions can be added within the control scheme. In order to design a controller with FRtool, the user does not need a detailed knowledge of the frequency-response background theory. Tools lessen the need for prior insights, but should provide a better understanding of the problem to let the user make better decisions. In figure 1, the PHC-curve corresponds to the loop Nichols curve, with a default controller equal to 1 (and in this example also H=1). Notice that the PHC-curve is above the critical point in the Nichols chart: -1+j0 – denoted by a *star* corresponding to an open-loop gain of 0dB and phase -180°. Consider now figure 2 and a transfer function available in the Matlab workspace:

$$P(s) = \frac{2500}{s(s+25)} e^{-0.2s} \tag{1}$$

It is obvious that transfer function (1) denotes a system which is not trivial to control: it is marginally stable due to the integrator and it has a significant dead-time, two aspects which make the control design a challenging task.

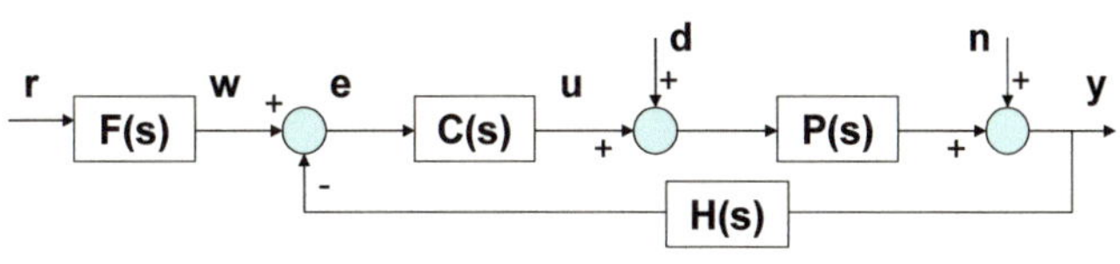

Fig. 2. General scheme of a control loop: r – reference, w – setpoint, e – error, u – the manipulated variable, d and n – disturbances, y – the controlled variable, F(s) is a pre-filtering transfer function and H(s) is a feedback transfer function; C(s) and P(s) denote the controller, respectively the process transfer function.

When imported in FRTool, the process from (1) with controller C=1 gives the result as depicted in figure 1. One may observe that the closed loop system will be unstable, and the user has then to *play with the controller's poles and zeros* to fulfill the specifications by pure visual inspection in the Nichols chart. Figures 3 and 4 depict various situations of zeros-poles placement, affecting the shape of the Nichols curve. Additionally, the user may choose to plot the Nichols grid (see dotted grid in figures 3-4), denoting the circles of Hall in the Nyquist plane (Nise, 1995). This grid shows the relationship between open-loop and closed-loop frequency responses.

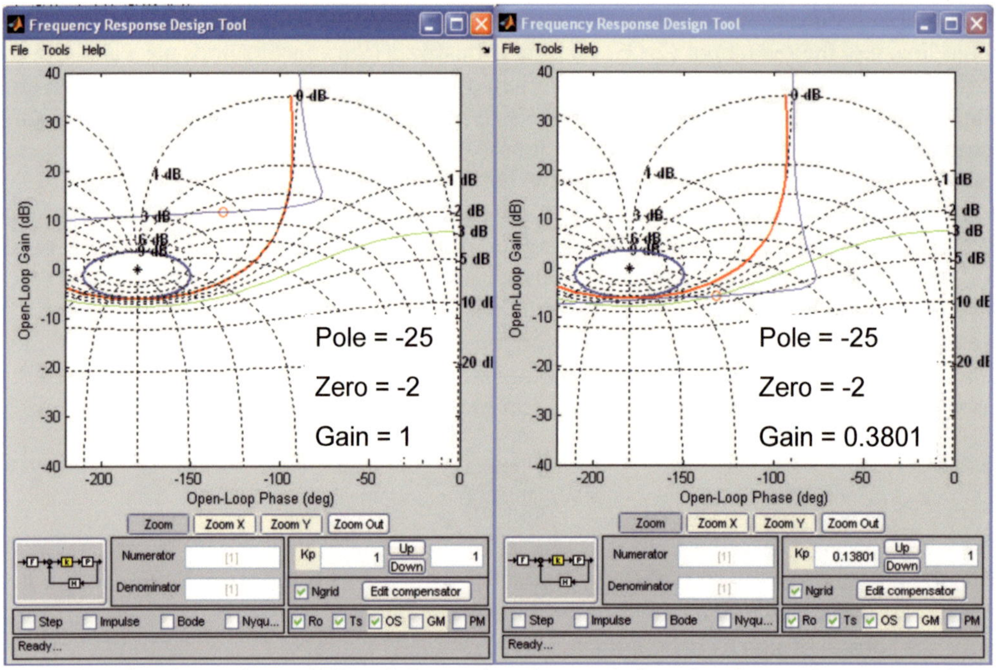

Fig. 3. Graphical interface of FRtool. It can be observed that the change in gain produces only a translation of the Nichols curve along the vertical axis, while its shape (dynamics) is influenced by the position of the controller's poles and zeros.

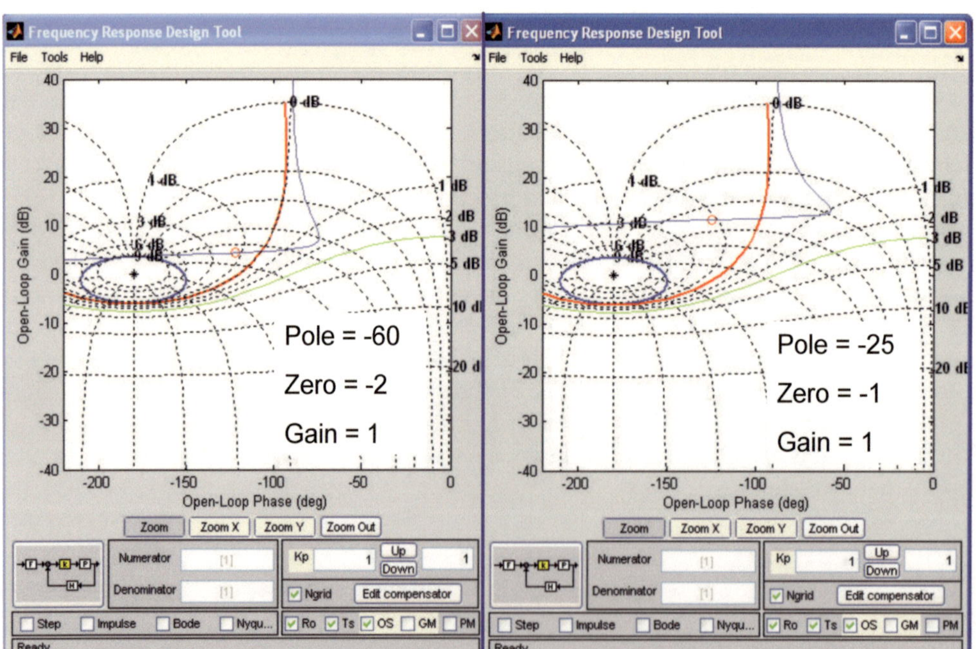

Fig. 4. Graphical interface of FRtool. Referenced to the pole/zero positions in figure 3, this picture illustrates the effect of a change in the pole position (left) and in the zero position (right).

3. Design Specifications

An important feature of a controller design tool is the possibility to define practically-meaningful design specifications – which will guide the designer in the tuning process. These specifications have to be converted to graphical restrictions to make the designer's job easier. Some of the *traditional* design specifications are gain margin and phase margin (Nise, 1995). However, these specifications have not necessarily a clear physical meaning to a potential user (unless this user is e.g. a control engineer) – they are based on mathematical insight and system theory. Therefore, more *practical* specifications - which can be easily interpreted by any user - are settling-time and overshoot of the closed-loop time response, and of course robustness of the design (Nise, 1995). In this section, the background theory on which these specifications are taken into account in FRtool is explained with reference to their graphical equivalents. The basic (textbook) transfer function of a PID is:

$$C(s) = K_p(1 + \frac{1}{T_i s} + T_d s) = K\frac{(s-z_1)(s-z_2)}{s} \tag{2}$$

with K_p the proportional gain, T_i the integrative and T_d the derivative constants, K the equivalent controller gain in zero-pole chart, z_1 and z_2 zeros. Similarly, in FRtool a *general form* of the compensator (filter) can be defined as the following transfer function:

$$C(s) = K\frac{(s-z_1)(s-z_2)...}{(s-p_1)(s-p_2)...} \tag{3}$$

Robustness is probably the most important design specification in practice. Since the controller tuning is done around a nominal operating point, the control performance should still be acceptable irrespective of model changes (e.g. in chemical plants) or model-mismatches (e.g. in mass-produced mechatronic devices such as DVD-players, hard-disks, etc). Denote $G(s)$ as the (open-)loop transfer function and $T(s)$ as the closed-loop transfer function, then the closed-loop sensitivity is defined as the closed-loop relative change over the open-loop relative change (the controller does not change, but the process may):

$$\frac{\partial T(s)/T(s)}{\partial G(s)/G(s)} = \frac{dT(s)}{dG(s)} \cdot \frac{G(s)}{T(s)} = \frac{1}{1+G(s)} \tag{4}$$

Thus the sensitivity should be as small as possible, resulting in $|1+G(s)|$ to be as big as possible. The equivalent representation in the complex plane is given in figure 5.

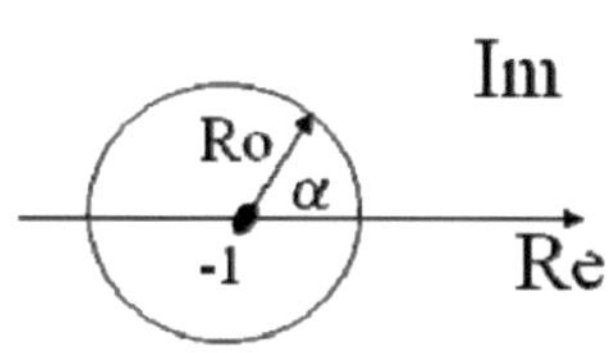

Fig. 5. Graphical representation of the robustness-function.

Robustness is described as how in-sensitive a closed-loop is to changes in the process. In FRtool, robustness (*Ro*) is a design parameter specified by the user, with value 0<*Ro*<1. It has the meaning of $|1+G(j\omega)|$, thus a larger *Ro*-value means more robustness. To fulfill the robustness spec, the Nyquist curve has to stay outside the circle with radius *Ro*.
Every point of this circle can be translated into the Nichols chart, leading to the ellipse-type blue curve in figures 2, 3 and 4. The inner part of this ellipse denotes a forbidden zone for the Nichols curve (with $\alpha = 0 \cdots 360°$):

$$\mathrm{R} = -1 + Ro * \cos(\alpha) \qquad \mathrm{I} = Ro * \sin(\alpha)$$
$$M_{dB} = 20\log\sqrt{\mathrm{R}^2 + \mathrm{I}^2} \quad \Phi_{\deg} = -180 + \arctan\left(\frac{\mathrm{I}}{\mathrm{R}}\right) \tag{5}$$

The other two specifications - overshoot (*%OS*) and settling time (T_s) – are derived from the dominant second order closed-loop transfer function:

$$T(s) \cong \frac{\omega_n^2}{s^2 + 2\xi\omega_n s + \omega_n^2} \tag{6}$$

From (6) the overshoot and settling time in time-domain are obtained via the damping factor (ξ) and the natural frequency (ω_n). Further on, given the user-defined specifications for *%OS* and T_s, it is straightforward to obtain ξ and ω_n from:

$$\%OS = 100e^{-\xi\pi/\sqrt{1-\xi^2}}$$
$$T_s \cong \frac{4}{\xi\omega_n} \tag{7}$$

Having (7), the time-domain specifications can be translated into frequency-domain specifications by using the following formulas (Nise, 1995):

$$M_p = \frac{1}{2\xi\sqrt{1-\xi^2}}$$
$$\omega_{BW} = \omega_n\sqrt{1 - 2\xi^2 + \sqrt{4\xi^4 - 4\xi^2 + 2}} \tag{8}$$

These parameters correspond then to the maximum closed-loop magnitude M_p (which is related to overshoot specification) and the closed-loop bandwidth ω_{BW} (which is related to the settling time specification).
From (7) and (8) it results that the designed controller should induce in the closed loop transfer function a peak-magnitude smaller than M_p, and the -3dB-bandwith frequency should be bigger than ω_{BW}. Notice in figure 2 the representation of M_p by the red curve indicated by *%OS*; the Nichols curve must stay below this *%OS* curve. The frequency ω_{BW} is denoted by the little red circle on the Nichols curve in figure 2; it must be above the green -3dB line in order to fulfill the specification.

4. Illustrative Examples

4.1 First Order Plus Integrator and Time-Delay

Given the challenging process (1), design a phase-lead controller so that the closed-loop will satisfy the specifications for overshoot $\%OS < 5\%$ and settling time $T_s < 0.8s$. Defining the system in the Matlab command window:

sys=tf(2500,[1 25 0],'InputDelay',0.2)

importing it in the FRtool P-block (as Process transfer function) and defining the given specifications, the Nichols curve will be the one shown in figure 2 (blue line), which represents the process and controller C=1. Suppose the user wants to design a phase-lead controller, whose transfer function is defined by:

$$C(s) = K\frac{s-z}{s-p} \tag{9}$$

where the condition $|p| > |z|$ is satisfied. The optimal situation with the corresponding phase-lead controller design that satisfies the specifications is given in figure 6 along with the corresponding step response of the closed-loop.

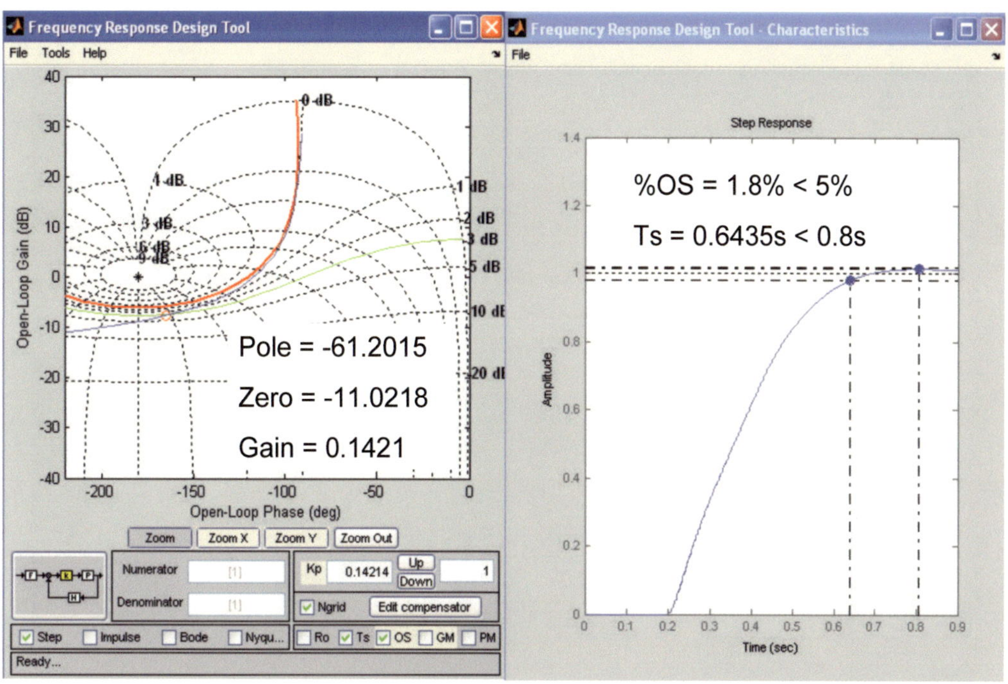

Fig. 6. Optimal phase-lead controller design fulfilling the required specifications and its step response for first example.

4.2 Second Order System

A second example is given to illustrate the robustness property of the designed controller. Consider a flight control system (angular) velocity control (it can be as well a servo-control system, antenna, disk drive, DVD, etc) represented by:

$$P(s) = \frac{32}{(s+4)(s+16)} \tag{10}$$

and the following specifications for a PI-controller design: robustness Ro>0.7 (a reasonably high robustness specification on a scale 0…1); overshoot %OS<10% and a *minimum* settling time T_s. The optimal PI-controller design and its corresponding step response are given in figure 7. The robustness can be evaluated in case the process model changes (the controller is fixed). To illustrate this case, consider the following transfer function, assuming that (10) has changed:

$$P^{*}(s) = \frac{48}{(s+5)(s+12)} \tag{11}$$

As it can be observed from (11), the changes do not affect only the gain (+50%), but also change the dynamics of the process quite significantly. In figure 8 can be evaluated the performance of the same PI-controller designed as in figure 7, but applied on the process model (11).

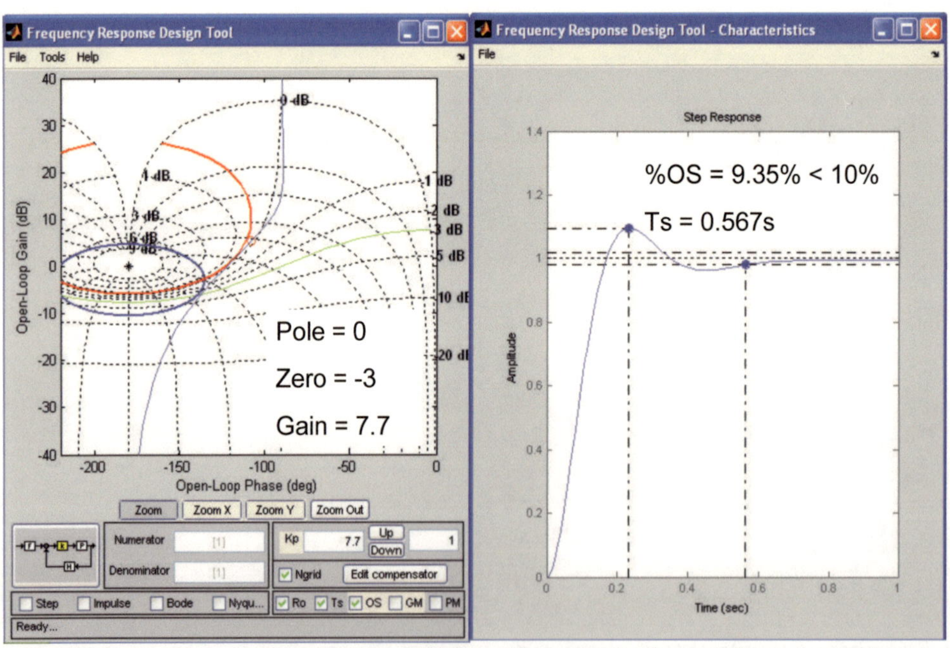

Fig. 7. Optimal PI-controller design fulfilling the required specifications and its step response for second example.

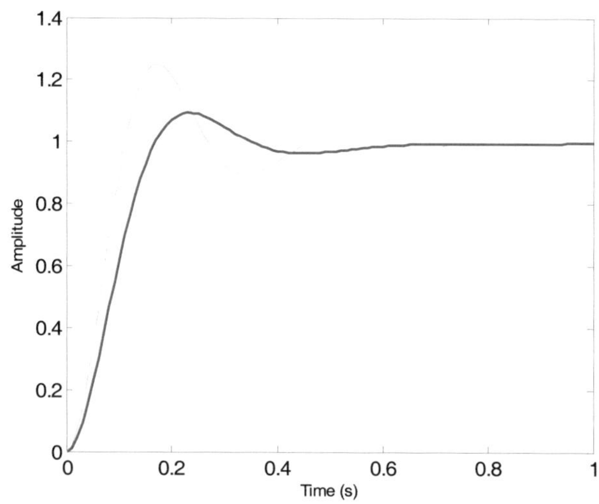

Fig. 8. Robustness evaluation of the PI-controller. The continuous line represents the nominal process model, and the dashed line represents the changed process model.

It can be concluded that the performance of the controller does not fulfill anymore the initial specifications (%OS>10%) but it has still a reasonably good behavior, taking into account the fairly large changes in the process transfer function. This is due to the fact that a relatively high robustness was asked in the specifications.

4.3 High Order + Poorly Damped System

Consider a mass-spring-damper system driven by an electrical motor, with two masses, three springs and one damper, given by the transfer function:

$$P(s) = \frac{800}{2.498s^4 + 16.65s^3 + 4473s^2 + 14400s + 1360000} \tag{12}$$

This system has two poorly damped eigenfrequencies $\omega_1 = 20.8$ rad/s and $\omega_2 = 39.1$ rad/s, with damping factors $\xi_1 = 0.08$ and $\xi_1 = 0.05$. Although this type of vibrational process should in practice be better controlled by a more sophisticated controller, it is possible to design with the CAD package, a suboptimal controller, of PID type. The result is then indicated in figure 9.

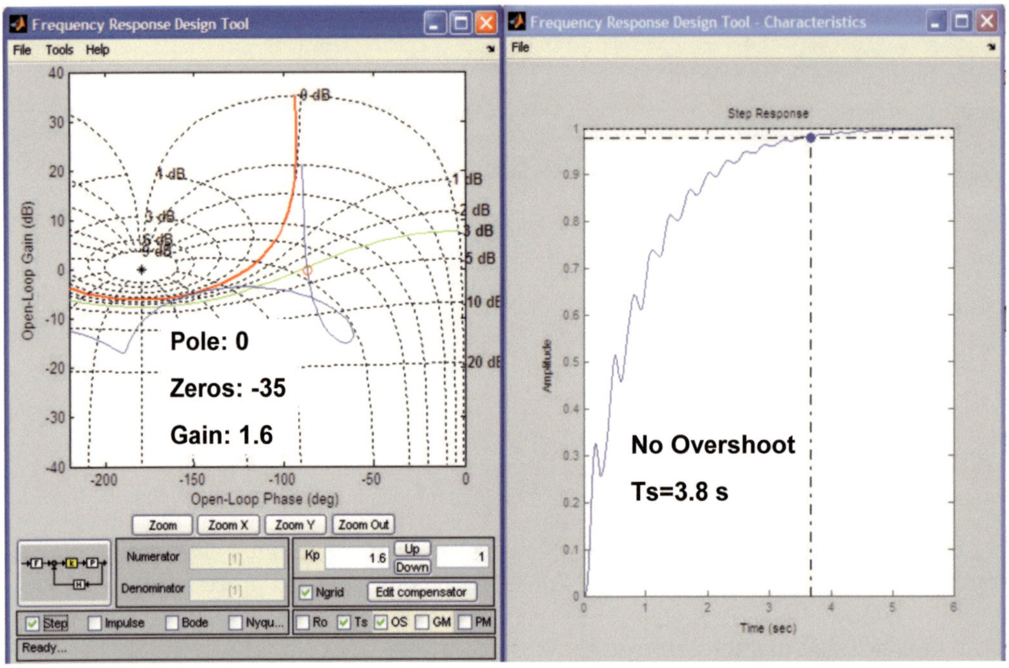

Fig. 9. Optimal PID-controller design fulfilling the required specifications and its step response for the high order plus poorly damped example.

4.4 High Order System

Consider the high order system presented by:

$$P(s) = \frac{1}{(s+1)^6} \tag{13}$$

and the specifications: phase margin PM=62°, overshoot %OS<20% and a the settling time T_s as small as possible. The PID controller design in FRTool is given in figure 10, along with the step response.

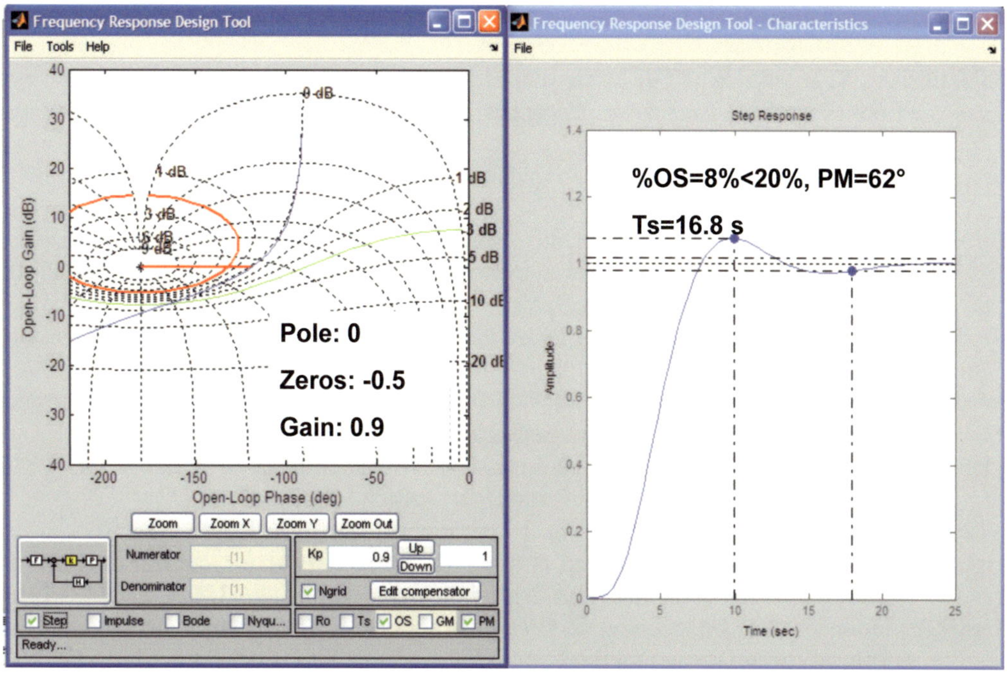

Fig. 10. Optimal PID-controller design fulfilling the required specifications and its step response for the high order example.

5. Conclusions

In this contribution, a novel controller design toolbox has been presented for the Matlab environment. It is based on the frequency response (Nichols chart) representation of systems and entitled FRtool - Frequency Response toolbox. The toolbox can perform controller design with given *practical* specifications such as overshoot, settling time, robustness (and also 'classical' gain and phase margins as an option). It can also deal with time-delay systems and it has been illustrated on four examples, of which two examples far from being second order systems (6th order, respectively, 4th order with poor damping).

Notice that the design procedure is extremely simple and close-at-hand, given the highly interactive graphical user interface of FRtool. Insight in all details of the underlying control engineering principles is not really required in order to use the CAD tool. This makes the toolbox attractive to students and engineers who are not control experts, and it offers an elegant solution for obtaining satisfactory results.

The CACSD tool has been used during five years by several hundreds of engineering students - not specializing in control engineering - in a *basic* control engineering course. The experience is that the majority of them are able to manage the tool and produce a good controller design within about fifteen minutes.

The software package is a development of Ghent University EeSA department; it consists of a set of Matlab files and is freely provided by email request.

6. References

Balakrihsnan, V. & Boyd S. (1994) Trade-offs in frequency-weighted H_∞-control, *Proceedings of the IEEE/IFAC Joint Symp. Computer Aided Control Systems Design,* Arizona, pp. 469–474

Bernstein, D. (2002) Feedback control: an invisible thread in the history of technology, *IEEE Ctrl Syst Mag,* 22(2), pp. 53-68

Dormido, S., Gordillo, F., Dormido-Canto, S. & Aracil J. (2002) An interactive tool for introductory nonlinear control systems education, *Proceedings of the 15th. IFAC World Congress* b'02, Barcelona, Spain

Dormido, S. (2004) Control Learning: Present and Future, *Annual Review in Control,* **28**, pp. 115-136

Johansson, M., Gäfvert, M., Åström, K. (1998) Interactive tools for education in automatic control, *IEEE Control Systems Magazine,* 18, pp. 33-40

Kheir, N., Åström, K., Auslander, D., Cheok, K., Franklin, G., Masten, M. & Rabins M. (1996) Control system engineering education, *Automatica,* **32**, pp. 147-166

Nise, N. (1995) *Control Systems Engineering,* 2nd edition, Addison-Wesley, chapter 10

Piguet, Y., Gillet D. (1997) Java-based remote experimentation for control algorithms prototyping, *Proc. of the American Control Confrence,* San Diego, U.S.A. pp. 1465-1469

Piguet, Y., Holmberg, U., Longchamp, R. (1999) Instantaneous performance visualization for graphical control design methods, *14th IFAC World Congress*, Beijing, China, 6p.

Poulis, D., Pouliezos, A. (1997) Computer assisted learning for automatic control, *IFAC Symposium on Advances in Control Education,* Estambul, Turquía, pp. 181-184

Satoh, T., Ishihara, T. & Inooka, H. (1994) Computer-aided control system design accounting pole-zero cancellations by the method of inequalities, *Proceedings of the IEEE/IFAC Joint Symp. Computer Aided Control Systems Design,* Arizona, pp. 481–488

Wittenmark, B, Häglund, H., Johansson, M. (1998) Dynamic pictures and interactive learning, *IEEE Control Systems Magazine,* 18, pp. 26-32

6

MATLAB – based software for modeling and studying grid – tied photovoltaic systems

Ali Assi and Mohammed Abdi Jama
UAE University
United Arab Emirates

1. Introduction

On-grid photovoltaic systems are well known and established systems in countries where solar energy is considered for residential buildings. MATLAB - based interactive software was developed to perform a quick and reliable design of grid - tied photovoltaic systems. The software is one of a kind, since it was the first time to build such a user-friendly comprehensive tool using MATLAB. The reason behind choosing MATLAB as a programming environment was primarily because of its powerful capabilities in numerical computation, data analysis and visualization. MATLAB also offers impressive and easy-to-use tools in applications development using Graphical User Interfaces (GUIs). The software was originally developed to serve educational purposes in the university domain, keeping in mind that MATLAB is considered a standard tool for tackling engineering problems. In the first stage of this project, the software was created by using simple script programming in m-files, and then these m-files were used later on with Graphical User Interface programming.

It's an essential step before installing a PV system, whether it is stand alone or grid-tied systems, to perform a detailed study which showcases its technical and economical feasibility. The technical validity of the PV system can be achieved by insuring that the system is working with a sufficient overall light-to-electricity conversion efficiency. This can be insured by a good selection of the system components such as PV panels, inverters, and cables, connecting the system components in a permissible manner, and a proper installation of the PV arrays in order to increase the sun light exposure and reduce surface temperatures.

The software was developed to perform a sequential task designing and planning procedure, which means that the design procedure consists of a number of dependent tasks that follow each other as shown in Figure.1. The software was equipped with a daily 13-year period meteorological database for number of cities in the United Arab Emirates (UAE) and PV system components database (i.e. PV modules, inverters, etc). MS Excel was used to build the databases, due to the simplicity of linking Excel to MATLAB routines and the ease of carrying out adjustments in the databases whenever necessary. The first task in the design procedure is to specify the site information and carry out the solar irradiance study. This is simply done by selecting the city of investigation, specifying the PV installation area orientation and inclination angle, and finally determining a proper reflectivity factor depending on the surrounding ground surfaces and structures (i.e. sand, grass, snow, etc).

In the next step, the designer is asked to give some details about the geometry of the installation area, such as the PV panels' alignment and dimensions. The designer will then move to do the building load profile study, in order to determine the building's annual energy requirements and decide how much the PV system will be responsible to cover. According to the aforementioned design steps, the software will suggest number of PV panels that would surely fit into the installation area. Upon the designer choice of the PV panel, the software will pick up number of DC/AC inverters according to their sizing factor.

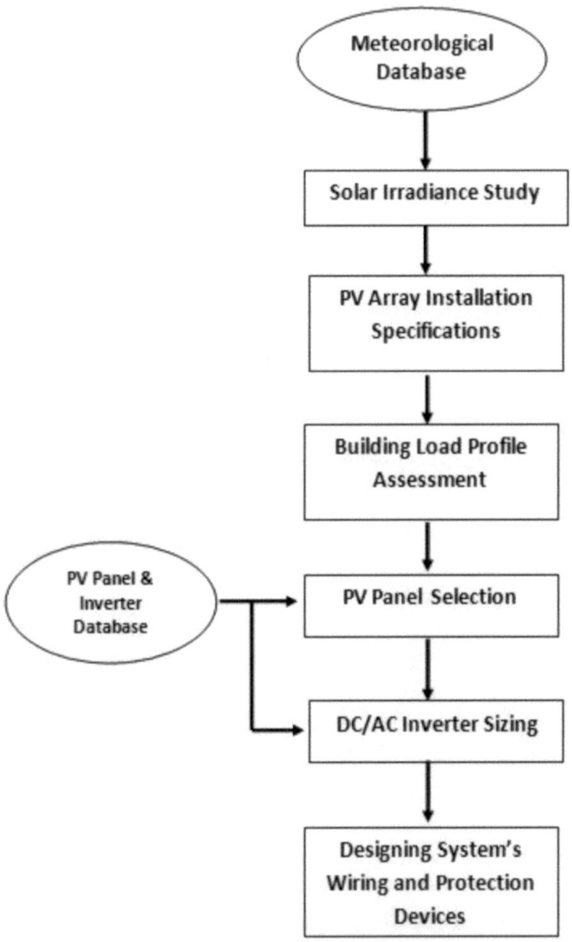

Fig. 1. The sequential design process used in the developed application

Up to this stage of the design procedure, the user can analyze the systems electrical performance graphically. The final design step is to select appropriate wiring and protection devices in such a way the planned system will be efficient and as safe as possible. A partitioned grid-tied PV system can be modeled and designed using the developed software. The partitioning feature is available in both DC and AC circuits of the PV system. The user can save his design at any stage of the design procedure, with the ability to load the saved file and perform adjustments whenever needed. Simplicity and clearance of the

software has been carefully preserved through creating the software in a one window multi panel fashion. Moreover, a user with minimum knowledge about PV systems can easily perform the designing procedure with the assistance provided by the guidance features of the software. These guidance means varies from providing quick and short explanation of some technical terminologies to providing the PV components datasheets.
The book chapter will mainly focus on the software capabilities and features and how MATLAB tools were used to create a reliable, simple, and user friendly software, that can be utilized to design, model, and predict grid-tied PV systems.

2. Background

The amount of carbon dioxide and sulfur oxides has increased rapidly, putting the whole world in a real battle with the resulting environmental problems (Ohnishi et al., 1995). In the light of that and in order for a future society to be sustainable while operating at or above our current standard of living, a shift away from carbon based energy sources must occur. Active PV energy technology can outline a partial solution for the environmental problems caused by accelerating global energy expenditure. Solar cells, since they convert solar light directly into electrical energy, are the most prominent candidates for a new and clean energy source. The research works on solar cells are moving fast worldwide. The technical, social, and economic benefits and limitations of PV technologies to provide electricity in both off-grid and on-grid applications are critically analyzed and it has been demonstrated that PV electrical production is a technologically feasible, economically viable, environmentally green, sustainable, and socially equitable solution to the energy needs in the near future (Pearce, 2002).
It is argued that in order to resolve the energy problems the world is facing today and to live comfortably in the 21st century, we must install photovoltaic power-generating systems in our homes, facilities, etc ..., and then build a global system with solar cells (Ohnishi et al., 1995).
Given this promising field of research all over the world, there is remarkably growing use of photovoltaic technologies in building design especially in housing. Unfortunately little research efforts have been devoted to the same sector in Arab countries in general and in the UAE in particular. According to the last general census in UAE for population, housing and establishments conducted by the Ministry of Economy on 6 December 2005, the total number of buildings in UAE reaches 336 thousand buildings and the number of residential buildings reaches about 60% of this number in Abu Dhabi and Dubai.
With the advances and enhancements in the quality of PV technologies, the electricity produced through utilizing these technologies in buildings is witnessing a noticeable increase. The spread of the use of PV technologies has and is still leading to a continuous decrease in the initial cost of installing PV systems. The situation is getting better with the current production of photovoltaic panels in Abu Dhabi. Consequently, it is thought that through the incorporation of photovoltaic technology in housing designs and BIPVs of the UAE, significant saving of energy will be achieved. This will help in realizing environmental sustainability in the housing sector in which the domestic use of electricity represents a significant level.
The integration of photovoltaic technologies into the design of typical housing might be generalized for the whole of the UAE. This may help the developed communities and the scattered ones in securing their electricity needs, or most of them, at a lower cost. Even with higher initial cost, PV systems are a good choice, considering the rising cost of fossil fuel - based electricity. This claim is supported by a recent research in the region (Egypt) which

proved that providing electricity for a family house in a rural zone using PV systems is very beneficial and competitive with other types of conventional energy sources, especially considering the decreasing prices of PV systems and their increasing efficiency and reliability. PV systems also have the advantage of maintaining a clean environment. The first solar village project in Abou-Sorra, Syria (Zein et al., 1998) showed that the generated power has been supplied to six households. The PV plant in this project has proved to be technically feasible and efficient. In comparison with a system based on diesel generator set, this PV system turned out to be more economically efficient for rural electrification of scattered houses and villages in sunny countries like Syria.

In addition, some research works have been conducted in the field of BIPV to tackle the issue of the practical and economic feasibility of adopting this system and how to overcome some inherited difficulties associated with its use. For example, in a study conducted by Omer et al. (2003) about a BIPV system installed on a detached house, using crystalline PV roof slates appropriate for domestic buildings, it has been found that the problems inherent in the design of roof slate integrated PVs result in elevated temperatures of cells. Therefore, the study suggested a modification to the way solar slates are built, and that is by providing airways and voids at the rear of the slates to allow air to pass between them, which would help to prevent any rise in cell temperature.

In the same study, in terms of economic justification, it was suggested that for the systems to be economically competitive, the array and labor costs need to be reduced. The researchers claim that this appears to be possible, given volume production and standardization of PV system components, which would drive down production costs, and reduce labor costs as installation experience becomes greater. Solar energy is already economically viable in many applications, and will continue to expand as production continues to increase in scale (Omer et al., 2003).

During recent years, interest in introducing the use of PV systems in the envelope of buildings (BIPV) has increased significantly. PV production has been doubling almost every 2 years, having increased by 48% since 2002 (Elgun & Shahrabi, 2008). The cumulative global PV power production was 12400 MW at the end of 2007 (Elgun & Shahrabi, 2008). UAE has strongly emerged in the PV market by launching its outstanding MASDAR initiative. This AED 15 billion initiative is expected to establish a strong renewable energy-dependent society in the country. This initiative is being directed to investments in a solution for the manufacture of future energy, as well as education and R&D, carbon management and sustainable development and planning.

Photovoltaic systems can be connected to the public electricity grid via suitable inverters. Energy storage (i.e. batteries) is not necessary in this case. On sunny days, the PV system provides power for the electrical appliances in a house. Excess energy is injected in the public grid. During the night and overcast days, power is drawn from the grid. PV systems operating parallel to the grid have great technological potential. However, without subsidies from the government or utilities, they are not yet financially competitive (Román et al., 2006).

Today, PV solutions form one of the basic concepts of smart homes, ensuring renewable, clean, and free-of-charge energy resource. Recently, the concept of a smart home has come to present this home not only as one that can provide a convenient and healthy life through the utilization of intelligent solutions mainly based on information and communication technologies, but also a home that can cover its energy requirements using renewable energy sources.

In this work, a MATLAB – based modeling tool to design, predict, and analyze grid- tied PV systems is presented. This tool offers a simple, quick, and accurate means for designing grid

-tied PV systems that can be used in smart homes. The simplicity of this modeling tool would probably make it a good tool for educational and research purposes. In comparison with the tools available in the market (i.e PVSol, PVSYST 4.37), this developed tool has some smart routines that classify and suggest suitable PV panels, while meeting both the power and installation area requirements, unlike other tools where either the output power or the installation area is considered. Besides, the user can easily design the cables and protection devices throughout all portions of the PV system. Such a feature is not available in other PV system design tools. In addition, the developed tool can be limited to records, such as weather records, of the UAE environment, or it may include weather records for tens of cities around the world. In section two all necessary background information is presented. The tool sections, the how-to-use and features of the proposed tool are discussed in section three. Section four presents the results and discussion of a case study, which was conducted to validate and show the features of the presented modeling tool.

3. Principle of Grid Tied Photovoltaic Systems

PV systems may be connected to the public grid. This requires an inverter for the transformation of the PV-generated DC voltage to the level of grid AC voltage. National and even regional regulations differ widely with respect to the policy of interconnection requirements and incentives for PV-generated electricity fed into the grid. In order to support the production of PV-generated power, some utilities offer a better price for the kWh fed into their grid than they charge for the kWh from the grid. In other locations a one-to-one ratio is applied which means the same kWh-price applies to both flow directions. The third option is to pay less for the generated PV power fed into the grid than for that sold to the consumer (Luque & Hudges, 2005). In comparing the rates, the fixed rates for the power connection also have to be considered. Depending on the kind of tariffs adopted, one or two electricity meters have to be used at the point of utility connection. Figure 2 shows a block diagram of a grid-connected PV system suitable for building integration. In grid-connected applications, photovoltaic systems must compete against the cost of the conventional energy source used to supply the grid. PV systems are particularly cost-effective when the utility load and solar resource profiles are well matched. This is, for example, the case in areas with high air-conditioning loads (such as the UAE) that have their peaks during the peak sunshine hours of the summer day.

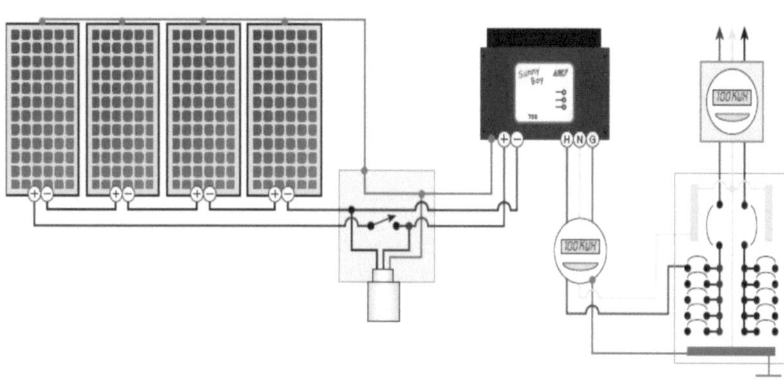

Fig. 2. Grid connected PV system schematic (source: www.homepower.com),

3.1 Conservation and Energy Efficiency

Renewable energy may seem to be a fascinating solution when you look at its benefits, but the main concern of someone willing to invest in renewable energy should be conservation and efficiency (Kerr, 2008). It is well known that renewable energy solutions are not yet economically competitive with exhaustible resources (i.e oil, coal and gas) especially for countries with low electricity tariffs like the UAE. Conservation involves changing your energy consumption behaviors from wasteful, inefficient habits (such as lighting places that should not be lighted) to energy-saving ones. Efficiency, on the other hand, is reducing energy consumption without changing your life-style by using efficient appliances (Livingston, 2007). Both conservation and efficiency work in parallel, because the more efficiency you have in your energy consumption the more money you will save when installing your renewable energy.

3.2 Principle of Building Load Assessment

Before designing a PV system for a building, whether it is a residential, commercial or public building, a full load assessment should be performed. The load assessment is described by a graph called the load profile. This graph shows the variation in the electrical load versus time (Woodfeden & Laforge, 2007). A load profile will vary according to the customer type (typical examples include residential, commercial and industrial), the temperature and the holiday seasons.

Figure 3 shows a typical load profile for a residential building (i.e. Villa) in Al Ain. Load profiles could be hourly, daily, monthly, or annually, depending on the nature of the analysis carried out and the level of precision required. The load assessment shows the power consumption behavior of people occupying the building, which is a vital step for planning and designing PV systems (Woodfeden & Laforge, 2007).

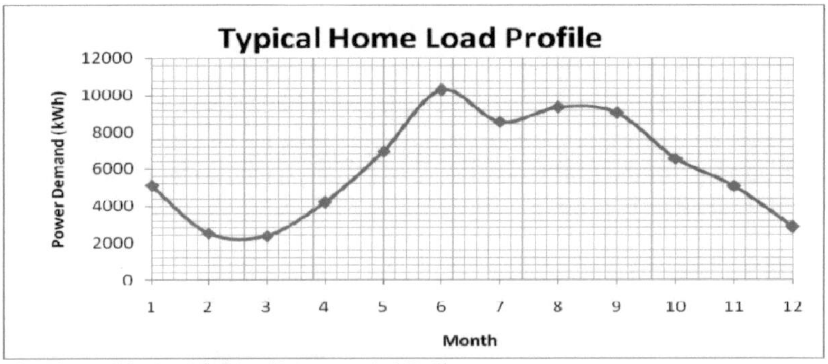

Fig. 3. Villa load profile in Al Ain (Source: AADC)

3.3 Grid Tied Inverters

In grid-connected PV systems, grid-tied inverters are used to convert the DC power from the PV generator (PV arrays) to AC power. The AC power is then delivered first to the home loads (i.e. household appliances), with any excess power fed to the grid as described in Figure 4.

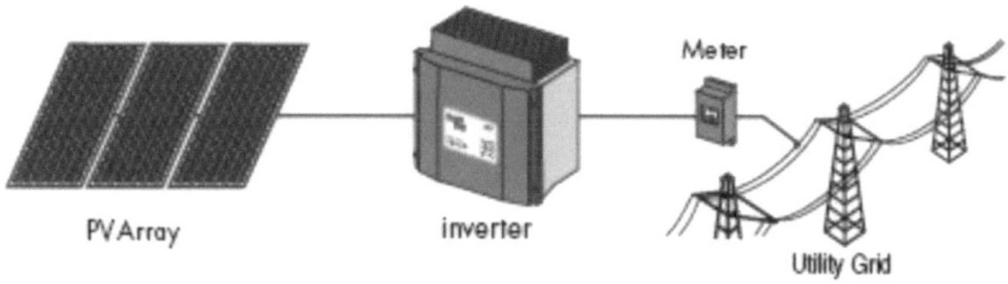

Fig. 4. Grid tied inverter connected between the PV generator and the utility grid

Most of the grid-tied inverters have a set of features that make them interactive with both the DC side (PV arrays) and the AC side (utility grid). These features improve the safety and reliability of the overall system. The inverters are equipped with an anti-islanding protection. Islanding occurs when the grid gets down and the inverter power output becomes in resonance with the power demand of home appliances (Woodfeden, 2007). This phenomenon may lead to some unwanted consequences if it lasts for a long time. To avoid this islanding, the inverter automatically switches off once it senses a utility outage. Another feature inverters should have is the ground fault detection system, which turns off the inverter until the fault is manually cleared. Some inverters can provide a string over- current protection by fixing fuses inside the inverter enclosure (SMA Sunny Boy, 2007).
The PV generator is connected to the grid via DC/AC inverters based on different technological concepts. There are three main topologies that can be followed in connecting the inverter to the PV generator. The first topology involves a number of modules connected in series (string), and a large number of parallel strings connected to one central inverter as shown in Figure 5 (Luque & Hedgus, 2005).

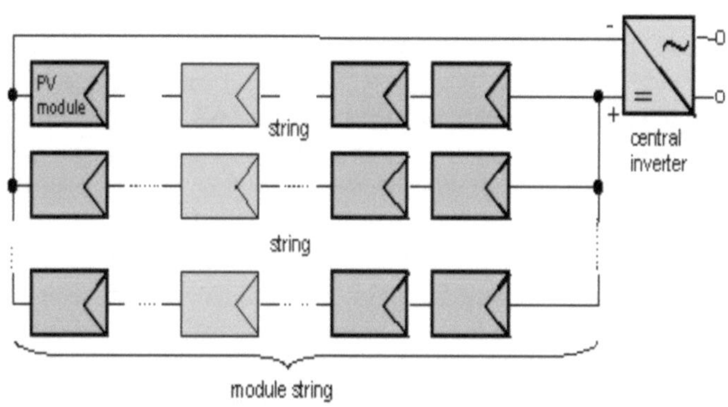

Fig. 5. Schematic of central inverter topology

Central inverter topology is mainly used for large PV systems (> 10kW), which is not the appropriate topology for residential building grid-tied PV system. Instead, the same central inverter topology is used but with a lower number of strings (< 4 strings); this topology is called multi-string inverter topology. The second topology is the string inverter topology, where each PV string is connected to one inverter, which is a good solution to minimize mismatch between strings and reduce losses due to shading as shown in Figure 6 (Luque & Hedgus, 2005).

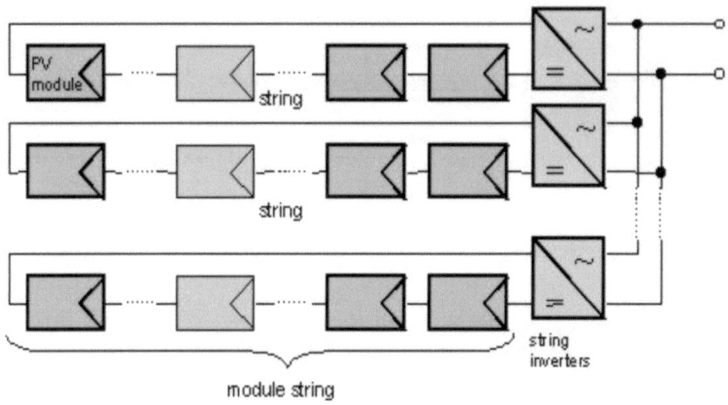

Fig. 6. Schematic of string inverter topology

String inverter topology was the first standard topology for utility–interactive systems. The third topology is a less popular topology, and that is the module integrated inverter, where each module has its own inverter. Module integrated inverter topology is used in relatively small PV systems (50 – 400 W), where a lower number of modules is involved. For large PV systems, module integrated inverter topology is avoided since it would make the system AC circuit drastically complex. These different types of inverters are all available in the market. The choice of the most appropriate inverter depends on the technical and economical feasibility (Luque & Hedgus, 2005).

3.4 PV System Sizing

The PV generator is designed in such a way that the output DC power, voltage and current match with the input DC ratings of the inverter used. This principle is very important from both technical and economical points of view, because if the PV system is optimally sized, the overall performance of the system would be improved. This means that the inverter is primarily picked according to the configuration of the PV generator. In other words, an oversized inverter will lead to a shorter inverter service life, which in turn may increase the maintenance cost of the system. On the other hand, an undersized inverter would cause an unjustified excess in the initial cost of the system (Luque & Hedgus, 2005). To determine the sizing status of the inverter, the inverter sizing factor is calculated, which is the ratio of the PV generator DC power output to the DC input power rating of the inverter. The inverter sizing factor ranges from 0 to 100%. The maximum and minimum sizing factors should be calculated to make sure that the inverter will remain optimally sized regardless of the DC power output of the PV generator throughout the year.

3.5 Balance of System

All components that make up the grid-tied PV system except the PV panels and the inverter are called Balance of the System (BOS). This includes wiring, protection devices (fuses and circuit breakers), enclosures, disconnects, installation equipment and power metering devices (Sick & Erge, 1996). Each of these components is designed and picked according to the system requirements and the code of the standard adopted in order to improve the system reliability, durability and safety.

3.5.1 Wiring and Cable Sizing

Every single conductor in the system is sized and picked to withstand the maximum possible operating currents and harsh weather conditions. The selection procedure is achieved through the corresponding standard code practices (IEEE P929, 1996). Cable sizing is the process of selecting the proper cable size (cross-sectional area) in a specific location of the system. The ampacity of the cable is calculated, which is the maximum current that a conductor can handle. Each cable has different ampacity values depending on the ambient temperature and cable insulation type (IEEE P929, 1996). Cable sizing includes the module interconnection cables, PV generator–inverter cables, inverter–utility grid cables and grounding cables.

3.5.2 Protection Devices

Like conductors, protection devices are sized according to their ampacity. The protection devices used in PV systems are mainly fuses and circuit breakers. The ratings of these devices are determined according to which part of the system these devices are protecting. The ampacity of a protection device should be smaller than that of the conductor it is directly connected to, while both should have the same insulation (National Electrical Code, 2005). Fuses and circuit breakers are encapsulated in enclosures that are usually equipped with a manual disconnect such as junction boxes.

3.5.3 DC and AC Disconnects

To improve the level of safety of the PV system, manual disconnects should be used in both DC and AC sides of the system, in such a way that it would be easy to isolate any portion of the system in case of a fault or for maintenance. At least one disconnect should be installed right between the PV generator and the inverter, while another disconnect should be placed between the inverter and the utility grid (IEEE P929, 1996).

3.5.4 Metering Devices

In grid-connected PV systems, power metering devices are an important part of the system. A wattmeter should be used to record the amount of energy the PV system is generating during the day, alongside the normal wattmeter that records the amount of energy bought from the utility company. Sometimes, one wattmeter could be used, in such a way that its needle spins in one direction when energy is bought and in the opposite direction when it is sold.

4. The Modeling Tool

This section presents all the methods, techniques and procedures applied to build a comprehensive PV tool that can be used to design, predict and analyze on-grid PV systems.

4.1 Site information & PV Array Installation

The first step in designing the grid-tied PV system is to specify the site information such as the city, the tilt angle and the reflectivity factor. These pieces of information are enough to calculate the daily average global irradiance, which is a very important parameter in the PV system as shown in Figure 7. The PV tool prompts the user to enter the dimensions of the array installation area (width and height) as shown in Figure 8.

Fig. 7. Site information section

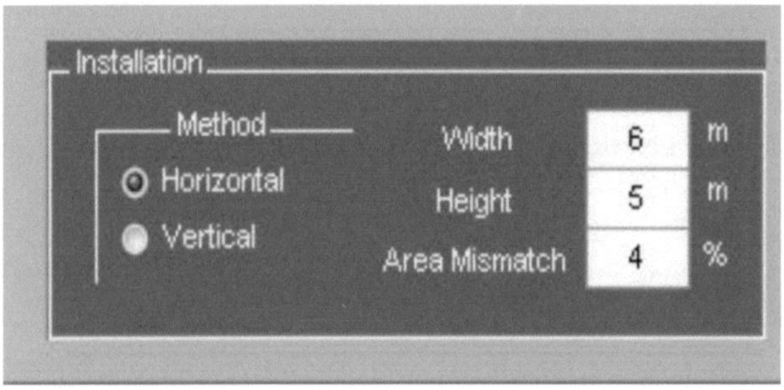

Fig. 8. Array installation parameters

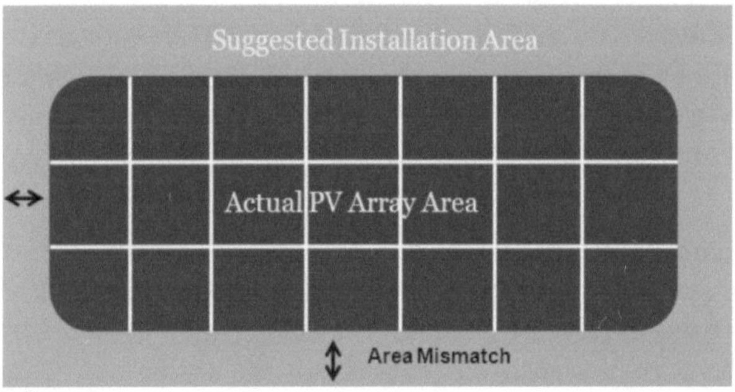

Fig. 9. Area mismatch

The tool will fit the module on the suggested area considering the space between modules in each string and between strings as well. The user will be able to control the accuracy of the installation area filling by adjusting the area mismatch variable, which is the allowed error margin between the suggested installation area and the actual PV array area as shown in Figure 8. The user can also specify whether the modules alignment is horizontal or vertical as shown in Figure 9. This feature has been added to make sure that the modules alignment matches with the shape of the installation area, hence ensuring a good appearance of the PV array as part of the building.

4.2 Load Profile Section

In the load profile section, the user will be able to select the load profile model from the pop-up menu shown in Figure 10. The menu includes three load profile models for residential buildings (villa). Each of these models represents a level of power demand behavior. For

example, model A represents the average power consumption, while model B and C represent the maximum and minimum power consumption respectively.
These three load profile models were developed by analyzing and studying a 13-year annual load profile for tens of villas in Al Ain. To develop a realistic and accurate power demand profile representing the environment and the life-style in Al Ain, a large number of load profiles were obtained from Al Ain Distribution Company (AADC). After selecting the proper load profile model, the user should specify the coverage factor as shown in Figure 10, which is the percentage the PV system is expected to cover from the annual home power demand. This way, the tool will give an indication message showing to what extent the designed PV system will cover the annual power demand.

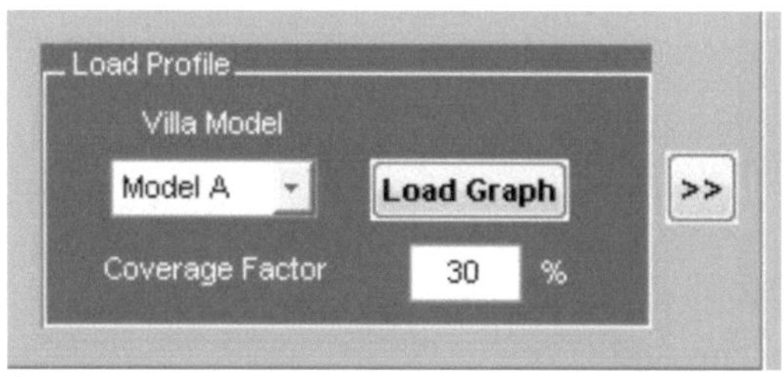

Fig. 10. load profile section

4.3 Modules Sorting Procedure

The database built for this tool includes various types of modules, each with different electrical and mechanical characteristics. To make the design procedure simpler and faster, the PV tool has some routines that sort out the most appropriate modules in terms of fitting the installation area, so instead of going through all modules, only the modules that would fit the suggested installation area will be displayed for the user as shown in Figure11.

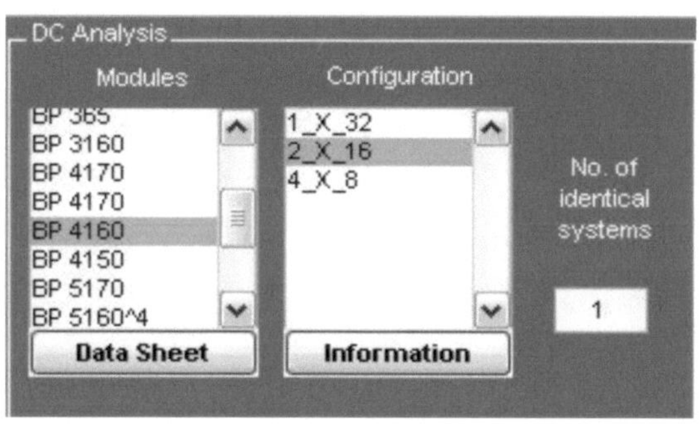

Fig. 11. load profile section

After confirming the installation area dimensions, the user can select from a group of modules based on the desired electrical behavior. Once the user selects one of the listed modules, the tool determines all possible PV array configurations: a number of parallel strings (group of modules in series) and a number of modules per string as shown in Figure 12.
The tool is designed to show all possible configurations, where the number of strings is less than the number of modules per string as shown in Figure 11. This is to limit the number of choices in front of the user and because of the fact that if the number of strings is greater

than number of modules per string, high overall current and low overall voltage will be obtained, which is not technically recommended (IEEE P929, 1996).

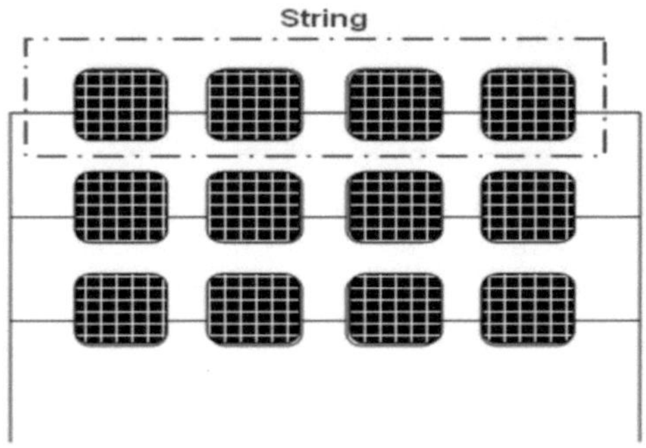

Fig. 12. PV generator configuration schematic

4.4 Inverter Selection Methodology

After the module and the PV generator configurations are selected, the tool searches the database of inverters for the inverters that would work properly with the designed PV array. The inverter searching procedure is performed by comparing the output voltage, current and power of the DC generator with the DC input ratings of the inverter. The tool lists all the inverters that can work properly from the technical point of view as shown in Figure 13. All selected inverters would probably work in all conditions such as maximum irradiance days (maximum current) and maximum ambient temperature days (minimum voltage).

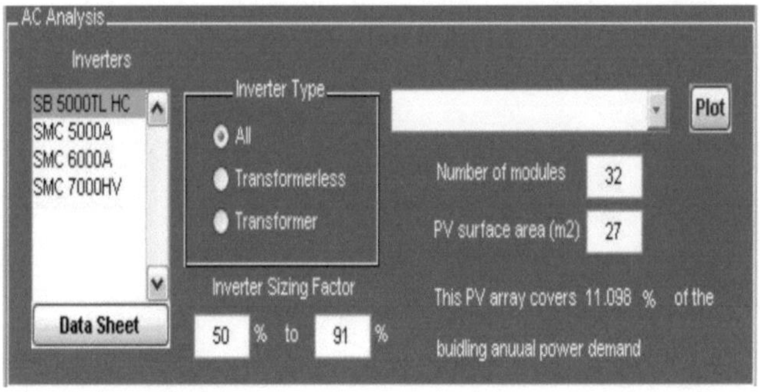

Fig. 13. Inverter selection section

Based on the budget and the preferred level of system reliability, the user can select the suitable inverter. The tool offers a helpful clue for the designer to select the best inverter based on the inverter sizing factor range as explained above. The higher the sizing factor range, the better the design would be. Practically, an inverter sizing factor criterion that ranges from 45 to 100 could be considered optimal (Antonio Luque and Steven Hedgus, 2005). In general, the inverter sizing factor range is calculated as shown in equation 1.

$$Sizing\ Factor\ Range = \frac{P_{Array}^{Min}}{P_{Inverter}^{Max}}\ to\ \frac{P_{Array}^{Max}}{P_{Inverter}^{Max}} \tag{1}$$

4.5 PV System Partitioning

The PV tool offers the opportunity of designing a partitioned grid-tied PV system. The partitioning feature is available for both DC and AC circuits of the PV system. For the DC side, if the system is composed of several PV generators located in different locations, while they all have the same design parameters and specifications, the user can design one PV generator and then specify a number of identical PV generators as shown in Figure 10. This feature duplicates the PV array and prevents the designer from going back and starting again from the beginning. The duplicated PV arrays are then connected to the same inverter, so the partitioning of the DC side is at the PV array level. For the AC side, the PV system can be divided into independent sub-systems, each subsystem with its own inverter. Then all the subsystems are combined together via a combiner enclosure to connect it to the home distribution panel as shown in Figure 14.

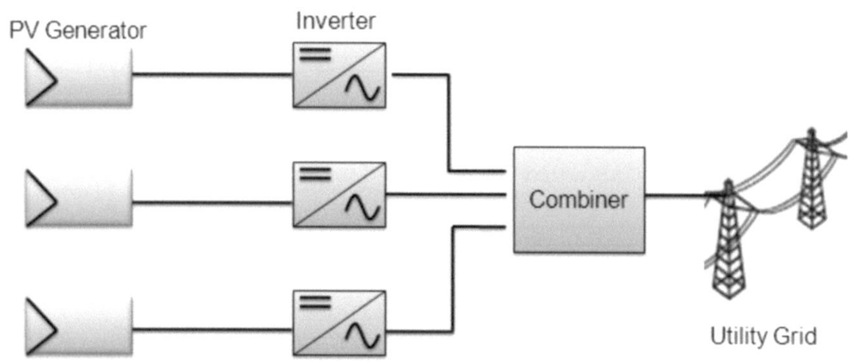

Fig. 14. Schematic of an AC partitioned grid tied PV system

4.6 Cable and Protection Devices Sizing Procedure

Picking the appropriate components for the PV system is very important to ensure a high level of reliability and safety. The PV tool computes the cable sizes at every spot in the system. In electrical power systems, most conductors are restricted from operating on a continuous basis at more than 80% of their rated ampacity. This principle also applies for over-current protection devices. However, the current-carrying conductors used in PV systems are further de-rated by a factor of 80% due to the manner in which PV modules generate power in response to sunlight and because the intensity of sunlight at noon may exceed the standard test conditions (IEEE P929, 1996). The ampacity of conductors and the sizing of over-current devices is an area that requires careful attention. Temperatures and wiring methods must be addressed for each site. Calculations start with the 125% of Isc value to comply with the UL 1703 requirements, and an additional 125% must then be used for code compliance (UL 1703, 2000). Finally, the cable ampacity is adjusted for temperature using the cable de-rating table. The user is requested to specify the ambient temperature of operation and the cable insulation type at a specific part of the PV system, and then the tool will determine the adequate cable size and protection device rating for that part as shown in Figure 15.

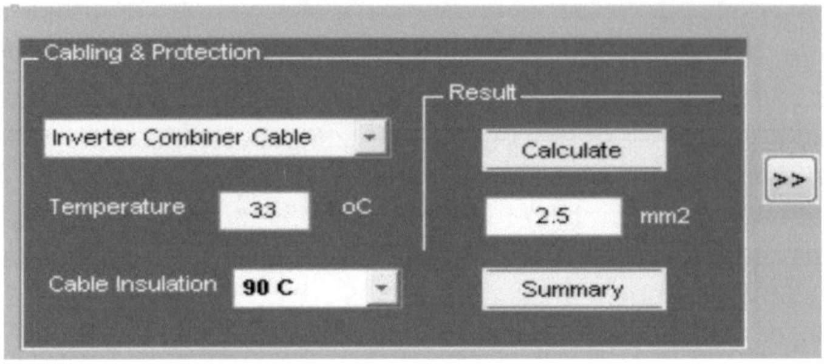

Fig. 15. Cabling and protection section

Regarding the cabling of the system, the tool is designed to determine the cable sizes at the following parts of the system:

- Module interconnection cabling
- DC combiner – Inverter cabling
- Inverter – AC combiner cabling (if more than one inverter is used)
- Equipment grounding cable
- DC grounding electrode cable

Grounding all PV system components is an important step to make the system immune to all kinds of hazards caused by electrical faults. After determining the cable size, the tool computes the proper protection device ratings to protect each cable and all attached equipment from any over-current that may occur.

4.7 Economical Assessment Procedure

The PV tool offers the opportunity to perform an economical assessment. The economical evaluation is based on two variables, the net present value (NPV) and the system payback period (P) (Jose L. Bernal-Agustın, Rodolfo Dufo-Lopez, 2005). Basically, both of these variables are strongly linked to one another because NPV shows whether the system will pay-off during its service life time or not, while the year in which the system pays-off will determine the payback period (P). To calculate the net present value (NPV), the system initial cost (S) should be calculated as shown in equation 2.

$$S = C_{investment} - C_{Subsidy} \tag{2}$$

The investment cost includes the PV system cost, which in turn includes all PV components such as modules, inverters and BOS equipments. The annual maintenance cost is also included in the investment cost. The initial cost of grid-tied PV systems is unfortunately very high, so these renewable solutions can be made economically competitive by applying subsidy programs. The subsidy programs can be offered and controlled by the government, who can pay a percentage of the initial investment cost or increase the price of the energy sold to the utility (Bernal-Agustın & Dufo-Lopez, 2005).

The net cash flow (Q) i.e. the difference between the cash input generated by the investment and the payment or cash output the investment requires) can be calculated for each year (j) as described in equations 3 & 4:

$$Q_j = (Cash\ Input)_j - (Cash\ Output)_j \tag{3}$$

$$Q_j = (p_b\ E_{PV-Aut} + p_S\ E_{PV-Inj}) - (\ C_M + C_{Ins}\ ) \tag{4}$$

where p_b and p_s are the prices of the energy bought from and sold to the utility respectively. E_{PV-Aut} is the annual energy generated by the PV system connected to the grid that is auto-consumed (i.e. not bought from the grid), and E_{PV-Inj} is the generated energy injected into the grid annually (Bernal-Agustın & Dufo-Lopez, 2005).
Furthermore, C_M and C_{Ins} are the annual costs attributed to the operation, maintenance and insurance. It should be taken into account that the income and expenditures may vary from year to year due to inflation. For PV systems connected to the grid, the maintenance costs and insurance increase with inflation. However, the income due to the sale of the energy does not necessarily have to increase. The effect of the inflation rate (g) is calculated as shown in equation 5.

$$Q_j = (p_b\ E_{PV-Aut} + p_S\ E_{PV-Inj}) - (\ C_M + C_{Ins}\ )(1+g)^j \tag{5}$$

In order to compare investments, it is necessary to consider the same period of time. If the cash flow is over various years, they should all be considered during the same period of time (normally at the start of the investment). This way, different investments can be compared using the Nominal Interest Rate and the Net Present Value. The Nominal Interest Rate (i) is the monetary price or the interest rate that allows different economic quantities to be referred to each other, transferred periodically over time, to the initial year of investment. The net present value of the investment is defined as described in equation 6.

$$NPV = -S + \sum_{J=1}^{N} \frac{Q_j}{(1+i)^j} \tag{6}$$

Where (NPV) is the duration of the investment (i.e. the service time of the PV system) and (i) is the nominal interest rate. In order to say that the generated benefits from the system are greater than the cost, NPV should be as large as possible and always positive (Jose L. Bernal-Agustın, Rodolfo Dufo-Lopez, 2005).
The Pay-Back Time (P) is the number of years, up to the present moment, needed to make the NPV of the cash flow equal to the initial outlay of the investment. It can be expressed as shown in equation 7.

$$-S + \sum_{J=1}^{N} \frac{Q_j}{(1+i)^j} = 0 \tag{7}$$

Based on this method of analysis, the shorter the Pay-Back time is, the better the investment. This is a criterion that values the availability more than the profitability and does not take into account the cash flow generated after the recuperation period (Bernal-Agustın & Dufo-Lopez, 2005).

4.8 Guidance and Documentation

The PV tool (Figure 16) is designed to be simple, clear and easy-to-use. To achieve these characteristics, guidance and help features were added so that the user will be able to understand all technical parameters and terminologies during the design process. All modules and inverters data sheets were added to help the user choose the most appropriate PV component. The tool also has the ability to provide a full and comprehensive summary of the designed system as final output documentation.

5. Results and Discussions

5.1 Design of a BIPV Villa in Al Ain – UAE

The developed PV software was used to design a grid-tied photovoltaic system for a residential building (villa) in Al Ain. Then the villa was prototyped to show how the PV array is integrated into the structure of the building. The system consists of three PV generators (subsystems). Each subsystem is oriented towards the south. The first subsystem is mounted on the southward-tilted parts of the building roof with an inclination angle of 30°. The second and third subsystems are located on the garage with an inclination angle of 15° as shown in Figure 17. Each subsystem was designed to be independent of both the DC and AC sides.

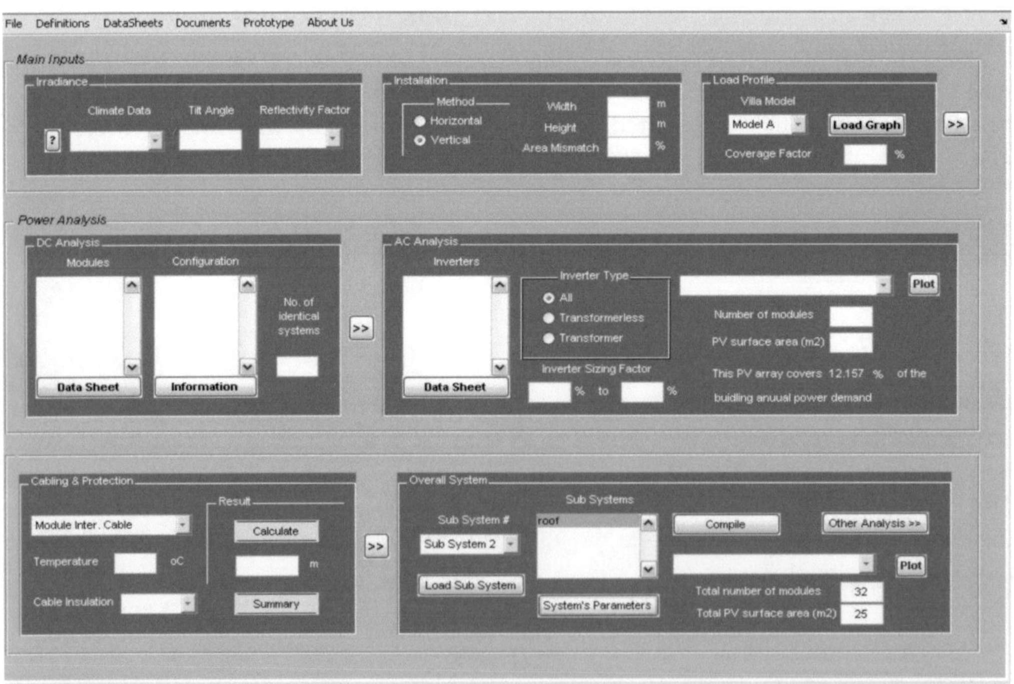

Fig. 16. PV Tool

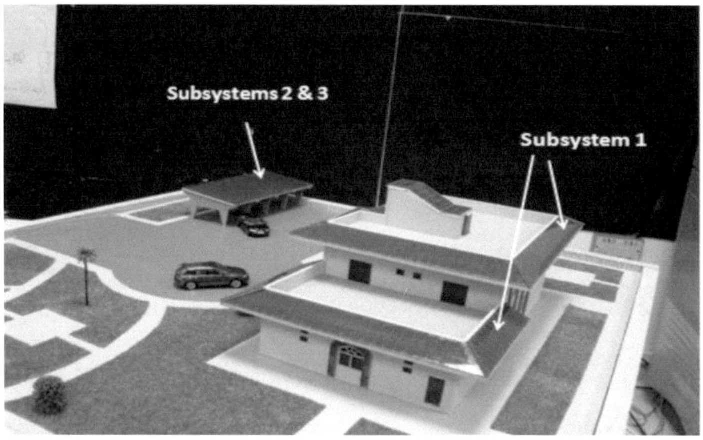

Fig. 17. Villa prototype

5.1.1 Roof Array (Subsystem 1)

The design of the PV system starts with the selection of a proper load profile. Model A load profile, which represents the average energy consumption of typical villas in Al Ain, was selected to be used in the design. Figure 18 shows the average monthly energy consumption for Model A.

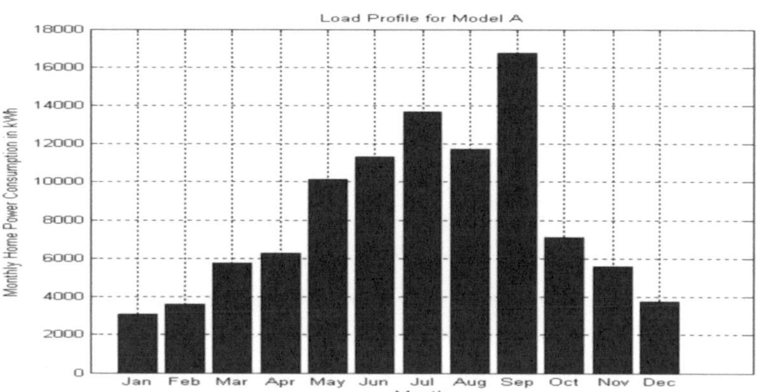

Fig. 18. Average monthly energy consumption

The south-facing roof is tilted at an angle of 30°. Figure 19 shows the daily average global irradiance distribution with reflectivity factor set to 0.2. The installation area dedicated to subsystem 1 was approximately 41 m^2 (26.5 x 1.70 m). To have a good- looking PV array, the modules were aligned vertically in order to suit the shape of the installation area.

Moreover, the aesthetical side was preserved by setting the area mismatch factor to 5%, so that the proposed installation area will be very close to the actual array area. The proper module was selected from a set of modules suggested by the tool, keeping in mind that all the suggested modules should fit into the installation area. BP SX 3200 was used as a module in subsystem 1 array with a rated maximum power of 200W. A total number of 29 modules were used with a configuration of 1 x 29, occupying an area of 44m2. Figure 20 demonstrates the daily DC analysis parameters of subsystem 1.

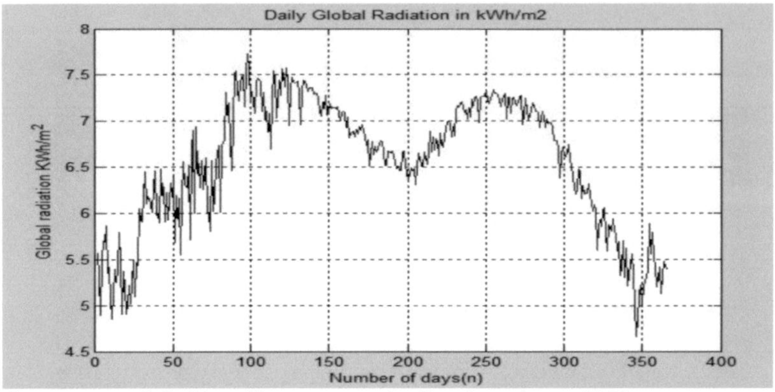

Fig. 19. Daily average global irradiance on an inclined surface of 30°

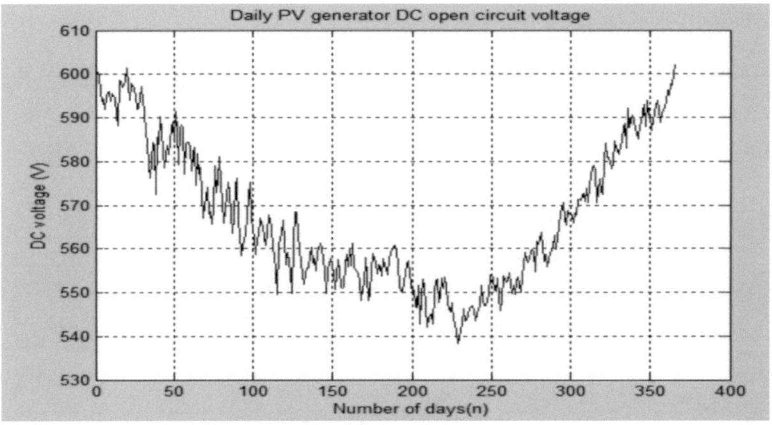

(a)

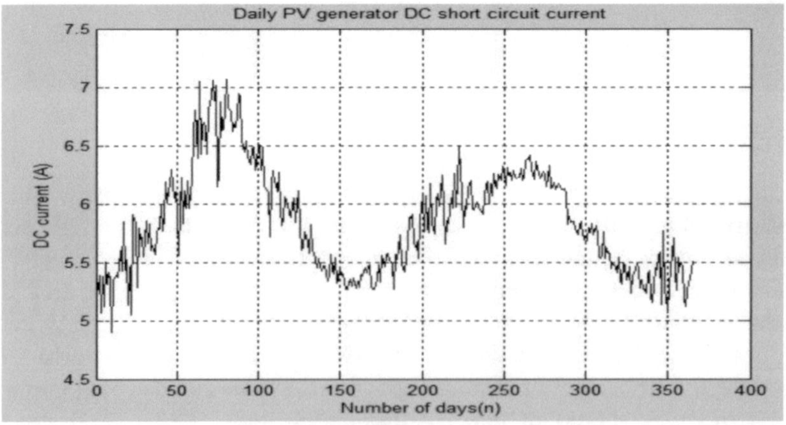

(b)

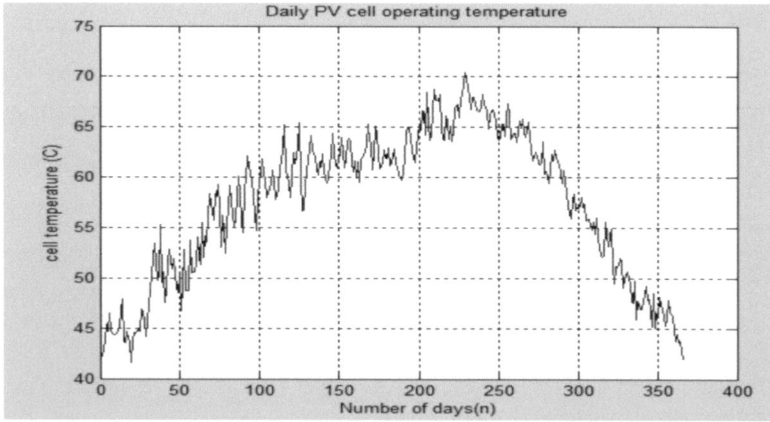

(c)

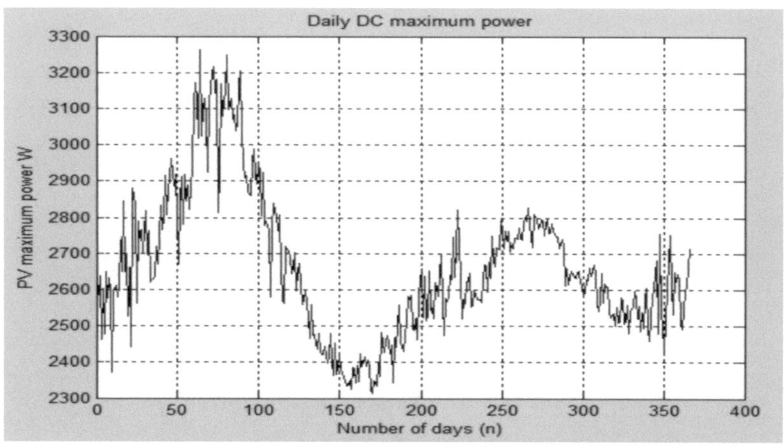

(d)

Fig. 20. (a) Daily DC open circuit voltage of the array (b) Daily DC short circuit current (c) Solar cell operating temperature along the year (d) Daily DC maximum power of the array

After completing the design of the PV generator, a proper grid-tied inverter was selected. SB 5000TL HC is the proper inverter for this design, since it has a sizing factor range of 53% - 86% (which is a permissible sizing factor range). The tool predicted the annual energy produced by subsystem 1 (approximately 12.3 MWh). Figure 21 shows the energy produced by subsystem 1.

After designing both the PV array and the grid-tied inverter, the next step is to size the cables and protection devices for all parts of the PV system. The module interconnection cable size is found to be 2.5mm^2 and it is protected by a 12A fuse located at the DC combiner enclosure (ambient temperature of 70° C and insulation of 90°C). Since subsystem 1 has a single string array, the array–inverter part has the same cable and fuse sizes as the previous part (PV array). The inverter–AC combiner cable is sized to be 6mm^2 (ambient temperature 60°C and insulation 90°C).

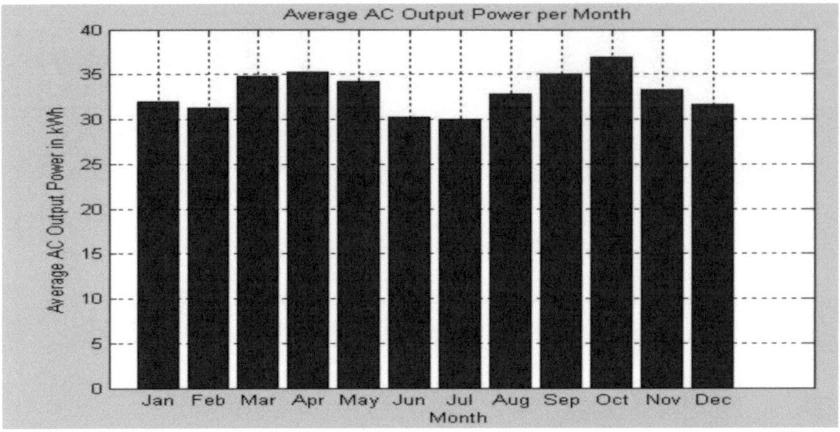

(a)

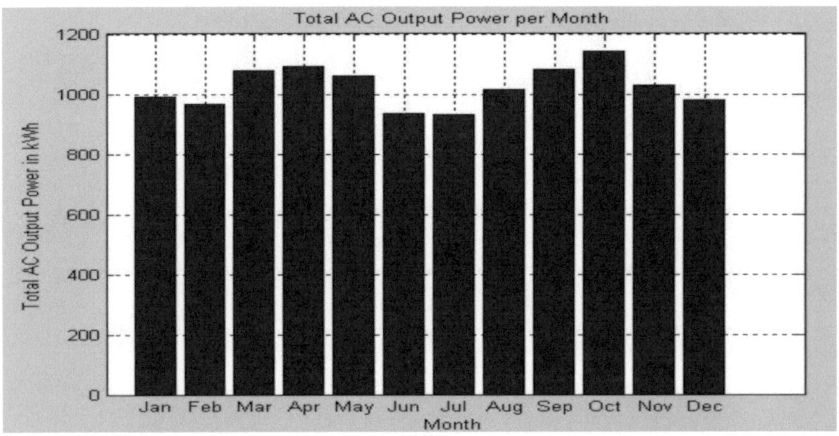

(b)

Fig. 21. (a) The average energy yield of sub-system 1 per month (b) The total energy output every month

5.1.2 Garage Array (Subsystem 2)

Subsystem 2 is located on the garage with dimensions of 6.25 x 3 and tilt angle of 15°. The selected module for this array was BP 175I with configuration of 2 x 7 and total gross PV array area of $10m^2$. The inverter SB 3300TL HC was selected as the most appropriate inverter with sizing factor range of 67 – 95 %. The DC analysis results of subsystem 2 are shown in Figure 22. The total monthly energy yield produced by this subsystem is shown in Figure 23.

The module interconnection cable was sized to be $2.5mm^2$ and it is protected with a 9A fuse located in the DC combiner enclosure (ambient temperature 70°C and insulation 90°C). The array- inverter cable was sized to be $4mm^2$ and it is protected with a 20A fuse located in the DC disconnect enclosure. The inverter–AC combiner cable size was designed to be $6mm^2$.

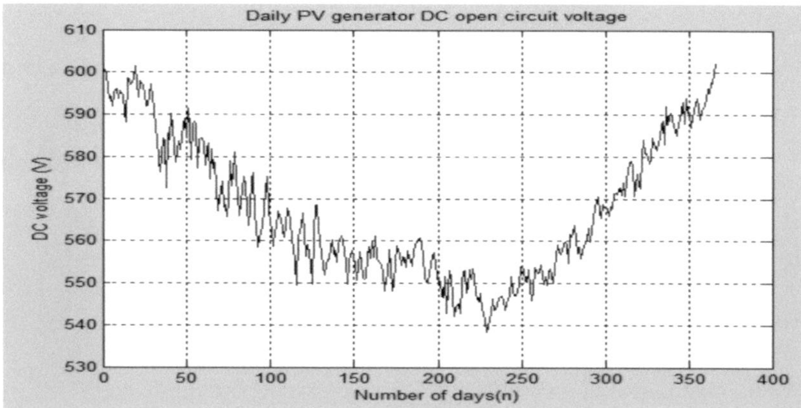
Daily PV generator DC open circuit voltage
DC voltage (V)
Number of days(n)
610
600
590
580
570
560
550
540
530
0
50
100
150
200
250
300
350
400

(a)

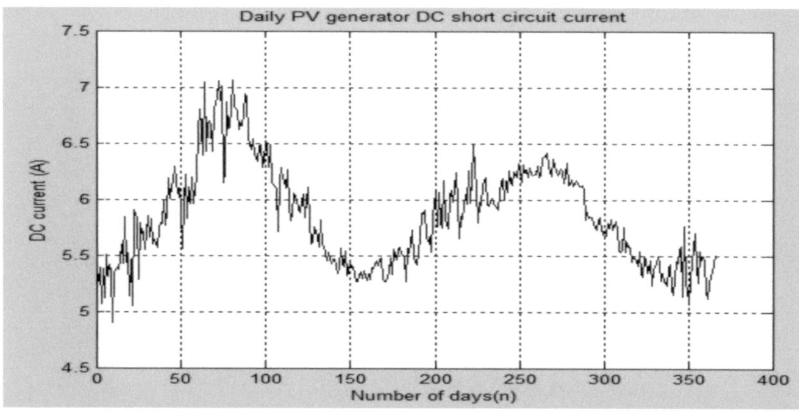
Daily PV generator DC short circuit current
DC current (A)
Number of days(n)
7.5
7
6.5
6
5.5
5
4.5
0
50
100
150
200
250
300
350
400

(b)

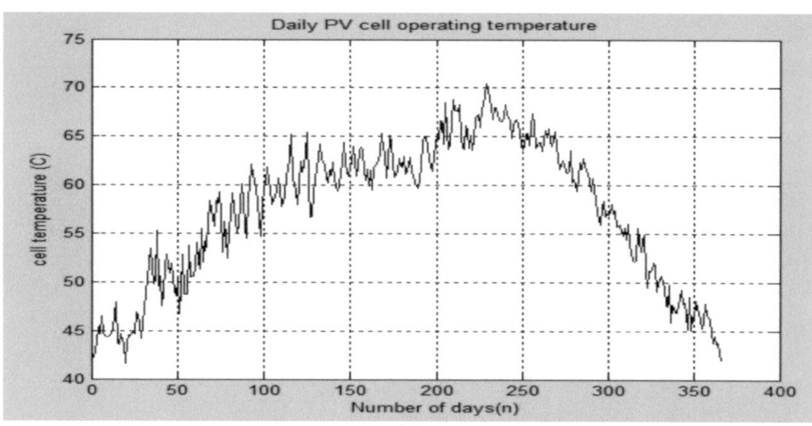
Daily PV cell operating temperature
cell temperature (C)
Number of days(n)
75
70
65
60
55
50
45
40
0
50
100
150
200
250
300
350
400

(c)

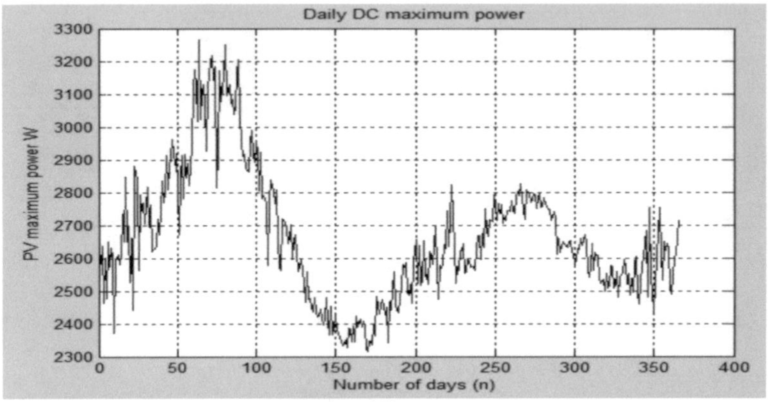

(d)

Fig. 22. (a) Daily DC open circuit voltage of the array (b) Daily DC short circuit current (c) Solar cell operating temperature along the year (d) Daily DC maximum power of the array

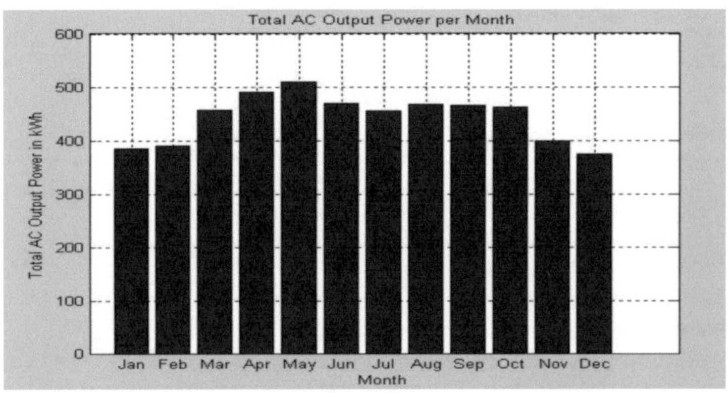

Fig. 23. Total energy yield per month of sub-system 2

5.1.3 Overall PV System

The overall coverage factor of the whole PV system was determined to be approximately 27%. Figure 24 shows the overall output energy of the combined PV system.

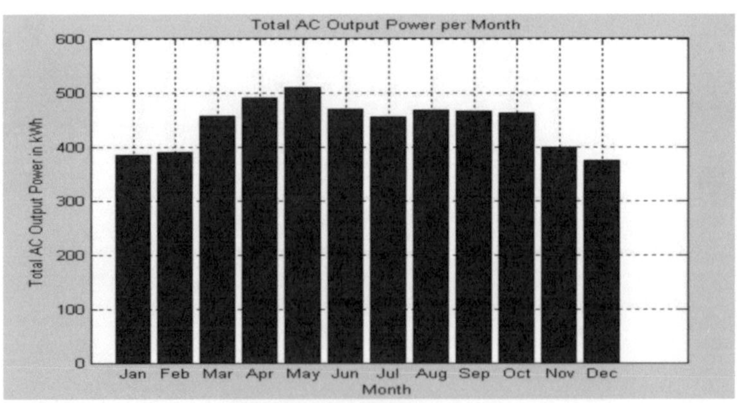

Fig. 24. Monthly maximum overall PV energy output

Figure 25 shows the monthly building energy consumption versus the monthly energy produced by the PV system.

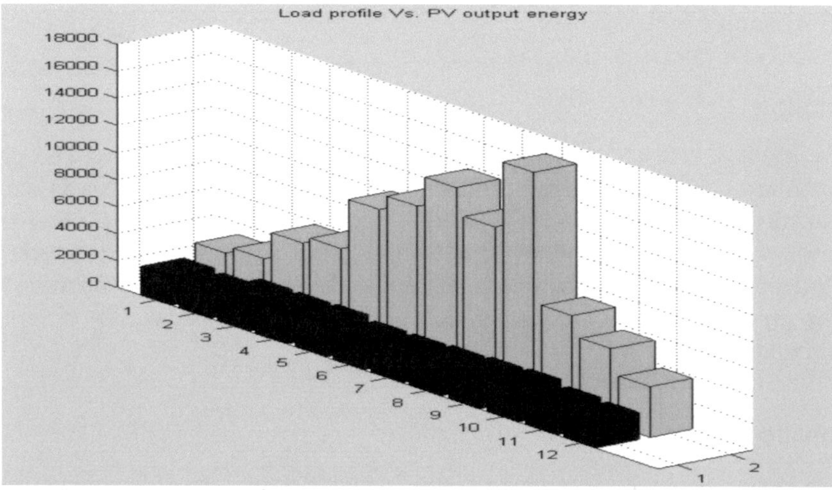

Fig. 25. Building energy consumption (grey columns) vs. PV energy output (black columns)

It is obvious that the monthly energy consumption values are much larger than the value of the energy produced by the PV system, which is an expected result. The PV system was basically designed to cover up to 25% - 30%, while the actual PV system coverage factor is approximately 28%, keeping in mind that the overall wiring losses comprise around 5% (typical value). It is known that the total PV energy production is divided into auto-consumed energy and injected energy. Figure 26 shows the total auto-consumed energy versus the total injected power.

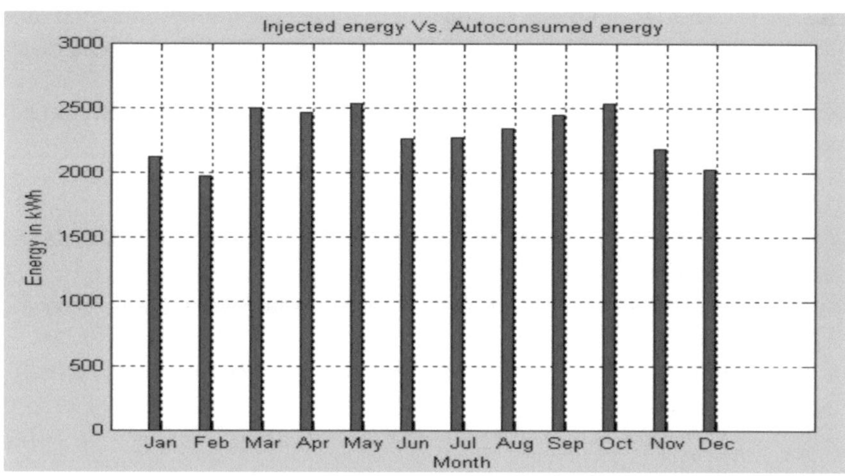

Fig. 26. Auto consumed energy vs. injected energy

The monthly total injected energy was equal to zero in all months, because all the generated PV power was consumed. So the green bars represent only the auto-consumed energy. The designed PV system has an overall system efficiency of 15%, which makes sense due to the large losses in the system, which are mainly due to the low light- electricity conversion efficiency of the crystalline-type panels used in this modeling tool and also the losses in the cables and wires used in the system.

6. Conclusion

This paper presents a MATLAB-based tool for the design of PV systems. The proposed modeling tool uses daily weather data and simple irradiance models that are as accurate as many other complex models. This tool is flexible enough to adapt quickly if other locations in the world are to be investigated. Besides, the tool offers a variety of PV products such as modules, inverters, cables, etc. The tool is still under development to include more features such as the prediction of the amount of CO_2 that can be reduced in case of replacing a traditional building by a BIPV.

7. Acknowledgments

The authors would like to thank engineers Sina Fattahi and Ibrahim Al Shehhi for their help in building various databases, Engineer Khaled Al-Kathairi for his help in developing the Matlab code, the National Center of Meteorology and Seismology (Abu Dhabi) for providing weather data, Al-Ain Distribution Company (AADC) for providing load profiles, and Mariam Assi from American University of Beirut (AUB) for revising the English language of the final manuscript. This work was financially supported by the UAE University under the contract no. 07-04-7-11/09.

8. References

Bernal-Agustın, J.L. and Dufo-Lopez, R. (2006). Economical and environmental analysis of grid connected photovoltaic systems in Spain. Renewable Energy, Vol. 31, pp.1107–1128.

Elgun, S.Z. and Shahrabi, K. (2008). Solar Airports. *IAJC – IJME International Conference*, 2008, No. 95.

IEEE P929 (1996). Recommended practice for utility interface of photovoltaic (PV) systems. Draft 9.

Kerr, A. (2008). Making PV Pay, It's Just a Good Business Sense. www.homepower.com. (accessed on 15 June 2008).

Livingston, P. (2007). First steps in renewable energy for your home. *Home Power Magazine*, April and May 2007 edition, pp.68–69.

Luque, A. & Hedgus, S. (2005). *Handbook of Photovoltaic Science and Engineering*, 1st ed, England.

National Electrical Code (2005). *Photovoltaic power systems (suggested practices)*, Articles 100, 110, 200, 240, 300 and 310. USA.

Ohnishi, M., Takeoka, A., Nakano, S. & Kuwano, Y. (1995). Advanced photovoltaic technologies and residential applications. *Renewable Energy*, Vol. 6, No. 3, pp.275–282.

Omer, S.A, Wilson, R. & Riffat, S.B. (2003). Monitoring results of two examples of building integrated PV (BIPV) systems in the UK. *Renewable Energy*, No. 28, pp.1387-1399.

Pearce, J.M. (2002). Photovoltaics - a path to sustainable futures. *Futures*, No. 34, pp.663-674.

Román, E., Alonso, R., Elorduizapatarietxe, S. & Ibáñez, P. (2006). Economic analysis of modular PV systems for building integration. *21st European Photovoltaic Solar Energy Conference*, 4-8 September, Dresden, Germany.

Sick, F. & Erge, T. (1996). *The Design Handbook for Architects and Engineers*, 1st ed., Freiburg, Germany.

SMA Sunny Boy (2006). Grid tied string inverter for PV systems. *Installation and Operation Manual*, pp.77-101.

UL 1703 (2000) Standard for Flat-Plate Photovoltaic Modules and Panels, 20 November. Woodfeden, I. (2007). Small scale system for an on grid island getaway. *Home Power Magazine*, February and March 2007 edition, pp.34-38.

Woodfeden, I. (2007). Small scale system for an on grid island getaway. *Home Power Magazine*, February and March 2007 edition, pp.34-38.

Woodfeden, I. & Laforge, C. (2007). Getting started with renewable energy - professional load analysis and site survey. *Home Power Magazine*, August and September 2007 edition, pp.44-46.

Zein, A. & Sarsar, W. (1998). Analysis of solar photovoltaic-powered village electrification at Abou-Sorra in Damascus Region. *Renewable Energy*, Vol. 14, Nos. 1-4, pp.119-128.

7

Modelling of DC-DC converters

Ovidiu Aurel Pop and Serban Lungu
Technical University of Cluj-Napoca
Romania

1. Introduction

The DC-DC converters are electrical circuits that transfer the energy from a DC voltage source to a load and regulate the output voltage. The energy is transferred via electronic switches, made with transistors and diodes, to an output filter and than is transferred to the load.

DC-DC converters are used to convert unregulated dc voltage to regulated or variable dc voltage at the output. They are widely used in switch-mode dc power supplies and in dc motor drive applications. In dc motor control applications, they are called *chopper-controlled drives.* The input voltage source is usually a battery or derived from an ac power supply using a diode bridge rectifier. These converters are generally either hard-switched PWM types or soft-switched resonant-link types.

These converters employ square-wave pulse width modulation to achieve voltage regulation. The output voltage is regulated varying the duty cycle of the power semiconductor switch driving signal. The voltage waveform across the switch and at the input of the filter is square wave in nature and they generally result in higher switching losses when the switching frequency is increased. Also, the switching stresses are high with the generation of large electromagnetic interference (EMI), which is difficult to filter. However, these converters are easy to control, well understood, and have wide load control range.

These converters operate with a fixed-frequency, variable duty cycle. This type of signal is called Pulse Width Modulated signal (PWM). Depending on the duty cycle, they can operate in either continuous current mode (CCM) or discontinuous current mode (DCM). If the current through the output inductor never reaches zero then the converter operates in CCM; otherwise DCM occurs.

The output voltage will be equal with the average value on the switching cycle of the voltage applied at the output filter. Due to the losses on the ON or OFF state of the ideal transistor are zero, the theoretical efficiency of the switching mode converters is up to 100%. But, considering the real switches, with parasitic elements, the efficiency will be a little bit lower, but higher than linear regulators.

Another advantage of switching mode converters consist in the possibility to use the same components but in other topology in order to obtain different values of the output voltages: positive or negative, lower or higher than input voltage.

There are various analysis methods of DC-DC converters. Throughout the chapter an extended analysis and modelling for DC-DC power converters is proposed. In this approach, the differential equations that describe the inductor current and capacitor voltage are determined and are solved according with the boundary conditions of the switching periods. The values of currents and voltages at the end of a period become initial conditions for the next switching period. This method is very accurate and produces a set of equations that require extensive computation.
In addition, for specified values of converter parameters (inductance and capacitor) we can calculate the maximum value of transistor and diode current and reverse voltage, in order to help user to choose the appropriate type of transistor and diode.

2. Buck converter

The buck (or step-down converter), shown in the figure 1, contain a capacitor and an inductor with role of energy storing, and two complementary switches: when one switch is closed, the other is open and vice-versa.

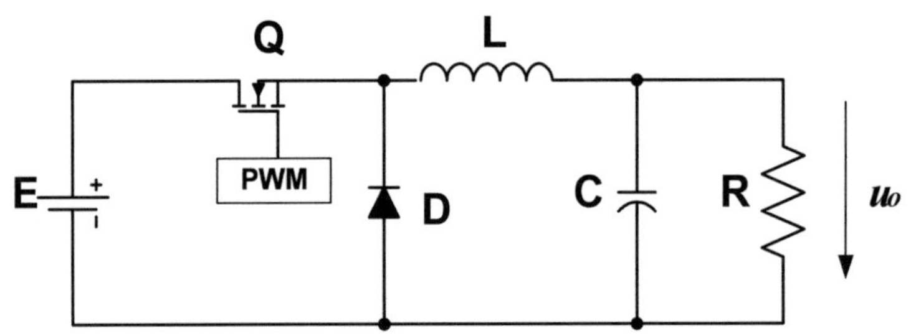

Fig. 1. The buck converter diagram

The switches are alternately opened and closed with at a rate of PWM switching frequency. The output that results is a regulated voltage of smaller magnitude than input voltage. The converter operation will be analyzed function of switches states.

The first time interval: The transistor is in ON state and diode is OFF.

During this time period, corresponding with duty cycle of PWM driving signal, the equivalent diagram of the circuit is presented bellow:

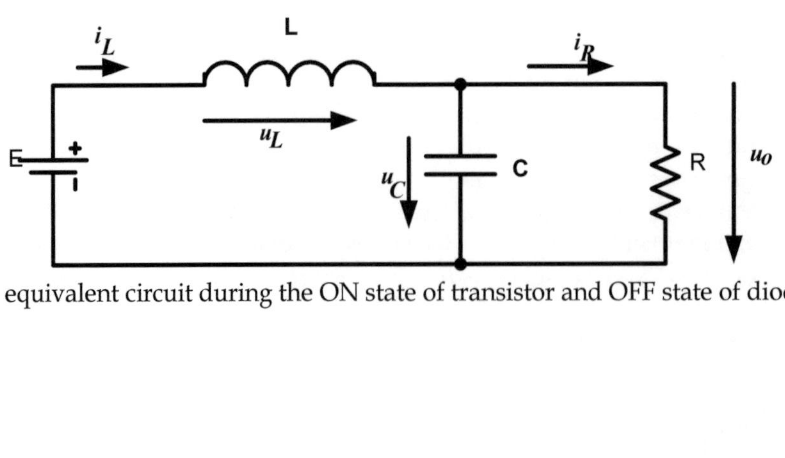

Fig. 2. The equivalent circuit during the ON state of transistor and OFF state of diode

For this equivalent circuit will write the equations that describe the converter operation:

$$\begin{cases} \dfrac{du_o}{dt} = (i_L - \dfrac{u_o}{R})\dfrac{1}{C}; \\ \dfrac{di_L}{dt} = \dfrac{E - u_o}{L}; \end{cases} \quad (1)$$

The second time period: the transistor is OFF and diode is ON

In the moment when the transistor switch in OFF state, the voltage across the inductor will change the polarity and the diode will switch in ON state. The equivalent diagram of converter during this period is shown in the bellow figure:

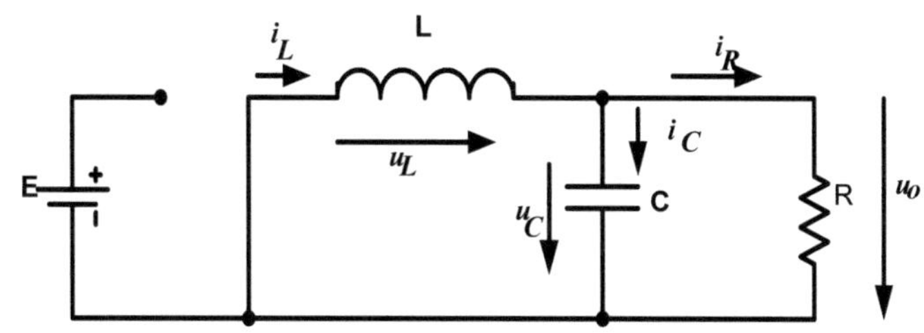

Fig. 3. The equivalent circuit for OFF state of transistor and ON state of diode

For this operation period, the output voltage u_O and the current through the inductor i_L satisfy the following equations:

$$\begin{cases} \dfrac{du_o}{dt} = \left(i_L - \dfrac{u_o}{R}\right)\dfrac{1}{C}; \\ \dfrac{di_L}{dt} = -\dfrac{u_o}{L}; \end{cases} \quad (2)$$

The third operation mode: The both transistor and diode are OFF

If the inductor current becomes zero before ending the diode ON period, both transistor and diode will naturally closed. This operation regime is called *discontinuous current mode*. The equivalent diagram of this operation regime is shown bellow.

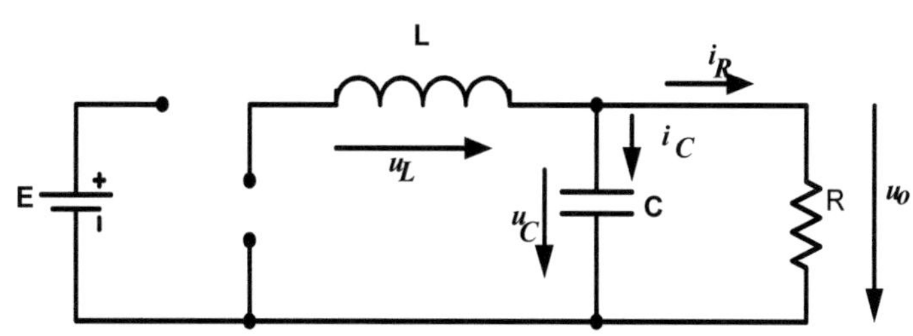

Fig. 4. The equivalent circuit with transistor and diode in OFF state

For this operation period, the output voltage u_o and the current through the inductor i_L satisfy the following equations:

$$\begin{cases} \dfrac{du_o}{dt} = -\dfrac{u_o}{R} \cdot \dfrac{1}{C}; \\ \dfrac{di_L}{dt} = 0; \end{cases} \tag{3}$$

2.1 CCM inductance

The minimum value of inductance for continuous current mode (CCM) operation is calculated from output voltage and inductor current equations.

Thus, the output voltage u_o and the current through the inductor i_L satisfies the following equations:

$$\begin{cases} u_L = E - Uo .... t \in (0, D \cdot T) \\ u_L = -Uo .... t \in (D \cdot T, T) \end{cases} \tag{4}$$

$$\begin{cases} i_L = \dfrac{E - Uo}{L} \cdot t .... t \in (0, D \cdot T) \\ i_L = -\dfrac{Uo}{L} \cdot t .... t \in (D \cdot T, T) \end{cases} \tag{5}$$

The waveforms of inductor voltage and current on a switching period are shown in the figure 5:

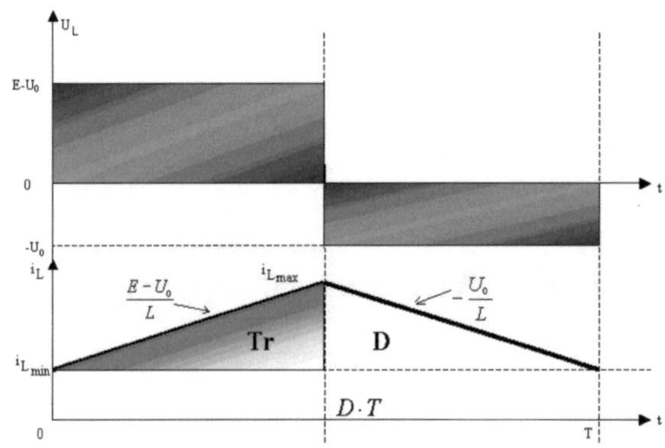

Fig. 5. The waveforms of output voltage and inductor current

In the steady state regime, the average value of voltage across the inductor is zero. Thus,

$$(E - Uo) \cdot D \cdot T = Uo \cdot T(1 - D) \Rightarrow Uo = D \cdot E \tag{6}$$

Based on the inductor current waveform, the following equation can be write:

$$I_{L\max} = I_{L\min} + \frac{E - Uo}{L} \cdot D \cdot T \tag{7}$$

The average value of the inductor current is equal with the output current:

$$\frac{I_{L\max} + I_{L\min}}{2} = \frac{U_o}{R} = I_o R \quad (8)$$

From the equations (7) and (8) results the minimum ad the maximum values of inductor current.

$$I_{L\min} = \frac{U_o}{R} - \frac{E - U_o}{2L} \cdot D \cdot T \quad (9)$$

$$I_{L\max} = \frac{U_o}{R} + \frac{E - U_o}{2L} \cdot D \cdot T \quad (10)$$

Thus:

$$\Delta i = I_{L\max} - I_{L\min} = \frac{E - U_o}{L} \cdot D \cdot T \quad (11)$$

From the equations (6) and (11) the inductor current ripple can be calculated.

$$\Delta i = \frac{E \cdot D \cdot (1 - D)}{L} \cdot T \quad (12)$$

From the condition, $I_{L\min} \geq 0$, it results:

$$\frac{2L}{RT} \geq 1 - D . \quad (13)$$

This relation can be used to determine the minimum value of inductance, when the switching frequency and load value are known.

$$L_{\min} = \frac{R \cdot T}{2} \cdot (1 - D) \quad (14)$$

2.2 The discontinuous current mode

In discontinuous current regime, the waveforms of inductor voltage and current are shown in the figure bellow:

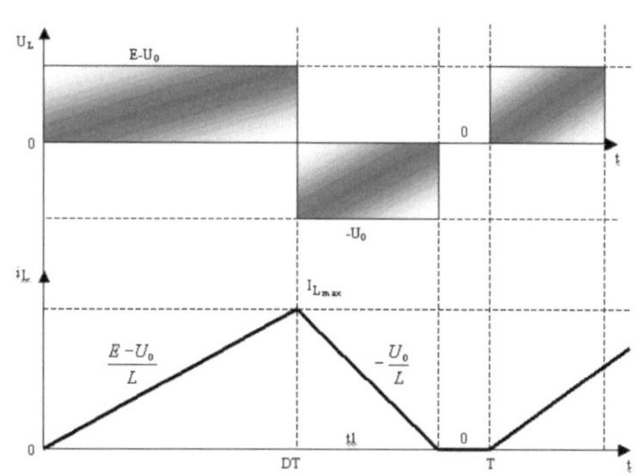

Fig. 6. The waveforms of voltage and inductor current in DCM

The average value of the input current is equal with the current through the switching transistor.

$$I_{iav} \cdot T = \frac{1}{2} \cdot D \cdot T \cdot I_{L\max} \tag{15}$$

$$I_{L\max} = \frac{E - U_o}{L} \cdot D \cdot T \tag{16}$$

From the above equations, it results:

$$I_{iav} = \frac{E - U_o}{2L} D^2 T \,. \tag{17}$$

Considering that there are no losses in the circuit, the input and the output powers are equals.

$$P_{in} = P_{out} \Leftrightarrow \frac{U_o^{\,2}}{R} = E \cdot I_{iav} \tag{18}$$

Thus,

$$\frac{U_o^{\,2}}{R} = E \frac{E - U_o}{2L} D^2 T \tag{19}$$

$$\frac{U_o^{\,2}}{E^2} = \frac{RT}{2L}\left(1 - \frac{U_o}{E}\right) D^2 \tag{20}$$

Denoting the circuit transfer ratio $\frac{Us}{E}$ =M:

$$M^2 + \frac{R \cdot T \cdot D^2}{2 \cdot L} \cdot M - \frac{R \cdot T \cdot D^2}{2 \cdot L} = 0 \tag{21}$$

Denoting $a = \frac{R \cdot D^2 \cdot T}{2 \cdot L}$, (22)

the solutions of the above equation are :

$$M = \frac{-a \pm \sqrt{a^2 + 4a}}{2} \,. \tag{23}$$

Analyzing those solutions, can be observed that the single valid solution is

$$M = \frac{-a + \sqrt{a^2 + 4a}}{2} \tag{24}$$

The variation of circuit transfer ratio M function of PWM signal duty-cycle D, for different values of $\frac{2L}{RT}$ parameters is shown in the figure:

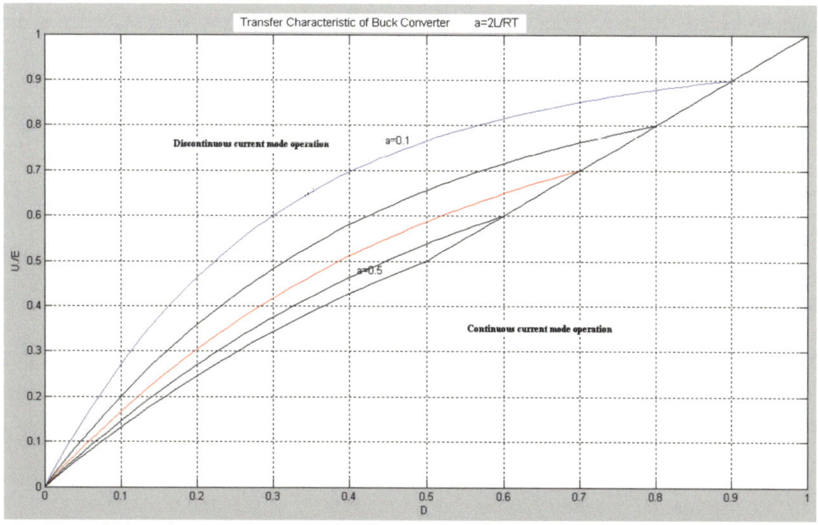

Fig. 7. Variation of circuit transfer ratio M function of PWM signal duty-cycle D

2.3 Filtering capacitor

Other important parameter that is important to be determined is the value of the output capacitor, in order to obtain a specific value of the output voltage ripple.

The capacitor charging current is equal with difference between the inductor current i_L and the output current i_O. Considering a constant output current, the electric charge stored in the capacitor during a switching period is equal with the shade area from the figure bellow:

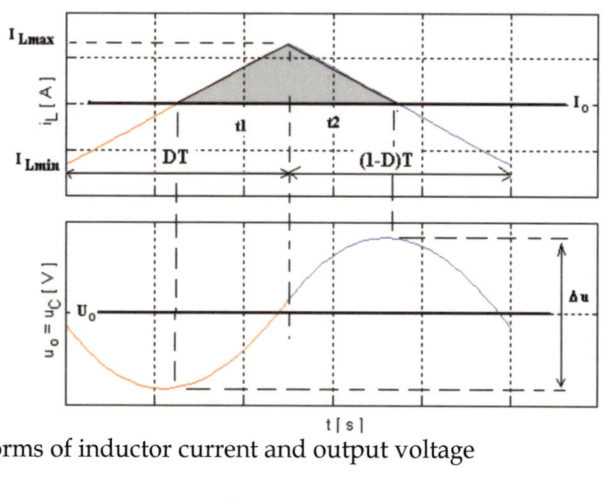

Fig. 8. The waveforms of inductor current and output voltage

$$Q = \Delta u \cdot C = \frac{1}{2}(I_{L\max} - I_O)(t_1 - t_2) \tag{25}$$

$$\frac{t_1}{DT} = \frac{t_2}{(1-D)T} = \frac{t_1 + t_2}{T} = \frac{I_{L\max} - I_O}{I_{L\max} - I_{L\min}} \tag{26}$$

Thus, the value of the output capacitor can be calculated with the following formula:

$$C = \frac{(E - U_O)DT^2}{8L\Delta u} = \frac{E(1-D)D}{8Lf^2\Delta u} \tag{27}$$

It can be seen in this formula that the capacitor value depends by the switching frequency. Increasing the switching frequency, the capacitor value will be smaller.

3. Boost Converter

The boost (or step-up converter), shown in the figure 9, contains, like the Buck converter, a capacitor and an inductor with role of energy storing, and two complementary switches. In the case of the boost converter, the output voltage is higher than the input voltage.

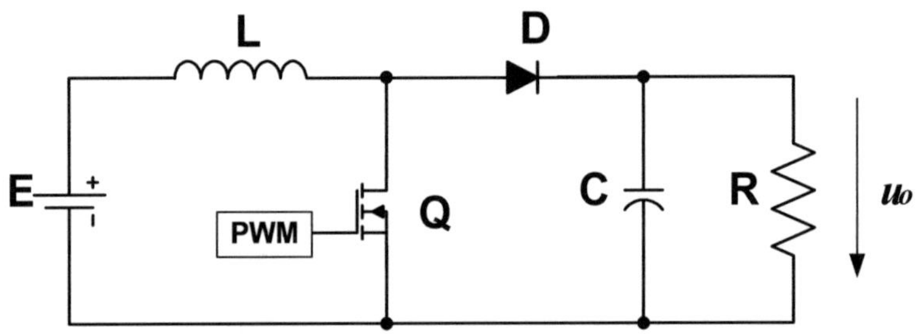

Fig. 9. The boost converter diagram

The switches are alternately opened and closed with at a rate of PWM switching frequency. As long as transistor is ON, the diode is OFF, being reversed biased. The input voltage, applied directly to inductance L, determines a linear rising current. When transistor is OFF, the load is supplied by both input source and LC filter. The output that results is a regulated voltage of higher magnitude than input voltage. The converter operation will be analyzed according with the switches states.

The first time interval: The transistor is in ON state and diode is OFF.

During this time period, corresponding with duty cycle of PWM driving signal, the equivalent diagram of the circuit is presented bellow. In this time period the inductance L store energy.

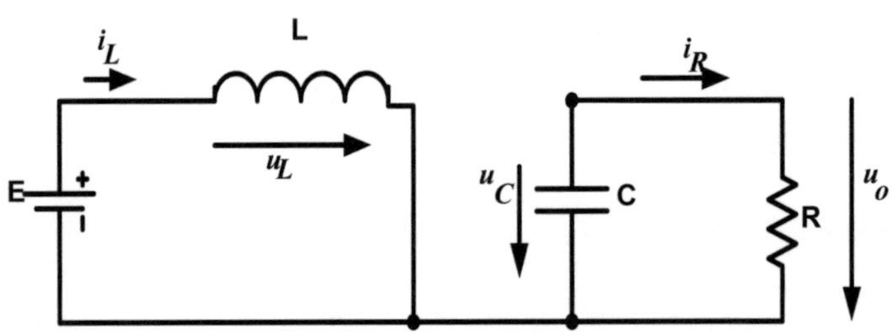

Fig. 10. The equivalent circuit during the ON state of transistor and OFF state of diode

For this operation period, the output voltage u_o and the current through the inductor i_L satisfies the following equations:

$$\begin{cases} \dfrac{di_L}{dt} = \dfrac{E}{L}; \\ \dfrac{du_o}{dt} = -\dfrac{u_o}{R \cdot C}; \end{cases} \tag{28}$$

The second time period: the transistor is OFF and diode is ON

In the moment when the transistor switch in OFF state, the voltage across the inductor will change the polarity and diode will switch in ON state. The equivalent diagram of converter during this period is shown in the bellow figure:

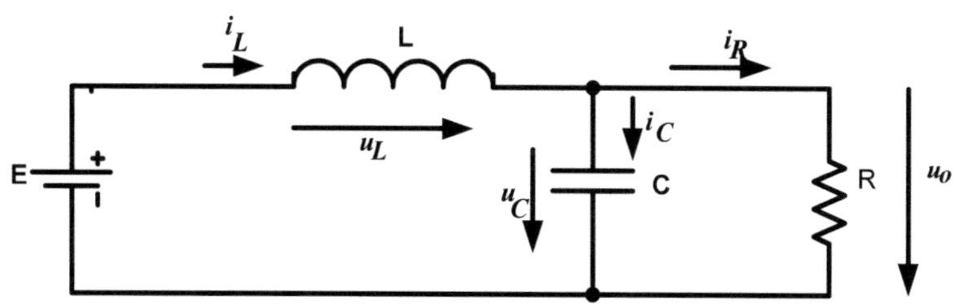

Fig. 11. The equivalent circuit for OFF state of transistor and ON state of diode

For this operation period, the output voltage u_o and the current through the inductor i_L satisfy the following equations:

$$\begin{cases} \dfrac{di_L}{dt} = \dfrac{E - u_o}{L}; \\ \dfrac{du_o}{dt} = \dfrac{1}{C}\left(i_L - \dfrac{u_o}{R}\right); \end{cases} \tag{29}$$

The third operation mode: The both transistor and diode are OFF

If the inductor current becomes zero before ending the diode conduction period, both the transistor and the diode will be in OFF state. Due to the diode current becomes zero, the diode will naturally close, and the output capacitor will discharge on the load. This operation regime is called *discontinuous current mode*. The equivalent diagram of this operation regime is shown bellow.

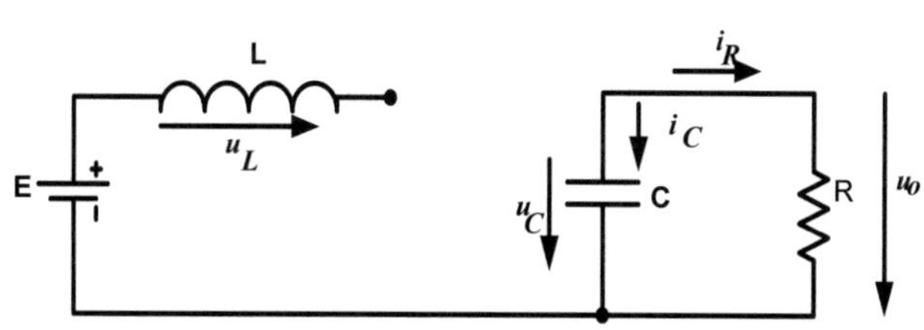

Fig. 12. The equivalent circuit with transistor and diode in OFF state

For this operation period, the output voltage u_o and the current through the inductor i_L can be calculated from the following equations:

$$\begin{cases} \frac{di_L}{dt} = 0; \\ \frac{du_o}{dt} = -\frac{u_o}{R \cdot C}; \end{cases} \tag{30}$$

3.1 CCM inductance

The minimum value of inductance for continuous current mode (CCM) operation is calculated from inductor current equation. In the steady state regime, the average value of voltage across the inductor is zero.

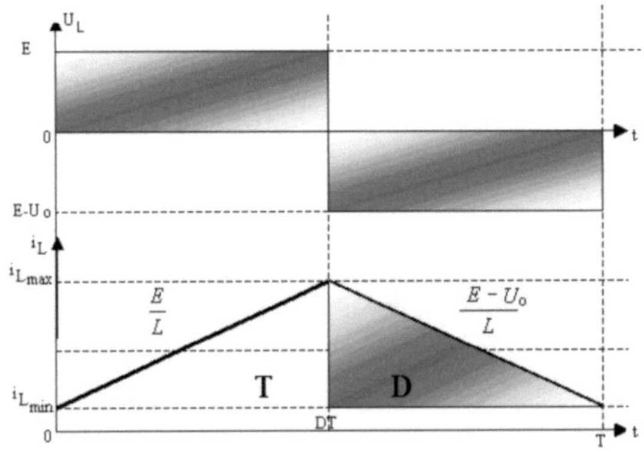

Fig. 13. The waveforms of inductor voltage and current in steady-state regime

Thus, the output voltage u_0 and the current through the inductor i_L satisfies the following equations:

$$E \cdot D \cdot T = T \cdot (1-D) \cdot (Uo - E); \Rightarrow Uo = \frac{E}{1-D} \tag{31}$$

Based on the above waveforms, the maximum value of the inductor current is:

$$i_{L_{\max}} = i_{L_{\min}} + \frac{E}{L} \cdot D \cdot T \tag{32}$$

The output current is equal with the diode average current:

$$\frac{i_{L\max} + i_{L\min}}{2} \cdot T \cdot (1-D) = \frac{U_o}{R} \cdot T \tag{33}$$

Based on the equations (32) and (33), results:

$$i_{L\max} = \frac{U_o}{R \cdot (1-D)} + \frac{E \cdot D \cdot T}{2 \cdot L} \tag{34}$$

$$i_{L\ \min} = \frac{U_o}{R\cdot(1-D)} - \frac{E\cdot D\cdot T}{2\cdot L} \tag{35}$$

Based on the equations (34) and (35), can be determined the inductor current ripple:

$$\Delta i = \frac{E\cdot D\cdot T}{L} \tag{36}$$

From the condition for continuous conduction mode, $i_{L_{\min}} \geq 0$, results:

$$\frac{2L}{R\cdot T} \geq D\cdot(1-D)^2 \tag{37}$$

This condition can be used to determine the minimum inductance value, for a specific switching period T and a specific load value R.

$$L_{\min} = \frac{R\cdot T}{2} D\cdot(1-D)^2 \tag{38}$$

3.2 The discontinuous current mode

In discontinuous conduction mode, the waveforms of the inductor voltage and current are shown in the figure bellow:

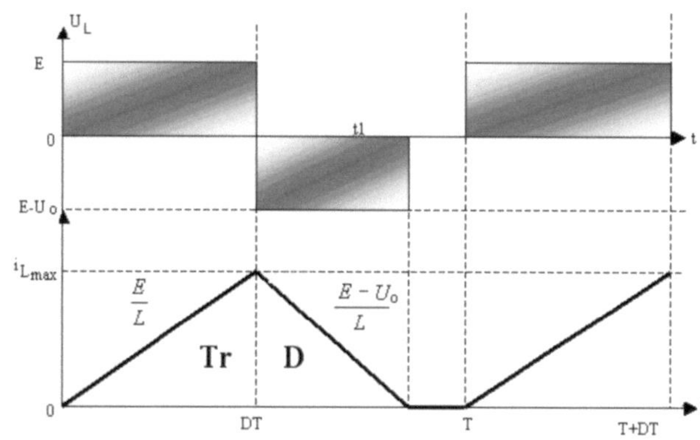

Fig. 14. The waveforms of voltage and inductor current in DCM

The average value of the input current is equal with the inductor average current.

$$I_{i_{av}} \cdot T = \frac{1}{2}\cdot I_{L_{\max}}\left(D\cdot T + t_1\right) \tag{39}$$

where

$$I_{L_{\max}} = \frac{E\cdot D\cdot T}{L}. \tag{40}$$

Based on the equations (39) and (40), results:

$$I_{i_{av}} = \frac{E\cdot D}{2\cdot L}\cdot\left(D\cdot T + t_1\right) \tag{41}$$

The average value of the inductor voltage during a switching period is zero.

$$E \cdot D \cdot T = t_1(Uo - E); \Rightarrow t_1 = \frac{E \cdot D \cdot T}{U_0 - E} \tag{42}$$

Replacing equation (42) in the equation (41), and also considering the input and the output power equals,

$$P_{in} = P_{out} \Leftrightarrow \frac{Uo^2}{R} = E \cdot I_{i_{av}} \tag{43}$$

it results:

$$\frac{Uo}{E}\left(\frac{Uo}{E} - 1\right) = \frac{D^2 \cdot T \cdot R}{2 \cdot L}. \tag{44}$$

Denoting the voltage transfer ratio with $M = \frac{Uo}{E}$, the equation (44) becomes:

$$M(M-1) = \frac{D^2 \cdot T \cdot R}{2 \cdot L} \tag{45}$$

The solution of this equation is:

$$M = \frac{1 + \sqrt{1 + \frac{4 \cdot D^2 \cdot T \cdot R}{2L}}}{2} \tag{46}$$

The variation of circuit transfer ratio M function of PWM signal duty-cycle D, for different values of $\frac{2L}{RT}$ parameters is shown in the figure:

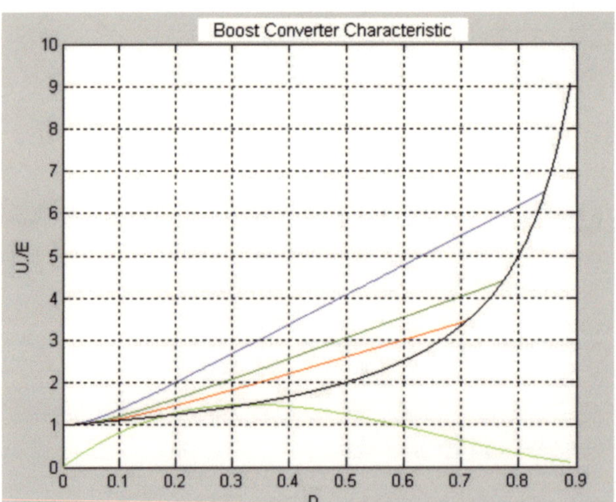

Fig. 15. Variation of circuit transfer ratio M function of PWM signal duty-cycle D

3.3 Filtering capacitor

Other important parameter that is important to be determined is the value of the output capacitor, in order to obtain a specific value of the output voltage ripple.
The capacitor charging current is equal with the difference between the diode current i_D and the output current i_o. Considering a constant output current, the electric charge stored in the capacitor during a switching period is equal with the shade area from the figure bellow:

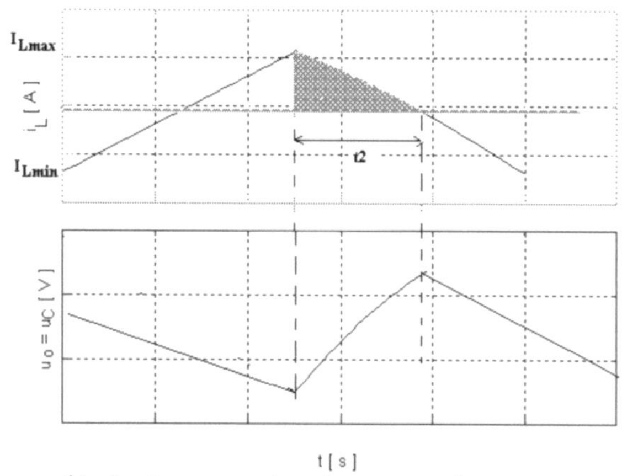

Fig. 16. The waveforms of inductor current and output voltage

$$Q = C \cdot \Delta u = \frac{1}{2}(I_{L\max} - I_o)t_2 \tag{47}$$

$$\frac{t_2}{T(1-D)} = \frac{I_{L\max} - I_o}{I_{L\max} - I_{L\min}} \tag{48}$$

Thus, the value of the output capacitor can be calculated with the following formula:

$$C = \frac{(I_{L\max} - I_o)^2 T(1-D)}{2(I_{L\max} - I_{L\min})} \tag{49}$$

4. Buck-Boost converter

The buck-boost converter (polarity inverter) is shown in figure 17.

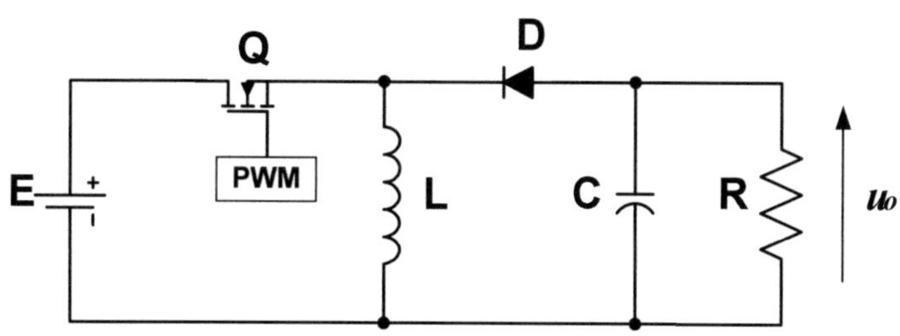

Fig. 17. Buck-Boost converter diagram

The switches are alternately opened and closed with at a rate of PWM switching frequency. As long as the transistor is ON, the diode is OFF, being reversed biased. The input voltage, applied directly to inductance L, determines a linear rising current. The capacitor is discharged on the load circuit. When the transistor is OFF, the load is supplied by LC filter. The output that results is a regulated voltage of smaller or higher magnitude than input voltage, depending on the value of duty cycle, but it has a reverse polarity. The converter operation will be analyzed according with the ON or OFF state of switches.

The first time interval: The transistor is in ON state and diode is OFF.

During this time period, corresponding with duty cycle of PWM driving signal, the equivalent diagram of the circuit is presented bellow. In this time period the inductance L stores energy. The load current is assured by the output capacitor.

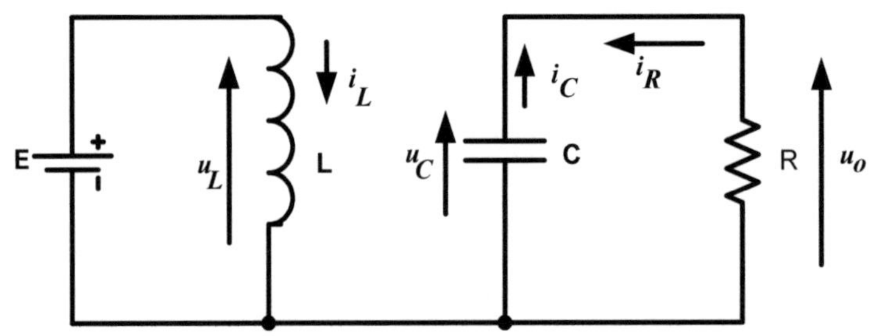

Fig. 18. The equivalent circuit during the ON state of transistor and OFF state of diode

For this operation period, the output voltage u_o and the current through the inductor i_L are given by the following equations system:

$$\begin{cases} \dfrac{di_L}{dt} = E \\ \dfrac{du_o}{dt} = -\dfrac{u_o}{R \cdot C} \end{cases} \tag{50}$$

The second time period: the transistor is OFF and diode is ON

In the moment when the transistor switch in OFF state, the voltage across the inductor will change the polarity and diode will switch in ON state. The energy stored in the inductor will supply the load. The equivalent diagram of converter during this period is shown in the figure bellow:

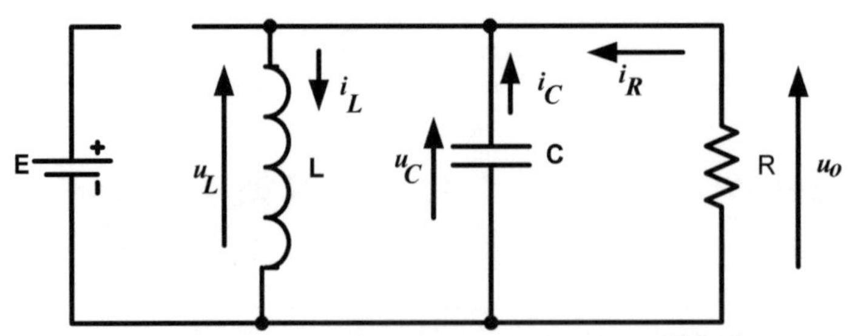

Fig. 19. The equivalent circuit during the OFF state of transistor and ON state of diode

For this operation period, the following equations for the output voltage u_o and the current through the inductor i_L can be written:

$$\begin{cases} \dfrac{di_L}{dt} = -\dfrac{u_o}{L} \\ \dfrac{du_o}{dt} = \left(i_L - \dfrac{u_o}{R}\right) \cdot \dfrac{1}{C} \end{cases} \tag{51}$$

The third operation mode : The both transistor and diode are OFF

If the inductor current becomes zero before ending the diode ON period, both the transistor and the diode will be OFF. Due to the diode current becomes zero, the diode will naturally close, and the output capacitor will discharge on the load. This operation regime is called *discontinuous current mode*. The equivalent diagram of this operation regime is shown bellow.

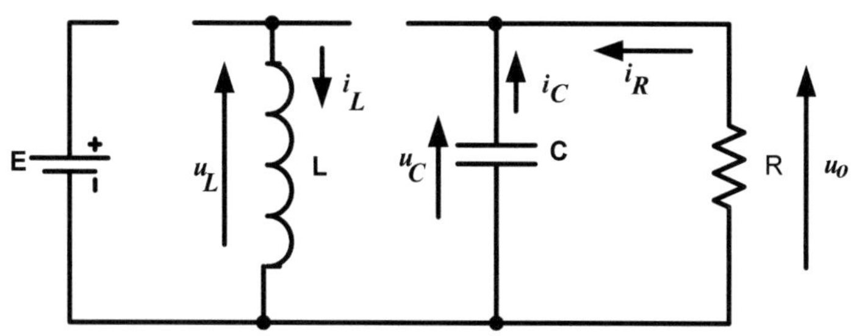

Fig. 20. The equivalent diagram for discontinuous conduction mode operation

For this operation mode, the output voltage u_o and the current through the inductor i_L can be calculated from the following differential equations:

$$\begin{cases} \dfrac{di_L}{dt} = 0 \\ \dfrac{du_o}{dt} = -\dfrac{u_o}{R \cdot C} \end{cases} \tag{52}$$

4.1 CCM inductance

The minimum value of the inductance for continuous current mode (CCM) operation is calculated from the the inductor current equations.

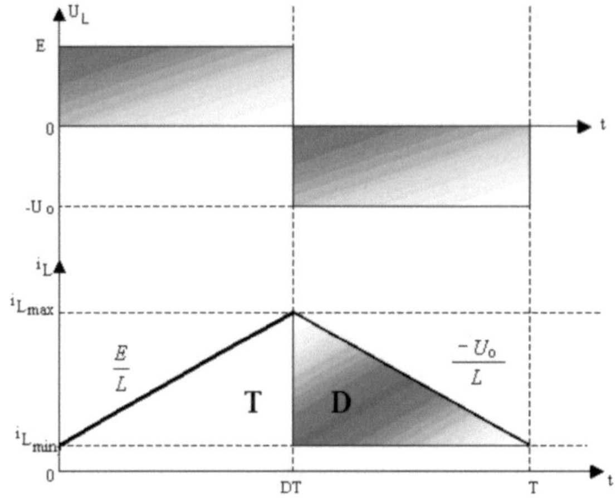

Fig. 21. The inductor voltage and current waveforms in steady-state regime

In the steady state regime, the average value of the voltage across the inductor is zero. From this condition, the output voltage *Uo* can be determined:

$$E \cdot D \cdot T = Uo \cdot T(1-D) \Rightarrow E \cdot D = Uo(1-D)$$
$$\Rightarrow Uo = \frac{E \cdot D}{1-D} \tag{53}$$

Based on the above waveforms:

$$I_{L\max} = I_{L\min} + \frac{E}{L} \cdot D \cdot T \tag{54}$$

Also, the average diode current is equal with the output current.

$$\frac{I_{L\max} + I_{L\min}}{2} \cdot T \cdot (1-D) = \frac{U_o}{R} \cdot T \tag{55}$$

Based on the equations (54) and (55), the maximum and the minimum value of the inductor current will be:

$$I_{L_{\max}} = \frac{U_o}{R \cdot (1-D)} + \frac{E \cdot D \cdot T}{2 \cdot L} \tag{56}$$

$$I_{L_{\min}} = \frac{U_o}{R \cdot (1-D)} - \frac{E \cdot D \cdot T}{2 \cdot L} \tag{57}$$

Thus, the inductor current ripple is:

$$\Delta i = \frac{E \cdot D \cdot T}{L} \tag{58}$$

From the condition for continuous conduction mode, $i_{L_{\min}} \geq 0$, results:

$$\frac{2L}{RT} \geq (1-D)^2 \tag{59}$$

This condition can be used to determine the minimum inductance value, for a specific switching period T and a specific load value R.

$$L_{\min} = \frac{R \cdot T \cdot (1-D)^2}{2} \tag{60}$$

4.2 The discontinuous current mode

In discontinuous conduction mode, the waveforms of the inductor voltage and current are shown in the figure bellow:

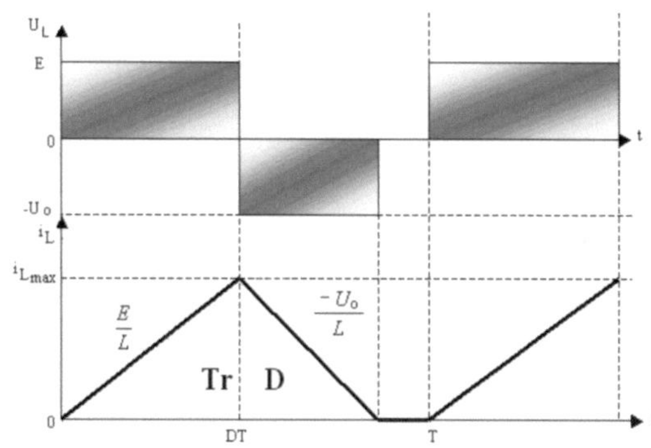

Fig. 22. The waveforms of voltage and inductor current in DCM

The average value of the input current is equal with the transistor average current.

$$I_{i_{av}} \cdot T = \frac{1}{2} \cdot I_{L\max} D \cdot T \tag{61}$$

where,

$$I_{L\max} = \frac{E \cdot D \cdot T}{L} \tag{62}$$

From the above equations results:

$$I_{i_{av}} = \frac{E \cdot D^2 T}{2 \cdot L} \tag{63}$$

Neglecting the losses in the circuit, the input power is equal with the output power.

$$P_{in} = P_{out} \Leftrightarrow \frac{U_o^2}{R} = E \cdot I_{i_{av}} \tag{64}$$

$$\frac{E^2 D^2 T}{2L} = \frac{U_o^2}{R} \tag{65}$$

Denoting the voltage transfer ratio $\frac{Uo}{E}$ =M , it results:

$$M = D\sqrt{\frac{R\,T}{2L}} \tag{66}$$

The variation of circuit transfer ratio M function of PWM signal duty-cycle D, for different values of $\frac{2L}{RT}$ parameters is shown in the figure:

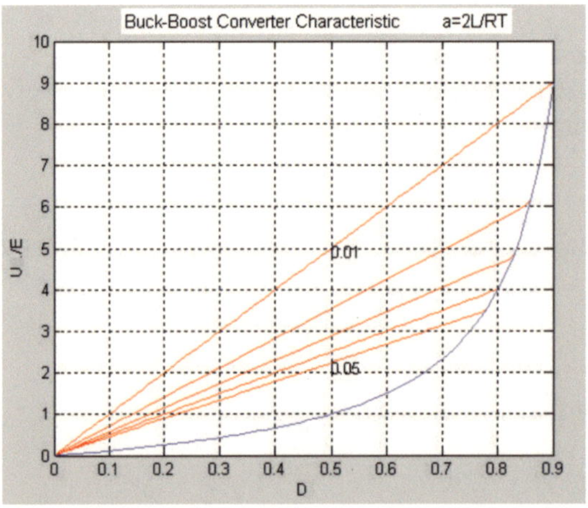

Fig. 23. Variation of circuit transfer ratio M function of PWM signal duty-cycle D

4.3 Filtering capacitor

Other important parameter that must be determined is the value of the output capacitor, in order to obtain a specific value of the output voltage ripple.

The capacitor charging current is equal with difference between the diode current i_D and the output current *io*. Considering a constant output current, the electric charge stored in the capacitor during a switching period is equal with the shade area from the bellow figure:

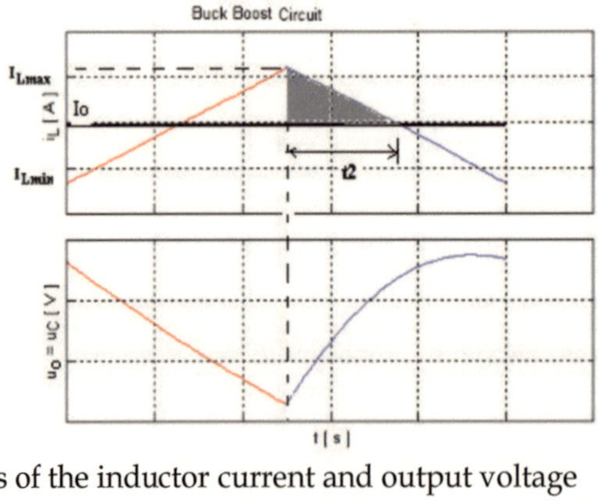

Fig. 24. The waveforms of the inductor current and output voltage

$$Q = C \cdot \Delta u = \frac{1}{2}(I_{L\max} - I_o)t_2 \tag{67}$$

$$\frac{t_2}{T(1-D)} = \frac{I_{L\max} - I_o}{I_{L\max} - I_{L\min}} \tag{68}$$

The value of the output capacitor can be calculated with the following formula:

$$C = \frac{\left(I_{L\max} - I_o\right)^2 T(1-D)}{2\left(I_{L\max} - I_{L\min}\right)} \tag{69}$$

5. Matlab Modeling of DC-DC Converters

In order to simulate the converters, the equations that describe the converter operation on each of the three possible operating stages are implemented in Matlab, and solved using Matlab facilities.

The program structure consists in two files. The first file initializes the default values of converter parameters: the input voltage E, the inductance value L, the capacitor value C, the load value R, the switching period T, the duty-cycle D and the number of periods to be displayed. All the parameters can be changed during the converters simulation. The structure of this file is:

<u>Listing for initialization of default parameters values</u>

```
clear all;
close;
E=10;     %input voltage value
L=1e-4;   %inductor value
C=10e-6;  %capacitor value
R=10;     %load value
%--------------------
Q=sqrt(L./C)./R;
T0=2.*pi.*sqrt(L.*C);
%-----------
T=50e-6;  %switching period
D=0.5;    %duty-cycle
N=20;     %numbers of periods to be displayed
%--------------
p=1;      % default plotting regime (transient)
%-------------------
type=1;   % default analyzed converter -Buck
%type=2;  % Boost
%type=3;  % Buck-Boost
%---------------
ed_converter(E,L,C,R,T,D,N,p,type);  % function for converters simulation
```

As it can be seen at the end of the file, the *ed_converter(E,L,C,R,T,D,N,p,type)* function is called. This function is implemented in a file with the same name, and had as arguments the converter parameters. In the first part of the file are created the buttons that allow to change the values of the converter parameters. Than, are implemented the functions that solve the differential equations that describe the converter operation and are calculated the critical values of inductor for continuous conduction mode operation and value of output voltage. Also, are defined the plots for output voltage and input current.
The structure of this file is presented bellow:

Listing of function file

```
function ed_converter(E,L,C,R,T,D,N,p,type);
%create a new figure;
Fig=figure('Name',' DC-DC Converters',...
      'Numbertitle','off', 'color', [1, 1, 1]);

% creating 7 text buttons B_T;

txt=['E [V]  L[ H]  C[ F] R[ohm]  T[ s]  D     N   '];
  for k=1:7
   B_T(k)=uicontrol('Style','text', ...
              'Units','normalized', ...
              'backgroundcolor',[1, 1, 1],...
              'Position',[0.91 0.95-0.1.*(k-1) 0.10 0.04], ...
              'String',txt((7.*(k-1))+1:7.*k), ...
              'Callback','close; ');
  end

% Creating 7 Edit buttons B_E ;
var=['E';'L';'C';'R';'T';'D';'N'];
val=[E;L;C;R;T;D;N];

 xc= '=str2num(get(gco,''String''));close;ed_converter(E,L,C,R,T,D,N,p,type)';
for i=1:7
 B_E= uicontrol('Style','edit',...
           'Units','normalized',...
           'backgroundcolor',[1, 1, 0],...
           'Position',[0.91 0.90-0.1*(i-1) 0.10 0.04],...
           'String',val(i),...
           'Callback',cat(2,var(i),xc));
end

%Creating the control buttons for selection of converter type: Buck, Boost or Buck-Boost
             Buck=uicontrol('Style','pushbutton',...
              'Units','normalized',...
              'Position',[0.05 0.01 0.17 0.04],...
              'String','Buck',...
```

```
        'backgroundcolor',[0, 1, 0.5],...
        'Callback','type=1,close;ed_converter(E,L,C,R,T,D,N,p,type)');
       Boost=uicontrol('Style','pushbutton',...
        'Units','normalized',...
        'Position',[0.25 0.01 0.17 0.04],...
        'String','Boost',...
        'backgroundcolor',[0, 1, 0.5],...
        'Callback','type=2,close;ed_converter(E,L,C,R,T,D,N,p,type)');
     Buck_Boost=uicontrol('Style','pushbutton',...
        'Units','normalized',...
        'Position',[0.45 0.01 0.17 0.04],...
        'String','BuckBoost',...
        'backgroundcolor',[0, 1, 0.5],...
        'Callback','type=3,close;ed_converter(E,L,C,R,T,D,N,p,type)');

 %----------------
      Bp=uicontrol('Style','pushbutton',...
        'Units','normalized',...
        'Position',[0.01 0.92 0.19 0.04],...
        'String','Steady-State Regime',...
        'backgroundcolor',[0, 1, 1],...
        'Callback','p=0;close;ed_converter(E,L,C,R,T,D,N,p,type)');
      if p==0
        set(Bp,'String','Transient Regime');
        set(Bp,'Callback','p=1,close;ed_converter(E,L,C,R,T,D,N,p,type)');
      end
% When a button is pushed, the callback will call again the function file with the
newer parameters
%Routine for solving the function ec_conv, that describes the converters operation
t=0;
y=[0 0];
for k=1:N
nt=length(t);
t0=(k-1).*T;
tf=t0+D.*T;
ci=y(nt,:);
interval=1;
[t,y]=ode45(@ec_conv,[t0,tf],[ci],[],E,R,L,C,type,interval);
nt=length(t);
%Setting the plots
subplot('Position',[0.10 0.55 0.80 0.35]);
plot(t,y(:,1),'r');grid on;hold on;
subplot('Position',[0.10 0.15 0.80 0.35]);
plot(t,y(:,2),'r');grid on;hold on;
%--------------------interval=2;
t0=(k-1).*T+D.*T;
```

```
tf=k.*T;
ci=y(nt,:);
interval=2;
options=odeset('Events',@conv_ev);
[t,y,te,ye,ie]=ode45(@ec_conv,[t0,tf],[ci],[options],E,R,L,C,type,interval);
nt=length(t);
%----------------------
 subplot('Position',[0.10 0.55 0.80 0.35]);
plot(t,y(:,1),'b');grid on;hold on;
subplot('Position',[0.10 0.15 0.80 0.35]);
plot(t,y(:,2),'b');grid on;hold on;
%---------------------------interval=3;
if te>0;
t0=t(nt);
tf=k.*T;
ci=y(nt,:);
interval=3;
[t,y]=ode45(@ec_conv,[t0,tf],[ci],[],E,R,L,C,type,interval);
%----------------------
subplot('Position',[0.10 0.55 0.80 0.35]);
plot(t,y(:,1),'g');grid on;hold on;
subplot('Position',[0.10 0.15 0.80 0.35]);
plot(t,y(:,2),'g');grid on;hold on;
%--------------------
end
    if (p==0)&(j<N-1)
            subplot('Position',[0.10 0.55 0.80 0.35]);
          hold off;
      end

    if (p==0)&(j<N-1)
            subplot('Position',[0.10 0.15 0.80 0.35]);
         hold off;
    end

end
%========================================
subplot('Position',[0.10 0.55 0.80 0.35]);
ylabel(['iL [ A ]']);
 switch type;
    case 1
Lm=R.*T.*(1-D)./2;   %Calculating the minimum value of inductance for Buck Converter
          if 2.*L./(R.*T)>=1-D
Uo=E.*D;                %Calculating the output voltage in Continuous conduction mode

          else
```

```
        z=0.5.*R.*D.^2.*T./L;
        v=0.5.*(sqrt(z.^2+4.*z)-z);
    Uo=v.*E;         %Calculating the output voltage in Discontinuous conduction mode
        end
    title(['Buck Converter',' Uo = ',num2str(Uo),' [ V ]',' Lm = ',num2str(Lm),' [ H ]']);

    case 2
    Lm=R.*T.*D.*(1-D).^2./2;     %Calculating the minimum value of inductance for
    Boost Converter
        di=E.*D.*T./L;

        if 2.*L./(R.*T)>=D*(1-D).^2
    Uo=E./(1-D);         %Calculating the output voltage in Continuous conduction mode

        else
    v=0.5.*(1+sqrt(1+2.*D.^2.*T.*R./L));
    Uo=v.*E;         %Calculating the output voltage in Discontinuous conduction mode
        end
    title(['Boost Converter',' Uo = ',num2str(Uo),' [ V ]',' Lm = ',num2str(Lm),' [ H ]']);

    case 3
          Lm=R.*T.*(1-D).^2./2, %Calculating the minimum value of inductance
    for Buck-Boost Converter
        if 2.*L./(R.*T)>=(1-D).^2
    Uo=E.*D./(1-D);  %Calculating the output voltage in Continuous conduction mode

        else
         v=D.*sqrt(0.5.*T.*R./L);
    Uo=v.*E;         %Calculating the output voltage in Discontinuous conduction mode
        end
title(['Buck-Boost Converter',' Uo = ',num2str(Uo),' [ V ]',' Lm = ',num2str(Lm),' [ H ]']);

   end

subplot('Position',[0.10 0.15 0.80 0.35]);
ylabel(['Uo = uC [ V ]']);
xlabel(['t [ s ]']);

%Function that describes the converters operation
function dy=ec_conv(t,y,E,R,L,C,type,interval);
dy=zeros(2,1);
switch type;

  case 1
    if interval==1
      a=1;b=1;c=1;
```

```
        elseif interval==2
            a=0;b=1;c=1;
        else
            a=0;b=0;c=0;
        end

    case 2
        if interval==1
            a=1;b=0;c=0;
        elseif interval==2
            a=1;b=1;c=1;
        else
            a=0;b=0;c=0;
        end

    case 3
        if interval==1
            a=1;b=0;c=0;
        elseif interval==2
            a=0;b=1;c=1;
        else
            a=0;b=0;c=0;
        end
end

            dy(1)=(a.*E-b.*y(2))./L;     % Current equation
            dy(2)=(c.*y(1)-y(2)./R)./C;  % Voltage equation

%=========================================================
function [value,isterminal,direction] =conv_ev(t,y,E,R,L,C,type,interval);
value = y(1);     % detect iL = 0
isterminal = 1;   % stop the integration
direction = -1;   % negative direction
```

As it can be seen in the converters description, for all types of converters, the equation that describes the operation has the same shape. The difference consists in the value of the coefficients. From this reason, the same equations are used for the simulation of the converters operation and from each converter only the value of *a*, *b*, and *c* coefficients are set. The equations system is:

$$\begin{cases} \dfrac{di_L}{dt} = \dfrac{a \cdot E - b \cdot u_o}{L} \\ \dfrac{du_o}{dt} = (c \cdot i_L - \dfrac{u_o}{R})\dfrac{1}{C} \end{cases} \tag{70}$$

The simulation results of the dc-dc converters are presented in the following figure:

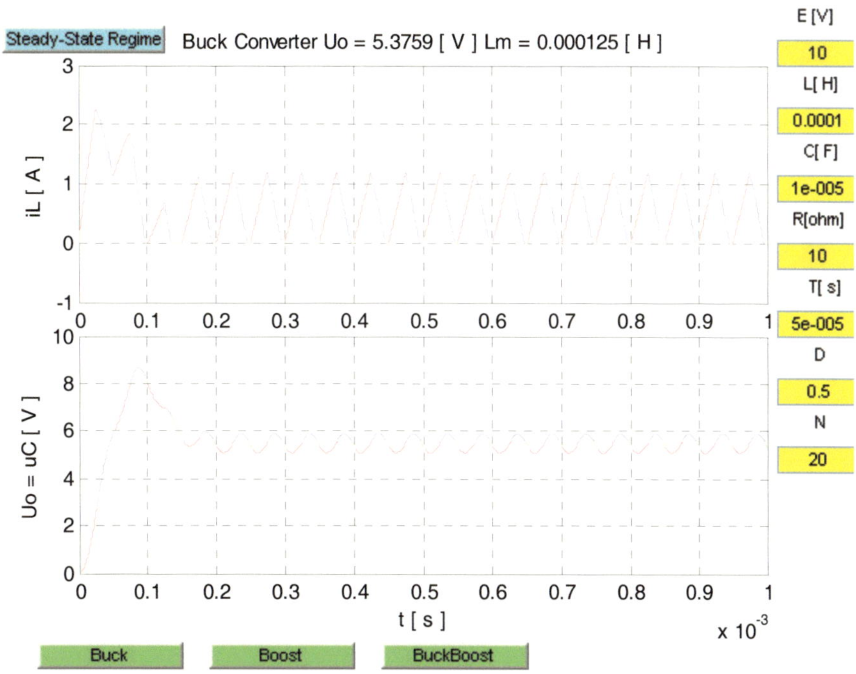

Fig. 25. The converters simulation results

As can be seen in the figure, from the upper left side button can be chosen the display mode: transient, when all the simulated periods are plotted or steady state regime when only the last simulated period is plotted.

From the right site editing buttons, all of the converter parameters can be set. From the bottom side it can be selected the desired converter: buck, boost or buck-boost. Also, for each converter type, the program displays the output voltage value and the minimum inductance value in order to obtain continuous current mode operation.

6. References

Attaway, S (2009). *Matlab: A Practical Introduction to Programming and Problem Solving*, 480 pages, Butterworth Heinemann, ISBN 978-0-7506-8762-1, USA

Attia, J. (1999). *Electronics and Circuits Analysis using Matlab*, 378 pages, CRC Press, ISBN 0-8493-1176-4, USA

Erickson, R.W. & Macksimovic, D. (2001). *Fundamentals of Power Electronics, Second ed.*, 920 pages, Kluver Academic Publisher, ISBN 0-7923-7270-0, USA

Mohan, N. & Undeland, T.M. (2003). *Power Electronics: Converters, Applications and Design. Third Ed.*, 802 pages, John Wiley & Sons, ISBN 0-4714-2902-2, USA

Lungu, S. & Pop, O.A. (2006). *Modelling of Electronics Circuits*, 133 pages, Science Books House, ISBN 978-973-686-975-4, Romania

Schaffer, R. (2007). *Fundamentals of Power Electronics with Matlab*, 384 pages, Charles River Media, ISBN 1-58450-853-3, USA

Matlab simulations for power factor correction of switching power

Ren Kaichun, He Chunhan, Su Dan, Wang Yongli, Zhang Xingqi
Liu Xiaojun, Gong Lihong, Zhao Ying and Liu Peng
Chongqing Communication College
China

Definition of Power Factor

Definition of power factor is:

$$PF = \frac{P}{S} = \frac{U_1 I_1 \cos\phi_1}{U_1 I_R} = \frac{I_1 \cos\phi_1}{I_R} = \gamma \cos\phi_1 \tag{1}$$

In formula (1), *PF* is power factor, *P* is active power, *S* is apparent power, I_1 is effective value of fundamental component of input current, I_R is effective value of AC power source current, $I_R = \sqrt{I_1^2 + I_2^2 + \cdots + I_n^2}$, I_1 , I_2 ,..., I_n are effective value of harmonic components of input current, U_1 is effective value of fundamental component of input AC voltage, γ is deformation factor of input current, ϕ_1 is the angel between the input AC voltage and fundamental component of the input current.

It is clear that the power factor *PF* is determined by γ and ϕ_1. The bigger the ϕ_1, the bigger the reactive power is, the bigger the wastage of conductive line wire and transformer is. The smaller the γ, the bigger the input current harmonics of is, which will cause current distortion, produce pollution to electric grid, and even damage the electric equipments if condition is serious.

Input Circuit and Its Power Factor of Single-Phase AC/DC Switching Power Supply

Single-phase AC/DC switching power replaces the low frequency transformer of traditional power source with high frequency transformer, so it has such advantages as light weight, small size, and high power density etc. At the same time, the switching power has higher

efficiency than the linearly-regulated DC power because its main power elements work as high frequency switches, so its application range is wider and wider.
The input circuit of traditional single-phased AC/DC switching power is demonstrated as Figure 1, after the mains supply(commercial power) is bridge rectified by D1~D4, it takes advantage of big electric capacity C to carry on smooth filtering to get DC voltage, and then transformed by DC/DC to realize insulation and voltage changing to supply the load. In simulation, use equivalent resistance R to replace the latter DC/DC and load as shown in the Figure 2.

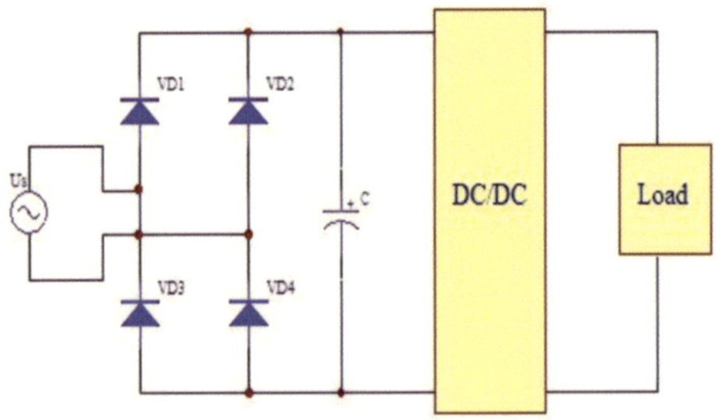

Fig. 1. Input circuit of AC/DC switch power supply

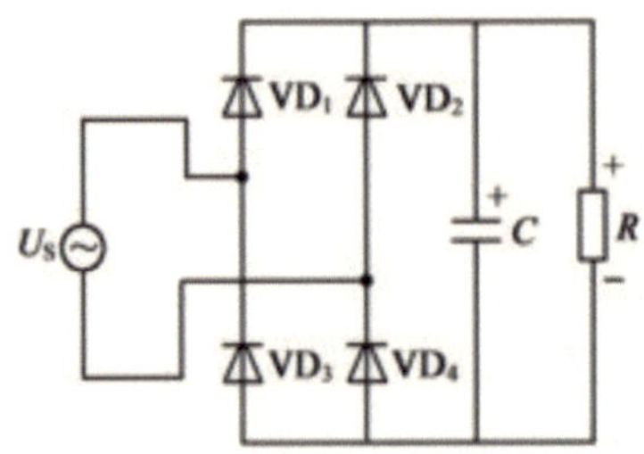

Fig. 2. Input equivalent electric circuit of AC/DC switching power supply

The emulated electric circuit that uses MATLAB structure is shown as Figure 3. The SCOPE module is used to observe the input voltage and current wave form; the current measuring module is used to check input current and then calculate the current effective value I_R, fundamental wave's effective value I_1 and included angel between input voltage and current fundamental component φ_1, and at last use formula (1) to calculate the power factor.

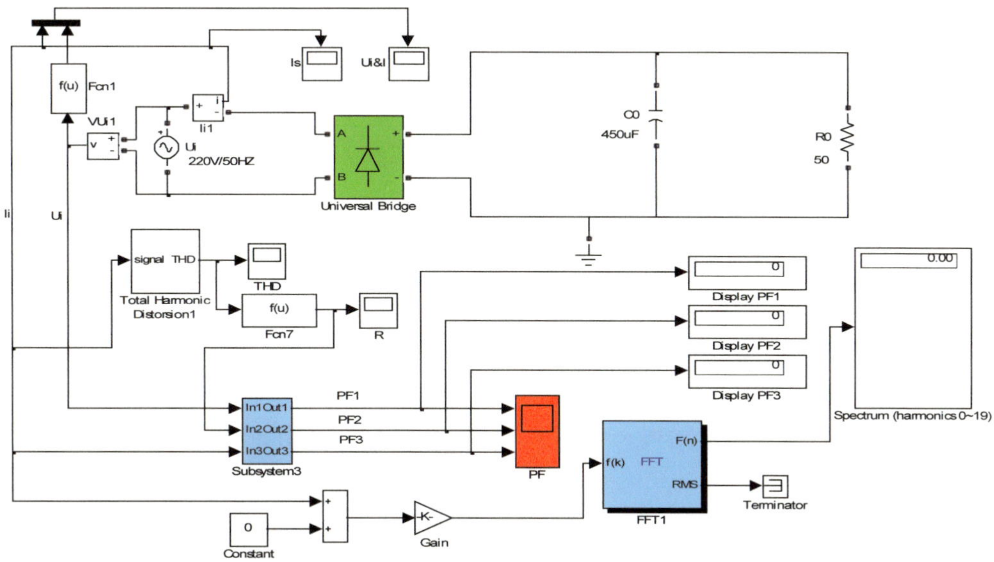

Fig. 3. Emulated circuit figure for input circuit of AC/DC switching power

The wave forms of input voltage and current are shown as Figure 4. There are current pass through the rectifier diode D1~D4 only when input alternating voltage bigger than the voltage between the two ends of filter capacitor, so the input current presents in sharp impulse form, the distortion factor of wave form γ is small, power factor PF is small, usually 0.6~0.7, and then the electric grid and other electric equipments are polluted and disturbed. In 1982, the IEC laid down a regulation IEC55-2 to limit higher harmonic (the later modified one is IEC1000-3-2), and made many power electronics technicians start to study harmonic filtering and PFC. The English full name for PFC is "Power Factor Correction".

There are two kinds of PFC, one is passive PFC, and the other is active PFC. Passive PFC(PPFC) only use capacitance, diode, inductance and other passive elements. The circuit is simple, and the cost is low, but the power factor of passive PFC is not very high that can only reach 0.7~0.8; APFC need to use transistor and controlling IC, the cost of which is much higher than that of PPFC. But the AC input current wave totally conform with such standard limits provision as IEC1000-3-2 etc. And can fundamentally realize unit power factor (when power factor is 1, it is called unit power factor). As a result, active BOOST correcting circuit is used much widely.

This following will introduce several kinds of passive PFC and active PFC.

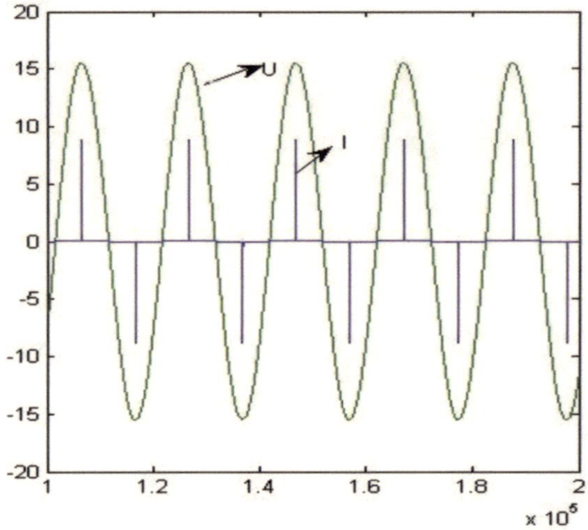

Fig. 4. Wave forms of input voltage and current

Correcting circuit of passive power factor with large inductance

Correcting circuit of passive power factor with large inductance is as Figure 5. The current and voltage wave form are shown as Figure 6, and its power factor is 0.898. If adopting infinite inductance, then the current wave form will be as Figure 7, and the power factor reaches to 0. 901.

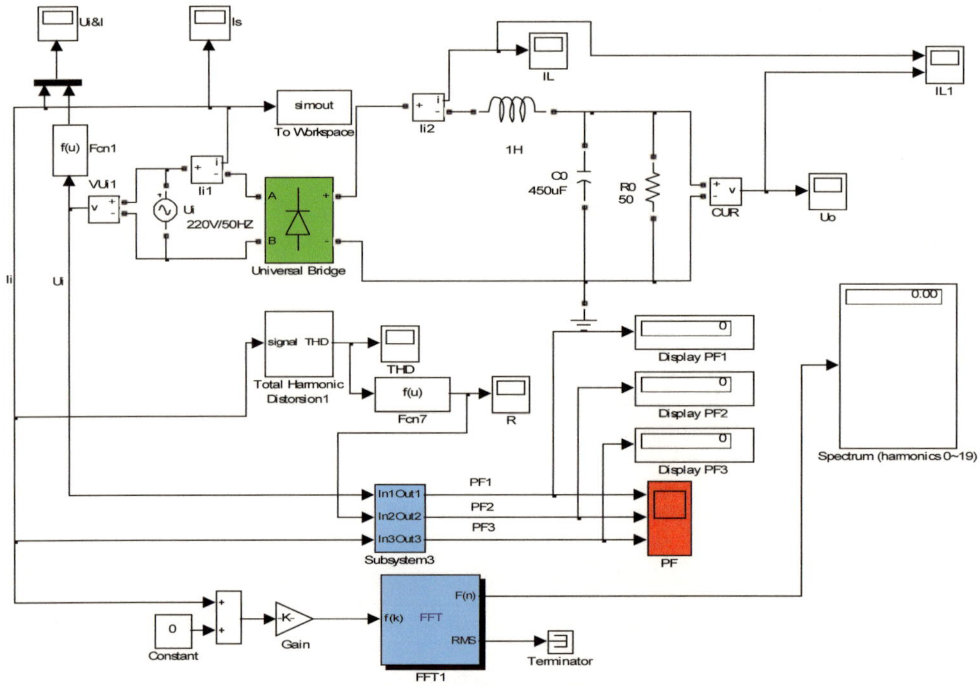

Fig. 5. Correcting circuit of passive power factor with large inductance

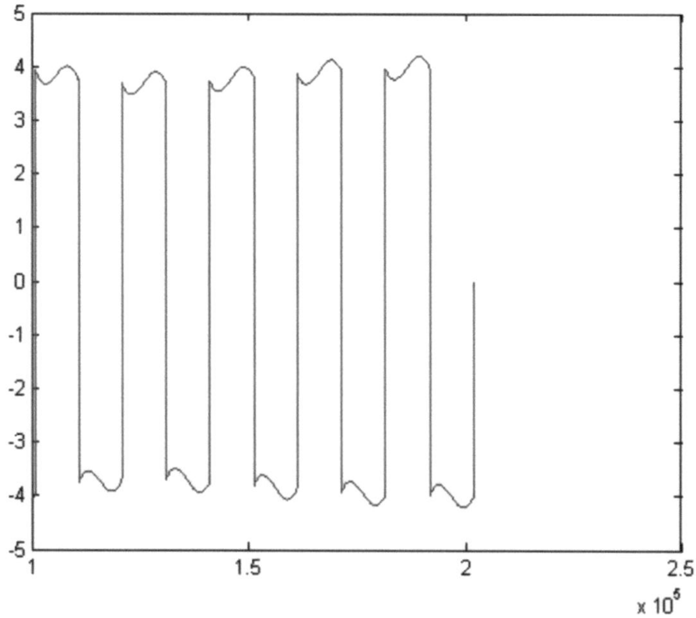

Fig. 6. Current wave form of large inductance

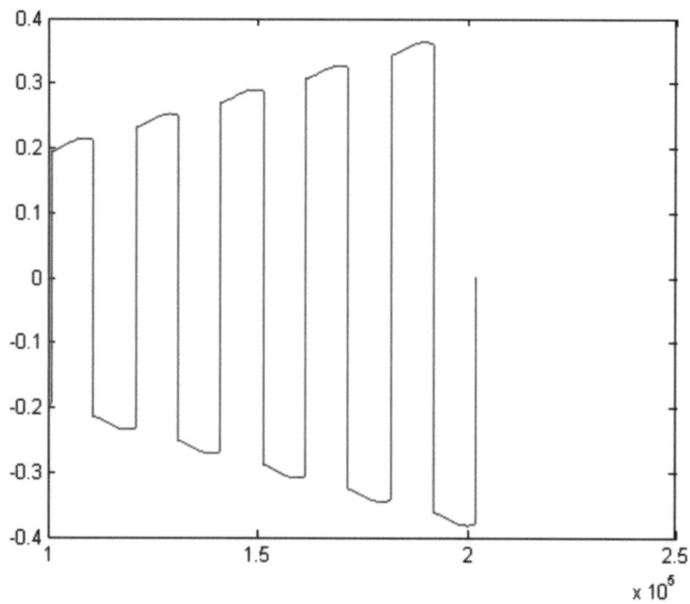

Fig. 7. Current wave form of infinite inductance

Using large inductance to correct power factor has such advantages as simple circuit, high reliability, and no extra frequency disturbing; But its drawback is it is cumbersome, the effect of power factor correcting is not very satisfied, and the correcting effect is inferior when the load range is relatively wide.

Correcting Circuit of Valley-filled Passive Power Factor

The basic structure of valley-filled PFC is demonstrated as Figure 8. When the input voltage is higher than the voltage between the two ends of the capacity, then the two capacities are charged in series; when the input voltage is lower than the voltage in the two ends of the capacity, the two capacities are discharging in parallel, which magnifies the conduction angle of diode, and then improves the current wave form and the power factor. The voltage and current waves by using MATLAB simulation are demonstrated as Figure 3. And the different power factors under different loads are shown as table 1.

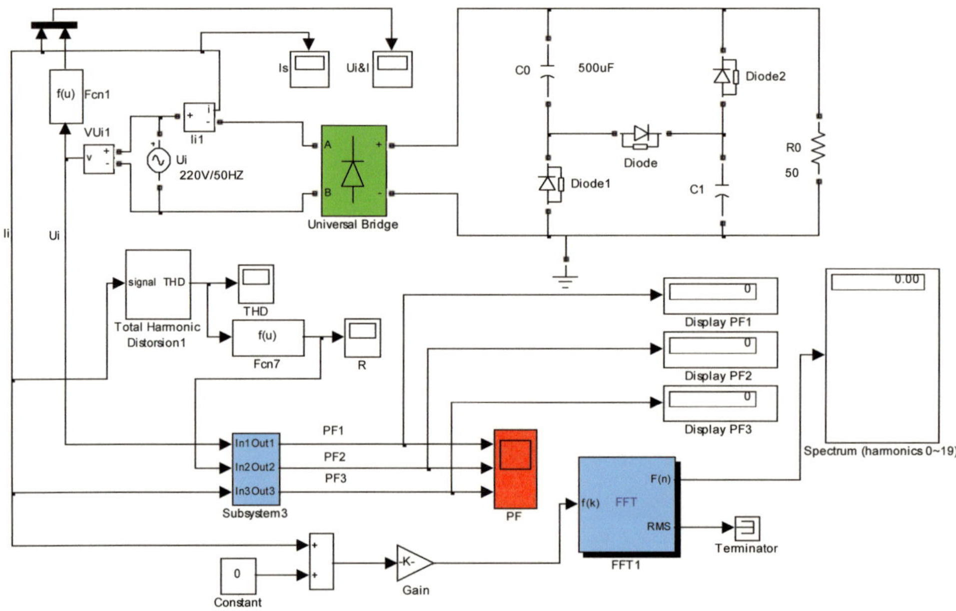

Fig. 8. Basic structure of valley-filled PFC rectification circuit

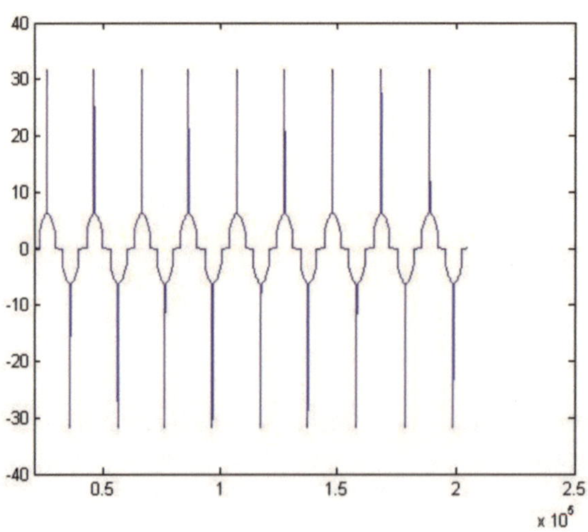

Fig. 9. Current wave form of valley-filled PFC

Load Resistance /Ohm	40	60	80	100	120	140	160	180
Power Factor	0.9112	0.8946	0.8836	0.8749	0.8644	0.8446	0.8442	0.8174

Table 1. Power factors of valley-filled PFC under different loads

From Figure 9, we can see that valley-filled PFC current wave form is still not very satisfied, so, literature 5 put forward a kind of improved circuit as Figure 10. Its current wave form demonstrates as Figure 11. Compared with Figure 9, the current wave form is improved evidently, and the power factor is also been improved, and its power factors under different loads are shown as in table 2.

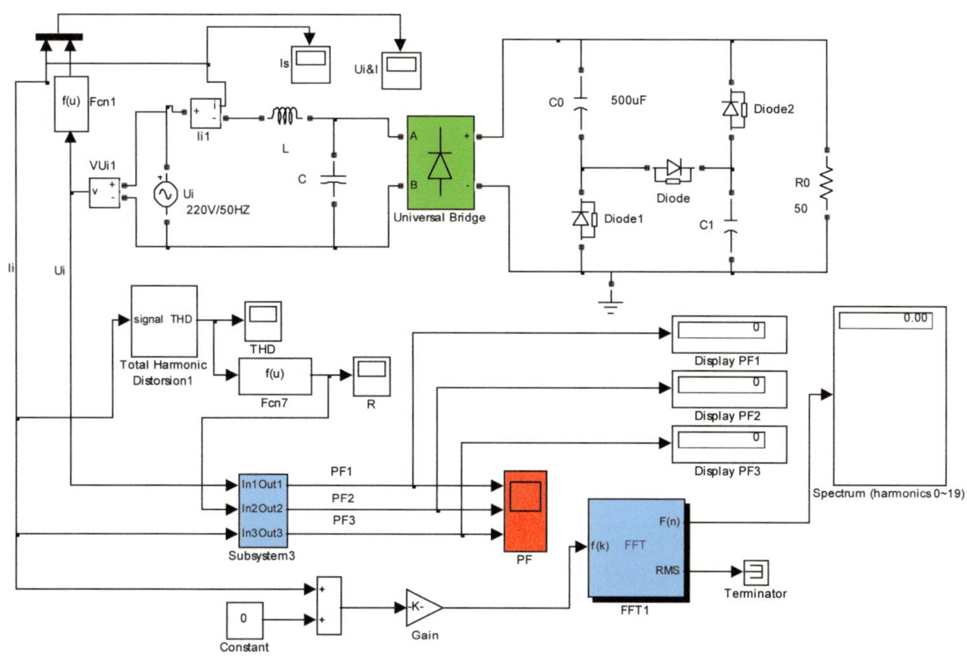

Fig. 10. An improved valley-filled PFC circuit

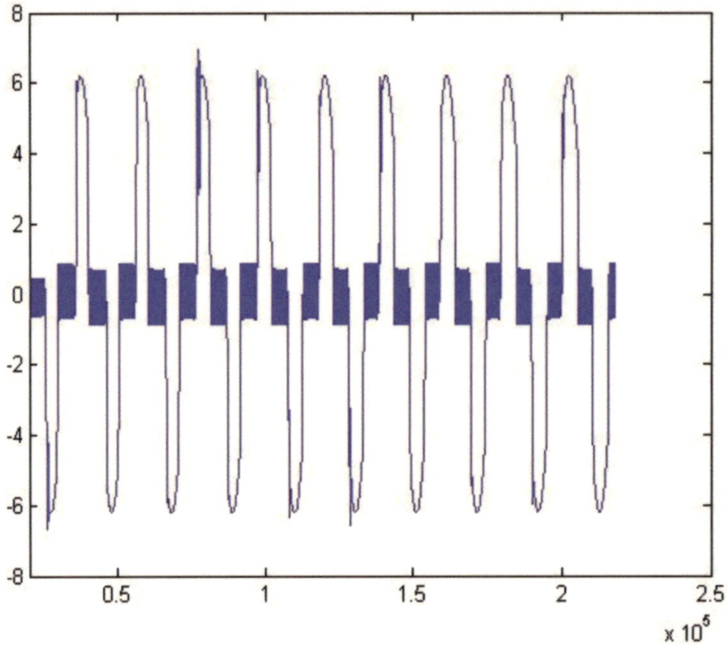

Fig. 11. an improved current wave form of valley-filled PFC circuit

Load Resistance /Ohm	40	60	80	100	120	140	160	180
Power Factor	0.9554	0.9502	0.9421	0.9396	0.9345	0.9304	0.9285	0.9202

Table 2. Power Factors of the improved valley-filled PFC under different loads

We can see that this kind of improved valley-filled PFC can evidently improve the power factors by comparing table 1 and table 2. Valley-filled PFC has been used in electronic ballast and other small electronic equipment, which can meet the requirements for power factor of low power electronic equipments of IEC1000-3-2 and other standards.

Correcting Circuit and its Limit Power Factor of Active Power based on BOOST Circuit[1]

BOOST active correcting circuit is demonstrated as Figure 12, U_A is sampled current, U_B is sampled full wave voltage and alternating voltage effective value, U_C is MOSFET driving impulse, and U_D is sampled output voltage. When the circuit operates in steady state, voltage U_B is similar to full wave voltage, current of inductance L is similar to full wave current, the current is similar to sine current, and is similar to mains supply voltage, of same frequency and phase, and then make switching power factor approached to unit one.

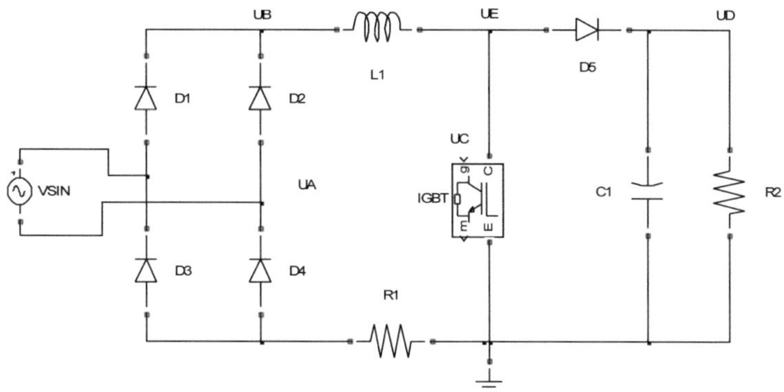

Fig. 12. BOOST active correcting circuit

BOOST active correcting circuit's power factor is smaller than 1. This conclusion is proved by counter evidence. i.e., assuming the circuit in Figure 12 has corrected the power factor to unit one, and then U_B should be full wave voltage, current of inductance L_1 should be full wave current, and same as U_B in wave form. Then the circuit can be emulated as Figure 13. This circuit uses current source (peak value is 12A) to replace, $IGTB$, D_5, C_1, R_2 in Figure 12, and this current source has same wave forms with inductive current. The R1 in Figure 13 is the resistance added in order to avoid iteration divergence, but it is evidently that the effect to emulation results can be ignored. The emulation results are shown as Figure 14. From Figure 14, we can see that V_{out} appears minus voltage that is obviously impossible. Because the peak value of U_E in Figure 12 is similar and almost equivalent to U_D, and its valley value is 0, the low frequency component of U_E e could not be minus. And thus it is proved that the BOOST active correcting circuit power factor of the BOOST active correcting circuit is always smaller than 1.

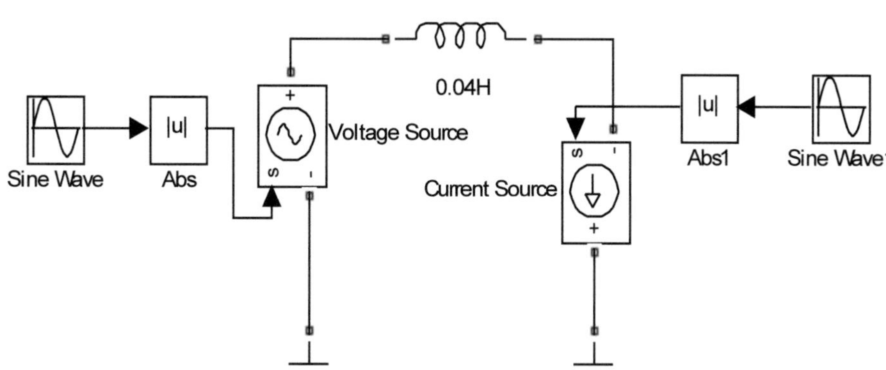

Fig. 13. Emulated circuit to prove the limit power factor of BOOST which is smaller than unit one

Now, we are going to calculate power factor's limit of BOOST active correcting circuit. The emulated circuit is demonstrated as in Figure 14, the diode D5 is added in order to delete the minus part of VOUT in Figure 13, and this conforms to actual application. Its voltage and current wave forms are demonstrated as the Figure 15. And we can see from the Figure that except the current wave near the zero point is "a little" deflected from the sine wave, all the other places are very close to it.

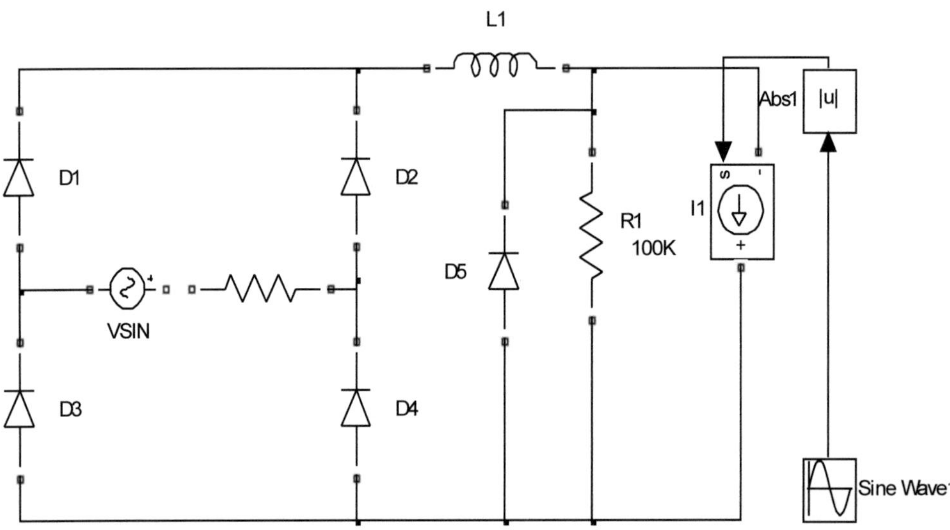

Fig. 14. Emulated circuit that calculating the power factor's limit of BOOST active correcting circuit

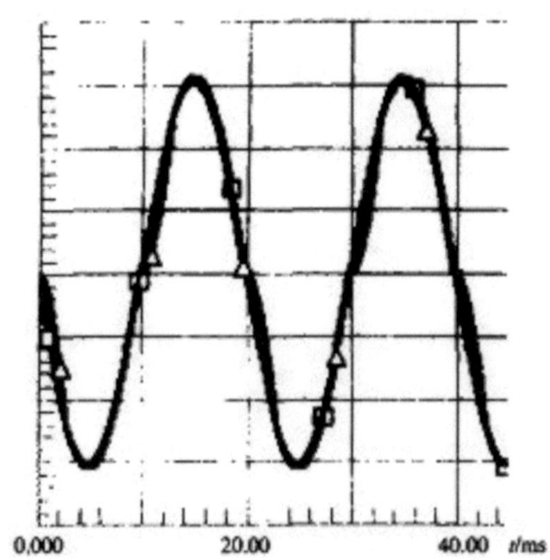

Fig. 15. Voltage and current wave form

Correcting Circuit of Active PFC based on BOOST Circuit

BOOST active correcting circuit is demonstrated as Figure 12, and its emulated circuit is demonstrated as Figure 16. The module Ii1 is used to detect current, the module Is is to display current, The module Vui1 is used to calculate voltage, the module Ui&I is to display voltage and current, the module Subsystem3 is used to calculate power factor according to formula (1), the module fft1 is used to calculate elements of harmonic wave, RS is current sampling resistor, the module Ii2 is to detect current of inductance, the module Subsystem is controlling module that adopts average current control mode. The module Subsystem3 is demonstrated as Figure 17.

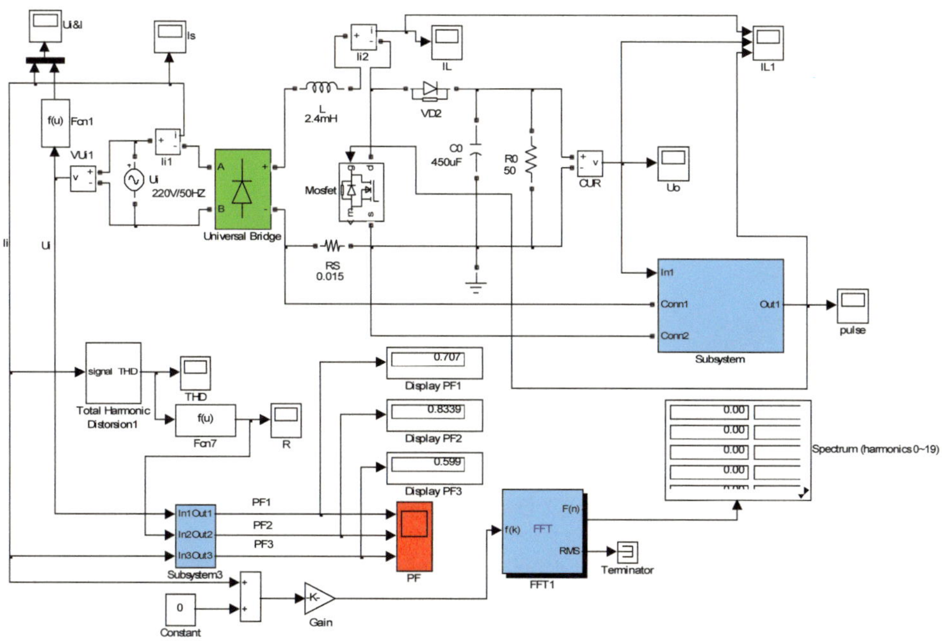

Fig. 16. BOOST active correcting circuit

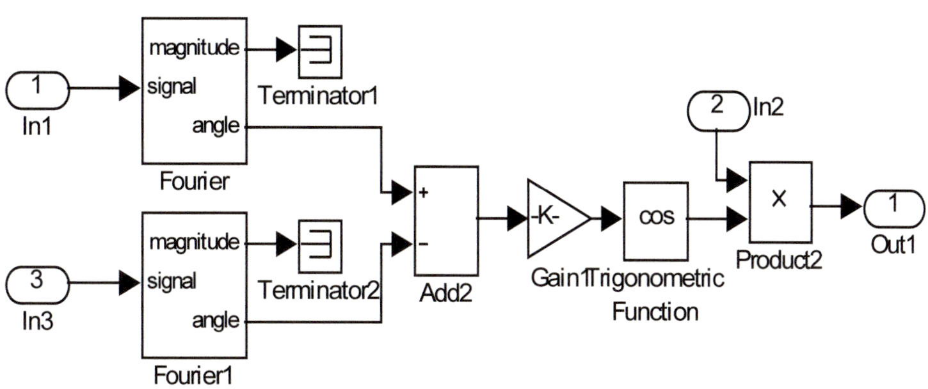

Fig. 17. The circuit of the module Subsystem3

The input voltage and current of BOOST active correcting circuit are shown in Figure 18, in which the power of factor is up to 0.99. BOOST active correcting circuit is mainly used on occasions of high and medium power.

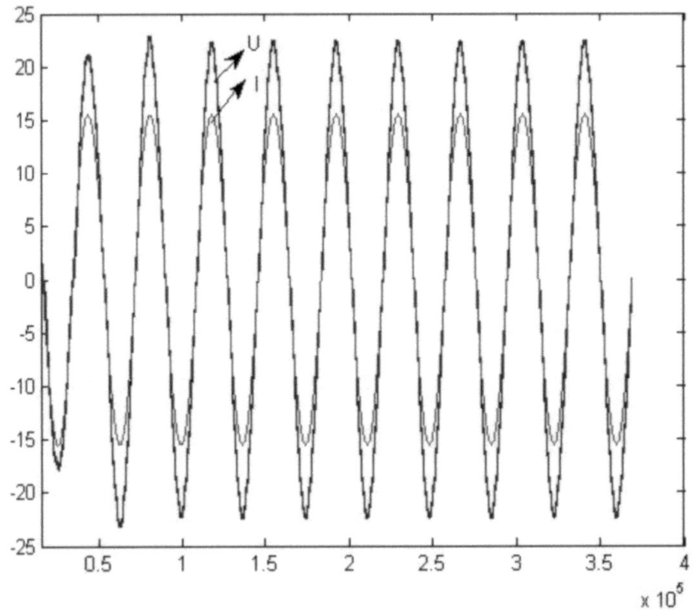

Fig. 18. Input voltage and current wave form of BOOST active correcting circuit

Soft-switching Correcting Circuit Based on BOOST Circuit[2]

By the use of active switch components, BOOST active correcting circuit drastically decreases the harmonic current in AC side, and increases power factor. But, with the use of active switch components, switch devices' off-losses increase, the stress of the voltage and current increases. In order to solve these problems, soft switch technology is introduced. The typical circuit of using soft switch technology is shown in Figure 19. The circuit is consisted of basic BOOST circuit and auxiliary resonant network. Auxiliary resonant network is comprised of auxiliary switch Q_2, resonant inductor L_a, resonant capacitor C_a and C_r, auxiliary diode D_a, D_b and D_c.

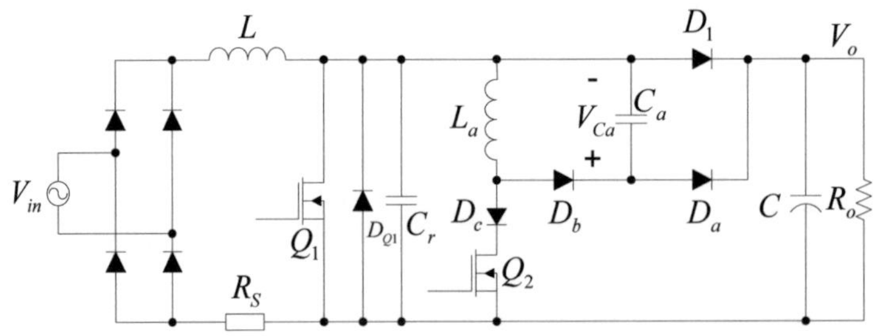

Fig. 19. Correcting circuit of typical soft-switching active power factor

Auxiliary resonant network supplies ZVS/Zero-voltage opening conditions for main switch Q_1. The working procedure can be divided into 6 steps as the following:

(1) Assuming main switch Q_1 is off, and diode D_1 is conducted, inductance L charges for capacitor C;

(2) When the main switch Q_1 is needed to be turned on, the auxiliary switch Q_2 is turned on in advance, the current of resonant inductance increases from zero linearly at the time. D_1 will be turned off when the current of L_a equals to the one of L;

(3) When D_1 is turned off, resonant inductance L_a and resonant capacitor C_r is to form resonant circuit, C_r voltage gradually decreases, and when it equals zero, the diode D_{Q_1} in the main switch Q_1 is inducted, the resonant circuit stops vibrating, and the voltage of the Q_1 equals zero;

(4) Switching on Q_1 to realize ZVS;

(5) When Q_1 is on, Q_2 is turned off, then L_a and C_a is to form resonant circuit, but for the initial value of C_a is zero, Q_2 is off at zero voltage; when voltage of C_a equals to output voltage, the diode D_a is conducted, and the current of La decreases linearly, when it decreases to zero, D_a and D_b are turned off;

(6) When the mains switch Q_1,is turned off ,the current of inductance L charges for C_a and C_r respectively, for the initial voltage of capacitor C_r is zero, the Q_1 is off under the condition of zero voltage; when the voltage of C_r increases to as same as the output voltage, the voltage of C_a already decreases to zero, diode D_a and diode D_1 is conducted.
Hereafter, repeating the front process.

Therefore, from the above analysis we can see that the main switch Q_1 is zero voltage turned on and turned off, which works in the mode of real ZVT model; auxiliary switch is zero current turned on and zero voltage turned off, which works on the model of the combination of ZCT（Zero Current Transition）and ZVT.

There are various controlling circuit of Boost power factor correction, among which, average current control is suitable to be used in occasions of high and medium voltage and it most widely used in APFC currently because that its THD（Total Harmonic Distortion）and EMI（Electro Magnetic Interference）is small, it is not sensitive to noise, the switching frequency is fixed, and the error between inductive current peak value and average value is small, it is a kind of controlling method that used most widely in APFC at present. So, in correcting circuits for soft-switching power factor, average current controlling is chose.

In order to make sure that the main switch keeps turning on under zero voltage, and the auxiliary switching tube maintains conducted when the time the resonance voltage on C_r

decrease to zero, a fixed period of delaying time can be added, this period of time $t_{ZVT} = \frac{I_{IN_P} L_a}{V_o} + \frac{\pi}{2}\sqrt{L_a C_r}$ equals to the transition time of zero voltage under the condition of input voltage low limit and full loading. This is also the advanced conduction time of auxiliary switching tube than main switching tube.
The selecting of parameters as is shown in table 3.

Boost Inductance L	Filter Capacitor C	Auxiliary Inductance L_a	Auxiliary Capacitor C_a	Sampling Resistance R_s	Output Load R_0
1.0mH	450μF	6μH	3.6nF	0.048Ω	160Ω

Table 3. the selecting of parameters of correcting circuit components of soft-switching power factor

Power factor is shown in Figure 20, wave forms of input voltage and current are shown in Figure 21, and wave form of output voltage is shown in Figure 22. We can see that when emulation time reaches to 0.024s, the circuit tends to stable, power factor is also stable and power factor approaches to 1. Although the power factor fluctuated after became stable, but the amplitude of fluctuation is very small.

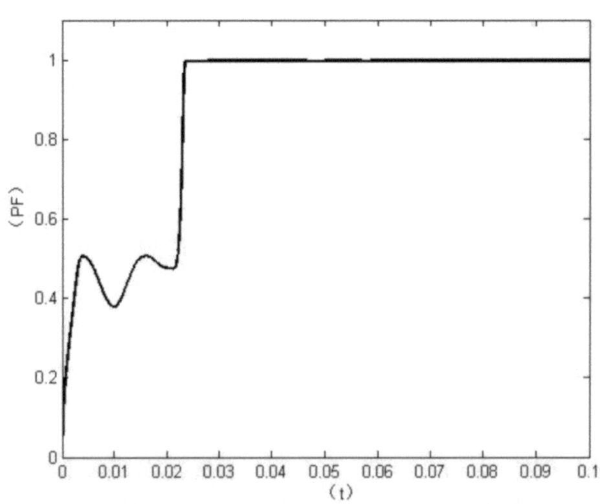

Fig. 20. The Power Factor of soft Switch BOOST

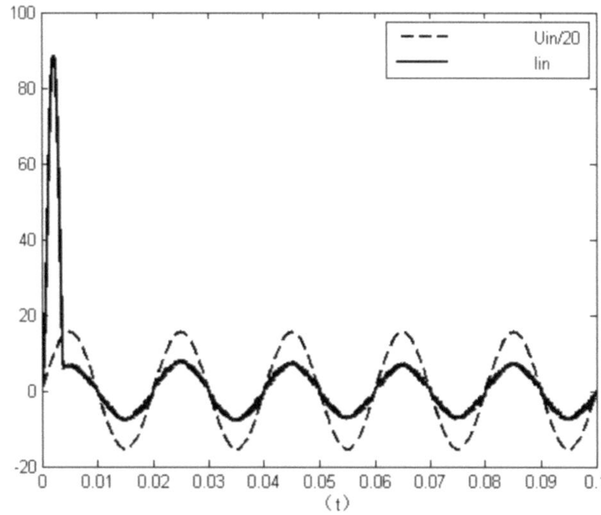

Fig. 21. Wave Forms of Input Voltage, Current of Soft Switch BOOST

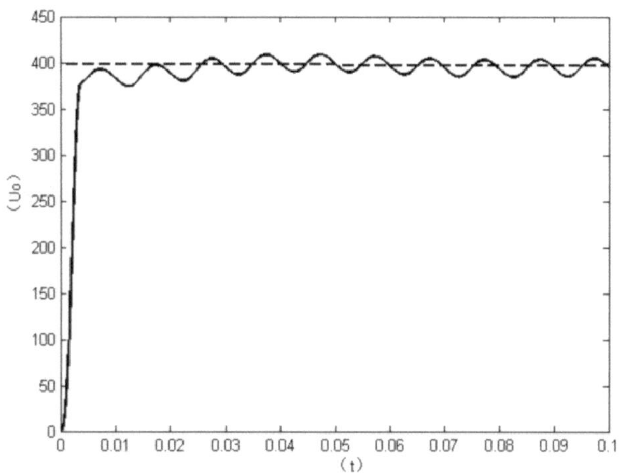

Fig. 22. Wave Form of Output Voltage

Figure 23 gives harmonic wave input current value of soft switching active power factor's correcting circuit and the comparing result with standard value of IEC61000-3-2A. We can see from the Figure that input current's 2、3……19 harmonic wave, the current values are all much smaller than standard value in IEC61000-3-2A.

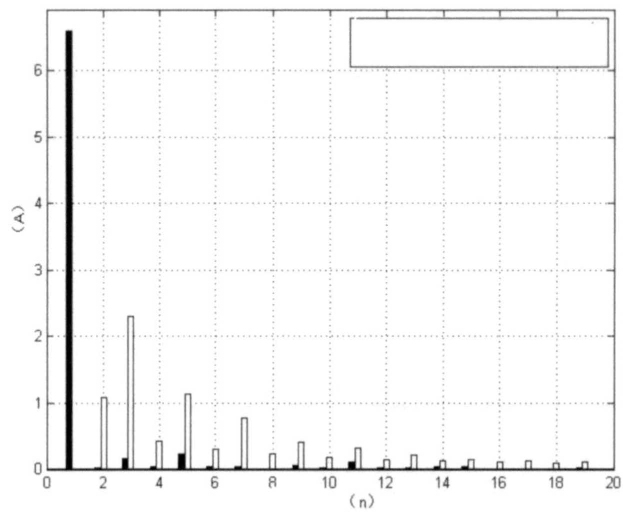

Fig. 23. Comparison of Circuit Input Harmonic Current Wave Value and Standard Value

Power factor of three-phase AC/DC switching power supply with the load of pure resistance

In single-phase uncontrolled rectifying circuit, if the load equivalent is a resistance, the input power factor is unit 1. But in three-phase uncontrolled rectifying circuit, even the load is a resistance (see Figure 24), its power factor is only about 0.94. The phase voltage and phase current wave form of the time being as are shown in Figure 25.

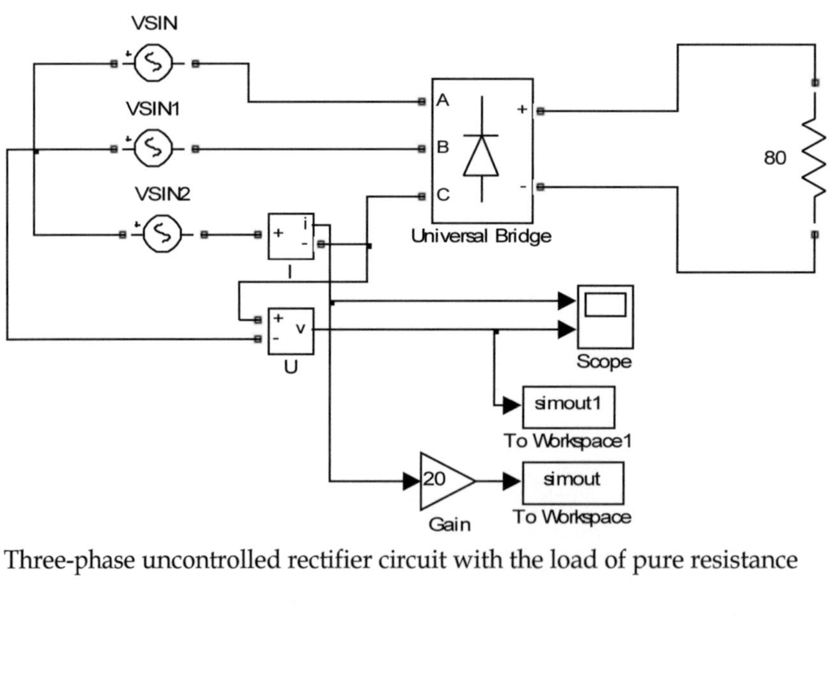

Fig. 24. Three-phase uncontrolled rectifier circuit with the load of pure resistance

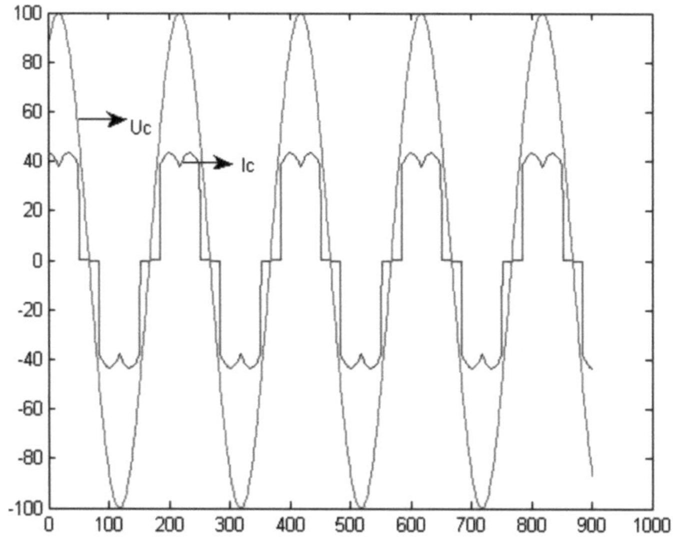

Fig. 25. Phase voltage and phase current wave forms of three-phase uncontrolled rectifier circuit with the load of pure resistance

Three-phase Passive PFC Circuit of Series Connected Large Inductance

Power factor correcting circuits of three phase AC/DC switch power source can be divided into passive PFC and active PFC. Active PFC can adopt three three-phase BOOST correcting circuit, but its application area is not as wide as the one of passive PFC. The most widely used of three-phase passive PFC is inductive circuit, the voltage and current of which are shown in Figure 26, and the power factor reach to 0.95.

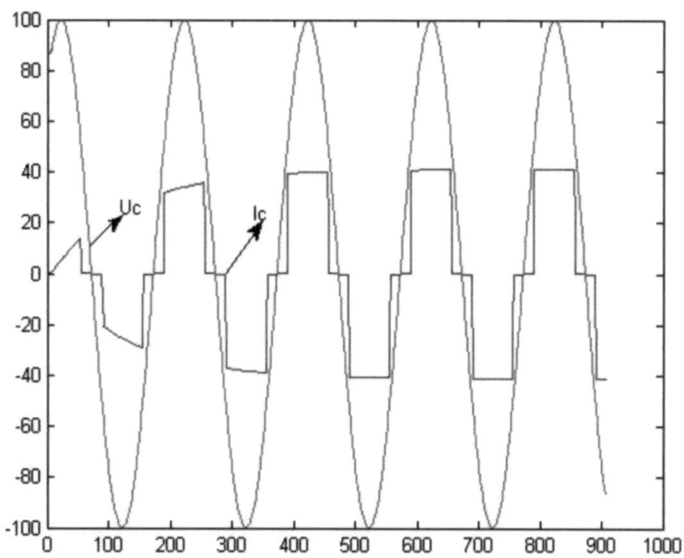

Fig. 26. Three-phase Current of Series Connected Large Inductance

An Improved Three-phase Passive PFC Circuit

Figure 27 is a kind of improved three-phase passive power factor's correcting circuit, the circuit parameters of which has been optimized by using MATLAB. Figure 28 is its phase voltage and phase current form, and the power factor of which reaches to 0.991.

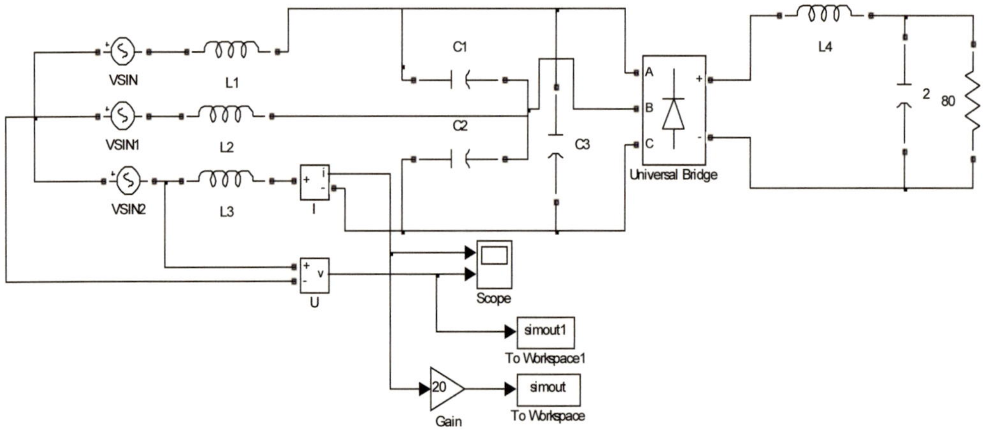

Fig. 27. The circuit of an improved three-phrase passive power factor correcting

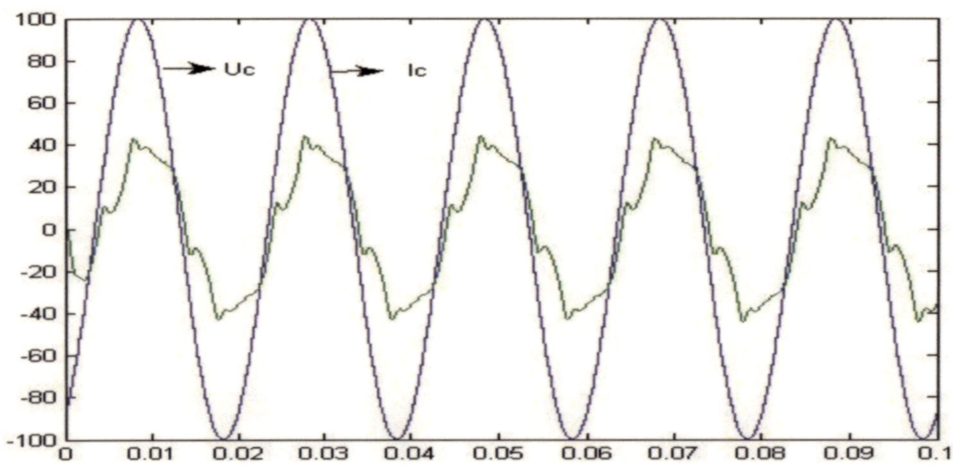

Fig. 28. The phase voltage and phase current form of an improved three-phase passive power factor's correcting circuit

References

Ren Kaichun, Zhang Xuanqi, Tu Yaqing. The Emulation for the Maximum Power Factor of BOOST Circuit. ELECTRIC ENGINEERING, 2003(10)

Ren Kaichun, Zhang Xuanqi, Tu Yaqing, etc. The PSPICE Simulation for the Power Factor of Three- phase-switching-power. ELECTROTECHNICAL JOURNAL, 2003(8)

Ren Kaichun, Zhang Xuanqi, Zhang Xiaoqing, etc. The PSPICE Simulation and Optimization for the Power Factor Correction of Single-phase Switching Power Supply. ELECTRICAL AUTOMATION, 2003(5)

Ren Kaichun, Yan Zhiqiang, Wang Yongmin. Soft-switching APFC circuit based on Matlab. ELECTRIC POWER AUTOMATION EQUIPMENT, 2007(8)

Wang Huitao, Ren Kaichun, Qiang Shengze, Jing Youquan. Imitation Analysis and Optimization of a Single-Phase Switch Electric Source Power Factor. ELECTRIC ENGINEERING, 2005(11)

Wang Yongmin, Ren Kaichun, Jing Youquan. The Caspoc Simulation Analysis and Optimization of a three-Phase Switching Power Supply PFC Circuit. ELECTRIC AGE,2006(11)

9

Simulation of numerical distance relays

Dr. Hamid H. Sherwali and Eng. Abdlmnam A. Abdlrahem
Al-Fatah University
Tripoli-Libya

1. Introduction

Utility engineers and consultants use relay models to select the relay types suited for a particular application, and to analyze the performance of relays that appear to either operate incorrectly or fail to operate on the occurrence of a fault. Instead of using actual prototypes, manufacturers use relay model designing to expedite and economize the process of developing new relays. Electric power utilities use computer-based relay models to confirm how the relay would perform during systems disturbances and normal operating conditions and to make the necessary corrective adjustment on the relay settings. The software models could be used for training young and inexperienced engineers and technicians. Researchers use relay model to investigate and improve protection design and algorithms. However, simulating numerical relays to choose appropriate settings for the steady state operation of over current relays and distance relays is presently the most familiar use of relay models (McLaren et al., 2001)

Numerical relay models can be divided into two categories. The models of the first category consider only the fundamental frequency components of voltages and currents. Phasor-based models were the first to be widely used to design and apply relays. The models of the second category take into consideration the high frequency and decaying DC components of voltages and currents in addition to the fundamental frequency components. These models are called transient models of relays. (McLaren et al., 2001)

The goal of this chapter is to explain the building process of MATLAB model of a distance relay and validating the relay behavior when the input data that describes the voltage and current signals at the relay location is generated by simulation of the power network using EMTP–ATP. Voltage and current signals during faults are severely distorted; this is why EMTP is used as a power simulator during faults. EMTP would present voltage and current signals during fault with their dc decaying components and high frequency oscillations. However the model was validated by a similar input data generated by the simulation of the power network using MATLAB. The validation process extended to include the cases where the measured impedance is changed due to a change of fault location, due to an existence of resistive faults or due to an existence of more than one in-feed.

The chapter began by introducing the principle of operation of distance relays and reviews the functionality of each of the internal modules of numerical relay such as, analog anti-aliasing filtering module, analog-to-digital conversion module, and phasor estimation algorithm.

2. Protective Relays

Fault current is the expression given to the current that flow in the circuit when load is shorted i.e. flow in a path other than the load. This current is usually very high and may exceed ten times the rated current of a piece of plant. Faults on power system are inevitable due to external or internal causes, lightning may struck the overhead lines causes insulation damage. Internal overvoltage due switching or other power system phenomenon may also cause an over voltage leads to deterioration of the insulation and faults. Power networks are usually protected by means of two main components, relays that sense the abnormal current or voltage and a circuit breaker that put a piece of plant out of tension. Power System Protection is the art and science of the application of devices that monitor the power line currents and voltages (relays) and generate signals to deenergize faulted sections of the power network by circuit breakers. Goal is to minimize damage to equipment and property that would be caused by system faults, if residues, and maintain the delivery of electrical energy to the consumers. Many types of protective relays are used to protect power system equipments, they are classified according to their operating principles; over current relay senses the extra (more than set) current considered dangerous to a given equipment, differential relays compare in and out currents of a protected equipment, while impedance relays measure the impedance of the protected piece of planet. For a good performance of a relay in a power system it must have the following characteristics; dependability, security, selectivity, sensitivity and speed.

Traditionally, power systems problems and applications have been solved by means of purely analog circuits, However the scenario have changed and power system area was one of the most benefited areas from the booming in area of digital and signal processing. Numerical relays are the result of the application of microprocessor technology in relay industry, they convert the measured voltages and currents from analog to digital values and calculates from these samples the relay protection criterium i.e. impedance (Ziegler, 1999). Due to processing capacity of numerical relays many protection criteria can be implemented. Protection relays, such as other monitoring and control equipments have taken the advantage from the increasing improvement of the semiconductor industry and the enormous number of digital signal processing and control algorithms. The latest generations of protective relays be provided with a large capacity of processing capabilities become more efficient and can perform a numerous number of functions such as fault locators, integrated monitoring and control functions.

Designing and modeling of numerical relay require establishing a generalized numerical relay structure, which is composed the more relevant and common internal modules employed by typical numerical relays.

3. Distance Relays

Distance relays, as the name sounds, should measure distance. In fact this is true, as in case of transmission line, distance relay measures the impedance between the relay point and the fault location. This impedance is proportional to the length of the conductor, and hence to the distance between the relaying point and the fault.

3.1 Principle of operation

The basic principle as illustrated in figure 1, involves the division of the voltage at the relaying point by the measured current. The apparent impedance is compared with the reach point impedance. If the measured impedance is less than the reach point impedance, it is assumed that a fault exists on the line between the relay and the reach point. The reach point of the relay is the point along the line impedance locus that is intersected by the boundary characteristics of the relay. Distance relay is the broader name of the different types of impedance relay.

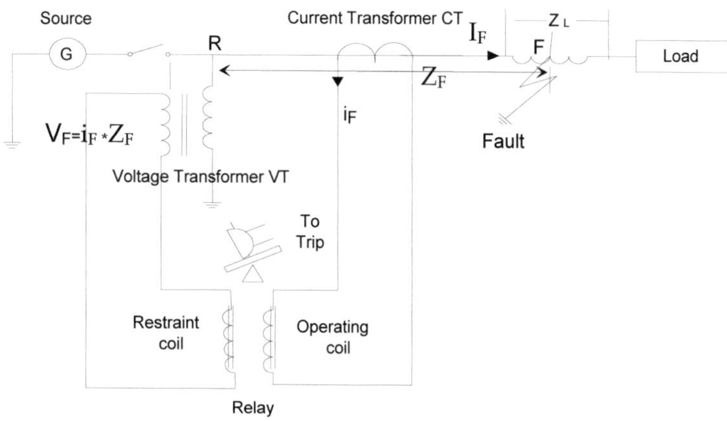

Fig. 1. Principle of operation of distance relay

The relay is connected at position, R and receives a secondary current, iF, equivalent to a primary fault current, IF. The secondary voltage, VF, is equivalent to the product of the fault current "IF" and impedance of the line up to the point of fault, ZF. The operating torque of this relay is proportional to the fault current "IF", and its restraining torque is proportional to the voltage "VF". Taking into account the number of turns of each coil, there will be a definite ratio of V/I at which the torque will be equal. This is the reach point setting of the relay. The relay will operate when the operating torque is greater than the restraining torque. Thus any increase in current coil ampere-turns, without a corresponding increase in the voltage coil ampere-turns, will unbalance the relay. This means the V/I ratio has fallen below the reach point. Alternatively if the restrain torque is greater than the operating torque, the relay will restrain and its contacts will remain open. In this case the V/I ratio is above the reach point. The reach of a relay is the distance from the relaying point to the point of fault. Voltage on the primary of voltage transformer, VT, is :

$$V = {}^{EZ_F}/_{(Z_s + Z_F)} \tag{1}$$

The fault current, I_F

$$I_F = {}^{E}/_{(Z_s + Z_F)} \tag{2}$$

The relay compare the secondary values of V and I, as to measure their ratio which is an impedance Zm ,

$$Z_m = \frac{V / V.T\ Ratio}{I / C.T.Ratio}$$

$$Z_m = ZF * \frac{C.T\ Ratio}{V.T\ Ratio} \tag{3}$$

Zm is the measured impedance called secondary impedance. (GEC, 1990)

3.2 Zones of protection

Basic distance protection will comprise instantaneous directional Zone 1 protection and one or more time delayed zones. Numerical distance relays may have up to five zones, some set to measure in the reverse direction. Numerical relays usually have a reach setting of up to 85% of the protected line impedance for instantaneous Zone 1 protection. The resulting 15% safety margin ensures that there is no risk of the Zone 1 protection over-reaching the protected line due to errors in the current and voltage transformers, inaccuracies in line impedance data provided for setting purposes and errors of relay setting and measurement. of the distance protection must cover the remaining 15% of the line.

The reach setting of the Zone 2 protection should be at least 120% of the protected line impedance. In many applications it is common practice to set the Zone 2 reach to be equal to the protected line section +50% of the shortest adjacent line. Zone 3 reach should be set to at least 1.2 times the impedance presented to the relay for a fault at the remote end of the second line section (GEC, 1990). Typical reach for a 3-zone distance protection are shown in Figure 2.

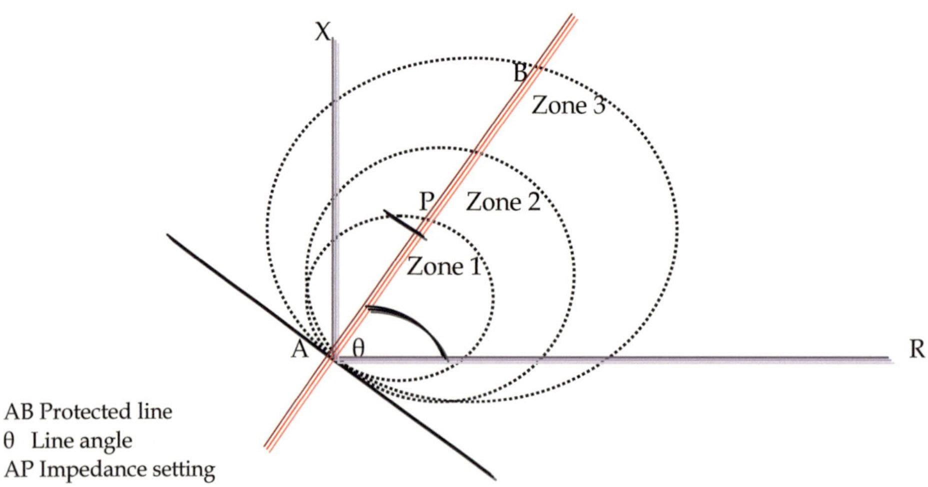

Fig. 2. Typical 3 zones distance protection

3.3 Residual factor

The measuring element of the distance relay is principally laid out such that for each fault type the line impedance of the fault loop is determined. In three phase system the zone-1 of the relay will have six elements responsible for detecting both phase and earth faults (Ziegler, 2006). For phase faults elements, the difference between the two relevant phase signals are used, e.g. a-b elements is supplied with samples of Va - Vb voltage and Ia _ Ib current. For earth elements, the relevant phase voltage is supplied e.g. Va, but the corresponding current is residually compensated. The earth faults compensation factor may be calculated considering the sequence-networks connection for the phase A-to-ground fault on a transmission line. Table (1) indicates calculation formula for phase and line to line faults. In order for the relay to be correctly operated, residual factor shall be introduced as shown in the following equations

$$R_K = \frac{V_K}{I_K + 3.\mathrm{Re}(K_0).I_{0K}} \qquad X_K = \frac{V_K}{I_K + 3.\mathrm{Im}(K_0).I_{0K}} \tag{4}$$

Where; K_0, is the compensation factor
I_0, is zero sequence current
V_k, I_k are the sampled voltage and current respectively

Distance Element	Voltage signal	Current signal
Phase A	V_a	$I_a + 3K_0I_0$
Phase A - Phase B	$V_a - V_b$	$I_a - I_b$

Table 1. Calculation formula for phase and line to line faults

3.4 Effect of fault resistance on relay coverage

The earth fault resistance reduces the effective earth-fault reach of a mho Zone 1 element to such an extent that the majority of faults are detected in Zone 2 time. Figure 3 illustrates the effect of arc resistance on the relay reach. The effect of fault resistance on the reach of distance relays is better discussed with the simulation results.

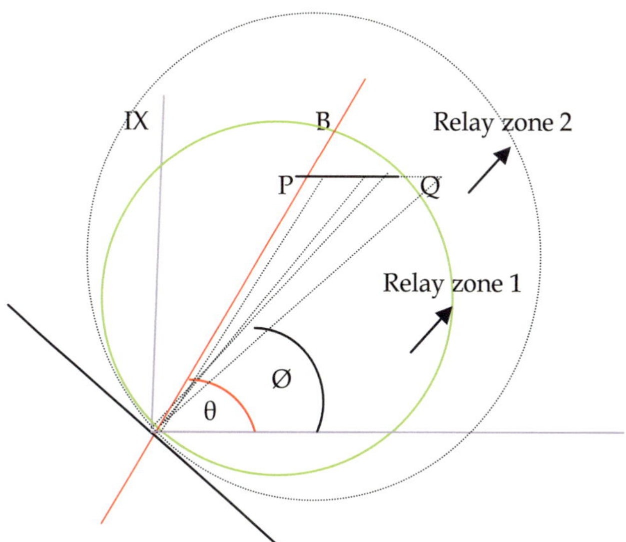

AB, Protected line,
θ, Line angle,
Ø, Relay characteristic angle setting
AP, Relay Impedance setting and
PQ, Arc (fault) resistance

Fig. 3. Effect of arc resistance on relay coverage

4. Numerical Relay Structure

Since their introduction on 1920, Classic distance relays based on electro-mechanical and then on static technology are still in wide use. However due to the booming in digital techniques, microprocessor-based relays were introduced. It is quite common to use term digital relay instead of numerical relay as the distinction between both rests on fine technical details. Others see numerical relays as natural developments of digital relays as a result of advances in technology. However, in US the term (digital distance protection) has always been used in the meaning of (numerical distance protection) (Ziegler, 1999). A general view of the typical digital relay is shown in figure 4.

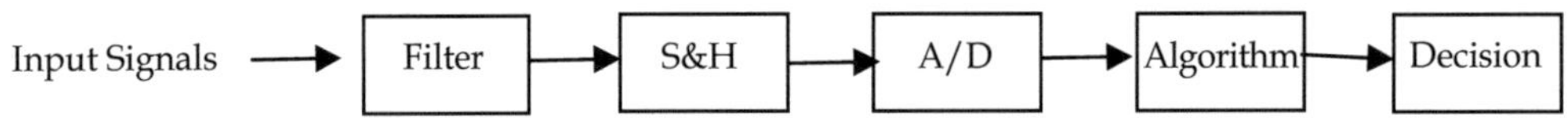

S&H, Sample and Hold, A/D, Analogue to digital convertor
Fig. 4. Block diagram of a typical digital relay.

The generalized numerical relay concept is directly derived from open system relaying (different relay functions can be obtained from the same hardware just by modifying microprocessor programming) (Sandro, 2006). The following hardware modules and functions constitute the generalized numerical relay.

4.1 Isolation and analog signal scaling

Current and voltage waveforms from instrument transformers are acquired and scaled down to convenient voltage levels for use in the digital and numerical relays.

4.2 Analog anti-aliasing filtering

Low-pass filters are used to avoid the phenomena of aliasing in which the high frequency components of the inputs appear to be parts of the fundamental frequency components. The analog inputs must be applied to low-pass filters and their outputs should be sampled and quantized. The use of low-pass filter is necessary to limit the effects of noise and unwanted components of frequencies. The filter is designed to remove any frequencies existing on the input signal which are greater than half the sampling frequency. The nature of the relaying task dictates the total amount of filtering required. Distance protection based on impedance measurements uses information contained in the sinusoidal steady state components of 50-60 Hz. Therefore, filtering must preserve the steady state components and reject other components. Common analog low-pass filters used in these relays are of third to fifth order with cutoff frequency of about 90 Hz. The cutoff frequency of 90 Hz implies that a sampling rate of at least three samples per cycle (180 Hz) must be used in order that the information needed to perform the distance relay functions is retained and errors due to aliasing are avoided. In practice, the sampling rate must be at least four samples per cycle (240 Hz) (Sandro, 2006).

4.3 Analog-to-digital conversion (ADC)

Because digital processors can process numerical or logical data only, the waveforms of inputs must be sampled at discrete times. To achieve this, each analog signal is passed through a sample- and-hold module, and conveyed, one at a time, to an Analog-to-Digital Converter (ADC) by a multiplexer (Mux), as shown in figure 5.

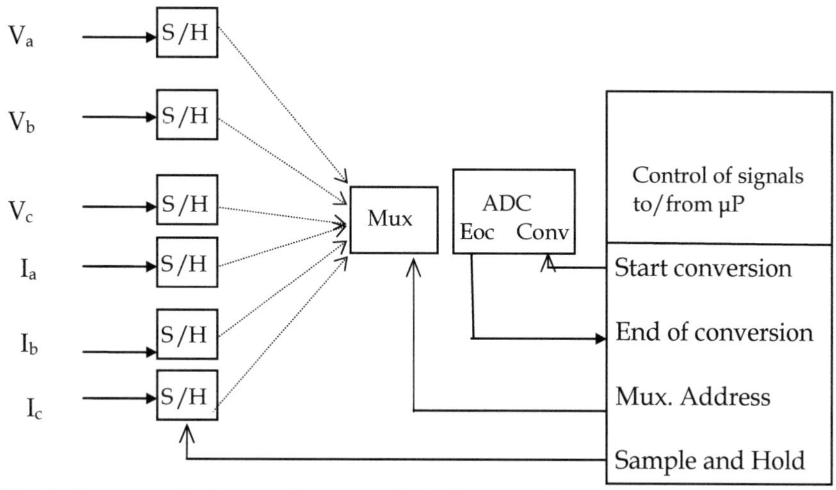

Fig. 5. Block diagram of relay analogue to digital conversion arrangement

The basic function of a sample-and-hold in an analog input system is to capture an input signal and hold it constant during the subsequent ADC conversion cycle. An analog-to-digital converter (A/D converter or ADC) takes the instantaneous value of an analog voltage and converts it into an n-bit binary number that can be easily manipulated by a microprocessor. A distance relay having a minimum set impedance of 4Ω, would have a highest current level for a voltage transformer of 110 V, equal to 110/4 = 27.5 A. Allowing for offset during faults,100%, this current could reach 55A. Suppose that the relay must operate for a minimum current level of 25 mA and this can be represented by I digital level. Hence the dynamic range for one polarity of the current is 55/0.025 =2200. Hence for bipolar signal the dynamic range is 4400. The ADC closest to this figure is 12 bit. In general, most high performance numeric relays use 12, 14 or 16 bit ADCs. (IEE, 1995). The n-bit number is a binary fraction representing the ratio between the input voltage and the full-scale voltage of the converter. A number of techniques can be used to achieve this conversion. The full-input voltage ranges for an ADC are typically 0 to +5 or 0 to +10 volts for unipolar operations, and -5 to +5 or -10 to +10 volts for bipolar operation (Sandro, 2006).

4.4 Quantizer

The Quantizer block passes its input signal through a stair-step function so that many neighboring points on the input axis are mapped to one point on the output axis. The effect is to quantize a smooth signal into a stair-step output. The output is computed using the round-to-nearest method, which produces an output that is symmetric about zero. The output y of the quantizer is given by:

$$y = q * round(u/q) \tag{5}$$

where u is the input, and q the Quantization interval.

4.5 Digital filter

Digital filters have, for many years, been the most common application of digital signal processors. There are two basic forms of digital filters, the Finite Impulse Response (FIR) filter and Infinite Impulse Response (IIR) filter. The main draw back to the use of IIR filters in digital protection relays is that the group delay cannot be specified in the design process. This makes their use in protection somewhat onerous, in general, FIR filters are usually the preferred type. (IEE, 1995). As this the case FIR filter will be briefly explained. As seen in the block diagram of figure 6, and the second order Finite Impulse (FIR) filter shown in figure 7, the input signal x(n) is a series of discrete values obtained by sampling an analogue signal. X(0) correspond to the input value at *t=0, x(1) at t=Ts, x(2) at t=2 Ts* and so on, where *Ts* is sampling period =1/*fs*. The three main blocks of FIR filters are:

(a) ***Unit delay***

Its purpose is to hold the input for a unit of time (physically equal to the sampling interval Ts) before it is delivered to the output. Mathematically, it performs the following operation.

$$y(n) = x(n-a) \tag{6}$$

Unit delay is depicted schematically in Figure 6(a). The letter D, indicating delay, sometimes is replaced by z-1, which is the delay operator in the z domain.
Unit delay can be implemented in software in a storage variable, which changes its value when instructed by the program.

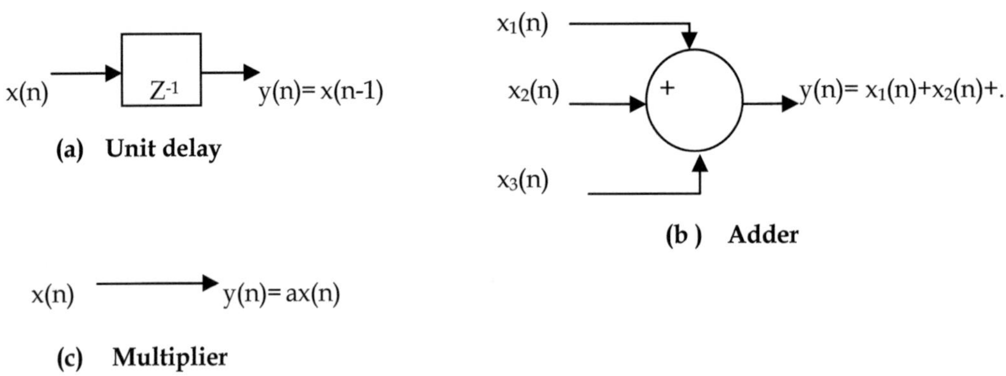

Fig. 6. Basic elements of Finite Impulse (FIR) digital filter.

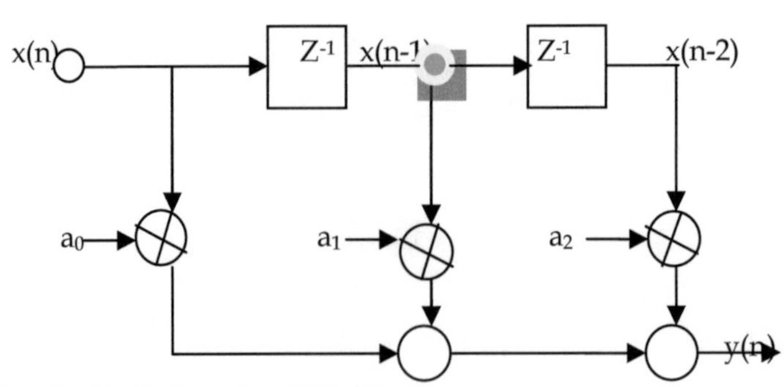

Fig. 7. Second order Finite Impulse (FIR) filter.

(b) ***Adder***

The purpose of the adder is to add two or more signals appearing at the input at a specific time. Mathematically, it performs the operations like the one shown in the following equation.

$$y(n) = x_1(n) + x_2(n) + x_3(n) + ... \tag{7}$$

An adder is depicted schematically in Figure 6(b).

(c) ***Multiplier***

The purpose of this element is to multiply a signal (a varying quantity) by a constant number, which takes the form;

$$y(n) = ax(n) \tag{8}$$

A multiplier is depicted schematically in Figure 6(c). There is no specific symbol for the multiplier, but to show its operation, a constant factor is placed above or besides the signal line.

4.6 Phasor estimation algorithm

A software algorithm implemented in a microprocessor estimates the amplitude and phase of the waveforms provided to the relay. More details are given in section 8, Impedance Estimation Algorithms.

4.7 Relay algorithm and trip logic

After microprocessor calculates the phasors representing the inputs, acquires the status of the switches, performs protective relay calculations, and finally provides outputs for controlling the circuit breakers, the result of the algorithm transported to the control part of the relay where the results is compared with the settings of the relay and trip signal may be generated. Trip signal has to be secured and it should not be released unless the fault is stable within the tripping zone. Since impedance measurement falling within the relay characteristic is not a reliable indication of fault, counter may be used to establish a decision scheme that decides the trip signal generation. One of the employed counters techniques increases when the impedance is in the tripping zone and decreases when outside the tripping zone, other, remaining the impedance values in the characteristic for a certain period of time before fault is reliably evaluated, i.e. a number of successive samples are in tripping zone. The processor may also support communications, self-testing, target display, time clocks, and other tasks (McLaren et al,. 2001).

5. Numerical Relays Operating Principles

When the distance relays receive discrete voltage and current signal, it converts it to a phasor. However faults on transmission lines cause the voltage and current signals to be severely distorted. These signals may contain decaying dc components, subsystem frequency transients, high frequency oscillation quantities, and etc. The higher frequency components can be eliminated using low pass anti-aliasing filters with appropriate cut-off frequency, but the anti-aliasing filters cannot remove decaying dc components and reject low frequency components. This makes the phasors very difficult to be quickly estimated and affects the performance of digital relaying. Therefore, the Discrete Fourier transform is usually used to remove the dc-offset components. DFT is a digital filtering algorithm that computes the magnitude and phase at discrete frequencies of a discrete time sequence.

6. Current and Voltage Signal During Faults

The voltage and current signals in resistance-inductance behavior of power network are as usual sinusoid with exponentially decaying offsets. The offsets can severely affect the currents but seldom affect the voltage. Figure 8, shows the shape of the fault current at the terminal of a synchronous machine (Nasser, 2008)

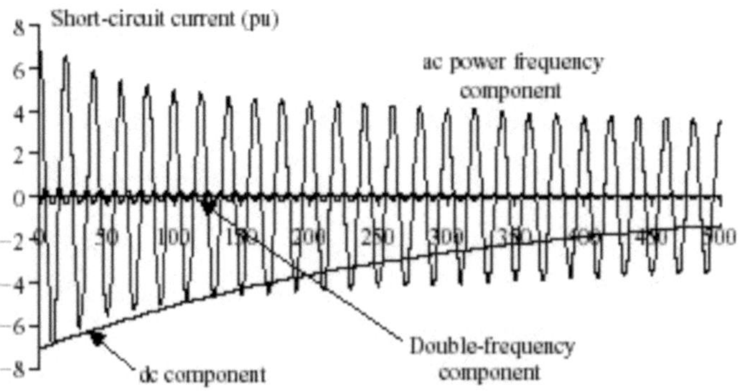

Fig. 8. Three-phase short-circuit fault at a synchronous machine terminals

Non-linear loads, power transformers and instrument transformers can produce harmonics. Figure 9 shows a composite harmonic waveform. (Barry, 2000). In addition to that, capacitive series compensation introduces subsystem frequency transients. This transient depends on the percentage of capacitive compensation. Attention has to be given to filters, no matter how they are built, they should have the following characteristics:-

Band pass response, about the system frequency, because all other components are of no interest.

Dc rejection to guarantee decaying- exponential are filtered out.

Harmonic attenuation or rejection to limit effects of nonlinear loads.

Reasonable bandwidth for fast response.

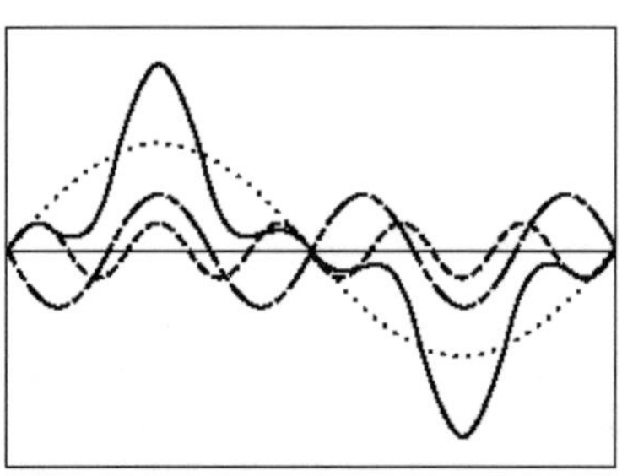

------ Fifth harmonic waveform .... Fundamental 60Hz waveform

_._._ Third harmonic waveform ____ Resultant nonlinear wave

Fig. 9. Composite harmonic waveform.

7. Relay Models

A successful relay model must produce the same output for the same inputs as its real counterpart. However, numerical relay models can be divided into two categories. First, the models that considers only the fundamental frequency components of voltages and currents. Phasor-based models were the first to be widely used to design and apply relays. The second category models take into consideration the high frequency and decaying DC components of voltages and currents in addition to the fundamental frequency components (McLaren,et,2001)

7.1 Transient relay models

Transient relay models mimic the behavior of numerical relays including their performance in the transient state and the impact of the transient components in the input signal. The availability of detailed information of the internal functioning of relays is critical in the process of producing a close-to-real transient relay model. According to the available information, transient models can be categorized in generic and detailed models (Sandro, 2006).

Generic models give considerable insight into the operation of the relay type but may not be suitable for marginal cases and precise timing. They may not have detailed logic provided in specific implementation of the generic principle in a specific relay. This logic is often applied to make specific functions interact with other functions to make a protection system. Because of this limitation generic model determine the best use for checking specific functions, rather than complete systems that are made up of numerous interacting functions.

Detailed models preserve all the advantages of being able to examine the internal operation of any function. Detailed models are more useful than generic models for checking the performance of complete systems since all logic is represented. Unfortunately, detailed models are not as readily available as the generic models because they may include trade secrets of the manufacturers.

Manufacturers are in position to design accurate transient models, particularly for new digital relays, for the reason that, in the designing process, the software model may precede the hardware design. Where algorithms and hardware are known in detail, very precise performance can be achieved in the modeling.

8. Impedance Estimation Algorithms

The estimated phasors of voltages and currents are used in the implementation of protection algorithms in numerical relays. A relay algorithm is a set of equations whose evaluation and comparison with certain predetermined levels determines the operation of the relay. A number of algorithms can be regarded as impedance calculations in that the fundamental frequency component of both voltages and currents are obtained from the samples. The ratio of appropriate voltages and currents then provide the impedance to the fault. The performance of all of these algorithms is dependent on obtaining accurate estimate of the fundamental frequency component of a signal from a few samples. The algorithm based on series R&L model has the apparent advantage of allowing all signals that satisfy the differential equations to be used in estimating the R and L of the model.(Phadke & Thorp, 1990). The equations and parameters that represent the relay algorithm of distance relays are simplified hereinafter. The algorithms are classified according to the approach used to calculate the impedance based on the voltage and current measurements.

8.1 Transmission Line Model

By assuming that the transmission line to which the relay is connected is composed of a series resistance and inductance, the fundamental equation is:

$$v(t) = Ri(t) + L\frac{di(t)}{dt} \tag{9}$$

where, R and L are the resistance and reactance of the fault loop (up to the fault point respectively).

Any sampled voltage and current signals taken at any time is considered to obey above equation.

To solve the equation (9) and calculate *R* and *L*, two equations are required. This can be achieved by measuring *v(t), i(t)* and *di/dt* at two different instants of time

$$v(t_n) = Ri(t_n) + L\frac{di(t_n)}{dt} \tag{10}$$

$$v(t_{n-1}) = Ri(t_{n-1}) + L\frac{di(t_{n-1})}{dt} \tag{11}$$

By solving equations (10) & (11), R and L may obtained from the following matrix

$$\begin{bmatrix} v(t_n) \\ v(t_{n-1}) \end{bmatrix} = \begin{bmatrix} i(t_n) & \dfrac{di(t_n)}{dt} \\ i(t_{n-1}) & \dfrac{di(t_{n-1})}{dt} \end{bmatrix} \cdot \begin{bmatrix} R \\ L \end{bmatrix}$$

$$\begin{bmatrix} R \\ L \end{bmatrix} = \frac{1}{D}\begin{bmatrix} \dfrac{di(t_{n-1})}{dt} & -\dfrac{di(t_n)}{dt} \\ -i(t_{n-1}) & i(t_n) \end{bmatrix} \cdot \begin{bmatrix} v(t_n) \\ v(t_{n-1}) \end{bmatrix} \tag{12}$$

where D is matrix determinant. The derivative of the current may be calculated from difference formula,

$$\frac{di(t_n)}{dt} = \frac{i(t_n) - i(t_{n-1})}{T} \tag{13}$$

It is obvious how sampled voltage and current signals can be combined to form the resistance and inductance of the fault loop.

8.2 Discrete Fourier Transform (DFT)

In this approach the estimation is based on equation $Z = {}^{v}\!/_{i}$. The sampled current and voltage signals are initially transformed in to phasor quantities (both direct and quadrature components). The estimation approach includes estimation of the first harmonic; calculation from equation $Z = {}^{v}\!/_{i}$ the impedance as a quotient of voltage and current phasors. Based on fault type (using residual factors as explained in section 3.3), the resistance and reactance up to the relay point is calculated.

Mathematical Background

Signal at any given time may be described by a phasor. Phasor actually is a vector rotating in the complex plane with a speed ω radian/sec , a snap-shot in time, the signal at that time, x(t)) is given in rectangular form by; (Marven & Gillian, 1993)

$$x(t)\big|_{t=T} = (realcoordinate) + j(imaginarycoordinate)$$

$$x(t) = a + jb \quad (14)$$

And in polar form by

$$x(t) = Ae^{j\omega t} \quad (15)$$

Considering the initial value at t=0,

$$x(0) = Ae^{j\alpha}$$

the general form of x(t)is;

$$x(t) = Ae^{j(\omega t+\alpha)}$$

$$e^{j\omega t} = \cos\omega t + j\sin\omega t \quad (15)$$

$$\cos\omega t = \frac{1}{2}(e^{j\omega t} + e^{-j\omega t}) \quad (16)$$

$$\sin\omega t = \frac{1}{2j}(e^{j\omega t} - e^{-j\omega t}) \quad (17)$$

Therefore, sine or cosine signal can be represented by two phasors form a conjugate pair, i.e. if, x(t)= $A\cos\omega t$, then x(t)may be written as;

$$x(t) = \frac{A}{2}(e^{j(\omega t+\alpha)} + e^{-j(\omega t+\alpha)}) \quad (18)$$

The above discussion is related to a simple cosine or sine functions of a single frequency, most signals are composed of many cosine and sine waves. Therefore any complex periodic signal can be described as sum of many phasors. Fourier series assumes that a set of phasors have frequencies which are multiples of some fundamental frequency, f_0, i.e.

$$x(t) = \sum_{k=-N}^{N} A_k e^{j(k\omega_0 t)} \tag{19}$$

The individual frequency components are known as harmonics.
If the complex signal is not periodic the phasor frequencies are not related, thus the Fourier general form may be written as;

$$x(t) = \sum_{k=-N}^{N} A_k e^{j(k\omega_k t)} \tag{20}$$

In digital domain (discrete time), replace the continuous function, t, with a function progresses in jumps of w_0 T_s, thus phasor description of single frequency signal would be;

$$\begin{gathered} x(n) = Ae^{j(n\omega T_s + \alpha)} \\ e^{j(n\omega T_s)} = \cos(n\omega T_s) + j\sin(n\omega T_s) \end{gathered} \tag{21}$$

where, Ts is the sampling interval
A real signal can be described using Fourier in discrete domain called (Discrete Fourier Series) as,

$$x(n) = \sum_{k=-N}^{N} A_k e^{j(k\omega_0 T_s n)} \tag{22}$$

which is a simple phasor model that describes a general discrete signal.
The discrete Fourier transform (DFT) is a digital filtering algorithm that computes the magnitude and phase at discrete frequencies of a discrete time sequence. Fast Fourier transforms are computationally efficient algorithms for computing DFTs. FFTs are useful if we need to know the magnitude and/or phase of a number individual or band of frequencies. The DFT is ideal method of detecting the fundamental frequency component in a fault signal. However, DFT, Least Error Square LES and Walsh Function algorithms are among the most popular phasor estimation techniques employed in numerical relays (Phadke & Thorp, 1990). As we are dealing with a 50-60 Hz signal that is sampled synchronously. This means that the sample interval is the inverse of an integer multiple of 50 or 60. We need to compute the DFT for the fundamental using equation (1), where, *k* equal to one for the fundamental and *n* is the coefficient subscript. Two digital filters are required, one to get the real part and one for the imaginary part.

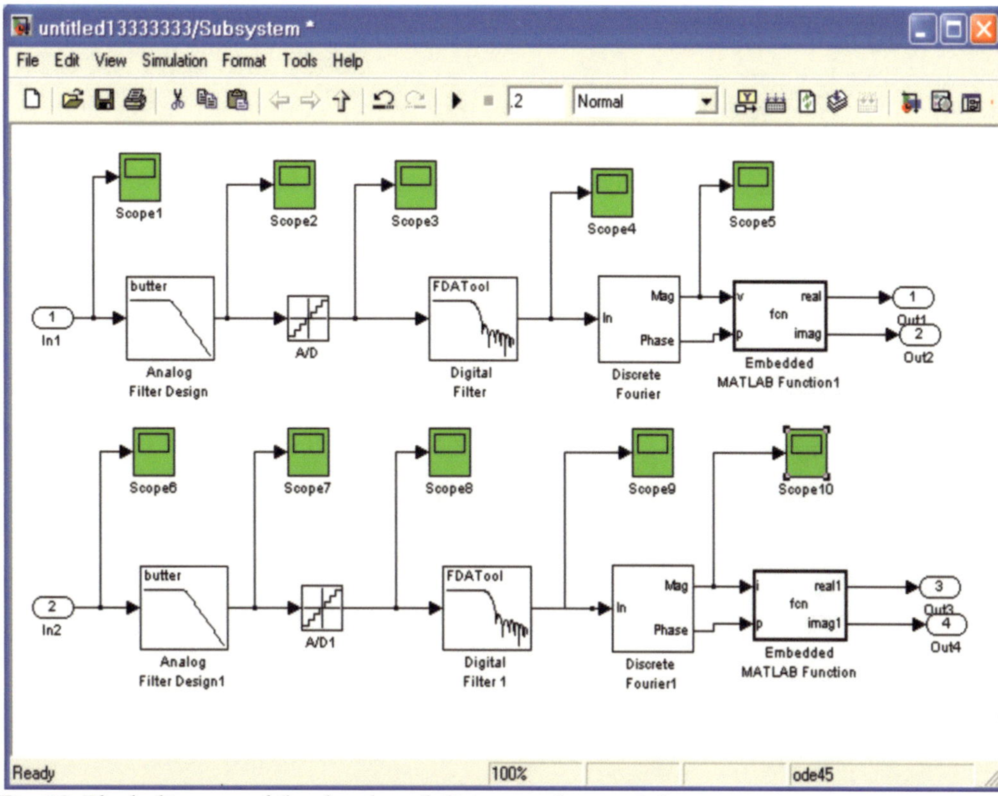

Fig. 10. Block diagram of the developed distance relay model

9. Developing Procedures of Distance Relay Model Using MATLAB

MATLAB development environment, is a set of tools to help the use of MATLAB functions and files (Matlab, 2006), where Simulink is an interactive tool for modeling, simulating and analyzing dynamic systems, including control and many complex systems. (Simulink, 2001) . MATLAB and Simulink were used to model the relay components such as ADC and digital filters. (Abdlmnam, 2007). Figure 10, shows block diagram for developed distance relay model. The voltage and current data are derived using the power simulator EMTP-ATP. It is possible to derive these values from any power system simulator such as MATLAB, EMTP, NEPLAN....etc. and converted to a MATLAB format. Simulation of electric power systems has been a common practice for more than thirty years. Computer models of major power system components have been used in software packages such as short circuit programs, load flow, stability programs, and electromagnetic transient programs. In most of the cases the power system is represented by a single line diagram which is representing either a three or single phase system. This may include three phase source, three phase transmission line (lines may be represented using π model), current transformers, voltage transformers and voltage and current measurements. The voltage and current input signals are inserted in a MATLAB window which is designed to set the distance relay parameters. As these signals generated by applying faults they may include a dc offset and a high frequency traveling waves which, if not suppressed, may lead to misjudgment to the fault location.

Figure 11 a&b shows a sample of a current and voltage waveform before, during and after fault, while Figure 12 a@b shows the Matlab window that contain the input signals as appeared after low pass filter. Thus data is passed through low pass filter to remove the effects, on the voltage and current signals, of the traveling waves instigated by the fault.

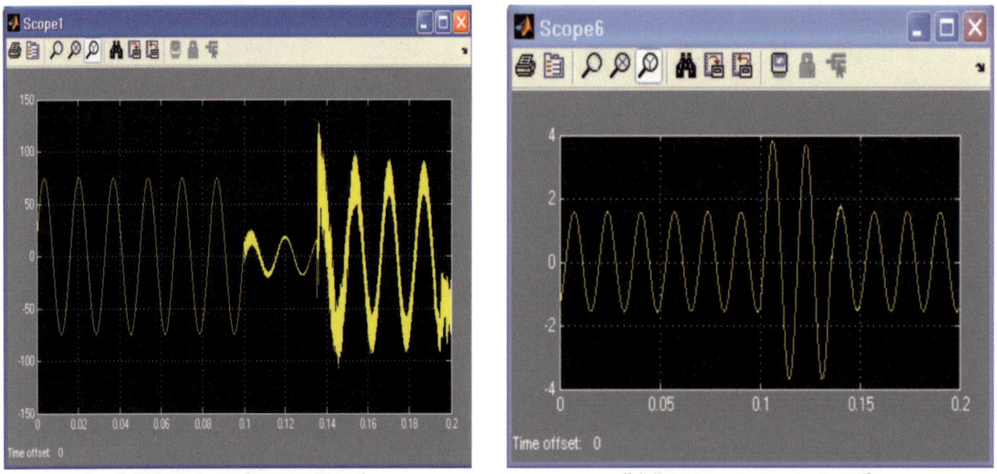

(a) Input voltage signals (b) Input current signals

Fig. 11. The input signals as resulted from a single line to ground fault.

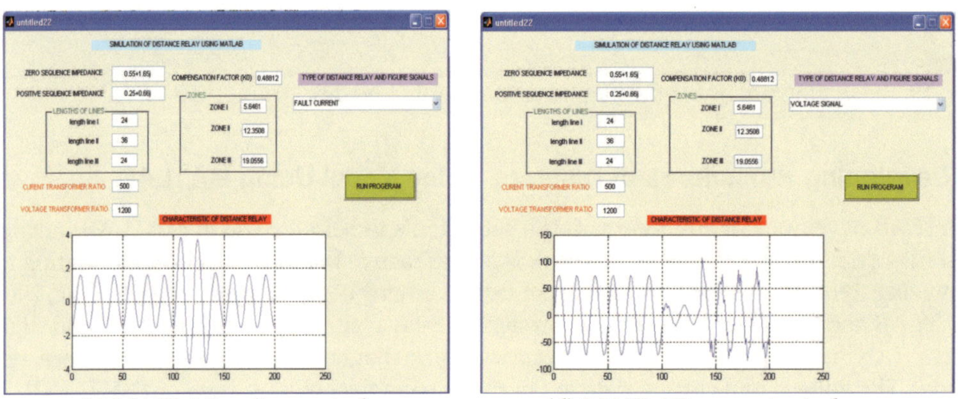

(c) MATLAB voltage window (d) MATLAB current window

Fig. 12. The Matlab window for the input signals as appeared after low pass filter.

The input filtered signals then passed through A/D convertor. Figure 13 shows the output signal of A/D convertor. The output signal becomes ready to be used by the Discrete Fourier Transformer. Figure 14 shows the input voltage and current signals amplitude as determined by Discreet Fourier Transform model. Data applied to the developed relay model, is then analyzed to evaluate the relay response i.e. whether the impedance trajectory of the relay during fault denotes to the proper zone. MATLAB program then used to plot the characteristic of mho distance relay, the behavior of Z during the sampled period. The results are presented in graphical form using an R-X diagram.

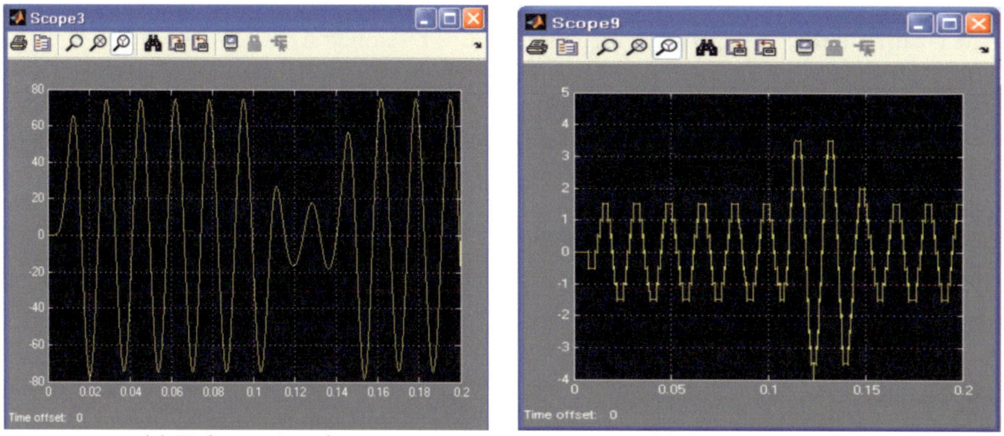

(a) Voltage signal (b) Current signal

Fig. 13. The signals as appeared after Analogue to Digital convertor.

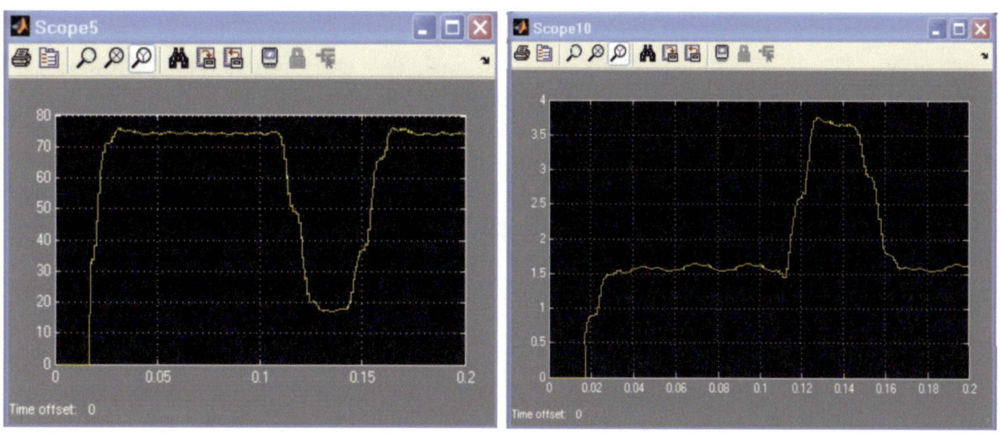

(a) Voltage signals amplitude (b) Current signals amplitude

Fig. 14. The input signals amplitude as determined by Discreet Fourier Transform model.

10. Simulation Results

The developed distance relay model is evaluated using data generated from power simulator. The output signals as resulted from faults set over a power network using EMTP are input to the MATLAB relay model. Evaluation extended to include different power networks at different fault locations. The faults were also set over the power network when fault resistances at different values were assumed. and when the power network consist of more than one in-feed. This is to evaluate performance of the developed model at different operating conditions and to check the effect of system conditions, fault resistance and load conditions on the performance of the developed distance relay model.

A Single line diagram representing a single 220 kV 50 Hz over head line connected to a single power source is shown in figures 15, where the overhead line is modeled as a lumped π model. The positive and zero sequence impedance of the source are:-

Zs0= 3.681+j24.515 Zs1=0.819+j7.757
The positive and zero sequence impedance of transmission line are
Z1= 0.09683 + 0.9034j Ω /km
Z0= 0.01777 + 0.4082j Ω /km
The current transformer ratio is 1000/1A and the voltage transformer ratio is 220kV/110V.

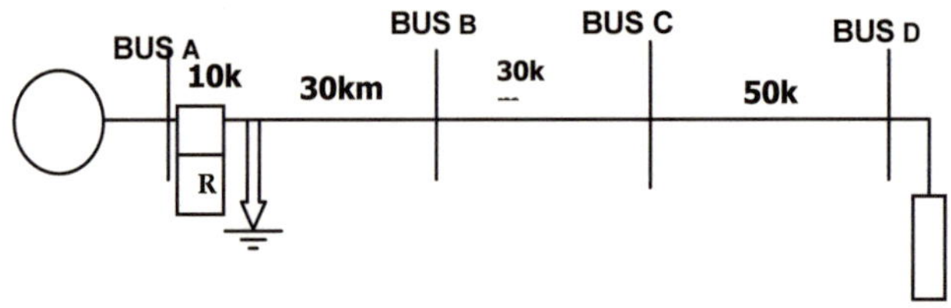

Fig. 15. The single line diagram of the simulated single in-feed power network.

10.1 Case one: Single line to ground faults at different distances from the relay location

Single line to ground faults were set on EMTP model of the power system shown in figure 13 at a distance of 10 Km, 20 Km and 35 Km from the location of bus-A. The distances representing 10% to 80% of line A-B length. Similarly few more Single line to ground faults were set at 5 Km, 10Km and 25 Km from the location of bus-B and bus-C. The selected distances are to check the relay behavior at faults that covers the different zones of protection of the relay. The voltage and current signal before and during fault were fed to the relay model. Figures 16, show the impedance trajectory for few samples of these cases. In all cases the output results which are the impedance trajectory of the digital distance relay model had the expected behavior where the impedance trajectory calculations start the trajectory from the load area, before fault, and end up at the proper zone.

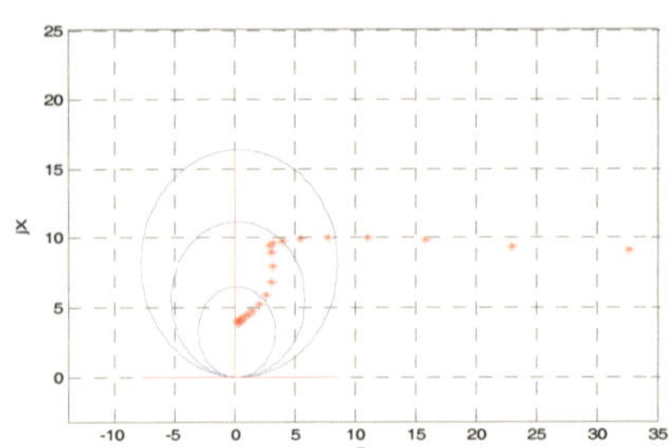

a) Fault at 10 Km from bus-A, Zone 1

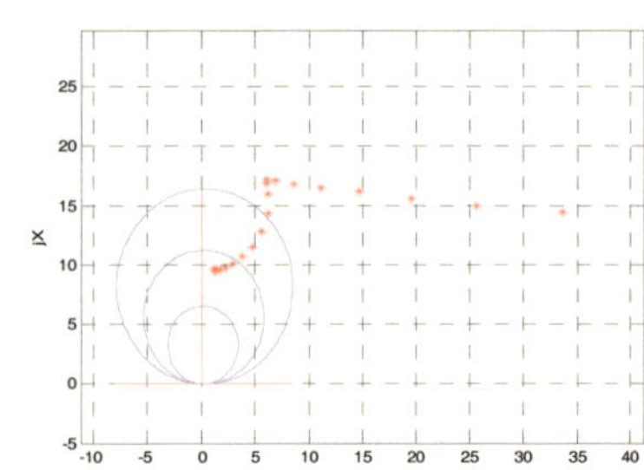

b) Fault at 20 Km from bus-B, Zone 2

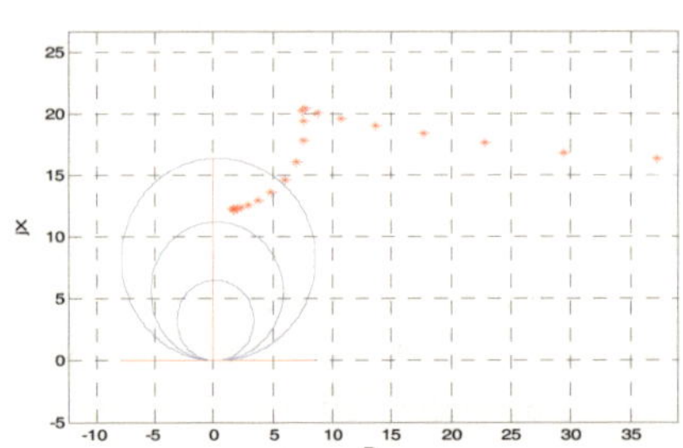

c) Fault at 10 Km from bus-C, Zone 3

Fig. 16. Impedance trajectory for faults at different locations, case 1.

10.2 Case two: Single line to ground faults with fault resistance

Single line to ground faults with different fault resistances were set on EMTP model of the power system shown in Figure 15 at different fault locations. Figure 17 show the impedance trajectory for two of these cases. The shown cases illustrate the behavior of the relay when fault resistance is 2Ω and 10Ω. (Abdlmnam & Sherwali, 2009)

In first case the relay detects the fault in zone 1 as the resistance value were not enough to change the reach of the relay, while in the second case the value of the resistance was enough to make the impedance presented to the relay lies in zone two, even though the fault were set in zone one. However, in all cases the output results which are the impedance trajectory of the digital distance relay model had the expected behavior where the effect of the arc resistance reflected on the value of the impedance seen by the relay. Impedance trajectory calculations start the trajectory from the load area, but due to the existence of fault resistance the relay judges the location of the fault considering the effect of arc resistance, as expected.

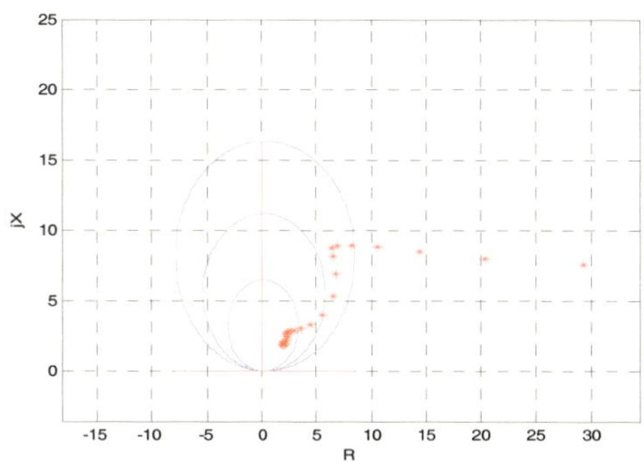

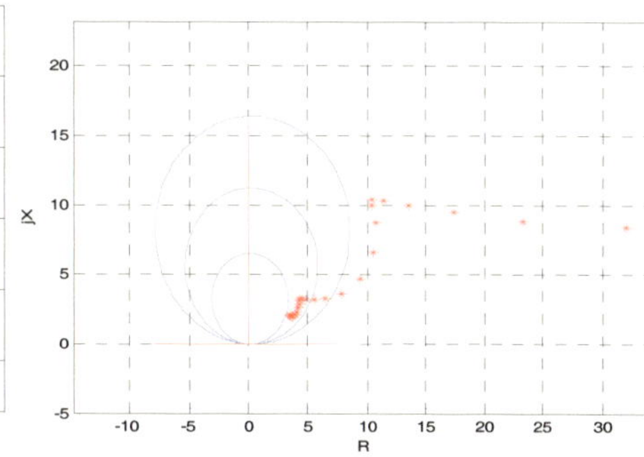

(a) Fault resistance of 2 Ω (b) Fault resistance of 10 Ω

Fig. 17. Impedance trajectory of the relay for faults accompanied by fault resistances.

10.3 Case three: Double circuit fed from more than one in-feed

A distance relay is said to under-reach when the impedance presented to it is apparently greater than the impedance to the fault. The main cause of underreaching is the effect of fault current in-feed at remote busbars. High voltage power system usually interconnected and run in double circuits for a reliable system. This usually implies an existence of more than one in-feed point which may cause the distance relay to under. EMTP-ATP is used to simulate the power system network shown in figure 18, to evaluate the developed model under this circumstance. Fault location is shown on the single line diagram and system data is as shown below:-

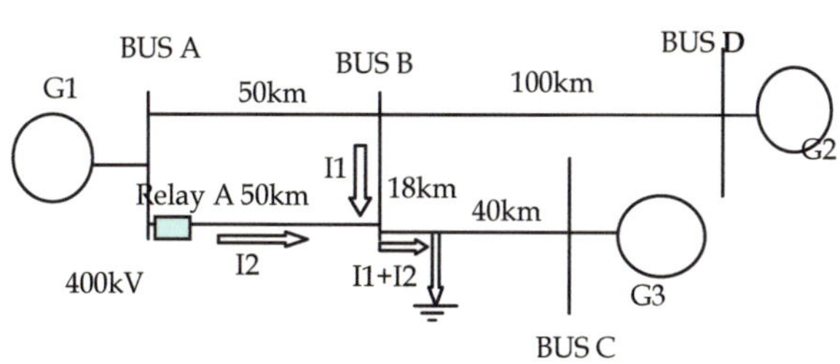

Fig. 18. Single line diagram of the simulated multi in-feed power network.

The positive and zero sequence impedance of the sources are
Zs1of G1=0.819+6.76j Zs1 of G2= 4.5+12.8j Zs1of G3= 1.4+8.8j
Zs0 of G1=3.48+22.515j Zs0 of G2=10.6+38.8j Zs0 of G3= 6.6+27.8j
The positive and zero sequence impedance of the transmission lines are
Z1= 0.09683 + 0.9034j Ω /km., Z0= 0.01777 + 0.4082j Ω /km.
Where the network voltage is 400kV, the current transformer ratio is 400/1A, the voltage transformer ratio is 400kV/110V and the setting of relay A is as follows:
Zone one = 1.79 ohm-secondary (80 % of the protected line).
Zone two = 3.55ohm-secondary (100% of the protected line + 50% of the shortest adjacent line).
Zone three = 7.64 ohm-secondary (120% of the impedance presented to the relay for a fault at the remote end of the longest adjacent line).
As seen in figure 19, the impedance trajectory moves into zone three not in zone two. If the fault impedance is calculated assuming a single in-feed the relay, A would see the fault within its zone two, however due to the under-reach caused by the in-feed from the parallel line, relay A sees the fault in zone three.

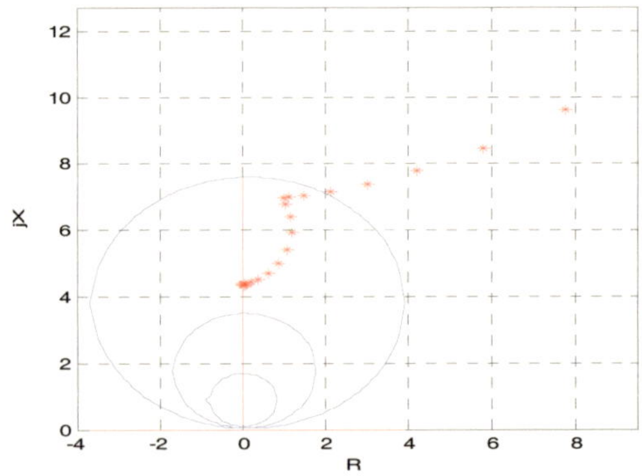

Fig. 19. Impedance trajectory for faults on multi in-feed power network

11. Future Research

Since the developed model was not provided with a decision scheme, work may be extended to include a comprehensive relay model including trip scheme. Work may be extended to incorporate algorithms used to improve the relay behavior when overhead lines are compensated by series capacitors or/and when the model is to be used to protect power systems incorporate power cables having a considerable capacitance.

12. Conclusions

As modern numerical relays are widely employed in protection systems nowadays and modeling of these types of relays is important to adjust and settle protection equipment in electrical facilities and to train protection personnel, the simulation of distance relays using MATLAB offers a good opportunity to perform these activities efficiently and with minimum cost. Another advantages is that, as MATLAB is a powerful tool rich with component models, any shape of relay characteristic (Impedance, mho, quadrilateral,..) can be employed. The simulation of numerical distance relay using MATLAB/SIMULINK was explained in details and the behavior of the developed relay model was tested under different onerous conditions. From impedance calculation point of view, the relay model was able to identify the proper zone of operation. In all of the cases presented to test the model, the model judged the fault location as expected including the cases were the measured impedance was changed due to a change of fault location, due to an existence of resistive faults and/ or due to the change in apparent impedance as a result of an existence of more than one in-feed. The impedance trajectory that reflects the behavior of the developed model under different fault locations and at different arc resistances, for few of the cases tested, was presented and discussed. However, trip signal was not generated since the model was not provided with a decision scheme that decides when to generate the trip signal.

13. References

Abdlmenam A. Abdlrahem, Modeling of distance relays for power system protection, M.Sc. dissertation, EE&E Dept., Faculty of Engineering, Al-Fatah University,Fall 2007.

Abdlmnam A. Abdlrahem & H.Sherwali. (2009), Modeling Of Numerical Distance Relays Using Matlab, Procedding of IEEE Symposium on Industrial Electronics and Applications, ISIEA 2009, October, 2009, Kuala Lumpur, Malaysia.

A Phadke and J G Thorp, Computer Relaying for Power Systems, John Wiley & Sons Inc, 1990, ISBN 0 471 92063 0.

ATP Draw for windows user's Manual, Version4.0p2, copyright 1998-2003, intef Energy Research, Norway.

Barry W. Kennedy, Power Quality Primer, McGraw-Hill Company,2000 (Barry, 2000)

Craig Marven & Gillian Ewers, A simple approach to digital signal processing, Texas Instruments, 1993, ISBN 0 904 047 00 8.

Electricity Training Association, Power System Protection, Volume 4: Digital Protection and Signaling", The Institution of Electrical Engineering, IEE, London 1995, ISBN 0 85296 838 8

GEC Alsthom ,Protective Relays Application Guide, GEC Alsthom Measurement limited, Erlangen, GEC England, Third edition, 1990.

Gerhard Ziegler, Numerical Distance Protection, Publicis Corporate Publishing, Erlangen, Siemens, second edition, 2006, ISBN 3 89578 266 1.

Nasser Tleis, Power System Modeling and fault analysis, Elsevier Ltd, 2008, ISBN 13 978 0 7506 8074 5

MATLAB User's guide, Math Works Inc., 2006.

P. G. McLaren, K. Mustaphi, G. Benmouyal, S. Chano, A. Girgis, C. Henville, M. Kezunovic, L. Kojovic, R. Marttila, M. Meisinger, G. Michel, M. S. Sachdev, V. Skendzic, T. S. Sidhu, and D. Tziouvaras, " Software Models for Relays", IEEE Transactions on Power Delivery, Vol. 16, No. 12, April 2001, pp. 238-45.

Sandro Gianny Aquiles Perez, "Modeling Relays for Power System Protection Studies", Thesis Submitted to the College of Graduate Studies and Research, Department of Electrical Engineering University of Saskatchewan, Saskatchewan, Canada, July 2006

SIMULINK 4.1, Reference Manual, MathWorks, Inc. 2001.

10

Evaluation of the Delta-Sigma modulator coefficients by MATLAB parallel processing

Michal Pavlik, Martin Magat, Lukas Fujcik and Jiri Haze
Brno University of Technology
Czech Republic

1. Introduction

The task of the ΔΣ modulator design is the fact that ΔΣ modulator is nonlinear discrete system. Thus, the calculation of the optimal transfer coefficients is difficult. There exist three main design approaches: utilization of the table values, calculation from signal transfer and noise transfer functions (*STF, NTF*) and by iteration methods. At first, it is necessary to define tests and test conditions for optimization of the modulator transfer coefficients. Test results are used for consequent optimization steps. Spectral analysis is used to calculation of the signal to noise ratio (*SNR*) of the ΔΣ modulator output. The Fast Fourier Transform (FFT) is used for calculations. Accuracy of the *SNR* calculation directly depends on number of the spectral lines of the input signal bandwidth. Unfortunately, increasing number of the spectral lines also leads to exponential increasing of time demand. The low frequency or band pass filter is used inside modulator structure. Due to *SNR* of modulator would be different for various frequencies of the input signal in input signal bandwidth. Logically the modulator *SNR* would be dependent on the input signal amplitude. It is crucial to get relevant test results to ensure appropriate test conditions and resolution.

It is possible to calculate coefficients of the ΔΣ modulator based on signal and noise transfer functions instead of utilizing of the table values. It allows calculating values of the ΔΣ modulator transfer coefficients. Nevertheless, the coefficients ensure modulator stable, they are not apparently optimal. We usually use interpolation methods to determinate optimal values of the transfer coefficients. However, the number of the interpolation steps issue appears at this point. If we suppose the second order CIDIDF ΔΣ modulator, we can optimize total eight coefficients. Next, if we use only 64 iteration steps to each of eight coefficients it leads to the total of 64^8 (approximately 3.10^{14}) combinations. It is also number of the necessary FFT analysis to calculate. In addition, if we would calculate with various frequencies and amplitudes of the input signal, the number of combinations would be higher. We can see that it is not possible to calculate each combination by using computing power of the common personal computers. That is why we are looking for faster calculation like another optimization methods.
There exist a lot of optimizing methods. We would like to deal with the aspects of mentioned application for optimal coefficients values calculation of the modulator ΔΣ,

namely for computers with one or more processor cores. Next, the possibility of the computation cluster using will be described and another parallelization methods and processes as well. General comparisons of each described parallelization methods will be introduced in this chapter.

2. The number of spectral components issue

2.1 SNR and THD calculation issue

There are two most important parameters defining the AD converter quality and area of the utilization: conversion rate and effective number of bits (*ENOB*). The dynamic parameters (including *ENOB*) are usually obtained for harmonic sinusoidal signal (IEEE, 2000), (Kester & Sheingold, 2004). We can write (Norsworthy et al. ,1997), (Geerts et al., 2002)

$$ENOB = \frac{SNDR_p - 1.76}{6.02} \tag{1}$$

where *SNDR* is signal to noise distortion ratio for sinusoidal signal with maximal amplitude. The *ENOB* parameter concerns the distortion due to nonlinear transfer characteristics and overload of the quantization stage. The *SNDR* is very important for ΔΣ modulators. Sometimes it is called *SINAD*. Therefore it must be calculated to obtain *ENOB* (Kester, 1999)

$$SINAD = 20\log\left(\frac{S}{N+D}\right) = -10\log\left[10^{-\frac{SNR}{10}} + 10^{-\frac{THD}{10}}\right] \tag{2}$$

where *S* is energy of the input signal, *N* is energy of the quantization noise, *D* is energy of the harmonic distortion, *SNR* is signal to noise ratio and *THD* is total harmonic distortion. The IEEE Std. 1241-2000 standard defines examination of the first 10 harmonic components. However the integrated circuits producers usually do not follow this definition, i.e. the Analog Devices company analyzes only first 6 harmonic components. The reason is very simple. When calculating *THD*, only first 5 harmonic components mainly influence this calculation. The error between calculations from first 10 or 5 harmonic components is only tenth of dB (Kester, 1999). The *THD* parameter is (Kester & Sheingold, 2004)

$$THD = 20\log_{10}\left(\frac{P_{sig}}{P_{noise} + P_{dis}}\right) = -10\log_{10}\sqrt{\sum_{i=2}^{n}\left[10^{-\frac{V_i}{20}}\right]^2} \tag{3}$$

where P_{dis} is energy of the input signal distortion and *Vi* is amplitude of the *i*-th harmonic component. The analysis of the *THD* and *ENOB* is simple. Fig. 1 shows frequency spectrum of the converter with sampling frequency of 100 MHz and input signal with frequency of 35 MHz. The first 10 harmonic components of signal fa are shown. Aliased harmonics of f_a fall at frequencies equal to

$$f_{hn} = \left| \pm Kf_s \pm nf_{in} \right| \tag{4}$$

where n is the order of the harmonic, and K = 0, 1, 2, 3,....

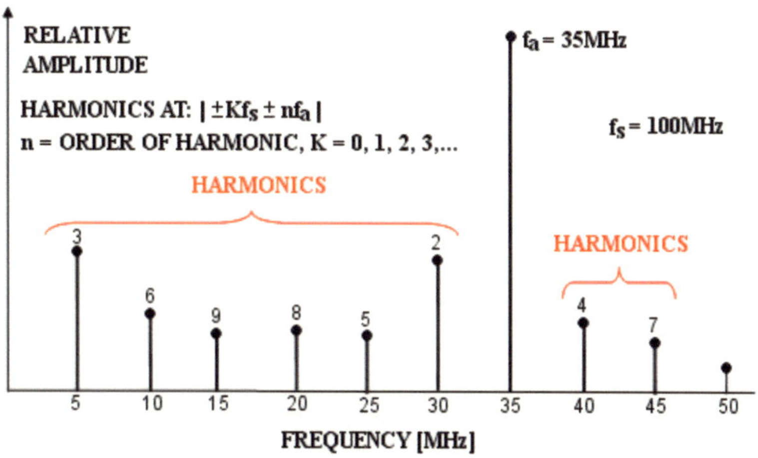

Fig. 1. Spectral analysis of the converter

It can be seen that for DFT (Discrete Fourier Transform) result 10.*i*, where i = 1,2,3,... of spectral components, the identification of the first 10 harmonic components is simple. The complicated situation is for mismatched spectral components and frequency of the harmonic components. The resulting error should be in tens of %. Nevertheless, when calculating *THD* it is possible to determine the number of spectral components in relation with input signal frequency to avoid the problem. The number of spectral components necessary for FFT (Fast Fourier Transform) is

$$M = D\left(\frac{f_s}{D(f_s, f_{in})}, 2^n \right) \tag{5}$$

where D is most common divisor. Unfortunately, the important disadvantage of the FFT algorithm is occasion of 2^n of spectral components.

The second parameter affecting *ENOB* of the AD converter is *SNR* (Kester, 1999)

$$SNR = \frac{P_{sig}}{P_{noise}} - 10 \log_{10}\left(\frac{f_s}{2.BW} \right) \tag{6}$$

where P_{sig} is energy of signal, P_{noise} is noise energy, f_s is sampling frequency and *BW* is bandwidth. Unfortunately this equation cannot be used for any case. The calculation error occurs for AD converters which spectral modulate quantization noise.

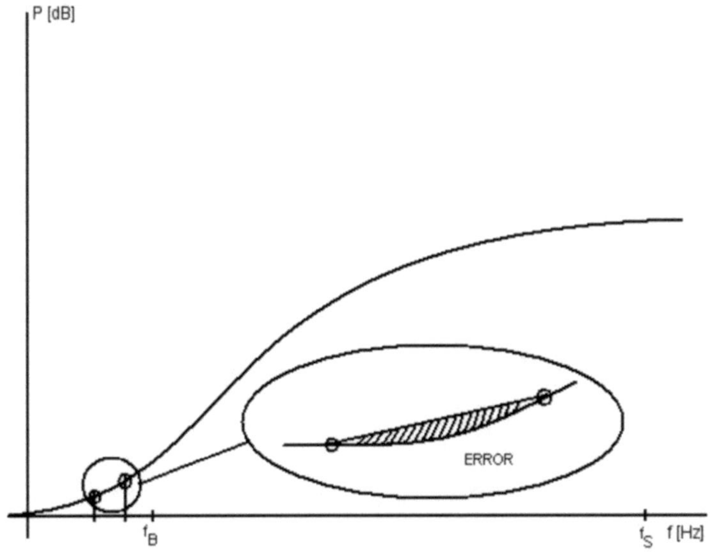

Fig. 2. The error of defining *SNR*

Several facts influence this error. There is mainly number of spectral components used for calculation, order modulator noise and oversampling ratio (*OSR*). It can be confirmed direct relation between growing number of spectral components and resulting accuracy of calculation.

The behaviour and function confirmation of ΔΣ modulators could be processed utilizing tools and scripts called SDtoolbox 2 (Brigati et al., 2004). It is very universal tool and the result of the calculation is value of *SNDR* (Malcovati et al., 2003). On the other hand, it is not able to differ contribution of particular errors on *spurious free dynamic range SFDR*

2.2 DFT leakage

The frequency analysis of the AD converter output signal should be done for calculation of both parameters (*SNR* and *THD*). It leads to calculation of DFT realized using FFT algorithm. However another problem occurs at this point. It is DFT leakage (Lyons, 2004). It is defined as energy distortion of one spectral component into its neighbour components. This situation arises when the ratio between frequency of sampling signal and input signal is not integer – Fig. 3. Nevertheless it is possible to set the frequency of input signal correctly during simulation. The AD converter must be able to process signals with any frequency in real situation.

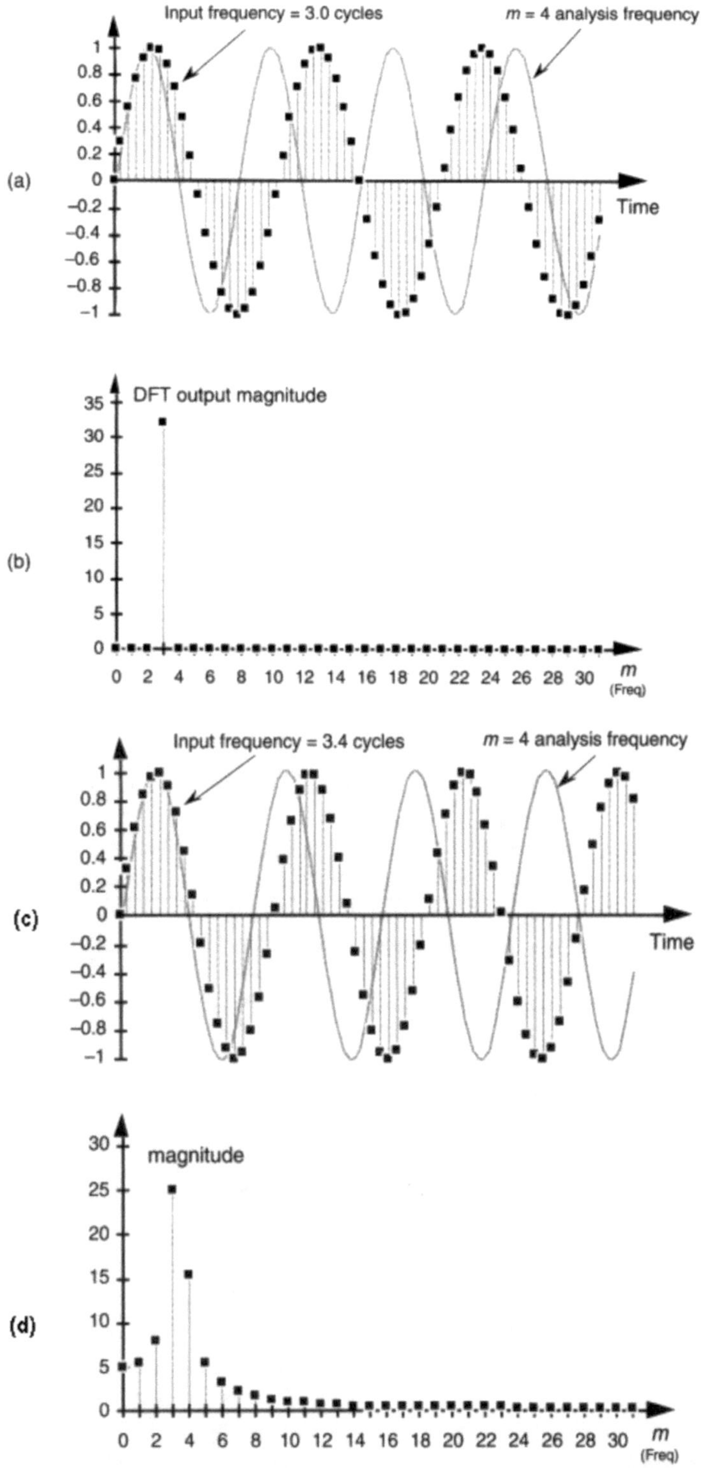

Fig. 3. Dependency of the DFT leakage

2.3 Computing time

The growing number of spectral components leads to the higher accuracy of *SNDR* calculation, but also grows computing time. This relation is exponential, but the deviation change caused by calculation decreases very fast.

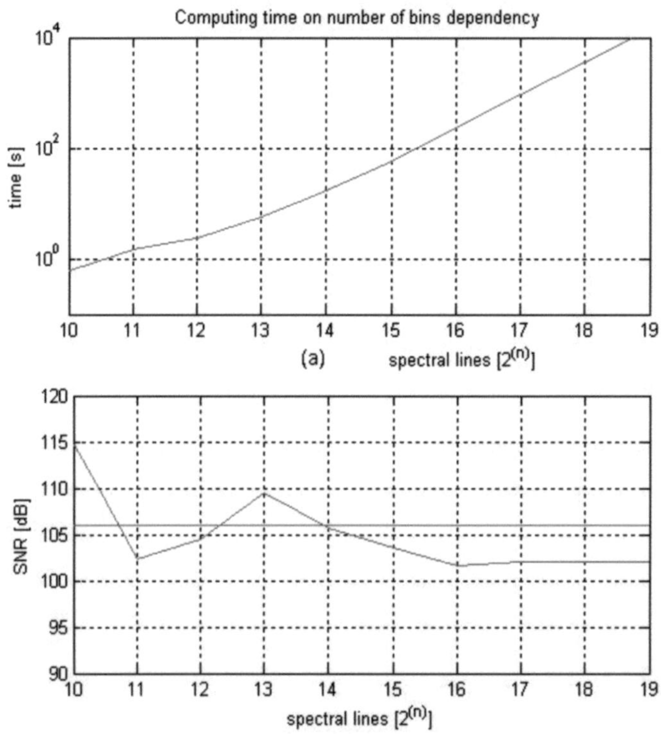

(b)

Fig. 4. Modulator *SNR* computing time consumption

The sufficient accurate result of simulation is obtained, when number of spectral components is higher than half of *OSR*.

3. Computing of the modulator transfer parameters

There exist three possibilities of determination of the ΔΣ modulator transfer parameters. They are:

- Utilization of table values,
- The calculation based on *STF* and *NTF*,
- Iteration methods.

The first method is useless due to its simplicity. The second is more complicated. It should be spited in two groups. One way uses fundamental behaviour of ΔΣ modulator with basic transform functions

$$STF = 1 \tag{7}$$

$$NTF = (z-1)^l \tag{9}$$

where l is order of the modulator.

The second way is utilization of table values of optimal transfer functions and transfer parameters calculation. This solution is universal and it should be applied on various types of DA modulators.

The third method is focused on observation of ideal ΔΣ modulator parameters by means of iteration. However, since the modulator is nonlinear system, the iteration is possible only by partial intervals. All appropriate constants must be iterated during transfer coefficients calculation. Fig. 5 shows the second order CIDIDF ΔΣ modulator, which were used in experiments.

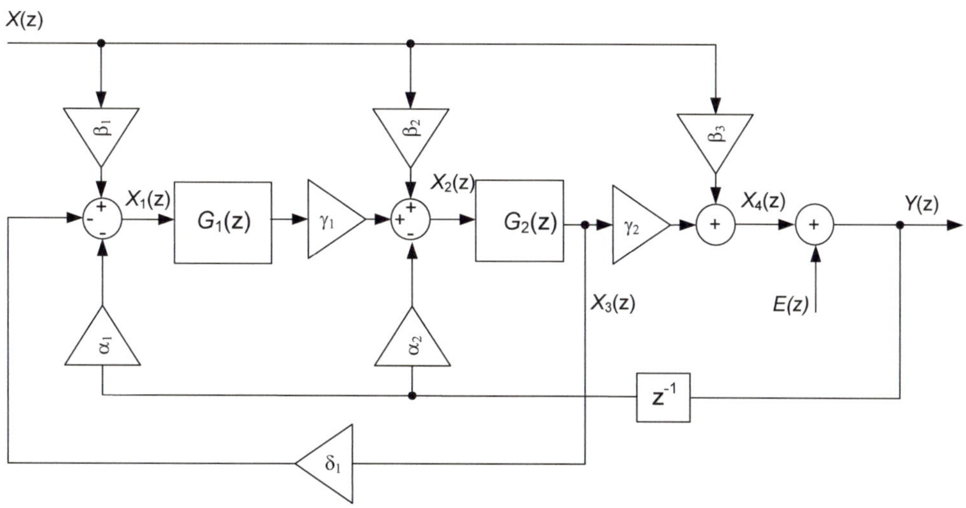

Fig. 5. Block scheme of the second order CIDIDF ΔΣ modulator

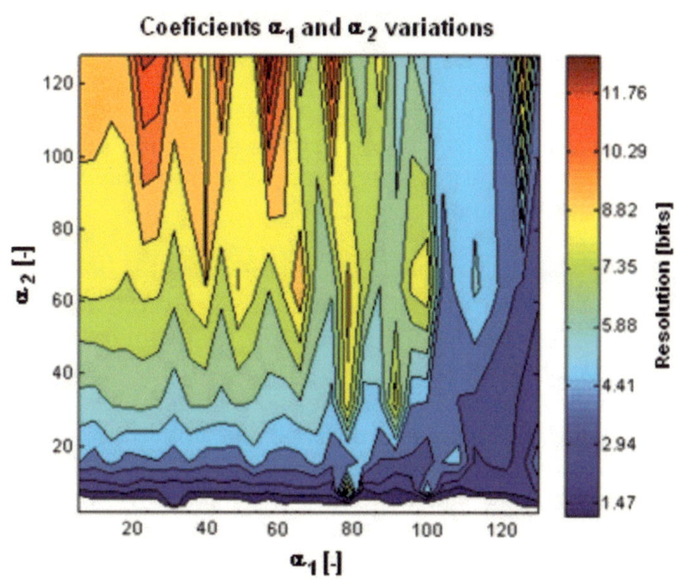

Fig. 6. *SNR* on coefficients α_1 and α_2 dependent

The input parameters are:

- *OSR*,
- bandwidth,
- limits of parameters,
- amplitude of the input signal.

It is possible to change eight parameters in this case. Their values affect each other. The example of simulation result for two parameters is shown in Fig. 6.

Consequently, it means that for iteration of i.e. 64x parameters, it is necessary to calculate $2{,}814.10^{14}$ times *SNR* of modulator. Therefore it is not possible to utilize this solution. The total computing time will take hundreds of years. That is why the optimization methods for iteration process must be used. One solution leads to several computing units utilization, which speed-up the calculation *n*-times. The second approach is genetic algorithm (GA) (Mitchell, 1996).

4. Computing cluster and its using in optimization methods

The aim of this chapter is not comparison of all computing parallelization methods. It describes the most useful method for our purpose. Since the computing tools for ΔΣ modulator simulation are created for MATLAB SIMULINK, we utilized this software.

There are many reasons why optimize methods, which use multi-results algorithm (e.g. GA, Particle Swarm Optimization (Kennedy & Eberhart, 1995), etc.). The first advantage is high efficiency of the solving of selected tasks accompanied with the fact that computing is very simple parallelizable as well. It gives a possibility to compute with multi-core systems if the algorithm is properly designed and parallelization is adequately processed. Additionally, the computing can be processed by any computer cluster that can be composed of many computers. It is simple and relatively cheap way, to enhance computing power and decrease the computing time.

4.1 Parallelization

There are many ways to parallelization of computing tasks in MATLAB. Unfortunately, methods like "parloop" or "matlab pool" are useable only for certain computing algorithms. Moreover, it speeds-up the computing minimally.

Another possibility of parallel computing is based on using of „Parallel computing toolbox"(PCT) (MATLAB, 2006). It enables parallel calculations on local station. Next method is utilization of „Distributed computing engine"(MDCE). It divides computing task into more computing stations. The main advantage of the MDCE against PCT is the fact that all parallel instances of the MATLAB are running and waiting for computing task instead of the PCT case, where MATLAB instances are started and stopped on request. If computing time is shorter than time needed to start MATLAB, the PCT method is useless. Moreover, using the PCT method in case of many quick tasks could bring significant delay during computing.

4.2 Computer cluster

The computer cluster was created to verify parallelization possibility of tasks which would be useful for the simulations of the ΔΣ modulator. The computer cluster was created and placed behind the Network Address Translation (NAT). The restriction was applied due to security reason. It is not necessary to connect computer cluster from outer network. If the situation is opposite the computer with main "job manager" would have public IP address to ensure that the "workers" will be able to connect to it from outer network. The block scheme of the computer connection is shown in Fig. 7.

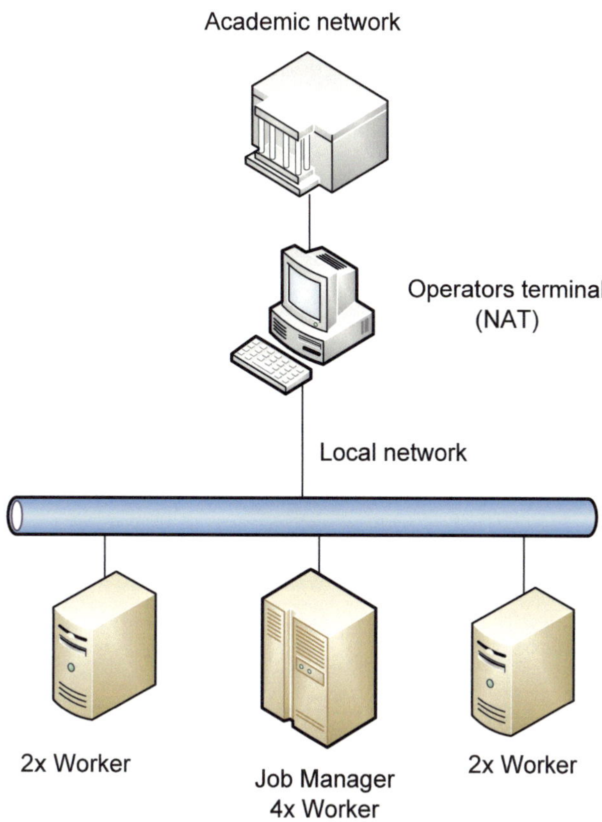

Fig. 7. The block scheme of the computer connection in the computer cluster

The crucial condition during MATLAB installation on computer connected into the network is proper MATLAB configuration on each connected computer. The MDCE could be executed from the system command line. First installation of the MDCE instance as "services" is necessary. The command "mdce install" serves for this purpose. Next the MDCE could be started by command "mdce start". Both commands should run from "bin" directory of the MDCE. It is usually "MATLAB\R2009b\toolbox\distcomp\bin". There is also "admin center" in same directory, which is executable in Windows operational system by command "admincenter.bat".

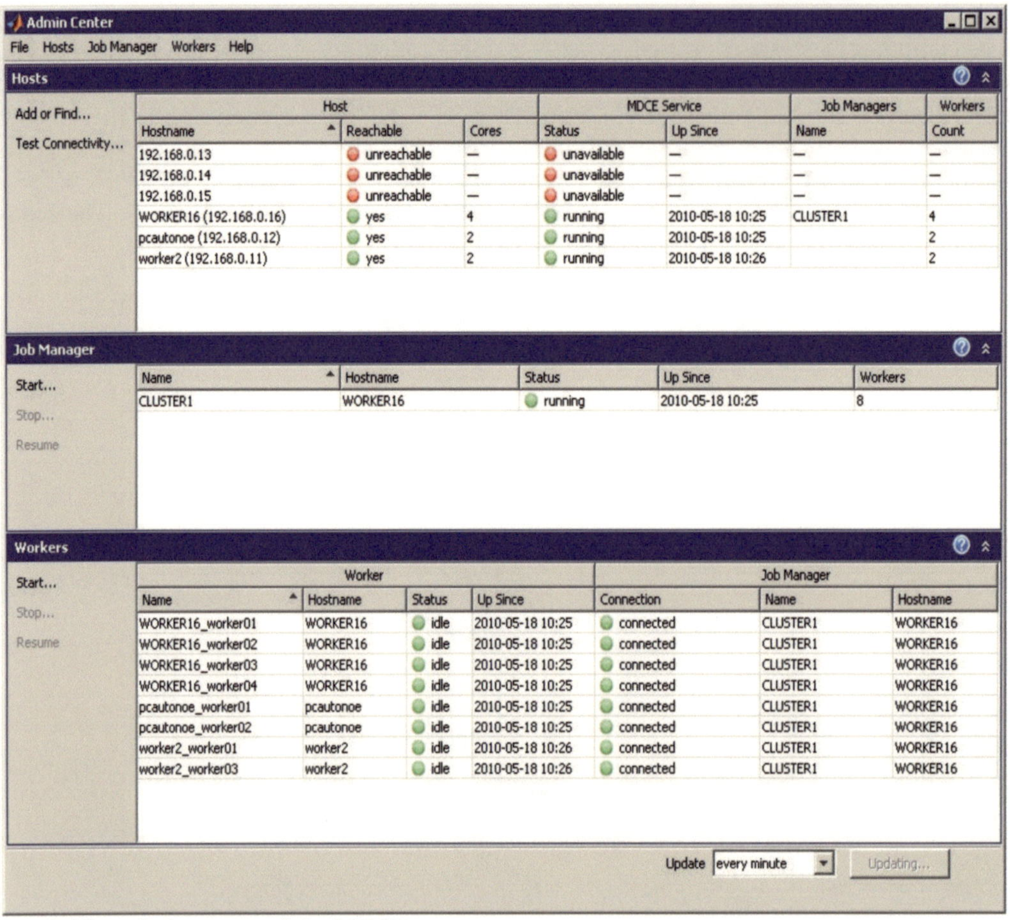

Fig. 8. The admin centre of the MDCE

Dialog window of the "admin centre" is divided into three parts placed underneath where the computer cluster is configured - Fig. 8. The connection of the each "worker" is controlled in the first part. There is displayed whether the "workers" are connected into the computer cluster and/or the MDCE runs there. The "job manager" is configured in the next part of the "admin centre". The "job manager" spreads computing tasks among the connected "workers".

Finally, the workers of the connected stations are executed in the third part of the "admin centre". It is an advantageous to run the same number of "workers" as a number of processor cores in the computer station.

Fig. 9 depicts the configuration of six computers in the cluster for our case. Three of them are temporary shut down. The figure shows the job manager "CLUSTER1" is configured on computer named "WORKER16". The running instances of the MDCE "workers" are doubled on computers "pcautonoe" and "wprker2" and four on computer "WORKER16". There are total 8 "workers" executed on three computers.

The block scheme of the MATLAB instances connected into the "job manager" is shown in Fig. 9.

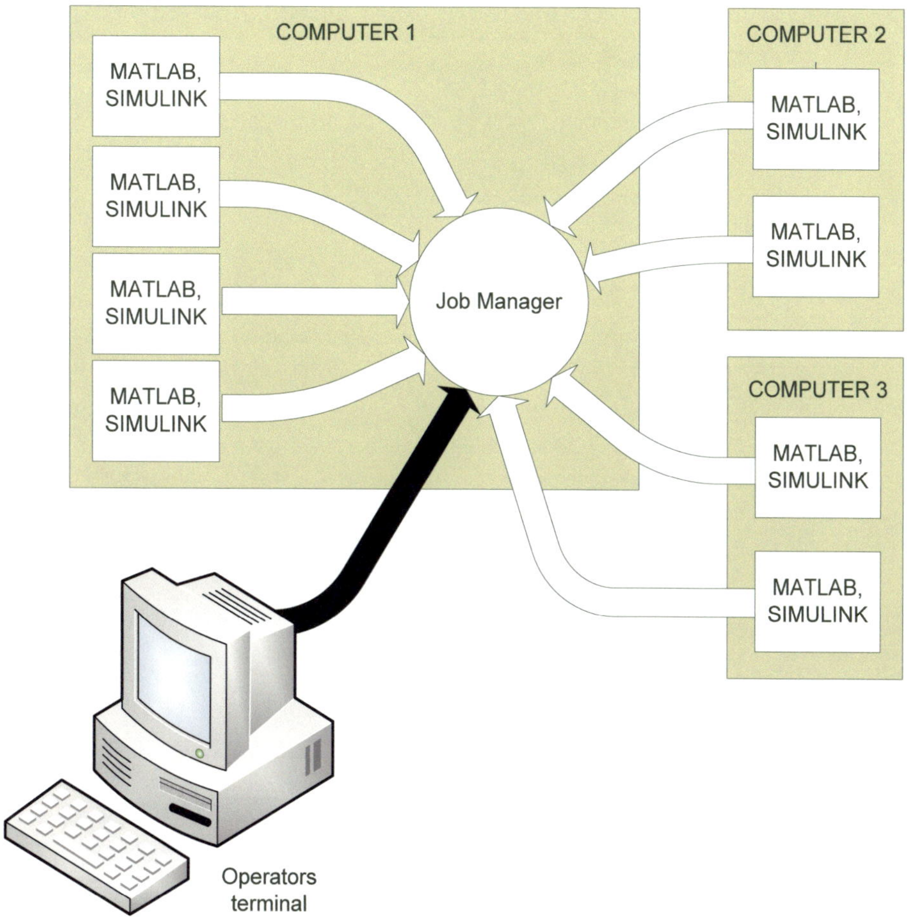

Fig. 9. The MATLAB instances connected into the "job manager"

There is also marked the connection of the operator computer in Fig. 9. The operator computer is sending calculation tasks. The MATLAB is configured to be as local "job manager". It is necessary to configure MATLAB to use cluster "job manager" to take advantage of the computer cluster - computer capacity. It is set in the bookmark "Parallel" of the MATLAB main menu. The new configuration of the "job manager" and IP address of the computer with running "job manager" of created computer cluster could be set in the "parallel" menu. The Fig. 10 shows the mentioned dialog box.

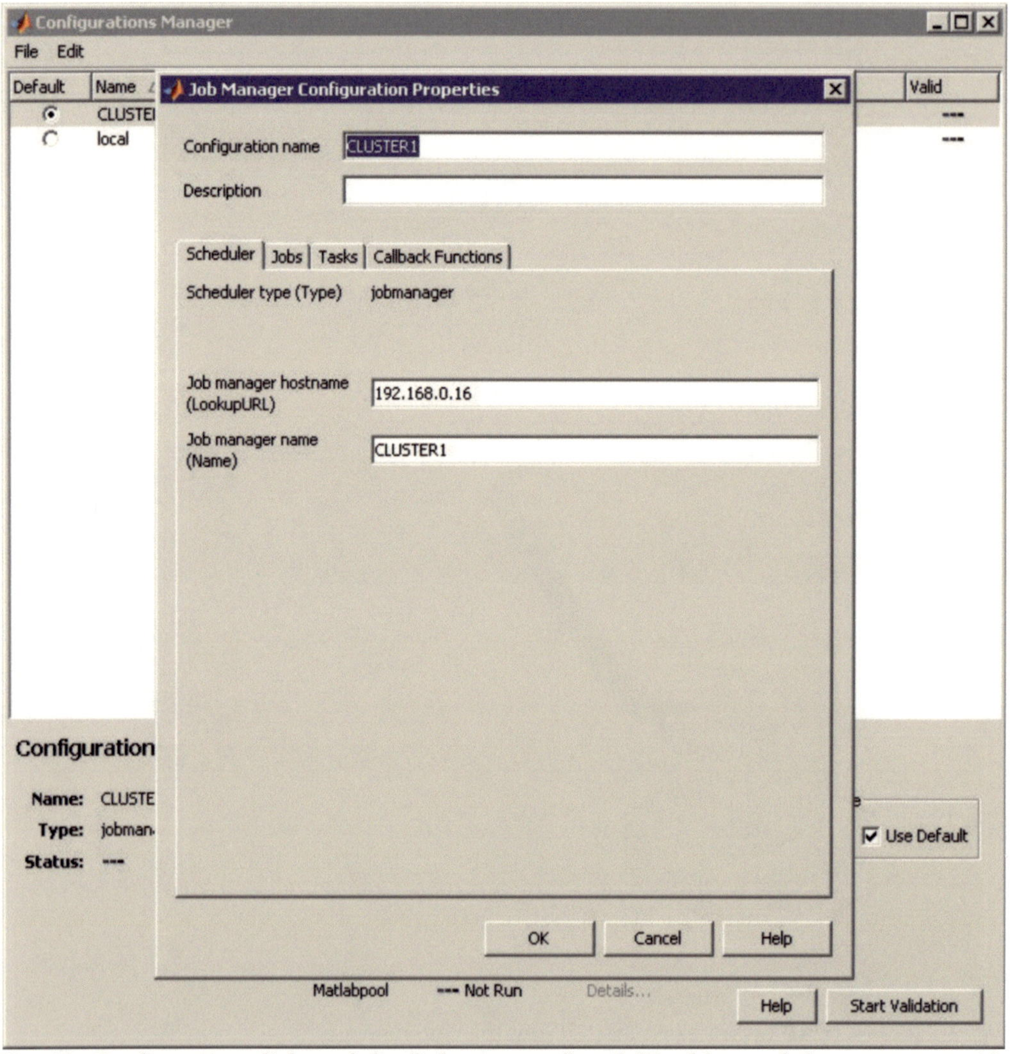

Fig. 10. Configuration dialog of the "job manager" and IP address of the computer with running "job manager" of created computer cluster

Next, the MATLAB must be configured for use of the new configuration to distribute computing task into the computer cluster.

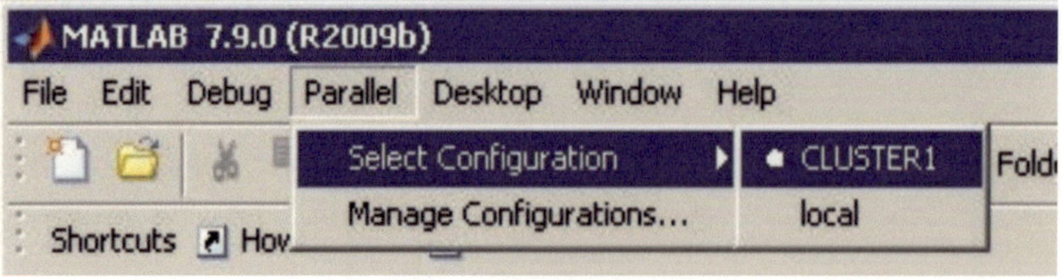

Fig. 11. MATLAB menu with the parallel computing items

4.3 Test of the computer cluster

The followed code was created to verify configuration and power of the computer cluster (soubor test_cluster_simulink.m , F_Test_Simulink.m). There is a function that uses the simulink for computing in the file F_Test_Simulink.m. The script described in test_cluster_simulink.m hundred times calculates function F_Test_Simulink in two configurations of the „job manager". In the first case the option is set as "local" (default settings) and in second case is set as "CLUSTER1" (the task is spread into the computer cluster). Computing time is measured in both cases.

```
test_cluster_simulink.m
clear all;
disp('start');

for i = 1:100
  p{i}=i;
end

startTime = tic;
a=dfeval(@F_Test_Simulink,p,'Configuration', 'CLUSTER1');
stopTime = toc(startTime);
fprintf('Cluster congiguration time: %g seconds.\n', stopTime);

startTime = tic;
a=dfeval(@F_Test_Simulink,p,'Configuration', 'local');
stopTime = toc(startTime);
fprintf('Local congiguration time: %g seconds.\n', stopTime);

disp('stop');
```

The result of this test is:

```
start
Cluster congiguration time: 14.9345 seconds.
Local congiguration time: 206.757 seconds.
stop
```

The test script was executed on the main computer of the computer cluster to obtain the most relevant result. It can be seen that the computing was 13-times faster in comparison with default settings. Note, it is remarkable result, especially considering the fact that the computation was calculated by eight computing threads. It is probably thanks to calculations processed without graphical interface (GUI) which requires the SIMULINK to be executed.

The function "dfeval" in mentioned code is used to parallelize the computation tasks. It is the simplest way how effectively executes tasks that have to be processed by PCT or MDCE. There are other methods to do it, but they are not useful for the $\Delta\Sigma$ modulator simulations. The main reason is that during parallelizing of GA task it is supposed all parameters of the functions are known before spreading computations of the criteria functions. The problem has to be solved in different way in difficult cases, especially in case of dynamic function.

5. Genetic algorithm

The GA is stochastic searching method based on the evolution algorithm. As a stochastic process the GA is always nondeterministic and cannot guarantee successful solution. The knowledge of the course of criteria (evaluative) function is not needed. It is main benefit of the GA technique. Next advantage of the GA is parallel computing possibility, since the algorithm operates with higher amount of results together. Finally, those are the main reasons why the GA was chosen and used for ΔΣ modulator coefficients evaluation.

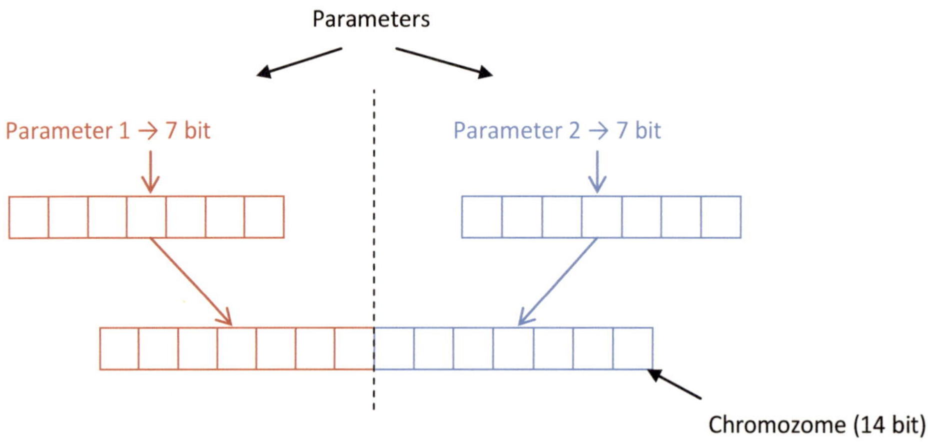

Fig. 12. Parameter coding

5.1 Parameters coding

The GA works with more results (subjects) which are collected into one generation. The subject represents sequence of bits, which is called chromosome. Parameters of the result are optimized and coded as a sequence of bits and put into the chromosome like a gene. Coding of the result parameters is shown in Fig. 12. Parameter coding is very interesting and provides coding also for unordinary types of parameters which would be difficult expressed by number g.e. smell or light colour.

5.2 Description of the genetic algorithm

The GA can be dividend into the six steps:

- Initialization of the starting population
- Coding of the solution parameters
- Gene creating from chromosome
- Subject evaluating of the population by criteria function
- Selecting of the best evaluated subjects
- Creating of the next generation based on the recombination and mutation of the selected subjects

Typical GA processing could be dividend into the three basic stages: Initialization, Reproduction and Exchange of the generations.

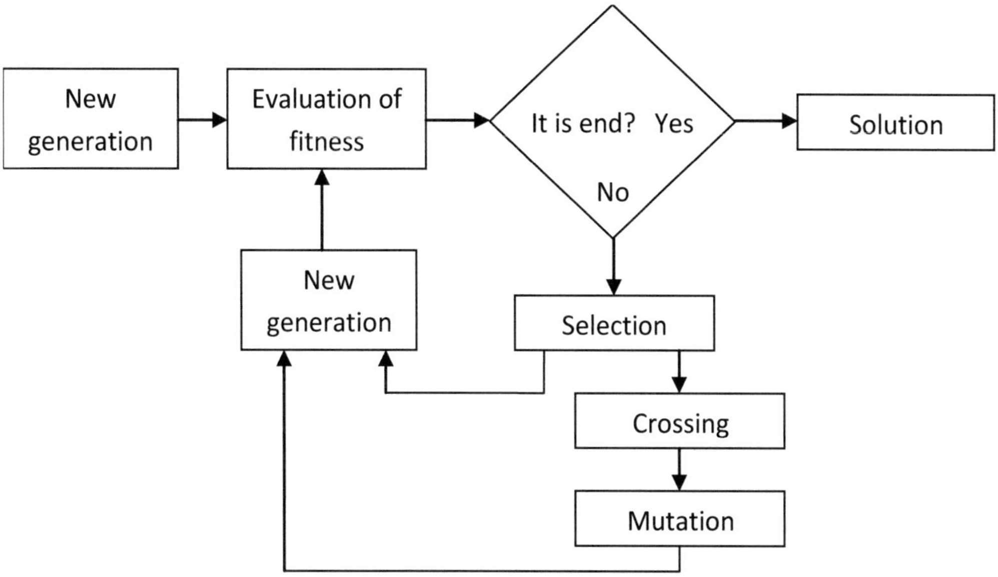

Fig. 13. Flowchart of the GA

The fundamental GA flowchart is shown in the Fig. 13. The first generation is filled by defined quantity of the randomly generated and coded unique subjects during the initialization. Each of the generated subjects represents one solution. The generated subjects are used as a new generation and consequently, each subject is evaluated by criteria function.

The new generation from older one is created during the reproduction phase. The reproduction means that the individual pair is selected. The selected pair serves like parents. Parents are hybridized and muted. They produce new pair called descendants. Consequently the descendants are placed into the new generation. Selection, hybridizing and mutations have to be processed until the sufficient amount of the descendants is generated for filling of the new generation.

5.3 Selection

The selection starts by the criteria function evaluating of the subjects. It uses results of the criteria function for each subject to determine the subject effectiveness. Nevertheless, selection is not only choosing the best subject, because the best subject need not be close to the optimal solution. The different selecting strategies are used depending on the concrete task. The most frequently used strategies are strategy of concurrent fight or tournament.

5.4 Hybridizing

The two parents are used to obtain two new descendants creating in operation of hybridizing. Many hybridizing methods are developed. One of the simplest is one-point hybridizing. The one-point hybridizing method is depicted in Fig. 14. It selects randomly place where the chromosomes of the parents are swapped.

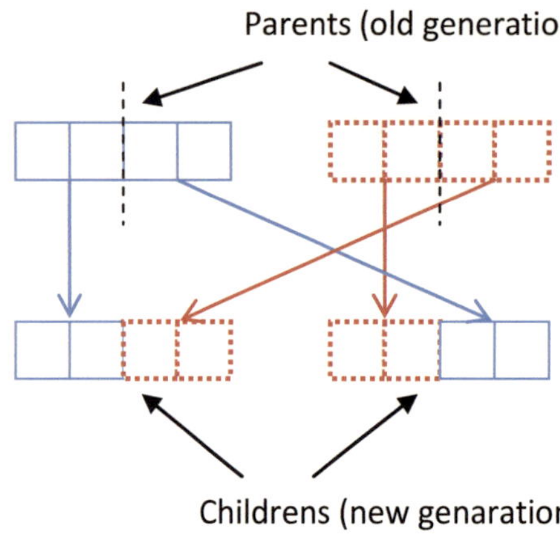

Fig. 14. Block scheme of the hybridizing process

5.5 Mutation

The chromosome is randomly chosen and arranged. The random bit is selected and inverted in the randomly selected chromosome. Example of the mutation is shown in Fig. 15.

5.6 Finalization of the genetic algorithm

The last step of the GA calculation is its finalization. The most frequently used method is displaying of the best searched solution after the defined number of GA runs.

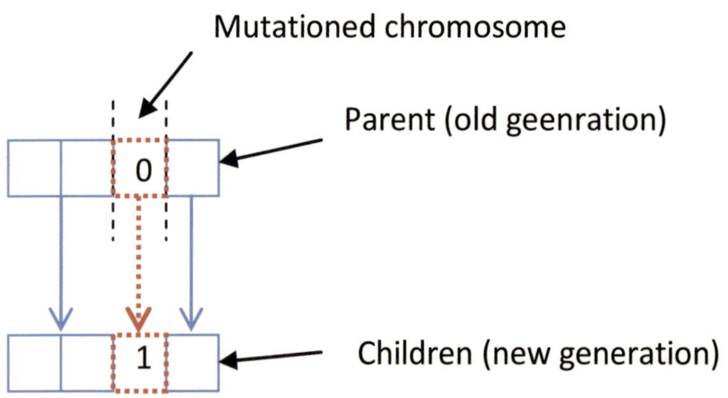

Fig. 15. The process of mutation

If the number of the algorithm solutions is not sufficient the possibility that the optimal solution would not be found exists. Alternative frequently finalizing method to terminate the GA algorithm is based on the computing termination when the solution with defined error is found. Since the GA is stochastic, the various results could be found. It is a serious problem of the GA. Due to the adequate number of the calculation runs and parameters for hybridizing and mutation have to be set as well.

6. Conclusion

The most important parameters, which affect this process, are conversion rate and effective number of bits (*ENOB*). The *ENOB* influences another features of the ΔΣ modulator such as signal to noise distortion ratio (*SNDR*) and total harmonic distortion (*THD*).
There are three methods of coefficients calculation – utilization of table values, the calculation based on signal and noise transfer function (*STF*, *NTF*) and iteration methods.
The article presents problems arising during MATLAB simulation of the ΔΣ modulator behaviour. It has been discussed the problem of finding of optimal spectral components number. Next, there have been depicted methods of determination of ΔΣ modulator transfer coefficients. The genetic algorithm has been presented in more details as one of the solution possibilities. The calculations require a lot of time. That is why the computer cluster has been made and its configuration and utilization have been presented. It has been shown how to find the optimal solution for certain task.

7. References

Brigati et al. (2004). A FourthOrder Single Bit Switched Capacitor ΣΔ Modulator for Distributed Sensor Applications; IEEE Transactions on Instrumentation and Measurement, Vol. 53, Issue 2, 2004, pp. 266 G270

Geerts et al. (2002) Design of Multi-Bit Delta-Sigma A/D Converters, The Springer International Series in Engineering and Computer Science, Vol. 686, 2002, 240 p., Hardcover ISBN: 978-1-4020-7078-5

IEEE (2000). IEEE Standard for Terminology and Test Methods for Analog-to-Digital Converters, IEEE 1241-2000

Johns & Martin (1997). Analog integrated circuit design; publisher John Wiley & Sons, Inc., USA; ISBN:0-471-14448-7

Kennedy & Eberhart (1995). "Particle Swarm Optimization". Proceedings of IEEE International Conference on Neural Networks. IV. pp. 1942-1948.

Kester & Sheingold (2004). Chapter 5: Testing Converters, Analog Devices

Kester (1999). Understand SINAD, ENOB, SNR, THD, THD + N, and SFDR so You Don't Get Lost in the Noise Floor, Analog Devices

Lyons (2004). Understanding Digital Signal Processing (2nd Edition), Prentice Hall PTR, Upper Saddle River, NJ, 2004

Malcovati et al. (2003). Bahavioral modelling of switched-capacitor Sigma–Delta modulators; IEEE Trans. Circuits Syst. I, vol. 50, no. 3, pp. 352–364, Mar. 2003.

MATLAB (2006) Parallel Computing Toolbox 4.3, MathWorks

Mitchell (1996). An Introduction to Genetic Algorithms. Cambidge, MA: MIT Press 1996

Norsworthy et al. (1997). Delta-Sigma Data Converters, Piscataway NJ, IEEE Press, 1997, 476 pages, ISBN 0-7803-1045-4

Roberts (2008). Test Methods For Sigma-Delta Data Converters and Related Devices; Proceedings of the 21st annual symposium on Integrated circuits and system design; publisher ACM New York, USA; ISBN:978-1-60558-231-3

Strle (2008). Efficient Testing of Σ-Δ A/D Converters; proceedings of 15th IEEE International Conference on Electronics, Circuits and Systems, 2008, ISBN:978-1-4244-2181-7, pp 1225-1228

Van de Plassche (2003). CMOS Integrated Analog-to-Digital and Digital -to-Analog Converters, 2nd Edition, publisher Kluwer Academic Publishers Dordrecht, Netherlands; ISBN:1-4020-7500-6

Zaplatílek & Doňar (2003). MATLAB pro začátečníky; publisher BEN Technická literatura, Praha, Czech republic; ISBN:80-7300-095-4

Zaplatílek & Doňar (2004). MATLAB tvorba uživatelských aplikací; publisher BEN Technická literatura, Praha, Czech republic; ISBN:80-7300-133-0

Zaplatílek & Doňar (2006). MATLAB začínáme se signály; publisher BEN Technická literatura, Praha, Czech republic; ISBN:80-7300-200-0

11

A Matlab/Simulink framework for PLC controlled processes

João Martins and Celson Lima
CTS, UNINOVA, Departamento de Engenharia Electrotécnica, Faculdade de Ciências e Tecnologia, Universidade Nova de Lisboa
Portugal

Herminio Martínez and Antoni Grau
College of Industrial Engineering of Barcelona (EUETIB), U.E. d'Electrònica Industrial
Technical University of Catalonia (UPC)
Spain

1. Introduction

Relevant literature recognises that the practical test of an automation and control process controlled by programmable logic controllers (PLC) is a well-known problem [1-3]. There are several solutions that can be implemented, such as scale models, batteries of led's and switches and Human Machine Interfaces (HMI), Supervisory Control and Data Acquisition (SCADA) systems, or simulation tools. The use of scale models of real processes is very expensive and difficult to adapt to different processes. There is no question that this is the best way to teach PLC controlled process, allowing project testing in an almost real environment, however their cost often prohibits its use. The use of leds and switches sets is extremely confusing end uninteresting. This approach, only valid when small processes are considered, severely reduces the motivation. Some HMI and SCADA systems allow this feature but there are very expensive, not intended for this purpose and usually consider property protocols.

The use of Matlab®/Simulink® [4] has not been a regular approach for teaching industrial automation and PLC controlled processes. Assuming that the model of the industrial process is implemented in the Matlab/Simulink, this chapter presents a tool that can be used to implement the PLC control program in Matlab/Simulink environment. The basic idea is to consider the PLC control program as a Matlab function block, within the Matlab/Simulink environment, that will control the model of the industrial process as long as the simulation runs. The main objective of the work described in this chapter is to automatically translate the PLC control program, written as an instruction list, into Matlab/Simulink software language.

2. State-of-the-art

Although *programmable logic controllers* (PLC) have many definitions, one can affirm that they are solid-state members of the computer family, using integrated circuits instead of electromechanical devices to implement control functions. They can be thought of in simple terms as industrial computers with specially designed architecture in both their central units (the PLC brain) and their input/output (I/O) interfacing circuitry with the real world. PLCs are capable of storing instructions, such as sequencing, timing, counting, logic, arithmetic, data manipulation, and communication, to control industrial machines and processes [5]. Fig. 1 shows a conceptual diagram of a PLC application.

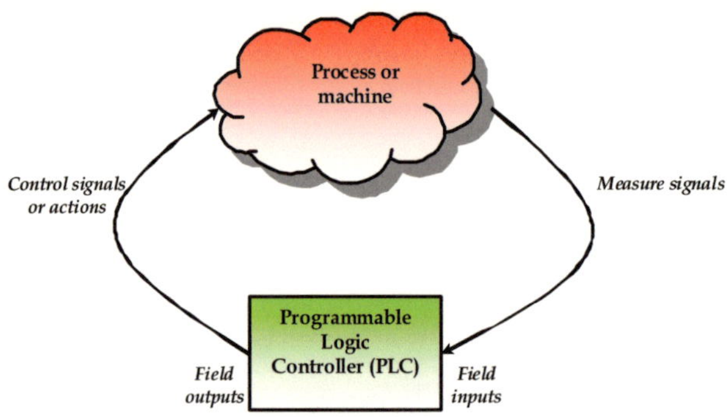

Fig. 1. Conceptual diagram of a PLC application.

The Hydramatic Division of the General Motors Corporation specified the design criteria for the first programmable controller in 1968. Their primary goal was to eliminate the high costs associated with inflexible, relay controlled systems. The specifications required a solid-state system with computer flexibility to survey in an industrial environment, be easily programmable and maintained by plant engineers and technicians, and be reusable. The first PLC had its first product models in 1969. These early controllers met the original specifications and opened the doors to the development of a new control technology. PLCs provided an easy way to *reprogram* the wiring rather than actually rewiring the control system. The first PLCs offered relay functionality, thus replacing the original hardwired relay logic. Notice that they were more or less just relay replacers: Their primary functions were to perform the sequential operations that were previously implemented with relays (ON/OFF control of machines and processes that required repetitive operations, such as transfer lines and grinding and boring machines). However, the first programmable controllers were a vast improvement over relays: They were easily installed, used considerably less space and energy, had diagnostic indicators that aided troubleshooting, and unlike relays, were reusable if a project should be modified.

2.1 Today's Programmable Logic Controllers

Many technological advances in the programmable controller industry continue today. These advances not only affect programmable controller design, but also the philosophical approach to control system architecture and programming. In fact, changes include both hardware (physical components) and software (control program) upgrades. Thus, the following list describes some recent PLC hardware enhancements:

- Faster scan times are being achieved using new, advanced microprocessor and electronic technology.
- Small, low-cost PLCs, which can replace four to ten relays, now have more power than their predecessor, the simple relay replacer.
- High-density input/output (I/O) systems provide space-efficient interfaces at low cost.
- Intelligent, microprocessor-based I/O interfaces have expanded distributed processing. Typical interfaces include PID (proportional-integral-derivative) controllers, network, CANbus, fieldbus, ASCII communication, positioning, host computer, and language modules (e.g., BASIC, Pascal).
- Mechanical design improvements have included rugged input/output enclosures and input/output systems that have made the terminal an integral unit.
- Special interfaces have allowed certain devices to be connected directly to the controller. Typical interfaces include thermocouples, strain gauges, and fast-response inputs.
- Peripheral equipment has improved operator interface techniques, and system documentation is now a standard part of the system.

All of these hardware enhancements have led to the development of programmable controller families. These families consist of a product line that ranges from very small "microcontrollers," with as few as 10 I/O points, to very large and sophisticated PLCs, with as many as 8000 I/O points and 128000 words of memory. These family members, using common I/O systems and programming peripherals, can interface to a local communication network.

The family concept is an important cost-saving development for users. Like hardware advances, software advances, such as the ones listed below, have led to more powerful PLCs:

- PLCs have incorporated object-oriented programming tools and multiple languages based on the IEC 1131-3 standard.
- Small PLCs have been provided with powerful instructions, which extend the area of application for these small controllers.
- High-level languages, such as BASIC and C, have been implemented in some controllers' modules to provide greater programming flexibility when communicating with peripheral devices and manipulating data.
- Advanced functional block instructions have been implemented for ladder diagram instruction sets to provide enhanced software capability using simple programming commands.
- Diagnostics and fault detection have been expanded from simple system diagnostics, which diagnose controller malfunctions, to include machine diagnostics, which diagnose failures or malfunctions of the controlled machine or process.
- Floating-point math has made it possible to perform complex calculations in control applications that require gauging, balancing, and statistical computation.
- Data handling and manipulation instructions have been improved and simplified to accommodate complex control and data acquisition applications that involve storage, tracking, and retrieval of large amounts of data.

Programmable controllers are now mature control systems offering many more capabilities than were ever anticipated. They are capable of communicating with other control systems, providing production reports, scheduling production, and diagnosing their own failures and those of the machine or process. These enhancements have made programmable controllers important contributors in meeting today's demands for higher quality and productivity. Despite the fact that programmable controllers have become much more sophisticated, they still retain the simplicity and ease of operation that was intended in their original design.

2.2 Programmable Logic Controllers and the Future

The future of programmable controllers relies not only on the continuation of new product developments, but also on the integration of PLCs with other control and factory management equipment. PLCs are being incorporated, through networks, into computer-integrated manufacturing (CIM) systems, combining their power and resources with numerical controls, robots, CAD/CAM systems, PCs, management information systems, and hierarchical computer-based systems. There is no doubt that programmable controllers will play a substantial role in the factory of the future.

New advances in PLC technology include features such as graphic user interfaces (GUIs), better operator interface (human-machine interfaces or HMIs), and more human-oriented man/machine interfaces (such as voice modules). They also include the development of interfaces that allow communication with equipment, hardware, and software that supports artificial intelligence, such as fuzzy logic controllers, etc.

2.3 Mechanical Configurations for PLC Systems

There are four common types of mechanical design for PLC systems:

- **Single-board PLCs** or **open frame PLCs.**
- **Compact PLCs** or **single-box PLCs** (sometimes referred to as a **brick PLCs** or **shoe-box PLCs**).
- **Semi-modularized PLCs**.
- **Modularized PLCs, modular PLCs** or **rack types**.

On the one hand, **single board PLCs** are basic PLCs available on a single printed circuit board. They are totally self-contained (normally with the exception of a power supply) and, when installed in a system, they are simply mounted inside a control cabinet on threaded standoffs [6]. Single board PLCs are very inexpensive, easy to program, small, and consume little power, but, generally speaking, they do not have a large number of inputs and outputs, and have a somewhat limited instruction set. They are best suited to small, relatively simple control applications.

On the other hand, PLCs are also available housed in a single case with all input and output, power and control connection points located on the single unit. In this case, they are known as **compact PLCs**. This kind of programmable controllers is generally chosen according to available program memory and required number and voltage of inputs and outputs to suit the application. The compact type is commonly used for small programmable controllers and is supplied as an integral compact package complete with power supply, processor, memory, and input/output units. Typically such a PLC might have 6, 8, 12, or 24 inputs and 4, 8, or 16 outputs and a memory that can store some 300 to 1000 instructions.

Some compact systems have the capacity to be extended to cope with more inputs and outputs by linking input/output boxes to them. This kind of PLCs is known as **semi-modularized units** [7].These systems generally have an expansion port (an interconnection socket) which will allow the addition of specialized units such as high speed counters and analog input and output units or additional discrete inputs or outputs. These expansion units are either plugged directly into the main case or connected to it with ribbon cable or other suitable cable.

Finally, systems with larger numbers of inputs and outputs and more sophisticated units, with a wider array of options, are likely to be modular and designed to fit in racks (**modularized PLCs**) [8]. The modular type consists of separate modules for power supply, processor, and the like, which are often mounted on rails within a metal cabinet. The rack type can be used for all sizes of programmable controllers and has the various functional units packaged in individual modules that can be plugged into sockets in a base rack. The mix of modules required for a particular purpose is decided by the user and the appropriate ones then plugged into the rack. Thus it is comparatively easy to expand the number of I/O connections by simply adding more input/output modules or to expand the memory by adding more memory units. The power and data interfaces for modules in a rack are provided by copper conductors in the backplane of the rack. When modules are slid into a rack, they engage with connectors in the backplane.

2.4 Scopes of Applications and Sizes for PLC Systems

Prior to evaluating the system requirements, the designer should understand the different ranges of programmable controller products and the typical features found within each range. This understanding will enable the designer to quickly identify the type of product that comes closest to matching the requirements of the application. Fig. 2 illustrates PLC product ranges divided into five major areas with overlapping boundaries. The basis for this product segmentation is the number of possible inputs and outputs the system can accommodate (I/O count), the amount of memory available for the application program, and the general hardware and software of the system structure. As the I/O count increases, the complexity and cost of the system also increase. Similarly, as the system complexity increases, the memory capacity, variety of I/O modules, and capabilities of the instruction set increase as well. Thus, PLC market or their scopes of applications can be segmented into five groups [5]:

- Micro PLCs.
- Small PLCs.
- Medium PLCs.
- Large PLCs.
- Very large PLCs.

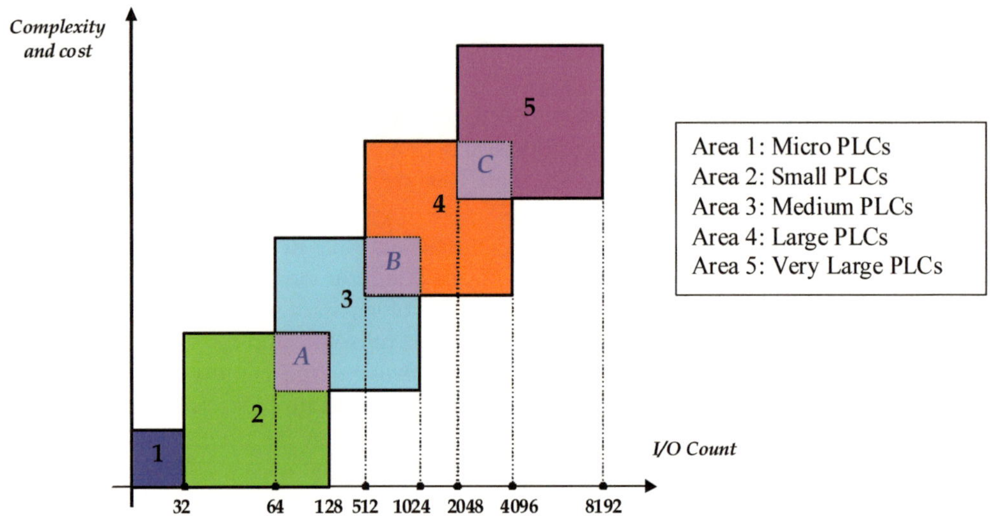

Fig. 2. PLC product ranges.

The shaded areas in Fig. 2, labeled *A*, *B*, and *C*, reflect the possibility of controllers with enhanced (not standard) features for a particular range. These enhancements place the product in a shady area that overlaps the next higher range. For example, because of its I/O count, a small PLC would fall into area 2, but it could have analog control functions that are standard in medium-sized controllers. Thus, this type of product would belong in area *A*. Products that fall into these overlapping areas allow the user to select the product that best matches the requirements of his/her application, without having to select the larger product, unless it is necessary. Thus, micro PLCs are used in applications controlling up to 32 input and output devices, 20 or less I/O being the norm. The micros are followed by the small PLC category, which controls 32 to 128 I/O. The medium (64 to 1024 I/O), large (512 to 4096 I/O), and very large (2048 to 8192 I/O) PLCs complete the segmentation.

In particular, **micro PLCs** (area 1) are used in applications that require the control of a few discrete I/O devices, such as domotic applications and small conveyor controls. Some micro PLCs can perform limited analog I/O monitoring functions (e.g., monitoring a temperature set point or activating an output).

Small PLCs (area 2) are mostly used in applications that require ON/OFF control for logic sequencing and timing functions. These PLCs, along with microcontrollers, are widely used for the individual control of small machines. Often, these products are single-board controllers. In addition, area *A* includes controllers that are capable of having up to 64 or 128 I/O, along with products that have features normally found in medium-sized controllers. The enhanced capabilities of these small controllers allow them to be used effectively in applications that need only a small number of I/O, yet require analog control, basic math, I/O bus network interfaces, LANs, remote I/O, and/or limited data-handling capabilities. A typical application of an area *A* controller is a transfer line in which several small machines, under individual control, must be interlocked through a LAN.

Medium PLCs (area 3) are used in applications that require more than 128 I/O, as well as analog control, data manipulation, and arithmetic capabilities. In general, the controllers in segment 3 have more flexible hardware and software features than the controllers previously mentioned. Area *B* contains medium PLCs that have more memory, table handling, PID, and subroutine capabilities than typical medium-sized PLCs, as well as more arithmetic and data-handling instructions.

Large PLCs (area 4) are used for more complicated control tasks, which require extensive data manipulation, data acquisition, and reporting. Further software enhancements allow these products to perform complex numerical computations. Area *C* includes the segment 4 PLCs that have a large amount of application memory and I/O capacity. The PLCs in this area also have greater math and data-handling capabilities than other large PLCs.

Very large PLCs (area 5) are used in sophisticated control and data acquisition applications that require large memory and I/O capacities. Remote and special I/O interfaces are also standard requirements for this type of controller. Typical applications for very large PLCs include steel mills and refineries. These PLCs usually serve as supervisory controllers in large, distributed control applications.

2.5 PLC Architecture

The typical blocks for a general programmable controller are [6]: The processor, the mounting rack, the input and output modules, the power supply and the programming unit.

The **processor** (also known as CPU), as in the self contained units, is generally specified according to memory required for the program to be implemented. The processor consists of the microprocessor, system memory, serial communication ports for printer, PLC LAN link and external programming device and, in some cases, the system power supply to power the processor and I/O modules. Notice that, in modularized versions, capability can also be a factor. This includes features such as higher math functions, PID control loops and optional programming commands.

The **mounting rack** is usually a metal framework with a printed circuit board backplane which provides means for mounting the PLC input/output (I/O) modules and processor. Mounting racks are specified according to the number of modules required to implement the system. The mounting rack provides data and power connections to the processor and modules via the backplane. For CPUs that do not contain a power supply, the rack also holds the modular power supply. There are systems in which the processor is mounted separately and connected by cable to the rack. The mounting rack can be available to mount directly to a panel or can be installed in a standard equipment cabinet. Mounting racks are "cascadable" so several may be interconnected to allow a system to accommodate a large number of I/O modules.

The **input and output** (I/O) modules are specified according to the input and output signals associated with the particular application. These modules fall into the categories of discrete, analog, high speed counter or register types. Discrete I/O modules are generally capable of handling 8 or 16 and, in some cases 32, on-off type inputs or outputs per module. Modules are specified as input or output but generally not both although some manufacturers now offer modules that can be configured with both input and output points in the same unit. The module can be specified as AC only, DC only or AC/DC along with the voltage values for which it is designed. Analog input and output modules are available and are specified according to the desired resolution and voltage or current range. As with discrete modules, these are generally input or output; however some manufacturers provide analog input and output in the same module. Analog modules are also available which can directly accept thermocouple inputs for temperature measurement and monitoring by the PLC. Pulsed inputs to the PLC can be accepted using a high speed counter module. This module can be capable of measuring the frequency of an input signal from a tachometer or other frequency generating device. These modules can also count the incoming pulses if desired. Generally, both frequency and count are available from the same module at the same time if both are required in the application. Register input and output modules transfer 8 or 16 bit words of information to and from the PLC. These words are generally numbers (BCD or Binary) which are generated from thumbwheel switches or encoder systems for input or data to be output to a display device by the PLC. Other types of modules may be available depending upon the manufacturer of the PLC and its capabilities. These include specialized communication modules to allow for the transfer of information from one controller to another.

The **power supply** specified depends upon the manufacturer's PLC being utilized in the application. As stated above, in some cases a power supply capable of delivering all required power for the system is furnished as part of the processor module. If the power supply is a separate module, it must be capable of delivering a current greater than the sum of all the currents needed by the other modules. For systems with the power supply inside the CPU module, there may be some modules in the system which require excessive power not available from the processor either because of voltage or current requirements that can only be achieved through the addition of a second power source. This is generally true if analog or external communication modules are present since these require ± DC supplies which, in the case of analog modules, must be well regulated.

The **programming unit** allows the engineer or technician to enter and edit the program to be executed. In its simplest form it can be a hand held device with a keypad for program entry and a display device (LED or LCD) for viewing program steps or functions. More advanced systems employ a separate personal computer which allows the programmer to write, view, edit and download the program to the PLC. This is accomplished with proprietary software available from the PLC manufacturer. This software also allows the programmer or engineer to monitor the PLC as it is running the program. With this monitoring system, such things as internal coils, registers, timers and other items not visible externally can be monitored to determine proper operation. Also, internal register data can be altered if required to fine tune program operation. This can be advantageous when debugging the program. Communication with the programmable controller with this system is via a cable connected to a special programming port on the controller. Connection to the personal computer can be through a serial port or from a dedicated card installed in the computer.

3. Industrial Process Modeling and Simulation

3.1 Why Modeling?

In order to study, analyze and control systems, it is necessary to know them very well and, thus, to have a mathematical model that describes them. This model can be used in a computer simulator tool (as MATLAB/Simulink), or for the analysis and design purposes of control systems.

On the one hand, in case a model is developed for a computer simulator, in general, such a model will be represented in a complex and complete way in order to describe as accurate and realistic as possible the real system behavior. On the other, in case a control is needed for the analysis or design purposes of a control system, a representation of this model will be required in its simplest manner, but always taking into account the essence of the model and its more characteristic behavior. Therefore, the goal in modeling techniques is to achieve models in a simple or complex manner depending on the application and objectives. In this Section, we will briefly focus on the development of control models that describe industrial processes that will be useful to controllers' tuning.

Models serve to represent and determine systems behavior and thus fulfill at least three purposes: Prediction, learning new rules and/or data compression. Models can be developed in two different ways or two basic approaches. Let us imagine in the need, in the other hand quite often, of crossing a closed door without knowing the direction of opening. A possibility to know the right direction of opening is to observe the arrangement of hinges; this would be a *theoretical approach*. The other possibility is to try to open the door choosing one of the directions; this would be the *experimental approach*. Following, there is the definition of both approaches:

- Theoretical approach: This approach consists of building a model from physical laws. Here, the engineer can find the difficulty of managing all the physical laws that take part, and in case the model is achieved, it could be very complex and thus difficult to manage. Moreover, another drawback of this approach is that real phenomena are not taken into account such as components wearing, tolerances, noise and disturbance effects...
- Experimental approach or identification: When a system is not suitable for the theoretical approach due to many reasons (such as its complexity, an incomplete knowledge of the system structure or due to an unpredictable variation of its features), it is necessary to resort to another approach that permits the achievement of valid and suitable models. This second approach consists of analyzing the system based on the study of its output signals in front of a well-known set of input signals. In this approach, to not adopt any hypothesis about the system's characteristics usually makes the study difficult, limiting its quality.

The experience demonstrates that the best solution is the combination of both approaches, whenever it is possible. In this case, two steps are usually carried out: The analysis stage and, then, the experimental stage. In the analysis stage, physical laws and work conditions (operation modes) will be taken into account in order to establish the hypothesis. In the experimental stage, starting from the hypothesis set in the analysis, the obtained experimental measures will be considered to determine the coefficients of the mathematical model.

In order to obtain the system's response, it is necessary to stimulate it thanks to the input variables that are generated from the environment of the system under study. There exist two kinds of system input variables: Those that can be controlled, and those that cannot be controlled and are automatically generated by the environment (known as disturbances, Fig. 3). The variables generated by the system are the output variables and they influence on the environment. Those variables are measurable and, sometimes, observable.

Suppose a system like the presented one in Fig. 3. Mainly, two problems can arise with this system:

- Direct problem or analysis: knowing (input, system), find (output). This problem has a unique solution and it is called a problem of analysis.
- Inverse problems:
    - Knowing (input, output), find (system). This problem does not have a unique solution but it has infinite correct solutions. This is a problem of

structure identification and state estimation, and it is called a problem of synthesis.

- Knowing (system, output), find (input). This is a problem of control (instrumentation).

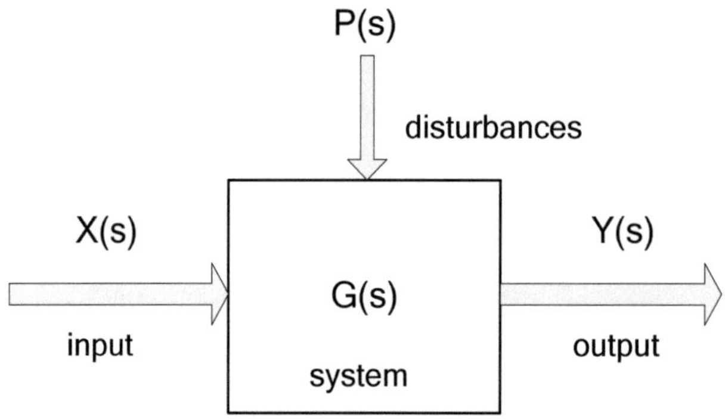

Fig. 3. System Diagram.

3.2 Modelling and simulation spectrum

A system can belong to different disciplines, and each one presents different aspects that should be taken into account when treating this system. The modeler can face a kind of systems that present only historical data, for instance, public opinion systems or social areas systems (see Fig. 4). Models can only be built from experimentation and the modeling technique is *identification* that is mainly used when the system structure is unknown. In this case, the models are call *black box models*, and they can be represented with differential equations.

In the real world, there exist many complex systems which evolution depends on various variables (time, space…) and the most suitable way to describe them is through Partial Differential Equations (PDEs) because they are systems with distributed parameters. In the field of Environmental Sciences is where those systems can be mainly found (Ecology, pollution, biodiversity…). The models developed in these systems are mostly for prediction and experimentation of management strategies.

Finally, there is another kind of systems that their physical laws are perfectly known, that is, the system structure is known and they can be built using *white box models*. From those models the differential equations are generated and, in the most of the cases, they are straightforward enough to be represented with Ordinary Differential Equations (ODEs) because normally their parameters are concentrated. For instance, electric and electronics circuits, chemical control processes, industrial control and aerospatial systems can be represented with white box models. In these cases, the obtained models are used to design a controller to manage the process.

As it can be seen in Fig. 4, from the black box models to white box models there are all the models that a modeler can find in the real world.

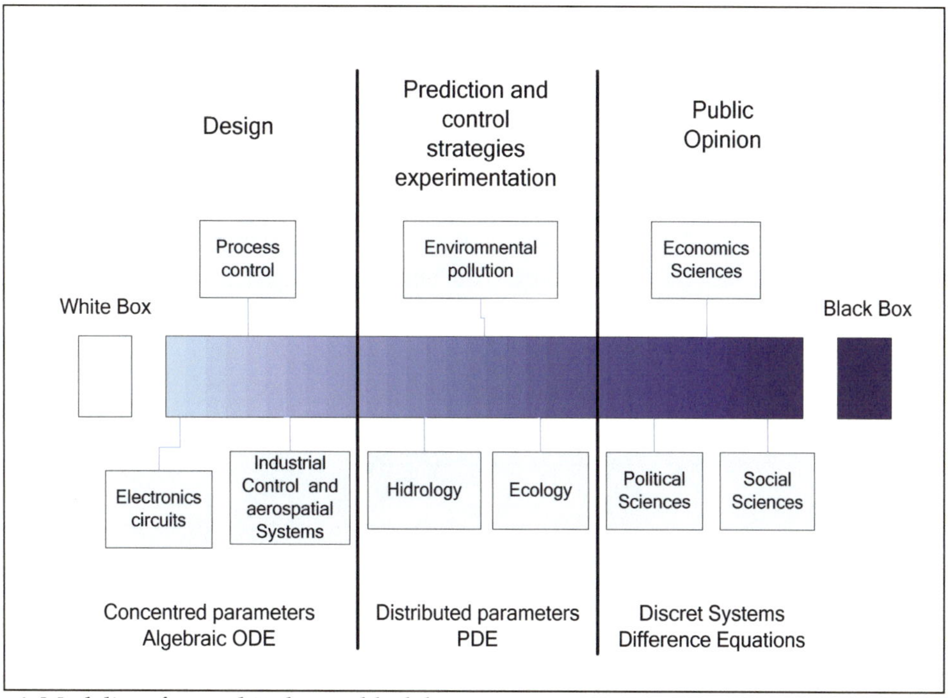

Fig. 4. Modeling: from white box to black box.

3.3 Mathematical model representation

Linear Time-Invariant (LTI) systems are represented by ODEs, but these expressions are too much complicated to manipulate. Thus, modelers use equivalent and easier expressions to represent these equations, for instance, Laplace transform. This representation permits to obtain the **transfer function** describing the system, mainly used in SISO (Single Input Single Output) systems. An alternative to represent a system is through the state space representation, mainly used in MIMO (Multiple Input Multiple Output) systems. The main feature of state space representation is that the internal system variables are represented (all the system's stated) whereas the transfer function only represents the relationship between output and input of the system.

In control engineering, a state space representation is a mathematical model of a physical system as a set of input, output and state variables related by first-order differential equations. To abstract from the number of inputs, outputs and states, the variables are expressed as vectors and the differential and algebraic equations are written in matrix form (the last one can be done when the dynamical system is linear and time invariant). The state space representation (also known as the "time-domain approach") provides a convenient and compact way to model and analyze systems with multiple inputs and outputs. With p inputs and q outputs, we would otherwise have to write down q x p Laplace transforms to encode all the information about a system. Unlike the frequency domain approach, the use of the state space representation is not limited to systems with linear components and zero initial conditions. "State space" refers to the space whose axes are the state variables. The state of the system can be represented as a vector within that space.

3.4 Steps for the simulation project

To choose the type of model to apply is important to know the objectives for which the model will be used. After chosen the model that best fits to the objectives, the system model is developed using the physical laws and/or identification, depending on the situation. Then, the model has to be implemented and validated using obtained real data (data base). To validate the model any error criterion is used, and if the model has goodness enough the process is over, in opposite case the model is reconsidered and the selection process starts again looking for the model that best fits with the system and all the process is repeated until we are satisfied with the chosen model. The whole process can be seen in Fig. 5.

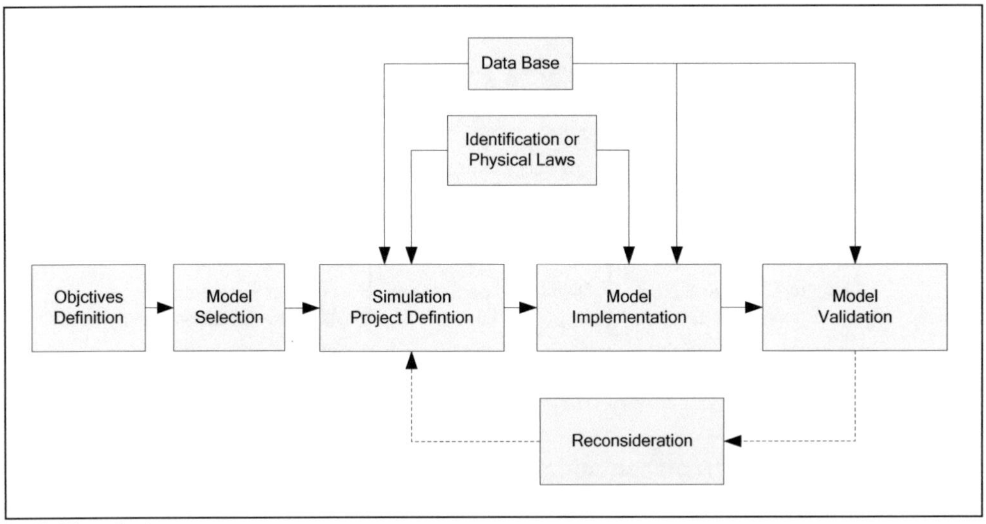

Fig. 5. Simulation steps.

3.5 Simulation Software

Mathematical modeling and simulation are emerging as key technologies in engineering. Relevant computerized tools, suitable for integration with traditional design methods are essential to meet future needs of efficient engineering.

Interactive simulation provides a flexible and user-friendly method to define the experiments performed on the model. During the interactive simulation run, the user can change the values of the model inputs (signals of interest or disturbances), system parameters and initial conditions of the state variables, perceiving instantly how these changes affect to the model dynamic. As a consequence, interactive simulation facilitates the development and improvement of the model performance and allows enhancing the understanding of the system behavior. This capability is especially useful when the model is being used for educational purposes [9].

3.5.1 Today's simulation tools

There is a large amount of simulation software on the market. All languages and model representations are proprietary and developed certain tools. There are general-purpose tools such as ACSL, MATLAB-Simulink, and System Build. They are based on the same modeling methodology, input-output blocks, as in the previous standardization effort, CSSL, from

1967. There are domain-oriented packages: electronic programs SPice, Saber, Multibody Systems, HADAMS, DADS, SIMPACKI, chemical processes (ASPEN Plus, SpeedUp), etc. In October 1996, an international effort started to design a new language for physical modeling. The language is called Modelica. The main objective is to make it easy to exchange models and model libraries and to allow users to benefit from the advances in object oriented modeling methodology [10].

On the other hand, there exists novel simulation software, for instance Easy Java Simulations (Ejs), that lastly is growing and widely used because it is a freeware, open source, Java-based tool intended to create interactive dynamic simulations [11]. Ejs was originally designed to be used by students for interactive learning, under the supervision of educators with a low programming level. As a consequence, simplicity was a requirement. Ejs guides the user in the process of creating interactive simulations. This process includes the definition of the *model* and the *view*.

The use of Ejs, together with Matlab/Simulink and Modelica/Dymola allows us to combine the best features of each tool. Ejs has the capability for building interactive user-interfaces composed of graphical elements, whose properties are linked to the model variables. Matlab/Simulink has the capability for modeling of automatic control systems and for model analysis. Modelica has the capability for physical modeling, and finally Dymola has the capability for simulating hybrid-DAE (differential-algebraic equations) models.

It is important to highlight that, with a few exceptions, all simulation packages are only strong in one domain and are not capable of modeling components in other domains reasonably. This is a major disadvantage since technical systems are becoming more and more heterogeneous with components from many engineering domains.

JMAG provides state of the art technology to encompass extensive physical phenomena accurately in the simulation model. JMAG's precise analysis supports superior electromechanical design. In addition, Spice, in its different versions (PSpice, HSpice, etc.), is the main simulation software in the field of Electronics and Electrical Engineering. PSIM is another simulation package specifically designed for power electronics and motor control.

Finally, apart from the industrial process software simulation software, there exists another line of simulators: The PLC simulator. In this field, developers can find software packages such as PC-SIM, a good option for PLC programming learning, because it has a very good graphical environment, among other features. Another tool is SIMTSX, a software package that enables debugging some PLC commercials brands without the presence of the machine or process and allows validate PLC programs and associated control command functions, and training for control and maintenance operators before taking charge of the equipment on site. Some PC-based process simulation tools have been developed, using microcontroller technologies and designed to work with any type of PLC [12]. The PLC modeling issue can be reduced to the emulation of the PLC control program and many approaches can be further taken regarding the PLC program. Several authors developed specific packages for the verification of the PLC program [13,14]. These packages verify the structure of the program using, among others, automata networks. Often these programs only verify the program structure without verifying if it achieves the desired control objectives. Other approach is the generation of the PLC program from other formalisms, such as Petri nets [15], state diagrams, or finite state machines. If the original formalism is error free this could be a valuable tool for developing PLC programs. Some authors developed software

packages to translate PLC programs to DSP code, so that it can be used in non-PLC hardware [16].
None of these approaches is intended to be used within the Matlab/Simulink environment. The proposed methodology approach will consider that the PLC is essentially modelled by emulating its control program, which interacts with the controlled industrial process itself, as presented in Fig. 1.

4. PLC/Matlab Translation Methodology

In order to fully understand the advantages of the proposed translation methodology, let us assume that the industrial process is already modelled in the Matlab/Simulink environment, as presented in Fig. 6.

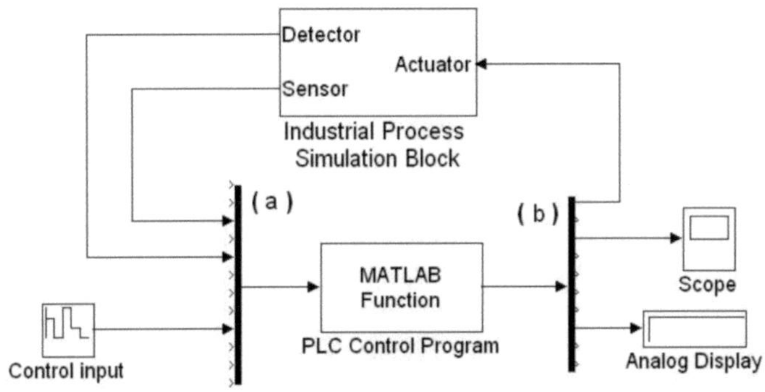

Fig. 6. PLC operation and Industrial Process interaction

The industrial PLC controlled process is simulated in a Matlab/Simulink block named 'Industrial Process Simulation Block'. This block outputs (sensors and detectors outputs) are the process sensors and detectors signals, which will be used as inputs to the Matlab/Simulink block named 'PLC Control Program'. This block will emulate the PLC operation and its outputs will correspond to the PLC outputs that will connect to the actuators input, in the 'Industrial Process Simulation Block'.
The block 'PLC Control Program' is the keystone of the proposed methodology. It will emulate the cyclic PLC operation. This function block is a Matlab *m*-file. In order to automatically build this block, the following procedures must be accomplished:

1. Assume a PLC-controlled process, which is already modelled in an already existing 'Industrial Process Simulation Block', developed in Matlab/Simulink environment;
2. Consider the functional specifications of this PLC-controlled process;
3. Consider a specific PLC to control the process;
4. Elaborate the respective PLC control program accordingly to the considered functional specifications, using for example the GRAFCET methodology [17];
5. Write down the PLC control program using one of the vendor's programming languages;

6. Save the PLC control program as a text-oriented programming language in a text file;
7. Run the developed PLC–Matlab/Simulink translation package in order to convert the PLC control program into the Matlab/Simulink language (the Matlab/Simulink *m*-file function block 'PLC control program' should be automatically produced);
8. Test the developed PLC control program with the considered PLC-controlled process model (Matlab/Simulink *m*-file function block 'Industrial Process Simulation Block');
9. Elaborate the required adaptations in order to put the program control to work properly.

The proposed PLC–Matlab/Simulink translation package, before automatically translate the PLC control program into Matlab/Simulink language, will require the following information:

1. Type of PLC;
2. PLC's number of inputs and outputs;
3. PLC control program file for translation.

4.1 Type of PLC

The choice of the PLC type is essential for establishing the translation rules accordingly to the manufacturer program syntax. Although they are all boolean logic based, each PLC manufacturer develops its own programming syntax. In this way the translation package should know the PLC manufacturer in order to apply the adequate translation rules.

4.2 PLC's number of Inputs and outputs

The number of PLC's Inputs and Outputs clearly defines the arguments of the Matlab/Simulink function 'PLC Control Program' (1). This function will be responsible for executing the PLC control program within the Matlab/Simulink environment, and will be created as a text *m*-file. Both di_1 to di_n denote the PLC's digital inputs, ai_1 to ai_m denote the PLC's analog inputs, do_1 to do_p denote the PLC's digital outputs and ao_1 to ao_q denote the PLC's analog outputs. n, m, p and q denote, respectively, the PLC's number of digital inputs, analog inputs, digital outputs and analog outputs.
It is important to note that $n+m$ define the dimension of the Mux block (a) in Fig. 6. Similarly $p+q$ define the dimension of the Demux block (b) in Fig. 6.

$$
\begin{aligned}
&function\left[output\right]=\\
&=PLC\ Control\ Program\left(di_1,\ldots,di_n,\ldots,ai_1,\ldots,ai_m\right)\\
&\ldots\\
&\begin{pmatrix} PLC\ Control\ Program \\ in\ Matlab\ /\ Simulink\ language \end{pmatrix}\\
&\ldots\\
&output=\left[do_1,\ldots,do_p,\ldots,ao_1,\ldots,ao_q\right]
\end{aligned}
\tag{1}
$$

4.3 PLC Control Program file for translation

The PLC control program can be written in a wide set of programming languages. The software model of PLC's and the referred set of languages are established and defined in the IEC standard 1131-3. Every manufacturer offers different kinds of suitable programming languages, resulting in a typical set of five programming languages:

- **Instruction List**: Very close to assembler can be considered as a low-level text programming language;
- **Ladder Diagrams**: Historically derived from electric circuits wiring does not allow complexity and modularity;
- **Sequential Functional Chart**: A Petri Net like graphical programming language it structures the internal elements of the PLC into steps (associated with actions) and transitions (between steps);
- **Function Block Diagram**: Another graphical language where function blocks process the several PLC's signals;
- **Structured Text**: Derived from Pascal programming language, it is a high level programming language that enables complexity and modularity.

The PLC control program is typically represented using a graphical language known as a ladder diagram. However, almost every PLC software-programming packages allows the use of text-oriented programming languages. Moreover, they allow the automatic conversion between ladder diagrams and text-oriented programming languages, and vice-versa. The proposed translation methodology will consider that the PLC control program is written as a text-oriented programming language, in a standard text file. This does not represent a problem because, as referred, almost every PLC software-programming package allows saving the PLC control program in this format. Fig 7 shows a simple PLC Control Program text file considering, as an example, a Siemens PLC.

```
//
// PROGRAM TITLE COMMENTS
//
NETWORK 1
LD      I 0.0
A       I 0.1
LD      I 0.2
A       I 0.3
OLD
=       Q 0.0
//
NETWORK 2
LD      I 0.4
LD      I 0.5
CTU     C5,+6
//
END
```

Fig. 7. PLC Control Program standard text file

The PLC control program translation package is a software tool, developed in Visual Basic, which automatically converts the PLC control program text file into a correspondent Matalb/Simulink *m*-file. This *m*-file, containing the PLC control program described in Matalb/Simulink language, holds the Matalb/Simulink function defined in (1). Knowing

the PLC's number of inputs/outputs, the conversion tool establishes the correct number of input and output arguments for function (1). The translation of the PLC Control Program itself relays on a set of translation rules applied to the set of PLC instruction list.
A full PLC instruction list can be roughly divided into:

- Boolean
- Comparison
- Output
- Timer
- Counter
- Math
- Increment/Decrement
- Moving/Shifting
- Program Control
- Other

Following some instructions conversion rules will be described, considering a Siemens PLC instruction list. Boolean instructions will be translated into Matlab/Simulink language using standard Matlab boolean functions, as presented in Table 1, where I x.y denotes a digital input and Q x.y denotes a digital output, x and y are, respectively, the byte and bit of the considered digital input/output. Furthermore, do_g is a Matlab variable denoting digital output g and di_h is a Matlab variable denoting the digital input h. The bollean state TRUE will be represented in Matalb environment by '1' and FALSE by '0'. Combinations of various Boolean instructions will be converted using the above rules. An example is shown on the last row of Table 1.

Boolean instruction	PLC instruction	Matlab/Simulink translation
AND	LD I a.b A I c.d = Q e.f	do_g = di_h&di_i
OR	LD I a.b O I c.d = Q e.f	do_g = di_h | di_i
NOT	LDN I a.b = Q c.d	do_g = ~ di_i
Combinations of various Boolean instructions	LD I 0.0 A I 0.1 LD I 0.2 OLD = Q 0.0	do_1 = (di_1 & di_2) | di_3

Table 1. Boolean Instructions Translation

PLC math instructions are usually boolean enabled. This implies the use of Matlab function 'if' in order to represent their behavior. As an example, consider the PLC integer adding instruction presented in Table 2. AIW0 and AQW0 represent, respectively, a PLC analog input and a PLC analog output. Variable ao_1 is a Matlab variable denoting the first analog output and ai_1 is a Matlab variable denoting the first analog input.

On the other hand, PLC control programs often use internal flags (bit and variable internal memories) to represent states or to store analog values. Whenever the translation package finds a PLC internal memory, automatically assigns a Matlab/Simulink variable to it. These variables are usually denoted as m or v, as they are digital or analog. The PLC multiply instruction (MUL) often involves the use of an auxiliary internal memory, as presented in Table 2, where the MOVW instruction (moving the value of one word variable - 16 bit - into another) is also used. Please, note that the PLC internal variable VD refers to a 32-bit word.

Instruction	PLC instruction	Matlab/Simulink translation
INCREMENT	LD I 0.0 +I AIW0 , AQW0	if di_1 ao_1 = ai_1 + ao_1 end
MULTIPLY	LD I 0.0 MOVW +6 , VD4 MUL +9 , VD4	if di_1 v_4 = +6 v_4 = +9 * v_4 end

Table 2. Non-Boolean Instructions Translation

PLC counter instructions (CTUD - counter up and down) can require several boolean inputs: One for counting up, other for counting down (if the case) and other for resenting the counter. Since the counting is only performed on the rising edge of the boolean input, the Matlab/Simulink translation should take into account the previous state of that boolean input. Table 3 presents a counting example, where di_1_prev is a Matlabb variable denoting the previous state of variable di_1. Previous state means the state in the previous PLC Control Program Cycle. In this example, by reaching counting 4 the counter boolean state changes to true. In Matlab environment c_10 denotes the boolean state of counter number 10, and c_10_value denotes the counting value of the same counter.
PLC timer instructions, such as on-delay timers, usually require only one digital input for counting. As Fig. 8 presents, the on-delay timer (T33 in the example) works whenever the respective digital input (I2.0 in the example) is enabled, and becomes Boolean TRUE when it reaches its preset time (3 seconds in the example).

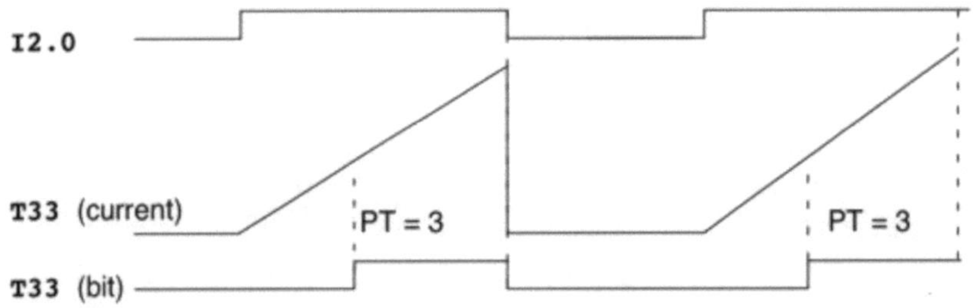

Fig. 8. On-delay timer operation

The previous timer translation is presented in Table 3. Whenever the timer starts (its corresponding digital input - di_20 –is TRUE and the timer has not started yet) the preset time (t33_start) is added to the actual clock value (clock_in) establishing the timer stopping time (t33_end_time). After reaching this stopping time the logical value of the timer (t1_bin) becomes true. The timer is restarted when its corresponding boolean input becomes FALSE.

Instruction	PLC instruction	Matlab/Simulink translation
COUNTER	LD I 0.0 // Count up LD I 0.1 // Count down LD I 0.2 // Reset counter CTUD C10, +4	if di_1 & ~ di_1_prev c_10_value = c_10_value + 1 end if di_2 & ~ di_2 c_10_value = c_10_value - 1 end if di_3 c_10_value = 0 c_10 = 0 end if c_10_value >= +4 c_10 = 1 end

TIMER	LD I 2.0
	TON T33, 3
		%Start timer
		if di_20 & t33_start==0
		t33_start=3;
		t33_end_time=clock_in+3;
		end
		%Timer ON
		if t33_start &clock_in>=t33_end_time
		t33_bin=1;
		end
		%Timer OFF
		if ~di_20
		t33_bin=0;
		t33_start=0;
		end

Table 3. Counter and Timer Instructions Translation

5. Application Examples

As a first illustrative application example let us consider pure Boolean. It is supposed to automate the sawmill presented on Fig. 9. After pressing the START pushbutton the cutting machine moves to the right. The blade must be connected before it reaches the logs and cut off after sawing them. At this time the blade should be raised. When the top position is reached the upward movement should stop and the machine must move to the left until it reaches its original position, where the blade should be lowered. In Fig. 9 are also depicted the limit switches (denoted as Si) that are used to control the machine actions.

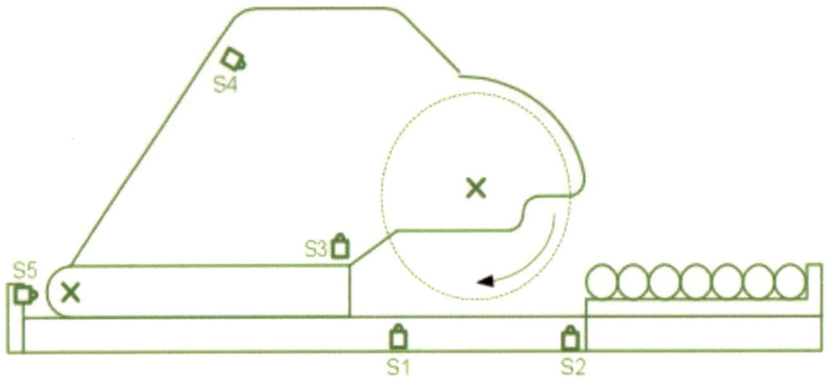

Fig. 9. Sawmill machine

Table 4 presents the PLC's list of the process inputs and outputs. It shows each signal description, its PLC address and the corresponding Matlab/Simulink assignment. For this automated process 6 digital inputs and 5 digital outputs are required. A standard SIEMENS S7-200 PLC with 8 digital inputs and 6 digital outputs is considered to perform the desired process control. The process control algorithm was elaborated accordingly to the GRAFCET, (Graphe Fonctionnel de Commande Étape Transition) or SFC (Sequential Function Chart) presented in Fig. 10.

Signal description	PLC I/O address	Notes	Matlab/ Simulink assignment
Start	I 0.0	Push button	di0
Switch on saw position	I 0.1	Limit switch - S1	di2
Switch off saw position	I 0.2	Limit switch - S2	di3
Machine lowered	I 0.3	Limit switch - S3	di4
Machine raised	I 0.4	Limit switch - S4	di5
Machine at start position	I 0.5	Limit switch - S5	di6
Left displacement	Q 0.0	Motor M1 - left	do1
Right displacement	Q 0.1	Motor M1 - right	do2
Saw rotating	Q 0.2	Motor M2	do3
Raise machine	Q 0.3	Motor M3 - up	do4
Lower machine	Q 0.4	Motor M3 - donw	do5

Table 4. Boolean Instructions Translation

From this GRAFCET the PLC control program is written as a text-oriented programming language, in a standard text file. Applying the developed PLC–Matlab/Simulink translation package to this text file, it automatically produces the Matlab/Simulink *m*-file function block 'PLC control program'. The type of PLC and the number of I/O were also considered as translation process package arguments. The obtained *m*-file, containing the PLC control program written in Matalb/Simulink language, holds the Matalb/Simulink version of the developed control program. It is presented in (2), where mi denotes each GRAFCET step and mi_a its previous boolean value.

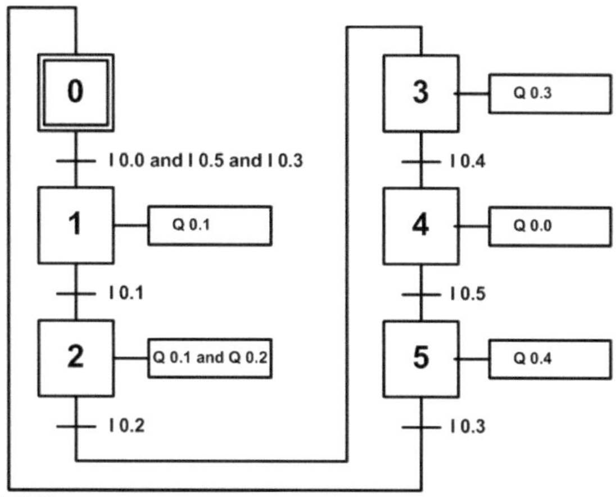

Fig. 10. Sawmill GRAFCET

```
function
[output]=cpu222(di1,di2,di3,di4,di5,di6,di7,di8,ai1,ai2,ai3,ai4,clock_in
)

global m0 m0_a m1 m1_a m2 m2_a m3 m3_a m4 m4_a m5 m5_a

%output initialization
aux=0; do1=aux; do2=aux; do3=aux; do4=aux; do5=aux; do6=aux;
ao1=aux; ao2=aux; ao3=aux; ao4=aux;

%grafcet step evolution
m0=(m5&di3) | (m0&~m5);
m1=(m0&di1&di6&di4) | (m1&~m0);
m2=(m1&di2) | (m2&~m1);
m3=(m2&di3) | (m3&~m2);
m4=(m3&di5) | (m4&~m3);
m5=(m5&di6) | (m5&~m4);
                                                            (2)
%Output generation
do1=m1;
do2=m2;
do3=m3;
do0=m4;
d04=m5;

%grafcet previous steps actualization
m0_a=m0;
m1_a=m1;
m2_a=m2;
m3_a=m3;
m4_a=m4;
m_a=m5;

output=[do1 do2 do3 do4 do5 do6 ao1 ao2 ao3 ao4];
```

The second example (including timer and counter operations) considers a water tank with a random flow of input water, whose level should be kept between 4 and 5 meters height (Fig. 11). In order to accomplish this goal an electric output valve (with 8 l/sec flow rate) is controlled by a PLC. The PLC controls this valve accordingly to the information provided by two level detectors (installed at 4 and 5 meter height respectively). In this example it is also desired to count the number of times that the output valve is actuated. Whenever this number reaches 8, two types of alarms should be produced: A light signal and a buzzer. The buzzer, however, should only be activated one second after the counter has reached 8. Additionally, for testing purposes, an external reset signal is considered at 3 and 12 seconds.

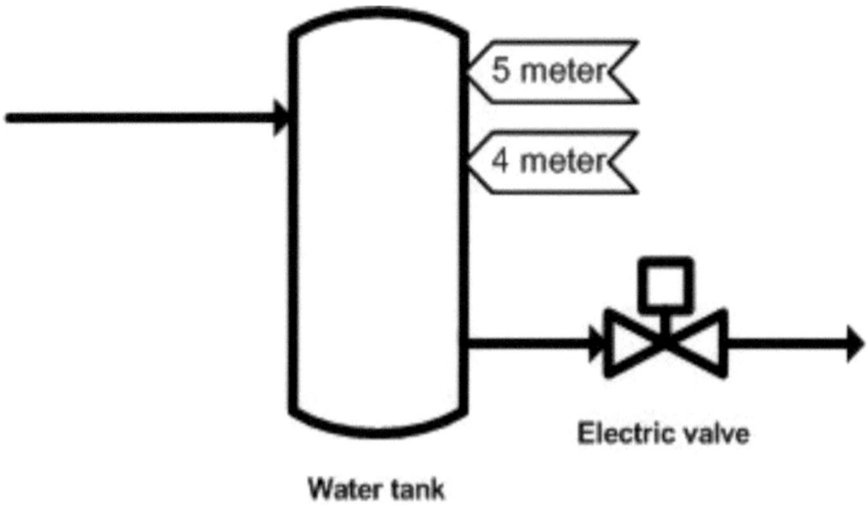

Fig. 11. Water tank level control

Fig. 12 presents the Matlab/Simulink environment for this application. The subsystem "Water Tank System" contains the simulated model of the water tank, with its detectors and actuators. The subsytem "PLC" contains the Matlab/Simulink version of the developed PLC program control. Actually this subsystem simulates the PLC action over the process. The PLC inputs are: "Maximum water level switch", "Minimum water level switch", and "External counter reset". The two first inputs are the signals provided by the two level detectors installed in the water tank. The PLC outputs are: "Output valve", "Counter=8?", "Counter Alarm" and "Valve counter". This last output is an analogue output with the number of times that the output valve has been operated.

The chosen PLC for this application was again a SIEMENS S7-200 with 8 digital inputs, 4 analog inputs, 6 digital outputs and 4 analog outputs. This automatically defines the number and type of input and output arguments of the Matlab/Simulink subsystem "PLC Control Program". The input arguments are the SIEMENS S7-200 inputs and the clock, while the subsystem output arguments are the SIEMENS S7-200 outputs. Table 5 defines the PLC's data and the respective representation in the Matlab/Simulink environment, where the description of each data variable is also presented.

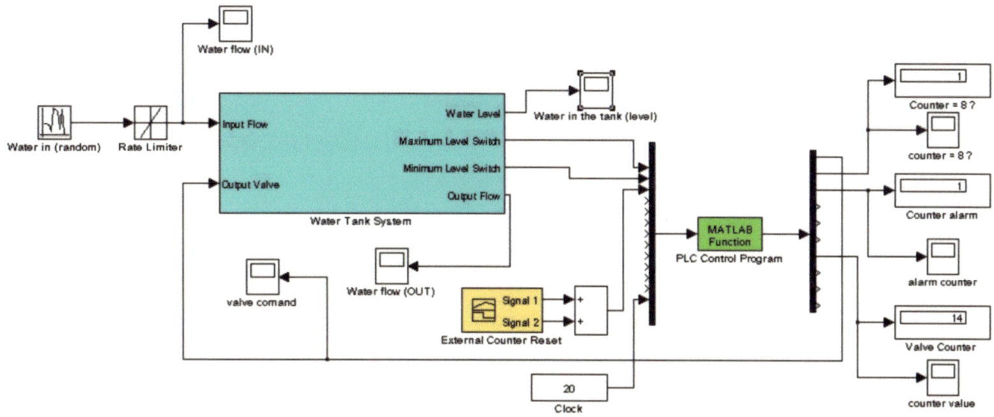

Fig. 12. Matlab/Simulink model of the controlled water tank system

Signal description	PLC signal	Notes	Matlab/ Simulink assignment
Maximum level	I 0.0	Switch	di1
Minimum level	I 0.1	Switch	di2
External counter reset	I 0.2	Pushbutton	di3
Valve	Q0.0	Electric valve	do1
Light signal alarm	Q0.0	Signals 8 valve operations	do2
Buzzer signal alarm	Q0.2	One second delay after light signal	do3
Counter value	QW10	Counter value	ao1
Valve operation counter	C1	Internal counter (CTU)	c1
Counter alarm timer	T1	Internal timer (on-delay)	t1
GRAFCET1 step 0	M10.0	Internal mark	m0
GRAFCET1 step 1	M10.1	Internal mark	m1
GRAFCET1 step 2	M10.2	Internal mark	m2
GRAFCET 2 step 0	M20.0	Internal mark	m10
GRAFCET 2 step 1	M20.1	Internal mark	m11

Table 5. Maltalb/Simulink representation of the water tank system PLC's data

In order to accomplish the desired specifications, two GRAFCETs were considered, one for the valve control and other for the counter reset. Additionally, the counter and the timer were also considered in the instruction list for signalling purposes. Using the previously described conversion rules, the SIEMENS PLC program control instruction list is converted into the Matlab/Simulink function presented in (3).

```
function [output]=cpu222(di1,di2,di3,di4,di5,di6,di7,di8,ai1,ai2,ai3,ai4,clock_in)
global m0 m0_a m1 m1_a m2 m2_a m3 m3_a m10 m10_a m11 m11_a c1 c1_bin t1_start
t1_end_time t1_bin
%output initialization
aux=0; do1=aux; do2=aux; do3=aux; do4=aux; do5=aux; do6=aux;
ao1=aux; ao2=aux; ao3=aux; ao4=aux;

%grafcet 1 (valve control)
m0=(m2) | (m0&~m1);
m1=(m0&di1) | (m1&~m2);
m2=(m1&~di2) | (m2&~m0);
%grafcet 2 (counter reset)
m10=(m11) | (m10&~m11);
m11=(m10&di3) | (m11&~m10);

%Counter Siemens (CTU)
%counter actualization
if m1==1 & ~m1_a
   c1=c1+1;
end
%counter set
if c1==8
   c1_bin=1;
end
%counter reset
if m11
   c1=0;
   c1_bin=0;
end
                                                                        (3)
%Timer SIEMENS (on-delay)
%Start timer
if c1_bin & t1_start==0
   t1_start=1;
   t1_end_time=clock_in+1;
end
%Timer ON
if t1_start &clock_in>=t1_end_time
   t1_bin=1;
end
%Timer OFF
if ~c1_bin
   t1_bin=0;
   t1_start=0;
end

%Output generation
do1=m1;
do2=c1_bin;
do3=t1_bin;
ao1=c1;
ao2=ai1;
%GRAFCET previous steps actualization
m0_a=m0;
m1_a=m1;
m2_a=m2;
m3_a=m3;
m10_a=m10;
m11_a=m11;
output=[do1 do2 do3 do4 do5 do6 ao1 ao2 ao3 ao4];
```

Function (3) is called in the subsystem "PLC Control Program" (see Fig. 6). Whenever the simulation runs this function acts as the PLC, controlling the water system process. Fig. 13 presents the random input water flow and the water tank level. One can see that the developed control program (implemented in the PLC simulation subsystem) is able to comply with the desired specifications, keeping the water level between 4 and 5 meter height.

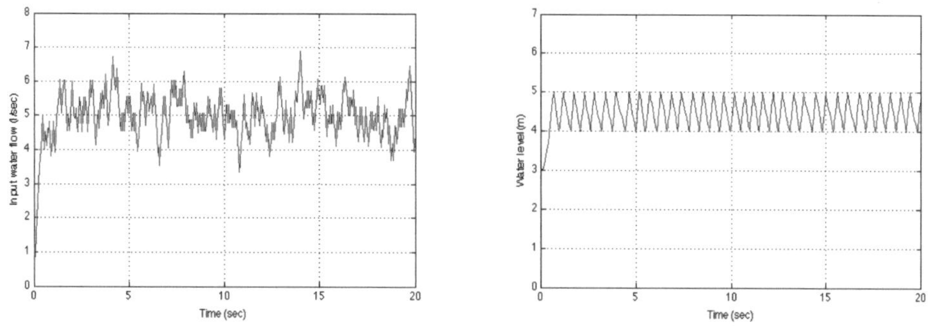

(a) (b)

Fig. 13. PLC controlled water tank system Matlab/Simulink simulation results. (a) Input water flow. (b) Water tank level.

Fig. 14 presents the cumulative counting of the valve operation and both of the considered alarms. One clearly sees the effect of the external reset counter (at 3 and 12 seconds), and the one second delay (due to timer operation) between the light alarm (gray thick line) and the buzzer alarm (black thin line).

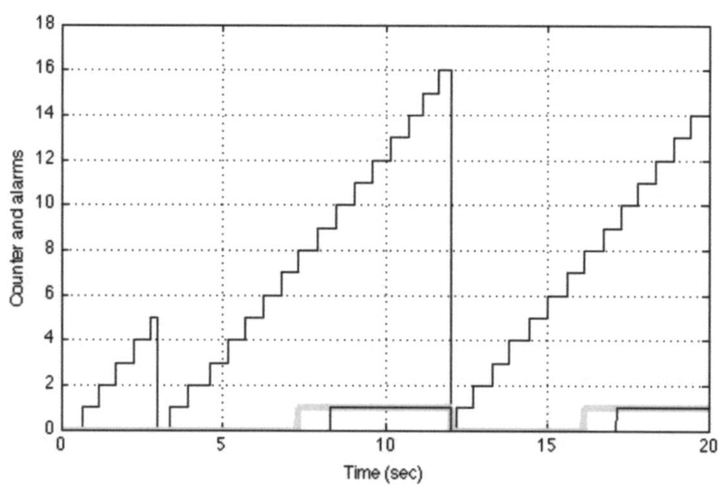

Fig. 14. PLC controlled water tank counter evolution and alarm generation

6. Conclusions

A new approach for testing PLC control programs for teaching automation and PLC-controlled processes was presented. This approach is based on the Matlab/Simulink software language. The PLC control program is translated into a Matlab function block, within the Matlab/Simulink environment, which will act over the model of the industrial process as long as the simulation runs. The developed translation package automatically translates the PLC control program, written as an instruction list, into Matlab/Simulink software language. The translation package produces a *m*-file, obtained by applying a set of translation rules that convert the PLC instruction list into Matlab language. This *m*-file is integrated into the Matlab/Simulink process simulation as a function block named 'PLC Control Program'.

7. Acknowledgements

Authors would like to thank Prof. Yolanda Bolea for her valuable help and suggestions in Section 3.

8. References

[1] Mikell P. Groover, Automation, Production Systems and Computer Integrated Manufacturing, Prentice Hall, 1987.
[2] Andrew Kusiak; Computational Intelligence in Design and Manufacturing, John Wiley & Sons, 2000.
[3] S. B. Morriss, Automated Manufacturing Systems, McGraw Hill, 1994.
[4] Matlab/Simulink, http://www.mathworks.com/
[5] L.A. Bryan and E.A. Bryan. '*Programmable Controllers. Theory and Implementation*'. Atlanta, Georgia, USA: Industrial Text Company Publication. 2nd Edition. 1997.
[6] John R. Hackworth and Frederick D. Hackworth, Jr. '*Programmable Logic Controllers: Programming Methods and Applications*'. Ed. Prentice Hall. 2004.
[7] Enrique Mandado, J. Marcos Acevedo, Celso Fernández, José I. Armesto and Serafín Pérez. '*Autómatas Programables. Entorno y Aplicaciones*' (in Spanish). Madrid: Ed. Thomson-Paraninfo. 2005.
[8] José Luís Romeral and Josep Balcells Sendra. '*Autómatas Programables*' (in Spanish). Barcelona: Ed. Marcombo. Boixareu Editores. 1996.
[9] C. Martin, F. Esquembre and J.L. Guzman, "Interactive Simulation of Object-oriented Hybrid Models by Combined Use of EJS, MATLAB/SIMULINK and MODELICA/DYMOLA", Proceedings 18th European Simulation Multiconference Graham Horton (c) SCS Europe, 2004.
[10] H. Elmqvist and S. E. Mattsson, "An Introduction to the Physical Modeling Language Modelica", Proc. of the 9th European Simulation Symposium, ESS'97, Oct 19-23, 1997.
[11] Ejs, Easy Java Simulations, http://fem.um.es/Ejs/
[12] V Pinto, S. Rafael, J: F: Martins; "PLC controlled industrial processes on-line simulator"; IEEE International Symposium on Industrial Electronics, ISIE 2007, June 2007, Vigo, Spain.

[13] G. L. Kim, P. Paul, Y. Wang, "UPPAAL in a nutshell", International Journal on Software Tools for Technology Transfer, 1, pp. 134-152, 1997.

[14] M. Chmiel, E. Hrynkiewicz, M. Muszynski, "The way of ladder diagram analysis for small compact programmable controller", Proceedings of the 6th Russian-Korean International Symposium on Science and Technology KORUS-2002, pp. 169-173, 2002.

[15] Gi Bum Lee, Han Zandong, Jin S. Lee, "Automatic generation of ladder diagram with control Petri Net", Journal of Intelligent Manufacturing, 15, 245±252, 2004.

[16] HyungSeok Kim, Wook Hyun Kwon, Naehyuck Chang; "A translation method for ladder diagram with application to a manufacturing process", Proceedings of the IEEE International Conference on Robotics and Automation, pp. 793-798, Detroit, USA, 1999.

[17] IEC, International Electrotechnic Commission, *Preparation of Function charts fos Control Systems*, publication 848, 1988.

12

Optimization and Scheduling Toolbox

Michal Kutil, Přemysl Šůcha, Roman Čapek and Zdeněk Hanzálek
Czech Technical University in Prague
Czech Republic

1. Introduction

TORSCHE (Time Optimization of Resources, SCHEduling) Scheduling Toolbox for Matlab is a freely (GNU GPL) available toolbox developed at the Czech Technical University in Prague. The toolbox is designed for researches in operational research or industrial engineering and for undergraduate courses. The current version of the toolbox covers the following areas: scheduling on monoprocessor/dedicated processors/parallel processors, open shop/flow shop/job shop scheduling, cyclic scheduling and real-time scheduling. Furthermore, particular attention is dedicated to graphs and graph algorithms due to their large interconnection with the scheduling theory. The toolbox offers a transparent representation of the scheduling/graph problems, various scheduling/graph algorithms, a useful graphical editor of graphs, interfaces for mathematical solvers (Integer Linear Programming, satisfiability of the boolean expression) and an interface to a MATLAB/Simulink based simulator and a visualization tool. The scheduling problems and algorithms are categorized by notation $(\alpha|\beta|\gamma)$ proposed by Graham and Błażewicz (Blazewicz et al., 1983). This notation, widely used in the scheduling community, greatly facilitates the presentation and discussion of scheduling problems.
The toolbox is supplemented by several examples of real applications, e.g. the scheduling of Digital Signal Processing (DSP) algorithms on a hardware architecture with pipelined arithmetic units, scheduling the movements of hoists in a manufacturing environment and scheduling of light controlled intersections in urban traffic. The toolbox is equipped with sets of benchmarks from the research community (e.g. DSP algorithms, the Quadratic Assignment Problem). TORSCHE is an open-source tool available at (`http://rtime.felk.cvut.cz/scheduling-toolbox/`)
In the off-line scheduling area, some tools for the development of scheduling algorithms already exist. The term *off-line* scheduling means all parameters of the scheduling problem are known a priori (Pinedo, 2008). A scheduling system developed at the Stern School of Business is called LEKIN (Pinedo et al., 2002). It was created as an educational tool and it provides six basic workspace environments: single machine, parallel machines, flow shop, flexible flow shop, job shop, and flexible job shop. Another tool is LiSA (Andresen et al., 2003). It is a software-package for entering, editing and solving off-line scheduling problems while the main focus is on shop-scheduling and one-machine problems. The graphical user interface is written in Tcl/Tk for machine and operating system independence. All algorithms are implemented externally while the parameters are passed through files. The commercial tool ILOG Scheduler from the software package ILOG CP Optimizer (ILOG, 2009) is based on

constraints programming. It provides extensions for scheduling problems in manufacturing, transportation and workforce scheduling.

There are more tools for on-line scheduling, where *on-line* means the parameters of the tasks become known on the task arrival/occur. One example is the MAST tool (Gonzalez et al., 2008) built to mainly support the timing analysis of real-time applications. A tool with close relationship to this category is TrueTime (Andersson et al., 2005), which is a Matlab/Simulink based discrete-events simulator mainly focused on real-time control systems.

The TORSCHE toolbox is mostly based on the existing well-known scheduling algorithms, but some of them were developed by our group. It is a very convenient platform for sharing ideas and algorithms among researchers and students. The toolbox has become part of a textbook for courses in scheduling (Pinedo, 2008). Our objective for developing TORSCHE was to fill the gap in the available tools for scheduling and optimization.

This chapter is organized as follows: Section 2 outlines the toolbox architecture. Section 3 summarizes the selected scheduling algorithms from the toolbox, with their practical applications. The first two algorithms are selected from the scheduling for the digital signal processing area. The first algorithm uses the problem formulation by satisfiability of the boolean expressions (SAT). The second one solves a cyclic scheduling problem by Integer Linear Programming (ILP). Moreover, the subsection demonstrates how the results of the scheduling can be simulated in Matlab Simulink using TrueTime. The third algorithm shows an original application of the minimum cost multi-commodity flow problem on the scheduling of light controlled intersections in urban traffic. The last application is focused on the graphic visualization of the scheduling results based on the Matlab Virtual Reality toolbox demonstrated on the hoist scheduling problem. Section 4 concludes the chapter.

2. Tool Architecture and Basic Notation

TORSCHE Scheduling Toolbox is written in the Matlab object oriented programming language (backward compatible with Matlab environment version 2007) and it is used in the Matlab environment as a toolbox. The toolbox includes two complementary parts. The first one is intended for solving problems from scheduling theory. Problems from this area or their parts can, very often, be reformulated to another problem which can be directly solved by a graph algorithm. For this purpose the second part of the toolbox is dedicated to graph theory algorithms.

2.1 Scheduling Part

The main classes of the scheduling part are *Task, PTask, Taskset* and *Problem*. The UML class diagram illustrating the class relationships is shown in Fig. 1. A task represented by the class of the same name is a unit of work to be scheduled on the given set of processors. The class includes task parameters as processing time, release date, deadline, etc. The instance of the class (variable `T1` depicted below) is returned by the constructor method, which has the following syntax rule:

```
T1 = task([Name,]ProcTime[,ReleaseTime[,Deadline ...
        [,DueDate[,Weight[,Processor]]]]])
```

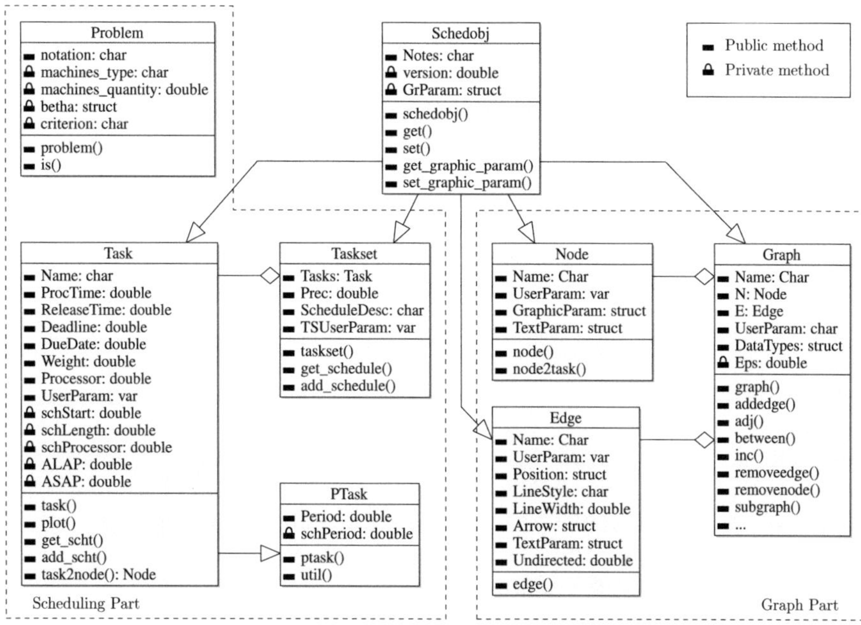

Fig. 1. TORSCHE architecture by the UML Class Diagram

Input variables correspond to the public class properties. Variables contained inside the square brackets are optional. The class *Task* provides the following properties (also graphically depicted in Fig. 2):

Processing time (`ProcTime`, p_j) is time necessary for task execution (also called computation time).

Release date (`ReleaseTime`, r_j) is the moment at which a task becomes ready for execution (also called the arrival time, ready time, request time).

Deadline (`Deadline`, $\widetilde{d}_j$) specifies a time limit by which the task has to be completed, otherwise the scheduling is assumed to fail.

Due date (`Duedate`, d_j) specifies a time limit by which the task should be completed, otherwise the criterion function is charged by a penalty.

Weight (`Weight`) expresses the priority of the task with respect to other tasks (also called the priority).

Processor (`Processor`) specifies the dedicated processors on which the task must be executed.

The resulting schedule is represented by the following properties:

Start time (`schStart`, s_j) is the time when the execution of the task is started.

Completion time (c_j) is the time when the execution of the task is finished.

Lateness $L_j = c_j - d_j$.

Tardiness $D_j = \max\{c_j - d_j, 0\}$.

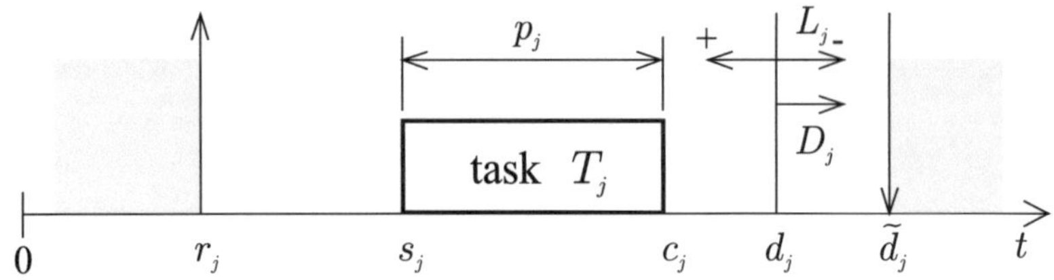

Fig. 2. Graphic representation of the task parameters

The private properties of the class *Task* are mainly intended for the final task schedule representation, which are set up inside the scheduling algorithms (e.g. by method `add_scht`). The values from the private properties are used, for example, by the method `plot` for the Gantt chart drawing.
Class *PTask* (see Fig. 1) is a derived class from the *Task* class in order to represent a periodic task in on-line scheduling problems (e.g. in response-time analysis). This class extends the *Task* class with support to store, plot and analyze the utilization methods.
The instances of the classes *Task* and *PTask* can be aggregated into a set of tasks. A set of tasks is represented by the class *Taskset* which can be obtained as the return value of the constructor `taskset`, for example:

```
TS = taskset(tasks[,prec])
```

where the variable `tasks` is an array of instances of the *Task* class. Furthermore, the relations between the tasks can be defined by precedence constraints in the optional parameter `prec`. The parameter `prec` is an adjacency matrix defining a graph where the nodes correspond to the tasks and the edges are precedence constraints between these tasks. For simple scheduling problems, the object *Taskset* can be directly created from a vector of the tasks processing times. In this case, the tasks are created automatically inside the object constructor. There are also other ways how to create an instance of the set of tasks in order to simplify the user interface as much as possible.
Another class, *Problem*, is used for the classification of deterministic scheduling problems in Graham and Błażewicz notation (Blazewicz et al., 1983). This notation consists of three parts $(\alpha|\beta|\gamma)$. The first part describes the processor environment (e.g. number and type of processors), the second part describes the task characteristics of the scheduling problem (e.g. precedence constrains, release time). The last part denotes the optimality criterion (e.g. schedule makespan minimization). The following example shows the notation string used as an input to the class constructor:

```
prob = problem('P|prec|Cmax')
```

This instance of the class *Problem* represents the scheduling problem on parallel identical processors where the tasks have precedence constraints and the objective is to minimize the schedule makespan.
All of the above-mentioned classes are designed to be maximally effective for users and developers of scheduling algorithms. The toolbox includes dozens of scheduling algorithms which are stored as Matlab functions with at least two input parameters and at least one output parameter. The first input parameter has to be an instance of the *Taskset* class containing the tasks to be scheduled. The second one has to be an instance of the *Problem* class describing

the required scheduling problem. The output parameter is an instance of the *Taskset* class containing the resulting schedule. A typical syntax of the scheduling algorithm call is:

```
TSout = algorithmname(TS,problem[,processors[,parameters]])
```

where:

`TSout`	is the instance of the *Taskset* with the resulting schedule,
`algorithmname`	is the algorithm name,
`TS`	is the instance of the *Taskset* to be scheduled,
`problem`	is the instance of the *Problem* class,
`processors`	is the number of processors to be used,
`parameters`	denotes additional parameters, e.g. algorithm strategy, etc.

The typical workflow of a scheduling problem solution is shown in a UML Interaction Overview Diagram (see Fig. 3). There are several sequence diagrams (sd) used. The first two "Create Taskset 1" and "Create Taskset 2" show the constitution of a *Taskset* instance by both of the above described ways. The third one, called "Classification", shows the constitution of a *Problem* instance. The following sequence diagram "Scheduling" presents the call of the scheduling algorithm. The scheduling algorithm is described separately in the "Scheduling Algorithm" diagram, which is divided into three parts. The first one is checking of the input parameters ("Read Properties"). The second one is constituted by the solver of a scheduling algorithm and the final part stores the resulting schedule into the instance of the *Taskset* ("Schedule to the Tasks"). The last diagram "Gantt Chart" presents the final schedule conversion to a Gantt chart, i.e. the graphical representation of a schedule.
Furthermore, the toolbox contains objects to handle problems like open shop, flow shop and job shop, it also supports limited buffers and transport robots. For more details please see the toolbox documentation (Kutil et al., 2007).

2.2 Graph Part

A number of scheduling problems can be solved with the assistance of the graph theory. Therefore, the second part of the toolbox is aimed at graph theory algorithms. All algorithms are available as a method of the main class *Graph* which is used to describe the directed graph. There are several different ways to create an instance of the class *Graph*. The graph is generally described by an adjacency matrix. In this case, the *Graph* object is created by the command with the following syntax:

```
G = graph('adj',A)
```

where the variable A is an adjacency matrix. Similarly, it is possible to create the *Graph* by an incidence matrix. Another way how to create the *Graph* object is based on a matrix of edge weights.
The toolbox is equipped with a simple but powerful editor of graphs called *Graphedit* based on the System Handle Graphics of Matlab. It provides a simple and intuitive way to construct directed graphs with various user parameters on nodes and edges. (see Fig. 4). The constructed graph can be easily used to create an instance of the class *Graph* which can be exported to the Matlab workspace or saved to a binary mat-file. In addition, *Graphedit* contains a system of plug-ins which allow one to extend its functionality by the user.

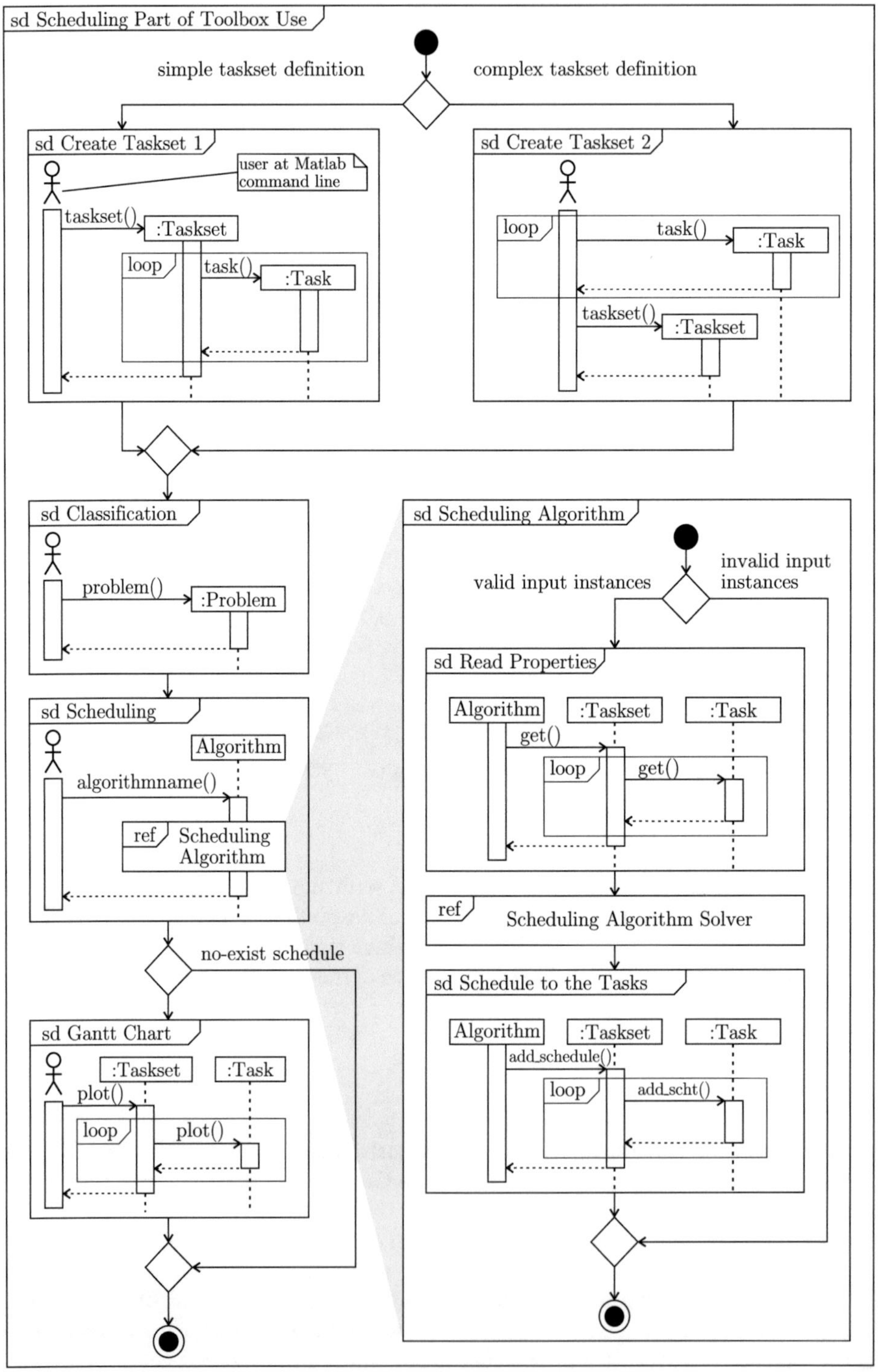

Fig. 3. UML Interaction Overview Diagram of a typical toolbox workflow of the scheduling problem solution

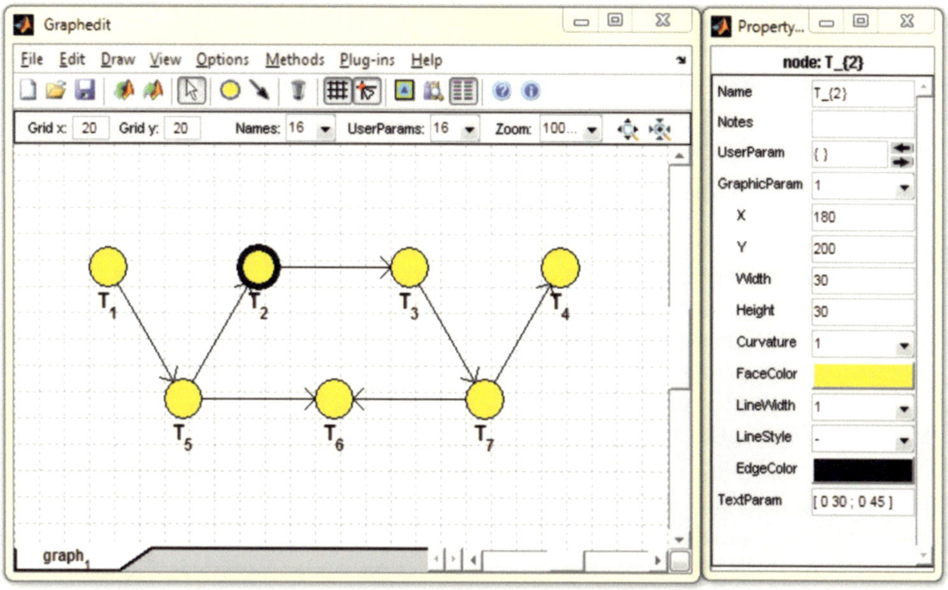

Fig. 4. Graphedit

Moreover, due to the close relationship between the scheduling and graph algorithms, each object *Graph* can be transformed to an object *Taskset* and vice versa. Obviously, the nodes from the graph are transformed to the tasks in the *Taskset* and the edges are transformed to the precedence constraints and vice versa according to the user specification.

3. Implemented algorithms

The biggest part of the toolbox is constituted by scheduling algorithms. There are a large variety of algorithms solving both simple problems (on a single processor) and practically oriented issues. This section shows several of them demonstrated on real applications.

3.1 List Scheduling Algorithm

List Scheduling (LS) is a basic and popular heuristic algorithm applicable on scheduling of set of tasks on a single and parallel processors as well. In this algorithm the tasks are ordered in a pre-specified list defining their priority. Whenever a processor becomes idle, the first available task on the list is scheduled and removed from the list. Where the availability of a task means that the task has been released and if there are precedence constraints, all its predecessors have already been processed (Leung, 2004). The algorithm terminates when all tasks from the list are scheduled. Its time complexity is $\mathcal{O}(n)$.

The accuracy of the algorithm depends on the order in which tasks appear on the list. There are many strategies defining the order of tasks in the list, e.g. the Earliest Starting Time first (EST), the Earliest Completion Time first (ECT), the Longest Processing Time first (LPT), the Shortest Processing Time first (SPT) etc. The appropriate choose of the strategy depends on the particular scheduling instance.

The List Scheduling algorithm is implemented in TORSCHE Scheduling Toolbox under function `listsch` which also allows to choice one of the implemented strategy defining the order of tasks. Furthermore, the algorithm steps can be displayed in the MABLAB workspace by enabling the verbose mode. Moreover, the last algorithm version is able to solve scheduling problems on unrelated parallel processors. The syntax of `listsch` function is:

```
TS = listsch(T, problem, processors[, strategy][, verbose])
TS = listsch(T, problem, processors[, option])
```

where:

`T`	is the instance of the *Taskset* class without schedule,
`TS`	is the instance of the *Taskset* class with schedule,
`problem`	is the instance of the *Problem* class,
`processors`	is the number of processors,
`strategy`	is the strategy (like LPT, SPT, EST, ...),
`verbose`	is a level of verbosity,
`option`	is the optimization option setting.

This subsection concludes by an example. The example solves a problem of a chair manufacturing by two workers (cabinetmakers). Their goal is to make four legs, one seat and one backrest of the chair and assembly all of these parts within minimal time. Release time of the task representing the backrest making is equal to 20 time units. Moreover, the assemblage is divided into two stages (assembly$_{1/2}$ and assembly$_{2/2}$). Fig. 5 shows the representation of the mentioned problem instance by a graph.

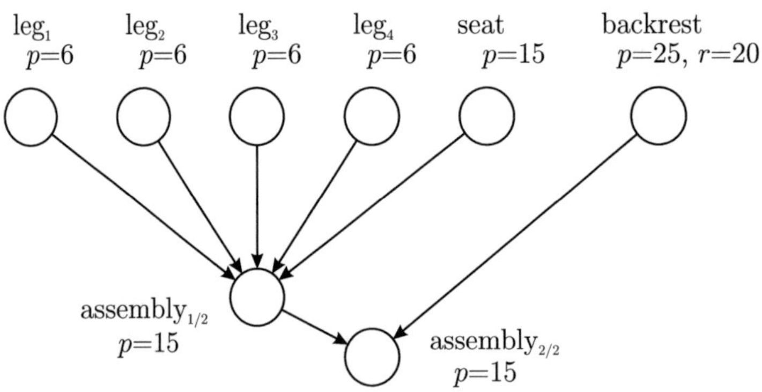

Fig. 5. Graph representing the chair manufacturing

Solution of the scheduling problem is shown in the following steps:

1. Create desired tasks.

```
>> T1 = task('leg1',6)
Task "leg1"
 Processing time: 6
 Release time:    0

>> T2 = task('leg2',6);
>> T3 = task('leg3',6);
>> T4 = task('leg4',6);
>> T5 = task('seat',6);
>> T6 = task('backrest',25,20);
>> T7 = task('assembly1/2',15);
>> T8 = task('assembly2/2',15);
```

2. Define precedence constraints by adjacency matrix `prec`. Matrix has size $n \times n$ where n is the number of tasks.

```
>> prec = [0 0 0 0 0 1 0 0;...
           0 0 0 0 0 1 0 0;...
           0 0 0 0 0 1 0 0;...
           0 0 0 0 0 1 0 0;...
           0 0 0 0 0 1 0 0;...
           0 0 0 0 0 0 0 1;...
           0 0 0 0 0 0 0 1;...
           0 0 0 0 0 0 0 0];
```

3. Create an object of taskset from recently defined objects.

```
>> T = taskset([T1 T2 T3 T4 T5 T6 T7 T8],prec)
Set of 8 tasks
 There are precedence constraints
```

4. Define solved problem.

```
>> p = problem('P|rj,prec|Cmax')
P|rj,prec|Cmax
```

5. Call the List Scheduling algorithm on taskset `T` where the scheduling problem is defined by object `p` and number of processors available for manufacturing is equal to 2. The algorithm use the Shortest Processing Time first (SPT) strategy.

```
>> TS = listsch(T,p,2,'SPT')
Set of 8 tasks
 There are precedence constraints
 There is schedule: List Scheduling
   Solving time: 0.1404s
```

6. Display the final schedule by standard plot function, see Fig. 6.

```
>> plot(TS)
```

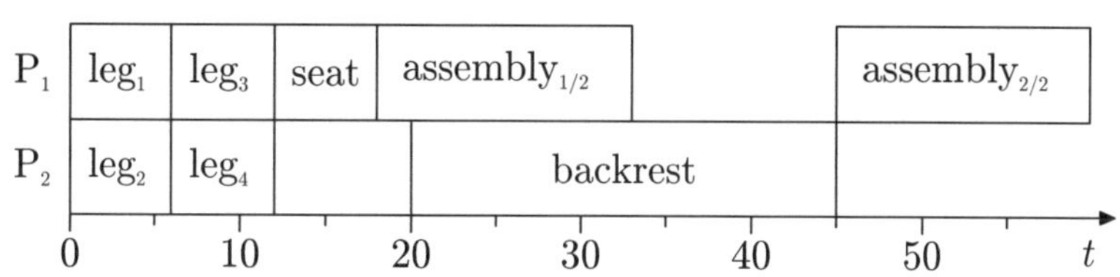

Fig. 6. The chair manufacturing schedule

3.2 Scheduling on Parallel Identical Processors

This section presents a SAT (satisfiability of boolean expression) based algorithm for the scheduling problem $P|prec|C_{max}$, i.e. the scheduling of tasks with precedence constraints on the set of parallel identical processors while minimizing the schedule makespan. The main idea is to formulate the scheduling problem in the form of CNF (conjunctive normal form) clauses (Crama & Hammer, 2006; Memik & Fallah, 2002).

In the case of the $P|prec|C_{max}$ problem, each CNF clause is a function of the boolean variables in the form x_{ijk}. If the task T_i is started at time unit j on the processor k then $x_{ijk} = true$, otherwise $x_{ijk} = false$. For each task T_i, where $i = 1 \ldots n$, there are $S \times R$ Boolean variables, where S denotes the maximum number of time units and R denotes the total number of processors.

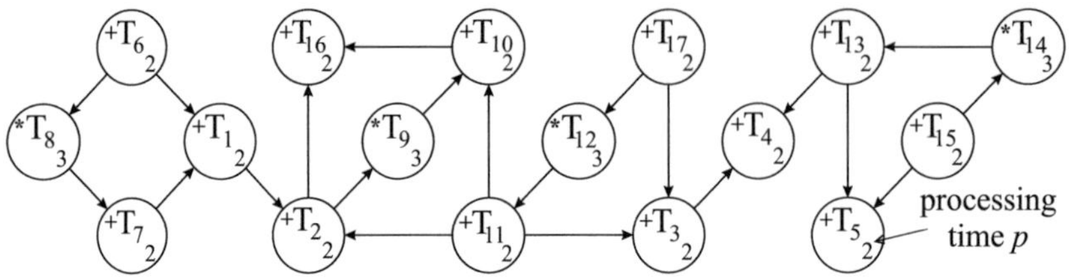

Fig. 7. Jaumann wave digital filter

```
>> procTime = [2,2,2,2,2,2,2,3,3,2,2,3,2,3,2,2,2];
>> prec = sparse([6,7,1,11,11,17,3,13,13,15,8,6,2, 9,11,12,17,14,15,2 ,10],...
                 [1,1,2, 2, 3, 3,4, 4, 5, 5,7,8,9,10,10,11,12,13,14,16,16],...
                 [1,1,1, 1, 1, 1,1, 1, 1, 1,1,1,1, 1, 1, 1, 1, 1, 1, 1, 1],17,17);
>> TS = taskset(procTime,prec);
>> TS = satsch(TS,problem("P|prec|Cmax"),2)
Set of 17 tasks
 There are precedence constraints
 There is schedule: SAT solver
   SUM solving time: 0.06s
   MAX solving time: 0.04s
   Number of iterations: 2
>> plot(TS)
```

Fig. 8. Solution of the scheduling problem $P|prec|C_{max}$ in the toolbox

The Boolean variables are constrained by the following three rules: 1. For each task, exactly one of the $S \times R$ variables has to be equal to *true*. 2. If there are precedence constraints such that T_u is the predecessor of T_v, then T_v cannot start before the execution of T_u is finished. 3. At any time unit, there is at most one task executed on a given processor. The rules result in a set of clauses in CNF generated by the algorithm in the toolbox that are consequently solved in a selected SAT solver.

The toolbox cooperates with the *zChaff* solver (Moskewicz et al., 2001) to decide whether the set of clauses is satisfiable. If it is, the schedule within S time units is feasible. An optimal schedule is found in an iterative manner. First, the List Scheduling algorithm is used to find the initial value of S. Then the algorithm iteratively decreases the value of S by one and tests the feasibility of the solution. The iterative algorithm finishes when the solution is not feasible. An example of the $P|prec|C_{max}$ problem can be taken from the digital signal processing area. A typical scheduling problem is to optimize the speed of a computation loop, e.g constituting the Jaumann wave digital filter (de Groot et al., 1992). The goal is to minimize the computation time of the filter loop, shown as a directed acyclic graph in Fig. 7. The nodes in the graph represent the tasks (i.e. operations of the loop) and the edges represent the precedence constraints. The nodes are labeled by the operation type ("+" or "$*$") and processing time p_i. The example in Fig. 7 considers two parallel identical processors, i.e. two general arithmetic units.

Fig. 8 shows the consecutive steps performed in the toolbox. The first step defines the set of the tasks with the precedence constraints for the scheduling algorithm `satsch`. The resulting schedule is displayed by the `plot` command. The optimal schedule is depicted in Fig. 9.

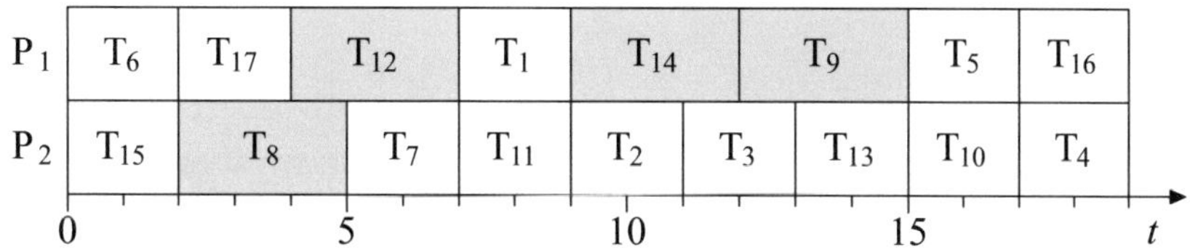

Fig. 9. The optimal schedule of the Jaumann filter

3.3 Cyclic Scheduling

The subsequent example has its application in digital signal processing (DSP) too but it uses a cyclic approach. *Cyclic scheduling* deals with a set of tasks (operations) that have to be performed an infinite number of times (Hanen & Munier, 1995). This approach is also applicable if the number of loop repetitions is large enough. If the execution of the operations belonging to different iterations can interleave, the schedule is called *overlapped*. An overlapped schedule can be more effective especially if processors are pipelined hardware units or precedence delays are considered. The *periodic schedule* is a schedule of one iteration that is repeated with a fixed time interval called a *period* (also called the *initiation interval*). The aim is then to find a periodic schedule with a minimum period (Hanen & Munier, 1995).

3.3.1 The Problem Outline

A DSP algorithm, used as an example, is a wave digital filter (LWDF) (Vesterbacka et al., 1994). Its computation loop, shown in Fig. 10(a), consists of five tasks. Their processing times are given by parameters of the used floating point arithmetic library for FPGA (Field-programmable gate array) circuits.

The operations in a computation loop can be considered as a set of n tasks $\mathcal{T} = \{T_1, T_2, \dots, T_n\}$ to be performed N times where N is usually very large. One execution of $\mathcal{T}$ labeled with the integer index $k \geq 1$ is called an *iteration*. The scheduling problem is to find a start time $s_i(k)$ of every occurrence T_i.

The data dependencies of this problem can be modeled by a directed graph $G(V, E)$. Each task (node in V) is characterized by the processing time p_i. Edge $(i, j) \in E$ from the node i to j is weighted by a couple of integer constants l_{ij} and h_{ij}. Length l_{ij} represents the minimal distance in clock cycles from the start time of the task T_i to the start time of T_j and is always greater than zero. Its value corresponds to the input-output latency of the used arithmetic

for k=1 **to** N **do**
  T_1: $a(k) = X(k) - c(k-2)$
  T_2: $b(k) = a(k) * \alpha$
  T_3: $c(k) = b(k) + X(k)$
  T_4: $d(k) = b(k) + c(k-2)$
  T_5: $Y(k) = X(k-1) + d(k)$
end

(a)

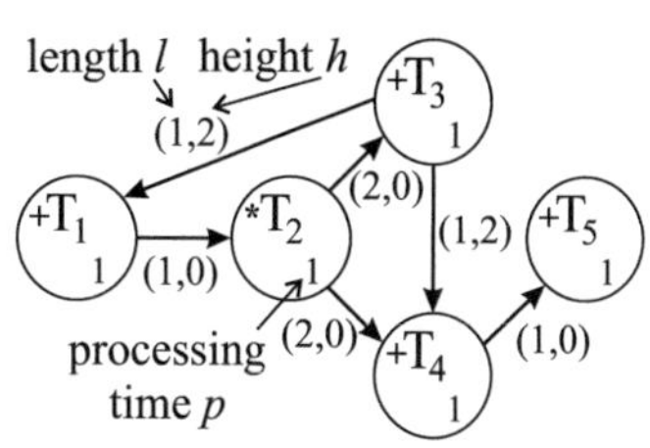

(b)

Fig. 10. Lattice wave digital filter (LWDF)

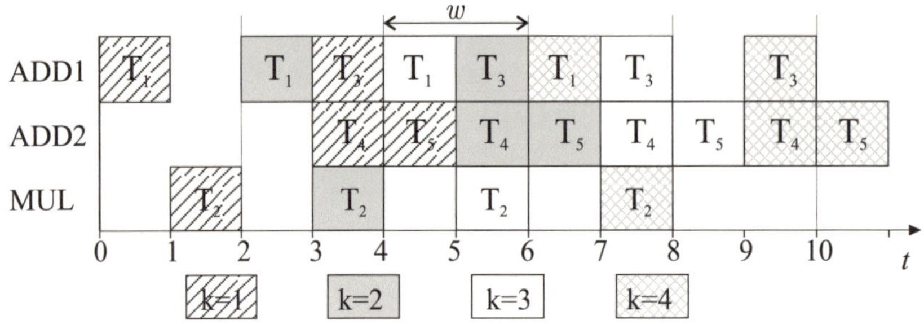

Fig. 11. An optimal schedule with period $w = 2$

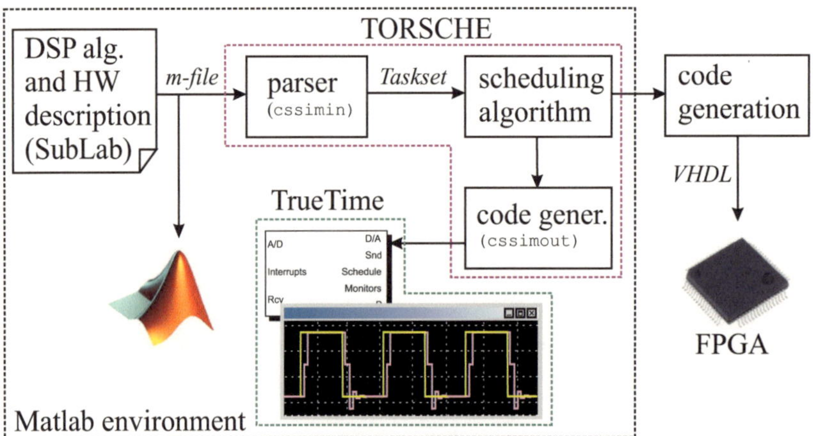

Fig. 12. Code to code generation

units. In our example in Fig. 10(b), the input-output latency of ADD (MUL) unit is 1 (2) clock cycles. On the other hand, the height h_{ij} specifies the shift of the iteration index (dependence distance) related to the data produced by T_i and read (consumed) by T_j.

Assuming a *periodic schedule* with the *period* w (i.e. the constant repetition time of each task), each edge $(i, j) \in E$ represents one precedence relation constraint $s_j - s_i \geq l_{ij} - w \cdot h_{ij}$, where s_i denotes the start time of task T_i in the first iteration. Fig. 10(b) shows the data dependence graph of the computation loop shown in Fig. 10(a). When the number of processors m is restricted, the cyclic scheduling problem becomes NP–complete (Hanen & Munier, 1995). An optimal solution of the example from Fig. 10 is shown in Fig. 11.

3.3.2 Solution in the Toolbox

In the toolbox, we formulate this scheduling problem as a problem of Integer Linear Programming (Šůcha & Hanzálek, 2009). In addition, the toolbox provides the possibility to simulate scheduled iterative loops in Matlab/Simulink using TrueTime tool (Andersson et al., 2005). The idea is depicted in Fig. 12. An instance of this scheduling problem (*Taskset* object) can be created manually but it can be generated automatically from a DSP algorithm and HW description in *SubLab*, a language compatible with Matlab. The main advantage of *SubLab* is that

```
function Y=lwdf(X)

%Arithmetic Units Declaration
struct('operator','+','number',2, ...
       'proctime',1,'latency',1);
struct('operator','*','number',1, ...
       'proctime',1,'latency',2);

struct('frequency',2000000);

%Variables Declaration
K = 10000;        alpha = 0.375;
a = zeros(1,K);   b = zeros(1,K);
c = zeros(1,K);   d = zeros(1,K);
Y = zeros(1,K);

%Iterative Algorithm
for k=3:K
    a(k) = X(k) - c(k-2);
    b(k) = a(k) * alpha;
    c(k) = b(k) + X(k);
    d(k) = b(k) + c(k-2);
    Y(k) = X(k-1) + d(k);
end
```

Fig. 13. LWDF algorithm in SubLab

```
>> [TS,m]=cssimin(dsvffile,schoptions);
>> prob=problem('CSCH');
>> TS=cycsch(TS, prob, m, schoptions);
>> plot(TS);
>> cssimout(TS,'simple_init.m','code.m');
```

Fig. 14. Solution of a cyclic scheduling problem in the toolbox

its code can be both transformed into the *Taskset* object and directly executed in the Matlab environment in order to check the iterative loops that were input (see Fig. 13).
Fig. 14 shows how the cyclic scheduling problem can be solved in the toolbox in three steps: input file parsing (function `cssimin`), cyclic scheduling (function `cycsch`) and True-Time code generation (function `cssimout`). The simulation is realized so that the scheduled code is time-exact executed by the *TrueTime Kernel* block which can be interconnected with other Matlab/Simulink blocks. It allows one to directly verify the behavior of the scheduled DSP algorithm interconnected with an appropriate model of the dynamic system.
Furthermore, the scheduling results can be used to generate parallel code for FPGAs in VHDL language. The concept is the same as for the simulation in TrueTime (see Fig. 12) but the output is a VHDL file which can be embedded into an FPGA design defining arithmetic units, interfaces, etc. FPGA code generation is not freely available in TORSCHE.

3.4 Minimum Cost Multi-commodity Flow Problem

Various optimization problems (e.g. routing) from the graph and network flow theory can be reformulated in terms of a minimum cost multi-commodity flow (MMCF) problem. The objective of the MMCF is to find the cheapest possible ways of sending a certain amounts of flows through the network. Therefore, TORSCHE includes a `multicommodityflow` function.

The MMCF problem is defined by a directed flow network graph $G(V, E)$, where the edge $(u, v) \in E$ from node $u \in V$ to node $v \in V$ has a capacity c_{uv} and a cost a_{uv}. There are ψ commodities $K_1, K_2, \ldots, K_\psi$ defined by $K_i = (source_i, sink_i, b_i)$ where $source_i$ and $sink_i$ stand for source and sink node of commodity i, and b_i is the volume of the demand. The flow of commodity i along the edge (u, v) is $f_i(u, v)$. The objective is to find an assignment of the flow $f_i(u, v)$ which minimizes the total cost $J = \sum_{\forall(u,v)\in E} \left(a_{uv} \cdot \sum_{i=1}^{\psi} f_i(u, v) \right)$ and satisfies the following constraints:

$$
\begin{array}{rcll}
\sum_{i=1}^{\psi} f_i(u,v) & \leq & c_{uv} & \forall(u,v) \in E, \\
\sum_{u\in V} f_i(u,w) & = & \sum_{v\in V} f_i(w,v) & w \in V \setminus \{source_i, sink_i\}, \\
 & & & \forall i = 1 \ldots \psi, \\
\sum_{w\in V} f_i(source_i, w) & = & \sum_{w\in V} f_i(w, sink_i) = b_i & \forall i = 1 \ldots \psi.
\end{array}
$$

The function `multicommodityflow` solves MMCF problem by the transformation to the linear programming problem (Korte & Vygen, 2006).

3.4.1 Example of the Urban Traffic Scheduling

As an example, we show how to find the time schedule for light-controlled intersections in a urban traffic region in Prague by the TORSCHE toolbox.

The light controlled intersections are characterized by several parameters: the number of light phases, phase split, offset time and a list of streets from which the vehicles flow (Guberinić et al., 2008). The term phase means state of traffic lights on the intersection. The number of phases and the list of streets are partially given by the urban architecture of the intersection and partially by the intersection control strategy (i.e. one-way street, directional roadway marking). Both of these parameters are constant. On the other hand, the split and offset can be changed dynamically during a day. The *split* τ_{vj} defines the time interval of phase j for which the vehicle flow can go through the intersection v from one or more streets (Papageorgiou et al., 2003). The *offset* φ_{uv} is a certain time delay between phases of two successive intersections u and v. When the offset is zero, all lights in the region turn on and off at the same time. It is called the synchronized strategy. In the *green wave* strategy, the traffic light changes with time delay between the light phases of two successive intersections. As a result, signals switch as the green wave (Nagatani, 2007).

The goal is to find the offset φ_{uv} respecting the green wave strategy and the split τ_{vj} which minimizes the total cost J and considers a constant *control period* $P_v = \sum_{\forall j} \tau_{vj}$ of intersection v such that $P_1 = P_2 = \cdots = P$.

For the first step, a traffic region is modeled as an oriented graph $G(V, E)$. Nodes V of the graph represent the intersections and edges E represent the streets. See Fig. 15 where the *Graphedit* tool of TORSCHE is utilized to construct the graph. Sink and source nodes are drawn as rectangles. The edges include two parameters; the first one is cost a_{uv} and the second one is capacity c_{uv} of the street (u, v). The cost is given by the street length in meters. The capacity of the street is given by the number of lanes ℓ_{uv} in the street as $c_{uv} = \ell_{uv} \cdot W_{uv}/l$ where W_{uv} is a maximal allowed vehicle speed in the street in ms^{-1} and l is the *unit vehicle* length including distance between vehicles. Let us assume that, in our case, the speed is $W_{uv} = 13.8\,\mathrm{ms}^{-1}$ ($50\,\mathrm{km/h}$) and the unit vehicle length is $l = 5\,\mathrm{m}$, then the capacity of one lane street is $2.8\,\mathrm{s}^{-1}$. The final graph is exported from the *Graphedit* tool to the Matlab workspace as graph object `G`.

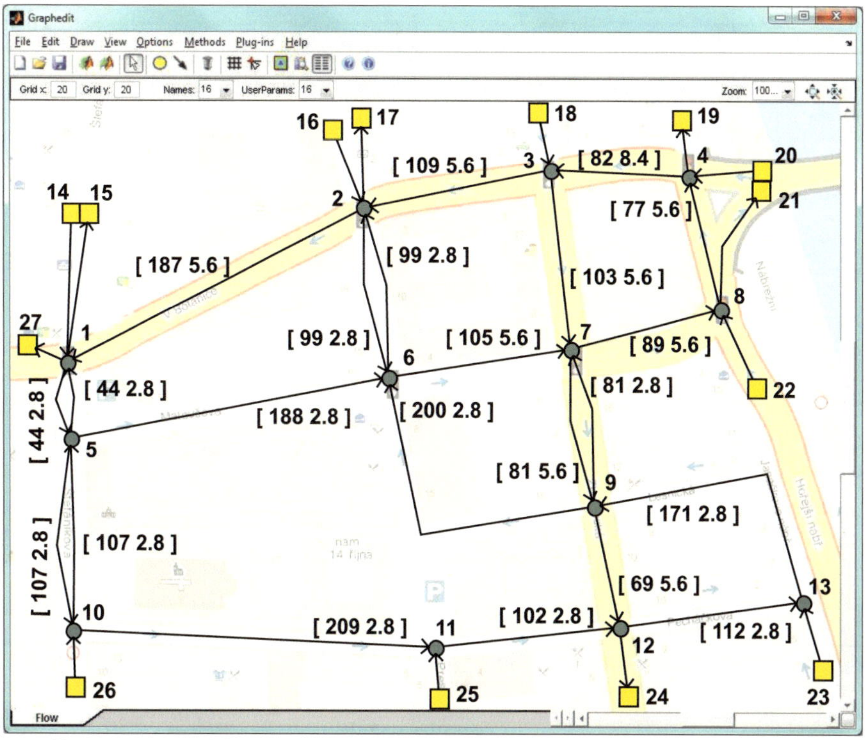

Fig. 15. Traffic region model

In the second step, the multicommodity flow method in the following form is called:

```
>> Gm = multicommodityflow(G,source,sink,b)
```

where the vectors `source`, `sink` and `b` define the required multi-commodity flow as is it described above. These variables are shown in Table 1. The graph `Gm` includes an assignment of optimal multi-commodity flow to the edges. We assume the drivers make their decision in a similar way. Table 2 shows a part of the assignment $f_i(u,v) : u = 6 \vee v = 6$. The complete result can be obtained from the *Graph* object by the command:

```
>> F = get(Gm,'edl')
```

3.4.2 Tasks Definition for Intersection

In the last step, the phase j split τ_{vj} and the offset φ_{uv} for each light controlled intersection $v \in V$ are found. Continuous vehicle flow from the street (u,v) over a given number of intersection phases can be formalized as one task T_{uv} from the scheduling theory point of view. The number of phases is given by the urban architecture of the intersection and by the intersection control strategy. The processing time p_{uv} of task T_{uv} is calculated by Algorithm 1 (Part of the Algorithm shows the solution of the consecutive steps in TORSCHE for intersection 6). This algorithm computes the processing time from the assignment of MMCF $f_i(u,v)$, from the control period P and from the precedence constraints of the tasks (defined by the intersection control strategy).

K_i	K_1	K_2	K_3	K_4	K_5	K_6	K_7	K_8
$source_i$	14	14	14	14	16	16	16	16
$sink_i$	24	17	21	27	24	21	15	27
$b_i[10^{-3}s^{-1}]$	4.9	1.9	3.1	30.1	10.1	12.1	1.2	6.6
K_i	K_9	K_{10}	K_{11}	K_{12}	K_{13}	K_{14}	K_{15}	K_{16}
$source_i$	18	18	18	18	18	20	20	20
$sink_i$	24	17	21	15	27	19	24	17
$b_i[10^{-3}s^{-1}]$	32.7	3.3	9.3	2.1	11.3	8.9	13.4	8.1
K_i	K_{17}	K_{18}	K_{19}	K_{20}	K_{21}	K_{22}	K_{23}	K_{24}
$source_i$	20	20	22	22	22	22	23	23
$sink_i$	15	27	19	21	15	27	24	17
$b_i[10^{-3}s^{-1}]$	7.9	41.7	11.7	88.5	4.7	25.1	8.6	4.3
K_i	K_{25}	K_{26}	K_{27}	K_{28}	K_{29}	K_{30}	K_{31}	K_{32}
$source_i$	23	23	25	25	26	26	26	26
$sink_i$	21	27	24	21	24	21	15	27
$b_i[10^{-3}s^{-1}]$	6.5	3.6	9.6	0.4	15.9	1.9	5.7	6.5

Table 1. Required traffic region multi-commodity flow instances

Algorithm 1 Processing time computation

1. Create tasks T_{uv}, each with temporary processing time $p'_{uv} = \sum_{i=1}^{\psi} f_i(u,v)$.

```
>> T56 = task('T(5,6)', 0.0069)
>> T26 = task('T(2,6)', 0.0222);
>> T96 = task('T(9,6)',0.0079);
```

2. Group the tasks into a *taskset* and add precedence constrains.

```
>> prec6 = [0 1 1; 0 0 0; 0 0 0];
>> TS6 = taskset([T56 T26 T96],prec6);
```

3. Compute a length of critical path CP_v by the *asap* (as soon as possible) function.

```
>> TS6.asap;
>> asapStart = asap(TS6,'asap');
>> CP6 = max(asapStart + TS6.ProcTime)
CP6 =
    0.0291
```

4. From the length of the critical path and control period P we obtain processing time p_{uv} as a linear proportion of flow: $p_{uv} = p'_{uv} \cdot P/CP_v$.

```
>> P = 90;
>> TS6.ProcTime = TS6.ProcTime * P / CP6;
```

	K_i	K_2	K_3	K_5	K_6	K_{24}	K_{26}	K_{30}	
u	v			$f_i(u,v)$ $[10^{-3}s^{-1}]$					$\sum_{i=1}^{\psi} f_i(u,v)$
2	6	0	0	10.1	12.1	0	0	0	22.2
5	6	1.9	3.1	0	0	0	0	1.9	6.9
9	6	0	0	0	0	4.3	3.6	0	7.9
6	2	1.9	0	0	0	4.3	3.6	0	9.8
6	7	0	3.1	10.1	12.1	0	0	1.9	27.2

Table 2. Multi-commodity flow assignment

3.4.3 Scheduling with Communication Delay

The intersection phase offset and split are computed for the green wave strategy. The green wave strategy, specified by the engineering skills, extends the tasks precedence constraints by the relationships between successive intersection tasks. Each of those relationships defines the offset φ_{uv} as a time, which a vehicle needs to pass from intersection u to intersection v. The φ_{uv} is given by the street length a_{uv} and vehicle speed W_{uv} as $\varphi_{uv} = a_{uv}/W_{uv}$.

The split can be found by an algorithm for scheduling with a communication delay (Chrétienne et al., 1995). The *scheduling with communication delay* problem extends the precedence constraints in the classical scheduling by the communication delay between dependent tasks assigned to distinct processors. In our case the communication delay is equal to the offset φ_{uv}.
Let `D` be a matrix of communication delays, where the elements are φ_{uv} in the case that the offset between intersections u and v is considered, and zero otherwise. We can classify our instances as tasks with precedence constraints in an out-tree form, communication delays, unlimited number of processors and no duplication of tasks. In Graham and Błażewicz notation it can be denoted as $P_\infty|out\text{-}tree, c_{jk}|C_{max}$. This problem can be solved in $\mathcal{O}(n)$ time by the allgorithm presented in (Chrétienne, 1989) which is implemented in the TORSCHE toolbox as a function `chretienne`.

Fig. 16 shows the problem solution in the toolbox for three intersections (6, 7 and 8).

```
>> T56 = task('T(5,6)', 21.3);
>> T26 = task('T(2,6)', 68.7);
>> T96 = task('T(9,6)', 24.4);
>> prec6 = [0 1 1; 0 0 0; 0 0 0];
>> TS6 = taskset([T56 T26 T96],prec6);
>> T67 = task('T(6,7)', 29.6);
>> T37 = task('T(3,7)', 60.4);
>> T97 = task('T(9,7)',  7.5);
>> prec7 = [0 1 1; 0 0 0; 0 0 0];
>> TS7 = taskset([T67 T37 T97],prec7);
>> T78 = task('T(7,8)',  18.4);
>> T228 = task('T(22,8)', 71.6);
>> prec8 = [0 1; 0 0];
>> TS8 = taskset([T78 T228],prec8);

>> TSall = [TS6 TS7 TS8];
>> TSall.Prec(1,4) = 1;
>> TSall.Prec(4,7) = 1;

>> D = zeros(size(TSall.Prec));
>> D(1,4) = 9.5;
>> D(4,7) = 8;

>> prob = ...
  problem('Pinf|prec,out-tree,cjk|Cmax');

>> TSall = chretienne(TSall,p,Inf,D);
>> plot(TSall);
```

Fig. 16. Solution of the scheduling problem in the toolbox

First, the taskset object `TSall` with eight tasks corresponding to the intersection control is defined. The tasks and precedence constraints among them are shown in Fig. 17(a). The precedence constraints given by the green-wave strategy are drawn as solid lines. Consequently, matrix `D` and the notation of the problem `prob` is defined. Finally, the scheduling problem

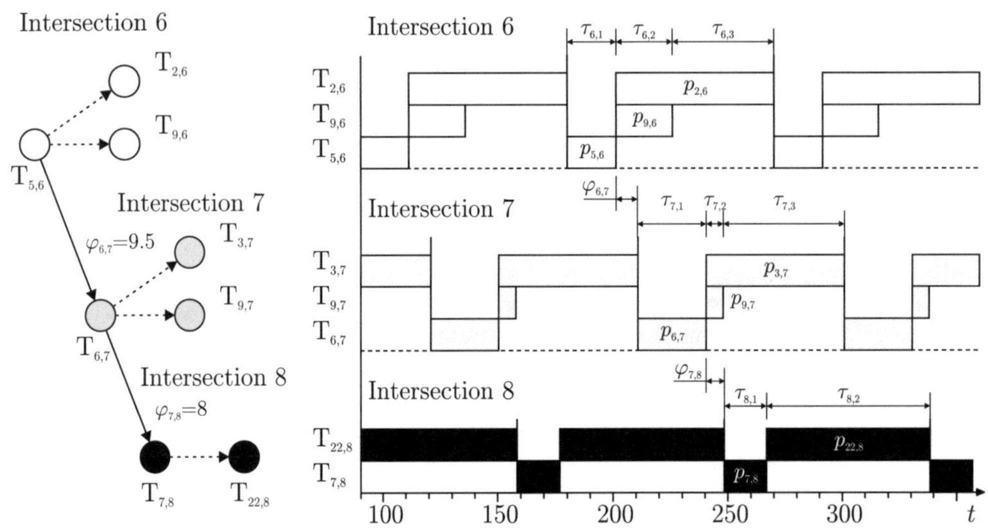

(a) Precedence constraints (b) Gantt chart for vehicle flow including split and offset mark

Fig. 17. The intersections (6, 7 and 8) control

is solved by the algorithm `chretienne` and the resulting Gantt chart is shown in Fig. 17(b). The figure shows the tasks for the three considered intersections including the processing time p_{uv}, split τ_{vj} and offset φ_{uv}. The split is given by the processing time of the scheduled tasks. The tasks are repeated with period P.

3.5 Visualization of the Scheduling Results

In the toolbox, there is a possibility to simulate or visualize the acquired scheduling results in the Matlab/Simulink environment through the use of the Matlab Virtual Reality toolbox, which is a standard part of Matlab. TORSCHE allows users to create their own project with 3-D animation in the Virtual Reality toolbox and interconnect it with a schedule obtained in TORSCHE. Consequently, both simulation and visualization are realized in Matlab/Simulink and in case of visualization, it is possible to capture any frame or a stream video file of the animation.

The hoist scheduling problem is chosen as an example for the visualization. The hoist scheduling problem (Manier & Bloch, 2003) deals with the problem how to schedule the hoist movements to perform a material handling between several tanks with elecrolyte solution, where the material is processed. The objective of this problem is to find a schedule which maximizes the processing throughput. The hoist scheduling problem can be solved by the `singlehoist` algorithm that is available in the TORSCHE toolbox. The problem is represented so that the tasks correspond with the movements of the hoist (load/unload station $\rightarrow$ Bath 1, Bath 1 $\rightarrow$ Bath 2, Bath 2 $\rightarrow$ Bath 3, Bath 3 $\rightarrow$ load/unload station).

The problem solution in the toolbox is shown in Fig. 18(a). The interconnection between the tasks and the project with 3-D animation is realized by a user defined text-file. Fig. 18(b) shows a fragment of the text-file containing the code that describes the movement of the hoist corresponding to the first task. The interconnection is performed in the function `adduserparam`. This function parses the code of the input-text file and

```
>> a = [0 70 70 30];
>> b = [0 100 200 75];
>> C = toeplitz([0 15 20 25]);
>> d = [36 36 36 51];
>> T = taskset(d);
>> T.TSUserParam.SetupTime   = C;
>> T.TSUserParam.minDistance = a;
>> T.TSUserParam.maxDistance = b;
>> TS = singlehoist(T);
>> adduserparam(TS,'onehoist.txt');
>> name  = 'onehoist.wrl';
>> ports = visiscontrolports('Output',
        'HoistArm',3,...
>> VRin  = vrports('Hoist','translation',...
>> taskset2simulink(name, TS, ports, VRin,
                    500, []);
```

(a) Solution in the toolbox

```
%File name: 'onehoist.txt'
task1
repeat 0:1:4
HoistArm(1) = HoistArm(1) + 1;
repeat 0:1:7
HoistArm(2) = HoistArm(2) - 0.5;
...
endparam

task2
repeat 0:1:5
HoistArm(1) = HoistArm(1) - 1;
repeat 0:1:9
HoistArm(2) = HoistArm(2) + 1;
...
endparam
```

(b) Visualization description (file: onehoist.txt)

Fig. 18. Matlab code for hoist scheduling visualization

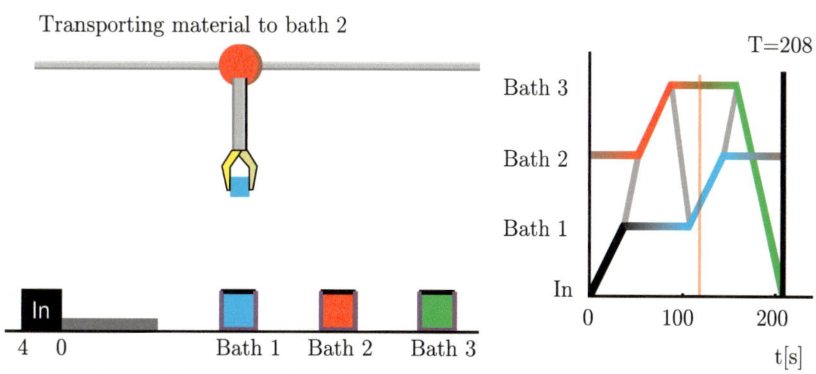

Fig. 19. Visualization of the hoist scheduling problem

assigns an appropriate code of visualization to each task. The visualization is subsequently performed by executing an automatically generated Matlab/Simulink file. The resulting problem visualization is shown in Fig. 19, and a video file can be found on `http://rtime.felk.cvut.cz/scheduling-toolbox/video`.

4. Conclusions

This chapter presents the TORSCHE Scheduling Toolbox for Matlab covering: scheduling on monoprocessor/dedicated processors/parallel processors, open shop/flow shop/job shop scheduling, cyclic scheduling and real-time scheduling. The toolbox includes scheduling algorithms that have been used for various applications as scheduling of Digital Signal Processing algorithms on a hardware architecture with pipelined arithmetic units, scheduling the movements of hoists in a manufacturing environment and scheduling of light controlled intersections in urban traffic. Moreover, the toolbox already has several real applications. It has been used for the development of a new method for re-configuration of the tasks or a process in an embedded avionics application (Muniyappa, 2009). Simulations in TORSCHE also helped to develop a method optimizing the jitter of tasks in a real-time system (Liu et al., 2009). Recently, TORSCHE has become a part of a textbook for courses in scheduling "Scheduling: Theory, Algorithms, and Systems" written by M. Pinedo (Pinedo, 2008). The actual version of the toolbox with documentation and screencasts is freely available at `http://rtime.felk.cvut.cz/scheduling-toolbox/`.

5. References

Andersson, M., Henriksson, D. & Cervin, A. (2005). *TrueTime 1.3–Reference Manual*, Department of Automatic Control, Lund University, Sweden, Lund University, Sweden. `http://www.control.lth.se/truetime/`.

Andresen, M., Bräsel, H., Engelhardt, F. & Werner, F. (2003). *LiSA - A Library of Scheduling Algortihms*, Otto-von-Guericke-Universität Magdeburg. `http://lisa.math.uni-magdeburg.de/`.

Blazewicz, J., Lenstra, J. & Kan, A. R. (1983). Scheduling subject to resource constraints. Classification and complexity, *Discrete Applied Mathematics* **5**(5): 11–24.

Chrétienne, P. (1989). A polynomial algorithm to optimally schedule tasks on a virtual distributed system under tree-like precedence constraints, *European Journal of Operational Research* **43**(43): 225–230.

Chrétienne, P., Coffman, E. G., Lenstraand, J. K. & Liu, Z. (eds) (1995). *Scheduling theory and its applications*, John Wiley & Sons Ltd, Baffins Lane, Chichester, West Sussex PO19 1UD, England.

Crama, Y. & Hammer, P. L. (2006). Boolean functions: Theory, algorithms and applications. `http://www.rogp.hec.ulg.ac.be/Crama/Publications/BookPage.html`.

de Groot, S. H., Gerez, S. & Herrmann, O. (1992). Range-chart-guided iterative data-flow graph scheduling, *Circuits and Systems I: Fundamental Theory and Applications, IEEE Transactions on* **39**: 351–364.

Gonzalez, M. et al. (2008). MAST (Modeling and Analysis Suite for Real-Time Applications), `http://mast.unican.es/`.

Guberinić, S., Šenborn, G. & Lazić, B. (2008). *Optimal Traffic Control: Urban Intersections*, CRC Press, 6000 Broken Sound Parkway NW, Suite 300, Boca Raton.

Hanen, C. & Munier, A. (1995). A study of the cyclic scheduling problem on parallel processors, *Discrete Applied Mathematics* **57**: 167–192.

ILOG (2009). *ILOG CP Optimizer*, IBM Corporation, ILOG Europe, 9 rue de Verdun, BP 85, 94253 Gentilly Cedex. `http://www.ilog.com/products/cpoptimizer/`.

Korte, B. H. & Vygen, J. (2006). *Combinatorial Optimization: Theory and Algorithms*, third edn, Springer-Verlag, Berlin, Heidelberg.

Kutil, M., Šůcha, P., Sojka, M. & Hanzálek, Z. (2007). *TORSCHE Scheduling Toolbox for Matlab: User's Guide*, Centre for Applied Cybernetics, Department of Control Engineering, Czech Technical University in Prague. `http://rtime.felk.cvut.cz/scheduling-toolbox/`.

Leung, J. Y.-T. (2004). *Handbook of Scheduling*, Chapman & Hall/CRC.

Liu, Z., Zhao, H., Li, P. & Wang, J. (2009). An optimization model for io jitter in device-level rtos, *ITNG '09: Proceedings of the 2009 Sixth International Conference on Information Technology: New Generations*, IEEE Computer Society, Washington, DC, USA, pp. 1528–1533.

Manier, M. A. & Bloch, C. (2003). A classification for hoist scheduling problems, *International Journal of Flexible Manufacturing Systems* **15**(1): 37–55.

Memik, S. O. & Fallah, F. (2002). Accelerated SAT-based scheduling of control/data flow graphs, *ICCD '02: Proceedings of the 2002 IEEE International Conference on Computer Design: VLSI in Computers and Processors*, IEEE Computer Society, Washington, DC, USA, p. 395.

Moskewicz, M. W., Madigan, C. F., Zhao, Y., Zhang, L. & Malik, S. (2001). Chaff: Engineering an Efficient SAT Solver, *Proceedings of the 38th Design Automation Conference (DAC'01)*, ACM, pp. 530–535.

Muniyappa, A. C. (2009). *Computer Safety, Reliability, and Security*, Springer, Berlin Heidelberg.

Nagatani, T. (2007). Vehicular traffic through a sequence of green-wave lights, *Physica A: Statistical Mechanics and its Applications* **380**: 503 – 511.

Papageorgiou, M., Diakaki, C., Dinopoulou, V., Kotsialos, A. & Wang, Y. (2003). Review of Road Traffic Control Strategies, *PROCEEDINGS - IEEE* **91**: 2043–2067.

Pinedo, M. (2008). *Scheduling: Theory, Algorithms, and Systems*, third edn, Springer, 233 Spring Street, NewYork, NY 10013, USA.

Pinedo, M. et al. (2002). *LEKIN® - Flexible Job-Shop Scheduling System*, Stern School of Business, NYU, New York University, Leonard N. Stern School of Business New York, NY. `http://www.stern.nyu.edu/om/software/lekin/`.

Šůcha, P. & Hanzálek, Z. (2009). A cyclic scheduling problem with an undetermined number of parallel identical processors, *Computational Optimization and Applications* . article in press.

Vesterbacka, M., Palmkvist, K., Sandberg, P. & Wanhammar, L. (1994). Implementation of fast dsp algorithms using bit-serial arithmetic, *National Conference on Electronic Design Automation, Stockholm*.

13

Designing antenna arrays using signal processing, image processing and optimization toolboxes of MATLAB

Joseph Sahaya Kulandai Raj and Joerg Schoebel
Braunschweig University of Technology
Germany

1. Introduction

An antenna array is a group of identical antenna elements arranged usually in a regular fashion. In a linear array, the elements are arranged along a straight line. They are arranged on a grid of points on a plane for a planar array. Generally the currents through the elements are of different amplitudes and phases in order to obtain greater control over the radiation pattern. Antenna arrays are important components of present day wireless communication systems. They have become ubiquitous. The current wireless standards include advanced antenna array concepts such as adaptive antenna arrays and MIMO (Multiple- Input and Multiple-Output) systems to improve the performance of the communication system. Therefore understanding and designing antenna arrays have become imperative.

Basically the antenna array design involves calculating the complex currents of the individual antenna elements and selecting an appropriate antenna element. The current excitations would largely determine how sharp the resultant radiation pattern is and how small the side lobe levels are in comparison to the main lobe. After calculating the current excitations, one would want to visualize the resultant radiation pattern to verify the design. MATLAB®, one of the languages of technical computing, has many built-in functions and visualization tools that would help the design process. Here we demonstrate how toolboxes such as signal-processing, image-processing and optimization toolboxes can help in designing an array and visualize its radiation pattern.

In addition to designing antenna arrays, the toolboxes can be effectively used in the teaching and learning process. Generally, the learning process involves augmenting one's existing knowledge with new concepts. Therefore, while teaching a new concept to students, their already acquired knowledge can be exploited to help them assimilate the concept. Explaining a new concept to students is made effective if we compare the new concepts to other concepts, with which the students are already familiar. The strong similarity between antenna theory and signal-processing theory can be used in this way. Students typically learn signal-processing theory earlier than antenna theory, and antenna educators can make use of the former to illustrate the latter. Though programs can be written in MATLAB without using the signal and image-processing toolboxes to analyze and synthesize antenna arrays, students can gain additional knowledge and insight by comparing signal and image-processing theories with antenna theory, using them. These toolboxes have many built-in functions for filter synthesis that are useful for array synthesis.

2. Use of Signal Processing Toolbox

The antenna array design process is fundamentally similar to the filter synthesis problem. This enables the use of the signal processing functions in antenna array analysis and synthesis.

2.1 Analysis

Given the currents on the radiating elements, calculating the radiation pattern and plotting it to visualize it is one of the tasks of antenna analysis. In this section, we will show how a built-in function of the signal processing toolbox is used in antenna analysis. The array factor of n isotropic point sources with different excitations placed along the x axis on the x-y plane is given by (Balanis, 2005)

$$AF = w_0 + w_1 e^{j\psi} + w_2 e^{j2\psi} + \ldots + w_{n-1} e^{j(n-1)\psi} \tag{1}$$

where

$$\psi = \beta d \cos \phi$$

the w_n are the complex currents of the elements, β is the wave number, d is the inter-element spacing and ϕ is the angular variable.The frequency response of a n point FIR filter is given by

$$H(j\omega) = h_0 + h_1 e^{-j\omega} + h_2 e^{-j2\omega} + \ldots + h_{n-1} e^{-j(n-1)\omega} \tag{2}$$

where h_n are the impulse-response coefficients of the FIR filter and ω is discrete angular frequency.

Equations (1) and (2) are of similar form, except for a minus sign in the power of the complex exponential. Therefore, the tool that is used for finding the frequency response can be used to find the array response as a function of direction ϕ. The built-in function `freqz` in the signal-processing toolbox of MATLAB evaluates the frequency response given the impulse-response coefficients (SP toolbox, 2010). The same function can be used to evaluate the radiation pattern of the array given the current excitations. For example, the current excitation of a four-element array is [1, 1.2, 1.2, 1]. Fig. 1 shows the pattern obtained by using `freqz` command. The following MATLAB code generates the radiation pattern of the four-element array of this example.

Code 1 To generate the pattern

```
phi=0:0.01:2*pi;             %0<phi<2*pi
shi=pi*cos(phi);             %For lambda/2 spacing
Currents=[1,1.2,1.2,1];      %Current excitations
E=freqz(Currents,1,shi);     %E for different shi values
polar2(phi,E);               %Generating the radiation pattern
```

As it is desirable to plot the radiation pattern of an array in dB scale, the built-in function `polar` is modified to plot in dB scale and is called as `polar2` in the code.

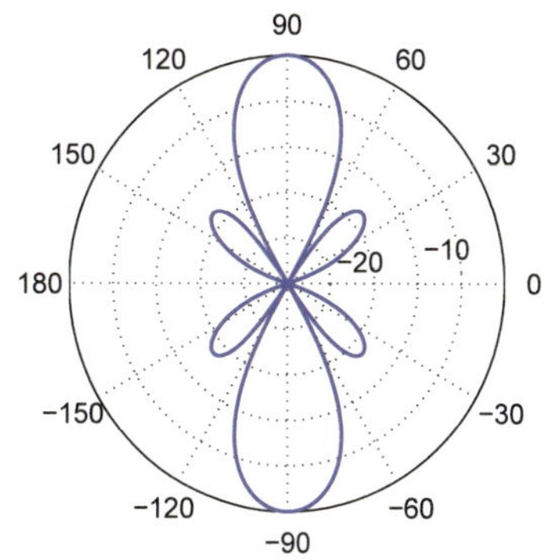

Fig. 1. The pattern of a four element array with current excitations [1, 1.2, 1.2, 1]

2.2 Synthesis

2.2.1 Least square method

One of the problems of array synthesis consists of finding the current excitations of the array elements, given the desired radiation pattern or some data about the radiation pattern. This synthesis problem is equivalent to the problem of finding the impulse response of a digital FIR filter for the desired frequency response, as follows from the explanation in the previous section. The MATLAB Signal-Processing Toolbox has the `firls` function for designing an one-dimensional FIR filter that is optimal in a least-squares sense (SP toolbox, 2010). The arguments of the function are:

- `N`, one less than the number of impulse response coefficients;
- `F`, a vector of frequency points, in ascending order between 0 and 1; 1 corresponds to half the sampling frequency;
- `A`, a real vector of the same size as F, which specifies the desired amplitude of the frequency response of the resultant filter.

If the function is given as `firls(N, F, A)`, it returns an FIR filter with N + 1 impulse-response coefficients that has the best approximation to the desired frequency response described by `F` and `A` in the least-squares sense. This function can be used to design an antenna array if a proper mapping is executed between the frequency variable, `F`, and the variable ψ, which in turn is related to ϕ. For a broadside array, if the spacing between the elements is $\lambda/2$, then $\psi = \pi \cos\phi$. In this case, when ϕ varies from 0 to π, ψ will vary from π to $-\pi$. Thus, for the `F` -vector values in the `firls` function to vary from 0 to 1 (the normalized range of ω), the corresponding ψ values will range from 0 to $-\pi$. This restricts the specification of $A(\phi)$ to be specified from $\pi/2$ to π. The normalized E-field values of the desired radiation pattern at the ψ vector values is given by `A`. `N` will now be equal to the number of elements in the array minus one. The values in the vector `F` should be in ascending order and normalized to unity. For instance, let us design an antenna array that will give an approximately bidirectional pattern as in Fig. 2 (indicated by the blue line). The pattern is defined by:

$$A(\phi) = \begin{cases} 0.1 & \text{if } 0 < \phi < \pi/3, \\ 1 & \text{if } \pi/3 < \phi < 2\pi/3 \\ 0.1 & \text{if } 2\pi/3 < \phi < \pi. \end{cases} \quad (3)$$

Using the above approach, for a 16 element linear array, respective current excitations were obtained. The pattern of the synthesized array is indicated by a blue line in Fig. 2.
The following MATLAB code synthesizes the array for a given specification.

Code 2 To synthesize a linear array in the least-squares sense

```
a=0:pi/315:pi/3;                    %Side lobe directions
b=pi/3:pi/315:2*pi/3;               %Main lobe directions
c=2*pi/3:pi/315:pi;                 %Side lobe directions
T=[a b c ];L=length(b);             %The direction variable
Spec=[0.1*ones(1,L),...
         ones(1,L),...              %Specifications
      0.1*ones(1,L)];
shi=pi*cos(T);
F=shi(((length(T))/2-1):-1:1)/pi;   %Sorting shi in ascending
                                    %order and normalizing to 1
A= Spec((length(T)/2-1):-1:1);      %Sorting in the order of shi
Currents=firls(15,F,A);             %Synthesis
E=freqz(Currents,1,shi);            %Analysis
EdB=20*log10(abs(E));               %dB scale conversion
plot(T*180/pi,EdB,'LineWidth',2);
axis([0 180 -25 10])
```

The values of the excitation currents can be found by displaying the variable `Currents`. The script for plotting the specification is excluded from Code 2.

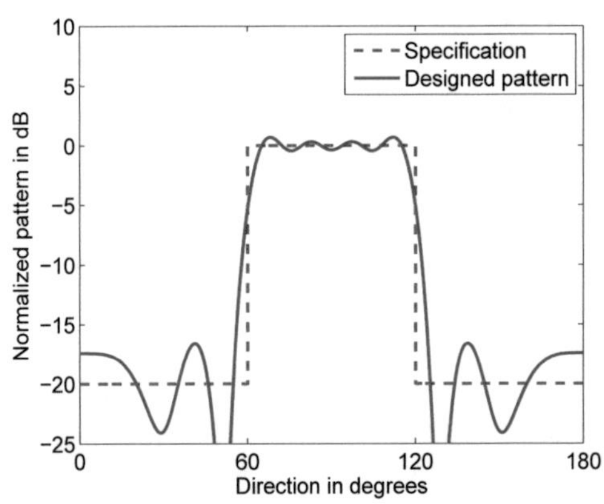

Fig. 2. Pattern of an array synthesized using least square method

2.2.2 Chebyshev and Taylor Syntheses

Another useful function regarding synthesis is `chebwin` (SP toolbox, 2010). For instance, if a six- element Chebyshev array is to be designed with a certain sidelobe level (SLL), the function `chebwin` available in the signal processing tool box can be used. The `chebwin(n,r)` returns a `n`-point Chebyshev window with side lobe level of `r` dB. The window values are the current excitations of the array elements. Discrete arrays having taylor patterns can also be synthesized in the same way using `taylorwin(N,Nbar,SLL)`. This function returns a Taylor window of `N`-points with side lobe level of `SLL` dB (SP toolbox, 2010). `Nbar` is a parameter of the window. The radiation patterns of the arrays synthesized using the window functions are shown in Fig. 3. The number of elements and the side lobe levels are taken to be 8 and -20dB respectively.

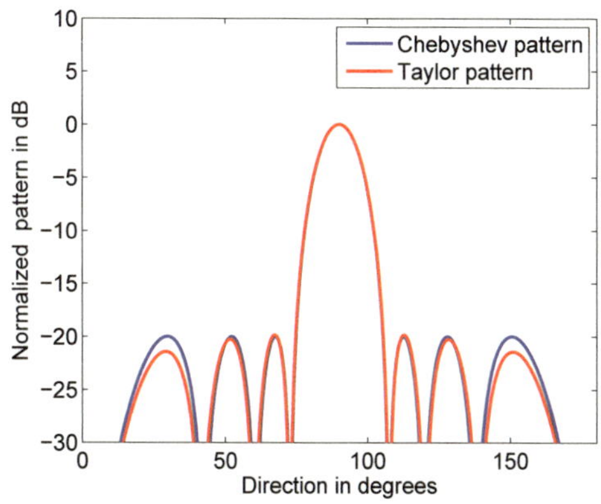

Fig. 3. Synthesized patterns of Chebyshev and Taylor arrays

The following code synthesizes a Chebyshev array and a Taylor array of eight elements with -20dB side lobe level.

Code 3 To synthesize Chebyshev and Taylor arrays

```
phi=0:0.01:2*pi;                          %0<phi<2*pi
shi=pi*cos(phi);                          %For lambda/2 spacing
Currents=chebwin(8,20);                   %Chebyshev Window values
E=abs(freqz(Currents,1,shi))              %E for different shi values
EdB(1,:)=20*log10(E/max(E));              %Converting into dB scale
Currents=taylorwin(8,3, -20);             %Taylow Window values
E=abs(freqz(Currents,1,shi))              %E for different shi values
EdB(2,:)=20*log10(E/max(E));              %Converting into dB scale
plot(phi*180/pi,EdB,'LineWidth',2)        %Generating the pattern
axis([0 180 -30 10])
```

2.2.3 Constrained least square method

In this section, we demonstrate the use of the `fircls` function in designing the antenna array. This function designs a FIR filter by minimizing the integral square error ($\|E(\omega)\|_2$) between the desired frequency response ($D(\omega)$)and the magnitude response of the filter ($A(\omega)$) subject to the constraint that the ripples of ($A(\omega)$) lie within the specified bounds. The minimization of ($\|E(\omega)\|_2$) is done until ($A(\omega)$) is within the bounds.The integral square error is:

$$\|E(\omega)\|_2 = \left(\frac{1}{\pi}\int_0^{\pi}(A(\omega) - D(\omega))^2\,d\omega\right)^{\frac{1}{2}}$$

In order to use this built-in function to design an array, proper mapping between the digital angular frequency (ω) and the angle variable must be accomplished as discussed in section 2.2.1. The arguments of the function are:

- `f` is a vector of transition frequencies in the range from 0 to 1, where 1 corresponds to the Nyquist frequency. The first point of `f` must be 0 and the last point 1. The frequency points must be in increasing order;
- `amp` is a vector describing the piecewise constant desired amplitude of the frequency response. The length of `amp` is equal to the number of bands in the response and should be equal to `length(f)-1`;
- `up` and `lo` are vectors with the same length as `amp`. They define the upper and lower bounds for the frequency response in each band.

If the function is given as `fircls(n,f,amp,up,lo)`, it generates a length n+1 linear phase FIR filter. According to equations (1) and (2), the range 0 to π of the angular digital frequency maps onto the range 0 to $-\pi$. This means that we can specify a pattern from $\phi = \pi/2$ to π. Since the frequency response of the digital filter is periodic, the magnitude response of a real filter in the range 0 to π is equal to 0 to $-\pi$. Therefore the pattern for the range 0 to $\pi/2$ is just the mirror image of the pattern for the range $\pi/2$ to π. The mapping between the filter frequency variables and the antenna angle variables are given in the following table.

Azimuth angle	ϕ	0	$\pi/2$	π
Progressive phase	ψ	π	0	$-\pi$
Angular frequency	ω	$-\pi$	0	π
Frequency	F	-0.5	0	0.5
Frequency (normalized to 1)	f	-1	0	1

Table 1. Mapping between filter and antenna variables

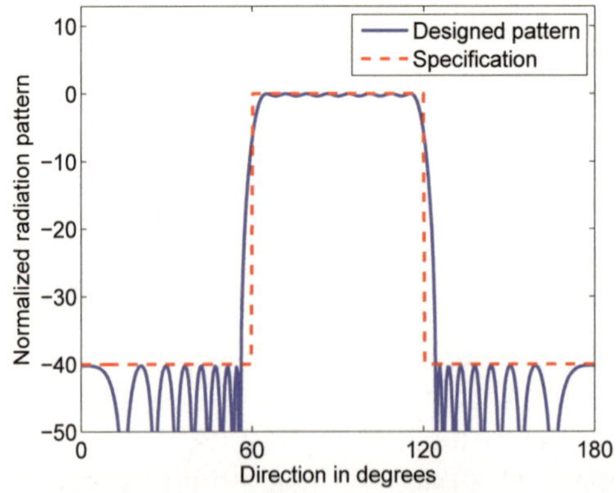

Fig. 4. Pattern of an array synthesized using constrained least square method

Supposing that a flat beam pattern antenna array is to be designed. The main lobe is between $\phi = \pi/3$ to $\phi = 2\pi/3$. The sidelobe level is -40 dB. The number of elements is n = 33. This would mean the main lobe is between $\pi/2$ and $-\pi/2$ in ψ domain. The corresponding filter passband ranges from $\omega = -\pi/2$ to $\omega = \pi/2$. In the normalized frequency domain, this is from -0.5 to 0.5. The built-in function requires the normalized frequency to be specified only from 0 to 1, as the magnitude response of a filter is symmetric about f=0. For this example, the normalized cutoff frequency is 0.5. The specification and the designed pattern are shown in Fig. 4. The script for plotting the specification is excluded from Code 4.

Code 4 To synthesize an array using constrained least square method

```
f=[0 0.5 1];amp=[1 0];                 %Specification
up=[1.02 0.01];lo =[0.98 -0.01];       %Bounds
phi=0:0.01:2*pi;                       %0<phi<2*pi
shi=pi*cos(phi);                       %For lambda/2 spacing
b = fircls(32,f,amp,up,lo);            %Sythesis
E=freqz(b, 1,shi);                     %E for different shi values
EdB=20*log10(abs(E)/max(abs(E)));      %Converting into dB scale
plot(phi*180/pi,EdB,'LineWidth',2)     %Generating the pattern
axis([0 180 -50 10])
```

3. Schelkunoff polynomial method

The array factor of a linear array (see (1)) can be rewritten as

$$AF = w_0 + w_1 z + w_2 z^2 + \ldots + w_{n-1} z^{n-1}$$

where

$$z = e^{j\beta d \cos\phi}$$

For an array with a real beam pattern, the array factor is given by

$$AF = w_0 + w_1 z + \ldots + w_1 z^{n-2} + w_0 z^{n-1} \quad (4)$$

For a real beam pattern, the excitations coefficients of an array are symmetric and the roots of the array factor occur in complex conjugate pairs. The Z transform of a symmetric discrete time sequence is given by

$$X(Z) = a_0 + a_1 z^{-1} + \ldots + a_1 z^{-(n-2)} + a_0 z^{-(n-1)} \quad (5)$$

The equations (4) and (5) are of similar form except for the minus sign. We can rewrite the Z transform equation as below to compare the array factor.

$$X(Z) = \frac{a_0 z^{n-1} + a_1 z^{n-2} + \ldots + a_1 + a_0}{z^{n-1}} \quad (6)$$

Exploiting this similarity, we may use a built-in function called `zplane` of the signal processing toolbox which is used to visualize the poles and zeros of a discrete filter to see the locations of the roots of a real beam pattern. Because of negative powers of the z terms in the Z transform, we would get $(n-1)$ poles at $z = 0$. For instance, we would like to see the roots of an array factor on the z plane. The array factor is given by

$$AF = z^3 - z^2 + z - 1$$

If we treat the above polynomial as the numerator of a Z transform of a sequence, then the function `zplane([-1 1 -1 1],1)` will give the locations of the roots of the array factor on the z plane in addition to three poles at the origin, which we can ignore (See Fig. 5). Although one can write a separate MATLAB code to find the roots of the array factor and then plot it on a rectangular graph using simple commands like `poly, roots and plot`, comparing the Schelkunoff polynomial with the Z transform would give more insight into the array factor dependence on the roots. One may also be interested in the Pole/Zero editor of the `fdatool` of the signal processing toolbox. This interactive editor allows the user to adjust the locations of the poles and zeros on the z plane and see the effect on the frequency response which is analogous to the array factor.

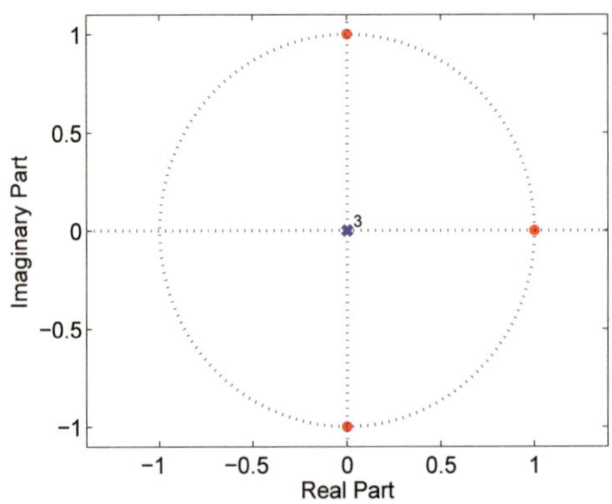

Fig. 5. Locations of the roots of the beam pattern (indicated in red)

4. Use of Image Processing Toolbox

4.1 Analysis

The array factor for an M×N rectangular array on the x-y plane (Ioannides & Balanis, 2005) is given by

$$AF(\theta,\phi) = \sum_{m=1}^{M}\sum_{n=1}^{N} w_{mn} e^{j[(m-1)\psi_x + (n-1)\psi_y)]} \tag{7}$$

where

$$\psi_x = kd_x \sin\theta \cos\phi$$
$$\psi_y = kd_y \sin\theta \sin\phi$$

where d_x and d_y are the spacings between the adjacent elements along the x axis and the y axis, respectively, and the w_{mn} are the current excitations. The frequency response of a two-dimensional filter is given by

$$H(j\omega_1, j\omega_2) = \sum_{m=1}^{M}\sum_{n=1}^{N} h_{mn} e^{-j[(m-1)\omega_1 + (n-1)\omega_2)]} \tag{8}$$

Equations (7) and (8) are of similar format, except for a minus sign in the power of the complex exponentials. Therefore, the tool that is used for finding the frequency response can be used to find the array response as a function of variables θ and ϕ. The image-processing toolbox of MATLAB has a function `freqz2` for finding the frequency response of two-dimensional filters. The same could be effectively used to evaluate the radiation pattern of the two-dimensional arrays (IP toolbox, 2010). The radiation pattern of the array on the x-y plane is shown in Fig. 6. For example, the code given below generates the radiation pattern of a 5 x 5 uniform rectangular array.
The following MATLAB function generates the three dimensional radiation pattern of a rectangular array. This requires three arguments:

- `Currents`, a matrix whose elements define the current distribution of the array;
- `theta`, an array having the θ directions in which the pattern is evaluated;
- `phi`, an array having the ϕ directions in which the pattern is evaluated .

The function `freqz2` requires the frequency variables to be normalized frequencies in the range -1.0 to 1.0, where 1.0 corresponds to half the sampling frequency, or π radians. Due to this, the progressive phase shifts ψ_x and ψ_y are normalized so that their limits are equal to the limits of the normalized frequencies of a two dimensional filter. The normalized values of the progressive phase shifts are defined as follows:

$$\begin{aligned} \psi_{nx} &= \sin\theta\cos\phi \\ \psi_{ny} &= \sin\theta\sin\phi \end{aligned} \tag{9}$$

Finally $E(\theta,\phi)$ is converted into $E(x,y)$ so that the three dimensional plotting function `mesh` can be used.

Code 5 To generate a three dimensional radiation pattern

```
function analyze2D(Currents,theta,phi)      %Function definition
[the,ph]=ndgrid(theta,phi);
shinx=cos(ph).*sin(the);                    %Normalized shinx
shiny=sin(ph).*sin(the);                    %Normalized shiny
E=freqz2(Currents,shinx,shiny);             %Analysis
x=abs(E).*sin(the).*cos(ph);                %Spherical to
y=abs(E).*sin(the).*sin(ph);                %rectangular
z=abs(E).*cos(the);                         %coordinate system
mesh(x,y,z)                                 %3D plot
```

4.2 Synthesis

Similarly, two-dimensional rectangular arrays can be synthesized using tools available in the image-processing toolbox. The tools are `fwindl`, `fsamp2`, `ftrans2`, and `fwind2` (IP toolbox, 2010). For example, `H=fwind2(FR,WIN)` designs a two-dimensional FIR filter `H` with frequency response `FR`. `fwind2` uses the two-dimensional window `WIN` to truncate the infinitely large impulse response required to meet the given frequency response, `FR`. `WIN` can be the `boxcar`(rectangular), `hamming`, `hanning`, `bartlett`, `blackman`, `kaiser`, or `chebwin` window functions of the signal processing toolbox. To synthesize the rectangular array, the `fwind2` function's argument `FR` is given by the desired radiation pattern samples in the θ and

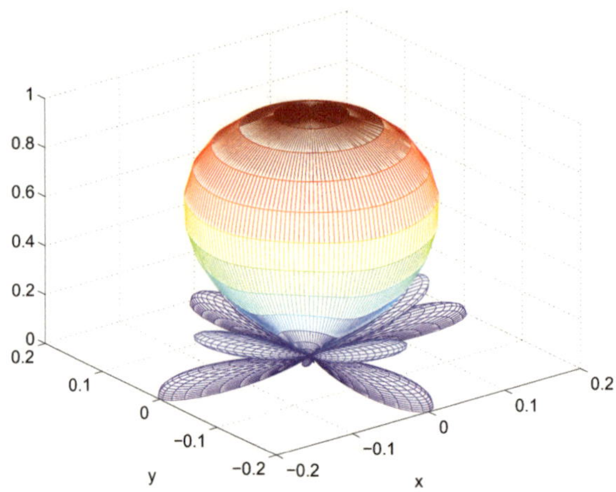

Fig. 6. The radiation pattern of a 5 × 5 uniform rectangular array

ϕ directions, and the dimension of `WIN` is given by N×N, the dimension of the array. The output, `H`, is the array excitations. Fig. 7(a) shows the desired pattern, and Fig. 7(b) shows the synthesized pattern, of the two-dimensional array.

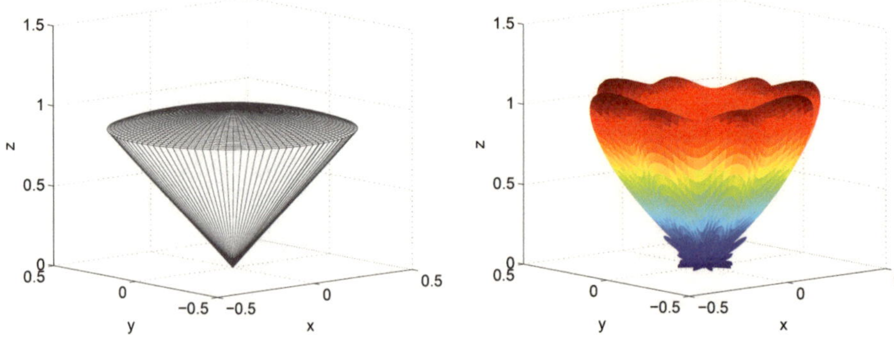

(a) The desired pattern (b) The synthesized pattern

Fig. 7. (a) The desired and (b) the synthesized pattern for the 10 x 10 two-dimensional array

The following MATLAB code synthesizes the array whose radiation pattern approximates a conical pattern (see Fig. 7) The code uses a built-in function called `freqspace`, which creates the two- dimensional normalized frequency vectors and returns a grid of values for each normalized frequency vector as if `meshgrid` is applied to the vectors. An intermediate variable is introduced to define the conic beam. Let the intermediate variable be r and is equal to

$$r = \sqrt{\psi_{nx}^2 + \psi_{ny}^2}$$

Using (9), $r = \sin\theta$ for all ϕ. The specification of the conic beam is

$$Espec(\theta) = \begin{cases} 1 & \text{if } 0 < \theta < \pi/6 \\ 0 & \text{if } \pi/6 < \theta < \pi/2. \end{cases}$$

Code 6 To synthesize a rectangular array

```
phi=2*pi*((0:1:100)/100);                    %0<phi<2*pi
theta=(pi/2)*((0:1:100)/100);                %0<theta<pi/2
[shix,shiy]=freqspace(101,'meshgrid');       %Frequencty points
r=sqrt(shix.*shix+shiy.*shiy);
Espec=ones(101);                             %Specifications
Espec(r>sin(pi/6))=0;
win=boxcar(10)*boxcar(10)';                  %Window
Currents=fwind2(Espec,win);                  %Synthesis
analyze2D(Currents,theta,phi)
```

5. Spacing and Sampling Rate

The effect on the array pattern of changing the spacing between the adjacent elements of the array is same as the effect on the frequency response of changing the sampling period of the FIR filter. To illustrate this point, the frequency responses of a 15-tap FIR filter with uniform impulse response coefficients for different sampling rates are compared with the array responses of a 15-element uniform linear array with different spacing. The frequency responses are plotted from -1 Hz to 1 Hz for the Nyquist rate (`Fs`), one-half the Nyquist rate, and one-quarter of the Nyquist rate in Fig. 8 (a), (b) and (c) respectively. It can be observed that the frequency response shrinks as the sampling frequency decreases (the sampling period increases). As a result, more main lobes creep into the fundamental range, which otherwise has only one main lobe.

In Fig. 9 (a), (b) and (c), the array responses for a 15-element uniform linear array are plotted to show the analogy. As the spacing between the elements is increased, more main lobes occur within the range of ϕ, just as in the frequency response of the FIR filter. This analogy can be used to explain the occurrence of grating lobes to the students, who have already come across the phenomenon of aliasing. Aliasing occurs when the signal is sparsely sampled. Aliasing is reflected in the frequency response of the filter, because it should respond in the same way for two different frequencies having the same identity. Similarly, aliasing of the pattern in the spatial domain occurs when the array elements are sparsely arranged. If the sampling rate is sufficiently high, the frequency response expands, and only the main lobe may occupy the entire fundamental range of -1 Hz to 1 Hz. In the same way, if the array elements are arranged densely enough, the extra grating lobes which would otherwise occur will disappear from the range of ϕ.

6. Convolution and Pattern Multiplication

Pattern multiplication is used to find the array pattern from the patterns of individual elements. This is analogous to multiplication of two frequency responses, corresponding to two

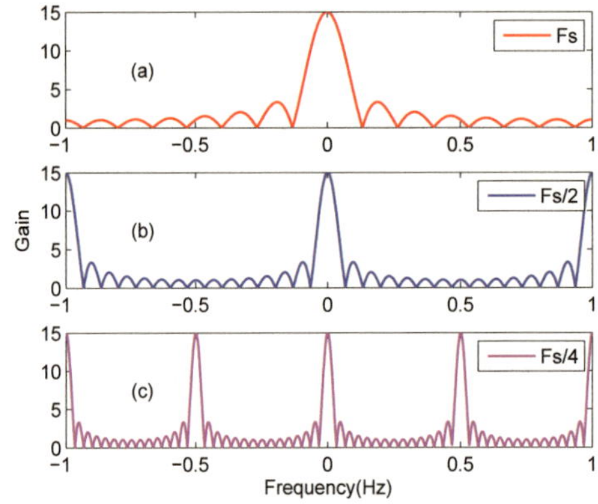

Fig. 8. (Top to bottom: a, b, and c) The frequency responses of a 15-tap FIR filter for different sampling rates.

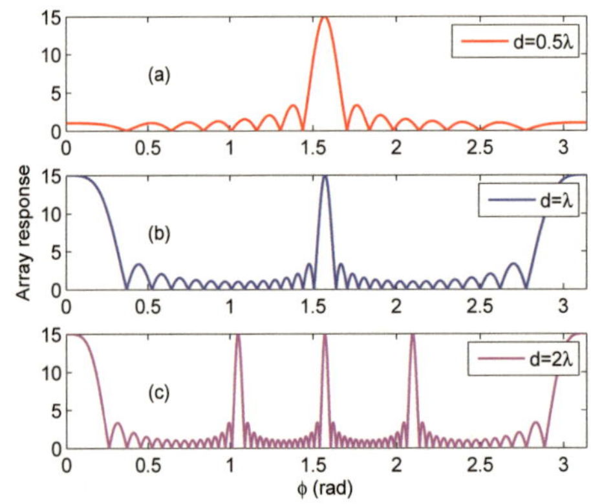

Fig. 9. (Top to bottom: a, b, and c) The array responses of a 15-point uniform linear array for different spacings between the elements.

discrete time sequences. The resultant frequency response obtained by multiplication is actually the frequency response of the resultant sequence obtained by convolving the two discrete time sequences. In the same way, an array for which the pattern is needed can be thought of as a result of convolution of two arrays, one comprising m individual elements of the array and the other comprising n elements. Each of the n elements is a combination of m elements.

For instance, to demonstrate the pattern-multiplication concept, a four-element isotropic array, shown in Fig. 10 (a) is considered here. The four element array is treated as a combination of two arrays of two elements each. Each two-element isotropic array can be regarded as a directional antenna. Then, the four-element array is equivalent to an array of two directional antennas separated by a distance $2d$. Now, by multiplying the pattern of the $2d$ -spaced two-element array with the pattern of the d-spaced two-element array, the pattern of the four-element array can be obtained.

The four-element array is comparable to a discrete time sequence having four unit samples with sampling period d. The two-element array separated by distance $2d$ is comparable to a sequence having two unit samples with sampling period $2d$, and so on. The discrete time sequence with $2d$ sampling period (Sequence 1) is `[1,0,1]` and with d sampling period (Sequence 2) is `[1,1]`. The resultant sequence (Sequence 3) is `[1,1,1,1]` which is obtained by the script `conv([1,0,1],[1,1]`. Just as the time sequence 3 can be considered as a result of a convolution of time sequences 1 and 2, as shown in Fig. 10 (b), the four-element array can be regarded as the result of a convolution of two arrays of two elements with spacing $2d$ and d distances. Since the convolution of two sequences in the time domain corresponds to multiplication of frequency responses in the frequency domain, the convolution of two arrays corresponds to multiplication of the radiation patterns of the respective two-element arrays (Raj & Kabilan, 2007).

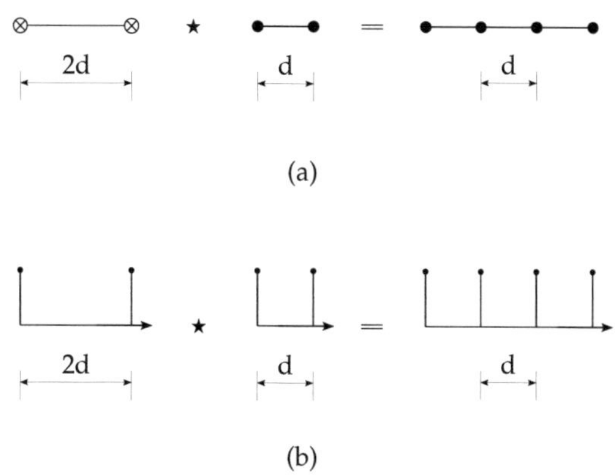

Fig. 10. (a) The convolution of two arrays of two elements with spacings of $2d$ and d, respectively. (b) The convolution of two sequences with sampling rates of spacings of $2d$ and d, respectively.

7. Use of Optimization Toolbox

Optimization is one of the main techniques that enable the designer to design an antenna array having asymmetric sidelobes and/or arbitrary main lobe, for example (Schoebel et al., 2005). In this section, we demonstrate how the optimization toolbox of MATLAB can be used to do antenna array optimization. Here we use the built-in function `fmincon` of the toolbox, as this function performs nonlinear constrained optimization (Optimization toolbox, 2010). This is suitable for the design of antenna array whose pattern is a nonlinear function of the direction variable and the pattern is constrained at various directions to meet the sidelobe requirement (Lebret & Boyd, 1997).

The problem that we consider for our demonstration is formulated as follows.

$$\begin{aligned} \min_{w_i} \quad & \left(\max_{m=1,\ldots,P} \ |AF(\phi_m)| \right) \\ \text{subject to} \quad & |AF(\phi_n)| \leq U_n,\ n = 1,\ldots,Q \\ & |AF(\phi_s)| = 1. \end{aligned} \tag{10}$$

- ϕ_m, directions in which the array factor is evaluated for the minimax problem;
- ϕ_n, directions in which the array factor is constrained to be equal to U_n;
- ϕ_s, angle at which the normalized gain is equal to 1.

The angles ϕ_m and ϕ_n will be within the two sidelobe regions. The original problem which involves complex numbers is cast into a formulation involving only real numbers. The weights w_i and the steering vector terms s_i are expressed as below.

$$\begin{aligned} w_i &= \Re(w_i) + i\Im(w_i) \\ e^{i\beta d_i \cos(\phi)} &= \Re(s_i) + i\Im(s_i). \end{aligned}$$

where d_i is the position of the ith element from the origin. Now we can write the array factor as

$$AF(w_i) = a_m{}^T x + i b_m{}^T x \tag{11}$$

where

$$\begin{aligned} x &= (\Re(w_1),\ldots,\Re(w_n),\Im(w_1),\ldots,\Im(w_n)); \\ RS &= (\Re(s_1),\ldots,\Re(s_n)); \\ IS &= (\Im(s_1),\ldots,\Im(s_n)); \\ a_m &= (RS,-IS); \\ b_m &= (IS,RS) \end{aligned}$$

Following (Lasdon et al., 1987), the problem in (10) is

$$\begin{aligned} \min_{w_i} \quad & z \\ \text{subject to} \quad & |AF(\phi_m)|^2 < z,\ m = 1,\ldots,P \\ & |AF(\phi_n)|^2 = U_n,\ n = 1,\ldots,Q \\ & |AF(\phi_s)|^2 = 1. \end{aligned} \tag{12}$$

The remaining section will show how to use `fmincon` function to the above optimization problem. The specification for the beam pattern is as follows:

```
phim=[0,44,57,72,106,122,140,180]*pi/180;
phin=[30,55,67,90,112,128,150]*pi/180;
goal=[0.01,0.01,0.01,1,0.02,0.02,0.02];
```

In this piece of code, `phin` vector has the values of the angles in which the magnitude square oof the array factor is constrained to be equal to the values in the vector `goal`. The goal is specified for the power pattern. The goal is equal to -20dB for the first three `phin` and is equal to -17 dB for the last three `phin` angles. When `phin`=90°, it is 0 dB. A separate function

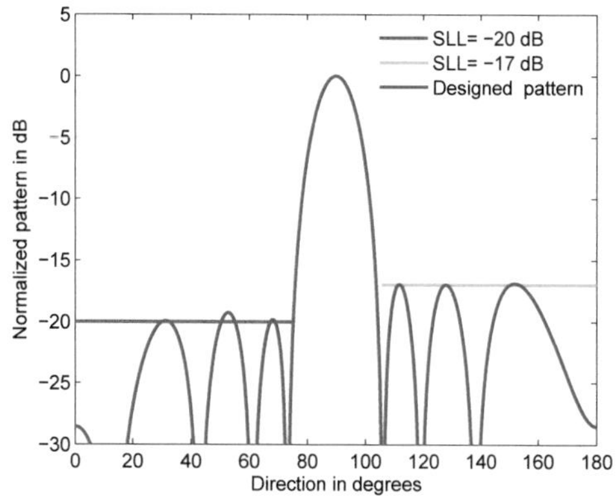

Fig. 11. Asymmetric pattern of an array of 8 elements with the specification indicated

must be written for the objective. This function returns the function value which is to be minimized. For our example, the argument is equal to the function value. The code for the objective function is given below.

```
function z=objfun(a0,goal,phim,phin)
%a0=[R(w1),...,R(wn),I(wn),...,I(w1),z]
z=a0(end);
%Since objective function is equal to the input argument.
```

Only the input `a0` is used in the objective function. The remaining arguments are not used but they must be included because the arguments of the objective function and the constraint function (described below) are the same. These arguments are passed by the optimization tool `fmincon` when it invokes the objective and constraint functions by their handles.
Similar to the objective function, the constraints are also stored as a separate MATLAB function. We show below the code for the constraint function.

```
function [c,ceq]=confun(a0,goal,phim,phin)
N=length(a0)-1;x=a0(1:1:N);phi=[phim,phin];
for n=1:length(phi)
AR=exp(-j*pi*(0:N/2-1)*cos(phi(n)));
RS=real(AR);IS=imag(AR);
a=[RS,-IS];b=[IS RS];
P(n)=(a*x').*(a*x')+(b*x').*(b*x');
end
Pnorm=P/max(P);
z=a0(end)*ones(1,length(phim));
c=Pnorm(1:length(phim))'-z';
ceq=goal'-Pnorm(length(phim)+1:end)';
```

In order to understand the variables of the above code, one may refer (11). The optimization tool is invoked as:

```
options = optimset('Algorithm','interior-point');
Wopt= fmincon('objfun',a0,[],[],[],[],...
lb,ub,'confun',options,goal,phim,phin);
```

As the problem does not have any linear constraints, the corresponding arguments must be empty. The arguments `lb` and `ub` define the bounds on the real and imaginary parts of the weight vector and the objective function input. Fig. 11 shows the normalized pattern of the array with sidelobe specifications.

8. Conclusion

Exploiting the similarity between signal-processing theory and antenna-array theory, it has been demonstrated that with little effort analysis of antenna arrays can be done using signal- and image-processing tools of MATLAB. The analogy between FIR filters and arrays can be effectively used to explain the concepts of the arrays to students. Also, synthesis of arrays, to a first approximation, can be carried out using signal-processing tools in the case of one-dimensional arrays, and image-processing tools in the case of two-dimensional arrays, ignoring the mutual coupling between the elements.It has been shown that the optimization toolbox of MATLAB can be used to design antenna arrays with asymmetric sidelobes.

9. References

Balanis, C. (2005). *Antenna Theory: Analysis and Design*, 3rd ed., Wiley and Sons, 047166782X, Hoboken, New Jersey, USA.

Ioannides, P. & Balanis, C.(2005). Uniform circular and rectangular arrays for adaptive beamforming applications, *IEEE Antennas Wireless Propag. Lett.* , vol.4, no., pp. 351- 354.

Image Processing Toolbox User's Guide. (2010), The MathWorks Inc.

Lasdon L. S. ; Plummer, J. ; Buehler, B. & Warren A. D. (1987). Optimal design of efficient acoustic antenna arrays, *Math. Programming*, vol.39, no. 2, pp. 131-155.

Lebret, H. & Boyd, S. (1997). Antenna array pattern synthesis via convex optimization, *IEEE Trans. Signal Process.* , vol. 45, no. 3, pp. 526-532.

Optimization Toolbox User's Guide. (2010), The MathWorks Inc.

Raj, J. S. K & Kabilan, A.P. (2007). Teaching and Designing Antenna Arrays Using Signal and Image-Processing. Toolboxes of MATLAB, *IEEE Antennas Propag. Mag.*, vol. 49, issue 4, pp. 184-190.

Schoebel, J.; Buck, T.; Reimann, M.; Ulm, M.; Hansen, T. & Schneider, M. (2005) Planar Phased Array Antenna Systems for W-Band Automotive Radar Sensors with Beam Steering Based on RF MEMS, *Frequenz*, vol. 59, No. 1-2, pp. 27-34.

Signal Processing Toolbox User's Guide. (2010), The MathWorks Inc.

14

Analysis, model parameter extraction and optimization of planar inductors using MATLAB

Elissaveta Gadjeva, Vladislav Durev and Marin Hristov
Technical University of Sofia
Bulgaria

1. Introduction

The rising development of the microelectronic integrated circuits and technologies requires effective and flexible tools for modeling and simulation. Modeling of the planar inductors is a key problem in microelectronic design and requires precise implementation of the corresponding models for simulation and optimization. The application of a general-purpose matrix based software like MATLAB and the proper model implementation for such software is of great importance in the RF designer's everyday work.
The on-chip planar inductor is a very important constructive component of the contemporary CMOS microelectronics. In the CMOS SoC RFs the use of the planar inductors in designs like VCOs, mixers, RF amplifiers, impedance-matching circuits is widespread. Many papers, devoted on the on-chip spiral inductors analysis, model parameter extraction and optimization were published in the recent years.
The MATLAB environment can be successfully used in the circuit analysis. The implemented symbolic representation of the equations is of a significant importance for the description and simulation of multiparameter models in microelectronics.
Genetic Algorithm (GA) optimization tools are already implemented in leading general-purpose system analysing software like MATLAB. This gives the users another opportunity for solving various design optimization problems. The GA is a stochastic global search method, which is based on a mechanism resemble the natural biological evolution mechanism. GA operates on a population of solutions and the fitness of the solutions is determined from the objective function of some specific problem. Only the best fitted solutions remain in the population after a number of predefined cycles. In microelectronic technologies and in the microelectronic design the problems are often presented as mathematical functions of multiple variables. The optimization of the values of these variables is in some cases a complex problem, especially when the amount of the variables is huge. The big advantage of GA is that these algorithms do not require derivative information or other knowledge. Only the objective function and the corresponding fitness levels influence the direction of search. This makes the GA an useful tool for parameter optimization in microelectronics and especially for geometric optimization of microelectronic components, when the parameters of the technology are known.

A method for optimal design and synthesis of CMOS inductors for use in RF circuits is proposed in (Hershenson et al., 1999). The method is based on formulating the design problem as an optimization problem using geometric programming. The physical dimensions of the inductor are defined as design parameters. A variety of specifications are introduced including the required inductance value, as well as the minimum allowed values of the self-resonant frequency and the quality factor. Geometric constraints that can be handled include the maximum and the minimum values for each of the design parameters and a limit on total area.
The wide-band spiral inductor model, proposed in (Gil & Shin, 2003) is simple and has an excellent accuracy in comparison to the measured results. The main advantage of this model compared to the models with geometry dependent parameters developed in (Ashby et al., 1994; Yue et al. 1996; Mohan et al., 1999) consists in the frequency independence of the model parameters. Moreover, the models in (Ashby et al., 1994; Yue et al. 1996; Mohan et al., 1999) can not predict the drop-down characteristics in the series resistance at higher frequencies. The wide-band model was widely accepted and several extraction procedures were published to aid the verification and the easy implementation in the microelectronic designs (Kang et al., 2005; Chen et al., 2008). Several modifications of the model are proposed in (Sun et al., 2004 ; Wen & Sun, 2006). The application of the simple parameter extraction method (Kang et al., 2005) and the systematic model parameter extraction approach (Chen et al., 2008) lead to very accurate results. However, the application of these procedures takes time and the need of having automated extraction procedures using an industrial standard environment like MATLAB is an important problem to solve.
A bandwidth extension technique of gigahertz broadband circuitry is applied in (Mohan et al., 2000) by using optimized on-chip spiral inductors. A global optimization method, based on geometric programming, is discussed. As a result, the optimized on-chip inductors consume only 15% of the total area. A fast Sequential Quadratic Programming (SQP) approach to optimize the on-chip spiral inductors is proposed in (Zhan & Sapatnekar, 2004). A robust automated synthesis methodology to efficiently generate spiral inductor designs using multi-objective optimization techniques and surrogate functions to approximate Pareto surfaces in the design space is developed in (Nieuwoudt & Massoud, 2005). The obtained results indicate that the synthesis methodology efficiently optimizes inductor designs based on the defined requirements with an improvement of up to 51% in key inductor design constraints. The need to develop analysis and optimizations in one and the same environment leads to the usage of MATLAB and the implemented optimization toolboxes and GA toolbox (Chipperfield et al., 1994).

2. Wide-band planar inductor model analysis in MATLAB

The enhanced model of spiral inductor (Gil & Shin, 2003) can be treated as a parallel combination of an upper and a lower subcircuits (Fig. 1a). Because of the DC blocking property of the oxide capacitors C_{ox1} and C_{ox2}, the spiral inductor model can be separated into two parts: upper subcircuit and lower subcircuit. The inductor can be approximately characterized by the upper subcircuit for lower frequencies and by the lower subcircuit for high frequencies.

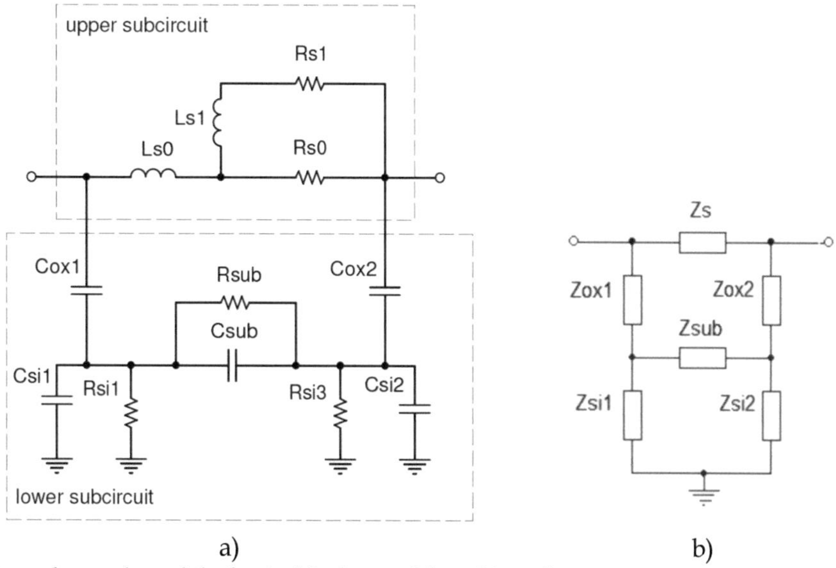

Fig. 1. The enhanced model of spiral inductor (a) and its schematic representation (b)

From the analysis point of view, the model can be represented using the equivalent schematic, shown in Fig. 1b (Durev et al., 2009). The following expressions can be written:

$$Z_{Ls0} = sL_{s0}\ ; \quad Z_{s1} = R_{s1} + sL_{s1}\ ; \quad Z_{Rs0} = R_{s0}\ ; \quad Z_s = Z_{Ls0} + \frac{1}{1/Z_{s1} + 1/Z_{Rs0}}, \tag{1}$$

$$Z_{ox1,2} = 1/sC_{ox1,2}\ ; \quad Z_{Rsi1,2} = R_{si1,2}\ ; \quad Z_{Csi1,2} = 1/sC_{si1,2}\ , \tag{2}$$

$$Z_{si1,2} = \frac{1}{1/Z_{Rsi1,2} + 1/Z_{Csi1,2}}\ ; \quad Z_{Rsub} = R_{sub}\ ; \quad Z_{Csub} = 1/sC_{sub}\ ; \quad Z_{sub} = \frac{1}{1/Z_{Rsub} + 1/Z_{Csub}}. \tag{3}$$

The Y-parameters can be found using equations (1), (2) and (3). The corresponding schematics are shown in Fig. 2 for both cases – $\dot{V}_2 = 0$ (Fig. 2a) and $\dot{V}_1 = 0$ (Fig. 2b). According to the two-port definition for the Y-parameters, Y_{11} and Y_{21} are defined for the case in Fig. 2a, and Y_{22} and Y_{12} – for the case, shown in Fig. 2b.

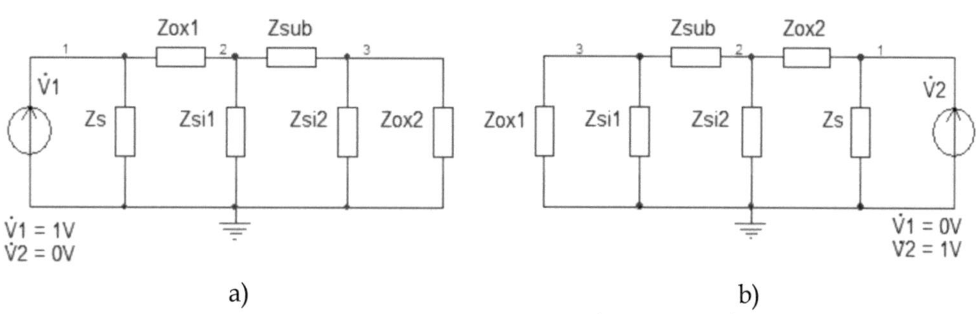

Fig. 2. Representation of the Y-parameter analysis: (a) $\dot{V}_2 = 0$; (b) $\dot{V}_1 = 0$

The equivalent impedance Z_{eqY11} for the schematic, shown in Fig. 2a can be found, using the following equations:

$$Z_{ox2si2} = \frac{1}{1/Z_{ox2} + 1/Z_{si2}}; \; Z_{subox2si2} = Z_{ox2si2} + Z_{sub} \; ; \; Z_{subox2si2si1} = \frac{1}{1/Z_{si1} + 1/Z_{subox2si2}}, \quad (4)$$

$$Z_{subox2si2si1ox1} = Z_{ox1} + Z_{subox2si2si1}; \qquad Z_{eqY11} = \frac{1}{1/Z_s + 1/Z_{subox2si2si1ox1}}. \quad (5)$$

The following expression for Y_{11} can be written:

$$Y_{11} = \dot{V}_1 / Z_{eqY11} \,. \quad (6)$$

The equivalent impedance Z_{eqY22} and Y_{22} are obtained similarly from the analysis of the schematic in Fig. 2b, when $\dot{V}_1 = 0$. The following expressions are valid:

$$Z_{eqY22} = \frac{1}{1/Z_s + 1/Z_{subox1si1si2ox2}} \; ; \quad Y_{22} = \dot{V}_2 / Z_{eqY22} \,. \quad (7)$$

Y_{21} can be easily expressed if the voltage $\dot{V}_{Zox2}$ across Z_{ox2} in Fig. 2a is known. It can be symbolically expressed using the symbolic analysis possibilities in MATLAB. If the input current, node voltages and admittances in Fig. 2 are declared as symbols using *syms*, the Modified Nodal Analysis (MNA) circuit matrix equation can be solved and the following expression can be written for $\dot{V}_{Zox2}$:

$$\dot{V}_{Zox2} = \frac{Y_{ox1} \cdot Y_{sub} \dot{V}_1}{(Y_{ox1} + Y_{si1}).(Y_{sub} + Y_{ox2} + Y_{si2}) + Y_{sub}.(Y_{ox2} + Y_{si2})} \,. \quad (8)$$

In order to obtain Y_{21}, the currents $\dot{I}_{Zox2}$ and $\dot{I}_s$ are expressed, using the following equations:

$$\dot{I}_{Zox2} = \dot{V}_{Zox2} / Z_{ox2} \; ; \; \dot{I}_s = \dot{V}_1 / Z_s \,. \quad (9)$$

Using the expressions (9) and the Y_{21} two-port definition, Y_{21} is expressed in the form:

$$Y_{21} = -\left(\dot{I}_s + \dot{I}_{Zox2}\right) / \dot{V}_1 \,. \quad (10)$$

Because of the symmetry of the model from Fig. 1b, the following expression is obtained for Y_{12} from the analysis of the circuit, shown in Fig. 2b when $\dot{V}_1 = 0$:

$$Y_{12} = -\left(\dot{I}_s + \dot{I}_{Zox1}\right) / \dot{V}_2 \quad (11)$$

3. Minimization the Parameter Extraction Errors Using GA

3.1. Purpose function and general structure

Once the basic circuit analysis and Y-parameter expressions are present, a GA approach can be applied to minimize the errors, coming from the parameter extraction procedure. The idea is to compare the Y-parameters, obtained for the model parameter values from the parameter extraction and the Y-parameters, obtained when the model parameter values are varied in a certain range. The actual comparison is done in the purpose function, which compares the absolute value for every frequency point of every two-port Y-parameter in one expression, using the sum of the least squares values:

$$G_{fun} = \sum_{i=1}^{n}\left(Y_{jk}(f_i) - Y_{jk}^{(m)}(f_i)\right)^2 , \tag{12}$$

where j, k = 1,2;

$Y_{jk}^{(m)}$ - measured Y-parameters;

Y_{jk} - simulated Y-parameters of the model;

n - number of the measured/simulated frequency points.

The GA optimization is done using 1000 iterations, generation gap of 0.7 for population of 200 individuals. (Durev, 2009). The function body contains two *for* cycles. The first cycle runs the calculations for every frequency point until the end (DATA_ROWS), and the second cycle runs the calculations for every generated individual (variable) for a given frequency point until the end (Nind).

3.2. Optimization procedure realized in MATLAB

The representation of equations (1 - 11) and the construction of the optimization procedure in MATLAB are shown below:

```
for i = 1:DATA_ROWS %Calculate the frequency response of the circuit
    s = j*2*pi*frequency(i);
for ix = 1:Nind
    ZLs0 = s.*Ls0(ix); Zs1 = Rs1(ix) + s.*Ls1(ix); ZRs0 = Rs0(ix);
    Zs = ZLs0 + ((Zs1.*ZRs0)./(Zs1 + ZRs0)); Zox1 = 1./(s.*Cox1(ix));
    Zox2 = 1./(s.*Cox2(ix)); ZRsi1 = Rsi1(ix); ZCsi1 = 1./(s.*Csi1(ix));
    Zsi1 = (ZRsi1.*ZCsi1)./(ZRsi1 + ZCsi1); ZRsi2 = Rsi2(ix); ZCsi2 = 1./(s.*Csi2(ix));
    Zsi2 = (ZRsi2.*ZCsi2)./(ZRsi2 + ZCsi2); ZRsub = Rsub(ix); ZCsub = 1./(s.*Csub(ix));
   Zsub = (ZRsub.*ZCsub)./(ZRsub + ZCsub);
    %Calculate Y11, V1 = 1, V2 = 0
    Zox2si2 = (Zox2.*Zsi2)./(Zox2 + Zsi2); Zsubox2si2 = Zox2si2 + Zsub;
    Zsubox2si2si1 = (Zsi1.*Zsubox2si2)./(Zsi1 + Zsubox2si2);
    Zsubox2si2si1ox1 = Zox1 + Zsubox2si2si1;
    ZeqY11 = (Zs.*Zsubox2si2si1ox1)./(Zs + Zsubox2si2si1ox1);
    Y11(ix, 1) = V1./ZeqY11;
    %Calculate Y22, V1 = 0, V2 = 1
    Zox1si1 = (Zox1.*Zsi1)./(Zox1 + Zsi1); Zsubox1si1 = Zox1si1 + Zsub;
    Zsubox1si1si2 = (Zsi2.*Zsubox1si1)./(Zsi2 + Zsubox1si1);
    Zsubox1si1si2ox2 = Zox2 + Zsubox1si1si2;
    ZeqY22 = (Zs.*Zsubox1si1si2ox2)./(Zs + Zsubox1si1si2ox2);
```

```
        Y22(ix, 1) = U2./ZeqY22;
        Ysub = 1./Zsub;  Yox1 = 1./Zox1;  Yox2 = 1./Zox2;  Ysi1 = 1./Zsi1; Ysi2 = 1./Zsi2;
        %Calculate Y12, V1 = 0, V2 = 1
        %Expressions taken from symmetry considerations with Y21
        VZox1 = (Yox2.*Ysub)./((Yox2 + Ysi2).*(Ysub + Yox1 + Ysi1) + Ysub.*(Yox1 + Ysi1));
        IZox1 = VZox1./Zox1;  Is = V2./Zs; I1 = Is + IZox1;  Y12(ix, 1) = -I1./U2;
        %Calculate Y21, V1 = 1, V2 = 0
        %Expressions taken from the symbolic extraction of Y21
        VZox2 = (Yox1.*Ysub)./((Yox1 + Ysi1).*(Ysub + Yox2 + Ysi2) + Ysub.*(Yox2 + Ysi2));
        IZox2 = VZox2./Zox2;  Is = V1./Zs;  I2 = Is + IZox2;
        Y21(ix, 1) = -I2./U1;
    end
    %Least squares sum of the difference between the modules of the required and the current
Y-parameters
    g_fun = g_fun + ((abs(Y11) - abs(Y11_req(i)))).^2 + ((abs(Y12) - abs(Y12_req(i)))).^2 +
((abs(Y21) - abs(Y21_req(i)))).^2 + ((abs(Y22) - abs(Y22_req(i)))).^2;
    end
```

The presented procedure for optimization of the model parameters of the wide-band on-chip spiral inductor model is verified according to the published data in (Gil & Shin, 2003; Chen et al., 2008). The relative percentage error for the modules of the extracted and the measured Y-parameters is used to estimate the accuracy of the optimization procedure for various geometry RF spiral inductors. The maximal relative percentage error is calculated for the modules of the Y-parameters in the form:

$$\mathrm{RelErr}_{Y\max} = 100.\max_{i}\left|1 - \frac{Y_{jk}(f_i)}{Y_{jk}^{(m)}(f_i)}\right|, \tag{13}$$

where j, k = 1,2;

$Y_{jk}^{(m)}$ - measured Y-parameters;

Y_{jk} - simulated Y-parameters of the model.

The obtained results for the relative errors from the extraction procedure and after the optimization procedure are compared and the error improvement for each of the Y-parameters is shown in Table 1. For example, the extracted values for the case of 4.5 x 30 x 14.5 x 2 geometry (Table 1) are: R_{s0} = 6.680 Ω, R_{s1} = 7.588 Ω, L_{s0} = 3.02 nH, L_{s1} = 1.183 nH, C_{ox1} = 119.57 fF, C_{ox2} = 112.745 fF, R_{si1} = 291.376 Ω, R_{si2} = 286.831 Ω, C_{si1} = 34.133 fF, C_{si2} = 32.993 fF, R_{sub} = 946.544 Ω and C_{sub} = 72.409 fF.

Dimension (N x R x W x S)*	Relative error improvement, %			
	Y_{11}	Y_{12}	Y_{21}	Y_{22}
2.5 x 60 x 14.5 x 2	15	19	19	16
4.5 x 60 x 14.5 x 2	32	33	33	43
6.5 x 60 x 14.5 x 2	14	9	9	7
4.5 x 30 x 14.5 x 2	61	34	34	36
3.5 x 60 x 9 x 7.5	29	37	37	14

* N: number of turns, R: inner radius (μm), W: metal width (μm), S: spacing (μm)

Table 1. Error improvement after the application of GA optimization procedure

The corresponding relative errors are: $RelErr_{Y11max} = 0.254$ %, $RelErr_{Y12max} = 0.062$ %, $RelErr_{Y21max} = 0.062$ %, $RelErr_{Y22max} = 0.239$ %. After the GA optimization, the following model parameter values are obtained: $R_{s0} = 6.697\ \Omega$, $R_{s1} = 7.558\ \Omega$, $L_{s0} = 3.02$ nH, $L_{s1} = 1.184$ nH, $C_{ox1} = 119.776$ fF, $C_{ox2} = 112.479$ fF, $R_{si1} = 292.638\ \Omega$, $R_{si2} = 285.733\ \Omega$, $C_{si1} = 33.997$ fF, $C_{si2} = 32.958$ fF, $R_{sub} = 944.4\ \Omega$ and $C_{sub} = 72.516$ fF.
The corresponding relative errors after the GA optimization are: $RelErr_{Y11max} = 0.099$ %, $RelErr_{Y12max} = 0.041$ %, $RelErr_{Y21max} = 0.041$ %, $RelErr_{Y22max} = 0.154$ %. Thus the improvement of the errors is 61%, 34%, 34% and 36% respectively. The improvement is achieved with 0.5% variation of the model parameter values. The proposed algorithm shows excellent agreement with the measured data over the whole frequency range.

4. Parameter extraction of the wide-band planar inductor model using MATLAB

Several extraction procedures for wide-band on-chip spiral inductor model are proposed in (Kang et al., 2005; Chen et al., 2008). An automated parameter extraction procedure using MATLAB is developed in (Gadjeva et al., 2009).
The input data is supplied to the MATLAB script as an Excel file .xls. The data is structured in columns, starting from the frequency column, followed by the real and imaginary parts of the measured two-port S-parameters: S_{11re}, S_{11im}, S_{12re}, S_{12im}, S_{21re}, S_{21im}, S_{22re} and S_{22im}.
The program has the option for the two-port Y-parameters to be the input data. In the most cases the input data are the measured S-parameters, which are easier to measure and the network analyzers provide this data. Once accepted from the .xls file, the S-parameters are converted to Y-parameters, as the parameter extraction procedure works with Y-parameters. The conversion is done using the MATLAB *s2y* function. Once converted, the input data is structured into five vectors: $[freq]_{n\times1}$, $[Y11]_{n\times1}$, $[Y12]_{n\times1}$, $[Y21]_{n\times1}$, $[Y22]_{n\times1}$, where n is the number of points, measured as input data. The input data can be represented as a matrix $[INPUT\_DATA]_{DATA\_ROWS\ x\ 9}$ for nine input data vectors – frequency vector matrix and the real and the imaginary parts vectors for the two-port S- or Y-parameters.
The enhanced model of spiral inductor (Gil & Shin, 2003) shown in Fig. 1a can be approximately characterized by the upper subcircuit for lower frequencies. Such an approximation has been widely applied to calculate the series resistance and inductance (Kang et al., 2005; Huang et al., 2006). To minimize the error, caused by the approximation, the upper frequency limit must be calculated and fixed in the parameter extraction program. For this reason, the spiral inductor model shown in Fig. 1a can be represented by the equivalent schematics in Fig. 3 (π-network).

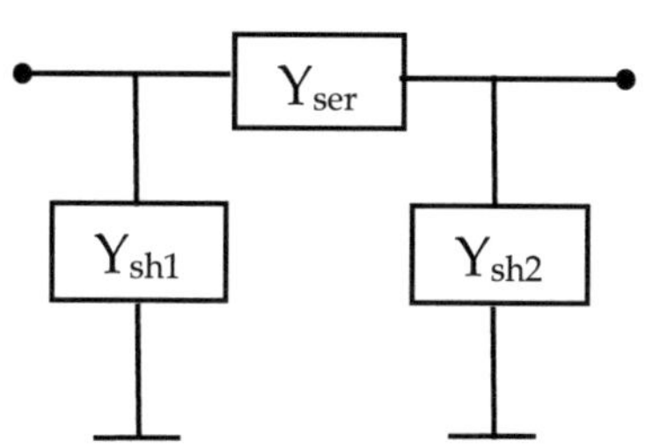

Fig. 3. Relation between the shunt and series admittances of the π-network for the spiral inductor model

In this network, the following expressions are valid (Chen et al., 2008):

$$Y_{ser} = -Y_{12}\ ; \quad Y_{sh1} = Y_{11} + Y_{12}\ ; \quad Y_{sh2} = Y_{22} + Y_{12}\ , \tag{14}$$

$$RAT_{1u} = 100\left|\frac{Y_{sh1}}{Y_{ser}}\right|; \quad RAT_{2u} = 100\left|\frac{Y_{sh2}}{Y_{ser}}\right|. \tag{15}$$

It is shown in (Chen et al., 2008) that the normalized magnitudes of the upper subcircuit RAT_{1u} and RAT_{2u} should be smaller than 1% in order to achieve accurate low frequency approximation. The frequency values in the $[freq]_{n\times1}$ data vector are in the range $[F_{min}; F_{max}]$. F_{min} is the start frequency and F_{max} is the end frequency at which the input two-port Y- or S-parameters are measured. The values of these two frequencies can be easily defined in MATLAB using *min* and *max* functions over the vector $[freq]_{n\times1}$:

```
Fmin = min(freq);
Fmax = max(freq);
```

The expressions (14) and (15), written as a MATLAB code are in the form:

```
Ysh1 = Y11 + Y12;   Ysh2 = Y22 + Y12;
rat1u = 100*abs(Ysh1./Y12);   rat2u = 100*abs(Ysh2./Y12);
```

The maximal frequencies, at which the normalized magnitudes of the vector components are less than 1%, can be found using the following code over the matrices $[freq]_{n\times1}$, $[RAT_{1u}]_{n\times1}$ and $[RAT_{2u}]_{n\times1}$:

```
for i = 1:DATA_ROWS
  if(rat1u(i) <= 1.0)
       freq_low_rat1u = freq(i);
  elseif(rat1u_min > 1.0)
       freq_low_rat1u = freq_low_rat1u_min;
       ErrorMsg
  end
  if(rat2u(i) <= 1.0)
       freq_low_rat2u = freq(i);
  elseif(rat2u_min > 1.0)
       freq_low_rat2u = freq_low_rat2u_min;
       ErrorMsg
  end
end
F1 = min(freq_low_rat1u, freq_low_rat2u);
```

Here n = DATA_ROWS and an error message ErrorMsg is written in case when there are no component values in $[RAT_{1u}]_{n\times1}$ and $[RAT_{2u}]_{n\times1}$, smaller than 1%. This occurs when the input data have not enough number of points or they are not precisely measured. The minimum values found in vectors $[RAT_{1u}]_{n\times1}$ and $[RAT_{2u}]_{n\times1}$ (freq_low_rat1u_min and freq_low_rat2u_min) are taken into account in this case and this could cause deviations in the calculations.

The frequency range, where the upper subcircuit from Fig. 1a represents the approximate behaviour of the spiral inductor model, is then fixed to [F_{min}; F_1], where F_1 is the minimal value of the frequencies freq_low_rat1u and freq_low_rat2u.
Once F_1 and F_{max} were calculated, the low and high frequency vectors: [freq_low]freq_low_rows x freq_low_columns and [freq_high]freq_high_rows x freq_high_columns can be found, which will be needed for the further indexing of the matrices in the calculations:

```
for i = 1:DATA_ROWS
  if(freq(i) <= F1)
      freq_low(i, 1) = freq(i);
  elseif(freq(i) <= Fmax)
      freq_high(i, 1) = freq(i);
  end
end
[freq_low_rows, freq_low_columns] = size(freq_low);
[freq_high_rows, freq_high_columns] = size(freq_high);
```

4.1. Extraction of L_{s0}, R_{s0}, L_{s1}, and R_{s1}

The equivalent resistance and inductance of the upper subcircuit are obtained for the frequency range [F_{min} ; F_1]:

$$R_{uf} = \Re[Z_u] \;\; ; \;\; L_{uf} = \frac{\Im[Z_u]}{\omega} \;\; ; \;\; Z_u = -1/Y_{12} \;. \tag{16}$$

The dc resistance and inductance R_{dc} and L_{dc} are calculated for $\omega = 0$. In the real case these values are calculated for $\omega = 2\pi F_{min}$ according to the following expressions:

$$R_{dc\max} = \max_i\left(\frac{R_{uf_i} F_{min}}{f_i}\right) \;\; ; \qquad L_{dc\max} = \max_i\left(L_{uf_i}\right). \tag{17}$$

The relation between the differences ΔR_{uf} and ΔL_{uf} gives the coefficient T from (Chen et al., 2008) defined in the form:

$$\Delta R_{uf} = R_{uf} - R_{dc\max} \;\; ; \;\; \Delta L_{uf} = L_{dc\max} - L_{uf} \;, \tag{18}$$

$$T = \frac{\Delta R_{uf}}{\Delta L_{uf}} \;\; ; \qquad T_{max} = \max_i\left(\frac{f_i}{F_1} . \frac{\Delta R_{uf_i}}{\Delta L_{uf_i}}\right). \tag{19}$$

The coefficient M and its maximal value M_{max} are obtained in the form (Chen et al., 2008):

$$M = \Delta R_{uf}\left(1 + T_\omega^2\right) ; \quad M_{max} = \max_i\left(\Delta R_{uf_i}\left(1 + T_{\omega_i}^2\right)\right) \;\; ; \;\; T_\omega = T/\omega \,. \tag{20}$$

The values of R_{s0}, R_{s1}, L_{s0} and L_{s1} are calculated directly from the obtained scalar values for R_{dcmax}, L_{dcmax}, T_{max} and M_{max} (Chen et al. , 2008):

$$R_{s0} = M_{max} + R_{dc\max} \;\; ; \quad R_{s1} = \frac{R_{s0} R_{dc\max}}{M_{max}} \;, \tag{21}$$

$$L_{s0} = L_{dc\,max} - M_{max}/T_{max}\ ;\quad L_{s1} = \frac{R_{s0} + R_{s1}}{T_{max}}. \tag{22}$$

Using the equations (16) – (21), the upper subcircuit parameter extraction can be done with the following MATLAB source code:

```
Zu = -1./Y12; Ruf = real(Zu([1 : freq_low_rows], 1)); Rdc = (Ruf*Fmin)./freq_low;
Luf = imag(Zu([1 : freq_low_rows], 1))./(w([1 : freq_low_rows], 1));
Rdc_max = max(Rdc) + 1.0e-15; Ldc_max = max(Luf) + 1.0e-15;
DRuf = Ruf - Rdc_max; DLuf = Ldc_max - Luf;
T = ((freq_low./F1).*DRuf)./DLuf; %Luf(x,x) = Ldc_max => Warning: Divide by zero.
T_max = max(T); Tw = T_max./w([1 : freq_low_rows], 1);
M = DRuf.*(1 + (Tw.*Tw)); M_max = max(M); Rs0 = M_max + Rdc_max;
Rs1 = (Rs0*Rdc_max)/M_max; Rt = Rs0 + Rs1; Ls0 = Ldc_max - (M_max/T_max);
Ls1 = (Rs0+Rs1)/T_max;
```

A small number of 1×10^{-15} is added to calculate R_{dcmax} and L_{dcmax} to avoid division by zero.

4.2. Extraction of C_{ox1} and C_{ox2}

Once the model parameters R_{s0}, R_{s1}, L_{s0} and L_{s1} are calculated, based on measured data in the frequency range [F_{min}, F_1], the equivalent series impedance Z_s and admittance Y_s of the upper subcircuit can be found using the following expressions:

$$Z_s = j\omega L_{s0} + \frac{1}{\dfrac{1}{R_{s0}} + \dfrac{1}{R_{s1} + j\omega L_{s1}}}\ ;\qquad Y_s = \frac{1}{Z_s}. \tag{23}$$

For frequencies greater than F_1 the lower subcircuit has to be taken into account. The Y-matrix of the lower subcircuit [Y_l] is obtained in the form:

$$[Y_l] = [Y] - [Y_s], \tag{24}$$

where [Y_s] is the admittance matrix of the upper subcircuit;
[Y] - admittance matrix of the entire model.

$$Y_{11l} = Y_{11} - Y_s\ ;\quad Y_{12l} = Y_{12} + Y_s\ ;\quad Y_{22l} = Y_{22} - Y_s\,. \tag{25}$$

The lower subcircuit from Fig. 1a can be represented again as a π-network. The following expressions are valid for this subcircuit (Chen et al., 2008):

$$Y_{sh\,1l} = Y_{11l} - Y_{12l}\ ;\qquad Y_{sh\,2l} = Y_{22l} - Y_{12l}\ ;\qquad Y_{serl} = -Y_{12l}\,, \tag{26}$$

$$RAT_{1l} = 100\left|\frac{Y_{serl}}{Y_{sh\,1l}}\right|;\qquad RAT_{2l} = 100\left|\frac{Y_{serl}}{Y_{sh\,2l}}\right|. \tag{27}$$

It is shown in (Chen et al., 2008) that the normalized magnitudes of the lower subcircuit RAT_{1l} and RAT_{2l} should be smaller than 5% in order to achieve accurate high frequency approximation.

The expressions (23) - (27), written as a MATLAB code, are in the form:

```
Zs = j*w*Ls0 + (1./((1/Rs0) + (1./(Rs1 + j*w*Ls1)))); Ys = 1./Zs; Y11l = Y11 - Ys;
Y12l = Y12 + Ys; Y22l = Y22 - Ys; Ysh1l = Y11l + Y12l; Ysh2l = Y22l + Y12l; Yserl = -Y12l;
rat1l = 100.*abs(Yserl./Ysh1l); rat2l = 100.*abs(Yserl./Ysh2l);
```

The maximal frequencies, at which the components of the vector of normalized magnitudes have values less than 5%, can be found using the following code over the matrices $[\text{frequency}]_{n\times 1}$, $[RAT_{1l}]_{n\times 1}$ and $[RAT_{2l}]_{n\times 1}$:

```
for i = 1:DATA_ROWS
  if(freq(i) >= F1)
    if(rat1l(i) <= 5.0)
        freq_low_rat1l = freq(i);
    elseif(rat1l_min > 5.0)
        freq_low_rat1l = freq_low_rat1l_min;
        ErrorMsg
    end
    if(rat2l(i) <= 5.0)
        freq_low_rat2l = freq(i);
    elseif(rat2l_min > 5.0)
        freq_low_rat2l = freq_low_rat2l_min;
        ErrorMsg
    end
  end
end
F2 = min(freq_low_rat1l, freq_low_rat2l);
```

ErrorMsg is written in case there are no component values in $[RAT_{1l}]_{n\times 1}$ and $[RAT_{2l}]_{n\times 1}$, smaller than 5%. The minimum values found in vectors $[RAT_{1l}]_{n\times 1}$ and $[RAT_{2l}]_{n\times 1}$ namely freq_low_rat1l_min and freq_low_rat2l_min are taken into account in this case and this could cause deviations in the calculations.

The frequency range, where the lower subcircuit from Fig. 1a represents the approximate behaviour of the spiral inductor model is then fixed to $[F_1; F_2]$, where F_2 is the minimal frequency between freq_low_rat1l and freq_low_rat2l.

Once F_2 is calculated, the middle frequency vector $[\text{freq\_mid}]_{\text{freq\_mid\_rows x freq\_mid\_columns}}$ can be found, which will be needed for the further indexing of the matrices in the calculations:

```
for i = 1:DATA_ROWS
  if(freq(i) <= F2)
      freq_mid(i, 1) = freq(i);
  end
end
[freq_mid_rows, freq_mid_columns] = size(freq_mid);
```

Then C_{ox1} and C_{ox2} can be extracted as maximal values in the range $[F_1; F_2]$ using the expressions from (Chen et al., 2008):

$$C_{ox1} = \frac{-1}{\omega\Im\left[1/\left(Y_{11l}+Y_{12l}\right)\right]}; \quad C_{ox2} = \frac{-1}{\omega\Im\left[1/\left(Y_{22l}+Y_{12l}\right)\right]}. \tag{28}$$

The following MATLAB source code is used for the calculation of C_{ox1} and C_{ox2}:

```
Cox1 = max(-1./(imag(1./(Y11l([freq_low_rows : freq_mid_rows], 1) + Y12l([freq_low_rows : freq_mid_rows], 1))).*w([freq_low_rows : freq_mid_rows], 1)));
Cox2 = max(-1./(imag(1./(Y22l([freq_low_rows : freq_mid_rows], 1) + Y12l([freq_low_rows : freq_mid_rows], 1))).*w([freq_low_rows : freq_mid_rows], 1)));
```

4.3. Extraction of R_{si1}, R_{si2}, C_{si1}, C_{si2}, R_{sub} and C_{sub}

The lower subcircuit represents the behavior of the model in the range $[F_2; F_{max}]$. It is analyzed for the extraction of R_{si1}, R_{si2}, C_{si1}, C_{si2}, R_{sub} and C_{sub} based on the relations between the lower subcircuit Y-parameters and the input and output voltages $\dot{V}_1$ and $\dot{V}_2$ using the previously extracted values for the model parameters C_{ox1} and C_{ox2}.

$$\dot{V}_{1a} = \left(1 - \frac{Y_{11l}}{j\omega C_{ox1}}\right)\dot{V}_1 \; ; \qquad \dot{V}_{2a} = \left(-\frac{Y_{12l}}{j\omega C_{ox2}}\right)\dot{V}_1 , \tag{29}$$

$$\dot{V}_{2b} = \left(1 - \frac{Y_{22l}}{j\omega C_{ox2}}\right)\dot{V}_2 \; ; \qquad \dot{V}_{1b} = \left(-\frac{Y_{12l}}{j\omega C_{ox1}}\right)\dot{V}_2 , \tag{30}$$

$$\Delta_V = \dot{V}_{1a}\dot{V}_{2a} - \dot{V}_{1b}\dot{V}_{2a} \; ; \qquad \Delta_{V1} = (Y_{11} + Y_{12})\dot{V}_{2b} - (Y_{22} + Y_{12})\dot{V}_{2a} , \tag{31}$$

$$\Delta_{V2} = (Y_{22} + Y_{12})\dot{V}_{1a} - (Y_{11} + Y_{12})\dot{V}_{1b} . \tag{32}$$

As a result, the model parameters R_{si1}, R_{si2}, C_{si1}, C_{si2} can be extracted directly as follows:

$$R_{si1} = \max_i\left(\frac{f_i/F_{max}}{\Re(\Delta_{V1}/\Delta_V)}\right) \; ; \; R_{si2} = \max_i\left(\frac{f_i/F_{max}}{\Re(\Delta_{V2}/\Delta_V)}\right) , \tag{33}$$

$$C_{si1} = \max_i\left(\frac{(f_i/F_{max})\Im(\Delta_{V1}/\Delta_V)}{\omega_i}\right) ; \qquad C_{si2} = \max_i\left(\frac{(f_i/F_{max})\Im(\Delta_{V2}/\Delta_V)}{\omega_i}\right) . \tag{34}$$

Expressions (29) – (34) are represented in MATLAB using the following code over matrices operations:

```
Zcox1 = 1./(j*w*Cox1); Zcox2 = 1./(j*w*Cox2); V1a = 1 - (Y11l.*Zcox1);
V2a = -(Y12l.*Zcox2); V2b = 1 - (Y22l.*Zcox2); V1b = -(Y12l.*Zcox1);
DV = (V1a.*V2b) - (V1b.*V2a);
DV1 = ((Y11 + Y12).*V2b) - ((Y22 + Y12).*V2a);
DV2 = (V1a.*(Y22 + Y12)) - (V1b.*(Y11 + Y12));
Rsi1 = max((freq([freq_mid_rows : freq_high_rows], 1)/Fmax)./real(DV1([freq_mid_rows : freq_high_rows], 1)./DV([freq_mid_rows : freq_high_rows], 1)));
Rsi2 = max((freq([freq_mid_rows : freq_high_rows], 1)/Fmax)./real(DV2([freq_mid_rows : freq_high_rows], 1)./DV([freq_mid_rows : freq_high_rows], 1)));
Csi1 = max((freq([freq_mid_rows : freq_high_rows], 1)/Fmax).*imag(DV1([freq_mid_rows : freq_high_rows], 1)./DV([freq_mid_rows : freq_high_rows], 1))./w([freq_mid_rows : freq_high_rows], 1));
```

```
Csi2 = max((freq([freq_mid_rows : freq_high_rows], 1)/Fmax).*imag(DV2([freq_mid_rows : freq_high_rows], 1)./DV([freq_mid_rows : freq_high_rows], 1))./w([freq_mid_rows : freq_high_rows], 1));
```

The following expression for the admittance Y_{sub} can be used to extract R_{sub} and C_{sub}:

$$Y_{sub} = \frac{\left(\Delta_{V2}/\Delta_V + j\omega C_{ox2}\right)}{\left(\dot{V}_{1a}/\dot{V}_{2a} - 1\right)}; \tag{35}$$

$$R_{sub} = \left\{\max_i\left[\left(f_i/F_{max}\right)\Re\left(Y_{sub}\right)\right]\right\}^{-1}; \qquad C_{sub} = \max_i\left(\frac{\Im\left(Y_{sub}\right)}{\omega_i}\right). \tag{36}$$

Expressions (35) and (36) are represented in MATLAB using the following code over matrix operations:

```
Ysub = ((DV2./DV) + j*w*Cox2)./((V1a./V2a) - 1);
Rsub = 1/max((freq([freq_mid_rows : freq_high_rows], 1)/Fmax).*
real(Ysub([freq_mid_rows : freq_high_rows], 1)));
Csub = max(imag(Ysub([freq_mid_rows : freq_high_rows], 1))./w([freq_mid_rows :
freq_high_rows], 1));
```

4.4. Results of the extraction procedure of the wide-band inductor model

The presented procedure for parameter extraction of wide-band on-chip spiral inductor model in MATLAB was verified according to the published data in (Gil & Shin, 2003). The relative error over the frequency range for the real and the imaginary part of the measured and the extracted Y-parameters is used to estimate the accuracy of the extraction procedure for various geometry RF spiral inductors. The maximal relative error is calculated over the modules of the Y-parameters, using formula (13). The obtained results are presented in Table 2. They are in agreement with the measured results from (Gil & Shin, 2003; Chen et al., 2008). The maximal relative error is less than 0.5% which makes the parameter on-chip spiral inductor parameter extraction procedure very accurate. For example the extracted values for the case of 4.5 x 30 x 14.5 x 2 geometry (Table 2) are: R_{s0} = 6.681 Ω, R_{s1} = 7.589 Ω, L_{s0} = 3.02 nH, L_{s1} = 1.183 nH, C_{ox1} = 119.571 fF, C_{ox2} = 112.745 fF, R_{si1} = 291.377 Ω, R_{si2} = 286.832 Ω, C_{si1} = 34.134 fF, C_{si2} = 32.994 fF, R_{sub} = 946.544 Ω and C_{sub} = 72.41 fF.

Dimension (N x R x W x S)	$RelErr_Y$, %			
	Y_{11}	Y_{12}	Y_{21}	Y_{22}
2.5 x 60 x 14.5 x 2	0.173	0.054	0.054	0.164
4.5 x 60 x 14.5 x 2	0.451	0.101	0.101	0.391
6.5 x 60 x 14.5 x 2	0.479	0.151	0.151	0.436
4.5 x 30 x 14.5 x 2	0.254	0.062	0.062	0.239
3.5 x 60 x 9 x 7.5	0.235	0.065	0.065	0.216

* N: number of turns, R: inner radius (μm), W: metal width (μm), S: spacing (μm)

Table 2. Error estimation of the extraction procedure

5. Parameter Extraction of Physical Geometry Dependent RF Planar Inductor Model

The physical model of planar spiral inductor on silicon (Yue et al., 1996) is a very popular model used in microelectronic design. Its model parameter values can be expressed directly using the geometry of the spiral inductor. The skin effect at high frequencies is modeled using a frequency dependent series resistance. Several extraction procedures are developed for the physical spiral inductor model – direct procedures (Shih et al., 1992), optimization based procedures (Post, 2000). A number of approaches to geometry optimization of spiral inductors are proposed based on geometric programming optimization (Wenhuan & Bandler, 2006), parametric analysis (Hristov et al., 2003), etc. An approach is developed in (Durev et al., 2010) to direct parameter extraction based on the measured S-parameters. The approach gives excellent results for frequencies around the working frequency. GA based approach is used to refine the simulated S-parameters and to minimize the post extraction errors for the full investigated frequency range.

5.1. Analysis of the spiral inductor model

The physical model of spiral inductor (Yue et al., 1996) is shown in Fig. 4. The model parameters are R_s, R_{si}, C_s, C_{ox}, C_{si} and L_s. The series resistance takes into account the skin depth of the conductor. L_s is the inductance of the spiral, C_{ox} represents the capacitance between the spiral and the substrate. R_{si} and C_{si} model the resistance and the capacitance of the substrate, and C_s models the parallel-plate capacitance between the spiral and the center-tap underpass. The presented extraction procedure is based on the measured two-port *S*-parameters.

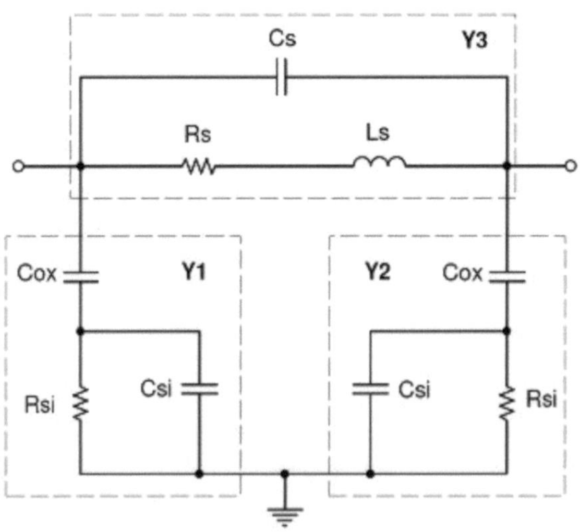

Fig. 4. Physical model of spiral inductor

As the model parameters can be easily expressed by the two-port *Y*-parameters, the measured S-parameters S_{ijm} are converted to Y-parameters Y_{ijm}, i, j = 1, 2. The parameter extraction procedure is based on determination of the admittances Y_1, Y_2 and Y_3 (Fig. 4) as a function of the two-port Y-parameters. The next step is to express the admittances Y_1 and Y_3 as well as the corresponding impedances Z_1 and Z_3 by the model parameters.

The parameters R_s , L_s , R_{si} and C_{ox} are obtained for lower frequencies ($f = f_l$). The parameter C_{si} is determined for high frequencies ($f = f_h$):

$$R_s = \Re(Z_{31}) \ ; \qquad L_s = \Im(Z_{31})/\omega_l \ ; \qquad R_{si} \approx \Re(Z_{11}), \tag{37}$$

$$C_{ox} \approx -\frac{1}{\omega_l \Im(Z_{11})}; \qquad C_{si} \approx -\frac{1}{\omega \Im(Z_{1h}) + \dfrac{1}{C_{ox}}}. \tag{38}$$

The series resistance R_{sw} is obtained for the working frequency f_w. C_s is obtained for the resonant frequency:

$$R_{sw} \approx (\omega_w L_s)^2 \Re(Y_{3w}) \ ; \qquad C_s \approx \frac{L_s}{(\omega_0 L_s)^2 + R_{sw}^2}. \tag{39}$$

The series resistance R_s in Fig. 4 is frequency dependent. If the geometry of the extracted spiral inductor is known, R_s can be calculated using the formula (Yue et al., 1996):

$$R_s = \frac{l}{\sigma w \delta \left(1 - e^{-t/\delta}\right)}, \tag{40}$$

where w is the width of the metal strips, δ is the skin-effect depth into the metal layers, σ is the conductivity of metal layers, l is the length of the spiral, t is the thickness of the metal layer of the spiral (Yue et al., 1996). In case when the geometry of the spiral inductor is not known, R_s can be calculated using the formula (Ashby et al., 1994):

$$R_s = R_0\left(1 + K_1 f^{K_2}\right), \tag{41}$$

where the coefficients K_1 and K_2 determine the frequency dependence of R_s.
The model parameters results after the application of the described direct extraction procedure are given in Table 3.

Model Param.	Extraction Results		
	(N x R x W x S) 6.5 x 60 x 14.5 x 2 f_w = 1.09GHz	(N x R x W x S) 4.5 x 60 x 14.5 x 2 f_w = 1.81GHz	(N x R x W x S) 3.5 x 60 x 9 x 7.5 f_w = 2.91GHz
$R_{s0}(\Omega)$	7.6	5.06	5.68
$R_{sw}(\Omega)$	9.08	6.351	5.7
L_s(nH)	11.9	5.67	3.56
C_{ox}(fF)	232.92	157.02	86.78
$R_{si}(\Omega)$	138.62	225.48	340.28
C_{si}(fF)	123.59	79.98	67.58
C_s(fF)	45.76	96.04	152.99

* N: number of turns, R: internal radius (μm), W: metal width (μm), S: spacing (μm)

Table 3. Model parameter values after the application of the direct extraction procedure

5.2. Error Estimation

The error estimation is given in Table 4. The relative RMS error is used over the investigated frequency range between the measured and the obtained S-parameters for three different geometries spiral inductors, published in (Gil & Shin, 2003):

$$RMSErr_S = 100 \times \sqrt{\frac{1}{n}\sum_{i=1}^{n}\left(1 - \frac{S_{jk}}{S_{jk}^{(m)}}\right)^2}, \tag{42}$$

where j, k = 1, 2; $S_{jk}^{(m)}$ – measured S-parameters (Gil & Shin, 2003);

S_{jk} - obtained S-parameters;

n – number of frequency points.

Geometry (N x R x W x S) Freq. range	RMSErrS, %	
	$\lvert S_{11} \rvert$	$\lvert S_{12} \rvert$
6.5 x 60 x 14.5 x 2 50MHz ÷ 1.3GHz	2.94	1.21
4.5 x 60 x 14.5 x 2 50MHz ÷ 2.1GHz	7.02	1.85
3.5 x 60 x 9 x 7.5 50MHz ÷ 3.2GHz	10.19	4.07

* N: number of turns, R: internal radius (μm), W: metal width (μm), S: spacing (μm)

Table 4. Error estimation of the direct extraction procedure

Because of the determination of C_s for the working frequency f_w the frequency ranges in Table 3 are limited. To enlarge the frequency ranges a GA approach is applied to optimize the model parameter values.

5.3. Optimization of the Model Parameters Based on GA

The model parameter values are varied in a certain range by the GA according to the value of its purpose function. This range is determined to be $\pm 20\%$ around the values from Table 3. As the capacitance C_s is determined at the working frequency, it is expected to decrease at high frequencies. This determines its broader range of variation. The purpose function minimizes the difference between the measured and the obtained Y-parameters:

$$G_{fun} = \sum_{i=1}^{n}\left|\Re[Y_k(f_i)] - \Re\left[Y_k^{(req)}(f_i)\right]\right| + \sum_{i=1}^{n}\left|\Im[Y_k(f_i)] - \Im\left[Y_k^{(req)}(f_i)\right]\right|, \tag{43}$$

where

$k = 1, 3;$

$Y_k(f_i)$ - current admittances;

$Y_k^{(req)}(f_i)$ - admittances obtained by S- to Y-transformation of the measured S-parameters;

n – number of frequency points.

The optimization procedure is realized using the GA Toolbox (Chipperfield et al., 1994) in MATLAB. The GA procedure has the following parameters: NIND = 300, MAXGEN = 200, NVAR = 5, PRECI = 200, GGAP = 0.7, where NIND is the number of individuals, MAXGEN is the maximal number of iterations, NVAR is the number of the optimized model parameters, PRECI is the precision factor, and GGAP is the generation gap (Chipperfield et al., 1994).

The obtained results are given in Table 5. As the model in Fig. 4 is verified up to 10GHz (Yue et al., 1996), the values of the optimized model parameters for geometries 6.5 x 60 x 14.5 x 2 and 4.5 x 60 x 14.5 x 2 preserve their dependence on the geometry of the inductor. The model parameters for geometry 3.5 x 60 x 9 x 7.5 are optimized in the frequency range 50MHz ÷ 14.4GHz and they do not preserve the dependence on the geometry of the inductor.

The comparison between the measured (Gil & Shin, 2003) and GA optimized results of S_{11} and S_{12} of 6.5 x 60 x 14.5 x 2 inductor is shown in Fig. 5. As a result of the GA optimization the obtained relative RMS error is less than 5%.

Model Param.	Extraction Results from MATLAB		
	(N x R x W x S) 6.5 x 60 x 14.5 x 2 f_w = 1.09GHz	(N x R x W x S) 4.5 x 60 x 14.5 x 2 f_w = 1.81GHz	(N x R x W x S) 3.5 x 60 x 9 x 7.5 f_w = 2.91GH
$R_{s0}(\Omega)$	Calculated using expression (40)		
L_s(nH)	11.7	5.48	3.5
C_{ox}(fF)	220	140	40
$R_{si}(\Omega)$	150	240	360
C_{si}(fF)	150	76.7	20
C_s(fF)	6.22	20	15.7

* N: number of turns, R: internal radius (μm), W: metal width (μm), S: spacing (μm)

Table 5. Model parameter values after the GA optimization in MATLAB

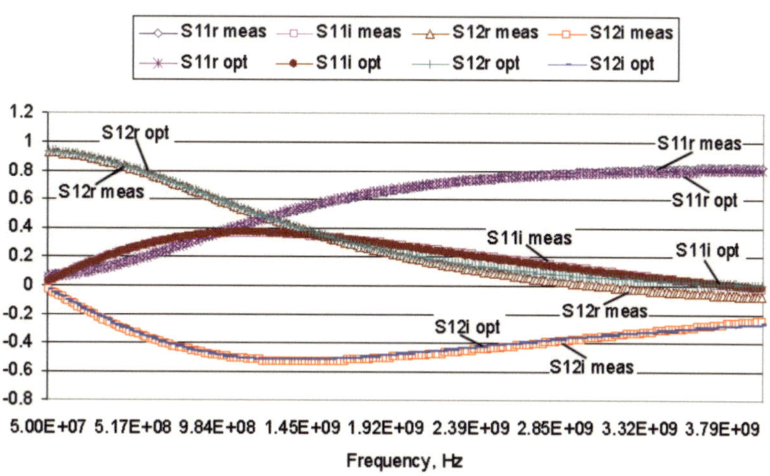

Fig. 5. Comparison between the measured (Gil & Shin, 2003) and GA optimized S-parameters of 6.5 x 60 x 14.5 x 2 inductor

6. Optimization of geometric parameters of spiral inductors using genetic algorithms in MATLAB

Based on the physical model for planar spiral inductors (Yue et al., 1996; Sieiro et al., 2002; Nieuwoudt et al., 2005) and the simple accurate expressions for the inductance (Mohan et al., 1999), a geometry optimization procedure is proposed in (Post, 2000). It allows the obtaining optimal trace width that maximizes the quality factor of the spiral inductor with a required inductance at a given frequency. Optimal design of the parameters of spiral inductors is proposed in (Gadjeva & Hristov, 2004), based on PSpice model and parametric analysis. Computer models are developed in (Gadjeva et al., 2006) using the possibilities of MATLAB and GA toolbox (Chipperfield et al., 1994). GA program designed using GA toolbox in MATLAB is used for optimization the geometric parameters of spiral inductors.

6.1. Optimal design of spiral inductors using GA

The optimal design of the spiral inductors is based on a precise mathematical model, which consists of multiple parameters - dependent and independent. The independent geometry parameters characterizing the spiral inductor are the number of turns n, the trace width w, the spacing sp, and the outer diameter D_{out} (Fig. 6).

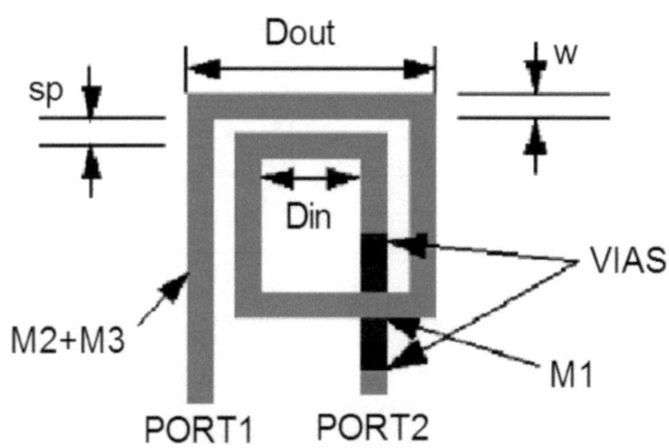

Fig. 6. The geometry parameters of a square spiral inductor

Each of the independent parameters has its own value range, which depends on the used microelectronic technology. The independent geometry parameters - number of turns n, the trace width w, the spacing sp, and the outer diameter D_{out} are fixed in the range:

n = 7 ±50%;
w = 13e-6 ±50%;
sp = 7e-6 ±50%;
Dout = 300e-6 ±50%;

The variables PERL and PERU fix the variation range to ±50%.
In MATLAB this is done in the following way (Chipperfield et al., 1994):
%Variation percent

```
PERL = 0.5; % lower limit
PERU = 1.5; % upper limit
%      %Dout            w               sp             n
FieldD = [PRECI         PRECI           PRECI          PRECI;
     300.0e-6*PERL  13.0e-6*PERL    7.0e-6*PERL    7.0*PERL;
     300.0e-6*PERU  13.0e-6*PERU    7.0e-6*PERU    7.0*PERU;
     1              1               1              1;
     0              0               0              0;
     1              1               1              1;
     1              1               1              1];
```

Based on these parameters, the dependent inductor parameters are calculated: the inner diameter D_{in}, the average diameter $D_{avg} = 0.5(D_{out} + D_{in})$, the trace length $l = 4nD_{avg}$, the area (Mohan et al., 1999; Post, 2000). The computer-aided design model is based on the two-port equivalent circuit of the spiral inductor shown in Fig. 4 (Yue et al., 1996). The parameters R_s, R_{si}, C_s, C_{ox} and C_{si} are in the form (Yue et al., 1996):

$$R_s = \frac{1}{\sigma w \delta \left(1 - e^{-t/\delta}\right)}; \qquad \delta = \sqrt{\frac{2}{\omega \sigma \mu_0}}, \tag{44}$$

$$C_s = \frac{\varepsilon_{ox} n w^2}{t_{oxM1,M2}}; \qquad C_{ox} = \frac{\varepsilon_{ox} l w}{2 t_{ox}}, \tag{45}$$

$$R_{si} = \frac{2}{G_{sub} l w}; \qquad C_{si} = \frac{C_{sub} l w}{2}, \tag{46}$$

where σ is the metal conductivity at dc, t is the metal thickness, δ is the metal skin depth, t_{ox} is the oxide thickness between spiral and substrate, $t_{ox\ M1\ M2}$ is the oxide thickness between spiral and centertap, l is the overall length of spiral, w is the line width, C_{sub} is the ubstrate capacitance per unit area, and G_{sub} is the substrate conductance per unit area.
The parallel equivalent circuit of the spiral inductor shown in Fig. 7 is used for calculating the quality factor Q of the inductor (Mohan et al., 1999):

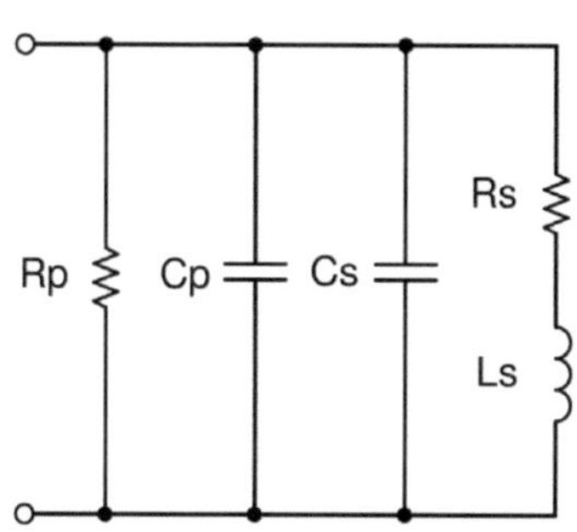

Fig. 7. The parallel equivalent circuit of the spiral inductor

$$Q = \frac{\omega L_s}{R_s} \cdot \frac{R_p}{R_p + \left[(\omega L_s/R_s)^2 + 1\right]R_s} \cdot \left[1 - \frac{R_s^2(C_s + C_p)}{L_s} - \omega^2 L_s (C_s + C_p)\right], \tag{47}$$

where

$$R_p = \frac{1}{\omega^2 C_{ox}^2 R_{si}} + R_{si}\left(1 + \frac{C_{si}}{C_{ox}}\right)^2, \tag{48}$$

$$C_p = C_{ox} \frac{1 + \omega^2 (C_{ox} + C_{si}) C_{si} R_{si}^2}{1 + \omega^2 (C_{ox} + C_{si})^2 R_{si}^2} . \tag{49}$$

The following monomial expression (Post, 2000) is used to model the inductance L_s:

$$L_s = \beta D_{out}^{\alpha 1} w^{\alpha 2} D_{avg}^{\alpha 3} n^{\alpha 4} sp^{\alpha 5} . \tag{50}$$

The dimensions are in μm and the inductance is in nH. The coefficients β, α_i, i = 1,2,...,5 depend on the inductor shape - square, hexagonal and octagonal (Mohan et al., 1999). The data for square inductor are β =1.62e-3, α_1= -1.21, α_2 = - 0.147, α_3 =2.4, α_4 =1.78, α_5 = - 0.03.
The expression ensures good accuracy and agreement between the calculated inductor value and the measured one (Mohan et al., 1999; Post, 2000).
The required inductance L_{sreq}, the frequency f_s , the technological parameters and the coefficients β, α_i , i = 1,2,...,5, are introduced as input data in MATLAB m-file. The optimization was done for L_{sreq} = 7.28 nH and f_s = 2 GHz.
The object function finds the global minimum g_fun for its expression:

$$g\_fun = Q_{req} + W . | L_S - L_{sreq} | , \tag{51}$$

where Q_{req} = 1/Q and W is a weighting coefficient. The minimum value of g_fun guarantees the maximal value for the Q-factor for Lsreq = 7.28 nH. The implementation of the procedure is done in the following way:

1. Introducing the input data:

```
mju = 1.256e-6; beta = 1.62e-3;
al1 = -1.21; al2 = -0.147; al3 = 2.4;
al4 = 1.78; al5 = -0.03; Eox = 3.45e-11;
toxM1M2 = 1.3e-6;
tox = 4.5e-6; Csub = 1.6e-6;
Gsub = 4.0e4; sigma = 1/3e-8;
ro_spec = 1/sigma; t = 1e-6;
frequency = 2e9; %2GHz
math_pi=3.1415965; omg = 2*math_pi*frequency;
delta = sqrt(2.0/(omg*mju*sigma));
Lsreq = 7.28e-9;
```

2. Explicitly enter the independent geometric parameters in order to be recognized from the GA:

```
Dout = Chrom(:,1)
w = Chrom(:,2)
sp = Chrom(:,3)
n = Chrom(:,4)
```

3. Enter the sequence of calcuations in order to obtain the members which take part in the expression for the objective function:

```
Din = (Dout - 2.0.*(n.*(sp + w) - sp));
Davg = 0.5.*(Dout + Din);
L = 4.0.*n.*Davg;
Cs = (n.*(w.^2).*Eox)./toxM1M2;
delta = sqrt(2.0/(omg*mju*sigma));
Cox = (0.5.*L.*w.*Eox)./tox;
Csi = 0.5.*L.*w.*Csub;
Rsi = 2.0./(L.*w.*Gsub);
Rs = L./(w.*sigma.*delta.*(1.0 - exp(-t./delta)));
Cs = (n.*(w.^2).*Eox)./toxM1M2;
Rp = (1./(omg.^2.*Cox.^2.*Rsi)) + (Rsi.*(Cox + Csi).^2)./Cox.^2;
Cp = Cox.*((1 + omg.^2.*(Cox + Csi).*Csi.*Rsi.^2)./(1 + omg.^2.*(Cox + Csi).^2.*Rsi.^2));
Ls = beta*((Dout*1.0e6).^al1).*((w*1.0e6).^al2).*((Davg*1.0e6).^al3).*(n.^al4).*
((sp*1.0e6).^al5).*1.0e-9;
Q = (omg.*Ls./Rs).*(Rp./(Rp + ((omg.*Ls./Rs).^2 + 1).*Rs)).*(1 - Rs.^2.*(Cs + Cp)./Ls -
omg.^2.*Ls.*(Cs + Cp));
Qrec = abs(1.0./Q);
```

4. Calculation the objective function:

```
g_fun = Qrec + 10e8*abs(Ls - Lsreq);
```

Fig. 8 represents the optimization of the Q-factor using the genetic algorithm in MATLAB, described above. After some itterations the GA finds the global minimum for its objective function, which gives the optimized value for the Q-factor.
The optimized geometry parameters using MATLAB GA are: $sp = 7.99\ \mu m$, $w = 13.15\ \mu m$, $n = 3.74$, $Dout = 365.64\ \mu m$.
The GA procedure has the following parameters: NIND = 100, MAXGEN = 100, NVAR = 4, PRECI = 100, GGAP = 0.7. The obtained results are in agreement with the simulated and test results obtained in (Mohan et al., 1999; Post, 2000; Gadjeva & Hristov, 2004).

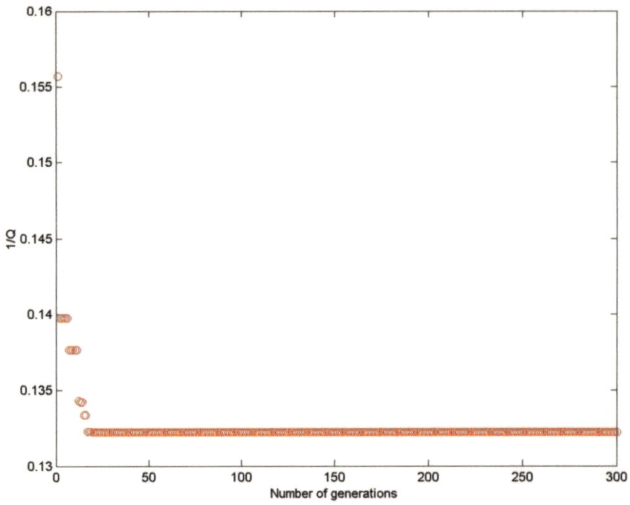

Fig. 8. Optimization of the Q-factor of the spiral inductor using GA in MATLAB

7. Conclusion

The extended possibilities of the general-purpose software MATLAB for modeling, simulation and optimization can be successfully used in RF microelectronic circuit design. Based on description of the device models, various optimization problems can be solved. Automated model parameter extraction procedure for on-chip wide-band spiral inductor model has been developed and realized in the MATLAB environment. The obtained results for the simulated two-port Y- and S-parameters of the spiral inductor model using extracted parameters are compared with the measurement data. The achieved maximal relative error is less than 0.5% which makes the developed parameter extraction procedure of the on-chip spiral inductor model very accurate.

Based on genetic algorithm and GA tool in MATLAB, optimization of geometric parameters of planar spiral inductors for RF applications is performed with respect to the quality factor Q. The optimization maximizes the Q-factor for a given value range of the input independent geometric parameters. The methodology is useful in microelectronics, as every mathematical technological model can be analysed in similar way, which gives an advantage in solving complex problems, based on the technology parameters optimization.

The automated approaches to model parameter extraction and optimizaton of on-chip spiral inductors in the MATLAB environment are universal and flexible and can be similarly applied to various passive and active microelectronic components such as planar transformers, MOSFETs, heterojunction transistors (HBT), etc.

The rich possibilities for analysis and optimization of MATLAB are of great importance in the design process of RF circuits at component and system level.

8. References

Ashby, K.; Finley, W.; Bastek, J.; Moinian, S. & Koullias, I. (1994). High Q inductors for wireless applications in a complementary silicon bipolar process, *Proc. Bipolar and BiCMOS Circuits and Technology Meeting, Minneapolis*, pp. 179-182, MN, USA, 1994, ISBN 0-7803-2117-0.

Chen, H.-H.; Zhang, H.-W.; Chung, S.-J.; Kuo, J.-T. & Wu, T.-C. (2008). Accurate Systematic Model-Parameter Extraction for On-Chip Spiral Inductors, *IEEE Transactions on Electron Devices*, pp. 3267–3273, Vol. 55, issue 11, Lausanne, Switzerland, Nov. 2008, ISSN 0018-9383.

Chipperfield, A.; Fleming, P.; Pohlheim, H. & Fonseca, C. (1994). *Genetic Algorithm TOOLBOX for use with MATLAB, User's Guide Version 1.2*, Department of Automatic Control and Systems Engineering, University of Sheffield, 1994.

Durev, V. P., Gadjeva, E. D. & Hristov, M. (2010). Parameter Extraction of Geometry Dependent RF Planar Inductor Model, *17-th International Conference Mixed Design of Integrated Circuits and Systems -MIXDES'2010*, Wroclaw, 24-26 June 2010, Poland.

Durev, V.P. (2009). Application of Genetic Algorithms in MATLAB to Parameter Extraction Errors Minimization of Wide-Band On-Chip Spiral Inductor Model, *XLIV International Scientific Conference Information, Communication and Energy Systems and Technologies ICEST 2009*, pp. 491-494, 25-27 June, 2009, Veliko Turnovo, Bulgaria. Vol. 2.

Durev, V.P., Gadjeva, E. D., Hristov, M.H. (2009). Wide-band Spiral Inductor Model Parameter Extraction Based on Genetic Algorithms, *15th International Symposium on Power Electronics - Ee 2009*, Novi Sad, Republic of Serbia, October 28-30, 2009.

Gadjeva, E. D., Durev, V. P. , Hristov, M. H. , Pukneva, D. I. (2006). Optimization of Geometric Parameters of Spiral Inductors using Genetic Algorithms, *Proc. of the 13th International Conference Mixed Design of Integrated Circuits and Systems MIXDES 2006*, Gdynia, Poland, pp. 518-521, 22-24 June, 2006, ISBN 83-922632-2-7.

Gadjeva, E.; Durev, V. & Hristov, M. (2009). Automated Procedure for Parameter Extraction of Wide-Band On-Chip Spiral Inductor Model in MATLAB, *16th International Conference Mixed Design of Integrated Circuits and Systems MIXDES'2009*, pp. 406-411, 25-27 June, 2009, Łódź, Poland, ISBN 978-1-4244-4798-5.

Gadjeva, E.D. & Hristov, M.H. (2004). Application of Parametric Analysis in RF Circuit Design, *11-th International Conference Mixed Design of Integrated Circuits and Systems - MIXDES'2004*, Szczecin, 24-26 June 2004, Poland.

Gil, J. & Shin, H. (2003). A simple wide-band on-chip inductor model for silicon-based RF ICs, *IEEE Transactions on Microwave Theory and Techniques*, Vol. 51, issue 9, pp. 2023–2028, Sept., 2003, ISSN 0018-9480

Hershenson, M.; Mohan, S. S.; Boyd, S. P. & Lee, T. H. (1999). Optimization of Inductor Circuits via Geometric Programming, *36th Annual Conference on Design Automation (DAC'99)*, pp. 994-998, 21-25 June 1999, ISBN: 1-58113-109-7.

Hristov, M.; Gadjeva, E. & Pukneva, D. (2003). Computer Modelling and Geometry Optimization of Spiral Inductors for RF Applications Using Spice, *The 10th International Conference Mixed Design of Integrated Circuits and Systems, MIXDES'2003*, 26-28 June 2003, Lodz, Poland.

Huang, F.; Jiang, N. & Bian, E. (2006). Characteristic-function approach to parameter extraction for asymmetric equivalent circuit of on-chip spiral inductors, IEEE Trans. Microw. Theory Tech., Scottsdale, AZ, USA, vol. 54, issue 1, pp. 115–119, Jan. 2006, ISSN: 0018-9480

Kang, M.; Gil, J. & Shin, H. (2005). A simple parameter extraction method of spiral on-chip inductors, *IEEE Transactions on Electron Devices*, pp.1976–1981, Vol. 52, issue 9, Sept. 2005, ISSN 0018-9383.

Mohan, S., Hershenson, M.; Boyd, S. & Lee, T.H. (1999). Simple Accurate Expressions for Planar Spiral Inductances, *IEEE Journal of Solid-State Circuits,* pp.1419-1424, Vol. 34, issue 10, Oct. 1999, ISSN 0018-9200.

Mohan, S.; Hershenson, M.; Boyd, S. P. & Lee, T. H. (2000). Bandwidth Extension in CMOS with Optimized On-Chip Inductors, *IEEE Journal of Solid-State Circuits*, pp. 346-355, Vol. 35, no.3, March 2000.

Nieuwoudt, A. & Massoud, Y. (2005). Robust Automated Synthesis Methodology for Integrated Spiral Inductors with Variability, *Proceedings of the 2005 IEEE/ACM International conference on Computer-aided design*, pp. 502-507, San Jose, CA, 2005, ISBN:0-7803-9254-X.

Nieuwoudt, A.; McCorquodale M. S.; Borno, R.T. & Massoud, Y. (2005). Efficient Analytical Modeling Techniques for Rapid Integrated Spiral Inductor Prototyping, *IEEE 2005 Custom Integrated Circuits Conference*, San Jose, California, pp. 281-284, Sept. 18-21, 2005.

Post, J. E. (2000). Optimizing the Design of Spiral Inductors on Silicon, *IEEE Trans. on Circuits and Systems - II: Analog and Digital Signal Processing*, pp. 15-17, Vol. 47, No 1, Jan. 2000.

Shih, Y.C.; Pao, C.K. & Itoh, T. (1992). A broadband parameter extraction technique for the equivalent circuit of planar inductors, IEEE MTT-S International Microwave Symposium Digest, pp. 1345-1348, 1992., Vol.3, 1-5 Jun 1992.

Sieiro, J. et al. (2002). A physical frequency-dependent compact model for RF integrated inductors, IEEE Trans. Microwave Theory Tech., pp. 384–392, Vol. 50, Jan. 2002.

Sivanandam, S. N. & Deepa, S. N. (2008). *Introduction to Genetic Algorithms*, Springer, 2008, ISBN 978-3-540-73189-4.

Sun, L.; Wen, J.; Yan, J. & Hu, J. (2004). Modeling and parameters extraction of spiral inductors for silicon-based RFICs, *Proceedings 7th International Conference on Solid-State and Integrated Circuits Technology*, pp. 224-227, Vol. 1, 18-21 Oct. 2004, ISBN 0-7803-8511-X.

Wen, J.-C. & Sun, L.-L. (2006). A Wide-Band Equivalent Circuit Model for CMOS On-Chip Spiral Inductor, *8th International Conference on Solid-State and Integrated Circuit Technology ICSICT '06*, pp. 1383-1385, Shanghai, China, 23-26 Oct. 2006, ISBN 1-4244-0160-7.

Wenhuan Yu & Bandler, J.W. (2006). Optimization of Spiral Inductor on Silicon Using Space mapping, *IEEE MTT-S*, pp. 1085-1088, June 2006.

Yue, C. P.; Ryu, C.; Lau, J.; Lee, T. H. & Wong, S. S. (1996). A Physical model for planar spiral inductors on silicon, *Proc. IEEE Int. Electron Devices Meeting Tech. Dig., San Francisco,* pp. 155-158., CA, Dec. 1996.

Zhan, Y. & Sapatnekar, S. S. (2004). Optimization of Integrated Spiral Inductors Using Sequential Quadratic Programming, *Proceedings of the conference on Design, automation and test in Europe,* P. 10622 , Vol. 1, 2004, ISBN:0-7695-2085-5-1.

Modelling and simulation of processes from an iron ore sintering plants

Corina Maria Diniş
Politechnica University Timişoara
ROMANIA

1. Introduction

Restructuring of metallurgical industry is strongly influenced by the modernization of manufacturing processes from the sintering plants. Sintering, as physical-chemical process of iron ores preparation and obtaining of a controlled situation, is of maximum importance because the resulted agglomerate allows the obtaining of quality cast-irons as they are required currently on the market. The current technology of cast-iron making imposes more and more rigorous conditions to the quality of the charge that should allow the optimization of the entire process, increasing the productivity and reducing the coke consumption.
In this respect, the major cast-iron producing countries are using iron ores previously prepared as agglomerate, meant to ensure the achievement of some charges with high iron content and homogeneous from chemical and grading viewpoint. From the processes with special influence on preparation, will be analyze: dosing, sintering and cooling (fig.1).
Dosing flow includes the quantitative dosing of the charge components, their pre-homogenization into the primary mixing drum (TAP) and the conveying flow of the mixture/blend from the dosing station into the main body to the charge bunker of the sintering machine. Materials extraction from the dosing station's bunkers and their further dosing is achieved by means of dozers with extracting belt. These are mounted in the bunker's entry and they extract the material from the bunker at the flow required by the charge recipe. The mixture, which is formed in accordance with the calculated recipe, is collected by the conveyor belts and transported to the TAP primary mixing station. During the process, to the dosed mixture is added further the hot return brought by the metallic belts to the return bunker (Diniş et al., 2008)
From the TAP, which has an inclination of 2 - 3^0, the charge mixture is overflowed on the conveyors and the transport is continued on other two conveyor belts towards the main section of the sintering plant from the charge bunker. The above description shows that the conveying process contains a multitude of working machines and is undergoing based on a complex algorithm, being suitable for organization into a hierarchical structure an a software-oriented control. The analyzed belt conveyor system in this work contains the following main elements: a main belt, a collector belt and two working belts. On the two working belts are delivered: the hot return from the return bunker (BRET) and the limestone, coke and iron ores from BKCM bunker (Aguilar et al., 2008).

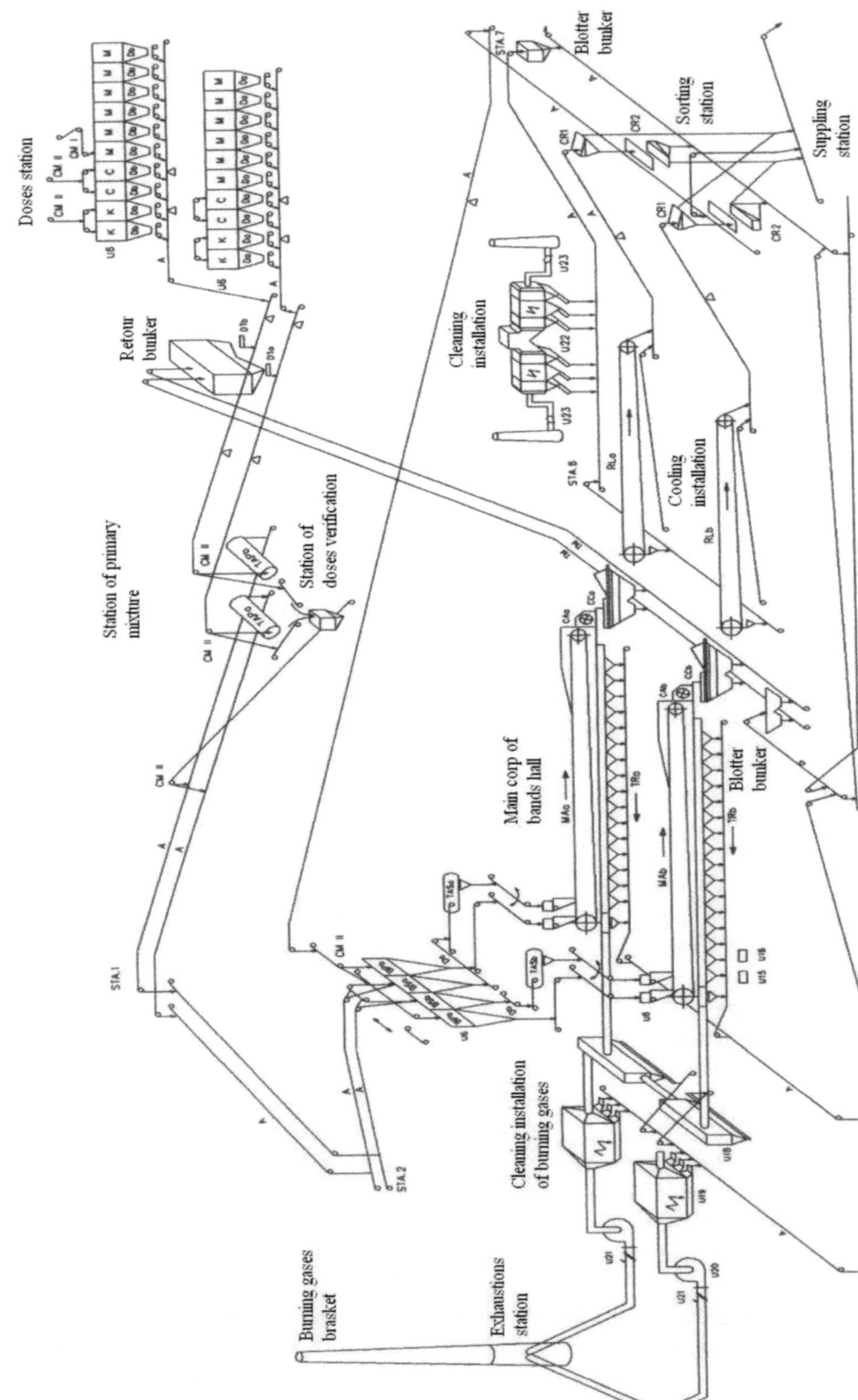

Fig. 1. Technological diagram of the sintering process

The entire charge mixture is discharged from the bus-belt into the charge bunker (BSRJ). The presence of these belts is controlled by level transducers. Each conveyor is served by three transducers: of speed, overflow and emergency and is driven by a motor, being present also a preventive signaling horn.

Sintering flow includes the following steps: mixing/blending, humectation and forming of micro-pellets in the secondary mixing drum (TAS); loading the mixture on the sintering machine's carriers; burning-up the charge; sintering of the mixture/blend; sizing of the agglomerate and recirculation of the return. The material from the charge bunker is extracted by a gravimetric dozer with extracting belt, and loaded further in the secondary mixing drum. Inside the TAS, the material is brought to the necessary humidity for the sintering process (7-10%), by adding water.

The humid material, homogenized and micro-palletized in TAS, is loaded on the sintering machine, uniformly on the entire machine's surface, by an oscillating belt. Repartition of the protection bed on the sintering machine's grills should be made in a uniform layer on the entire width of the machine.

The height of the layer on the sintering machine is adjusted by changing the position of the shield against the machine's grills and is established depending on the material's gas permeability.

Cooling flow includes the following steps: cooling of the agglomerate after the hot screening; conveying in cold condition to the screening station; conveying to the furnaces silos and to the agglomerate's shipment station.

Cooling of the agglomerate is made on two linear coolers, one for each sintering machine. The cooling air is supplied by 5 fans with an air flow of 200000 m^3/h, blow by each fan. At the entrance on the cooler, the agglomerate has a temperature of 700-800^{0}C and leaves the cooler with 80-100^{0}C, fact which allows it to be transported by some special rubber belts. Each cooling machine is served by an auxiliary belts flow, with the role to collect and convey the material which is returning on the inferior line of the linear cooler and the one which falls under the cooling machines (Diniş et al., 2008).

Each cooling machine is served by an auxiliary belts flow, with the role to collect and convey the material which is returning on the inferior line of the linear cooler and the one which falls under the cooling machines.

The continuous transportation process using belt conveyors is one of the most used solutions in various activity fields, starting with sorting of substances from industrial shops, going further with material processing from the sintering plants and ending with flexible robotized lines or the conveyors flow from airports.

As overview, the control of such transportation flow is very complex, both concerning the necessary hardware equipment and the implementation of control algorithms. Nowadays, the major part of conveyors' control systems is hardware-oriented. These contain many hardware components, such as: electromechanical elements, logical and analogical devices, discrete components, power electronics, etc. The control program is reduced to minimum and is implemented, usually, on the microcontroller (Ho & Ranky, 1997)

A microcontroller is an integrated circuit that achieves many of a typical computing system's functions. This contains in a single chip a microprocessor as central processing unit, memories, counters, converters, input-output peripherals. One of the advantages of the systems with microcontroller is using the software to replace a complex logic, without modifying anything in the hard structure. Another advantage is that it uses software

instead of some complex and expensive hardware components. Thus, by using microcontrollers are saved the costs due to some expensive hardware components, and the necessary physical space is much more reduced. In many cases, the hardware equipment reduces the reliability and flexibility of the entire system.
On the other hand, this control system, together with the power electronics, is higher in volume and price than the working machine itself.
Development of computerized technologies emphasized that very many control elements, controls, automation, etc. of mechanical, electrical and electronically nature can be achieved by program, reducing the complexity and saving materials and labor, with positive effect on cost and safety in operation.
Thus has been developed a new trend, which is currently dominant in designing of technical systems, called „software-oriented technology". This technology contains maximum of integrated software resources in product (software-embedded) and minimum of hardware resources, the software resources being in fact products of human intelligence, materialized in programs and included in the equipment, forming its artificial intelligence. In chapter is presenting a software-oriented control system, hierarchically distributed and conceived for a belt conveyors flow, with application for material dosing (Ho & Ranky, 1997).

2. Modelling and simulation of sub-processes from an iron ore sintering plant

In the dosing process from the sintering plants will be taken into account the following conditions:
- the materials supplied for sintering are wet;
- the supplied material quantities are bigger by about 0.5%, percents which represent the losses from manipulation $m_a\,\%$;
- if M is the quantity of wet material (iron ore) that should reach to dosing, the quantity M_a of supplied material is:

$$M_a = \frac{M}{(1 - m_a)} \tag{1}$$

where;

$$m_a = \frac{m_a\%}{100} \tag{2}$$

- the quality of the dosed materials is given in anhydrous condition (dry), therefore, to determine the account of iron, basic oxides and acid oxides, is taken as basis the dry material. Having $w\%$ the humidity percent, the calculation with wet materials will be made by bringing them to the dry condition. The dry iron ore will be:

$$M_{uscat} = (1 - w) \cdot M \tag{3}$$

where;

$$w = \frac{w\%}{100} \tag{4}$$

- the dosed charge is formed by the total of wet iron ores which are taken as unit or 100% and against which are reported the other additions: coke, limestone, return, as percentages against the total iron ores, or as proportion against the total iron ores, these being also in wet condition;
- a part of the iron ores, before reaching the sintering plant, are passed through the raw materials preparation sector, where are mixed and homogenized, having as result the iron ore

mixture called currently "homogenized" which has the deviations at Fe, SiO_2, CaO within the limits of ±0.5%. This homogenized is dosed separately as a self-sustained component;

- by the sintering process, the materials are calcinated and, knowing the calcinations percent "p%", the quantity of material found in agglomerate will be:

$$A_i = (1 - w_i) \cdot M_i \cdot (1 - p_i) \tag{5}$$

where

$$p_i = \frac{p_i\%}{100} \quad i = 1,2,\ldots, n; \tag{6}$$

- the coke C_i, after burning, participates in the agglomerate by its ash. For each coke C_i knowing the ash $Ce_i\%$, it results the account of ash in the agglomerate:

$$Ce = \sum_{i=1}^{n} (1 - w_{C_i}) \cdot C_i \cdot Ce_i \tag{7}$$

- the quantity of coke and return is reported to the total iron ore charge

$$M = \sum_{i=1}^{n} M_i \tag{8}$$

- the total coke quantity is

$$C = \sum_{i=1}^{n} C_i \tag{9}$$

$$c_0 = \frac{C}{M} = \sum_{i=1}^{n} \frac{C_i}{M} = \sum_{i=1}^{n} c_i \tag{10}$$

$$\Rightarrow$$

$$\begin{cases} C_i = c_i \cdot M \\ C = M \cdot \sum_{i=1}^{n} c_i = M \cdot c_0 \end{cases} \tag{11}$$

- the total ash quantity is:

$$Ce = M \cdot \sum_{i=1}^{n} (1 - w_{C_i}) \cdot c_i \cdot Ce_i \tag{12}$$

- the return results: from the hot screening, having $w_{r_1} = 0$ (R_1); from the cold screening, having $w_{r_2} = 0$ (R_2) and from the screening from the blast-furnace's day-shift bunkers, which is wet for not causing dust $w_{r_3} = 0 \div 1\%$ (R_3);

- for all three types of return will be considered $w_r = 0$, and the total return is:

$$R = R_1 + R_2 + R_3 \tag{13}$$

$$r_0 = \frac{R}{M} = \frac{R_1 + R_2 + R_3}{M} \tag{14}$$

where: R_1 does not pass through dosing, but is discharged on the conveyor belt from the burdening downstream and R_2 and R_3 are dosed through the dosing bunkers.

The limestone quantity is not dosed by a given average ratio, but determined by the need of basic oxides account, so that in the agglomerate's participation assembly the sum of basic oxides reported to the sum of acid oxides to be in a prescribed ratio, called basicity ratio I.

$$I = \frac{\sum_{i=1}^{n}(CaO + MgO)}{\sum_{i=1}^{n}(SiO_2 + Al_2O_3)} \tag{15}$$

The dosed iron ores charge is (400 ÷ 500) t/h at daily productions of (8000 ÷ 10000) tons of agglomerate/day. The ratio between the quantity of the produced agglomerate and the iron ore charge is sensitively around value 1, because at basicity I = 1.2 ÷ 1.4 as are prescribed the iron ores' calcinations losses, they are compensated by the participation of limestone into agglomerate plus the coke's ash, the return having a null effect, because it's a constant quantity that recirculates (Σoutputs = Σinputs).
The mathematic model of the dosing sub-process is described by the following equations:

$$K = M \cdot \frac{N}{(k_k - Is_k)} \tag{16}$$

$$S = M + K + C + R \tag{17}$$

$$M = S \cdot \frac{1}{1 + c_0 + r_0 + \frac{N}{(k_k - Is_k)}} \tag{18}$$

$$K = S \cdot \frac{\frac{N}{(k_k - Is_k)}}{1 + c_0 + r_0 + \frac{N}{(k_k - Is_k)}} \tag{19}$$

$$R = S \cdot \frac{r_0}{1 + r_0 + c_0 + \frac{N}{(k_k - Is_k)}} \tag{20}$$

$$C = S \cdot \frac{c_0}{1 + r_0 + c_0 + \frac{N}{(k_k - Is_k)}} \tag{21}$$

where: $$N = \sum_{i=1}^{n} m_i(Is_i - k_i) + c_0 Ce(Is_{Ce} - k_{Ce}) + r_0(Is_r - k_r) \tag{22}$$

$$s_i = \sum(SiO_2 + Al_2O_3)_i \tag{23}$$

$$s_{Ce} = \sum(SiO_2 + Al_2O_3)_{Ce} \tag{24}$$

$$s_r = \sum(SiO_2 + Al_2O_3)_r \tag{25}$$

$$s_k = \sum(SiO_2 + Al_2O_3)_k \tag{26}$$

$$k_i = \sum(CaO + MgO)_i \tag{27}$$

$$k_{Ce} = \sum(CaO + MgO)_{Ce} \tag{28}$$

$$k_r = \sum(CaO + MgO)_r \tag{29}$$

$$k_k = \sum(CaO + MgO)_k \tag{30}$$

In the above equations: M – represents the iron ore flow; K – limestone flow; R – return flow; C – coke flow; S – charge flow; I – basicity ratio; s_i, k_i – lime and silica from the iron ores; s_k, k_k – lime and silica from the limestone ; s_{Ce}, k_{Ce} – lime and silica from the coke ashes; s_r, k_r – lime and silica from the return; r_0 – the return participation against the total iron ore ; c_0 – the coke participation against the total iron ore. In case when is taken into account the humidity of the charge components, we have the following mathematic model:

$$K = M \cdot \frac{N'}{(k_k - Is_k)} \tag{31}$$

$$M = S \cdot \frac{1}{1 + c_0 + r_0 + \dfrac{N'}{(k_k - Is_k)}} \tag{32}$$

$$K = S \cdot \frac{\dfrac{N'}{(k_k - Is_k)}}{1 + c_0 + r_0 + \dfrac{N'}{(k_k - Is_k)}} \tag{33}$$

$$R = S \cdot \frac{r_0}{1 + r_0 + c_0 + \dfrac{N'}{(k_k - Is_k)}} \tag{34}$$

$$C = S \cdot \frac{c_0}{1 + r_0 + c_0 + \dfrac{N'}{(k_k - Is_k)}} \tag{35}$$

$$\begin{aligned} N' = &\sum_{i=1}^{n}(1 - w_i) \cdot m_i \cdot (Is_i - k_i) + \\ &+ [(1 - w_{c0}) \cdot c_0 \cdot Ce(Is_{Ce} - k_{Ce}) + r_0 \cdot (Is_r - k_r)] \end{aligned} \tag{36}$$

Maximization of the good-quality agglomerate production is based on the optimization of the sintering machine's speed. The mathematic model contains equations for calculating the necessary corrections for the value of the sintering machine's speed, respectively for the carbon quantity in the charge, by which is adjusted the quantity of the produced ore fines.
Optimization of the sintering machine's speed v_m is based on the coincidence principle of the longitudinal sintering front's length L_a with the machine's working length L_u.
The mathematic model of the sintering sub-process is described by the following equations.
In the above equations intervene the following quantities: v_m - sintering machine's prescribed speed; H_s - layer's height; k - proportionality factor; B - sintering machine's width; T_n, T_{n-1}, T_{n-2} - temperatures in the last three suction chambers; r = R/M - proportion of the return against the total iron ore; $r_0 = R_{mp}/M$ - proportion of the fine-grained produced against the total iron ore; a, b - constants which are determined statistically for each installation in part; w - speed agglomeration in layer; t_a - agglomeration time; Q_{at} - total agglomeration flow; ρ_v - sinter density; η_a - agglomeration yield (Meré et al., 2005).

$$v_{m\ opt} = v_m \cdot \frac{L_u}{L_{n-1} + 0{,}5 \cdot p_c \cdot \dfrac{T_{n-2} - T_n}{T_{n-2} - 2T_{n-1} + T_n}} \tag{37}$$

$$\Delta v_m = v_m \cdot \left(\frac{L_u}{L_{n-1} + 0{,}5 \cdot p_c \cdot \dfrac{T_{n-2} - T_n}{T_{n-2} - 2T_{n-1} + T_n}} - 1 \right) \tag{38}$$

$$\Delta C = 1.25 \cdot \Delta c \cdot M \tag{39}$$

$$\Delta c = (a - b \cdot r_0) - (a - b \cdot r) \tag{40}$$

$$S = k \cdot v_{m\ opt} \cdot H_s \cdot B \tag{41}$$

$$v_{m\ min} = \frac{L_u}{H_s} \cdot w_{min} \cdot 10^{-3}\ [m/min] \tag{42}$$

$$v_{m\ max} = \frac{L_u}{H_s} \cdot w_{max} \cdot 10^{-3}\ [m/min] \tag{43}$$

$$t_a = \frac{L_u}{v_{med}} = \frac{H_s}{w_{med}} = 10 \ldots 20\ [min] \tag{44}$$

$$Q_{at} = B \cdot H_s \cdot (1 - c) \cdot \eta_a \cdot \rho_v \cdot v_{med} \cdot 60\ [t/h] \tag{45}$$

$$\rho_v = 1.6\ [t/m^3];\ \eta_a = 0.93 \ldots 0.96;\ c = 0.06 \ldots 0.13 \tag{46}$$

Based on the mathematic model and using the Simulink program from Matlab environment, were executed the diagrams that achieve the simulation of the dosing sub-process of the sintering ores, as well as the simulation of the iron ores' sintering sub-process. The subsystem from fig. 2 makes the calculation of the material flow that compose the sintering charge, e.g.: the iron ore flow, limestone flow, coke flow and the return flow considering that in the agglomerate's manufacturing recipe enter four types of iron ore : Romanian iron ore (iron ore 1), Krivoi-Rog iron ore (iron ore 2), Brazilian iron ore (iron ore 3) and scale (iron ore 4), each with its own chemical composition, i.e. with different lime and silica. Based on the laboratory analysis, are established the values of the following input measures: silica and lime of iron ores, silica and lime of the limestone, as well as the silica and lime from the coke ashes.

Other input measures are prescribed measures, i.e.: basicity ratio (I), coke ashes' proportion (Ce%), c_0 – ratio between coke and iron ore, r_0 – ratio between the return and iron ore, m_1 – proportion of iron ore 1 against the total iron ore, m_2 – proportion of iron ore 2 against the total iron ore, m_3 – proportion of iron ore 3 against the total iron ore and m_4 – proportion of iron ore 4 against the total iron ore. Because in the sintering charge the total iron ore is considered 100%, it should be fulfilled the condition $m_1+m_2+m_3+m_4 = 1$, where :

$$m_1 = \frac{M_1}{M};\ m_2 = \frac{M_2}{M};\ m_3 = \frac{M_3}{M};\ m_4 = \frac{M_4}{M} \tag{47}$$

M_1 – Romanian iron ore flow; M_2 – Krivoi-Rog iron ore flow; M_3 – Brazilian iron ore flow; M_4 – scale flow; M – total iron ore flow.

The input measures s_r (silica in return) and k_r (lime in return) is calculated with a separate subsystem presented in fig. 3.

Because the return is in fact fine-grained agglomerate which is recycled in the process, the silica and lime from the return is equal with the silica and lime of the agglomerate.
The subsystem from fig. 3 makes the calculation of the silica and lime from the return based on the following formulas:

$$S \cdot s_r = M \cdot \sum m_i \cdot s_i + M \cdot c_0 \cdot Ce \cdot s_{Ce} + K \cdot s_k + M \cdot r_0 \cdot s_r \tag{48}$$

$$s_r = \frac{M \cdot \sum m_i \cdot s_i + M \cdot c_0 \cdot Ce \cdot s_{Ce} + K \cdot s_k}{S - r_0 \cdot M}; \; k_r = s_r \cdot I \tag{49}$$

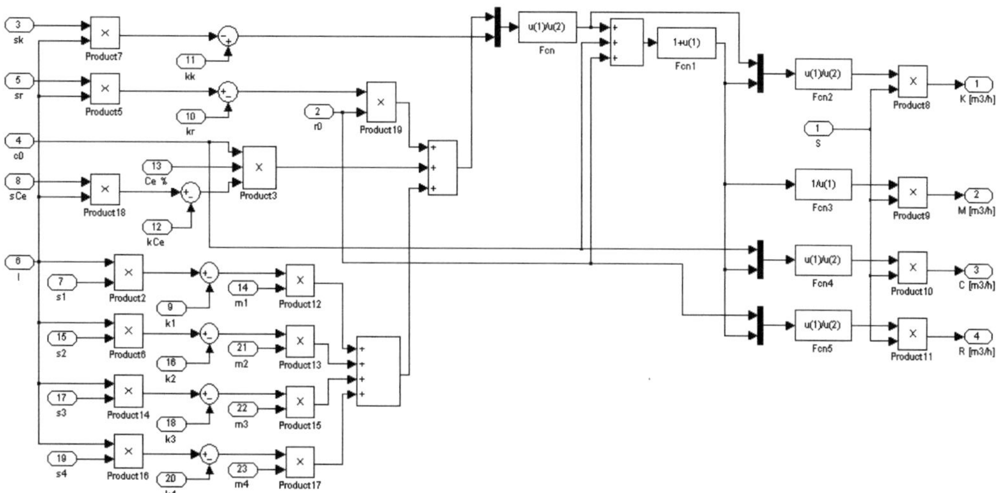

Fig. 2. Block diagram for calculation of the material flows from the charge [m³/h]

Using the Simulink program from Matlab environment it was determined the sintering machine's optimal speed variation.
The simulation allowed also to computing the carbon correction from the charge, as well as the charge flow (Diniş et al., 2009). The calculation subsystem of the sintering machine's optimal speed from fig. 4 has as input measures the following: temperatures in the last three suction chambers (T_n, T_{n-1}, T_{n-2}), the sintering machine's useful length (L_u), the length up to the penultimate suction chamber (L_{n-1}) and the suction chambers' distance (p_C).
The sintering machine's useful length, the length up to the penultimate suction chamber and the suction chambers' distance are considered constant measures (L_u=42 m, L_{n-1}=40 m, p_C=2 m), and the temperatures in the last three suction chambers are considered measures that take different values at certain moments of time.
The sub-system from fig. 5 calculates the carbons correction (coke) that should be made at dosing, in order that the fine-grained return produced in the sintering process (which is scaled) to be equal with the return which is introduced in the sintering charge at dosing. This sub-system is achieved based on the equations (39) and (40).
The input measure S (the sintering charge's flow) is calculated with a separate subsystem presented in fig. 6 based on the following parameters: the sintering band's speed, the sintering layer's height and the sintering band's width. The calculation subsystem of the charge flow presented in fig. 6 is achieved based on the equation (41).

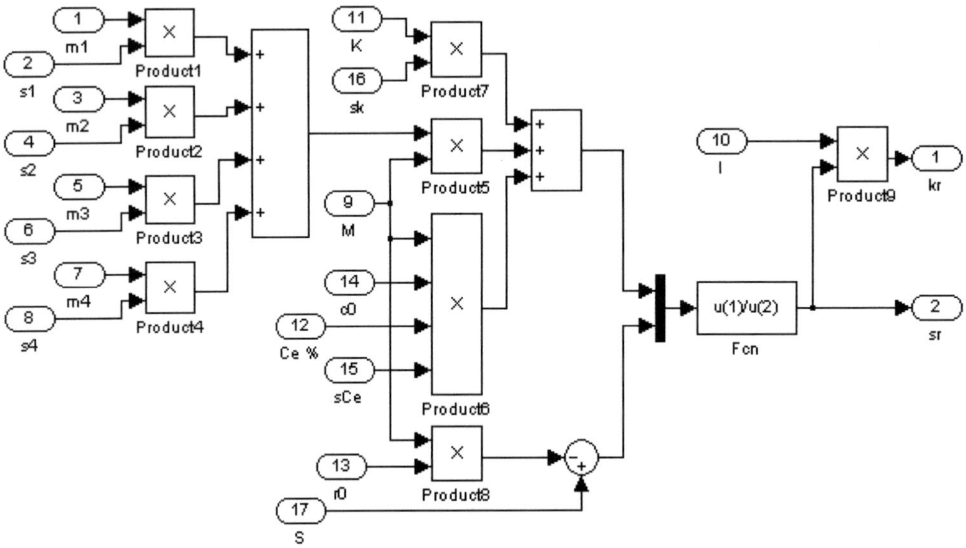

Fig. 3. Block diagram for calculation of the lime and silica from the return

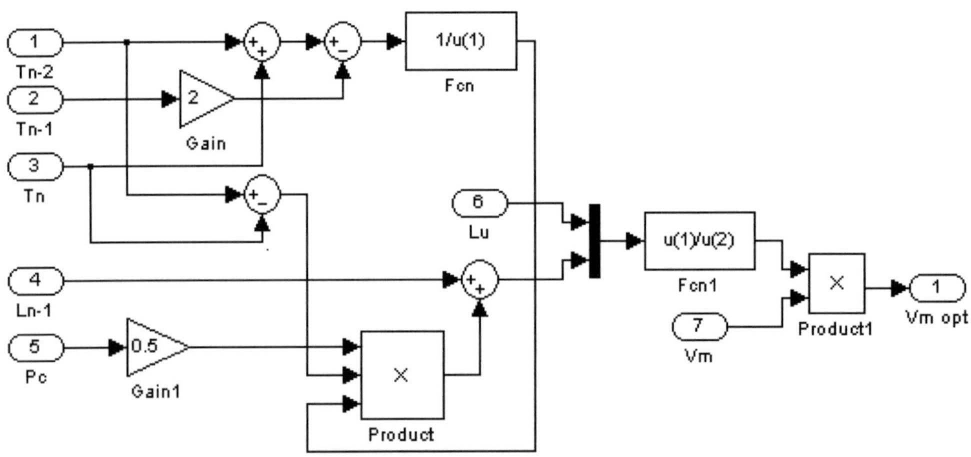

Fig. 4. Block diagram for calculation of the sintering line's optimal speed

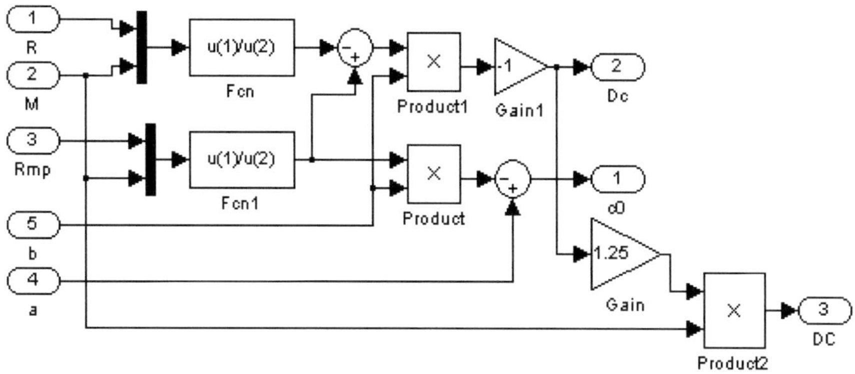

Fig. 5. Block diagram for calculation of the coke content's variation from the charge

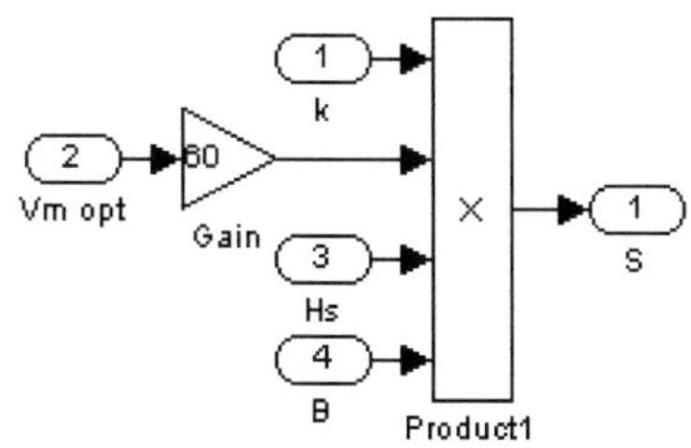

Fig. 6. Block diagram for calculation of the charge flow

For the temperature values T_{n-2}, T_{n-1} and T_n (the temperatures in the last three suction chambers of the sintering band) expressed at different moments of time, will be obtained the variation curve of the sintering machine's optimal speed. This time-variation curve of the sintering machine's optimal speed can be used successfully for the optimal control of the process from the sintering band (Diniş et al., 2009).
The temperature values T_{n-2}, T_{n-1} and T_n at different moments of time can be modified, obtaining, depending on these and the other subsystem's inputs, other time-variation curves of the sintering machine's optimal speed.

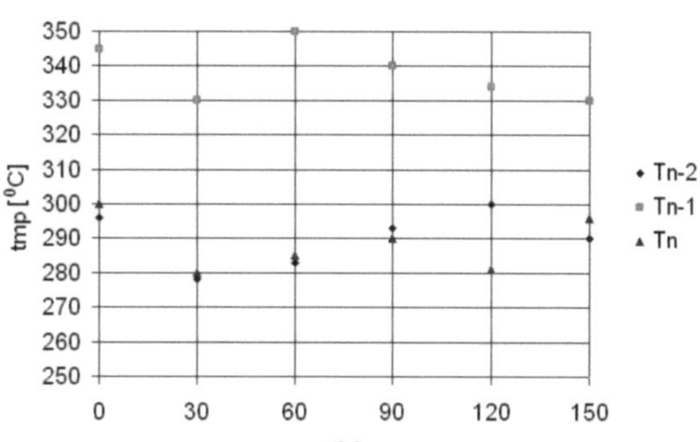

Fig. 7. The temperature values for the three suction chambers, in time, for the simulation from fig.8

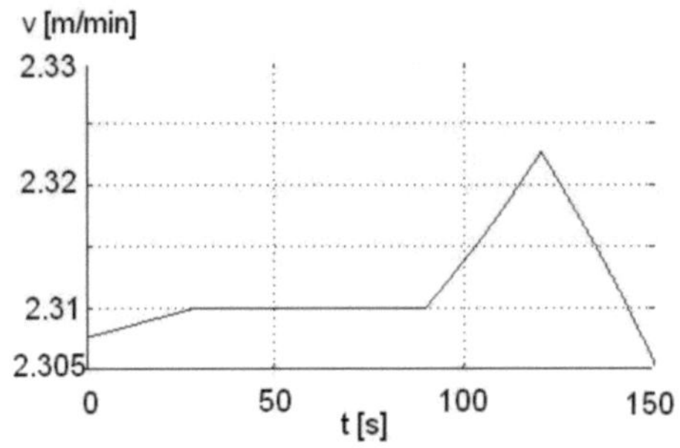

Fig. 8. Variation of the sintering machine's optimal speed – case 1

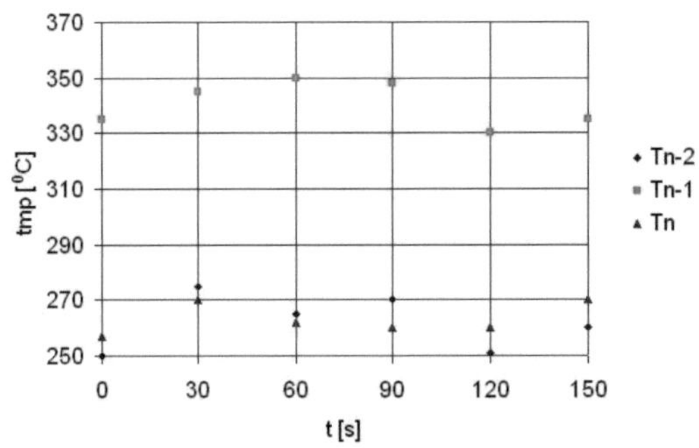

Fig. 9. The temperature values for the three suction chambers, in time, for the simulation from fig.10

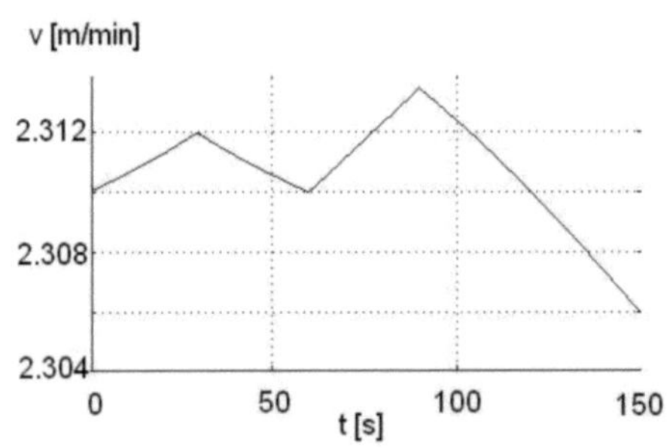

Fig. 10. Variation of the sintering machine's optimal speed – case 2

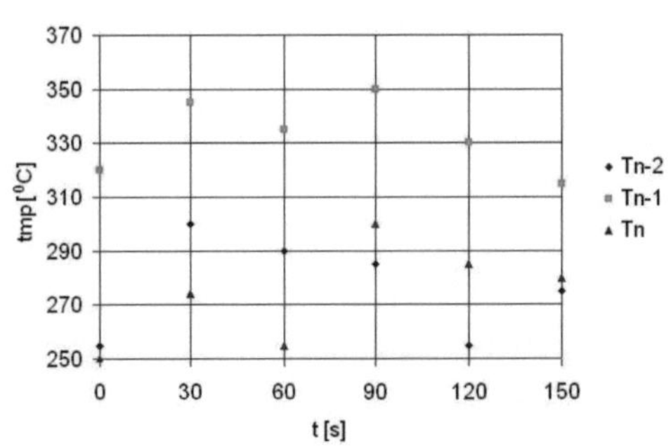

Fig. 11. The temperature values for the three suction chambers, in time, for the simulation from fig.12

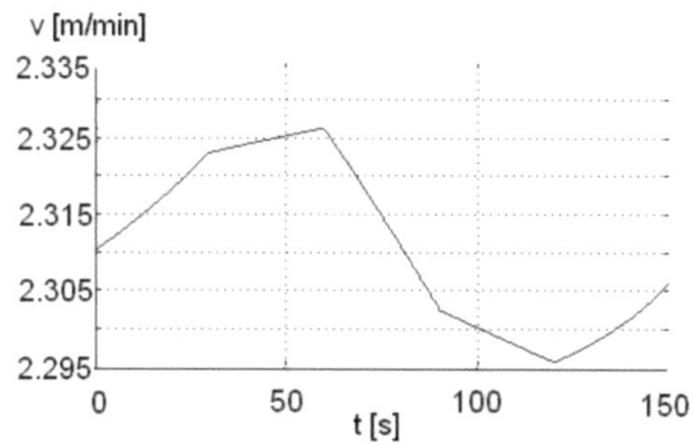

Fig. 12. Variation of the sintering machine's optimal speed - case 3

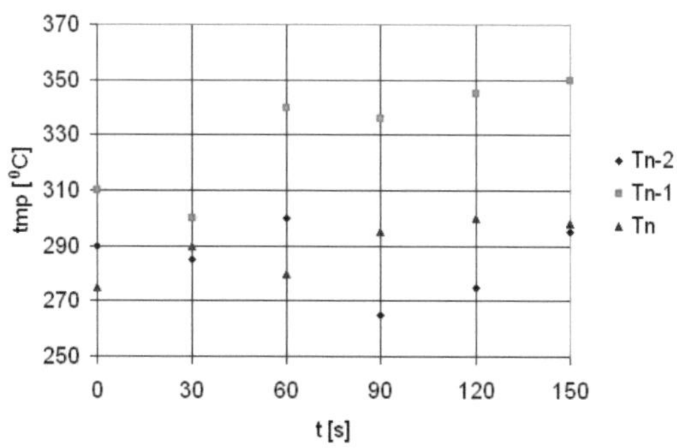

Fig. 13. The temperature values for the three suction chambers, in time, for the simulation from fig.14

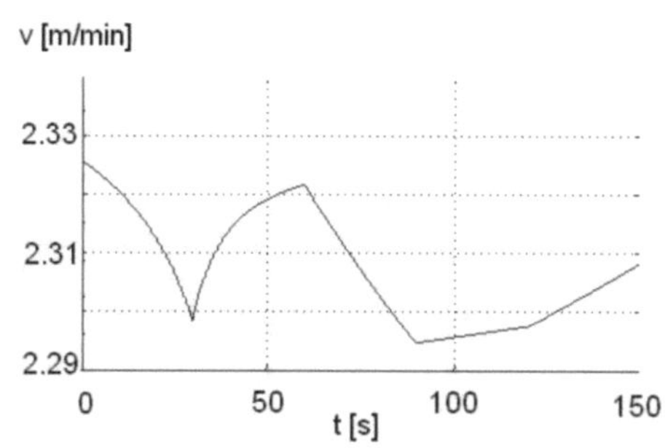

Fig. 14. Variation of the sintering machine's optimal speed - case 4

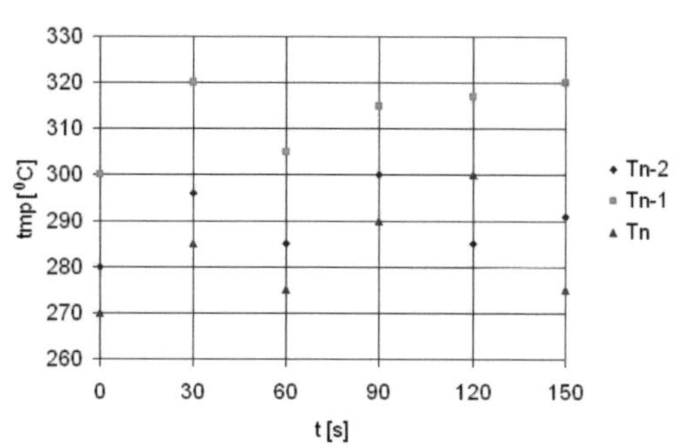

Fig. 15. The temperature values for the three suction chambers, in time, for the simulation from fig.16

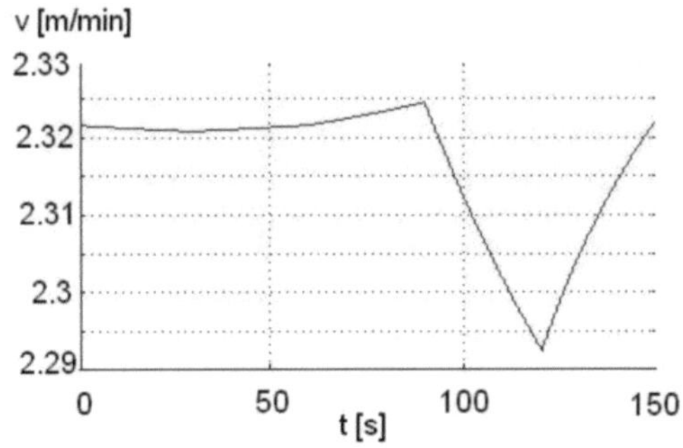

Fig. 16. Variation of the sintering machine's optimal speed – case 5

In fig. 8, 10, 12, 14, 16 are presented the variations of the sintering machine's optimal speed for different distributions of the iron ore's temperatures on the sintering band.
The temperature distributions in time, for the last three suction chambers of the sintering machine (T_{n-2}, T_{n-1}, T_n) are given under vectorial form and are presented in fig. 7, 9, 11, 13, 15. The prescribed speed (for the simulations from fig. 8, 10, 12, 14, 16) for the adjustment system is 2.2 m/s. The temperatures are considered to be measured each with a temperature transducer for each chamber. The simulation time is 150 s, and the temperature readings are made from 30 to 30 s. The measurement of the material's temperature on the sintering band is a difficult operation.
From practice, are known the temperature domains for each suction chamber: $T_{n-2} \in$ [250-300] ^{0}C; $T_{n-1} \in$ [300-350] ^{0}C; $T_n \in$ [250-300] ^{0}C.
Depending on the temperatures measured (fig.17) in the suction chambers, the adjustment system imposes a certain modification of the sintering band. For simulations were used the experimental data from fig.17 (graph 3, 40 cm layer).

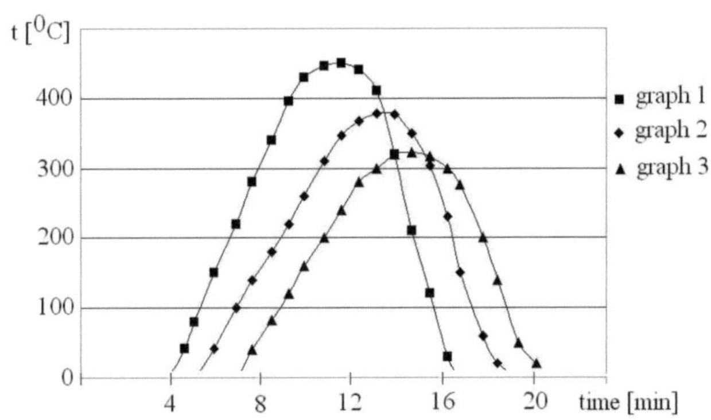

Fig. 17. Distribution temperatures, under the layer: graph 1: 20 cm layer; graph 2: 30 cm layer; graph 3: 40 cm layer

3. Control of a belt conveyors system, with MC68HC05B6 – Motorola microcontroller

Microcontroller MC68HC05B6 (Motorola) is an HCMOS integrated circuit, which has the following resources:
- 8-bit arithmetic and logical unit, which can execute adding, subtracting, multiplying, incrementing, decrementing, logical and rotating operations;

- 176 RAM 8-bit;
- 8 Kbytes EEPROM for programming;
- 256 EEPROM 8-bit;
- 16 bi-directional inputs/outputs;
- counter of 16 bits;
- 2 capture inputs;
- software reset of the main counter;
- 8 channels for 8-bit analogue-digital conversion;
- 2 conversion channels 8-bit digital-analogue;
- serial asynchronous communication interface

The conveyor belts T_2 and T_3 are supplied with material from silos S_1 and S_2. These are discharging the charge on the basic belt T_1. The transport flows on the belt system are on directions T_{a1}-T_2-T_1, respectively T_{a2}-T_3-T_1 indicated by arrows.
The power part contains five motors (M_{T1}, M_{T2}, M_{T3}, M_{Ta1}, M_{Ta2}) for driving each conveyor belt and belt feeders (fig.18). Each motor is protected by fusible fuses (F_{12}, F_{22}, F_{32}, F_{42}, F_{52} against short-circuits) and by thermo-bimetallic relays (F_1, F_2, F_3, F_{a1}, F_{a2} for overload protection). As commutation elements are used contactors (K_1, K_2, K_3, K_{a1}, K_{a2}). The contactors' coils are supplied at 380 V c.a., being controlled by the normally open contacts of the micro-relays K_{11}, K_{21}, K_{31}, K_{a11}, K_{a21} by the system with microcontroller (fig.19).

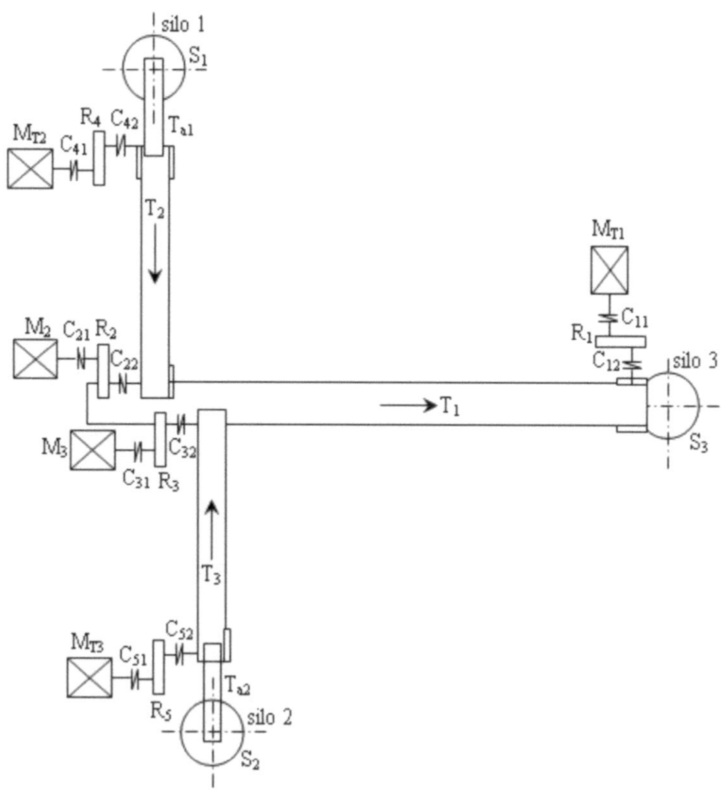

Fig. 18. Branched system of conveyor belts

Micro-relays K_{11}, K_{21}, K_{31}, K_{a11}, K_{a21} are controlled by 1 logic. The system by microcontroller is supplied at 5V. All components were connected at the first 16 digital ports (P_1,…,P_{16}). The normally closed contacts of the thermal protections (F_1, F_2, F_3, F_{a1}, F_{a2}) were connected by resistances of 10 kΩ to 5V. Thus, if the protections don't act, their normally closed contacts do not open and the microcontroller interprets this status as 0 logic. If a protection is actuating, the related contact is open and on the respective input is applied signal 1 logic.
The two flows can be controlled separately: flow 1 (T_1-T_2-T_{a1}) and flow 2 (T_1-T_3-T_{a2}). Flow 1 is started by button S_{p1}, and flow 2 by button S_{p2}. Flows' stopping is made by the stop buttons S_{o1}, respectively S_{o2}. If the buttons are not actuated, it's interpreted 1 logic, and if they are closed, is interpreted 0 logic. There are also connected two LEDs – LED1 and LED 2- that indicates the operation of flow 1 respectively flow 2. The LEDs' control is made by 1 logic.

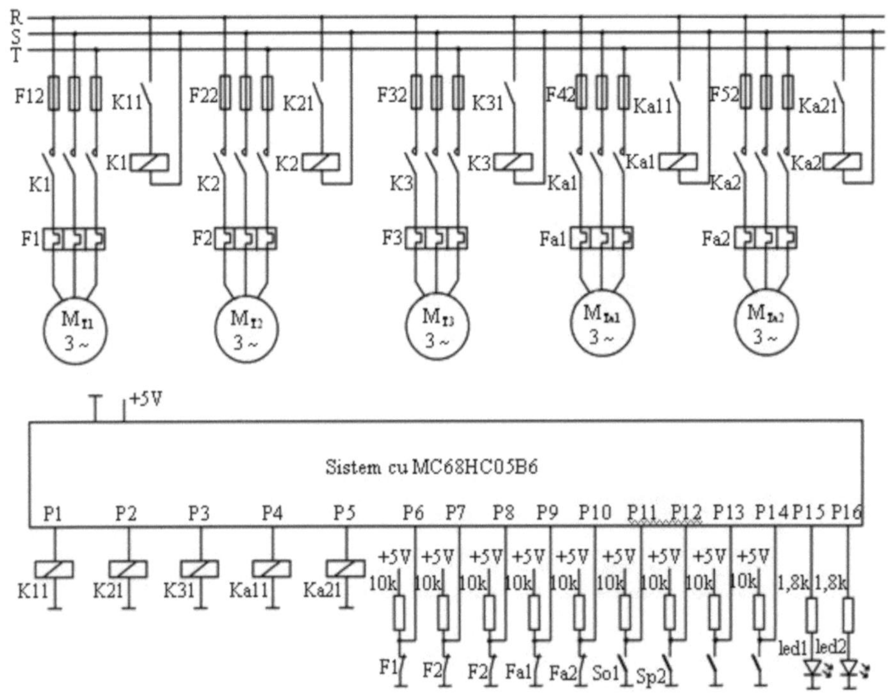

Fig. 19. The power and control diagram of the conveyor belt system

Is presented the control program's listing of the conveyor belt system achieved in CCBasic.
'Program for controlling the conveyor belts
define ports wordport [1] 'Ports 1 - 16
define t1 port [1] 'Port command contactor K1, for conveyor T1
define t2 port [2] 'Port command contactor K2, for conveyor T2
define t3 port [3] 'Port command contactor K3, for conveyor T3
define ta1 port [4] 'Port command contactor Ka1, for feeder Ta1
define ta2 port [5] 'Port command contactor Ka2, for feeder Ta2
define f1 port [6] 'Port thermal protection motor conveyor T1
define f2 port [7] 'Port thermal protection motor conveyor T2

```
define f3 port [8] 'Port thermal protection motor conveyor T3
define fa1 port [9] 'Port thermal protection motor feeder Ta1
define fa2 port [10] 'Port thermal protection motor feeder Ta2
define sp1 port [11] 'start-up button flow 1
define so1 port [12] 'shut-down button flow 1
define sp2 port [13] 'start-up button flow 2
define so2 port [14] 'shut-down button flow 2
define led1 port [15] 'LED operation flow 1
define led2 port [16] 'LED operation flow 2
'Main Program
'Initializations
ports = off
10      if sp1=off then led1=on
        if sp1=off then gosub flow1
        if so1=off then led1=off
        if so1=off then ta1=off
        pause 25
        if so1=off then t2=off
        pause 25
        if so1=off then t1=off
        if f1=on or f2=on or fa1=on then ta1=off
        if f1=on or f2=on or fa1=on then t2=off
        if f1=on or f2=on or fa1=on then t1=off
        if f1=on or f2=on or fa1=on then ta2=off
        if f1=on or f2=on or fa1=on then t3=off
        if sp2=off then led2=on
        if sp2=off then gosub flow2
        if so2=off then led2=off
        if so2=off then ta2=off
        pause 25
        if so2=off then t3=off
        pause 25
        if so2=off then t1=off
        if f1=on or f3=on or fa2=on then ta2=off
        if f1=on or f3=on or fa2=on then t3=off
        if f1=on or f3=on or fa2=on then t1=off
        if f1=on or f3=on or fa2=on then ta1=off
        if f1=on or f3=on or fa2=on then t2=off
        goto 10
        'Subroutine flow1
        #flow1
        t1=on
        pause 100
        if f1=on then t1=off
        if f1=on then led1=off
        if f1=on then goto 10
```

```
t2=on
pause 100
if f2=on then t2=off
if f2=on then t1=off
if f2=on then led1=off
if f2=on then goto 10
ta1=on
pause 100
if fa1=on then ta1=off
if fa1=on then t2=off
if fa1=on then t1=off
if fa1=on then led1=off
return
'Subroutine flow2
#flow2
t1=on
pause 100
if f1=on then t1=off
if f1=on then led2=off
if f1=on then goto 10
t3=on
pause 100
if f3=on then t3=off
if f3=on then t1=off
if f3=on then led2=off
if f3=on then goto 10
ta2=on
pause 100
if fa2=on then ta2=off
if fa2=on then t3=off
if fa2=on then t1=off
if fa2=on then led2=off
return
```

4. Hierarchical control of a belt conveyors system

To achieve the control by software orientation method, will be used a hierarchical structure on three levels, having at the superior level an industrial PC, at the middle level a number of PLCs, one for each conveyor, an date execution and feedback level the working machines and the process transducers (Da Silveira & Combacau, 2006). To achieve control software, after orientation method, is used for each belt conveyor a PLC, made with development board Keil MCB167-NET (fig.20) having the following characteristics: 5 ports I/O, 1 input port, two serial communication channels (asynchronous serial channel/synchronous ASC0 and a high-speed synchronous serial channel SSC), 1 x RS232 Interface, 2 x CAN Interfaces, 1 x Ethernet Controller. Local display of belt conveyor operation is achieved by a liquid crystal panel (LCD) (Diniş et al., 2008)

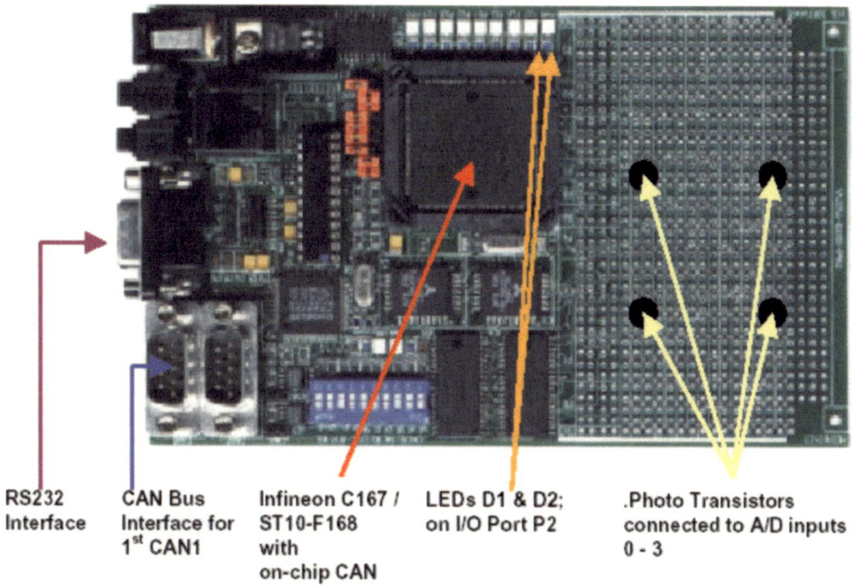

Fig. 20. Development board Keil MCB167-NET

In figure 21 is shown the block-diagram of the PLC_i afferent to the "i" conveyor and the elements which it serves. For a T_i conveyor have been made the following notes: VIT_i - speed transducer; DEV_i - overflow transducer (filling-up); AVR_i - emergency transducer (in-line); SER_i - serial communication between PLC and PC; $START_i$ - start signal for PLC_i; $STOP_i$ - stop signal for PLC_i; $START_{i+1}$ - start signal for the upstream conveyor; $STOP_{i+1}$ - stop signal for the downstream conveyor; CLX_i - control signal for the horn; MOT_i - control signal for starting the motor or motors group.

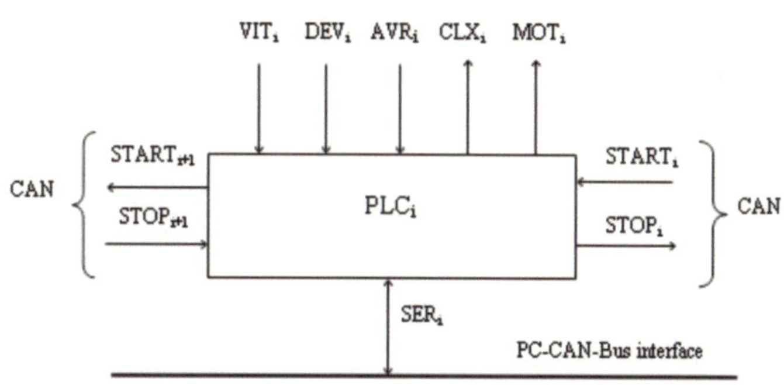

Fig. 21. Block-diagram PLC_i

The control algorithm implements the following 14 conditions: 1) Completely automatic operation with acoustic and graphic signaling in real-time; 2) At commissioning, the correctness of its integrity is tested; 3) Starting-up is made on the routes depending on the material's presence transducer; 4) Starting-up of a conveyor is made only after it was made the preventive acoustic signaling; 5) The minimum value of the material from the bunker stops the route in the direct sense of the material flow; 6) The duration of a conveyor's

starting-up is controlled by the speed transducer through the watchdog; 7) The upstream conveyor starts-up after the one from the downstream has started; 8) If a conveyor has stopped, all the others which overflow on it will stop also; 9) The upstream conveyor will be stopped if the downstream bunker has filled-up; 10) The conveyor will stop if the emergency transducer AVR_i is actuated; 11) If the watchdog has been actuated, the conveyor will stop; 12) Emergency detection produces the locking-up of starting the belt until the remedy of the defect; 13) Signaling of the system's condition is ensured at superior and local level; 14) Signaling of the transducers condition is ensured at superior and local level.
Structure of the hierarchical control system is presented in figure 22 and can be extended for any configuration by cascade connections (CASC).

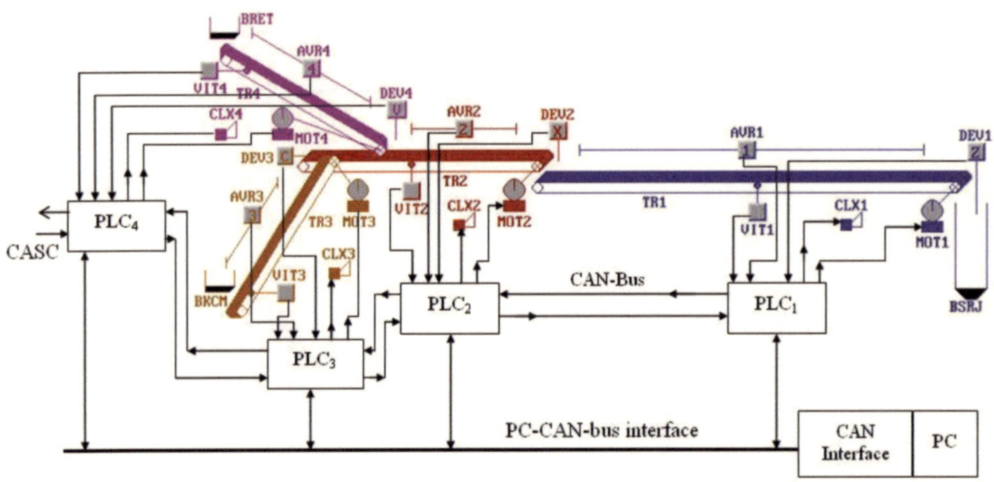

Fig. 22. Structure of the hierarchical control system

5. Modelling and implementation of the hierarchical control software

Testing of the control system's feasibility was done at the beginning by modeling and simulation of PLCi in the MatLab-Simulink. In this chapter, was developed the mathematic model which was used as basis for development of Simulink model from figure 23. In the chapter is presented the simulations results for individual PLC. Based on the model and the simulation results, it started the development and implementation of the hierarchical control software (Diniş et al., 2008).
The hierarchical control software at high level was achieved in I80X86 assembling language and contains about 8000 instruction lines. The program ensures a real-time graphic interface on PC's screen from the dispatcher, with the following elements: representing of the transportation flow in real time; real condition of the transducers; the condition of each belt; automatic or manual control; choosing a route in automatic mode, depending on the material from bunkers (Zamai et al., 1998). Further are shown few program sequences, i.e. the data segment and the main control routine.

```
.model small
.stack
.data
```

```
titleApp            db      " Control a conveyors system",0
titleKeys           db      " Keys used:",0
titleMessages       db      " Messages:",0
titleState          db      " State transducers:",0
trsp1               db      " TR1",0
trsp2               db      " TR2",0
trsp3               db      "  TR3",0
trsp4               db      "  TR4",0
damage              db      " AVR:",0
discharge           db      " DEV:",0
speed               db      " VIT:",0
MesDamage           db      " DAMAGE",0
MesSintering        db      " SINTERING",0
MesSpeeding         db      " SPEEDING",0
MesSpeedNormal      db      " NORMAL SPEED",0
MesSpeedAbnormal    db      " ABNORMAL SPEED",0
MesRest             db      " REST",0
MesBNCfull          db      " FULL",0
MesBNCempty         db      " EMPTY",0
MesBNCprocessed     db      " MEDIUM",0
keys02              db      " BKCM",0
keys03              db      " BRET",0
keys1               db      " Higher level (START):",0
keys2               db      " Lower level (STOP) :",0
keys32              db      " Q",0
keys33              db      " W",0
keys42              db      " A",0
keys43              db      " S",0
keys10              db      " ESC = exit program",0
cmdCLX              db      00001011b        ; port control = 37ah
cmdMOT              db      00000000b        ; port date = 378h
flagM1              db      0        ; 0=stop & 1=start
flagM2              db      0        ; 0=stop & 1=start
flagM3              db      0        ; 0=stop & 1=start
flagM4              db      0        ; 0=stop & 1=start
. code
; main program
start:    call portzero     ; initial state
call getcar
call getcar8x16
mov ax,@data
mov ds,ax
call far for whichvga
call svgamode
call doInitScreen           ;virtual instruments
call MainLoop               ; monitoring
```

```
exitDOS: call portzero        ; initial state
call txtmode
mov ax,4c00h
int 21h
end start
```

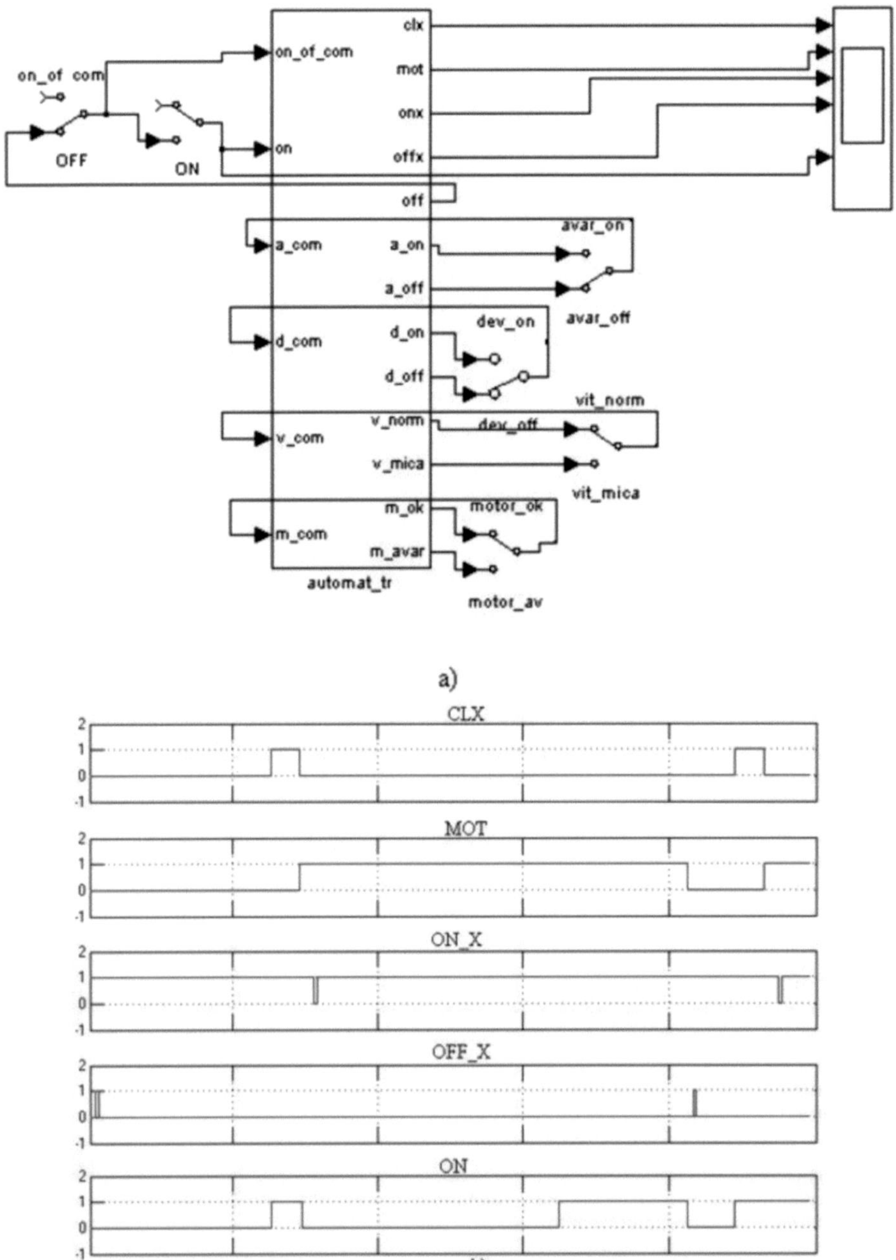

Fig. 23. Simulink model for PLC_i

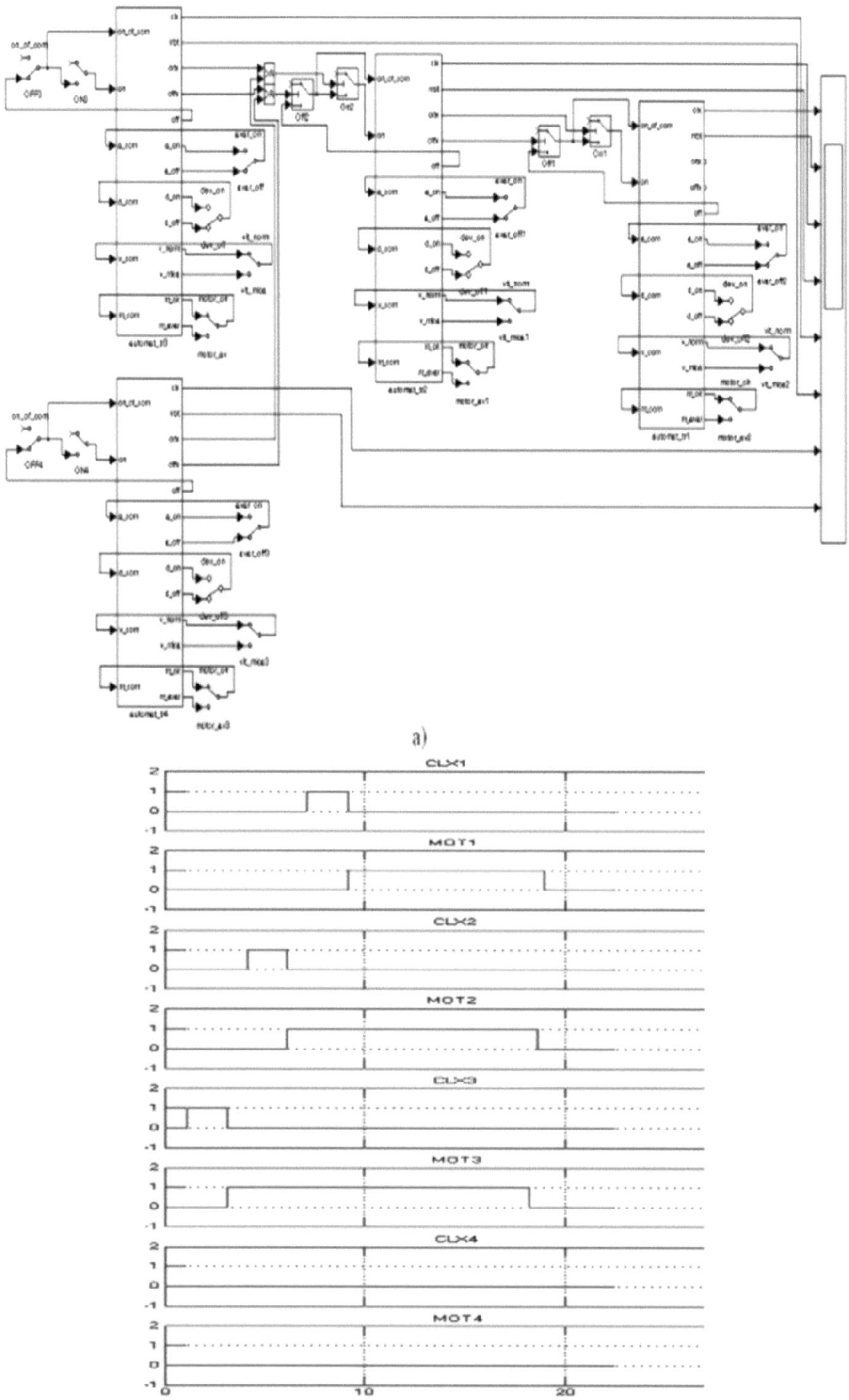

Fig. 24. Simulink model for simulations

In fig. 24 are shown the results of modeling the conveying flow in MatLab-Simulink. One can see the variation in time of the control and feedback signals, in accordance with the imposed technological conditions (Lupu et al., 2008). In fig. 25 is shown the work screen of the PC from the superior level in start regime for a configuration of 4 conveyors from a sintering plant.
When the materials' presence transducer detects the superior level in the BRET return bunker or in the mixing bunker of limestone, coke and iron ores BKCM, the conveyors system starts as follows:
- PLC1 gives the preventive acoustic warning command to the CLX1 horn, then is given the start command for MOT1 motor, which drives the conveyor 1 (TR1);
- The speed transducer VIT1 detects the normal operation regime of the TR1 conveyor, and PLC1 will give the START command for PLC2;
- PLC2 controls the preventive acoustic warning by CLX2 horn, then is given the start command for MOT2 motor of the conveyor 2 (TR2);
- The speed transducer VIT2 detects the normal operation regime of the TR2 conveyor, and PLC2 will give the START command for PLC3 and the process continue;
- Any emergency detected by the transducers generates the initiation of STOP subroutines, by displaying the condition on the PC screen.

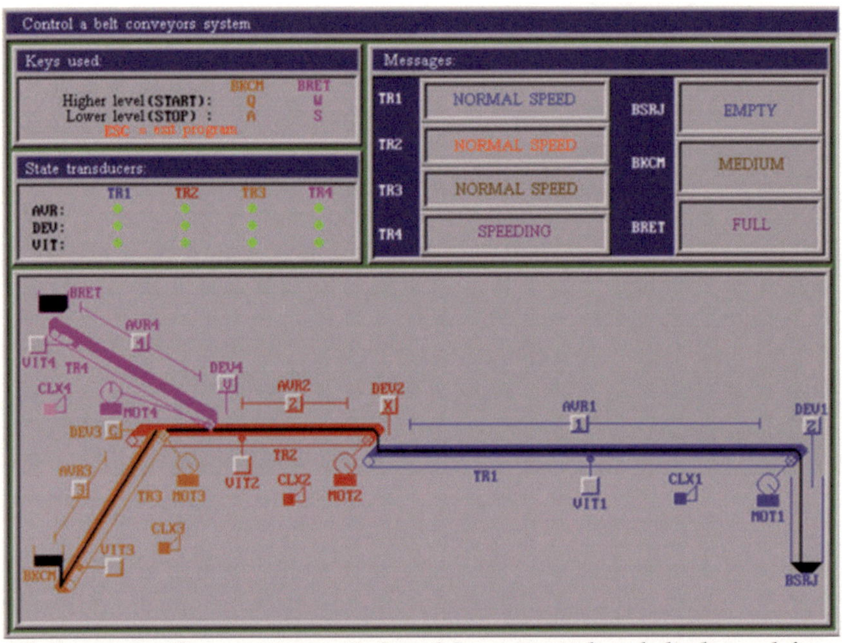

Fig. 25. Work screen when conveyors 1, 2 and 3 are started and discharged from BKCM bunker

6. Conclusion

The model achieved in Matlab/Simulink and its simulation allows the determination of the material flows in the charge, either at the variation of their chemical composition, or at variation of the reference values of the parameters S, I, r_0, c_0. The value of the charge flow S varies as result of the transitory adjusting regime of the sintering machine's speed.

The values r_0 and c_0 are established by independent criteria, e.g.: balancing the ore fines circulation, respectively ensuring the optimal compromise, between the agglomerate production on one side and the coke specific consumption on the other side, and between the agglomerate's reducibility and resistance.
Also, the achieved model allows the visualization of the optimal speed in time, which leads to the optimal charge of the sintering machine from the viewpoint of the charge's chemical and mineralogical composition. The obtained results are in accordance with the practical ones, and the model can be implemented to a real installation (Diniş et al., 2009).
The current technology of cast-iron making imposes more and more rigorous conditions to the quality of the charge that should allow the optimization of the entire process, increasing the productivity and reducing the coke consumption.
As regards the modernization of the iron ores' sintering plants, will be considered the following research directions:
- Development of an expert system for correcting the sintering belt's speed based on fuzzy logic;
- Development of computerized control systems for adjusting the water quantity in the raw materials and the agglomerate's chemical composition;
- Implementation of a surveillance system in the iron ores' sintering process.
Without the control systems by contacts and relays or by logical gates, the control by microcontroller ensures flexibility in programs' achievement and is achieved by programming without intervene upon the hard components.
It were designed and made a transport control flexible system on the basis of software orientation technology (Antipov & Malov, 2005). It was made a hierarchical control structure of the transport flux, that was modeled and simulated in Matlab/Simulink with good results. Based on the model, was conceived a hierarchical control software of the belt conveying process, adaptable to any configuration in space of the conveyors.
The obtain results may be a support for revamping the belt conveying flows used in sintering plants, lignite quarries or for the distribution conveyors from the robotic manufacturing cells, etc.

7. References

Aguilar, J.; Cerrada, M.; Hidrobo, F.; Chacal, J. & Bravo, C. (2008). Specification of a multiagent system for planning and management of the production factors for automation based on the SCDIA framework and MASINA methodology. *WSEAS Transactions on Systems and Control,* Vol. 3, Issues 2, (February 2008) page numbers (79-88), ISSN 1991-8763

Antipov, A.L. & Malov, N.A. (2005). Model of an adaptive hierarchical control system, *Proceedings of SPIE,* pp. 209-212, ISSN 0277-786X, Volume 5851 Fundamental Problems of Optoelectronics and Microelectronics II, June 2005

Da Silveira, M.R. & Combacau, M. (2006). Supervision and control of heterarchical discrete event systems. *Controle & Automação,* Vol. 17, No. 1, (Janeiro, Fevereiro e Março 2006) page numbers (1-9), ISSN 0103-1759

Diniş, C.M.; Pop, E.; Iagăr, A. & Popa, G.N. (2008). Researches upon the hierarchical control of a conveyor belt system from the sintering plants. *Metalurgia International,* Vol. XIII, No. 9, (August 2008) page numbers (54-61), ISSN 1582-2214

Diniş, C.M.; Popa, G.N. & Iagăr, A. (2008). Modeling and simulation of processes from an iron ore sintering plant. *Proceedings of the 7th WSEAS International Conference on SYSTEM SCIENCE and SIMULATION in Engineering*, pp. 119-124, ISBN 978-960-474-027-7, Italy, November 21-23 2008, Venice

Diniş. C.M.; Popa, G.N. & Iagăr, A. (2009). Mathematical modeling and simulation in Matlab/Simulink of processes from iron ore sintering plants. *WSEAS Transaction on Systems,* Volume 8, Issue 1, (January 2009) page numbers (34-43), ISSN 1109-2777

Ho, J.K.L. & Ranky, P.G. (1997). Object oriented modeling and design of reconfigurable conveyors in flexible assembly systems. *International Journal of Computer Integrated Manufacturing*, Vol. 10, Issue 5, (September 1997) page numbers (360-379), ISSN 1362-3052

Lupu, C.; Popescu, D. & Udrea, A. (2008). Real-time control application for nonlinear processes based on adaptive control and the static characteristic. *WSEAS Transaction on Systems and Control*, Vol. 3, Issues 6, (June 2008) Page Numbers (607-616), ISSN 1991-8763

Meré, J.O.; Elías, F.A.; Gonzáles, A.M.; Limas, M.C. & Ascacíbar, F.J.M.P. (2005). Data mining and simulation processes as useful tools for industrial processes, *Proceedings of the 5th WSEAS Int. Conf. on Simulation, Modeling and Optimization,* pp. 243-249, ISBN 960-8457-32-7, Greece, August 17-19 2005, Corfu

Zamai, E.; Chaillet-Subias, A. & Combacau, M. (1998). An architecture for control and monitoring of discrete events systems. *Computers in Industry*, Vol. 36, Issues 1-2, (30 April 1998) page numbers (95-100), ISSN 0166-3615

16

Fired process heaters

Hassan Al-Haj Ibrahim
Al-Baath University
Syria

1. Introduction

Furnaces are a versatile class of equipment where heat is liberated and transferred directly or indirectly to a solid or fluid mass for the purpose of effecting a physical or chemical change. In industrial practice many and varied types of furnaces are used which may differ in function, overall shape or mode of firing, and furnaces may be classified accordingly on the basis of their function such as smelting or roasting, their shape such as crucibles, shafts and hearths or they may be classified according to their mode of firing into electrical, nuclear, solar, and combustion furnaces. Combustion furnaces are of two general types: fired heaters and converters. A converter is a type of furnace in which heat is liberated by the oxidation of impurities or other parts of the material to be heated. Fired heaters, on the other hand, are furnaces that produce heat as a result of the combustion of fuel. The heat liberated is transferred to the material to be heated directly (in internally-heated furnaces) or indirectly (in externally-heated furnaces). Examples of internally-heated furnaces include submerged heaters and blast furnaces where a solid mass is heated by a blast of hot gases. Externally-heated furnaces include ovens, fire-tube boilers and tubular heaters.

In tubular or pipe-still heaters process fluids flowing inside tubes mounted inside the furnace are heated by gases produced by the combustion of a liquid or gaseous fuel. Such heaters were first introduced in the oil industry by M. J. Trumble. Two advantages were thereby gained, viz. the achievement of continuous operation and the reduction of foam formation. These heaters are widely used for heating purposes in petroleum refining, petrochemical plants and other chemical process industries. The calculation and design of fired heaters in petroleum refineries in particular remains one of the most important applications of heat transfer.

Tubular fired heaters are generally built with two distinct heating sections: a radiant section, variously called a combustion chamber or firebox, and a convection section followed by the stack. The hot flue gases arising in the radiation section flow next into the convection section where they circulate at high speed through a tube bundle before leaving the furnace through the stack. A third section, known as a shield or shock section, separates the two major heating sections. It contains those tubes close to the radiation section that shield the remaining convection section tubes from direct radiation. The shield section normally consists of two to three rows of bare tubes that are directly exposed to the hot gasses and flame in the radiant section, but the arrangement varies widely for the many different heater designs. In certain fired heater designs, known as the all-radiant type, there is no separate convection section.

The functions served by fired heaters in chemical plants are many ranging from simple heating or providing sensible heat and raising the temperature of the charge to heating and partial evaporation of the charge, where equilibrium is established between the unvaporised liquid and the vapour. The charge leaves the furnace in the form of a partially evaporated liquid in equilibrium. Fired heaters may also be used to provide the heat required for cracking or reforming reactions. In this case the furnace would be divided into two parts: a heater, where the temperature of the charge is raised, and a soaker, where heat is provided in order to maintain a constant temperature. The soaker may be a part of either the radiation or convection sections. Radiation soakers are generally to be preferred to convection soakers for better control of heat input.

Fired heaters are usually classified as vertical cylindrical or box-type heaters depending on the geometrical configuration of the radiant section.

In box-type heaters, the radiant section has generally a square cross section (as in older furnaces, where the reduced height is compensated for by a larger construction site) or a rectangular cross section (with its height equal to 1.5 to 2.5 times its width) as in cabin-type heaters. The configuration of the cabin type heater with horizontal tubes may have a so-called hip, or the radiant section may be just a rectangular box.

The tubes in the radiant section may be arranged horizontally or vertically along the heater walls including the hip and the burners are located on the floor or on the lower part of the longest side wall where there are no tubes. A fire wall is often built down the centre of the combustion chamber in heaters fired from the sides.

Box-type furnaces are best suited for large capacities and large heat duties. This makes such furnaces particularly suitable for topping units where it is possible to increase tube length in both the radiation and convection sections reducing thereby the required number of headers or return bends. It is possible in such furnaces to open the headers for cleaning, something which makes cleaning the tubes in the radiation section easier; this is especially significant in furnaces used to heat easily-coking oils.

In the cylindrical-type furnace, the radiation section is in the shape of a cylinder with a vertical axis, and the burners are located on the floor at the base of the cylinder. The heat exchange area covers the vertical walls and therefore exhibits circular symmetry with respect to the heating assembly. In the radiant section, the tubes may be in a circular pattern around the walls of the fire box or they may be in a cross or octagonal design which will expose them to firing from both sides. Older designs have radiating cones in the upper part of the radiant section as well as longitudinal fins on the upper parts of tubes. The shield and convection tubes are normally horizontal.

Cylindrical heaters with vertical tubes (Fig. 2) are commonly used in hot oil services and other processes where the duties are usually small, but larger units, 100 million kJ/hr and higher, are not uncommon.

Cylindrical heaters are often preferred to box-type heaters. This is mainly due to the more uniform heating rate in cylindrical heaters and higher thermal efficiency. Furthermore, cylindrical heaters require smaller foundations and construction areas and their construction cost is less. High chimneys are not essential in cylindrical furnaces because they normally produce sufficient draught.

2. Analysis and evaluation of heat transfer

In the usual practice, the process fluid is first heated in the convection section preheat coil which is followed by further heating in the radiant section. In both sections heat is transferred by both mechanisms of heat transfer, viz. radiation and convection, where radiation is the dominant mode of heat transfer at the high temperatures prevalent in the radiant section and convection predominates in the convection section where the average temperature is much lower. Most of the heat transferred to the process fluid takes place in the radiant section while the convection section serves only to make up the difference between the heat duty of the furnace and the part absorbed in the radiant section. Roughly-speaking, about 45-55% of the total heat release in the furnace is transferred to the process fluid in the radiant section, leaving about 25-45% of the total heat release to be either transferred to the process fluid in the convection section or carried by the flue gases through the stack and is lost.

Generally speaking, the chief mechanism by which heat is transferred to the process fluid is radiative heat transfer. In the radiant section the process fluids are mainly heated by direct radiation from the flame. About 70-90 % of the heat absorbed by the tubes in the radiant and shield sections of a furnace is transferred by radiation. This clearly indicates that heat transfer by radiation is of particular significance for the thermal analysis and design of fired heaters in general. Furthermore, the fundamental understanding of heat transfer by radiation is essential for a better appraisal of the expected effects of any modifications of existing heaters or suggestions for possible future developments. Heat transfer by radiation can not however be considered in isolation, but it must be considered in conjunction with other mechanisms of heat transfer such as conduction and convection, in addition to heat liberation by such chemical reactions as may take place inside heater tubes.

The heat-absorbing surface in both sections of the heater is the outside wall of the tubes mounted inside the heater. The overall thermal efficiency of the fired heater is dependent to a large extent on the effectiveness of the recovery of heat from the flue gases, which depends in turn on the size of the heat exchange surface area in the furnace. In order to increase the heat transfer area and thus further increase the overall efficiency of the heater, finned or studded tubes are normally used in the convection section. By this means it is often possible to attain heat flux in the convection section comparable to that in the radiation section.

Different methods are available for the calculations involved in the thermal evaluation and design of fired heaters and some of these methods may be based in theory on fundamental considerations, but more usually the calculation of heat transfer in heaters is based on empirical methods and the construction of such units precedes in general theoretical developments. The validity and significance of a method is determined to a large extent by its general application for different furnace designs. Such a method would take into consideration a larger number of variables that affect the process of heat transfer.

While some of the empirical methods available are simplified methods that can be used for an overall evaluation of the heater in a relatively simple and rapid manner, other methods are more rigorous where it is possible to obtain a better approximation, but the application of such methods requires more information and longer time, and would in fact require the use of a computer. Using computer programmes greatly simplifies the procedure for the computations involved in fired heaters' evaluation and analysis and makes it possible to use more rigorous methods giving better and more accurate results. Most computer programmes available in the literature are written in Basic, but there are also some programmes written in other more advanced computer languages such as Matlab, a programming language which is widely used in all scientific fields and in engineering sciences in particular.

The use of computer simulation and modelling for the optimization of fired heaters operation and design can be a powerful tool indispensable to combustion researchers, furnace designers and manufacturers in their efforts to develop and design advanced heaters with higher performance and efficiency and lower pollutant emissions. Modelling in most cases, however, involves the use of numerical methods and simplifying assumptions which may lead if not approached with care to serious errors, given in particular the complexity of the problems involved.

In most methods available in the literature for the modelling and design of fired heaters, the heater is divided into surface and volume (gas) zones of different heights where each gas zone is treated as well-stirred and completely mixed and temperatures may be calculated at the inlet and outlet to each zone. For a rough analysis of heat transfer by radiation, the surface zones may be assumed to be black bodies and the volume zones grey gases, but for more accurate work the surface zones may have to be considered as grey and the volume zones as real gases.

In the stirred furnace model, which is an early design method, three zones are assumed: two surface zones (the sink and the refractory) and a gas zone comprising the combustion products. This is a simple and approximate method which may be further refined for greater accuracy by increasing the number of zones, particularly where significant changes in gas temperature and composition and in the surface temperature and emissivity are expected. Dividing the furnace into a series of well stirred zones approximates to the long furnace model where plug flow and radial radiation are assumed, with no axial radiation and negligible back mixing. In the Monte Carlo model, on the other hand, the zone model may also be refined by the appropriate choice of the shape of the zones so that they fit the heater geometry. In this method radiative exchange between zones is calculated by tracing "parcels" of radiation moving along random paths.

The basic objection to the zone model in the considered opinion of many designers is that it assumes discontinuous changes from one homogenous gas zone to the next. This makes this model not a very realistic one. The flux model which allows for variation in gas properties as a smooth function throughout space would be a more realistic model than the zone model. The flux method should be used when accuracy demands that continuous changes in gas temperature or optical properties cannot be represented by discrete homogeneous gas zones. In the flux method radiative transfer through gases is considered as beams of photons which are absorbed and scattered according to the laws of astrophysics.

Modelling of fired heaters is generally based on the two heater sections, namely the radiation and the convection sections. Within each section three heat transfer elements need to be considered. These are the flue gas, the process fluid and the heat exchange surfaces including the tubes and the refractory walls of the heater. In addition to the calculation of heat exchange areas and heat transfer rates to the process fluid, other key variables serve as a basis for the determination of heater performance. These include:
(1) Process fluid and flue gas temperatures.
(2) Flame and tube skin or tube wall temperatures.
(3) Process fluid flow rate.
(4) Fuel flow rate and composition.
(5) Process fluid pressure drop and the pressure profile in the heater and stack.

For most furnace designers and operators, however, the thermal efficiency remains the most important single performance factor. This is particularly so in view of the current trend of rising fuel costs and environmental concerns. The successful design and operation of a fired heater must aim first and foremost at the highest possible thermal efficiency with due regards to other performance and pollution considerations.

3. Heat transfer in the radiant section

Heat transfer by radiation is governed in theory by the Stefan-Boltzman law for black body radiation, $Q_R = \sigma T^4$. In practice, the mathematical solution of radiative heat transfer is more complicated however as it involves the calculation of heat exchange factors as a function of the furnace geometry and the calculation of the absorptivity and emissivity of the combustion gases. There are also other factors to be considered such as the emissivities of the surface and the effects of re-radiation of the tubes.

There are two primary sources of heat input to the radiant section, the combustion heat of fuel, Q_{rls}, and the sensible heat of the combustion air, Q_{air}, fuel, Q_{fuel} and the fuel atomization fluid (for liquid fuel when applicable), Q_{fluid}. Part of this heat input liberated in the radiant section is absorbed by the tubes in the radiant Q_R and shield Q_{shld} sections, while the remaining heat is either carried as sensible heat by the exiting flue gas, $Q_{flue\ gases}$ or is lost by radiation through the furnace walls or casing, Q_{losses}. The temperature of the flue gas can then be calculated by setting up a heat balance equation.

Radiation heat losses through furnace walls depend on the size of the furnace, where greater heat losses are to be expected in small furnaces as the ratio between the walls area and the volume of the radiation section decreases with furnace size increase. For furnaces of 10 MW or more, they range from 2 to 5% of the net calorific value. Apart from furnace size, however, radiation heat losses depend also on the material composing the insulating refractory lining and its thickness, and these losses may be low for an economically optimum insulating lining.

For the radiant section, the heat balance equations are:

$$Q_{in} = Q_{rls} + Q_{air} + Q_{fuel} + Q_{fluid} \quad (1)$$

$$Q_{rls} = m_{fuel} \times NCV \quad (2)$$

$$Q_{air} = m_{air} \times Cp_{air} \times (T_{air} - T_{datum}) \quad (3)$$

$$Q_{fuel} = m_{fuel} \times Cp_{fuel} \times (T_{fuel} - T_{datum}) \quad (4)$$

$$Q_{fluid} = Cp_{fluid} \times (T_{fluid} - T_{datum}) \quad (5)$$

$$Q_{out} = Q_R + Q_{shld} + Q_{losses} + Q_{flue\ gases} \quad (6)$$

$$Q_R = Q_r + Q_{conv.} \quad (7)$$

$$Q_r = \sigma \times (\alpha \times A_{cp}) \times F \times (T_g^4 - T_w^4) = \text{radiant heat transfer} \quad (8)$$

$$Q_{conv} = h_{conv} \times A_t \times (T_g - T_w) \quad (9)$$

= convective heat transfer in the radiant section

$$Q_{shld} = \sigma \times (\alpha \times A_{cp})_{shld} \times F \times (T_g^4 - T_w^4) \quad (10)$$

$$Q_{losses} = (2\text{-}5)\% \times m_{fuel} \times NCV = \text{Radiation heat losses} \quad (11)$$

$$Q_{flue\ gases} = m_{flue\ gases} \times Cp_{flue\ gases} \times (T_g - T_{datum}) \quad (12)$$

The heat balance equation is:

$$Q_{rls} + Q_{air} + Q_{fuel} + Q_{fluid} = Q_R + Q_{shld} + Q_{losses} + Q_{flue\ gases} \quad (13)$$

4. Calculation of Flame and Effective Gas Temperatures.

Flame and effective gas temperatures are key variables that need to be accurately determined before analysis of the heat transfer in the radiant section of fired heaters can be meaningfully undertaken.

Flame temperature is the temperature attained by the combustion of a fuel. This temperature depends essentially on the calorific value of the fuel. A theoretical or ideal flame temperature may be calculated assuming complete combustion of the fuel and perfect mixing. But even when complete combustion is assumed, the actual flame temperature would always be lower than the theoretical temperature. There are several reasons for this, chiefly the dissociation reactions of the combustion products at higher temperatures (greater than about 1370°C), which are highly endothermic and absorb an enormous amount of heat, and heat losses by radiation and convection to the walls of the combustion chamber.

Some work has been done on the calculation of flame temperature, including work by Stehlik and others who studied furnace combustion and drew furnace temperature and enthalpy profiles. Vancini wrote a programme in assembly language for the calculation of the average flame temperature, taking into account dissociation at higher temperatures.

A simple heat balance normally serves as the basis for calculating the flame temperature. The increase in enthalpy between the unburned and burned mixtures is assumed to be equal to the heat produced by the combustion. When the fuel is fired, the heat liberated raises the temperature of the combustion products from t_1 to t_2 so that the following relationship is satisfied:

$$Q_{combustion} = \sum_{i=1}^{5} W_i \times \int_{t_1}^{t_2} Cp_i \cdot dt \tag{14}$$

Where:
$Q_{combustion}$ = Heat of combustion of fuel based on the gross calorific value.
W_i = Mass of a flue gas component. The five components considered are CO_2, N_2, O_2, SO_2 and water vapour.
Cp_i = Molar heat of a flue gas component.
t_1 and t_2 = Initial and final temperatures.
The use of Equation (14) allows the calculation of the flame temperature by iteration using a programmable calculator. The variation of Cp_i with temperature can be approximated by a polynomial, having the obvious advantage of being integrated easily. Using a third-degree polynomial, Cp_i can be written as:

$$Cp_i = a_i + b_i \times t + c_i \times t^2 + d_i \times t^3 \tag{15}$$

Where, a_i, b_i, c_i and d_i are constants dependent on the nature of the gas. Assuming t_1 to be negligible (= 0), Equation (14) thus becomes:

$$Q_{combustion} = \sum_{i=1}^{5} W_i \times \int_{0}^{t} \left(a_i + b_i \times t + c_i \times t^2 + d_i \times t^3\right) \cdot dt \tag{16}$$

Integrating:

$$Q_{combustion} = \sum_{i=1}^{5} W_i \times \left(a_i + \frac{b_i \times t}{2} + \frac{c_i \times t^2}{3} + \frac{d_i \times t^3}{4} \right) \times t \tag{17}$$

It is customary to call the parenthetic term in Equation (17) the mean molar heat:

$$Cp_{m,i} = a_i + \frac{b_i \times t}{2} + \frac{c_i \times t^2}{3} + \frac{d_i \times t^3}{4} \tag{18}$$

By taking mean molar heats instead of true molar heats, the integration of Equation (14) may be dispensed with. The molar heats at constant pressure for air and flue gases are given in Table (1).

For heat transfer at constant pressure:

$$Q_{combustion} = \sum_{i=1}^{5} W_i \times Cp_{m,i} \times (t_2 - t_1) \tag{19}$$

Equation (19) allows the calculation of the theoretical flame temperature, t_2, by iteration via a programmable calculator. In order to compensate for the factors that tend to lower the theoretical flame temperature, the heat of combustion is usually multiplied by an empirical coefficient. The values normally used for this coefficient are only estimates; this is why the temperature calculated with any method can only approximate actual values. For an accurate calculation of the actual flame temperature, account must be taken of heat losses through the casing by setting up heat balance equation for fuel gas as follows:

$$Q_{combustion} - Q_{losses} = \sum_{i=1}^{5} Wi \times Cp_{m,i} \times (t_2 - t_1) \tag{20}$$

Where:

$$Q_{combustion} = M_{fuel} \times GCV \tag{21}$$

$$Q_{losses} = 5\% \times Q_{combustion} \tag{22}$$

The Newton-Raphson method is used to solve the heat balance equation and determine the actual flame temperature, for which two Matlab programmes are written (Appendices 1 and 2).

Gas	Molar heat (kJ/ kmol.K)	Temp. Range
Air	$33.915 + 1.214 \times 10^{-3} \times T$	50-1500 K
CO_2	$43.2936 + 0.01147 \times T - 818558.5/T^2$	273-1200 K
N_2	$27.2155 + 4.187 \times 10^{-3} \times T$	300-3000 K
O_2	$34.63 + 1.0802 \times 10^{-3} \times T - 785900/T^2$	300-5000 K
SO_2	$32.24 + 0.0222 \times T - 3.475 \times 10^{-6} \times T^2$	300-2500 K
$^*H_2O_{(g)}$	$34.42 + 6.281 \times 10^{-4} \times T + 5.611 \times 10^{-6} \times T^2$	300-2500 K

$^*H_2O_{(g)}$ is gas phase

Table 1. Molar heats at constant pressure for air and flue gases

The effective gas temperature is the temperature controlling radiant transfer in the heater radiant section. For most applications complete flue gas mixing in the radiant section is normally assumed and the effective gas temperature is taken to be equal to the bridgewall temperature, i.e. the exit temperature of the flue gases leaving the radiant section. This is normally assumed in most methods used for the estimation of the effective gas and other radiant section temperatures, including the widely-used Lobo-Evans method. In general, this is an acceptable assumption with the notable exception of high temperature heaters with tall narrow fireboxes and wall firing where longitudinal and transverse temperature gradients may not be ignored and the effective gas temperature may be 95 to 150°C higher than the bridgewall temperature. In this and other cases where the two temperatures differ widely and an adjustment may be necessary, the use of a more accurate gas temperature

may have to be considered. The usual approach is to divide the radiant section into zones for the energy balance calculations, or temperature gradients in the fired heater may be evaluated in order to predict the bridgewall and effective gas temperatures.
The average tube wall temperature is given by:

$$T_W = 100 + 0.5\left(\frac{T_{in} + T_{out}}{2}\right) \tag{23}$$

The Newton-Raphson method is then used to solve the heat balance equation (Eq. 13) and determine the effective gas temperature, for which two Matlab programmes are written (Appendices 2 and 3).

To illustrate the use of the above programmes, an example is worked out for an actual crude oil heater used in an atmospheric topping unit at the Homs Oil Refinery (Cabin 43-5-16/21 N). In this example, fuel gas is fired with 25% excess air. Ambient temperature = 15°C, exit gas temperature = 400°C. Table (2) shows the geometrical characteristics for the heater, and Table (3) shows its Process data sheet and the characteristics of the fuel (natural gas), flue gas, process fluid and air.

External Dimensions of heater (m)	20.000×4.800×19.650
Total Number of tubes	100
Weight of heater (kg)	307000
Weight of refractory (kg)	298000
Geometrical Characteristics of Radiant Section	
Number of passes	2
Number of tubes	60
Overall tube length (m)	20.824
Effective tube length (m)	20.024
Tube spacing, centre-to-centre (mm)	394
Tube spacing, centre-to-furnace wall (mm)	220
Outside diameter of tube (mm)	219
Wall thickness of tube (mm)	8
Tube materials	Stainless steel 18 Cr-8 Ni, Type AISI 304
Geometrical Characteristics of Convection Section	
Total number of tubes	40
Number of passes	2
Number of shield tubes	8
Overall tube length (m)	20.824
Effective tube length (m)	20.024
Tube spacing, centre-to-centre (mm)	250
Outside diameter of tube (mm)	168
Wall thickness of tube (mm)	8
Tube materials	Stainless steel 18 Cr-8 Ni, Type AISI 304

Table 2. Geometrical Characteristics of Box-Type Fired Heater.

Design thermal load (Duty) (kJ/h)	8.482×10^7
Unit process conditions	
Process fluid	Heavy Syrian Crude oil
Fluid flow rate (kg/h)	225700
Specific gravity at 15 °C	0.9148
UOP K	12.1
Molecular weight	105.183
Specific heat (kJ/kg. K)	2.5744
Inlet conditions	
Temperature (°C)	210
Pressure (bar)	Max 19.5
Liquid density kg/m^3	914.8
Liquid viscosity (cst at 70°C)	30
Percentage of weight of vapour	0.0
Outlet conditions	
Temperature (°C)	250 from convection 355 from radiant section
Pressure (Mpa)	0.91
Percentage of weight of vapour	0.0
Design conditions	
Minimum calculated efficiency %	75.78
Radiation losses %	5.0
Flue gas velocity though convection	2.677 (kg/m^2.s)
Fuel characteristics	
Type of fuel	Natural gas
Nett calorific value (kJ/kmol)	927844.41
Molar heat (kJ/kmol.K)	39.26
Temperature (°C)	25
Flow of fuel (kmol/h)	120
Molecular weight (kg/kmol)	19.99
Composition (% mol)	CH_4 (80.43), C_2H_6 (9.02), C_3H_8 (4.54), iso-C_4H_{10} (0.20), n-C_4H_{10} (0.32), iso-C_5H_{12} (0.04), n-C_5H_{12} (0.02), CO_2 (3.52), H_2S (0.09), N_2 (1.735).
Air characteristics	
Molar heat (kJ/kmol.K)	$33.915+1.214\times10^{-3}\times T$
Flow of air (kmol/h)	1589.014
Air temperature (°C)	25
Percentage of excess air	25%
Flue gas characteristics	
Molar heat (kJ/kmol.K)	$29.98+3.157\times10^{-3}\times T$
Specific heat(kJ/kg.K)	$1.0775+1.1347\times10^{-4}\times T$
Flow of flue gas (kmol/h)	1720.9
Molecular weight (kg/kmol)	27.82336
Composition (% mol)	CO_2 (8.234), H_2O (15.968), O_2 (3.82), N_2 (71.79), SO_2 (0.188)

Table 3. Process data sheet for box-type fired heater.

The flame temperature equation, derived using programme (1), has the following form:

$$F(t_f)=a\times t_f+b\times t_f^2+c\times t_f^{-1}+d\times t_f^3+e \quad (24)$$

The first derivative of the flame temperature equation is:

$$\frac{dF(t_f)}{dt_f}=a+2\times b\times t_f-c\times t_f^{-2}+3\times d\times t_f^2 \quad (25)$$

Where a, b, c, d and e are constants estimated dependent on the type of fuel and its gross calorific value, the percentage of excess air and the operating conditions of the fired heater. These constants can then be estimated using Programme 2 as follows (Table 4):

$$F(t_f)=29.9825\times t_f+0.0021\times t_f^2+9.7421\times 10^4 t_f^{-1}+2.9648\times 10^{-7}\times t_f^3-6.4657\times 10^4 \quad (26)$$

$$\frac{dF(t_f)}{dt_f}=29.9825+0.0042\times t_f-9.7421\times 10^4\times t_f^{-2}+8.8943\times 10^{-7}\times t_f^2 \quad (27)$$

These equations were solved by the Newton-Raphson method using programme 2 to give the actual flame temperature of 2128 K.

The effective gas temperature equation, derived using programme (3), has the following form:

$$F(Tg)=C\times Tg^4+D\times Tg-B \quad (28)$$

The first derivative of the effective gas temperature equation is:

$$\frac{dF(Tg)}{dTg}=4\times C\times Tg^3+D \quad (29)$$

where B, C and D are constants dependent on the type of fuel, percentage of excess air, operating conditions and geometrical characteristics of the fired heater. These constants can then be estimated using Programme 2 as follows (Table 5):

$$F(Tg)=9.0748\times 10^{-5}\times Tg^4+7.9153\times 10^4\times Tg-1.5533\times 10^8 \quad (30)$$

$$\frac{dF(Tg)}{dTg}=3.6299\times 10^{-4}\times Tg^3+7.9153\times 10^4 \quad (31)$$

These equations were solved by the Newton-Raphson method in programme (2) to give an effective gas temperature in the fire box equal to 1278 K.

Flow rate of fuel (kmol/h) = 120
Flow rate of flue gases (kmol/h) = 1720.9
Percentage of heat losses = 0.05
Gross calorific value of fuel (kJ/kmol) = 976029.6
Molar fraction of CO_2 = 0.08234
Molar fraction of H_2O = 0.15968
Molar fraction of N_2 = 0.7179
Molar fraction of O_2 = 0.382
Molar fraction of SO_2 = 0.00188

Table 4. Data for the determination of flame temperature equation.

Inlet temperature of process fluid (°C) = 210
Outlet temperature of process fluid (°C) = 355
Stack temperature (°C) = 400
Flow rate of fuel (kmol/h) = 120
Flow rate of combustion air (kmol/h) = 1589.014
Flow rate of flue gases (kmol/h) = 1720.9
Number of tubes in radiation section = 60
Number of shield tubes = 8
Effective tube length (m) = 20.024
External diameter of tube in convection section (m) = 0.219
Centre-to-Centre distance of tube spacing (m) = 0.394
Net Calorific Value of fuel (kJ/kmol) = 927844.41
Molar heat of fuel (kJ/kmol.K) = 39.26

Table 5. Data for determination of the effective gas temperature equation.

5. Simulation of Heat Transfer in the Convection Section

The bases for the calculation of heat transfer in the convection section were laid for the first time by Monrad. Subsequently Schweppe and Torrijos developed a method based on the work done by Lobo and Evans on the radiation section. Other work done on the heat transfer in the convection section includes work by Briggs and Young and the work of Garner on the efficiency of finned tubes.

Heat transfer in the convection section is composed in general of the following:
1. Direct convection from the combustion gases.
A film coefficient based on pure convection for flue gas flowing normal to a bank of bare tubes may be estimated using an equation developed by Monrad:

$$h_c = 0.018 \times C_{P_{fluegas}} \times \frac{G_{\max}^{2/3} \times T_{avg}^{0.3}}{D_o^{1/3}} \tag{32}$$

where $Cp_{flue\ gas}$ is the average specific heat of flue gas, and can be determined using equation (33):

$$Cp_{flue\ gas}=1.0775+1.1347+3.157\times10^{-4}\times T_{qvg} \tag{33}$$

2. Direct radiation from the combustion gases.
An approximate value for the radiation coefficient of the hot flue gas may be obtained using the following equation:

$$h_{rg} = 9.2\times10^{-2}\times T_{avg} - 34 \tag{34}$$

3. Radiation from refractory walls.
Re-radiation from the walls of the convection section usually ranges from 6 to 15% of the total heat transfer by both direct convection and radiation from the combustion gases. A value of 10% represents a typical average, i.e. 0.1 (h_c + h_{rg}).

Based on the above equations the total convection heat transfer coefficient can be calculated from the following equation:

$$h_o = (1.1)\times(h_c + h_{rg}) \tag{35}$$

and the coefficient of overall heat transfer by convection and radiation (overall heat exchange coefficient, U_c) can then be determined using the following equation:

$$\frac{1}{U_c} = \frac{1}{h_i} + f\,(e,\lambda) + \frac{1}{h_o}\times\frac{S_i}{S_o} \tag{36}$$

where

$$f\,(e,\lambda) = \frac{R_i}{\lambda}\times\frac{R_o}{R_i} \tag{37}$$

and λ is the thermal conductivity of the tube wall which can be determined using an equation derived by curve-fitting thermal conductivity data for tube wall materials.

$$\lambda = -0.157\times10^{-4}\times T_w^{\,2} + 79.627\times10^{-3}\times T_w + 28.803 \tag{38}$$

The value of h_i for turbulent flow, 10000<Re<120000, and $L/D_o \geq 60$, is given by equation 39:

$$h_i = 0.023\times\frac{k}{D_i}\times \Pr^{1/3}\times \mathrm{Re}^{0.8}\times\left(\frac{\mu}{\mu_w}\right)^{0.14} \tag{39}$$

where k is the thermal conductivity of the process fluid which can be estimated using an equation derived by curve-fitting thermal conductivity data of the process fluid.

$$k = 0.49744-29.4604\times10^{-5}\times t \tag{40}$$

$$\ln(\mu) = -0.2207 \times \ln^2(t) + 0.5052 \times \ln(t) - 11.8201 \tag{41}$$

Equation (41) was also obtained by curve-fitting viscosity values of the process fluid.
4. Radiation escaping from the combustion chamber into the shield section. This can be estimated using the general equation for radiation heat transfer:

$$Q_f = \sigma \times \left(\alpha \times Acp_{shld}\right) \times F \times \left(T_g^4 - T_w^4\right) \tag{42}$$

where:

$$Acp_{shld} = N_{(tube)_{sld}} \times S_{tube} \times L_{tube} \tag{43}$$

and T_w is the mean tube wall temperature which can be estimated in terms of the inlet and outlet process fluid temperatures, T_{in} and T_{out}, respectively using equation 23.
Since all heat directed towards the shield tubes leaves the radiant section and is absorbed by these tubes, the relative absorption effectiveness factor, α , for the shield tubes can be taken to equal one.

Total heat transfer in the convection section is then equal to the sum of the total heat transferred by convection and radiation into the tubes and the escaping radiation across the shield section, if applicable.

$$Q_c = Q_f + U_c \times A_c \times LMTD \tag{44}$$

Where:
Q_c= total heat transfer in the convection section.
Q_f= Escaping radiation.
A_c= Area of heat transfer.

$$LMTD = \frac{(T_1 - t_1) - (T_2 - t_2)}{\ln \frac{(T_1 - t_1)}{(T_2 - t_2)}}$$ = Log mean temperature difference

A method proposed by Davalos, Fernandez and Vallejo for the simulation of cylindrical fired heaters may be used for predicting the overall behaviour of the convection section without giving information on the heat flux and temperature gradients. Such information may, however, be obtained by carrying out calculations for each layer or segment of the tubes in the convection section. This implies the use of iterative methods. A pre-requisite for such heat transfer analysis is the determination of the flue gas and process fluid temperatures in the zone separating the convection and the radiation sections, which may be calculated by solving the heat balance equation given above (Eq. 13) using the Newton-Raphson method, as previously mentioned. The intermediate flue gas and process fluid temperatures can then be calculated and the results presented in the form of temperature profiles for the combustion gases, tube walls and process fluid.

The following algorithm may be used for the calculation of the intermediate flue gas and process fluid temperatures.

1. Assume heat absorption by the first layer of tubes.
2. Calculate the flue gas and process fluid temperatures by means of an appropriate heat balance.
3. Calculate the log mean temperature difference.
4. Calculate the heat transfer coefficient for convection and radiation from the flue gas.
5. Determine the contributions of escaping radiation if the tubes in the convection section are close to the combustion chamber.
6. Compare the calculated heat absorption with the assumed value, and if close agreement found, proceed to the following layer of tubes. The total heat absorption in the convection section is determined by the summation of the amounts of heat absorbed in all layers.

Based on the above analysis, a Matlab computer programme (Appendix 4) was written for the convection section of the box-type fired heater used for heating crude oil at Homs Oil Refinery. The results obtained by this analysis are given in Table 6.

Fig. 1 shows a flow sketch for the furnace in which are indicated the combustion products, mass balance and overall energy balance and heat losses. Fig. 2 shows the temperature profiles for the process fluid, flue gas and tube wall and the amount of heat absorbed per layer in the convection section.

Outlet temperature of radiation gases (°C)	800
Outlet temperature of convection gases(°C)	400
Process fluid at radiation inlet (°C)	250
Heat liberated by combustion (kJ/h)	1.1193×10^{8}
Calculated heat absorption (kJ/h)	8.821×10^{7}
Heat absorbed in radiation section (kJ/h)	6.182×10^{7}
Heat absorbed in convection section (kJ/h)	2.30×10^{7}
Flow of fuel (kmol/h)	120
Transfer area required (m^2)	464.77
Number of required shield tubes	8

Table 6. Results of the Box-Type Heater heat transfer Simulation.

6. Thermal Efficiency

Furnace thermal efficiency is usually defined as the percent ratio of the total heat absorbed by the process fluid to the total heat input. The total heat input is the sum of the calorific value of the fuel (gross or net) and the sensible heat of all incoming streams including combustion air, fuel and atomization steam (if used). Heat losses calculated from the difference between the heat input and heat absorbed comprise both stack heat losses and radiation heat losses through furnace walls.

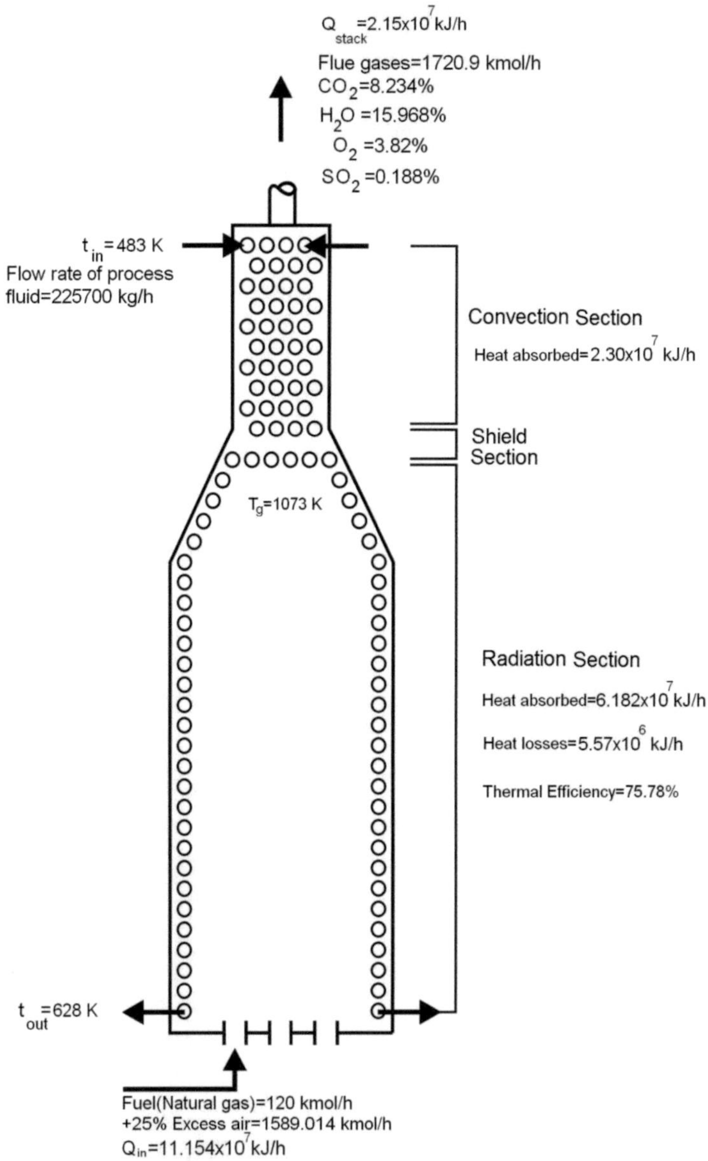

Fig. 1. Flowsketch of fired process heater

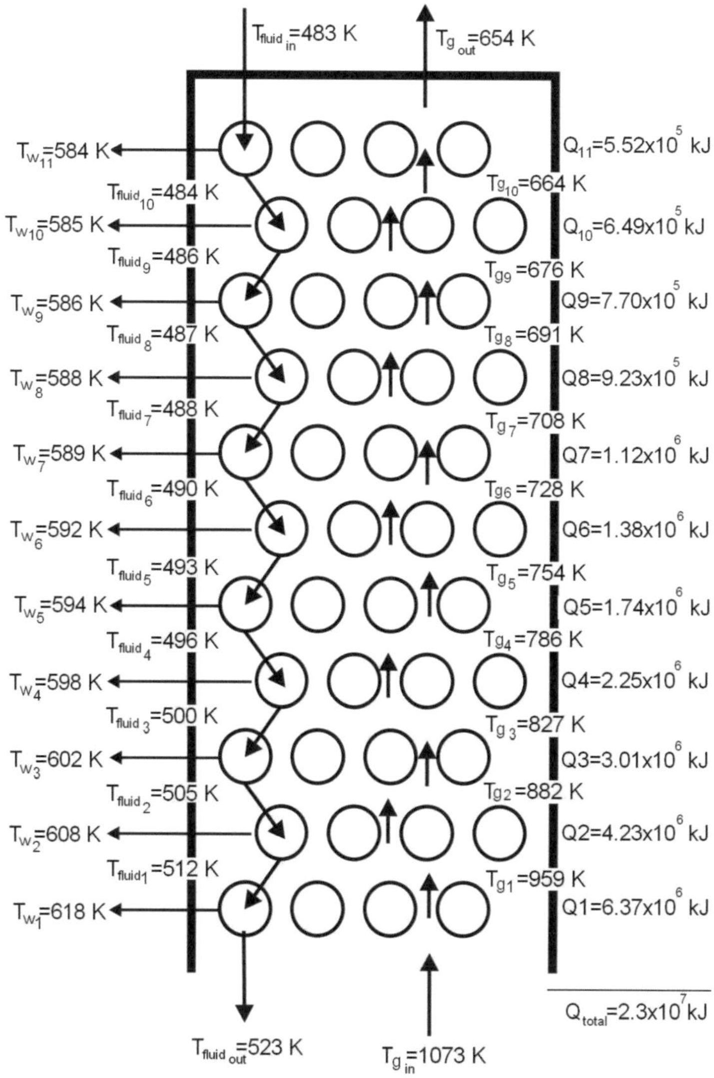

Fig. 2. Temperature profiles for combustion gases, tubewall and fluid process and absorbed heat per layer in the convection section

Stack heat losses are sensible and latent heats carried by the hot flue gases discharged through the stack. They are a function of the flue gas flow rate and temperature. Of these two factors, flue gas temperature is the main factor in furnace heat losses, and the thermal efficiency may be greatly improved if the flue gases are cooled before being discharged from the chimney. In order to cool the flue gases, a cold fluid must be available that needs to be heated. Flue gas cooling is limited, however, by corrosion problems caused by sulphuric acid condensation due to the presence of sulphur compounds in the fuels burned. If the fluid to be heated is at a temperature that is too high to give a sufficiently low flue gas temperature, i.e. a satisfactory thermal efficiency, either one of these two solutions may be used: (1) Steam production, which does not reduce fuel consumption, but is advantageous if the steam can be exploited, (2) Recycling the flue gas and utilizing its heat for preheating the combustion air. Preheating the combustion air allows a thermal efficiency of approximately 90% of the net calorific value, but this requires an air blower.

While flue gas temperature is the main factor in furnace heat losses, the effect of flow gas rate is by no means negligible. This depends to a large extent on the excess air ratio, and for higher efficiency the furnace should operate with the least possible excess air while ensuring at the same time complete combustion of the fuel. Operation with too little excess air may lead to unburned fuel losses that may be greater than the efficiency gained by reducing the excess air. Incomplete combustion is undesirable not only on account of calorific value loss, but also because of fouling problems often associated with the unburned fuel. If the flue gases are cooled, excess air will no longer have any importance since all the heat transferred to the excess air will be recovered from it.

For efficiency calculation either of two main methods may be used. These are: the input-output or direct method and the heat-loss or indirect method. The input-output method is based on the ratio of useful heat output (heat absorbed by the process fluid) to the heat input, where the net calorific value is used. It is an elaborate and detailed method involving complete mass and heat balances for which accurate measurements of the fuel calorific value as well as the quantities of incoming streams (fuel, air, steam) and outgoing combustion products are required. In the heat loss method, on the other hand, the gross calorific value is used and percentages of all losses occurring in the heater as a result of incomplete combustion and radiation and flue-gas heat losses are calculated and subtracted from the total of 100%. With this method it is possible to gain insight where the losses in efficiency occur and then be able to reduce such losses to increase the efficiency. For heat loss determination the ASME Power Test Code heat method is often used. Of the two methods available for the calculation of the thermal efficiency, the direct method is often preferred because of its many advantages for it is a quick and easy method for assessing the efficiency of fired heaters where laboratory facilities or analysis are not required for the computations involved. Its main disadvantage, however, is that there is no breakdown of losses by individual streams, and no clues are provided as to the causes of a lower heater efficiency.

The results of the heat balances carried on fired heaters are often represented by means of Sankey diagrams where all the heat transfers in the heater are summarized and represented by means of arrows or lines whose thicknesses are proportional to the amount of heat transfer. Sankey diagrams are widely used in technology where material and energy balances can be easily visualized making it easier to fully understand all the process steps and their interrelationships.

The heat balance equations for the input-output method are:

$$Q_{in} = Q_{rls} + Q_{air} + Q_{fuel} + Q_{flu} \quad (45)$$

$$Q_{out} = Q_u + Q_{losses} + Q_{stack} \quad (46)$$

Where:

Q_u = Heat duty or heat absorbed by the heated fluid

Q_{stack} = Sensible heat of the flue gases which include CO_2, H_2O, SO_2, N_2 and excess O_2 and the atomization fluid if applicable.

The thermal efficiency of the fired heater can then be written as:

$$E = \frac{Q_u}{Q_{in}} \times 100$$

A Matlab programme (Appendix 5) based on the direct method may be used to calculate a complete energy balance for all types of fuel.

A detailed procedure for calculating the fired heater efficiency using the indirect method is given below.
Step 1: Calculate the theoretical air requirement:
Theoretical air requirement
$= [(11.43\times C)+\{34.5\times(H_2-O_2/8)\}+(4.32\times S)]/100$ Kg/Kg of fuel
Step 2: Calculate the percentage of excess air supplied (EA):

$$EA = \frac{O_2 \times 100}{(21 - O_2\%)}$$

Step 3: Calculate the actual mass of air supplied per Kg of fuel (AAS)
AAS = (1+EA/100)×theoretical air
Step 4: Estimate all heat losses: The following equations are used to determine the losses in a fired heater after combustion calculations are performed.

1. Dry gas loss, $L_1=100\times M_{dg}\times 0.96\times(t_g-t_a)/GCV$
   Where: M_{dg} = mass of dry products of combustion/kg of fuel + mass of N_2 in fuel on 1 kg basis + mass of N_2 in actual mass of air supplied
2. Percentage heat loss due to the evaporation of moisture present in the fuel.
   $L_2=100\times M_{moist}\times(2445.21+1.88\times(t_g-t_a)/GCV$
3. Loss due to moisture formed by the combustion of H_2.
   $L_3=100\times 9\times H_2\times(2445.21+1.88\times(t_g - t_a)/GCV$

Where $9\times H_2$ is used for fuel oil. For gases it must be calculated

4. Loss due to moisture in the air supplied.
   $L_4=100\times 1.88\times$humidity factor $\times AAS\times (t_g-t_a)/GCV$
5. Unburned fuel loss, L_5: This is a figure based on experience, excess air used, type of furnace, burner design, unit size, etc. Poor design or combustion results in a lot of unburned fuel, especially coal, to go along with ash to the bottom of the heater or to be carried away with flue gases. This is normally negligible for oil and gaseous fuels, but for coals it varies from 0.25 to1.0%. However, field data from similar units give good guidance.
6. Loss due to radiation, L_6: Since it is impossible to prevent any insulated surface from radiating energy to a lower-temperature source such as ambient air, some losses are inevitable. Heater surfaces, although insulated, are 15 to 25 °C above ambient temperature. ABMA has published a chart that gives the radiation losses.
7. Unmeasured losses, L_7: Each manufacturer must take care of certain normally unmeasured losses. CO formation leads to some losses, though low. Ash in the ash pit and flue gases is heated to the temperature at the pit and the stack temperature respectively by the energy in the fuel, which is a loss.

If CO is formed instead of CO_2, it is a loss of 24,656 KJ/Kg. This is the difference between the heat of reactions of : $C + O_2 \rightarrow CO_2$ and $C + ½ O_2 \rightarrow CO$. Loss due to CO formation L_7 is given by:

$$L_7 = \frac{CO'}{CO' + CO_2'} \times 10{,}160 \times C$$

The thermal efficiency can be calculated by subtracting the heat loss fractions from 100 as follows:

$$E = 100-(L_1+L_2+L_3+L_4+L_5+L_6+L_7)$$

A Matlab programme (Appendix 6) based on the indirect method may be used to calculate all heat losses and the thermal efficiency for all types of fuel. Two examples are given below in order to illustrate the use of the programmes.

Example #1: Fuel oil is fired with 40% excess air in a horizontal, box-type crude oil heater in an atmospheric distillation unit. Ambient temperature =15°C, exit gas temperature = 446°C and relative humidity is 40%.
Ultimate analysis of fuel oil (by weight): 83% C, 10% H, 5% S, 1% N and 1% O.
Flow rate of fuel (kg/h): 12000
Sp. gr. of fuel at 15°C/15°C: 0.969
Temperature on burner inlet: 100~120°C
NCV (kJ/kg): 38456
Flow rate of air (kg/h): 222965.572
Superheated steam for atomization of fuel oil at 8.5 bars and 190° C, flow rate: 4200 kg/h.
On running the program the screen asks for the fuel type used in the heater, where INPUT (a=1) is selected for fuel oil and INPUT (a=2) for fuel gas. Other data are given in Table 7, and the results shown in Table 8.

Net Calorific Value of fuel, kJ/kg: 38520.4
Flow rate of fuel, m1, kg/h: 12000
Specific heat of fuel, kJ/kg.K: 1.7
Flow rate of steam, m2 ,kg: 4200
Enthalpy of steam, kJ/g: 2777
Mass of flue gas, m3, kg: 239165.73
Mass of Wet air, kg: 222965.572
Percentage of excess air:.4
Humidity of air ,kg of water vapor/kg of wet air:.4
Molar fraction of water is equivalent to humidity of air:.015
Mass fraction of CO_2,XCO_2=.1527
Mass fraction of H_2O,XH_2O=.0715
Mass fraction of O_2,XO_2=.062
Mass fraction of N_2,XN_2=.709
Mass fraction of SO_2,XSO_2=$.502\times10^{-2}$
Temperature of combustion air °C: 40
Temperature of fuel °C: 25
Flue gas temperature °C:446

Table 7. Data for example 1

Example #2: Natural gas is fired with 25% excess air in a horizontal, box-type crude oil heater. Ambient temperature=15°C, exit gas temperature= 446°C and relative humidity is 40%.
Fuel composition: 80.43 % CH_4, 9.02 % C_2H_6, 4.54 % C_3H_8, 0.20 % iso-C_4H_{10}, 0.32 % n-C_4H_{10}, 0.04 % iso-C_5H_{12}, 0.04 %n-C_5H_{12} , 3.61 % CO_2 and 1.73 % N_2
NCV (kJ/kmol): 927844.41
Temperature on burner inlet: 100~120°C
Data for fuel gas are given in Table 9, and the results shown in Table 10.
Sankey diagrams for both examples are shown in figures 3 and 4.

Heat value of fuel is 4.62e+008 kJ/h
Sensible heat of fuel is 2.04e+005 kJ/h
Sensible heat of wet air is 6.60e+006 kJ/h
Sensible heat of steam 1.17e+007 kJ/h
Energy Input is 4.81e+008 kJ/h
Sensible heat of Combustion gases is 1.03e+008 Kcal/h
Heat losses is 2.31e+007 kJ/h
Useful energy is 3.55e+008 kJ/h
Thermal efficiency = 73.81 %

Table 8. Results for example 1

Net calorific value of fuel, kJ/Kmol= 927844.41
Molar heat of gas fuel, kJ/Kmol.K = 39.26
Molar flow rate of gas fuel Kmol/h = 120
Molar flow rate of entering air to fired heater, Kmol/h = 1589.014
Molar flow rate of combustion gases exiting from stack, Kmol/h = 1720.9
Percentage of excess air =.25
Humidity of air, kg of water vapor/kg of wet air = .4
Molar fraction of water is equivalent to humidity of air =:.015
Molar fraction of CO_2, XCO_2 =.08234
Molar fraction of H_2O, XH_2O =.15968
Molar fraction of O_2, XO_2 =.0382
Molar fraction of N_2,XN =.7197
Molar fraction of SO_2,XSO_2=6.276×10^{-5}
Temperature of combustion air °C = 25
Temperature of burner fuel °C = 25
Flue gas temperature °C = 446

Table 9. Data for example 2

Heat value of fuel is 1.11e+008 kJ/h
Sensible Heat of fuel is 3.93e+002 kJ/h
Sensible Heat of air is 5.39e+005 kJ/h
Sensible Heat of Combustion gases is 2.15e+007 kJ/h
Heat Losses are 5.57e+006 kJ/h
Energy Output is 2.71e+007 kJ/h
Useful Energy is 8.48e+007 kJ/h
Thermal efficiency = 75.78 %

Table 10. Results for example 2

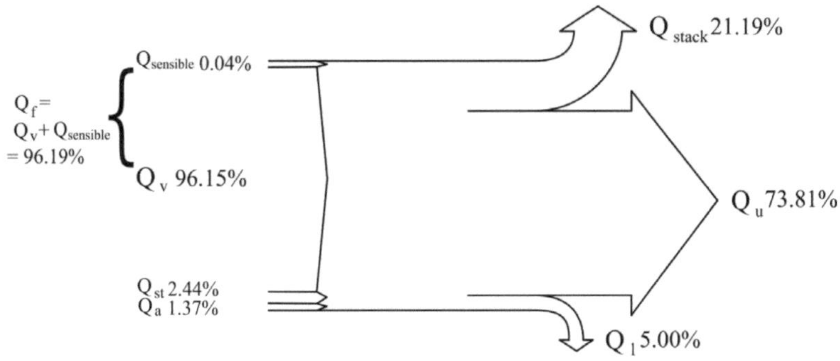

Fig. 3. Sankey diagram for the energy balance of a fuel oil fired heater of example 1

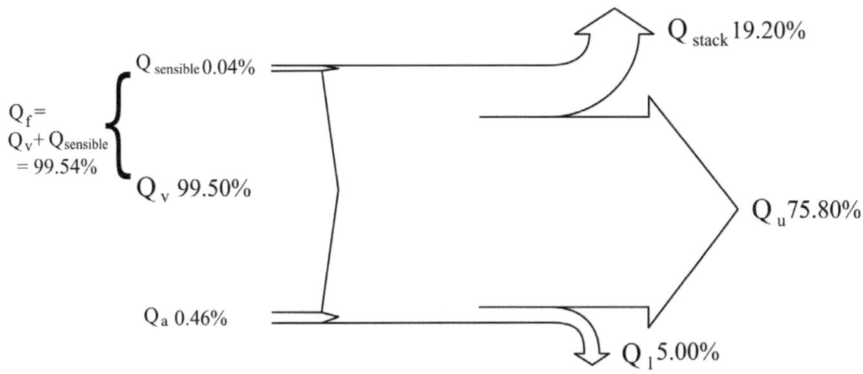

Fig. 4. Sankey diagram for the energy balance of a natural gas fired heater of example 2

7. Nomenclature

A_c	Area of tubes bank in convection section (m^2)
A_{cp}	Cold plane area of tubes bank in radiation section (m^2)
$A_{cp\ shld}$	Cold plane area of shield tubes bank (m^2)
A_t	Area of tubes bank in Radiation section (m^2)
AAS	Actual mass of air supplied per Kg of fuel
C_{Pair}	Molar heat of combustion air (kJ/kmol.K)
Cp_{fluid}	Specific heat of atomization fluid (kJ/kg.K)
$Cp_{flue\ gas}$	Average specific heat of flue gases flowing to a bank of bare tubes (kJ/kg.K)
C_{Pfuel}	Specific heat of fuel (kJ/kg.K)
Cp_i	Molar heat of a flue gas component (kJ/kmol.K)
D_i	Inside diameter of tube (mm)
D_o	Outside diameter of tube (mm)
E	Thermal efficiency %
EA	Percentage of excess air

F	Exchange factor
GCV	Gross calorific value of fuel (kJ/h)
G_{max}	Mass velocity of flue gas at minimum cross section (kg/m^2.h)
h_c	Convection film coefficient (kJ/m^2.K.h)
h_i	Convection coefficient between process fluid and the inside wall of the tubes (kJ/m^2.K.h)
h_c	Pure convection film coefficient (kJ/m^2.K.h)
h_o	Total convection heat transfer coefficient (kJ/m^2.K.h)
h_{rg}	Gas radiation coefficient (kJ/m^2.K.h)
k	Thermal conductivity of process fluid (kJ/m.K.h)
L_1	Dry gas heat loss %
L_2	Heat loss due to moisture in fuel %
L_3	Heat loss due to moisture formed by the combustion of H_2 %
L_4	Heat loss due to moisture in air supplied %
L_5	Unburned fuel heat loss %
L_6	Heat loss due to radiation %
L_7	Unmeasured heat losses %
L_{tube}	Effective tube length (m)
LMTD	Log mean temperature difference (°C)
m_{air}	Flow rate of combustion air (kg/h)
M_{dg}	Dry flue gases produced (Mass of dry flue gas in kg /kg of fuel)
$m_{flue\ gas}$	Flow rate of flue gas (kg/h)
m_{fuel}	Flow rate of fuel (kg/h)
M_{moist}	% moisture in 1 kg fuel
$N_{(tube)shld}$	Number of shield tubes
NCV	Net calorific value of fuel (kJ/h)
Pr	Prandtl number at the process fluid temperature ($Pr = \frac{C_p}{\mu \times k}$)
Q_{air}	Sensible heat of combustion air (kJ/h)
Q_C	Total heat transfer (kJ/h)
$Q_{combustion}$	Combustion heat of fuel based on the gross calorific value (kJ/h)
Q_{conv}	Convective heat transfer in the radiant section (kJ/h)
Q_f	Radiation escaping into the shield section (kJ/h)
$Q_{flue\ gas}$	Sensible heat of flue gas leaving radiant section (kJ/h)
Q_{fluid}	Sensible heat of atomization fluid (kJ/h)
Q_{fuel}	Sensible heat of fuel (kJ/h)
Q_{losses}	Assumed radiation heat loss through furnace casing (kJ/h)
Q_R	Total heat transferred to radiant tubes (heat absorbed by radiant tubes) (kJ/h)
Q_r	Radiant heat transfer (kJ/h)
Q_{rls}	Combustion heat of fuel based on the net calorific value (kJ/h)
Q_{shld}	Radiant heat to shield tubes (kJ/h)
Q_{stack}	Sensible heat of the flue gases (kJ/h)
Q_u	Heat duty or useful heat (kJ/h)
Re	Reynolds number at the process fluid temperature

R_i	Inside radius of tube (mm)
R_o	Outside radius of tube (mm)
S_i	Inside heat surface area of tube (m^2)
S_o	Outside heat surface area of tube (m^2)
S_{tube}	Tube spacing (m)
t_a	Ambient temperature (°C)
T_{avg}	Average flue gases temperature (K)
t_f	Flame temperature (°C)
T_f	Flame temperature (K)
t_g	Flue gas temperature (°C)
T_g	Effective gas temperature in firebox (K)
T_w	Average tube-wall temperature (K)
T_{in}, T_{out}	Inlet and outlet process fluid temperatures, respectively (K)
U_c	Over all heat exchange coefficient (kJ/m^2.K.h)
W_i	Mass of flue gas component (kmol/h)
α	Relative effectiveness factor of the tubes bank
λ	Thermal conductivity of tube wall (kJ/m.K.h)
ρ	Density of process fluid (kg/m^3).
σ	Stefan-Boltzman constant = 2.041×10^{-7} kJ/m^2.K^4.h
μ	Viscosity of process fluid at the average temperature (Pa.s)
μ_w	Viscosity of process fluid at the tube-wall temperature (Pa.s)

8. References

Al-Haj Ibrahim, H., Daghestani, N.; Petroleum Refinery Engineering (in Arabic), Vol. 3, Al-Baath University, Homs, 1999.

Al-Haj Ibrahim, H., Al-Qassimi, M. M.; Matlab program computes thermal efficiency of fired heater, Periodica Polytechnica, Chemical Engineering, Vol. 52, No. 2, pp. 61-69, 2008.

Al-Haj Ibrahim, H., Al-Qassimi, M. M.; Simulation of Heat Transfer in the Convection Section of Fired Process Heaters, Periodica Polytechnica, Chemical Engineering, Vol. 54, No. 1, pp. 33-40, 2010.

Baukal, J. R.; Heat transfer in Industrial Combustion, CRC Press, New York, 2000.

Berman, H. L.; Fired Heaters II, Construction Materials Mechanical Features, Performance Monitoring, Chemical Engineering, July 31, Vol. 85, No. 17, pp.87-96, 1978.

Berman, H. L.; Fired Heaters III, How Combustion Conditions Influence Design and Operation, Chemical Engineering, Aug. 14, Vol. 85, No. 18, pp.129-140, 1978.

Briggs, D. E, Young, E.H.; Convection Heat Transfer and Pressure Drop of Air Flowing Across Triangular Pitch Banks of Finned Tubes; 5th National Heat Transfer Conference, AIChE-ASME, Houston, Texas, August, 1962.

Chapra, Steven C.; Applied Numerical Methods with MATLAB for Engineers and Scientists, 1st edition, McGraw-Hill Companies, Inc, 2005.

Cross, A.; Evaluate Temperature Gradients in Fired Heaters, Chemical Engineering Progress, Vol. 98, No.6, pp. 42-46, 2002.

Davalos, H.R., Fernandez, A. P. and Vallejo, V. B.; Simulacion De Calentadores A Fuego Directo Cilindricos Verticales, Revista Del Instituto Mexicano Del Petroleo, Vol. 19, No.2, April, 1987.

Gardner, K. A.; Efficiency of Extended surface, Trans. Am. Soc. Mech. Engrs., 67, 621, 1945.

Ganapathy, V.; Applied Heat Transfer, 1st Edition, Pennwell Publishing Co., Tusla, Oklahoma, pp.34-44, 1982.

Lobo, W. E., Evans, J. E.; Heat Transfer in Radiant Section of Petroleum Heaters, Trans. Am. Inst. Chem. Engrs. 35, pp.748-778, 1939.

Monrad, C.C., Heat Transmission in Convection Section of Pipe Stills, Ind. Eng. Chem., Vol. 24, 505, 1932.

Nelson, W. L., Tube-still Heaters, Petroleum Refinery Engineering, 4th ed. McGraw-Hill, New York, 1958.

Perry, Robert H., Green, Don W.; Perry's Chemical Engineers' Handbook, 8th Edition, McGraw-Hill Publishing, 2008.

Schweppe, J. L., Torrijos, C.Q.; How to Rate Finned-Tube Convection Section in Fired Heaters. Hydrocarbon Processing and Petroleum Refiner, Vol.43, Num.6, pp.159-166, June, 1964.

Stehlik, P., et al.; Furnace integration into process justified by detailed calculation using a simple mathematical model, Chemical Engineering and Processing, 34, pp. 9-23, 1995.

Trambouze P. (ed.), Petroleum Refining, Vol. 4, Materials and Equipment, Institut français du pétrole publications, Editions Technip, Paris, 2000.

Vacini, C., A.; Program calculates flame temperature, Chemical Engineering, pp.133-136, March 22, 1982.

Walas, S. M.; Fired heaters, Chemical Process Equipment, Selection and Design, Butterworth-Heinemann, 1990.

Wuithier, P. (Ed.), Raffinage et génie chimique, L'institut français du pétrole, Paris, 1972.

ASME power test code, Performance Test Code for Steam Generating Units, PTC 4.1, 1974.

Direct Radiation in The Shield Section, Available at: www.firedheater.com

Effective gas temperature in firebox, Available at: www.firedheater.com.

Heat Balance in The Radiant Section, Available at: www.firedheater.com.

Geriap Technical Updates, Performance Evaluation of Boilers, August, 2004, Available at: www.geriap.org/documents/Technical%20Update%201%20%20Boiler%20Performance.pdf

Sankey diagram, available at: http://en.wikipedia.org/wiki/Sankey_diagram

Sankey guide, available at: http://pie.che.ufl.edu/guides/energy/sankey.html

Appendix 1:

```
% Programme for determination of flame temperature equation.
% Input:
% Flow rate of fuel (kmol/h)
% Flow rate of flue gases (kmol/h)
% Molar Composition of flue gases: XCO2, XH2O, XN2, …
% XO2 and XSO2
% Molar heats of flue gases (kJ/kmol.K)
% Percentage of heat losses
% Output:
% Flame temperature (K)
Mfuel=input('Flow rate of fuel(kmol/h)=:');
Mfluegas=input('Flow rate of flue gases(kmol/h)=:');
X=input('percentage of heat losses=:');
GCV=input('Gross calorific value of fuel (kJ/kmol)=:');
XC=input('Molar fraction of CO2=:');
XH=input('Molar fraction of H2O=:');
XN=input('Molar fraction of N2=:');
XO=input('Molar fraction of O2=:');
XS=input('Molar fraction of SO2=:');
td=15;  % Datum temperature (C)
% Molar heats at constant pressure for flue gases
% CpCO2=43.2936+0.01147*T-818558.5*T^(-2)
% CpH2O=34.42+6.281*10^(-4)*T+5.611*10^(-6)*T^2
% CpN2=27.2155+4.187*10^(-3)*T
% CpO2=34.63+1.0802*10^(-3)*T-785900*T^(-2)
% CpSO2=32.24+0.0222*T-3.475*10^(-6)*T^(2)
% Heat evolved by fuel during combustion (kJ/h)
Q=GCV*Mfuel;
% Heat losses (kJ/h)
Qloss=X*Q;
Qt=Q-Qloss;
syms tf
CpCO2=43.2936+0.01147*tf-818558.5*tf^(-2);
CpH2O=34.42+6.281*10^(-4)*tf+5.611*10^(-6)*tf^2;
CpN2=27.2155+4.187*10^(-3)*tf;
CpO2=34.63+1.0802*10^(-3)*tf-785900*tf^(-2);
CpSO2=32.24+0.0222*tf-3.475*10^(-6)*tf^(2);
% Integration of mean molar heats
Cpm=int(XC*CpCO2+XH*CpH2O+XN*CpN2+XO*CpO2+XS*CpSO2);
H=Cpm-Qt/Mfluegas;
disp('Equation of actual flame temperature')
func=H
% Finding of first derivative of flame temperature equation.
disp('Finding of first derivative of flame temperature equation')
dfun=diff(func)
```

Appendix 2:

```
% Solution of effective gas and flame temperature by ...
% Newton Raphson method
function root=newtraph(func,dfunc,xr,es,maxit)
% newtraph(func,dfunc,xguess,es,maxit):
% Uses Newton-Raphson method to find a function
%  input:
% func=name of function
% dfunc=name of derivative of function
% xguess=initial guess
% es=(optional) stopping maximum allowable iterations
% output:
% root =real root
% if necessary, assign default values
if nargin<5, maxit=50; end  % if maxit blank set to 50
if nargin<4, es=0.001; end  % if es blank set to 0,001
% Newton-Raphson
iter=0;
while (1)
xrold=xr;
xr=xr-func(xr)/dfunc(xr);
iter=iter+1;
if xr~=0, ea=abs((xr-xrold)/xr)*100; end
if ea<=es | iter>=maxit, break, end
end
root=xr;
if root>1300
root=root+273;
fprintf('The actual flame temperature is %8.0f K\n',root)
else root=xr+273;
fprintf('The Effective gas temperature is%8.0f K\n',root)
end
```

Appendix 3:

```
% Program for determination of effective gas temperature.
% Qin=Qrls+Qair+Qfuel
Tin=input(' Inlet temperature of process fluid(C)=');
Tin=Tin+273;
Tout=input(' Outlet temperature of process fluid(C)=');
Tout=Tout+273;
ts=input('Temperature of stack (C)=');
mfuel=input(' Flow rate of fuel(kmol/h)=');
mair=input(' Flow rate of combustion air (kmol/h)=');
mflue=input(' Flow rate of flue gases (kmol/h)=');
N=input (' Number of tubes in radiation section=');
Nshld=input(' Number of shield tube=');
L=input (' Effective tube length(m)=');
Do=input(' External diameter of tube in convection section(m)=');
C=input(' Center-to-Center distance of tube spacing(m)=');
NCV=input('Net Calorific Value of fuel(kJ/kmol)=');
Cpfuel=input(' Molar heat of fuel(kJ/kmol.deg.)=');
% Consrtant :
Sigma=2.041056*10^(-7); % Stefan-Boltzman Constant(kJ/h.m2.K4
F=0.97; % Exhange factor
alpha=0.835; % Relative effectiveness factor of the tubes bank
% Heat input to the radiant section
% Combustion heat of fuel
Qrls=mfuel*NCV;
% Q=mair*Cpair*(tair-tdatum)
tair=25;
tdatum=15;
% Molar heat of air
Cpair=33.915+1.214*10^(-3)*(tair+tdatum)/2;
% Sensible heat of air
Qair=mair*Cpair*(tair-15);
% Qfuel=mfuel*Cpfuel*(tfuel-tdatum)
tfuel=25;
% Sensible heat of fuel
Qfuel=mfuel*Cpfuel*(tfuel-tdatum);
Qin=Qrls+Qair+Qfuel;
% Heat is taken out of the radiant section
% Qout=QR+Qshld+Qlosses+Qflue
% Heat absorbed by radiant tubes
% QR=Qr+Qconv
% Radiant heat transfer
% Qr=sigma+(alpha*Acp)*F*(Tg^4-Tw^4)
% Tw = Average tube wall temperature in Kelvin
% Tg = Effective gas temperature in Kelvin
Tw=100+0.5*(Tin+Tout);
```

```
% Cold plane area of the tube bank
Acp=N*C*L;
% Qconv=hconv*At*(Tg-Tw)
At=N*pi*Do*L;    % Area of the tubes in bank
hconv=30.66;  % Film convective heat transfer coefficeint; (kJ/h.m2.c)
% Radiant heat to shield tubes
% Qshld=Nshld*sigma*(alpha*Acp)shld*F*(Tg^4-Tw^4)
% alpha=1, for the shield tubes can be taken to be equal to one.
Acpshld=Nshld*C*L;
% Qshld=Nshld*sigma*(1*Acpshld)*F*(Tg^4-Tw^4)
% Heat losses through setting
Qlosses=0.05*Qrls;
% Qflue=mflue*Cpflue*(Tg-Tdatum)
Tdatum=tdatum+273;
% Molar heat of flue gases
Ts=ts+273;
Cpflue=29.98+3.157*10^(-3)*(Ts-Tdatum);
% Sensible heat of flue gases
% Qflue=mflue*Cpflue*(Tg-Tdatium)
A=Qin-Qlosses;
A=A+Sigma*F*(alpha*Acp+Acpshld)*Tw^4+hconv*At*Tw-mflue*Cpflue*Tdatum;
B=Sigma*F*(alpha*Acp+Acpshld);
D=hconv*At+mflue*Cpflue;
syms Tg
% Equation for effective temperature.
y=B*Tg^4+D*Tg-A
func=y;
% Finding of first derivative of effective gas temperature equation.
dfunc=diff(func)
```

Appendix 4:

```
% Simulation of convection section of fired heater
% Program calculates heat duty, working fluid, flue gas and ...
% tube wall temperature and draft profiles for convection bank on ...
% a row-by-row basis
% Input data required for simulation:
t1=input('Inlet temperature of working fluid for heating ,C=');
t2=input('Outlet temperature of working fluid from convection section ,C=');
T1=input('Leaving flue gas temperature from radiation section ,C=');
T2=input('Leaving flue gas temperature from convection section, C=');
Cpf=input('average specific heat of process fluid, Kj/kg.C=');
td=15;                          % datum temperature (c)
Cpav=1.0775+1.1347*10^(-4)*(T2+td)/2;   % average specific heat of flue gases
Mfluid=input('Flow rate of process fluid ,kg/h=');
Mgases=input('Flow rate of flue gas ,kg/h=');
ru=input('density of process fluid ,kg/m3=');
G=input('Flue gas velocity through convection section ,kg/m2.s=');
L=input('Effective tube length ,m=');
Do=input('External diameter of tube ,m=');
Di=input('Internal diameter of tube ,m=');
n=input('Number of tubes in a layer=');
Nshld=input('Number of shield tubes=');
c=input('Center-to-center distance of tube spacing ,m=');
N=input('Number of tube layers=');
% ntube=input('Number of tubes at each row of tubes in convection section =');
% Assumed heat absorption by the first layer of tubes
Qs=input('Assumed heat absorption by the first layer of tubes, Kj/h =');
% Constants
sigma=2.041*10^(-7);  % Boltzman Constant
alpha=1;              % Relative effectiveness factor of the shield tubes
F=0.97;               % Exchange factor
for I=1:N
% Calculation of cold plane area of shield tubes
Acpshld=Nshld*c*L;
% Calculation of inside tube surface area
Si=pi*Di*L;
% Calculation of outside tube surface area
So=pi*Do*L;
% Calculation heat exchange surface area at each layer of tubes
S=n*Si;
% From the assumed heat absorption ,calculate the temperatures of...
% the flue gas process fluid by means of appropriate balances ...
% at each tube layer
% Qs=Mgases*Cpav*(T1-T)
Qc=0;
while abs(Qc-Qs)>=0.001;
```

```
if Qc~=0
Qs=Qc;
end
T=T1-Qs/(Mgases*Cpav);
% Qs=Mfluid*Cpf*(t2-t)
% x=0.01;
% H=286.8;
t=t2-Qs/(Mfluid*Cpf);
% Calcualtion of the log mean temperature difference (LMTD)
Def1=T1-t2;
Def2=T-t;
LMTD=(Def1-Def2)/log(Def1/Def2);
% Calculation of Escaping radiation
% Caculation tubewall temperature at tube layer
Tw=100+0.5*(t+t2)+273;
Qe_rad=sigma*alpha*Acpshld*F*((T+273)^4-Tw^4);
% Calculation of overall heat exchange coefficient :
% 1/U=(1/hi)+fy+(1/ho)*(Si/So)
% Calculation of convection coefficient between the process fluid and ...
% the inside wall of the tubes
% hi=0.023*(k/Di)*pr^(1/3)*Re^0.8*(u/uw)^0.14
% Let u/uw=1.0 for small variation in viscosity between ...
% bulk and wall temperatures
% k is thermal conductivity of oil(process fluid)
k=0.49744-29.4604*10^(-5)*(t2+t)/2;
% Calculation of Reynolds number ,Re=Di*w*ro/u
% u is viscosity of process fluid at average temperatute of process fluid
u=-0.1919*log((t2+t)/2)*log((t2+t)/2)+0.2295*log((t2+t)/2)-2.9966;
u=u/3600;
u=exp(u);
ri=Di/2;
ro=Do/2;
w=Mfluid/(pi*ri^2*ru);
Re=Di*w*ru/u;
% Calc of prandtl number at the average temperature of process fluid
pr=Cpf*u/k;
hi=0.023*(k/Di)*pr^(1/3)*Re^0.8;
% Calculation of radiation and convection coefficient .....
% between the flue gases and the outside surface of the tubes:
% Estimating of a film coefficient based on pure convection...
% for flue gas flowing normal to a bank of bare tubes
% hc=0.018*Cpg*G^(2/3)*Tgai^0.3/Do
% Tga is average flue gas temperature at each a tybe layer
Tga=(T1+T)/2;
Cpav=1.0775+1.1347*10^(-4)*(T1+T)/2;
hc=0.018*Cpav*G^(2/3)*Tga^0.3/Do;
```

```
% Estimating of a radiation coefficient of the hot gases :
hrg=9.2*10^(-2)*Tga-34;
% Estimating of the total heat-transfer coefficient for the bare tube...
% convection section :
ho=1.1*(hc+hrg);
% calculation of f(e,lampda)=fy:
% fy=(ro/lampda)*log(ro/ri)
% Lampda is thermal coductivity of the tube wall:
lampda=-0.157*10^(-4)*(Tw)^2+79.627*10^(-3)*(Tw)+28.803;
% Assume uniform distribution of the the flux over ...
% the whole periphery of the tube.
fy=(ro/lampda)*log(ro/ri);
% Calculation of the overall heat exchange coefficient:
% 1/U=(1/hi)+fy+(1/ho)*(Si/So)
K=1/((1/hi)+fy+(1/ho)*(Si/So));
% U=1/K;
% Uc=U;
Uc=K;
% The heat transferred by convection and radiation ...
% into the tubes:
% Qc=Qe_rad+Uc*Atubes*LMTD
% Atube is exchange surface are at each raw of tubes
Atubes=S;
Qc=Qe_rad+Uc*Atubes*LMTD;
end
I
Tg=T+273;
fprintf('The temperature of the flue gas is %5.1f Kelvin \n\n',Tg)
t;
Tf=t+273;
fprintf('The temperature of the process fluid is %5.1f Kelvin \n\n',Tf)
Tw=Tw;
fprintf('The tube wall temperature is %5.1f Kelvin \n\n',Tw)
Qc;
fprintf('Heat absorbed by heated fluid is %10.2e kJ/h\n',Qc)
if t==t1
T==T2
break
else
t2=t;
T1=T;
Cpav=1.0775+1.1347*10^(-4)*(T2+T)/2;
end
end
```

Appendix 5:

Direct method programme for determining the thermal efficiency for fired heaters

```
function directmethod=directeficiency
% The direct Method for determining the thermal efficiency
% Input :The data required for calculation of fired heater efficiency ...
% using the direct method are:
% Temperature of fuel tf
% Flow rate of fuel
% Temperature of combustion air ta
% percentage of exsess air
% Humidity of air
% Flue gas temperature tg
% Net Calorific Value (NCV)of fuel
% output:
% Thermal Efficiency
char('if you use liquid fuel then let s(select)=1 or if you use gas fuel then s(select)=2')
a=input('if you use liquid fuel then let [a=(select)=1] or of you use gas fuel then [a=(select)=2]')
if a==1
NCV=input('Net Calorific Value of fuel ,kJ/kg=:');
m1=input('flow rate of fuel ,m1=kg/h:');
Cpf=input('specific heat of fuel,=kJ/kg.K:');
m2=input('flow rate of steam ,m2 ,kg=:');
Hs=input('Enthalpy of steam ,kJ/g=:');
m3=input('Mass of flue gas ,m3 ,kg=:');
mairwet=input('Mass of Wet air ,kg=');
airper=input('percentage of excess air=:');
hum=input('humidity of air ,kg of water vapor/kg of wet air=:');
Xh=input('molar fraction of water is equivalent to humidity of air =:');
% Input :Composition of flue gas
xc=input('Mass fraction of CO2,Xco2=');
xh=input('Mass fraction of H2O,XH2O=');
xo=input('Mass fraction of O2,Xo2=');
xn=input('Mass fraction of N2,XN=');
xs=input('Mass fraction of SO2,Xso2=');
td=15;    % Datum temperature
ta=input('temperature of combustion air ,C=:');
tf=input('temperature of fuel ,C=:');
tg=input('flue gas temperature ,C=:');
% Energy balance of furnace
% Energy input
Qv=m1*NCV;    % heating value of fuel
fprintf('Heat value of fuel is %10.2e kJ/h\n',Qv)
Qseniseble=m1*Cpf*(tf-15);  % Sensible heat of fuel
fprintf('sensible heat of fuel is %10.2e kJ/h\n',Qseniseble)
Qf=Qseniseble+Qv;
```

```
% Calculation of Molecular weight of wet air
Mwair=(1-Xh)*28.84+Xh*18;
Mair=mairwet/Mwair;  % Molar mass of wet air
Cpa=33.915+1.214*10^(-3)*(ta+15)/2 ;  % Molar heat of dry air
% Molar heat of water as humidity in air
Cphum=34.42+6.281*10^(-4)*(ta+15)/2+5.6106*10^(-6)*((ta+15)/2)^2 ;
Ha=((1-Xh)*Cpa+Xh*Cphum)*(ta-15);
% Enthalpy of wet air
Qa=Mair*Ha;
fprintf('sensible heat of wet air is %10.2e kJ/h\n',Qa)
% Sensible of steam at 8.5 bar and 190 C
Qs=m2*Hs;
fprintf('sensible heat of steam %10.2e kJ/h\n',Qs)
Qin=Qf+Qa+Qs;
fprintf('Energy Input is %10.2e kJ/h\n',Qin)
% Energy output
% Molar heat of CO2
Cpco2=43.2936+0.0115*(tg+15)/2-818558.5/((tg+15)/2)^2;
Nco2=xc*m3/44;
% Sensible heat of carbon dioxide
HCO2=Nco2*Cpco2*(tg-15);
% Molar heat of O2
Cpo2=34.627+1.0802*10^(-3)*(tg+15)/2-785900/((tg+15)/2)^2 ;
No2=xo*m3/32;
% Sensible heat of excess O2
HO2=No2*Cpo2*(tg-15);
% Molar heat  of N2
Cpn2=27.2155+4.187*10^(-3)*(tg+15)/2 ;
NN2=xn*m3/28;
% sensible heat of N2
HN2=NN2*Cpn2*(tg-td);
% Molar heat of H2O
Cph2o=34.417+6.281*10^(-4)*(tg+15)/2-5.611*10^(-6)*((tg+15)/2)^2 ;
NH2O=xh*m3/18;
% Sensible heat of H2O
HH2O=NH2O*Cph2o*(tg-15);
% Molar heat of SO2
Cpso2=32.24+0.0222*(tg+15)/2-3.475*10*10^(-6)*((tg+15)/2)^2 ;
Nso2=xs*m3/64;
% Sensible hear of SO2
HSO2=Nso2*Cpso2*(tg-15);
Qstack=HCO2+HO2+HN2+HH2O+HSO2;
fprintf('Sensible Heat of Combustion gases is %10.2e Kcal/h\n',Qstack)
% Percentage heat losses  due to radiation and other unaccounted loss ...
% for a fired heater ,These losses are between 2% and 5%
% Ql=percentage of heating value of fuel
```

```
Ql=0.05*m1*NCV;
fprintf('Heat Losses is %10.2e kJ/h\n',Ql)
Qout=Qstack+Ql;
% The useful energy or heat absorbed by heated fluid
Qu=Qin-(Qstack+Ql);
fprintf('Useful Energy is %10.2e kJ/h\n',Qu)
% calculation of thermal efficiency
E=100*Qu/Qin;
fprintf('thermal efficiency %8.2f %%\n',E)
end
if a~=1
NCV=input('Net calorific value of fuel ,kJ/Kmol=:');
Cpf=input('Molar heat of gas fuel,=kJ/Kmol.K:');
n1=input('Molar flow rate of gas fuel Kmol/h=:');
n2=input('Molar flow rate of entering air to fired heater ,Kmol/h=:');
n3=input('Molar flow rate of combustion gases exiting from stack,Kmol/h=:');
airper=input('percentage of excess air=:');
hum=input('humidity of air ,kg of water vapor/kg of wet air=:');
Xh=input('molar fraction of water is equivalent to humidity of air =:');
% Input :Composition of flue gas
XCO2=input('Molar fraction of CO2,Xco2=');
XH2O=input('Molar fraction of H2O,XH2O=');
XO2=input('Molar fraction of O2,Xo2=');
XN2=input('Molar fraction of N2,XN=');
XSO2=input('Molar fraction of SO2,Xso2=');
td=15;    % Datum temperature ©
ta=input('temperature of combustion air ,c=:');
tf=input('temperature of burner fuel ,c=:');
tg=input('flue gas temperature ,c=:');
% Energy balance of furnace
% Energy input
Qv=n1*NCV ;    % heating value of fuel
fprintf('Heat value of fuel is %10.2e kJ/h\n',Qv)
Qsensible=Cpf*(tf-15);  % Sensible heat of fuel
fprintf('Sensible Heat of fuel is %10.2e kJ/h\n',Qsensible)
Qf=Qv+n1*Qsensible;
% Calculation of Molecular weight of wet air
Mwair=(1-Xh)*28.84+Xh*18;
% Molar heat of dry air
Cpa=33.915+1.214*10^(-3)*(ta+15)/2;
% Molar heat of water as humidity in air
Cphum=34.42+6.281*10^(-4)*(ta+15)/2+5.6106*10^(-6)*((ta+15)/2)^2 ;
% Sensible heat of wet air
Ha=((1-Xh)*Cpa+Xh*Cphum)*(ta-15);
Qa=n2*Ha;
fprintf('Sensible Heat of air is %10.2e kJ/h\n',Qa)
```

```
Qin=Qf+Qa;
% Energy output
% Molar heat of CO2
CpCO2=43.2936+0.0115*(tg+15)/2-818558.5/((tg+15)/2)^2;
QCO2=XCO2*n3*CpCO2*(tg-15);
% Molar heat of O2
CpO2=34.627+1.0802*10^(-3)*(tg+15)/2-785900/((tg+15)/2)^2 ;
QO2=XO2*n3*CpO2*(tg-15);
% Molar heat  of N2
CpN2=27.2155+4.187*10^(-3)*(tg+15)/2 ;
QN2=XN2*n3*CpN2*(tg-15);
% Molar heat of H2O
CpH2O=34.417+6.281*10^(-4)*(tg+15)/2-5.611*10^(-6)*((tg+15)/2)^2 ;
QH2O=XH2O*n3*CpH2O*(tg-15);
% Molar heat of SO2
CpSO2=32.24+0.0222*(tg+15)/2-3.475*10^(-6)*((tg+15)/2)^2 ;
QSO2=XSO2*n3*CpSO2*(tg-15);
Qstack=QCO2+QO2+QN2+QH2O+QSO2;
fprintf('Sensible Heat of Combustion gases is %10.2e kJ/h\n',Qstack)
% Percentage heat losses  due to radiation and other unaccounted loss ...
% for a fired heater ,These losses are between 2% and 5%
Ql=0.05*n1*NCV;
fprintf('Heat Losses is %10.2e kJ/h\n',Ql)
Qout=Qstack+Ql;
fprintf('Energy Output is %10.2e kJ/h\n',Qout)
% The useful energy or heat absorbed by heated fluid
Qu=Qin-Qout;
fprintf('Usful Energy is %10.2e kJ/h\n',Qu)
% calculation of thermal efficiency
E=100*Qu/Qin;
fprintf('thermal efficiency %8.2f %%\n',E)
end
```

Appendix 6:

The indirect method programme for the determination of the thermal efficiency of fired heaters

```
function indirectmethod=indirectefficiency
% The indirect Method for determining the thermal efficiency of fired heat
% Input :
% The required data for calculation of fired heater efficiency...
% by using the direct method are :
% Ultimate analysis of fuel (H ,O ,C ,S) , moisture content and ash content
% Percentage of Oxygen or CO2 in flue gas
% Flue gas temperature tf in C
% Ambient temperature ta in C
% Humidity of air in kg/kg of dry air
% Gross calorific value of fuel in kJ/kg (GCV)
% Mass of dry flue gas in kg/kg of fuel
% Output :
% L1 percentage heat losses due to dry flue gas
% L2 Heat loss to evaporation of water formed ...
% due to H2 in fuel
% L3 Heat loss due to moisture present in air
% L4 Percentage heat loss due to evaporation of moisture present if fuel
% moisture present if fuel
% L5 Percentage heat loss due to radiation and other unaccounted loss ...
%  for a fired heater ,These losses are between 2% and 5%
% Thermal efficiency of fired heater
tf=input('Flue gas temperature in C,tf=:');
ta=input('Ambient temperature in  C,ta=:');
GCV=input('Gross Calorific Value of fuel ,kJ/kg=:');
H=input('percentage of H in fuel by weight ,H=');
C=input('percentage of C in fuel by weight ,C=');
O=input('percentage of O in fuel by weight ,O=');
S=input('percentage of H in fuel by weight ,S=');
M=input('moisture content in 1 kg of fuel ,M=:');
mfuel=input('mass of fuel supplied ,(mfuel)=:');
h=input('humidity of air ,h=:');
% calculate the theoretical air requirement
air=((11.43*C)+(34.5*(H-O/8))+(4.32*S))/100
% calculate the % excess air supplied (EA)
 EA=O*100/(21-O)
% calculate actual mass of air supplied /kg of fuel (AAS)
AAS=(1+EA/100)*air
% calculate mass of dry flue gas in kg /kg of fuel
% m(total of lue gas)=mass of actual air supplied(ASS) + ...
% mass of fuel supplied (mfuel)
m=AAS+mfuel
% Output :
```

```
% Estimate all heat losses
% percentage heat losses due to dry flue gas
L1=m*0.96*(tf-ta)*100/GCV;
fprintf('percentage heat losses due to dry flue gas %10.2e kJ/h\n',L1)
% Heat loss to evaporation of water formed due to H2 in fuel
L2=0.09*H*(2445.2+1.884*(tf-ta))*100/GCV;
fprintf('Heat loss due to evaporation of water formed due to H2 in fuel %10.2e kJ/h\n',L2)
% Heat loss due to moisture present in air
L3=AAS*h*1.9*(tf-ta)*100/GCV ;
fprintf('Heat loss due to moisture in air %10.2e kJ/h\n',L3)
% Percentage heat loss due to evaporation of moisture present in fuel
L4=M*(2445.21+1.8842*(tf-ta))*100/GCV;
fprintf('Heat loss to evaporation of water formed due evaporation of moisture present in fuel %10.2e kJ/h\n',L4)
% Percentage heat loss due to radiation and other unaccounted loss ...
% for a fired heater ,these losses are between 2% and 5%
L5=5;
fprintf('Heat losses due to radiation and other unaccounted loss %10.2e kJ/h\n',L5)
% calculate thermal efficiency by indirect method
E=100-(L1+L2+L3+L4+L5);
fprintf('thermal efficiency %8.2f %%\n',E)
```

17

Finite difference solutions of MFM square duct flow with heat transfer using MatLab program

Mohammed Al-Khawaja and Mohamed Selmi
Qatar University
Doha, State of Qatar

1. Introduction

Many researchers are interested in magneto-hydro-dynamics MHD since the last century due to its important applications. For example, MHD steam plants and MHD generators are used in the modern power plants. The basic concept of the MHD generator is to generate electrical energy from the motion of conductive liquid that is crossing a perpendicular magnetic field. Carnot efficiency is improved by the presence of MHD unit. Another example is the MHD pumps and flow meters. In this type of pumps, the electrical energy is converted directly to a force which is applied on the working fluid. MHD separation in metal casting with superconducting coils is another important application.

A very useful proposed application which involves MHD is the lithium cooling blanket in a nuclear fusion reactor. The high-temperature plasma is maintained in the reactor by means of a toroidal magnetic field. The liquid-lithium circulation loops, which will be located between the plasma and magnetic windings, are called lithium blankets. The lithium performs two functions: it absorbs the thermal energy released by the reaction (and subsequently used for power generation) and it participates in nuclear reactions in which tritium is produced. The lithium blanket is thus a very important reactor component. On other hand, the blanket will be acted upon by an extremely strong magnetic field. Consequently, to calculate the flow of liquid metal in channels or pipes situated at different angles to the magnetic field, and to determine the required pressure drop, heat transfer, etc., a knowledge of the appropriate MHD relationships will be necessary.

Magnetohydrodynamics (MHD) has been studied since the 19th century, but extensive investigations in this field accelerated only at the beginning of the 20th century. The first theoretical and laboratory studies of MHD flows in pipes and ducts were carried out in the 1930s. Williams published results of experiments with electrolytes flowing in insulated tubes. The tubes were placed between the poles of a magnet, and the potential difference across the flow was measured using wires passed through the walls. Hartmann and Lazarus made some very comprehensive theoretical and experimental studies of this subject. They performed their experiments with mercury which has an electrical conductivity 100,000 times greater than that of an electrolyte. This made it possible to observe a wider range of phenomena than in the experiments by Williams. In particular, Hartmann and Lazarus were

able to investigate the change in drag (friction) and, indirectly, the suppression of turbulence caused by magnetic field. Hartmann obtained the exact solution of the flow between two parallel, non-conducting walls with the applied magnetic field normal to the walls.
Shercliff, in 1956, has solved the problem of rectangular duct, from which he noticed that for high Hartmann numbers M the velocity distribution consists of a uniform core with a boundary layer near the walls. This result enabled him to solve the problem for a circular pipe in an approximate manner (a first approximation which gives rise to errors of order M^{-1}) for large M assuming walls of zero conductivity and, subsequently, walls with small conductivity. In 1962, Gold and Lykoudis has obtained an analytical solution for the MFM flow in a circular tube with zero wall conductivity while in 1968, Gardner and Lykoudis have acquired experimentally some results for circular tube with and without heat transfer. The MFM flow is also examined numerically by Al-Khawaja et al. for the case of circular tube with heat transfer and for the case of uniform wall heat flux with and without free convection. The solution for MFM square duct flow is obtained using spectral method by Al-Khawaja and Selmi for the case of uniform wall temperature.
Also, the MFM combined free-and-forced convection duct flow was considered by many researchers. Chang & Lundgren considered the effect of wall conductivity for this problem. Gold analytically solved the MHD problem in a circular pipe with zero wall conductivity. His solution was an infinite series of Bessel functions, which was approximated for large M with the first few terms. For the same problem, Shercliff used the second approximation (which gives rise to errors of order M^{-2}) to get the solution for large M. Gardner used Gold's solution to evaluate the exact solution for temperature profile, which turned out to be very complex. Then, he approximated velocity profile for small to moderate M with a polynomial form from which he calculated the Nusselt number Nu. For large M, he used Gold's approximation to determine Nu. Gardner and Lykoudis experimentally studied MFM turbulent pipe flow in a transverse magnetic field with and without heat transfer. Gardner and Lo tried to solve the problem of a circular pipe flow with combined forced-and-free convection analytically using a perturbation technique in which the solutions were generated in inverse powers of the Lykoudis number, Ly. They obtained only the distribution of stream function and azimuthal velocity for some small Hartmann numbers M. Weiss studied a nonlinear two-dimensional magnetoconvective flow in a Boussinesq fluid with a series of numerical experiments. Tabeling and Chabrerie analyzed the secondary laminar flows in annular ducts of rectangular cross-section subjected to a constant axial magnetic field. They considered the cases for high M and treated the equations of flow by a perturbation method involving an infinite series expansion. In addition, some researchers investigated the case of non-uniform magnetic field. Petrykowski and Walker examined the liquid-metal flows in rectangular ducts having electrically insulating top and bottom walls and perfectly conducting sides and in the presence of strong, polar, non-uniform, transverse magnetic field. They presented solutions for the boundary layers adjacent to the sides that are parallel to the magnetic field. Singh and Lal have calculated numerically the temperature distribution for steady MHD axial flow through a rectangular pipe with discontinuity in wall temperature. Mittal, Nataraja and Naidu obtained a numerical solution of the equations governing the flow of an electrically conducting, viscous, compressible gas with variable fluid properties in the presence of a uniform magnetic field. They analyzed the velocity and temperature distributions for subsonic and supersonic flows as these occur in the duct of an MHD generator. Setayesh

and Sahai studied numerically the effect of temperature-dependent transport properties on the developing magnetohydrodynamic flow and heat transfer in a parallel-plate channel whose walls are held at constant and equal temperatures.
In addition, the problem of the combined free-and-forced convection in horizontal tubes in the absence of magnetic field was investigated considerably in the 1960s. Morton solved the problem of laminar convection in uniformly heated horizontal pipes at low Rayleigh numbers Ra using a perturbation method to obtain a formula for Nusselt number Nu which is valid only for ReRa = 3,000. Here, Re and Ra are Reynolds and Rayleigh numbers based on diameter, respectively. Mori, Futagami, Tokuda and Nakamura analyzed the same problem experimentally for air but for high Ra, and they noticed that Nusselt numbers would be about twice as large as those calculated by neglecting the effect of the secondary flow caused by buoyancy at ReRa = 4×10^5. They concluded that buoyancy has little effect on the velocity and temperature fields in turbulent flow. The critical Reynolds number (laminar-turbulent transition) was, however, affected by the secondary flow. Later, Mori and Futagami, investigated this problem theoretically on a fully developed laminar flow. On the assumption of a boundary layer (by making the velocity and temperature distributions are affected only by viscosity and thermal conductivity) along the tube wall and by use of the boundary-layer integral method, they obtained (after assuming the velocity and temperature fields are affected only by the secondary flow in the core region) the relations between Nusselt number and ReRa(= 10^4) for Prandtl number Pr not far from unity. Faris and Viskanta examined this problem analytically using a perturbation method. They presented approximate analytical solutions as well as average Nusselt numbers graphically for a range of Prandtl and Grashof numbers of the physical interest. Eckert and Peterson measured the temperature profile along the vertical diameter and calculated Nusselt number as a function of Peclet number Pe for the problem of the heat transfer to mercury in laminar flow through a horizontal tube with a constant heat flux. Siegwarth and Hanratty, measured the fully developed temperature field and axial velocity profile for Prandtl number Pr = 80 at the outlet of a long horizontal tube which is heated electrically. They also solved this problem by finite difference techniques to obtain the secondary flow pattern as well as the temperature field and axial velocity field. Newell and Bergles, formulated a numerical investigation of the effects of free convection on fully developed laminar flow in horizontal circular tubes with uniform heat flux. They obtained solutions for heat transfer and pressure drop, with both heating and cooling, for water with two limiting tube-wall conditions: low thermal conductivity (glass tube) and infinite thermal conductivity. They found that the infinite-conductivity tube exhibits higher Nu and friction factor f than the glass tube, with Nu being over five times the Poiseuille value at Grashof number (based on the difference of wall and bulk mean temperatures) ~ 10^6 . Yousef and Tarasuk, investigated experimentally the influence of free convection due to buoyancy on forced laminar flow of air in the entrance region of a horizontal isothermal tube for a narrow range of Grashof numbers (based on logarithmic mean temperature difference) from 0.8×10^4 to 8.7×10^4. That same year, Hishida, Nagano and Montesclaros, published numerical solutions without the aid of a large Prandtl number assumption for combined free-and-forced laminar convection in the entrance region of a horizontal pipe with uniform wall temperature. Chou and Hwang, studied numerically, without the aid of the large Prandtl number assumption, the Graetz problem with the effect of natural convection in a uniformly heated horizontal tube by a relatively novel vorticity-velocity method. They showed the variations in local

friction factor and Nusselt number with Rayleigh number for Prandtl numbers Pr = 5, 2 and 0.7. Rustum and Soliman, investigated numerically the steady, fully-developed, laminar, mixed convection in horizontal internally-finned tubes for the case of uniform axial heat input and circumferentially uniform wall temperature. At Pr = 7 and for modified Grashof number varies from 0 to 2×10^6, they obtained numerical results which include the secondary flow (velocity) components, axial velocity and temperature distributions, wall-heat flux, friction factor and average Nusselt number for different fin geometries. Finally, Al-Khawaja, Agarwal, and Gardner considered numerically the problem of MFM combined-free-and-forced convection pipe flow using modified third-order-accurate upwind scheme to handle the problem of high Grashof number. However, for high Hartmann number, they refined the mesh near the boundary.

2. Background

The problem considered herein is one of the forced convection in a horizontal, circular pipe of radius a in a uniform, vertical, transverse magnetic field B_0. A homogeneous, incompressible, viscous, electrically-conducting fluid flows through a horizontal circular pipe and is subjected to a uniform surface temperature and a uniform surface heat flux. In conjunction with defining this problem, the following assumptions are made:

a) All fluid properties are constant (the fluid considered is incompressible) and independent of the temperature.
b) The pipe is sufficiently long that it can be assumed the flow and heat transfer are fully developed and entrance or exit effects can be neglected. Further, it can be deduced that none of the variables except pressure and temperature vary linearly with axial direction.
c) The contributions of viscous and Joulean dissipation in the energy equation are small and can be neglected. This assumption has been shown to be applicable to a similar problem when no external electric field is imposed on the flow.
d) The induced magnetic field produced as a result of interaction of applied field, B_0, with either main or secondary flow, will be assumed negligibly small compared to B_0. This assumption follows from the fact that the magnetic Reynolds number based on the flow is much smaller than unity under conditions found in typical applications.

3. Basic Conservation Equations

For incompressible newtonian liquid metal fluid and steady-state conditions, the modified Navier-Stokes equations under the effect of magnetic field body force including induction and energy equations in vector forms are, respectively,

$$\rho(V \cdot \nabla)V + \nabla(p + \mu \frac{|H|^2}{2}) = \mu_f \nabla^2 V + \mu(H \cdot \nabla)H \quad (1)$$

$$\nabla^2 H + \mu\sigma[(H \cdot \nabla)V - (V \cdot \nabla)H] = 0 \quad (2)$$

and

$$\rho c\,(V \cdot \nabla)\,T = k\nabla^2 T + \mu_f \Phi + \frac{|J|^2}{\sigma} \tag{3}$$

in addition to solenoidal conditions on the two vectors

$$\nabla \cdot V = 0 \quad \text{and} \quad \nabla \cdot H = 0 \tag{4}$$

For very small magnetic Reynolds number R_M (i.e. the induced magnetic field produced as a result of interaction of applied field, B_0, will be assumed negligibly small compared to B_0), the induction equation, Eq. (2), can be derived from Maxwell's equations along with the two solenoidal conditions, Eqs. (4). The last two terms in the right hand of the energy equation, Eq. (3), represent the viscous and Joulean dissipations, respectively. Those terms can be neglected compared to the other ones in the equation.
After many simplifications by assuming fully developed flow, i.e. 2-D problem (See Fig. 1), and since the flow is laminar due to damping of the fluctuations of turbulence in the presence of magnetic field, the dimensionless governing equations for this flow become

$$\nabla^2 w^* - M\frac{\partial H^*}{\partial x^*} = 1 \tag{5}$$

$$\nabla^2 H^* - M\frac{\partial w^*}{\partial x^*} = 0 \tag{6}$$

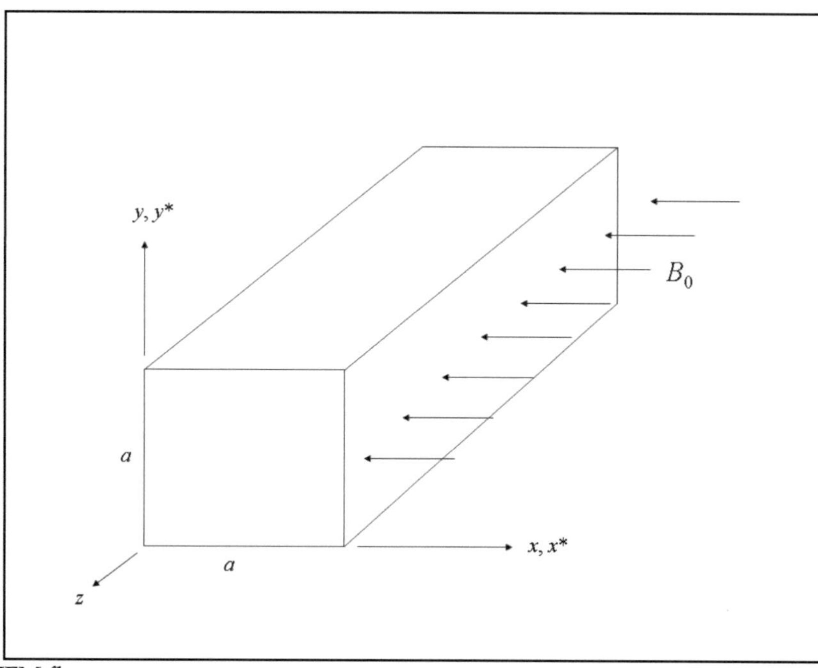

Fig. 1. MFM flow geometry

$$\nabla^2\theta + 4\text{Nu}\, w\theta = 0 \tag{7}$$

and

$$\nabla^2\theta - 4w = 0 \tag{8}$$

Where the negative dimensionless pressure gradient γ is related to w* by

$$\gamma = \frac{1}{\int_0^1 \int_0^1 w^* dx^* dy^*} \tag{9}$$

From the force and energy balances one can show, respectively, that fRe = −2γ and Nu = $-1/\theta_m$. Where the mean dimensionless temperature is given by

$$\theta_m = \frac{\int_0^1 \int_0^1 \theta w dx^* dy^*}{\int_0^1 \int_0^1 w dx^* dy^*} \tag{10}$$

Definitions of other dimensionless variables are described in the notation section. The boundary conditions are $w^* = 0$ (from no-slip condition), $H^* = 0$ (from electrically insulated surface), and θ = 0 (for isothermal surface and constant surface heat flux).

4. Numerical Investigations

4.1 Finite Difference Schemes

The partial differential equations considered here are of the elliptic type because of the steady state behavior of those equations. Some important schemes must be introduced in order to discretize those equations and get a system of linear algebraic equations with reasonable accuracy and stability if they are solved using one of the iterative methods that will be discussed below.

4.1.1 Central Difference Scheme

Central difference schemes are very well known and have been used extensively for elliptic equations, particularly, Laplace's and Poisson's equations. This scheme, for 2-D, can be represented by five-points formula, diagonal five formula, or nine-point formula, etc.. Unfortunately, these schemes do not work with all types of the elliptic equations since, for example, the numerical solutions of steady Navier-Stokes equations by relaxation methods using central difference scheme may become unstable and fail to converge if the grid Reynolds number exceeds the value 2. This instability occurs when both the convective and diffusion terms in the Navier-Stokes equations are central-differenced. The standard central-difference of the convective terms destroys the ellipticity of the difference equations at high Reynolds numbers because of loss of diagonal dominance in the resulting matrix.

4.1.2 First-Order and Second-Order-Accurate Upwind Schemes

The first-order-accurate upwind scheme has been used by many researchers to handle stability problem in the convective terms for high Reynolds number (in the present case is the square root of Grashof number). The diffusion operator and the source terms could be left as central-differenced.

There are two main disadvantages of employing these difference operators. First, the introduction of large artificial diffusion in the direction of the bias, thereby resulting in considerable loss of accuracy. Second, the overall accuracy of the algorithm being $O(\{Gr\}^{1/2}h)$, at high Grashof number, even with a reasonably fine mesh, the error of $O(\{Gr\}^{1/2}h)$ may become so dominant as to obscure the effects of physical diffusivity on the flow. Here, Gr is the Grashof number and h is the mesh size. Although considerable grid refinement, in principle, can alleviate the problem, the necessary degree of refinement is often impractical because of computer-time and storage limitations. For flow problem in a two-dimensional driven-square cavity (this flow structure has become a standard test case for evaluating the accuracy, stability and efficiency of various Navier-Stokes algorithm), only few investigators have computed the flowfield beyond Reynolds numbers of 1000.

Atias, Wolfshtein and Israeli employed a second-order-accurate upwind scheme to discretize the convective terms in the vorticity transport equation.

The overall accuracy of this scheme is $O(Re\ h^2)$, based on Reynolds number. However, Atias, Wolfshtein and Israeli on the basis of Von Neumann type stability analysis for the linearized vorticity equation, find that a Gauss-Seidel solution of the second-order upwind scheme is stable if the mesh Reynolds number is less than $2+(8)^{1/2}$ (compared with value 2 for a central difference scheme).

4.1.3 Third-Order-Accurate Upwind Scheme

This scheme was first introduced by Agarwal for computing Navier-Stokes solutions at high Reynolds numbers. He used this scheme to solve for example, flow in a 2-D driven square cavity, 2-D flow in a channel with sudden symmetric expansion, 2-D flow in a channel with a symmetrical placed blunt base, the flowfield of a 2-D impinging jet and 3-D flow in a driven cubic box. For all cases, he obtained a good agreement with computations of other investigators as well as with available experimental data. He obtained a highly accurate solution for Reynolds numbers up to 10,000 for flow in a 2-D driven square cavity. However, this scheme suffers from two main disadvantages. First, the numerical treatment of the boundary conditions requires extra care because the algorithm uses a five-point difference formula instead of the standard three-point formula for the first derivatives. Second, the solution by line relaxation requires a pentadiagonal matrix inversion.

4.1.4 Modified Third-Order-Accurate Upwind Scheme

A modification to the third-order upwind scheme also was presented by Agarwal which makes the scheme second-order-accurate, but frees it from the disadvantages discussed above. The new algorithm has low artificial diffusion compared to the second order upwind scheme.

4.2 Iterative Methods for Solving Systems of Linear Algebraic Equations

Methods for solving systems of linear algebraic equations are classified as either direct or iterative. Direct methods are those which give the solution (exactly, if round-off error does not exist) in a finite and predeterminable number of operations using an algorithm which is often quite complicated. Iterative methods consist of a repeated application of an algorithm which is usually quite simple. They yield the exact answer only as a limit of a sequence, but, if the iterative procedure converges, one can come within ε (small value) of the answer in a finite but usually not predeterminable number of operations. Thus, the iterative methods will be used. This class of methods is sometimes referred to by relaxation methods. Those methods are broken into point- (or explicit-) iterative methods and block- (or implicit-) iterative methods. In brief, for point-iterative methods, the same simple algorithm is applied to each point where the unknown function is to be determined in successive iterative sweeps whereas in block iterative methods, subgroups of points are singled out for solution by elimination (direct) schemes in an overall iterative procedure.

4.2.1 Point-Gauss-Seidel Iteration

overall This method is explicit and the steps which summarize the application of the point Gauss-Seidel iteration on a general system of algebraic equations would be as following,
(a) Make initial guesses for all unknowns.
(b) Solve each equation for the unknown whose coefficient is largest in magnitude (to satisfy stability criteria as it will be seen later), using the guessed values initially and the most recently computed values thereafter for the other unknowns in each equation.
(c) Repeat iteratively the solution of the equations in this manner until changes in the unknown become small.

4.2.2 Sufficient Condition for Convergence of The Gauss-Seidel Procedure

The point-Gauss-Seidel iterative method is simple but only converges under certain conditions related to diagonal dominance of the matrix of coefficients. Fortunately, the differencing of many steady-state conservation statements provides this diagonal dominance. Then, the sufficient condition for convergence of this method which is applied on a system of algebraic equations can be if the system is irreducible (cannot be arranged so that some of the unknowns can be determined by solving less than m equations) and if the resulting matrix of coefficient from the difference equation has a property of diagonal dominance. This is a sufficient condition which means that the convergence may sometimes be observed when the above condition is not met.
Now, the above iterative convergence criteria can be related to the system of algebraic equations, which results from differencing the elliptic equations. By inspection, it can be shown that the coefficient largest in magnitude belongs to $s_{i,j}$, where s is dependent variable. Then, those equations would establish a sparse matrix which has a property of the diagonal dominance, and hence, the Gauss-Seidel iteration would converge.

4.2.3 Successive Over-Relaxation (SOR)

Successive over-relaxation is a technique which can be used to accelerate any iterative procedure but it is proposed here primarily as a refinement to the Gauss-Seidel method.

Successive under-relaxation (SUR) appears to be most appropriate when the convergence at a point is taking on an oscillatory pattern and tending to overshoot the final solution. Over-relaxation is usually appropriate for numerical solutions to Laplace's equation with Dirichlet boundary conditions. Under-relaxation is sometimes called for in elliptic problems when the equations are nonlinear. Occasionally, for nonlinear problems, under-relaxation is even observed to be necessary for convergence.

In general, there is no specific formula which determines the optimum value of relaxation factor. Sometimes the determination of optimum factor could be obtained by numerical experiments.

4.2.4 Line-Iterative Relaxation Method

Line-iterative relaxation algorithm sometimes is referred to as block-iterative method and since this method has an implicit nature, then it is known as implicit-iterative method. Although this procedure is workable with almost any iterative algorithm, it makes sense to work within the framework of the Gauss-Seidel method with SOR or SUR.

Again, over-relaxation or under-relaxation can be used here. There are many alternative ways in applying SOR or SUR.

5. Solution

In this paper, the MFM problem for two heat transfer limits; constant temperature and constant heat flux boundary conditions, is investigated numerically for square duct (See Fig. 1). The modified dimensionless Navier-Stokes equations with uniform-temperature-condition having energy equation (Eq. 7), and uniform-heat-flux-condition having energy equation (Eq. 8) are transferred into finite-difference equations (using the central-difference scheme) and given as

$$w^*_{i-1,j} + w^*_{i+1,j} + w^*_{i,j-1} + w^*_{i,j+1} - 4w^*_{i,j} - \frac{1}{2} M\Delta x^* (H^*_{i+1,j} - H^*_{i-1,j}) = (\Delta x^*)^2 \quad (11)$$

$$H^*_{i-1,j} + H^*_{i+1,j} + H^*_{i,j-1} + H^*_{i,j+1} - 4H^*_{i,j} - \frac{1}{2} M\Delta x^* (w^*_{i+1,j} - w^*_{i-1,j}) = 0 \quad (12)$$

$$\theta_{i-1,j} + \theta_{i+1,j} + \theta_{i,j-1} + \theta_{i,j+1} - 4\theta_{i,j} + 4(\Delta x^*)^2 \mathrm{Nu}\, w_{i,j} \theta_{i,j} = 0 \quad (13)$$

and

$$\theta_{i-1,j} + \theta_{i+1,j} + \theta_{i,j-1} + \theta_{i,j+1} - 4\theta_{i,j} - 4(\Delta x^*)^2 w_{i,j} = 0 \quad (14)$$

with the following definitions of dimensionless pressure gradient and mean dimensionless temperature given, respectively, as

$$\gamma = \frac{1}{\sum_{i=0}^{I} \sum_{j=0}^{J} w^*_{i,j} (\Delta x^*)^2} \quad (15)$$

and

$$\theta_m = \frac{\sum_{i=0}^{I}\sum_{j=0}^{J} \theta_{i,j} w_{i,j} (\Delta x^*)^2}{\sum_{i=0}^{I}\sum_{j=0}^{J} w_{i,j} (\Delta x^*)^2} \tag{16}$$

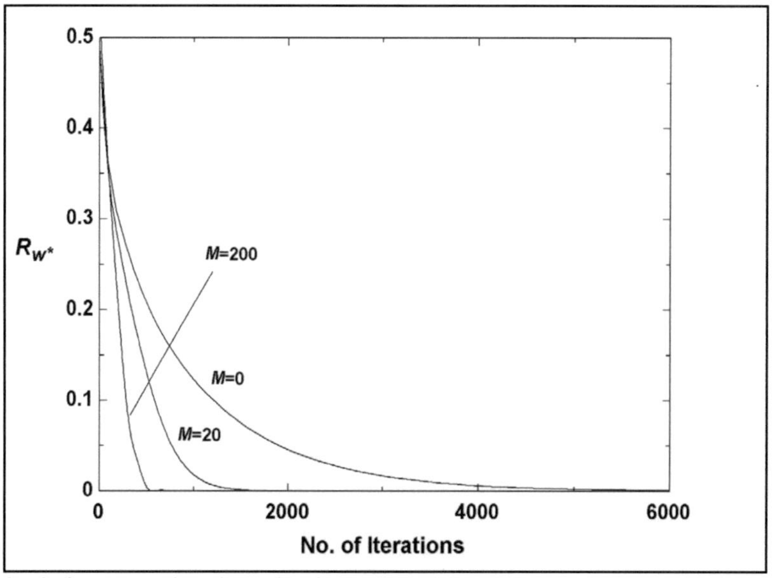

Fig. 2. Residuals for normalized axial velocity

Beside the following boundary conditions: $H^* = 0$ (for electrically insulated wall), $w^* = 0$ (from no-slip condition), and $\theta = 0$ (from the definition of dimensionless temperature). The last boundary condition is valid for the two heat transfer limits as given in the reference. It should be noted that the above finite-difference equations are derived by making the mesh size (either in x or y direction) to be uniform and to have the same value for both directions.
The non-linear energy equation (Eq. 13) for constant temperature condition or the linear equation (Eq. 14) for constant heat flux condition is solved simultaneously with the axial momentum (Eq. 11) and induction (Eq. 12) equations using Gauss-Seidel iterative method. The program utilized to achieve this task is MatLab software. For low to moderate Hartmann number ($M = 0$ to 100), a uniform 101 by 101 mesh is used while for high Hartmann number ($M = 200$), a uniform 201 by 201 mesh is used. The convergence of the solution is tested by using root-mean-square residual R (defined in the nomenclature section given below). The significance of this residual R is that once it reaches a very small number compared to unity, then the solution will be acceptable. As shown in Fig. 2, the convergence of normalized axial velocity residuals increases as the Hartman number increases. The residual at $M = 200$ reaches 10^{-3} after 500 iterations while the residual, without magnetic field, reaches 10^{-3} after 5800 iterations. The same behavior can be said for the normalized magnetic field residuals (See Fig. 3). The situation will be different for the dimensionless temperature. There are two cases. First, the residual for uniform temperature case converges more slowly, particularly, for $M = 200$. In this Hartmann number a value of 10^{-3} for the

residual can be reached if the number of iterations exceeds 29500. However, the number of iterations, at M = 0, should approach 7700 to have a residual value of 10^{-3} (See Fig. 4). Second, the residual for uniform heat flux condition, converges to 10^{-3} if number of iterations reaches 33800 for M = 200, while at M = 0, the residual will converge to same value if number of iterations exceeds 10600 (See Fig. 5).

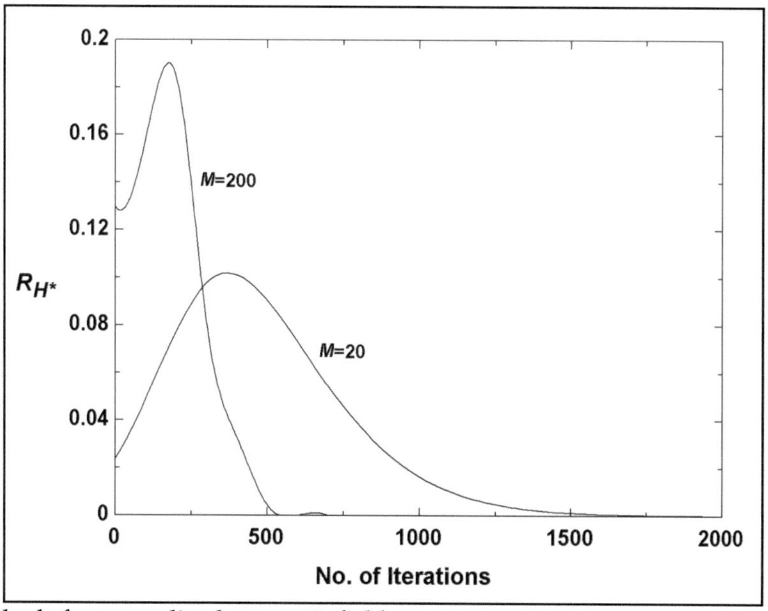

Fig. 3. Residuals for normalized magnetic field

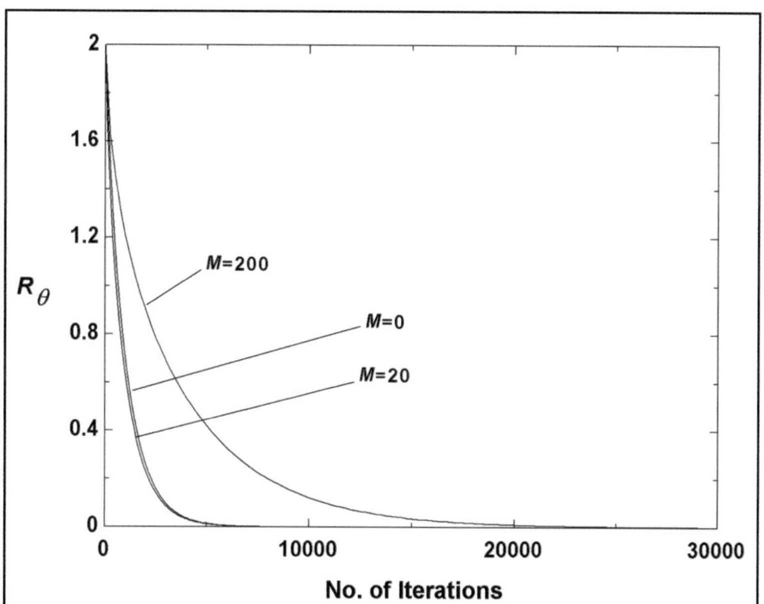

Fig. 4. Residuals for dimensionless temperature with uniform temperature boundary condition

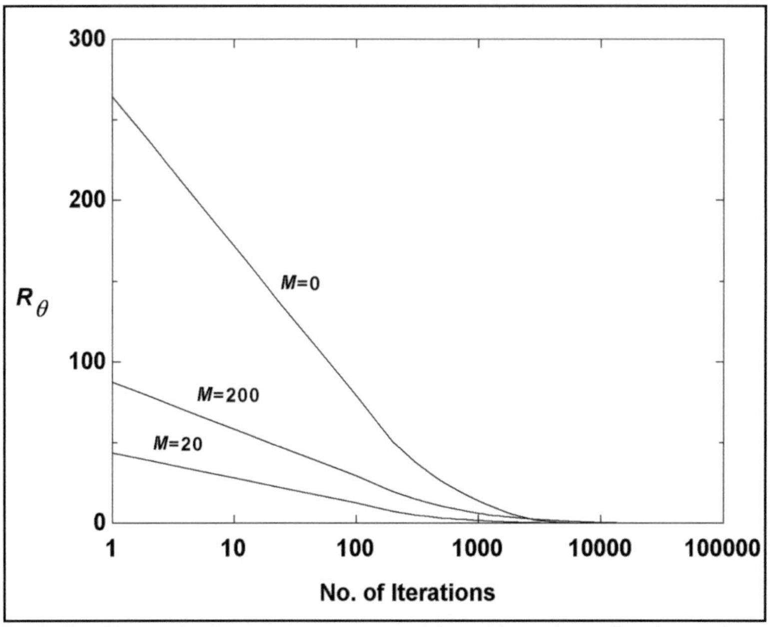

Fig. 5. Residuals for dimensionless temperature with uniform heat flux boundary condition

6. Results

Some noticeable heat transfer results are obtained for the MFM square duct flow with uniform temperature and heat flux boundary conditions. The flow (velocity and pressure) was studied so extensively in reference for the same flow conditions. For more details, the reader should refer to reference to notice, in the provided figures, the flattening of the axial velocity (due to the presence of the magnetic field) and the increase of the friction factor with the field. The negative dimensionless temperature distributions at the mid-plane (either along or normal to the magnetic field) always decrease as the Hartmann number increases for both boundary condition limits, See Figs. 6, 7, and 8. This is because the temperature distributions are more homogenous as the magnetic field is turned on. This can be seen from the results presented in and is due to the fact that velocity profile becomes more flattened as M increases, particularly along the direction of the magnetic field. Also we notice that the temperature distributions along and normal to the field are almost identical for any Hartmann number. This is supported by the color bands shown in Figs. 9. Figures 9 (a), (b), and (c) are the color bands for the case of uniform heat flux boundary conditions, whereas Figs. 9 (d), (e), and (f) show the color bands for uniform temperature boundary condition. The uniformity of the temperature across the duct is greater for the former case. This explains the reasons why this case has higher Nusselt number for any Hartmann number as will be further explained in the next paragraph.

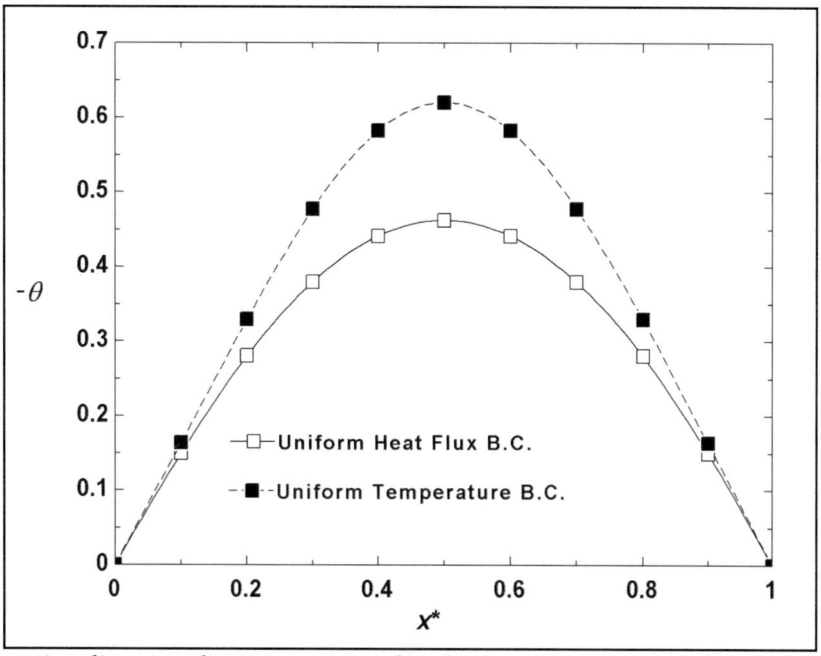

Fig. 6. Negative dimensionless temperature distribution along magnetic field and at the mid plane ($y^* = 0.5$) for both thermal boundary conditions with M = 0

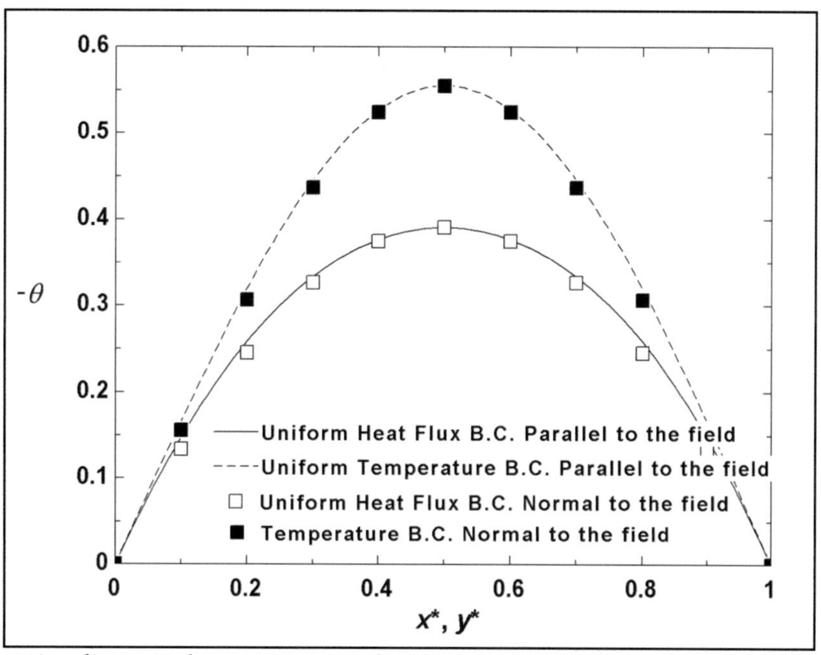

Fig. 7. Negative dimensionless temperature distribution along and normal to magnetic field and at the mid plane for both directions and for both thermal boundary conditions with M = 20

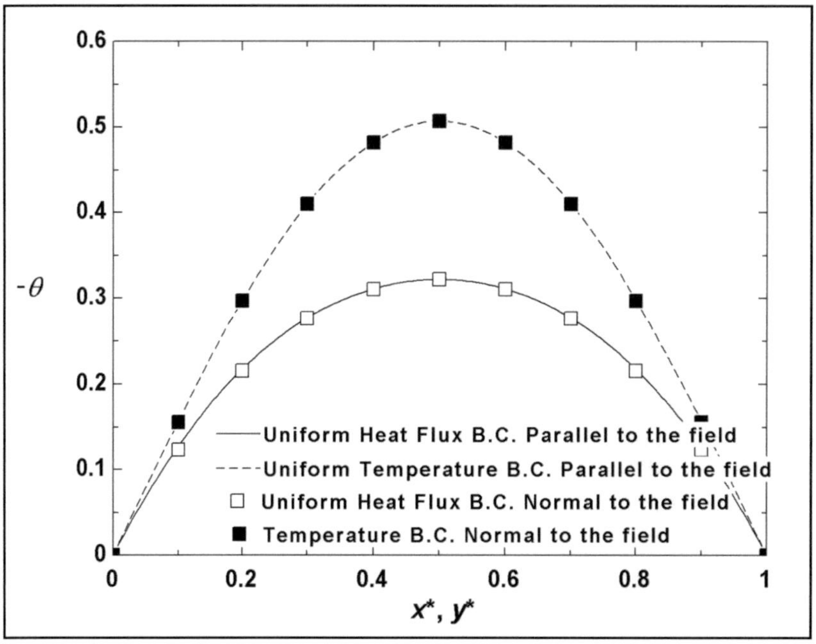

Fig. 8. Negative dimensionless temperature distribution along and normal to magnetic field and at the mid plane for both directions and for both thermal boundary conditions with M = 200

Finally, as expected the Nusselt number, Nu, increases as M increases for both cases of constant wall temperature and constant heat flux boundary conditions. Starting from conventional flow (M = 0), results for Nu coincide well with those obtained by the analytical approach given in reference for both boundary conditions. The present work gives values for Nu as 3.606 and 2.977 for constant heat flux and constant temperature boundary conditions, respectively, while the analytical Nu values for the same conditions are 3.61 and 2.98. For any Hartmann number M, the highest Nusselt number is shown by the results to correspond always to the case of circular tube with constant heat flux taken from reference, whilst the case of square duct with uniform temperature has the lowest Nu values (See Fig. 10). The solution for the present work agrees very well with the reference where spectral method was used for the case of uniform temperature boundary condition.

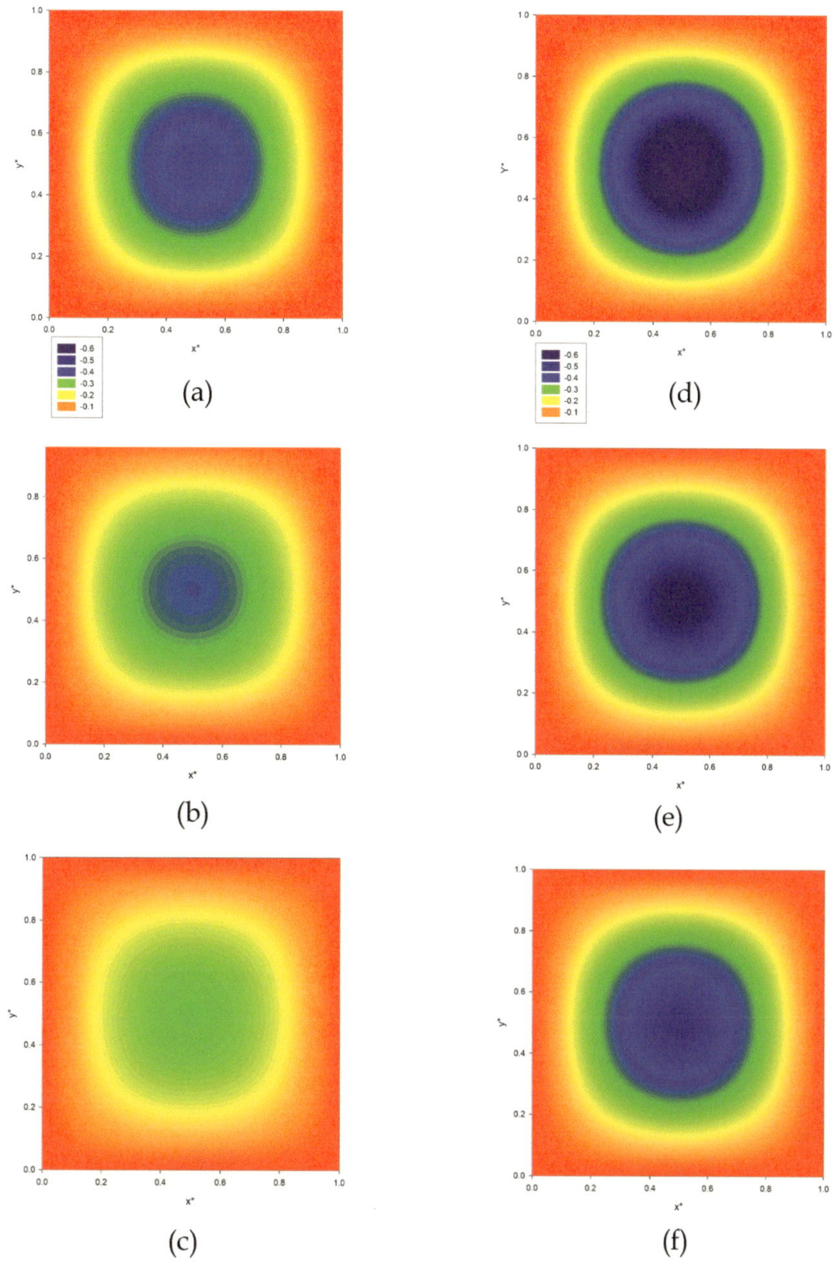

Fig. 9. Dimensionless temperature color bands. (a) M = 0, uniform heat flux; (b) M = 20, uniform heat flux with the same contour value shown in a; (c) M = 200, uniform heat flux with the same contour value shown in a; (d) M = 0, uniform temperature; (e) M = 20, uniform temperature with the same contour value shown in d; (f) M = 200, uniform temperature with the same contour value shown in d

7. Conclusion

The problem considered here is a square duct flow with electrically conducting fluid and with two heat transfer limits. The problem is analyzed numerically when a uniform transverse magnetic field is applied to the duct. The assumption of laminar flow is mostly valid in MFM flows since the turbulences will be damped out due the opposing force induced in the flow.

In reference, the fluid mechanic part of this problem was considered extensively and the results were shown using the spectral method. Also, the heat transfer results for only uniform temperature boundary condition were shown. In the present work, we consider two heat transfer limits (uniform heat flux and temperature boundary conditions) numerically using iterative Gauss-Seidel method, and the software package MatLab is utilized to achieve this approach. The results obtained for the case of constant temperature condition agree very well with reference.

In future, we can extend this work to include the aspect ratio (i.e. general rectangular cross section). This ratio will be added to the problem as dimensionless independent parameter beside Hartmann number M. Also, it is a good idea to include the natural convection, which makes us to be concerned with a problem of combined forced-and-free convection flow in a transverse magnetic field. Off course, it will be highly non-linear and we must employ an accurate and stable algorithm. This dilemma will add extra complexity to the problem, beside the independent Grashof number will appear in the governing equations.

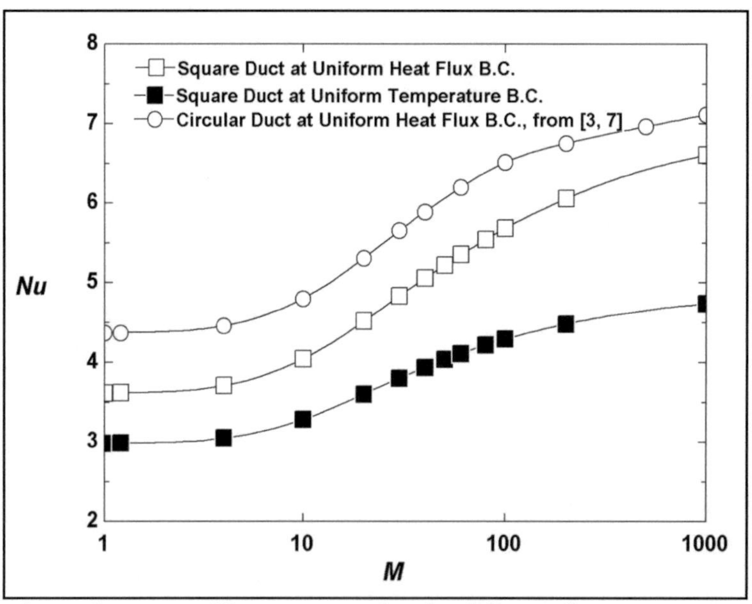

Fig. 10. Nusselt number versus Hartmann number for different flow geometries

8. References

Al-Khawaja, Mohammed J., Selmi, Mohamed (2006). Highly Accurate Solution of a Laminar Square Duct Flow in a Transverse Magnetic Field With Heat Transfer Using Spectral Method, *Journal of Heat Transfer*, Vol. 128, 2006, pp. 413-417

Cengel, Y. A. (2007). *Heat and Mass Transfer: A Practical Approach*, McGraw-Hill, ISBN-13: 978-007- 125739-8 Hightstown, NJ 08520, University of Nevada-Reno

Gardner, R. A. (1968). Laminar Pipe Flow in a Transverse Magnetic Field with Heat Transfer. *Int. J. Heat Mass Transfer*", Vol. 11, 1968, pp. 1076-1081

Gardner, R. A. and Lykoudis, P. S. (1971). Magneto-Fluid-Mechanic Pipe Flow in a Transverse Magnetic Field Part Two. Heat Transfer. *J. Fluid Mech.*, Vol. 48, Part 1, 1971, pp. 129-141

Gold, R. [1962]. Magnetohydrodynamic Pipe Flow. *J. Fluid Mech.*, Part 1, Vol. 13, 1962, p. 505

M. J. Al-Khawaja, R. A. Gardner, R. Agarwal (1994). Numerical Study of magneto-fluid-mechanics Forced convection Pipe Flow. *Engineering Journal of Qatar University*, Vol. 7, 1994, pp. 115-134

M. J. Al-Khawaja, R. K. Agarwal, R. A. Gardner (1999). Numerical study of magneto-fluid-mechanic combined free-and-forced convection Heat Transfer. *Int. J. Heat Mass Transfer*, Vol. 42, 1999, pp. 467-475

Ozizik, N. M. (1985). *Heat Transfer: A Basic Approach*, McGraw-Hill, ISBN 0-07-047982-8, North Carolina State University, pp. 289-291, Chap. 7

Shercliff, J. A. (1956). The Flow of Conducting Fluids in Circular Pipes under Transverse Magnetic Field. *J. Fluid Mech.*, Vol. 1, 1956, p. 644

Shercilff, J. A. (1962). Magnetohydrodynamic Pipe Flow, part 2 High Hartmann Number. *J. Fluid Mech.*, Vol. 13, 1962, p. 513

9. Appendix

The four basic dimensionless equations were simplified using the finite difference scheme to get a system of algebraic equations. The central difference approximation was used since it is more accurate than the forward and backward differences. Equations 5, 6, 7 and 8 represent the four basic dimensionless equations, which are transformed equations 11, 12, 13 and 14, respectively. We used 101 by 101 mesh size for low and moderate Hartmann number M (from 0 to 100). For high Hartmann number (= 200), we used 201 by 201 mesh size. The algebraic equations were solved numerically using the MatLab software. Equations 11 and 12 were solved simultaneously by employing Gauss Seidel method. Then γ is determined (from Eq. 9) once w^* is obtained. The double integration was approximated by the summation in both x^* and y^* directions as given in Eq. 15. For the constant surface heat flux boundary condition, Eq. 14 (linear) is solved by employing the iterative Gauss Seidel method. Also θ_m can be obtained once θ is determined. θ_m is found from Eq. 10. The double integration was approximated by the summation in both x^* and y^* directions as given in Eq. 16.

For constant surface temperature boundary conditions, an initial guess for Nusselt number Nu was assumed, then Eq. 14 (non linear) was solved using successive substitution. From Eq. 10, θ_m is obtained and a more accurate Nu is found, then another approximation of θ was solved using the new value of Nu. This process was repeated until the error becomes very small.

In our calculations, we used the root mean square residuals R (defined in the program) to check the convergence for each flow variable. Once $R< 10^{-7}$, then the iterations are stopped. From the definition of θ, the thermal boundary condition at the surfaces, for both the uniform surface heat flux and constant surface temperature, is $\theta = 0$.
The problem was solved by many researchers and they employed different software packages to solve the resulting simultaneous algebraic equations. They used, for example, Fortran and C++ languages and spectral method. But here, the matLab is employed and noticed that this program is so efficient and powerful for solving such problem.
The Matlab programs for uniform surface heat flux and uniform surface temperature are presented below.

9.1 Uniform Surface Heat Flux

```
%Solution for MHD flow inside square duct for const. heat flux B.C.'s
% a<x<b , c<y<d
% M = Hartmann number
% n = number of subintervals for x
% m = number of subintervals for y
% h = delta x*
% k = delta y*
% Note: In this program delta x = delta y
a=0; b=1; c=0; d=1; num_iter=20000; M=100;
n=100; m=100; h=(b-a)/n; k=(d-c)/m;
c1=1/4;   c2=(h*M)/8;  c3=(h^2)/4;
% ws = negative normalized axial velocity (w*)
% Hs = normalized induced axial magnetic field (H*)
ws=zeros(n+1, m+1);
Hs=zeros(n+1, m+1);
%B.C.'s at the four corners for w*(no slip conditions) & H* (electrically insulated surface)
  ws(1,1)=0;
  ws(n+1,1)=0;
  ws(1,m+1)=0;
  ws(n+1,m+1)=0;
  Hs(1,1)=0;
  Hs(n+1,1)=0;
  Hs(1,m+1)=0;
  Hs(n+1,m+1)=0;
%B.C.'s at the four sides for w*(no slip conditions) & H* (electrically insulated surface)
  for i=2:n
    ws(i,1)=0;
    ws(i,m+1)=0;
    Hs(i,1)=0;
    Hs(i,m+1)=0;
  end
  for j=2:m
    ws(1,j)=0;
    ws(n+1,j)=0;
```

```
      Hs(1,j)=0;
      Hs(n+1,j)=0;
   end
   for it=1:num_iter
   wsave=w;
   Hsave=H;
   Rws=0;
   RHs=0;
  % Solution for w* & H*
   for i=2:n
      for j=2:m
     ws(i,j)= c1*(ws(i,j+1)+ws(i,j-1)+ws(i+1,j)+ws(i-1,j))-c2*(Hs(i+1,j)-Hs(i-1,j))-c3;
     Hs(i,j)= c1*(Hs(i,j+1)+Hs(i,j-1)+Hs(i+1,j)+Hs(i-1,j))-c2*(ws(i+1,j)-ws(i-1,j));
         % Rws = Root mean square residuals for w*
         % RHs = Root mean square residuals for H*
         Rws=Rws+sqrt((w(i,j)-wsave(i,j))^2);
         RHs=RHs+sqrt((H(i,j)-Hsave(i,j))^2);
      end
   end
  Rwss(it,1)=Rws;
  RHss(it,1)=RHs;
   if (RHs<1e-8 & Rws<1e-8)
      break
   end
end
% gamma = Non-dimensional pressure gradient
% w = Dimensionless axial velocity
% H = Dimensionless induced axial magnetic field
% f = friction factor
gamma=1/sum(sum(ws*h^2));
w=ws*gamma;
H=Hs*gamma;
f=-2*gamma;
% t = Dimensionless temperature (theta)
t=zeros(n+1,m+1);
%B.C.'s at the four corners for theta (uniform surface heat flux)
   t(1,1)=0;
   t(1,m+1)=0;
   t(n+1,1)=0;
   t(n+1,m+1)=0;
%B.C.'s at the four sides for theta (uniform surface heat flux)
   for i=2:n
       t(i,m+1)=0;
       t(i,1)=0;
    end
   for j=2:m
```

```
        t(1,j)=0;
        t(n+1,j)=0;
    end
for itt=1:num_iter
    tsave=t;
    Rt=0;
    % Solution for theta
    for i=2:n
        for j=2:m
            t(i,j)=1/4*(t(i-1,j)+t(i+1,j)+t(i,j-1)+t(i,j+1))-h^2*w(i,j);
            % Rt = Root mean square residuals for theta
            Rt=Rt+sqrt((t(i,j)-tsave(i,j))^2);
        end
    end
    Rtt(itt,1)=Rt;
        if Rt<1e-8
        break
    end
 end
% thetam = Mean dimensionless temperature
% nu = Nusselt number (Nu)
thetam=(sum(sum(t.*w*h^2)))/(sum(sum(w*h^2)));
nu=-1/thetam;
% Display solution with x from left to right
ws=[ws'];
w=[w'];
Hs=[Hs'];
H=[H'];
t=[t'];
x= a:h:b; y=c:k:d;
```

9.2 Uniform Surface Temperature

```
%Solution for MHD flow inside square duct for const. temperature B.C.'s
% a<x<b , c<y<d
% M = Hartmann number
% n = number of subintervals for x
% m = number of subintervals for y
% h = delta x*
% k = delta y*
% Note: In this program delta x = delta y
a=0; b=1; c=0; d=1; num_iter=20000; M=100;
n=100; m=100; h=(b-a)/n; k=(d-c)/m;
c1=1/4;   c2=(h*M)/8;  c3=(h^2)/4;
% ws = negative normalized axial velocity (w*)
% Hs = normalized induced axial magnetic field (H*)
ws=zeros(n+1, m+1);
```

```
Hs=zeros(n+1, m+1);
%B.C.'s at the four corners for w*(no slip conditions) & H* (electrically insulated surface)
  ws(1,1)=0;
  ws(n+1,1)=0;
  ws(1,m+1)=0;
  ws(n+1,m+1)=0;
  Hs(1,1)=0;
  Hs(n+1,1)=0;
  Hs(1,m+1)=0;
  Hs(n+1,m+1)=0;
  %B.C.'s at the four sides for w*(no slip conditions) & H* (electrically insulated surface)
  for i=2:n
    ws(i,1)=0;
    ws(i,m+1)=0;
    Hs(i,1)=0;
    Hs(i,m+1)=0;
  end
  for j=2:m
    ws(1,j)=0;
    ws(n+1,j)=0;
    Hs(1,j)=0;
    Hs(n+1,j)=0;
  end
  for it=1:num_iter
  wsave=w;
  Hsave=H;
  Rws=0;
  RHs=0;
  % Solution for w* & H*
  for i=2:n
    for j=2:m
   ws(i,j)= c1*(ws(i,j+1)+ws(i,j-1)+ws(i+1,j)+ws(i-1,j))-c2*(Hs(i+1,j)-Hs(i-1,j))-c3;
   Hs(i,j)= c1*(Hs(i,j+1)+Hs(i,j-1)+Hs(i+1,j)+Hs(i-1,j))-c2*(ws(i+1,j)-ws(i-1,j));
      % Rws = Root mean square residuals for w*
      % RHs = Root mean square residuals for H*
      Rws=Rws+sqrt((w(i,j)-wsave(i,j))^2);
      RHs=RHs+sqrt((H(i,j)-Hsave(i,j))^2);
    end
  end
 Rwss(it,1)=Rws;
 RHss(it,1)=RHs;
  if (RHs<1e-8 & Rws<1e-8)
    break
  end
end
% gamma = Non-dimensional pressure gradient
```

```
% w = Dimensionless axial velocity
% H = Dimensionless induced axial magnetic field
% f = friction factor
gamma=1/sum(sum(ws*h^2));
w=ws*gamma;
H=Hs*gamma;
f=-2*gamma;
% t = Dimensionless temperature (theta)
t=zeros(n+1,m+1);
%B.C.'s at the four corners for theta (uniform surface temperature)
  t(1,1)=0;
  t(1,m+1)=0;
  t(n+1,1)=0;
  t(n+1,m+1)=0;
%B.C.'s at the four sides for theta (uniform surface temperature)
  for i=2:n
     t(i,m+1)=0;
     t(i,1)=0;
   end
  for j=2:m
     t(1,j)=0;
     t(n+1,j)=0;
   end
for itt=1:num_iter
   tsave=t;
   Rt=0;
   % Solution for theta
   for i=2:n
      for j=2:m
         t(i,j)=(t(i-1,j)+t(i+1,j)+t(i,j-1)+t(i,j+1))/(4-4*h^2*nu*w(i,j));
         % Rt = Root mean square residuals for theta
         Rt=Rt+sqrt((t(i,j)-tsave(i,j))^2);
      end
   end
   % thetam = Mean dimensionless temperature
   % nu = Nusselt number (Nu)
   thetam=(sum(sum(t.*w*h^2)))/(sum(sum(w*h^2)));
   nu=-1/thetam;
   Rtt(itt,1)=Rt;
      if Rt<1e-8
     break
  end
 end
 % Display solution with x from left to right
 ws=[ws'];
 w=[w'];
```

```
Hs=[Hs'];
H=[H'];
t=[t'];
x= a:h:b; y=c:k:d;
```

9.3 Derivation of the Energy Equations

The detailed derivation of the simplified energy equation are given in the literature and the key behind this derivation is to neglect the last two terms, in Eq. 3, which represent the viscous and Joulean dissipations, respectively, and to apply the energy balance given by:
Heat supply to fluid from surface = Energy removed by fluid by convection
Then the simplified dimensionless energy equations, Eqs. 15 and 16 given above , can be obtained if the above assumptions are applied, the axial conductive term is omitted, and proper dimensionless variables are defined.

18

Toolbox for GPS-based attitude determination: An implementation aspect

Zhen Dai, Stefan Knedlik and Otmar Loffeld
Center for Sensor Systems, University of Siegen
Germany

1. Introduction

The global positioning system (GPS) is known as its positioning and timing applications. Besides that, GPS multi-antenna system has become a high-accurate approach for attitude determination(Cohen et al. 1994; Van Grass and Braasch 1991). In comparison with the traditional inertial sensors, the GPS multi-antenna system provides attitude results without drift effects, and it has the advantages due to the cost-effectiveness and the flexible installation. The drawback is that GPS signals can be interfered or blocked in some shadow environments. Also, resolving the carrier phase ambiguity is another challenging task for single-frequency receiver and real-time applications.

This MATLAB toolbox is developed for attitude determination using GPS code data, which is partly introduced in (Dai et al. 2008). However, the implementation aspects will be highlighted herein. Some development details will be stressed and some problems occurred during the development procedure will also be presented in the following parts. It derives the attitude parameters based on the double-differenced (carrier phase smoothed) C/A code measurement. After the baselines between the antennas have been calculated, two algorithms can be invoked to determine the attitude: a direct computation method and a least-squares estimation approach(Lu 1995). The motivation of developing such a toolbox is not to provide a powerful and reliable software package for real applications, but to present the basic functions needed for GPS-based attitude determination.
It should be pointed out that this toolbox contains no functions to resolve double-differenced integer phase ambiguities. However, there is already some source code available (Chang and Zhou 2007; Jonge de and Tiberius 1996), so that those who want to employ the phase measurement to achieve a precise attitude result can choose the proper source code and combine it with our programs. As an example, we provide a demo program with a set of resolved ambiguities to show the results based on carrier phase.

In the following parts, we will first introduce the theoretical background of the attitude determination using GPS multiple antenna system, and then the implementation aspects will be highlighted. The test results will be presented to show the performance of the toolbox. Finally this study will be summarized and the future work will be suggested.

2. Coordinate frames and general mathematic model

In this section, the coordinate frames involved in the attitude determination system will be first explained. Then the attitude parameterization based on the Euler angles will be introduced. The general mathematic model for attitude determination will be presented.

2.1 Coordinate frames

In order to clarify the attitude determination using GPS multiple antennas, several coordinate frames needs to be distinguished, including the Earth-Centered-Earth-Fixed (ECEF) frame, the Local Level Frame (LLF), the Antenna Body Frame (ABF)

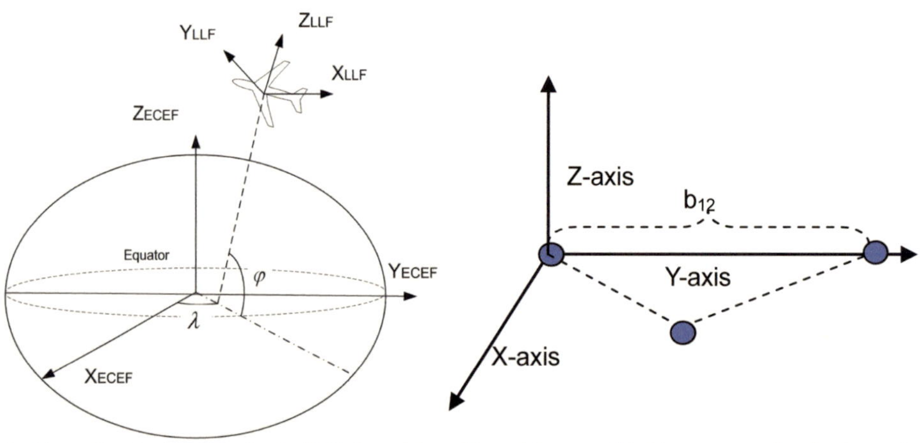

Fig. 1. Coordinate frames (Left: ECEF and local level frame; Right: antenna body frame)

The ECEF, also referred to as terrestrial equatorial system, is defined as follows: the origin is the geocenter; X_{ECEF} is located in the equatorial plane and points towards then Greenwich meridian; Z_{ECEF} is the rotation axis of the earth; Y_{ECEF} completes the right-handed Cartesian system along with Z_{ECEF} and X_{ECEF}.

The local level frame (LLF) describes the local coordinates of a point with respect to a reference point, and it is usually expressed in East-North-Up directions. The origin of LLF is chosen as the reference point. X_{LLF} points to ellipsoidal east and Y_{LLF} to north; Z_{LLF} is along with the ellipsoidal norm and points upwards. LLF is usually adopted as the reference frame in the attitude determination frame.

The antenna body application (ABF) is formed by the GPS antennas. Here we assume that the antennas are mounted on a rigid platform, i.e. the relative distances between the antennas remain unchanged. One antenna is chosen as the master antenna, and the other antennas are called slave antennas. Actually, three antennas are sufficient to determine the antenna body frame. The origin is chosen as the position of the phase center of antenna 1, namely the master antenna. Y_{ABF} is assumed along with the baseline from antenna 1 to antenna 2. X_{ABF} is perpendicular with Y_{ABF} and lies in the plane defined by antenna 1, 2 and 3. Z_{ABF} is perpendicular to both of the X_{ABF} and Y_{ABF} axis and points upwards.

2.2 Euler angles

A three-dimensional rotation can be decomposed into three individual rotations with each around a single axis. Euler angles represent the rotation angles with respect to three axes and usually comprise of yaw, pitch and roll angles, as shown in Fig. 2. Note that in the right-handed frame, the Euler angles describe counter-clockwise rotations when viewed from the end of the positive axes and clockwise rotation when viewed from the origin of the positive axes.

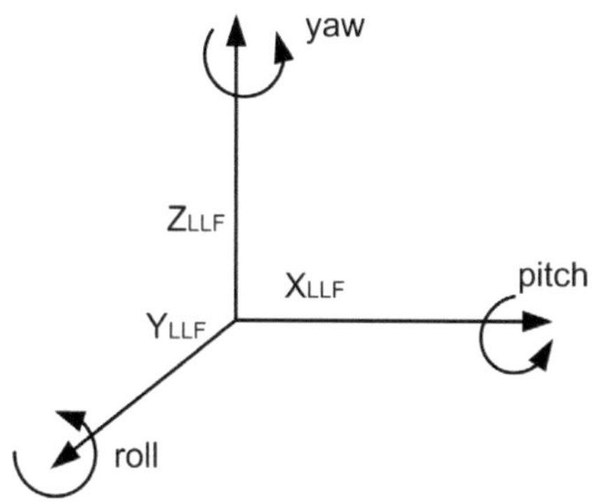

LLF=Local Level Frame

Fig. 2. Euler angles

Each rotation can be described by a Direction Cosine Matrix (DCM). A three-dimensional rotation can be obtained by multiplying the three DCMs into a specific order, yielding the combined rotation matrix. An example using the yaw-pitch-roll sequence is given below

$$\mathbf{x}_{ABF} = \begin{bmatrix} c(r)c(y)-s(r)s(p)s(y) & c(r)s(y)+s(r)s(p)c(y) & -s(r)c(p) \\ -c(p)s(y) & c(p)c(y) & s(p) \\ s(r)c(y)+c(r)s(p)s(y) & s(r)s(y)-c(r)s(p)c(y) & c(r)c(p) \end{bmatrix} \mathbf{x}_{LLF} \quad (1)$$

where y, p and r are short-hand notations for yaw, pitch and roll angles, respectively; c and s denote the cosine and sine operators, respectively.

3. Algorithms used for attitude determination in the toolbox

In section 2, the general mathematic model for attitude determination is presented. However, how to resolve the attitude parameters using this model is still an issue. In this section, we will introduce two algorithms, the direct attitude computation and least-squares attitude determination.

3.1 Least-squares attitude determination

In order to resolve the three dimensional unknown Euler angles using the nonlinear model given in (1), more than three equations are needed, or in other words, more than three baseline vectors are needed. Each master-slave antenna baseline provides three baseline vectors, and hence we need a minimum of two non-collinear slave antennas. Based on the linearization of the DCM around the proper attitude parameters y_0, r_0 and p_0, we have the following model to construct the least-squares attitude estimation (Lu 1995):

$$\begin{bmatrix} \mathbf{A}_2 \\ \mathbf{A}_3 \\ \cdots \\ \mathbf{A}_n \end{bmatrix} \begin{bmatrix} \Delta y \\ \Delta p \\ \Delta r \end{bmatrix} + \begin{bmatrix} [\mathbf{R}_0 \ \ \mathbf{-I}] & \mathbf{O} & \cdots & \mathbf{O} \\ \mathbf{O} & [\mathbf{R}_0 \ \ \mathbf{-I}] & \cdots & \mathbf{O} \\ \cdots & \cdots & \cdots & \cdots \\ \mathbf{O} & \mathbf{O} & \cdots & [\mathbf{R}_0 \ \ \mathbf{-I}] \end{bmatrix} \left(\begin{bmatrix} \mathbf{l}_2 \\ \mathbf{b}_2 \\ \mathbf{l}_3 \\ \mathbf{b}_3 \\ \cdots \\ \mathbf{l}_n \\ \mathbf{b}_n \end{bmatrix} - \begin{bmatrix} \Delta\mathbf{l}_2 \\ \Delta\mathbf{b}_2 \\ \Delta\mathbf{l}_3 \\ \Delta\mathbf{b}_3 \\ \cdots \\ \Delta\mathbf{l}_n \\ \Delta\mathbf{b}_n \end{bmatrix} \right) = 0 \tag{2}$$

In order to describe the matrix $\mathbf{A}_i$ for i=2,3,…,n, we express the combined rotation matrix R in terms of row vectors, i.e. $\mathbf{R}=[\mathbf{r}_1\ \mathbf{r}_2\ \mathbf{r}_3]^T$, then the matrix $\mathbf{A}_i$ has the form:

$$\mathbf{A}_i = \begin{bmatrix} \frac{\partial(\mathbf{r}_1\mathbf{l}_i)}{\partial y} & \frac{\partial(\mathbf{r}_1\mathbf{l}_i)}{\partial p} & \frac{\partial(\mathbf{r}_1\mathbf{l}_i)}{\partial r} \\ \frac{\partial(\mathbf{r}_2\mathbf{l}_i)}{\partial y} & \frac{\partial(\mathbf{r}_2\mathbf{l}_i)}{\partial p} & \frac{\partial(\mathbf{r}_2\mathbf{l}_i)}{\partial r} \\ \frac{\partial(\mathbf{r}_3\mathbf{l}_i)}{\partial y} & \frac{\partial(\mathbf{r}_3\mathbf{l}_i)}{\partial p} & \frac{\partial(\mathbf{r}_3\mathbf{l}_i)}{\partial r} \end{bmatrix} \tag{3}$$

In model (2), R_0 is the DCM at y_0, r_0 and p_0; $\Delta\mathbf{b}_i$ and $\Delta\mathbf{l}_i$ are the errors contained in the antenna body frame and the local level frame of the antenna i, respectively; **I** denotes the identity matrix and **O** the zero matrix. A detailed $\mathbf{A}_i$ can be seen below:

$$\begin{aligned}
\mathbf{A}_i(1,1) &= \frac{\partial(\mathbf{r}_1\mathbf{l}_i)}{\partial y} = \left[-c(r)x_{i,l} - s(r)s(p)y_{i,l}\right]s(y) + \left[-s(r)s(p)x_{i,l} + c(r)y_{i,l}\right]c(y) \\
\mathbf{A}_i(1,2) &= \frac{\partial(\mathbf{r}_1\mathbf{l}_i)}{\partial p} = \left[s(r)z_{i,l}\right]s(p) + \left[-s(r)s(y)x_{i,l} + s(r)c(y)y_{i,l}\right]c(p) \\
\mathbf{A}_i(1,3) &= \frac{\partial(\mathbf{r}_1\mathbf{l}_i)}{\partial r} = \left[-c(y)x_{i,l} - s(y)y_{i,l}\right]s(r) + \left[-s(p)s(y)x_{i,l} + s(p)c(y)y_{i,l} - c(p)z_{i,l}\right]c(r) \\
\mathbf{A}_i(2,1) &= \frac{\partial(\mathbf{r}_2\mathbf{l}_i)}{\partial y} = \left[-c(p)y_{i,l}\right]s(y) - \left[c(p)x_{i,l}\right]c(y) \\
\mathbf{A}_i(2,2) &= \frac{\partial(\mathbf{r}_2\mathbf{l}_i)}{\partial p} = \left[s(y)x_{i,l} - c(y)y_{i,l}\right]s(p) + \left[z_{i,l}\right]c(p) \\
\mathbf{A}_i(2,3) &= \frac{\partial(\mathbf{r}_2\mathbf{l}_i)}{\partial r} = 0 \\
\mathbf{A}_i(3,1) &= \frac{\partial(\mathbf{r}_3\mathbf{l}_i)}{\partial y} = \left[-s(r)x_{i,l} + c(r)s(p)y_{i,l}\right]s(y) + \left[c(r)s(p)x_{i,l} + s(r)y_{i,l}\right]c(y) \\
\mathbf{A}_i(3,2) &= \frac{\partial(\mathbf{r}_3\mathbf{l}_i)}{\partial p} = \left[-c(r)z_{i,l}\right]s(p) + \left[c(r)s(y)x_{i,l} - c(r)c(y)y_{i,l}\right]c(p) \\
\mathbf{A}_i(3,3) &= \frac{\partial(\mathbf{r}_3\mathbf{l}_i)}{\partial r} = \left[-s(p)s(y)x_{i,l} + s(p)c(y)y_{i,l} - c(p)z_{i,l}\right]s(r) + \left[s(y)y_{i,l} + c(y)x_{i,l}\right]c(r)
\end{aligned} \tag{4}$$

where the subscript l indicate the local level frame. Based on this model, the least-squares adjustment can be carried out. The correction values for the three Euler angles corresponding to a rotation matrix $\mathbf{R}_0$ are computed by:

$$\begin{aligned}[\Delta y \quad \Delta p \quad \Delta r]^T = &-\left[\sum_{i=2}^{n} \mathbf{A}_i^T \left(\mathbf{R}_0^T Cov(\mathbf{l}_i)\mathbf{R}_0 + Cov(\mathbf{b}_i)\right)^{-1} \mathbf{A}_i\right]^{-1} \\ &\times \left[\sum_{i=2}^{n} \mathbf{A}_i^T \left(\mathbf{R}_0^T Cov(\mathbf{l}_i)\mathbf{R}_0 + Cov(\mathbf{b}_i)\right)^{-1} (\Delta\mathbf{l}_i - \Delta\mathbf{b}_i)\right]\end{aligned} \tag{5}$$

where the short-hand notation $Cov(\cdot)$ denotes the error covariance matrix. The least-squares adjustment proceeds until the correction values converge to a certain threshold or the maximal iteration number is reached.

3.2 Direct attitude computation approach

Another fast algorithm for attitude determination is referred to as direct attitude computation approach. Based on the definition of antenna body frame, the coordinates of the slave antenna in the antenna body frame can be expressed as $\mathbf{b}_2=[0 \ b_{12} \ 0]^T$, where b_{12} is the magnitude of baseline from the master antenna (antenna 1) to the slave antenna (antenna 2), as shown in Fig. 1. Substituting the antenna body frame coordinate of the slave antenna into model (1) and using the orthogonality of the rotation matrix yields the local level frame coordinate of slave antenna:

$$\begin{bmatrix} x_{2,l} \\ y_{2,l} \\ z_{2,l} \end{bmatrix} = b_{12} \begin{bmatrix} -c_p s_y \\ c_p c_y \\ s_p \end{bmatrix} \tag{6}$$

After that, the yaw angle and pitch angle can be directly obtained as:

$$\begin{aligned} yaw &= -\tan^{-1}\left(\frac{x_{2,l}}{y_{2,l}}\right) \\ pitch &= \sin^{-1}\left(\frac{z_{2,l}}{b_{12}}\right) = \tan^{-1}\left(\frac{z_{2,l}}{\sqrt{x_{2,l}^2 + y_{2,l}^2}}\right) \end{aligned} \tag{7}$$

From both of the expressions of pitch given in (7) it can be seen that the pitch angle is acquirable using only the local level frame coordinate of the slave antenna instead of using the baseline length b_{12}. This reveals a significant advantage of the direct attitude computation that the magnitude of baseline length does not need to be measured in advance.

The coordinate of antenna 3 in the local level frame is then required to fix the value of roll. We can first rotate the antenna 3 by yaw and pitch resulted from (7) in order to obtain the rotation matrix including roll:

$$\begin{bmatrix} x'_{3,l} \\ y'_{3,l} \\ z'_{3,l} \end{bmatrix} = \begin{bmatrix} 1 & 0 & 0 \\ 0 & c(p) & s(p) \\ 0 & -s(p) & c(p) \end{bmatrix} \begin{bmatrix} c(y) & s(y) & 0 \\ -s(y) & c(y) & 0 \\ 0 & 0 & 1 \end{bmatrix} \begin{bmatrix} x_{3,l} \\ y_{3,l} \\ z_{3,l} \end{bmatrix} \tag{8}$$

Then following relationship holds by employing the coordinate of antenna 3 into the antenna body frame:

$$\begin{bmatrix} x_{3,b} \\ y_{3,b} \\ 0 \end{bmatrix} = \begin{bmatrix} \cos(r) & 0 & -\sin(r) \\ 0 & 1 & 0 \\ \sin(r) & 0 & \cos(r) \end{bmatrix} \begin{bmatrix} x'_{3,l} \\ y'_{3,l} \\ z'_{3,l} \end{bmatrix} \tag{9}$$

Note that the first two scalars $x_{3,b}$ and $y_{3,b}$ in the body frame vector are not to be explicitly specified, from the scalar 0 in body frame of the antenna 3 we can simply derive the roll angle:

$$r = -\tan^{-1}\left(\frac{z'_{3,l}}{x'_{3,l}}\right) \tag{10}$$

The direct attitude computation and least-squares approaches apply to different scenarios. If the baselines are not given in advance, the direct attitude computation can still yield the attitude results. However, it does not take all the measurement into calculation and hence leads to a non-optimal solution.

4. Implementation aspects

The flowchart of the toolbox is given in Fig. 3. Some key points at each step will be highlighted in each subsection.

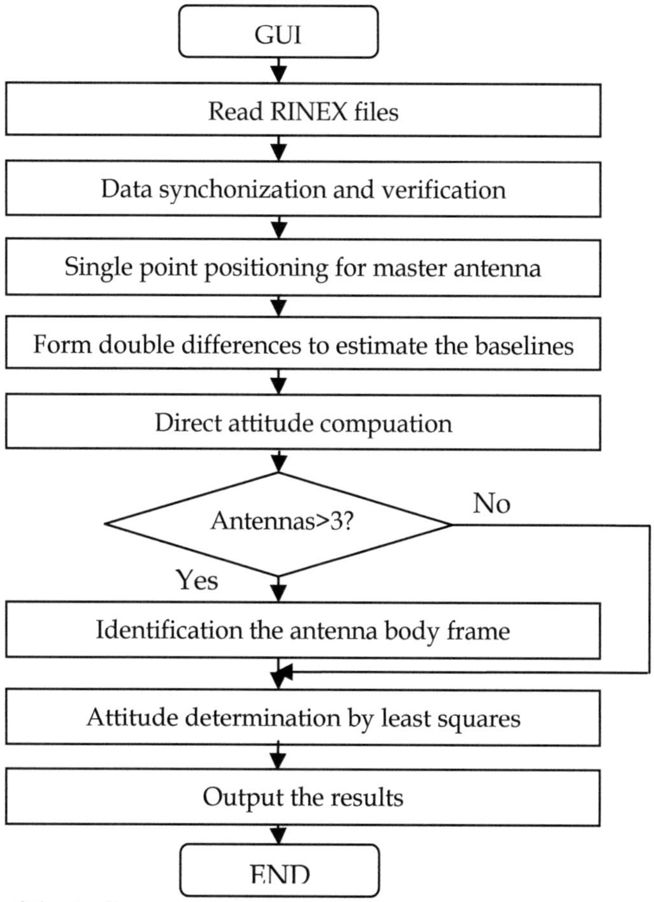

Fig. 3. Flowchart of the toolbox

4.1 Graphic user interface

After copying all the files into a directory and loading the main program *ControlPanel()* into the MATLAB environment, the toolbox can be executed. Shown first is the GUI for setting the application scenarios and assigning the relevant parameters.

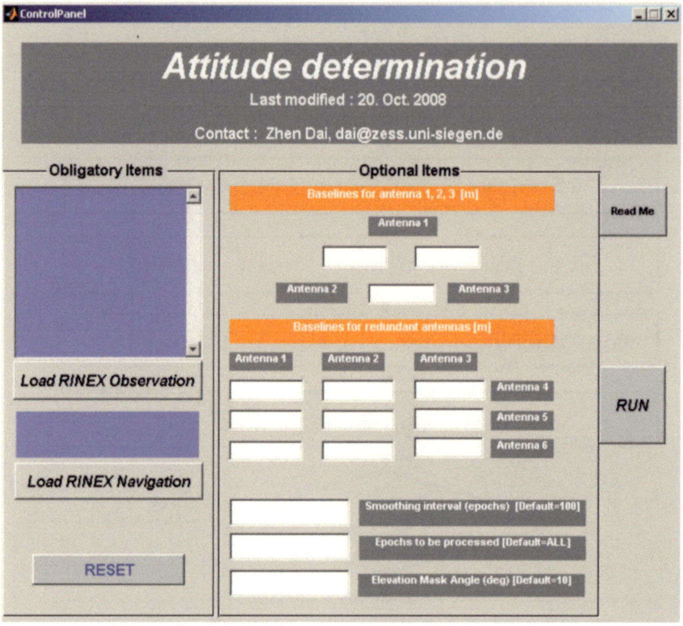

Fig. 4. Graphical user interface for toolbox

The layout of the GUI is composed of three columns. In the left column, the user can choose the RINEX observation files (upper) and navigation file (lower). Note that only the navigation file of an antenna is needed because all the antennas were receiving the satellite information simultaneously. In the upper parts of the middle column, the user can input the magnitude of the baselines between antennas in units of meters. In the lower parts, three parameters can be assigned, including a) the smoothing interval which determines the length of epochs for code data smoothing, b) the processed epochs which allows the user to process the data at a certain length in a large data set, and c) the elevation mask angle which excludes some low angle satellites due to the their potential large troposphere error and multipath error. Note that the parameters in the middle column are only optional items. The user can leave them blank, and in this case, only the direct attitude computation will be carried out and the default values of the parameters will be used instead. In the right column there are two buttons for viewing the readme file and starting the calculation.

4.2 Processing of RINEX data

Receiver Independent Exchange Format (RINEX) is a standard format widely accepted by the receiver manufactures to record the GPS navigation and measurement messages. However, there are slight differences in the files outputted from different receivers. A robust program should take these differences into account in order to expand the application scenarios. The main program for reading and analyzing the RINEX data can be seen from the function *ProcessRINEX()*. This function will invoke two functions *LoadRinexNav()* and *LoadRinexOBS()* to read the navigation file and the observation file, respectively.

This toolbox is dedicated to the post-processing, so that the data will be analyzed and saved into MATLAB data files (.MAT file). The RINEX navigation file contains the ephemeris data and is mainly used to calculate the information related to the satellites, like the satellite coordinates. The RINEX observation file is mainly composed of the available GPS measurement of each time epoch.

As the first task for analyzing the RINEX observation data, the head part should be read. The head part includes some global information, like the available measurement types supported by this receiver and their corresponding orders recorded in the following paragraphs. Only the C/A code data and carrier phase data on L1 signal are used in this toolbox. The carrier phase data will not be directly used for positioning, but can smooth the code data to reduce the potential multipath error and improve the quality of code data. Another important factor is the starting and end time of the data records, as well as the sampling interval. Based on these information, the total epochs involved can be calculated. In this toolbox the measurement of each antenna is recorded in a matrix with the first order being the time index and second order being the measurement type. After knowing the total number of epochs and measurement types, the matrix can be predefined. However, the starting and end epoch are not always available for some receivers. In this case, the matrix has to be extended dynamically epoch by epoch, and this can significantly reduce the processing efficiency for a large data set.

Each paragraph of the RINEX observation file represents the measurement of each epoch. The fist line of the paragraph indicates the visible satellites. Due to the all-in-view function and the integration of GPS with other GNSS system like GLONASS, a single line might not be enough to identify all the satellites in view, so that the an additional line(s) follows, like the following example from a GPS/GLONASS receiver:

08 11 20 14 56 36.0000000 0 16G19G 8G 3G22G18G 6G15G 7G16G21R 7R14
R22R13R21R 6

This case must be taken into account in order to prevent the ignorance of the satellites. In this toolbox, only GPS data will be used and the other GNSS data are excluded.

When processing the GPS ephemeris data, more than one ephemeris data for a satellite might appear in a single navigation file. In this case, the ephemeris data close to the current epoch will be utilized. This is realized in the function *SeekEpheEpoch()*.

Each line of a standard RINEX file should be composed of exactly 80 characters. However, in some lines without meaningful words at the end, the line terminator always appears before the 80th character. This always causes the problem when analyzing the RINEX data. We use a function *Getline80()* to solve this problem. This function first invokes the function *fgetl()* to read each line and add space characters to the end if the length of the line is less than 80 characters.

4.3 Data synchronization and verification

The data synchronization is to collect the GPS measurement of the common satellites acquired at the same time epoch. In most receivers, the time can be accurate to the second level or deci-second level. Nevertheless, some low cost receivers output the time with a slight floating part. For example the data at the same epoch from two different receivers with 1 Hz sampling rate:

08 11 20 14 16 35.0000000 0 11G03G06G07G15G16G18G19G21G22G25G26
08 11 20 14 16 35.0040000 0 07G03G07G15G18G19G21G25

The slight floating part can be seen from the second receiver (*35.0040000 s*). Both data cannot be synchronized due to the slight time difference. For this reason, it is recommended to use the receivers of the same model and the same manufacture. The synchronization manifests itself also in the search for the common satellites. The common satellites herein mean the satellites tracked simultaneously by all the receivers. According to the different tracking abilities, different receivers might not track the same number of satellites, especially at the first several epochs. However, only the common satellites will be employed.

The data verification is mainly to check if the measurement of a receiver is continuously available. If the receiver is working properly, the measurement from more than 4 satellites should be always acquirable in an open-air environment. The sampling rate is needed to check the data interruption. If the sampling interval is identified in the RINEX file, it will be directly used; otherwise the program will calculate this quantity from the first several epochs. Once the data of the current epoch is available, the data of the next epoch with the known time interval should also be presented, otherwise the data interruption can be concluded. In this case, the program should warn the user regarding this issue and the data will be synchronized again from the next common epochs. The data synchronization and verification are implemented in the function *ProcessRINEX()*.

4.4 Single point positioning for master antenna

The position of the master antenna serves as the reference point for the coordinate transformation from the ECEF to the local level frame(Hofmann-Wellenhof et al. 2001). The master antenna can be positioned by the single point positioning. Although the single point positioning yields only an accuracy of several meters to several tens of meters, it will bring just millimeter error to the transformed coordinate of the slave antennas(Lu 1995).

As the first step, the GPS code data will be smoothed by the carrier phase data in order to reduce the potential multipath error and thermal noise(Hatch 1982), and this is done by the function *Smoothing()*. The length of data sequence for smoothing can be identified in advance in the GUI. A zero-valued length means that the code will be directly used for positioning without smoothing. For simplicity, the ionosphere correction and troposphere correction are not implemented in the algorithm for single point positioning.

Another operation of the single point positioning is to obtain the satellite coordinates at each epoch. These coordinates will be saved and further used for the differential positioning applied later because these satellites can be tracked by all the receivers. A key satellite with the highest elevation angle will be identified and used for the differential positioning. However, if the carrier phase data will be used, this criterion for key satellite selection can be changed to choosing the satellite having the longest observation time. This is done in the function *SinglePointGPS()*.

4.5 Differential positioning for each master-slave antenna baseline estimation

The baseline between the master and slave antennas needs to be determined precisely. Here we apply the double-differential positioning to determine the baseline. The resulted baseline should be at the decimeter level for high-level receiver and smoothed code data. Related information can be seen in the function *DGPS_code*().

4.6 Selection of the algorithms for attitude determination

In this toolbox, the user can fix the baseline length between antennas once this has been measured in advance using other sensors or approaches. A simple way to determine the baseline is to collect the GPS data for a long observation session and perform the differential GPS technique using carrier phase data. There are also some free internet services for this purpose, like AUSPOS and CSRS-PPP services. However, inputting the baseline is not a prerequisite for resolving the attitude from GPS data. As stated before, the direct attitude computation approach does not need the premeasured baseline. If the baselines are not identified, the direct attitude computation will be the only approach. One drawback of this approach is that the measurements are not fully utilized so that it yields non-optimal estimates. Once the baselines are given by the user, the least-squares attitude determination will also be performed. The user can input the GPS data from 3 or more redundant receivers. The redundant data can only be employed once the corresponding baselines are provided.

4.7 Attitude determination

The baseline between each master-slave antenna pair is obtained initially in ECEF frame and will be project into the local level frame using the function *ECEF2ENU()*. After that, the aforementioned approaches can be carried out to determine the attitude. Both can be seen in the function *AD_Direct()* and *AD_LSQ()*, respectively. The least-squares adjustment needs an initial guess of the Euler angles. The initial values can be chosen freely using the value like zeros. The attitude results obtained from the direct approach can also be used to initialize the least-squares adjustment in order to reduce the iteration number. The range of the Euler angles should be fixed, and in this toolbox the Euler angles can range from -180 to 180 degrees.

Before applying the least-squares approach, the antenna body frame needs to be fixed from the given baselines, and this can be seen from the function *GetBodyCoordinates()*. If we have three antennas, the antenna body frame can be simply calculated according to the definition. Once more than three antennas are available, the coordinate of the redundant antennas in the antenna body frames can be fixed based on the least-squares principle. As the coordinates of the first three antennas have been obtained, and the distance between the redundant antenna to the first three antennas are known, the coordinate of the redundant antenna should result in the minimal least-squares residuals. However, this is a multiple-solution problem, as we cannot explicitly calculate the sign of the Z value of the coordinate of the slave antenna, namely we do not know whether the redundant antenna is above or under the X-Y plane. However, taking the redundant antennas into calculation should yield a compatible result with the results from other algorithms. For this reason, the attitude parameters can be first resolved by applying the direct attitude computation or the least-squares approach involving only the first three antennas. The resulted attitude parameters are then used to identify the sign of the Z-value of the redundant antenna in the antenna body frame.

4.8 A demo example using carrier phase data

The only difference between the attitude determination using code data and carrier phase data lies in the integer ambiguity resolution. Although the ambiguity resolution algorithm is not included in the toolbox, we still provide a set of resolved integer ambiguities to demonstrate the attitude results using carrier phase data. The ambiguity set is recorded into the file *ambiguity.mat* and only corresponds to the test data embedded in the toolbox. Note that the ambiguity is related to a common key satellite during the entire observation session. The differential positioning based on carrier phase is implemented in the function *DGPS_phase()*, where the ambiguity appears in the variable statements of the function.

5. Results

In the toolbox, a set of RINEX files obtained from a static experiment is provided to demonstrate the performance of the toolbox. The GPS measurements are acquired by using a NovAtel® DL-4 receiver and IFEN NavX® RF GPS simulator. The GPS simulator will generate the GPS RF signals according to the antenna position in ECEF frame specified by the user. The signals are then transferred to the GPS receiver and the measurements will be outputted in RINEX format. By setting four antenna reference points we can obtain an antenna frame composed of four distributed antennas, and we also know the true baselines. The observation session takes about 10 minutes with 1 Hz data rate. The reference coordinates of four antennas in ECEF and the true values of yaw, roll and pitch are given in Table 1.

Ant.	X (m)	Y (m)	Z (m)	Attitude
1	3991096.821	563014.827	4927065.332	Yaw=51.6656°
2	3991081.107	562998.402	4927061.001	Roll=26.1822°
3	3991081.400	563019.756	4927065.029	Pitch=-39.1834°
4	3991093.445	563007.247	4927059.915	

Table 1. True antenna coordinates and attitude parameters

Depicted below are two sets of results, one is based on the C/A coda data and the other one is based on the carrier phase data with resolved phase ambiguities. Both results are obtained using least-squares attitude determination approach.

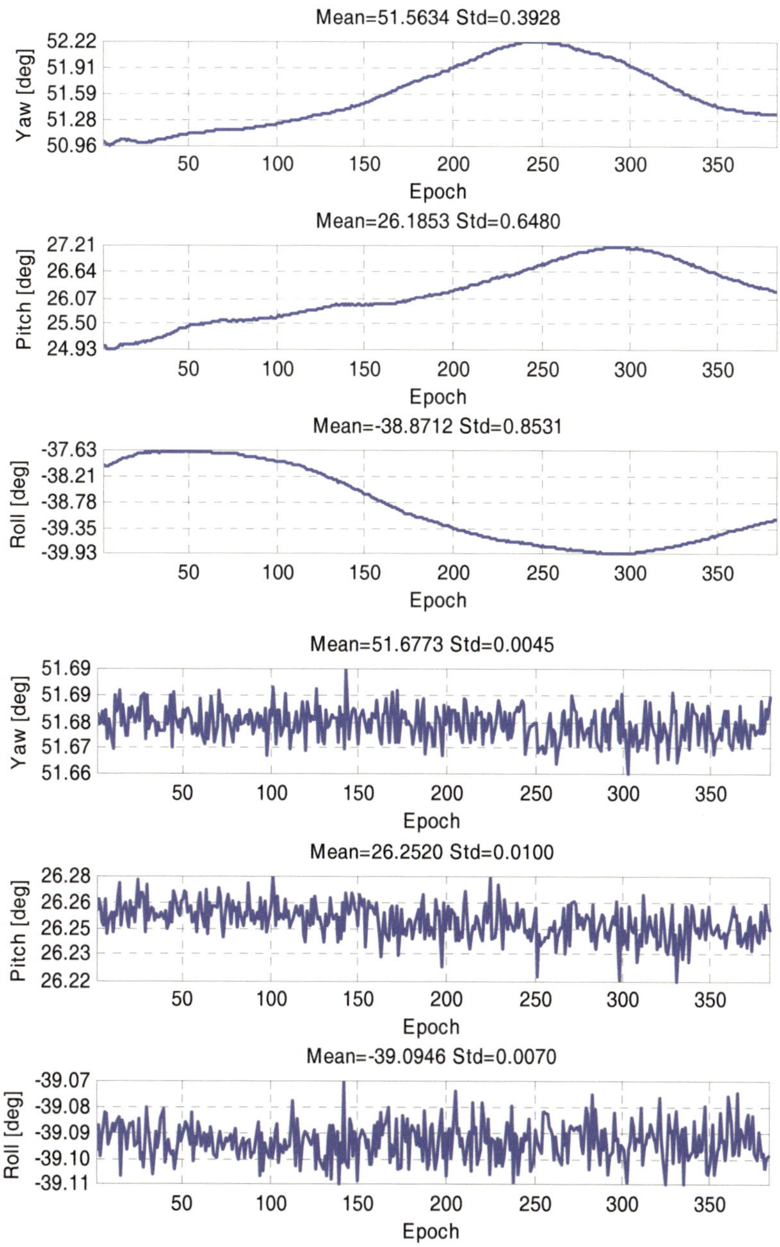

Fig. 5. Result based on C/A code (upper) and phase data (lower)

In the plotted attitude results, the X-axis shows the epochs and the Y-axis shows the estimated Euler angles in units of degrees. The title for each subplot also shows the mean value and the standard deviation of the results. It can be seen that the attitude results from the carrier phase data are more precise than that from code data.

Besides the attitude results, the magnitude of the errors contained in the estimated baselines are also outputted. The baseline is a fixed value for the rigid platform and hence can be used to evaluate the positioning error from GPS. The function is only activated if the baseline lengths are already given in the toolbox. Examples for code data and carrier phase data are given in Fig. 6.

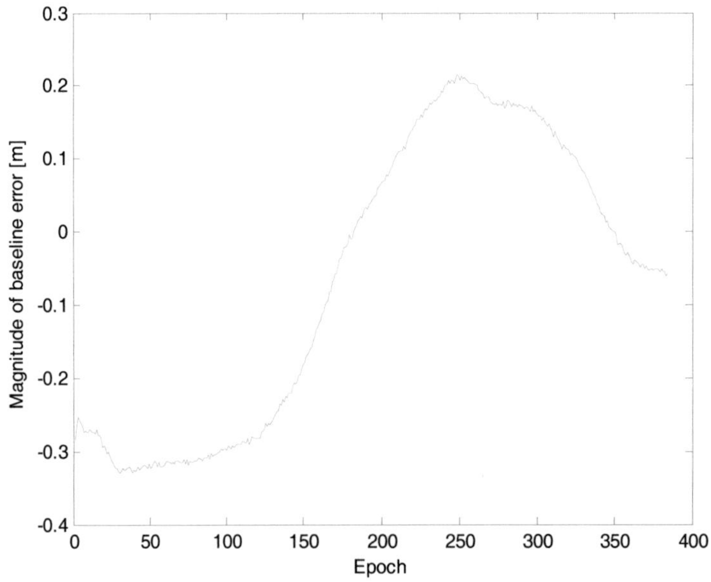

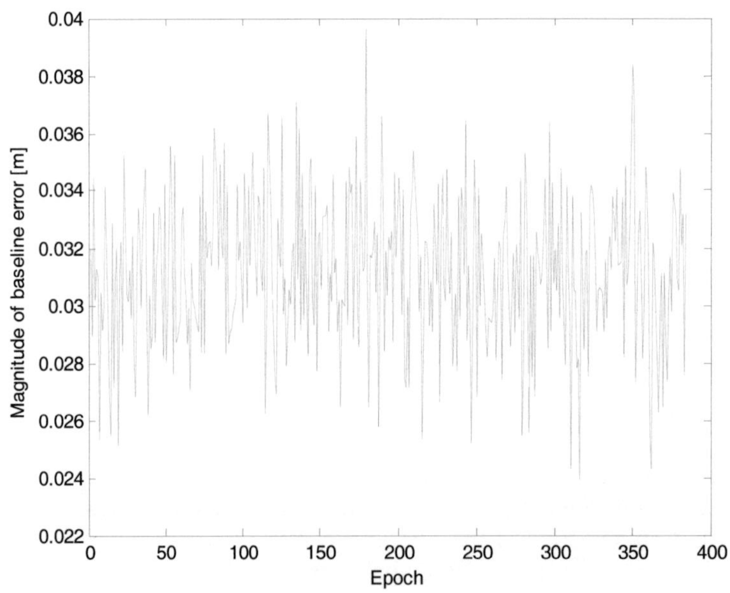

Fig. 6. Baseline length estimated by code data (upper) and carrier phase data (lower)

The accuracy of the estimated magnitude of the baseline error from carrier phase data is at centimeter level, whereas the results from code data are at decimeter level.

Following the user manual the user can also process other data set by using the toolbox. The result will be saved into a data file *results.txt* for further analysis, as shown below:

……

At Epoch 2006.10.29 01:44:30.00 -> YAW=50.875 ROLL=24.440 PITCH=-38.319

At Epoch 2006.10.29 01:44:31.00 -> YAW=50.886 ROLL=24.484 PITCH=-38.332

……

6. Conclusion

This MATLAB toolbox presents some basic functions needed for the attitude determination of a rigid non-dedicated GPS multiple antenna system. Since RINEX observation and navigation files are required, this toolbox can only be used for post-processing. This toolbox is oriented to the (smoothed) GPS C/A code. If the baseline between antennas are not measured in advance, the direct attitude computation approach offers a rapid solution. If the baselines are identified, the least-squares attitude estimation provides an optimal solution based on the pre-defined antenna body frame.

As is already mentioned in (Dai et al. 2008), dual-frequency data processing and ambiguity resolution technique should be added into the toolbox. These functions are currently under the development in order to fully extend this toolbox to the processing of carrier phase data. Besides that, a robust cycle-slip detection algorithm for carrier phase data per satellite should be implemented and the attitude results based on float ambiguities should also be provided. Also, the source code given in this toolbox can be further refined by using more efficient mathematical or MATLAB internal functions.

The toolbox can be accessed via the website of ZESS (http://www.zess.uni-siegen.de/cms/upload/navigroup/AttDet_16_3_2009.zip). Any suggestions, corrections, or comments about this toolbox are sincerely welcomed and can be emailed to dai@zess.uni-siegen.de. Other contact information can be read from the user manual in the toolbox.

7. Acknowledgment

This work was funded in part by the German Research Foundation (DFG) under grant number KN 876/1-1 and KN 876/1-2, which is gratefully acknowledged.

8. References

Chang, X., and Zhou, T. (2007). "MILES: MATLAB package for solving Mixed Integer LEast Squares problems." *GPS Solutions*, 11(4), 289-294.

Cohen, C. E., Lightsey, E. G., Parkinson, B. W., and Feess, W. A. (1994). "Space Flight Tests of Attitude Determination using GPS." *International Journal of Satellite Communications*, vol. 12, pp. 427-433.

Dai, Z., Knedlik, S., and Loffeld, O. (2008). "A Matlab toolbox for attitude determination with GPS multi-antenna systems." *GPS solutions*. vol.13, no. 3, pp.241-248

Hatch, R. "The synergism of GPS code and carrier measurements." Presented at *International Geodetic Symposium on Satellite Doppler Positioning*, Las Cruces, NM.

Hofmann-Wellenhof, B., Lichtenegger, H., and Collins, J. (2001). "*GPS: Theory and practice*". Wien: Springer Verlag.

Jonge de, P., and Tiberius, C. (1996). "The LAMBDA method for integer ambiguity estimation: implementation aspects." *Delft Geodetic Computing Centre LGR Series*, vol. 12.

Lu, G. (1995). *Development of a GPS Multi-Antenna System for Attitude Determination.* PhD. Thesis, University of Calgary, Calgary.

Van Grass, F., and Braasch, M. (1991). "GPS Interferometric Attitude and Heading Determination: Initial Fhght Test Results." *Journal of the Institute of Navigation*, vol.38, no.3, pp. 297-316.

19

Seismic model-based inversion using Matlab

Emilson Pereira Leite
Institute of Geosciences – University of Campinas
Brazil

1. Introduction

This chapter presents a workflow to invert post-stack seismic reflection data into acoustic impedance through the sequential use of several Matlab® codes. Acoustic impedance is defined as the product of density and seismic velocity and, as such, it is an intrinsic physical property of rocks. This physical property is closely related to variables that are of fundamental importance in the context of hydrocarbon reservoir characterization, such as lithology, porosity and, in some cases, water or oil saturation.

The basic premise of the vast majority of seismic inversion methods is the local validity of the 1-D convolutional model. Recursive methods were developed first in the late 70s (*e.g.* Lavergne and Willm, 1977; Lindseth, 1979) while sparse-spike methods were developed in the 80s. The later consists of techniques that use an additional premise that the reflections occur as sparsely distributed spikes within a layered Earth (*e.g.* Russell, 1988). Nowadays both methods are still widely jointly used even in sophisticated commercial seismic processing packages. Two well known methods that fall in this category are the L_1-norm sparse-spike inversion (*e.g.* Sacchi and Ulrych, 1996) and the maximum likelihood inversion (*e.g.* Hampson and Russell, 1988). When the sparse-spike inversion is constrained by a low-frequency model derived from acoustic impedance well logs or geologic models, it is commonly referred to as model-based inversion (Russel, 1988).

The idea of the proposed workflow is to apply a L1-norm sparse-spike inversion algorithm in the time domain, followed by a recursive inversion performed in the frequency domain. A low-frequency impedance model estimated at well-logs is incorporated as constraints during the recursive process. While it is clear that a similar inversion methodology can readily be applied using commercial packages, there is no consistent workflow designed for this type of application in low-cost scientific platforms such as Matlab. Therefore, the processing and visualization tools presented here are potentially useful especially for academic users of seismic data aiming at reservoir characterization.

2. Seismic-Well Tie

Before applying seismic inversion, an accurate depth-to-time conversion must be performed in order to make the vertical scale of the well log *AI* data match the vertical scale of the seismic data so as to allow spatial correlation. This conversion is carried out by using the sonic log and the initial two-way travel time for the first log sample that provides the

highest correlation coefficient between synthetic and observed trace. This is commonly known as seismic-well tie (e.g White and Hu, 1998).
Synthetic traces are calculated using the convolutional model given by Equation 1. This requires knowledge of the wavelet that represents the seismic pulse. By writing Equation 1 as a linear system and solving for $w(t)$, a deterministic wavelet extraction is conducted (Broadhead, 2008).

3. Model-Based Seismic Inversion

The fundamental premises behind all seismic inversion methods in the context of this work are: (i) the Earth can be represented locally by a stack of plane and parallel layers with constant physical properties; (ii) the seismic trace $s(t)$ can be represented by the convolution of the reflectivity coefficient series $r(t)$ with a band-limited wavelet $w(t)$ and the addition of a random noise $n(t)$:

$$s(t) = r(t) * w(t) + n(t) . \tag{1}$$

For zero incident angles, $r(t)$ is directly related to the contrast in the acoustic impedance (AI) of superposed layers through a simple equation that, after some algebraic manipulations and mathematical approximations, leads to the expression

$$AI_M = AI_1 \exp\left(2\sum_{j=2}^{M} r_j\right), \tag{2}$$

which is the equation used in practice for recursive inversion with the aim of transform reflectivities into impedances. AI_1 is the known acoustic impedance in the top layer and AI_M is that of the Mth layer. r_j is the reflection coefficient of the jth layer. This approximation is valid for most of the practical cases where $r_j \le |0.3|$ (*e.g.* Berteussen & Ursin, 1983).
The low-frequency AI model is obtained by estimating the AI values over the entire seismic volume through ordinary kriging of the AI values at the wells. The AI values at the wells are obtained by simple multiplication of the measured density values and the inverted sonic logs (i.e. interval transit time). For a properly usage of the recursive inversion, the seismic traces should be deconvolved into reflectivity series as suggested by Equation 2. To accomplish that, one has to apply a constrained sparse-spike optimization procedure that minimizes the objective function

$$J(\mathbf{r}) = \alpha \sum_{j=1}^{M} |r_j| + \frac{1}{2}\left\| \frac{1}{\sigma}(\mathbf{s} - \mathbf{Wr}) \right\|^2 \tag{3}$$

using, for example, a conjugate-gradient algorithm. The first term of Equation 3 minimizes the L_1-norm of the reflectivities where α controls the sparsity of the solution. The second term minimizes the difference between the synthetic seismic traces (**Wr**) and the observed traces (**s**). **W** is a wavelet coefficient matrix and σ is the standard deviation of the seismic data noise.

After estimating **r** from the seismic amplitudes, then **r** is inverted into *AI* according to the following sequential steps (Ferguson and Margrave, 1996):

(1) compute the linear trend of a spatial correspondent *AI* vector and subtract it, obtaining a residual AI_{res} vector;
(2) compute the Fourier spectra of AI_{res};
(3) apply Equation (2) to the reflectivity series, obtaining a relative AI_{rel} vector;
(4) compute the Fourier spectra of AI_{rel};
(5) determine a scalar α to match the mean power of AI_{rel} and AI_{res};
(6) multiply the spectra of AI_{rel} by α;
(7) low-pass filter AI_{res} and add to the result of step *(6)*;
(8) inverse Fourier transform the result of step *(7)*; and
(9) add the low-frequency trend from step *(1)* to the result of step *(8)*.

For the particular dataset used in this work, the wells are sparsely distributed through the oil field (Figure 1). Thus, the low-frequency trend of step *(1)* was extracted from the spatial correspondent *AI* trace estimated by kriging. A low cut-off for coupling the low frequency trend and a high cut-off is defined by finding where the energy content of the original seismic traces approaches to zero in the amplitude spectrum. This characterizes the band-limited nature of the seismic data. The basic workflow is presented in Figure 2.

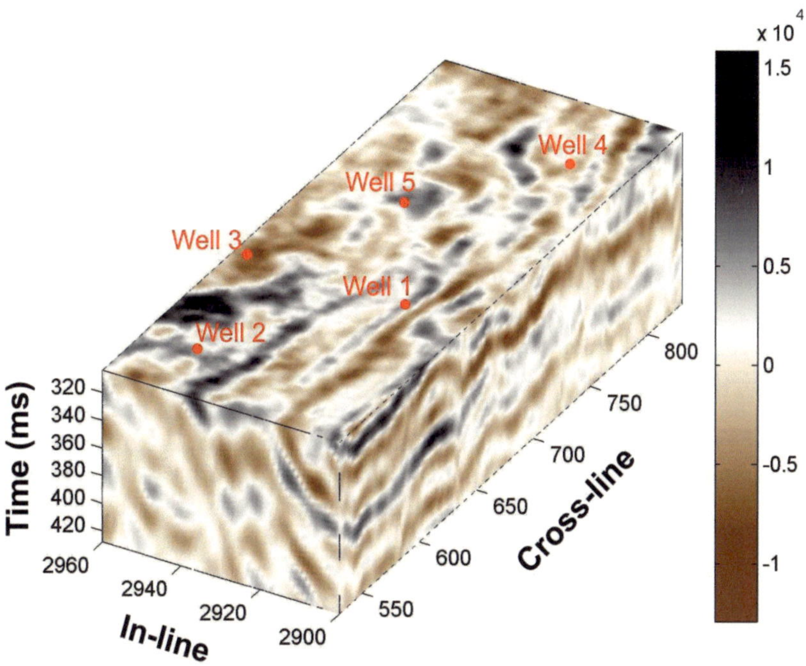

Fig. 1. 3D seismic data and spatial location of wells. Size of 3D matrix is 301 x 61 x 375. In-lines and cross-lines are spaced of about 13 and 27 m, respectively. Time interval is equal to 4 ms.

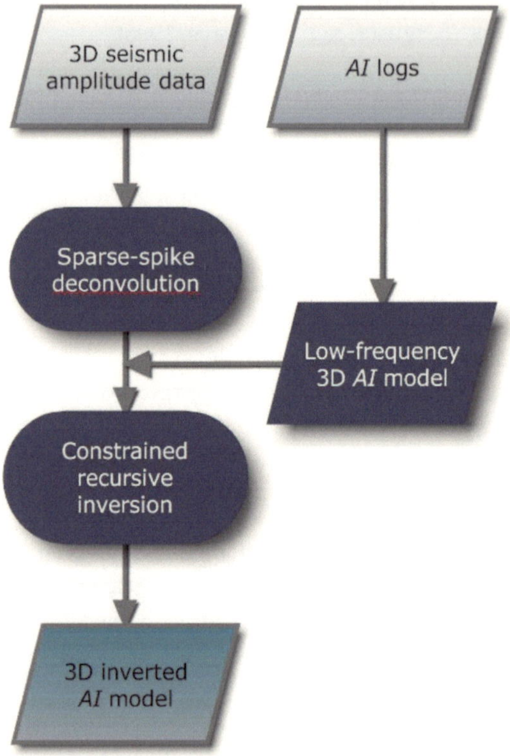

Fig. 2. Flowchart of the proposed inversion methodology. Each *AI* log is obtained by multiplying density log and inverted sonic log.

4. Matlab Algorithms

Seismic-well tie is conducted using functions from Seislab 3.01[1]. The core functions are *l_depth2time* and *s_wavextra*. The former computes two-way travel time by inverting and integrating sonic log starting from a given depth and a given time. Because at the beginning of the process we do not know the correct depth/time pair to be used, a range of values must be tested. The later performs deterministic wavelet extraction, as long as a reflectivity series and an observed seismic trace around the well are provided. The reflectivity series is obtained by rearranging Equation 2 and solving for each *r(t)*. *s_wavextra* also outputs a synthetic trace and the correlation coefficient with respect to the observed trace. The best depth/time pair is that for which this correlation coefficient is higher.
Sparse-spike inversion is applied by using the function *sparse_decon* from SeismicLab package[2]. This function performs L_1 regularization with Iterative Reweighted Least Squares (Sacchi, 1997). In this step, a reflectivity series is obtained from an observed seismic trace and a wavelet for each vertical column of seismic data.

---

1 http://www.mathworks.fr/matlabcentral/fileexchange/15674
2 http://www-geo.phys.ualberta.ca/saig/SeismicLab/index.html

To generate low-frequency models from known *AI* values at the wells, ordinary kriging is applied using mGstat[3] function *krig*. mGstat is a very flexible package for geoestatistical analysis and also provides interfaces to GSTAT, VISIM and SGeMS.
In the last step, recursive inversion is employed in order to map *AI(t)* from *r(t)*. The *blint* function from CREWES[4] group is used. This function calculates the summation that appears in Equation 2 in the frequency domain. Domain conversion is applied by using Matlab® native functions *fft* and *ifft* with few adaptations. Low and high frequency cut-offs must be provided and the integration filter rolls off as a smoth gaussian. This is not a problem because the seismic data is inherently of band-limited nature, so the task of the interpreter is to find these cut-offs.
To incorporate the low-frequency *AI* model, firstly log trends are subtracted from the *AI* logs. These log trends correspond to the lowest frequencies of the *AI* spectrum and they are simply fitted polynomials whose coefficientes are calculated by using native Matlab® *polyfit* function. Its value for a given time is obtained by *polyval*, which is also a native Matlab® function. Having removed the trends, the logs are converted to the frequency domain and a low-pass filters are applied to them. Finally, the results are merged with the band-limited outputs from *blint* by using *mergetrcs* function. After merging, the output log is converted back to time domain and the log trends are restored.
Visualizations can be performed using functions *s_wplot* and *s_cplot* for 2D seismic data, *s_volume_browser* for 3D seismic data and *l_plot* for well log data. These are powerful functions found in SeisLab.

5. Application Example

An example of depth-to-time conversion for Well 2 can be visualized in Figure 3, where it is shown the acoustic impedance log, the estimated reflectivity, the synthetic traces and the observed traces. Seismic-well ties were conducted by adjusting five traces around each well and retaining the local means. A global mean was calculated and used for inversion of the traces away from the wells.
Figure 4 shows the spectral content of the reflectivity, the wavelet, the synthetic traces and the observed traces. The spectral content of the other four wells is similar and low and high cut-offs were defined as 5 Hz and 60 Hz respectively.
In this case, the hydrocarbon reservoir top and base is estimated from well log markers allowing the definition of a minimum and maximum time values, thus establishing vertical boundaries for the seismic 3D grid. Lateral boundaries is defined so as to embrace wells that were previously found to have some hydrocarbon content. The 3D *AI* inverted model is shown in Figure 5. The average correlation coefficient of a synthetic seismic model calculated from this inverted model and the observed seismic data is equal to 0.95.

[3] http://mgstat.sourceforge.net/
[4] http://www.crewes.org/

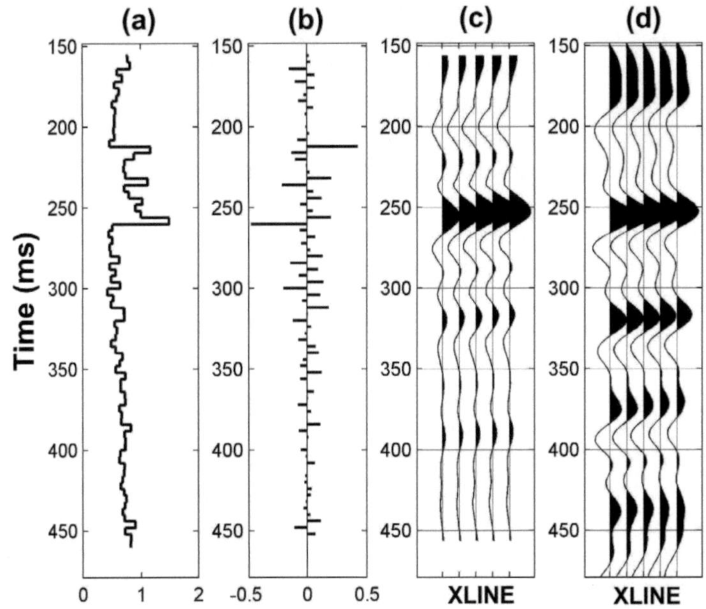

Fig. 3. Example of seismic-well tie for Well 2. (a) Impedance log converted to two-way time and resampled to the interval of 4 ms (values in m/s x g/cm³ x 10⁴). (b) Reflectivity. (c) Synthetic traces. (d) Observed traces.

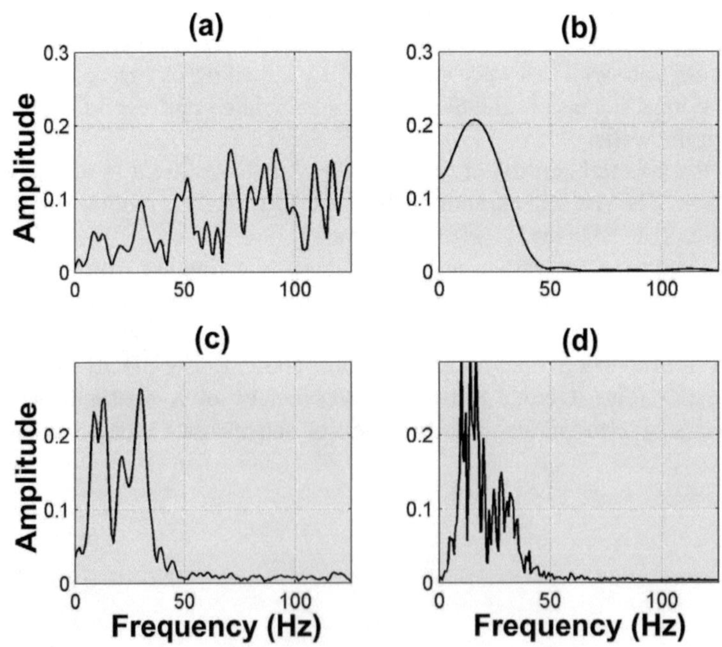

Fig. 4. Normalized Amplitude spectrum of (a) reflectivity; (b) wavelet; (c) synthetic traces; and (d) observed traces near Well 2.

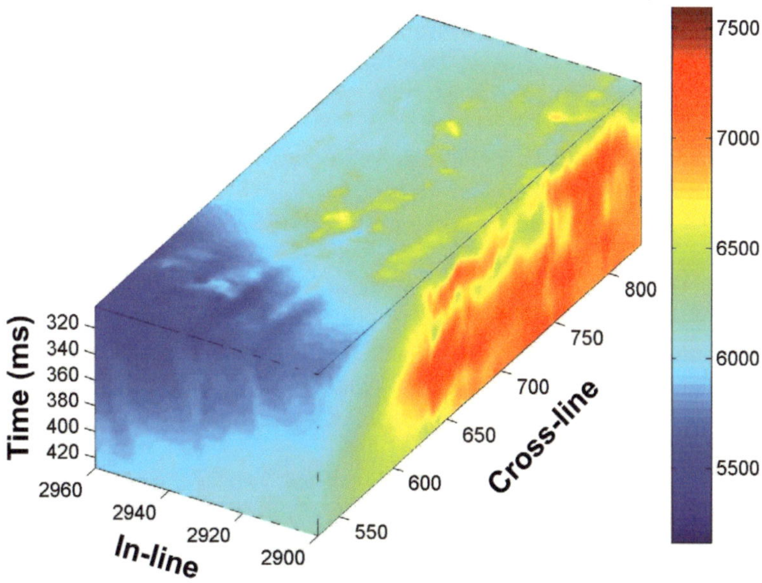

Fig. 5. *AI* obtained through the proposed inversion methodology.
Color bar is in m/s x g/cm^3.

6. Conclusions and recommendations

A simple methodology for mapping acoustic impedance and effective porosity from 3D seismic amplitude data using Matlab® was presented. This methodology can be used for a quick evaluation of reservoir properties, especially when powerful commercial programs are not available. An example with real data was also presented, showing that consistent 3D acoustic impedance models can be obtained if well-logs and 3D seismic data are available. A further improvement would be to obtain the low-frequency model by taking into account stratigraphic horizons, i.e., trend surfaces extracted from seismic data. This can be performed through universal kriging, or kriging with a trend. In Matlab®, universal kriging can be applied, for example, from mGstat toolbox. The use of stratigraphic horizons would allow the creation of low-frequency models that are spatially more consistent with the geological layering of a given reservoir area. Hopefully a Graphical User Interface will be developed in the near future integrating all this functions building a complete framework for performing seismic model-based inversion.

7. Acknowledgments

I gratefully acknowledge Petrobras - Petróleo Brasileiro SA for the financial support to this research. I am also indebted to Eike Rietsch for helping me with the use of his Seislab package for Matlab®.

8. References

Berteussen, A. K., and Ursin, B., 1983, Approximate computation of the acoustic impedance from seismic data: *Geophysics*, **41**, 882-894.

Broadhead, M. K., 2008, The impact of random noise on seismic wavelet estimation: *The Leading Edge*, **27**, 226-230.

Ferguson, R. J., and Margrave, G. F., 1996, A simple algorithm for band-limited impedance Inversion: The CREWES Research Report, **8**, 1-9.

Hampson, D., and Russell, B., 1985, Maximum-likelihood seismic inversion, 12th Annual International Meeting, CSEG, Abstract nº SP-16.

Lavergne, M., and Willm, C., 1977, Inverston of seismograms and pseudo-velocity logs. *Geophysical Prospecting*, **25**, 232-250.

Leite, E.P., and Souza Filho, C.R., 2009, TEXTNN—A MATLAB program for textural classification using neural networks. *Computers & Geosciences*, **35**, 2084-2094.

Lindseth, R. O., 1979, Synthetic sonic logs: a process for stratigraphic interpretation: *Geophysics*, **44**, 3-26.

Russell, B. H., 1988, *Introduction to seismic inversion methods*: Society of Exploration Geophysicists, Course Notes Series, 02, ISBN 978-0-931830-65-5.

Sacchi, M. D., and Ulrych, T. J., 1996, Bayesian Regularization of some seismic operators, In: *Maximum Entropy and Bayesian Methods*, K.M. Hanson and R. N. Silver (eds.): Kluwer Academic Publishers, **79**, 425-436.

Sacchi, M. D., 1997, Re-weighting strategies in seismic deconvolution. Geophysical Journal International, **129**, 651-656.

White, R. E., Hu, T., 1998, The Leading Edge, **17**, 1065-1071.

20

Computational and mathematical methods in portfolio insurance - A MATLAB-based approach

Vasilios N. Katsikis
General Department of Mathematics,
Technological Education Institute of Piraeus,
12244 Athens
Greece

1. Introduction

Portfolio insurance is based on the principal of risk transfer i.e., one person's protection is another person's liability. The cost of portfolio insurance is the mechanism to equilibrate its demand with supply. In the theory of finance minimum-cost portfolio insurance has been characterized as a very important investment strategy. In this chapter, we discuss the investment strategy called minimum-cost portfolio insurance as a solution of a cost minimization problem and we propose computational methods that translate the economics problem into the language of computing. This strategy not only enables an investor to avoid losses but also allows him/her to capture the gains at the minimum cost. In general, it is well known that the minimum-cost insured portfolio depends on security prices. The cases where it is price-independent (i.e., it does not depend on arbitrage-free security prices) are very important not only because the insured portfolio can be selected without knowledge of current security prices but also because we can present it in a simple form. Market structures in which minimum-cost portfolio insurance is price-independent relies on the theory of vector lattices (Riesz spaces). In particular, we focus our study in two very important classes of subspaces of a vector lattice, namely vector sublattices and lattice-subspaces. Vector lattices have been used by Brown & Ross (1991) and by Green & Jarrow (1987) in the framework of options markets. Also, Ross (1976) gave a characterization of complete markets by observing that derivative markets are complete if and only if the asset span is a vector sublattice of $\mathbb{R}^k$. Completeness of derivative markets is a sufficient but not necessary condition for the minimum-cost portfolio insurance to be price-independent. Let us denote by X the subspace of payoffs of all portfolios of securities; then in Aliprantis et al. (2000) it is proved that the minimum-cost insured portfolio exists and is price-independent for every portfolio and at every floor if and only if X is a lattice-subspace of $\mathbb{R}^k$. An equivalent necessary and sufficient condition so that X is a lattice-subspace is the existence of a positive basis for X, that is a basis of limited liability payoffs such that every marketed limited liability payoff has a unique representation as a nonnegative linear combination of basis payoffs. The notion of a positive basis for X is a generalization to incomplete markets of a basis of Arrow securities for complete markets. From the previous discussion, it is evident that the mathematical theory of lattice-subspaces has been used in order to provide a characterization of market structures in which the cost minimizing portfolio is price-independent. In general, the theory of lattice-subspaces has been extensively used in the last years in Mathematical Economics, especially in the areas of incomplete markets and portfolio insurance (e.g., Aliprantis et al. (1997; 2000; 2002); Polyrakis (2003)) as well as in completion of security markets (Kountzakis & Polyrakis (2006)). The study of finite-dimensional lattice-subspaces is important since many economic models are finite, such as, for example, the well-known Arrow-Debreu model. Additional applications of lattice-subspaces in economics appear in Aliprantis et al. (1998); Henrotte (1992). In this chapter, the main advantage of the computational techniques that we present is that we are able to solve the minimization problem without making use of any linear programming method. This is possible by using the theory of positive bases in vector lattices; specifically, we are able to provide a practical numerical way to check whether a subspace X is a lattice-subspace or a vector sublattice.

In Polyrakis (1996; 1999), lattice-subspaces and vector sublattices are studied in the space of continuous real valued functions $C(\Omega)$ defined on a compact Hausdorff topological space Ω. In the case where Ω is finite, for example $\Omega = \{1, 2, \ldots, k\}$, then $C(\Omega) = \mathbb{R}^k$ and the results of Polyrakis (1996; 1999) can be applied for the determination of the lattice-subspaces and vector sublattices of $\mathbb{R}^k$. In particular, in Polyrakis (1996) it is provided a solution to the problem of whether a finite collection of linearly independent positive functions in $C(\Omega)$ generates a lattice-subspace. In addition, he proposed an algorithm under which one can check whether the vector subspace[1] $X = [x_1, ..., x_n]$ is a lattice-subspace, where $x_1, ..., x_n$ are linearly independent positive functions in $C(\Omega)$. Another approach to the same problem of whether X forms a lattice-subspace of $\mathbb{R}^k$ is presented in Abramovich et al. (1994).

In Katsikis (2007), based on Abramovich et al. (1994), a computational solution is given to the problem of whether a finite collection of linearly independent, positive vectors of $\mathbb{R}^k$ generates a lattice-subspace. In addition, in Katsikis (2007), applications to the cost minimization problem that ensures the minimum-cost insured portfolio are discussed. The same reference concludes with a Matlab function which is an elegant and accurate tool in order to provide whether or not a given collection of vectors forms a lattice-subspace.

Also, in Katsikis (2008), a different computational method is presented based upon the Polyrakis algorithm (1996), in order to solve the corresponding problem in $C[a, b]$. This computational method implements a general algorithmic process and when slightly modified, this process can also be used in the case of lattice-subspaces of $\mathbb{R}^k$. Following this remark, Katsikis (2009) presents the translation followed by the implementation of this algorithm in $\mathbb{R}^k$ within a Matlab function. This function provides an important tool in order to investigate lattice-subspaces and vector sublattices of $\mathbb{R}^k$ with direct applications to portfolio insurance. Finally, the results of Katsikis (2009) can be applied in completion of security markets and the theory of efficient funds.

The material in this chapter is spread out in 8 sections. Section 2 gives the fundamental properties of lattice-subspaces and vector sublattices of $\mathbb{R}^k$ together with the solution to the problem of whether a finite collection of linearly independent, positive vectors of $\mathbb{R}^k$ generates a lattice-subspace or a vector sublattice. Section 3 studies, in detail, from the computational point of view the mathematical problem stated in Section 2 and presents an efficient computational method in order to solve it. Comparison results with other existing computational methods are also provided. Section 4 studies finite dimensional lattice-subspaces of $C[a, b]$ and presents the solution to the problem stated in Section 2, in the case where the initial space is $C[a, b]$. Section 5 presents computational methods in order to determine finite dimensional lattice-subspaces of $C[a, b]$. Section 6 provides the most important interrelationship between lattice-subspaces and the minimization problem of minimum-cost portfolio insurance. Also,

[1] $[x_1, ..., x_n]$ denotes the n-dimensional vector subspace generated by $x_1, ..., x_n$.

the reader will find in this Section a study that involves the computational techniques presented in Section 3 and Section 5 in order to calculate the minimum-cost insured portfolio both in the case of $\mathbb{R}^k$ and $C[a,b]$. Section 7 provides a computational technique, based on Section 3, in order to solve the problem of completion by options of a two-period security market in which the space of marketed securities is a subspace of $\mathbb{R}^k$. Methods on computing the efficient funds of the market are also presented. Conclusions and research directions are provided in Section 8.
In this chapter, all the numerical tasks have been performed using the Matlab 7.8 (R2009a) environment on an Intel(R) Pentium(R) Dual CPU T2310 @ 1.46 GHz 1.47 GHz 32-bit system with 2 GB of RAM memory running on the Windows Vista Home Premium Operating System.

2. Lattice-subspaces and vector sublattices of $\mathbb{R}^k$

In this section, a brief introduction is provided to the theory of lattice-subspaces and vector sublattices of $\mathbb{R}^k$. In addition, we present the solution to the problem of whether a finite collection of linearly independent, positive vectors of $\mathbb{R}^k$ generates a lattice-subspace or a vector sublattice.

2.1 Preliminaries and notation

We view $\mathbb{R}^k$ as an ordered space, then the *pointwise order* relation in $\mathbb{R}^k$ is defined by

$$x \leq y \textit{ if and only if } x(i) \leq y(i), \textit{ for each } i = 1, ..., k.$$

The positive cone of $\mathbb{R}^k$ is defined by $\mathbb{R}^k_+ = \{x \in \mathbb{R}^k | x(i) \geq 0, \textit{ for each } i\}$ and if we suppose that X is a vector subspace of $\mathbb{R}^k$ then X ordered by the pointwise ordering is an *ordered subspace* of $\mathbb{R}^k$ with positive cone X_+ defined by $X_+ = X \cap \mathbb{R}^k_+$. For a two-point set $S = \{x, y\}$, we denote by $x \vee y$ $(x \wedge y)$ the *supremum* of S i.e., its least upper bound (the *infimum* of S i.e., its greatest lower bound). Thus, $x \vee y$ $(x \wedge y)$ is the componentwise maximum (minimum) of x and y defined by

$$(x \vee y)(i) = \max\{x(i), y(i)\} \; ((x \wedge y)(i) = \min\{x(i), y(i)\}), \textit{ for all } i = 1, ..., k.$$

An ordered subspace X of $\mathbb{R}^k$ is a *lattice-subspace* of $\mathbb{R}^k$ if it is a vector lattice in the induced ordering, i.e., for any two vectors $x, y \in X$ the supremum and the infimum of $\{x, y\}$ both exist in X. Note that the supremum and the infimum of the set $\{x, y\}$ are, in general, different in the subspace than the supremum and the infimum of this set in the initial space. An ordered subspace Z of $\mathbb{R}^k$ is a *vector sublattice* or a *Riesz subspace* of $\mathbb{R}^k$ if for any $x, y \in Z$ the supremum and the infimum of the set $\{x, y\}$ in $\mathbb{R}^k$ belong to Z. Suppose that X is an ordered subspace of $\mathbb{R}^k$ and $B = \{b_1, b_2, ..., b_m\}$ is a basis for X. Then B is a *positive basis* of X if the positive cone X_+ of X has the form,

$$X_+ = \{x = \sum_{i=1}^{m} \lambda_i b_i | \lambda_i \geq 0, \textit{ for each } i\}.$$

Therefore, if $x = \sum_{i=1}^{m} \lambda_i b_i$ and $y = \sum_{i=1}^{m} \mu_i b_i$ then $x \leq y$ if and only if $\lambda_i \leq \mu_i$ for each $i = 1, 2, ..., m$. The existence of positive bases is not always ensured, but in the case where X is a vector sublattice of $\mathbb{R}^k$ then X has always a positive basis. Moreover, it holds that an ordered subspace of $\mathbb{R}^k$ has a positive basis if and only if it is a lattice-subspace of $\mathbb{R}^k$. If $B = \{b_1, b_2, ..., b_m\}$ is a positive basis for a lattice-subspace (or a vector sublattice) X then the lattice operations in X, namely $x \nabla y$ for the supremum and $x \triangle y$ for the infimum of the set $\{x, y\}$ in X, are given by

$$x \nabla y = \sum_{i=1}^{m} \max\{\lambda_i, \mu_i\} b_i \text{ and } x \triangle y = \sum_{i=1}^{m} \min\{\lambda_i, \mu_i\} b_i,$$

for each $x = \sum_{i=1}^{m} \lambda_i b_i, y = \sum_{i=1}^{m} \mu_i b_i \in X$. A vector sublattice is always a lattice-subspace, but the converse is not true as shown in the next example.

Example 0.1. Let $X = [x_1, x_2, x_3]$ be the subspace of $\mathbb{R}^4$ generated by the vectors $x_1 = (6, 0, 0, 1), x_2 = (6, 4, 0, 0), x_3 = (8, 4, 2, 0)$. An easy argument shows that the set $B = \{b_1, b_2, b_3\}$ where

$$\begin{bmatrix} b_1 \\ b_2 \\ b_3 \end{bmatrix} = \begin{bmatrix} 2 & 0 & 2 & 0 \\ 12 & 8 & 0 & 0 \\ 6 & 0 & 0 & 1 \end{bmatrix}$$

forms a positive basis of X therefore X is a lattice-subspace of $\mathbb{R}^4$. On the other hand, let us consider the vectors $y_1 = 2x_1 + x_2 = (18, 4, 0, 2)$ and $y_2 = x_3 - x_2 = (2, 0, 2, 0)$ of X. Then, $y_1 \vee y_2 = (18, 4, 2, 2)$ and since $y_1 = \frac{1}{2}b_2 + 2b_3, y_2 = b_1$, it follows that $y_1 \nabla y_2 = b_1 + \frac{1}{2}b_2 + 2b_3 = (20, 4, 2, 2)$. Therefore, X is not a vector sublattice of $\mathbb{R}^4$, since the supremum on the subspace X is different than the supremum on the whole space.

For an extensive presentation of lattice-subspaces, vector sublattices and positive bases the reader may refer to Abramovich et al. (1994); Polyrakis (1996; 1999).

2.2 The mathematical problem

Suppose that $\{x_1, x_2, ..., x_n\}$ is a collection of linearly independent, positive vectors of $\mathbb{R}^k$. The problem is, under what conditions the subspace $X = [x_1, x_2, ..., x_n]$ is a lattice-subspace or a vector sublattice of $\mathbb{R}^k$?
Let us denote by β the *basic function* of $x_1, x_2, ..., x_n$, that is, $\beta : \{1, 2, ..., k\} \to \mathbb{R}^k$ such that

$$\beta(i) = \left(\frac{x_1(i)}{z(i)}, \frac{x_2(i)}{z(i)}, ..., \frac{x_n(i)}{z(i)} \right),$$

for each $i \in \{1, 2, ..., k\}$ with $z(i) > 0$, where $z = \sum_{i=1}^{n} x_i$. The set

$$R(\beta) = \{\beta(i) | i = 1, 2, ..., k, \text{ with } z(i) > 0\},$$

is the *range* of the basic function and the *cardinal number*, $cardR(\beta)$, of $R(\beta)$ is the number of different elements of $R(\beta)$. Let $cardR(\beta) = m$ then it is clear that $n \leq m \leq k$. Denote by K the convex hull of $R(\beta)$. Since K is the convex hull of a finite subset of $\mathbb{R}^k$ it is a polytope with d vertices and each vertex of K belongs to $R(\beta)$ therefore $n \leq d \leq m$.
Suppose that $R(\beta) = \{P_1, P_2, ..., P_m\}$ such that, under a proper enumeration, the vertices $P_1, P_2, ..., P_n$ are linearly independent and $P_1, P_2, ..., P_d$ are the vertices of K, i.e.,

$$R(\beta) = \{ \overbrace{\underbrace{P_1, P_2, ... P_n}_{\text{linearly independent}}, P_{n+1}, ... P_d}^{\text{vertices of } K}, ..., P_m \}.$$

The following theorem, from (Polyrakis, 1999), provides a full answer to the stated problem.

Theorem 0.1. *Suppose that the above assumptions are satisfied. Then,*

(*i*) *X is a vector sublattice of* $\mathbb{R}^k$ *if and only if* $R(\beta)$ *has exactly n points (i.e.,* $m = n$*) and a positive basis* $\{b_1, b_2, ..., b_n\}$ *for X is defined by the formula*

$$(b_1, b_2, ..., b_n)^T = A^{-1}(x_1, x_2, ..., x_n)^T,$$

where A is the $n \times n$ *matrix whose ith column is the vector* P_i*, for each* $i = 1, 2, ..., m$.

(*ii*) *X is a lattice-subspace of* $\mathbb{R}^k$ *if and only if the polytope K has n vertices (i.e.,* $d = n$*) and a positive basis* $\{b_1, b_2, ..., b_n\}$ *for X is defined by the formula*

$$(b_1, b_2, ..., b_n)^T = A^{-1}(x_1, x_2, ..., x_n)^T,$$

where A is the $n \times n$ *matrix whose ith column is the vector* P_i*, for each* $i = 1, 2, ..., d$.

2.3 The algorithm

The basic steps of an algorithmic process that will accurately implement the ideas of Theorem 0.1 are the following:

(1) Determine $R(\beta)$.

(2) Compute the number $m = card R(\beta)$, and the number d of vertices of the polytope K.

(3) If $n = m$ (vector sublattice case) or $n = d$ (lattice-subspace case) then, determine a positive basis for X.

Based on a theorem of Edmonds, Lovász and Pulleybank in Edmond et al. (1982), we close this section with some remarks on the existence of a polynomial-time decision procedure, in order to decide whether the collection of vectors $\{x_1, x_2, ..., x_n\}$ generates a lattice-subspace or a vector sublattice. We shall present this result, in a suitable form for our analysis, as it is presented in Aliprantis et al. (1997).

Theorem 0.2. *There exists a polynomial-time algorithm that for any polytope, P, defined as the convex hull of a given finite set of vectors, determines the affine hull of P. Specifically the algorithm finds affinely independent vertices* $u_0, u_1, ..., u_\ell$ *of P such that*

$$\mathit{aff}(P) = \mathit{aff}(\{u_0, u_1, ..., u_\ell\}).$$

Recall that, algorithms which have a polynomial or sub-polynomial time complexity (that is, they take time $O(g(n))$ where $g(n)$ is either a polynomial or a function bounded by a polynomial), are practical. Such algorithms with running times of orders $O(\log n), O(n)$, $O(n \log n), O(n^2), O(n^3)$ etc. are called polynomial-time algorithms. There are several arguments to support the thesis that "polynomial" is a synonym to practical and the general conclusion is that a problem can be considered "efficiently solved" when a polynomial-time algorithm has been found for it.

In order to implement algorithm 2.3, we shall use the Quickhull algorithm from Barber et al. (1996) for computing the convex hull of a given set of points. According to Barber et al. (1996) (Theorem 3.2) if d is the dimension, n is the number of input points, r the number of processed points, and f_r the maximum number of facets of r vertices ($f_r = O(r^{\lfloor \frac{d}{2} \rfloor} / \lfloor \frac{d}{2} \rfloor !)$ then the worst-case complexity of Quickhull is $O(n \log r)$ for $d \leq 3$ and $O(n f_r / r)$ for $d \geq 4$.

3. The computational method

3.1 Method presentation

In this section we present the translation followed by the implementation of algorithm 2.3 within a Matlab function named `SUBlatSUB` from Katsikis (2009). This function provides an important tool in order to investigate lattice-subspaces and vector sublattices of $\mathbb{R}^k$ since we are able to perform fast testing for a variety of dimensions and subspaces. Recall that, the numbers n, m, d, k denote the dimension of X, the cardinality of $R(\beta)$, the number of vertices of the convex hull of $R(\beta)$ and the dimension of the initial Euclidean space, respectively.
The function `SUBlatSUB` first checks if the given collection of vectors generates a vector sublattice by examining the validity of condition (i) of Theorem 0.1. In the case of a vector sublattice, i.e., $m = n$, the program responds with the output:

```
vector sublattice
```

followed by a $n \times k$ matrix whose rows are the vectors of the positive basis.
If, instead, the collection does not generate a vector sublattice, that is $m \neq n$, then the function `SUBlatSUB` checks if the given collection generates a lattice-subspace by examining the validity of condition (ii) of Theorem 0.1. In the case of a lattice-subspace, i.e., $d = n$, the program responds with the output:

```
lattice-subspace
```

followed by a $n \times k$ matrix whose rows are the vectors of the positive basis.
If $m \neq n$ and $d \neq n$ then the program responds with the output:

```
not a lattice-subspace
ans=
     []
```

So, in order to decide whether a given collection of linearly independent, positive vectors generates a lattice-subspace or a vector sublattice of $\mathbb{R}^k$, we construct a matrix whose columns are the vectors of the given collection and then we apply the function `SUBlatSUB` on that matrix. It is possible to produce the numbers n, m, d, k, with this order, as a 4×1 matrix with the following code,

```
>> [positivebasis,dimensions]=SUBlatSUB(a)
```

where a is the matrix whose columns are the given vectors.

3.2 Numerical examples

In order to describe the most important features of `SUBlatSUB`, we illustrate some examples featured in Katsikis (2007) for various collections and dimensions. Also, we close this section with comparison results of the `SUBlatSUB` function and the alternative function, namely **K** function, presented in Katsikis (2007).

Example 0.2. Consider the following 7 vectors $x_1, x_2, ..., x_7$ in $\mathbb{R}^{10}$,

$$\begin{bmatrix} x_1 \\ x_2 \\ x_3 \\ x_4 \\ x_5 \\ x_6 \\ x_7 \end{bmatrix} = \begin{bmatrix} 1 & 0 & 0 & 0 & 0 & 0 & 0 & 0 & 0 & 0 \\ 0 & 1 & 0 & 0 & 0 & 0 & 0 & 1 & 0 & 0 \\ 0 & 0 & 1 & 0 & 0 & 0 & 0 & 0 & 0 & 0 \\ 0 & 0 & 0 & 1 & 0 & 0 & 0 & 0 & 0 & 0 \\ 1 & 0 & 0 & 0 & 1 & 1 & 0 & 0 & 1 & 0 \\ 0 & 0 & 0 & 0 & 0 & 0 & 1 & 0 & 0 & 0 \\ 0 & 1 & 0 & 0 & 0 & 0 & 1 & 0 & 0 & 1 \end{bmatrix}$$

According to the definition of the β function, the rows of the following matrix u are the different elements of $R(\beta)$,

```
u =
  0    0    0    0    0    0    1
  0    0    0    0    0    0.5  0.5
  0    0    0    0    1    0    0
  0    0    0    1    0    0    0
  0    0    1    0    0    0    0
  0    0.5  0    0    0    0    0.5
  0    1    0    0    0    0    0
  0.5  0    0    0    0.5  0    0
```

Thus, $m = 8$ and it is clear that rows $u(1), \ldots, u(5), u(7), u(8)$ of u are linearly independent. This means that these vectors belong to the convex hull of $R(\beta)$. Also, it is easy to see that row $u(6)$ of u is a convex combination of the other rows. Therefore, $d = 7$ and $X = [x_1, x_2, x_3, x_4, x_5, x_6, x_7]$ is a lattice-subspace.
For a numerical solution, we invoke the `SUBlatSUB` function by typing in the command window of the Matlab environment:

```
>> [positive basis,dimensions]=SUBlatSUB(a)
```

The results, then, are as follows:

```
lattice-subspace
positivebasis =
  0    1    0    0    0    0    0    0    0    1
  0    0    0    0    0    0    2    0    0    0
  0    0    0    0    1    1    0    0    1    0
  0    0    0    1    0    0    0    0    0    0
  0    0    1    0    0    0    0    0    0    0
  0    1    0    0    0    0    0    1    0    0
  2    0    0    0    0    0    0    0    0    0
dimensions =
           7
           8
           7
          10
```

We conclude with some comments based on the results of the `SUBlatSUB` function. A positive basis is unique in the sense of positive multiples since each element of the basis is an extremal[2] point of the positive cone of the subspace. If we denote by $\{b_1, b_2, ..., b_7\}$ the positive basis that we obtained by using the **K** function (see Katsikis (2007)) and by $\{B_1, B_2, ..., B_7\}$ the positive basis we found with the `SUBlatSUB` function then it holds

$$(B_1, B_2, B_3, B_4, B_5, B_6, B_7) = (b_7, 2b_5, b_4, b_3, b_2, b_6, 2b_1).$$

Example 0.3. Consider the following 7 vectors $x_1, x_2, ..., x_7$ in $\mathbb{R}^{10}$,

$$\begin{bmatrix} x_1 \\ x_2 \\ x_3 \\ x_4 \\ x_5 \\ x_6 \\ x_7 \end{bmatrix} = \begin{bmatrix} 2 & 2 & 4 & 3 & 0 & 0 & 0 & 0 & 1 & 1 \\ 0 & 0 & 1 & 1 & 2 & 3 & 1 & 3 & 4 & 4 \\ 3 & 3 & 0 & 0 & 0 & 0 & 4 & 0 & 0 & 0 \\ 1 & 1 & 0 & 1 & 0 & 1 & 0 & 1 & 0 & 0 \\ 0 & 0 & 1 & 0 & 1 & 0 & 1 & 0 & 1 & 1 \\ 0 & 0 & 0 & 0 & 0 & 0 & 6 & 0 & 0 & 0 \\ 0 & 0 & 0 & 0 & 0 & 0 & 0 & 0 & 6 & 6 \end{bmatrix}$$

where following the same procedure, as before, one gets

```
vector sublattice
positivebasis =
  0      0      0      0      0      0     12      0      0      0
  0      0      0      0      3      0      0      0      0      0
  0      0      0      0      0      4      0      4      0      0
  0      0      0      0      0      0      0      0     12     12
  6      6      0      0      0      0      0      0      0      0
  0      0      0      5      0      0      0      0      0      0
  0      0      6      0      0      0      0      0      0      0
dimensions =
           7
           7
          10
```

If we denote by $\{b_1, b_2, ..., b_7\}$ the positive basis that we obtained by using the **K** function and by $\{B_1, B_2, ..., B_7\}$ the positive basis we found with the `SUBlatSUB` function then it holds

$$(B_1, B_2, B_3, B_4, B_5, B_6, B_7) = (12b_6, 3b_4, 4b_5, 12b_7, 6b_1, 5b_3, 6b_2).$$

Example 0.4. Consider the following 5 vectors $x_1, x_2, ..., x_5$ in $\mathbb{R}^{10}$,

$$\begin{bmatrix} x_1 \\ x_2 \\ x_3 \\ x_4 \\ x_5 \end{bmatrix} = \begin{bmatrix} 1 & 1 & 1 & 1 & 1 & 1 & 1 & 1 & 2 & 1 \\ 1 & 1 & 1 & 2 & 1 & 1 & 1 & 2 & 1 & 2 \\ 1 & 1 & 1 & 2 & 1 & 1 & 1 & 2 & 1 & 1 \\ 1 & 1 & 1 & 1 & 1 & 1 & 1 & 2 & 2 & 1 \\ 2 & 1 & 2 & 1 & 1 & 1 & 1 & 1 & 1 & 1 \end{bmatrix}$$

For the above set, the program yields

[2] A nonzero element x_0 of X_+ is an *extremal point* of X_+ if, for any $x \in X, 0 \leq x \leq x_0$ implies $x = \lambda x_0$ for a real number λ.

```
lattice-subspace
positivebasis =
  0      0      0    0    0      0      0      8    0    0
  0      7/4    0    7    7/4    7/4    7/4    0    0    0
  6      3/2    6    0    3/2    3/2    3/2    0    0    0
  0      0      0    0    0      0      0      0    0    6
  0      7/4    0    0    7/4    7/4    7/4    0    7    0
dimensions =
                 5
                 6
                 5
                10
```

In this case it holds

$$(B_1, B_2, B_3, B_4, B_5) = (8b_3, 7b_2, 6b_1, 6b_5, 7b_4).$$

For the purpose of monitoring the performance, we present in Table 1 the execution times of the `SUBlatSUB` function and the method presented in Katsikis (2007) (**K** function).

Matlab functions	Example 0.2	Example 0.3	Example 0.4
`SUBlatSUB`	0.052	0.030	0.035
K	0.516	0.828	0.969

Table 1. Time in seconds

3.3 The case of coplanar points

The correct performance of the `SUBlatSUB` function requires the use of the **convhulln** Matlab function which is based on Qhull[3] and Qhull implements the Quickhull algorithm (Barber et al. (1996)) for computing the convex hull of a given set of points. Suppose that a denotes the matrix whose rows are the coefficients of the given points, then the **convhulln** function returns the indices of the points in a that comprise the facets of the convex hull of a. The **convhulln** function is facing problems during the calculation of the convex hull of points that lie in a q-manifold, with $q \leq n-1$, in the n-dimensional space of the given data. So, we cannot use **convhulln** to solve our problem directly.
We illustrate the details in this case through the following example and we also provide an improvement technique to solve the resultant problem in this particular case.

Example 0.5. Consider the following four vectors x_1, x_2, x_3, x_4 in $\mathbb{R}^7$,

$$\begin{bmatrix} x_1 \\ x_2 \\ x_3 \\ x_4 \end{bmatrix} = \begin{bmatrix} 1 & 2 & 1 & 0 & 1 & 1 & 4 \\ 0 & 1 & 1 & 1 & 1 & 0 & 2 \\ 2 & 1 & 0 & 1 & 1 & 1 & 2 \\ 1 & 0 & 1 & 1 & 1 & 0 & 0 \end{bmatrix}.$$

Following the second step of algorithm 2.3, the calculation of the convex hull of $R(\beta)$ is required to check whether $X = [x_1, x_2, x_3, x_4]$ is a lattice-subspace or a vector sublattice of $\mathbb{R}^7$.

[3] For information about Qhull see http://www.qhull.org/

In this case, and after the necessary calculations it is clear that $R(\beta) = \{P_1, P_2, P_3, P_4, P_5, P_6\}$ where

$$\begin{bmatrix} P_1 \\ P_2 \\ P_3 \\ P_4 \\ P_5 \\ P_6 \end{bmatrix} = \begin{bmatrix} 0 & \frac{1}{3} & \frac{1}{3} & \frac{1}{3} \\ \frac{1}{4} & 0 & \frac{1}{2} & \frac{1}{4} \\ \frac{1}{2} & 0 & \frac{1}{2} & 0 \\ \frac{1}{3} & \frac{1}{3} & 0 & \frac{1}{3} \\ \frac{1}{2} & \frac{1}{4} & \frac{1}{4} & 0 \\ \frac{1}{4} & \frac{1}{4} & \frac{1}{4} & \frac{1}{4} \end{bmatrix}.$$

Therefore, in order to determine the convex hull of $R(\beta)$ we have used the **convhulln** function. In this case the **convhulln** function yields with the following warning message:

```
??? qhull precision warning: The initial hull is narrow (cosine of
min. angle is 1.0000000000000002). A coplanar point may lead to a
wide facet.
```

If we use the following simple rank test:

```
>> y=[0 1/3 1/3 1/3;1/4 0 1/2 1/4;1/2 0 1/2 0;1/3 1/3 0 1/3;

1/2 1/4 1/4 0;1/4 1/4 1/4 1/4];
>> rank(bsxfun(@minus,y,y(6,:)))
```

then one gets

```
ans =
     3
```

Thus, by our previous analysis it is clear that the points $P_1, P_2, P_3, P_4, P_5, P_6$ of $\mathbb{R}^4$ lie in a 3-manifold and we cannot use **convhulln** to solve our problem directly. A solution to this problem can be given under the following methodology:

- Translate the points to a hyper-plane that passes through the origin.
- Determine a set of basis vectors for the subspace.
- Transform the points into an equivalent lower dimensional space.
- Form the convex hull triangulation in the lower dimensional space.

Let us describe, in detail, the procedure for this particular example. First, one has to translate the given points to a hyper-plane that passes through the origin by subtracting one of the vectors from the others,

```
>> ytrans = bsxfun(@minus,y,y(6,:))
ytrans =
  -0.2500    0.0833    0.0833    0.0833
        0   -0.2500    0.2500         0
   0.2500   -0.2500    0.2500   -0.2500
   0.0833    0.0833   -0.2500    0.0833
   0.2500         0         0   -0.2500
        0         0         0         0
```

Then, we form an orthonormal basis for the range of `ytrans`.

```
>> rot = orth(ytrans')
rot =
   0.5  -0.64505   0.28967
   0.5  -0.28967  -0.64505
  -0.5   0.64505  -0.28967
   0.5   0.28967   0.64505
```

Recall that, if $\{v_1, v_2, \ldots, v_r\}$ is an orthonormal basis for a finite dimensional subspace W of an inner product space V and u is any vector of V, then the projection of the vector u in W is given by the formula $proj_W u = < u, v_1 > v_1 + \ldots + < u, v_r > v_r$.
Now, we project the points into an equivalent lower dimensional space where `rot` is a basis for this space. Hence,

```
>> yproj = ytrans*rot
yproj =
   0.16667  0.21502    -0.096557
  -0.25     0.23368     0.088845
  -0.5      3.0531e-16 5.5511e-17
   0.16667 -0.21502     0.096557
  -0.25    -0.23368    -0.088845
   0        0           0
```

Note that, the rows of `yproj` matrix are the coordinates of the initial points in terms of the basis in the lower dimensional space.
Finally, we form the convex hull triangulation in the projected subspace `yproj`. That is,

```
>> tri = convhulln(yproj)
tri =
     1 2 3
     2 4 3
     4 2 1
     5 1 3
     4 5 3
     5 4 1
```

Since we are only interested for the number of vertices of the convex hull of $R(\beta)$, we can only determine the number of vertices of the convex hull in the projected subspace. Therefore,

```
>> length(unique(tri(:)))
ans =
     5
```

So, there are 5 vertices in the hull. This procedure is included in the `SUBlatSUB` function therefore, for a direct answer in the previous example, one can apply the `SUBlatSUB` function directly to the given collection by using the code,

```
>> [positive basis,dimensions]=SUBlatSUB(a)
```

the results, then, are as follows:

```
not a lattice-subspace
positivebasis =
                []
dimensions =
            4
            6
            5
            7
```

where a denotes a matrix that has the vectors $x_i, i = 1,2,3,4$ as columns.

3.4 Comparison results

In this section, we compare the performance of the `SUBlatSUB` function to that of the **K** function. The numerical method, based on the introduction of the `SUBlatSUB` function, enables us to perform fast and accurate estimations of the lattice-subspace or the vector sublattice for a finite collection of positive, linearly independent vectors of $\mathbb{R}^k$ for a variety of dimensions. For this purpose we have used the Matlab function **rand** in order to produce 50 full rank matrices for each rank $n, n = 3, ..., 30$. The cumulative results are presented in Figure 1 (Figure 1 shows the time efficiency curves, i.e., the rank of the 50 tested matrices versus the total computation time (in seconds)) and in Table 2. From the previous results (see Figure 1,Table 2) it is evident

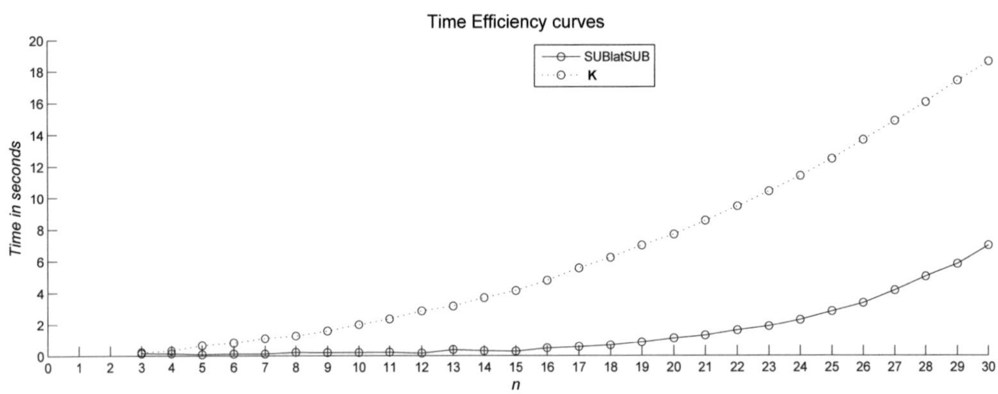

Fig. 1. Time efficiency curves for the **K** function and the SUBlatSUB function

that using the `SUBlatSUB` function the interested user can reach a fast computational solution using a reduced amount of computational resources.

4. Finite dimensional lattice-subspaces of $C[a, b]$

In what follows we shall denote by $C[a, b]$ the space of all continuous real functions defined on the interval $[a, b]$. As in the case of $\mathbb{R}^k$, lattice-subspaces of $C[a, b]$ are subspaces which are vector lattices in the induced ordering, i.e., for any two vectors x, y of the subspace the supremum and the infimum of the set $\{x, y\}$ both exist in the subspace. Recall that the supremum and the infimum of the set $\{x, y\}$ are, in general, different in the subspace than the supremum and the infimum of this set in the initial space. In this section we present a brief introduction to the theory of lattice-subspaces in $C[a, b]$. In addition, we describe in detail the construction of a powerful and efficient package for the translation, into the language of computing, of the

Rank	SUBlatSUB (Time in seconds)	K (Time in seconds)	Rank	SUBlatSUB (Time in seconds)	K (Time in seconds)
3	0.141	0.205	17	0.553	5.548
4	0.140	0.322	18	0.665	6.230
5	0.073	0.641	19	0.853	6.992
6	0.115	0.805	20	1.100	7.681
7	0.113	1.090	21	1.290	8.545
8	0.207	1.257	22	1.620	9.457
9	0.191	1.572	23	1.882	10.420
10	0.198	1.980	24	2.292	11.382
11	0.209	2.358	25	2.823	12.470
12	0.153	2.858	26	3.353	13.662
13	0.371	3.161	27	4.154	14.854
14	0.308	3.694	28	5.030	16.040
15	0.272	4.135	29	5.815	17.384
16	0.477	4.781	30	6.978	18.617

Table 2. Results for 50 tested full rank matrices for each rank n, $n = 3, ..., 30$.

mathematical problem of whether the vector subspace $X = [x_1, ..., x_n]$ is a lattice-subspace of $C[a,b]$, where $x_1, ..., x_n$ are linearly independent positive functions in $C[a,b]$.

4.1 Preliminaries and notation

Let $C[a,b]_+$ be the positive cone of $C[a,b]$ and assume that X is a subspace of $C[a,b]$. The *induced ordering* on X is the ordering defined by $X_+ = X \cap C[a,b]_+$ (induced cone of X). An *ordered subspace* of $C[a,b]$ is a subspace of $C[a,b]$ under the induced ordering. A *lattice-subspace* of $C[a,b]$ is an ordered subspace X of $C[a,b]$ which is a vector lattice in its own, that is, for each $x, y \in X$ the supremum and the infimum of the set $\{x,y\}$ exists in X. If X is a lattice-subspace of $C[a,b]$ then we will denote by $x \nabla y$ the supremum of the set $\{x,y\}$ in X. Similarly, $x \vartriangle y$ stands for the infimum of the set $\{x,y\}$ in X. If $x \vee y$ denotes the supremum and $x \wedge y$ the infimum in E of the set $\{x,y\}$ and we suppose that $x \vartriangle y, x \wedge y, x \vee y, x \nabla y$ exists, then it follows that

$$x \vartriangle y \leq x \wedge y \leq x \vee y \leq x \nabla y \tag{1}$$

For example, consider $C[0,1]$, the space of all continuous real functions in the interval $[0,1]$ and $X = \{ax + b | a, b \in \mathbb{R}\}$. Then X is a lattice-subspace of $C[0,1]$ and (1) holds for each $x, y \in X$ (Figure 2).

One of the most serious difficulties in the study of lattice-subspaces comes from the fact that the supremum and the infimum depend both on the subspace.

For a general definition of a positive basis, let E be a (partially) ordered Banach space. Then a sequence $\{e_n\}$ of positive vectors of E is a *positive basis* if it is a Schauder basis of E and

$$E_+ = \{x = \sum_{i=1}^{\infty} \lambda_i e_i \in E | \lambda_n \geq 0, \textit{ for all } n \in \mathbb{N}\}.$$

Equivalently, one can say that $\{e_n\}$ is a positive basis of E if

$$x = \sum_{i=1}^{\infty} \lambda_i e_i \geq 0 \Leftrightarrow \lambda_n \geq 0, \textit{ for all } n \in \mathbb{N}.$$

Let Y be a closed subspace of $E = C[a,b]$ with basis $\{b_n\}$ (not necessarily positive). Fix $t \in [a,b]$ and $m \in \mathbb{N}$. Following the terminology introduced in Polyrakis (1996), if $b_m(t) \neq 0$ and

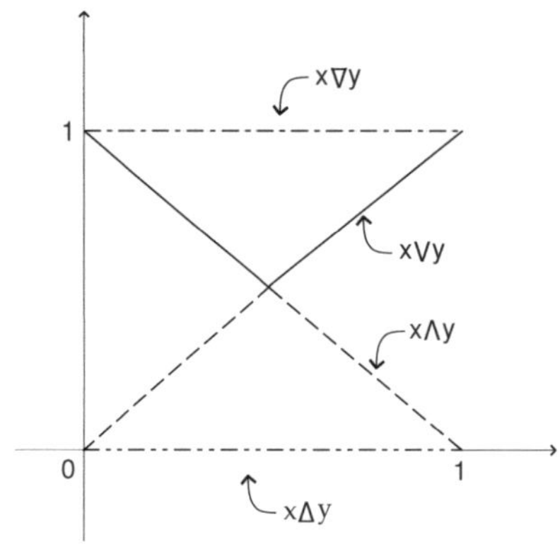

Fig. 2. Relation (1) for x=t, y=1-t,t∈[0,1].

$b_n(t) = 0$ for each $n \neq m$, then we shall say that the point t is an *m-node (or simply a node)* of the basis $\{b_n\}$. If for each n there exists an n-node t_n of the basis $\{b_n\}$, then we shall say that $\{b_n\}$ is *a basis of Y with nodes* and that t_n is *a sequence with nodes* of $\{b_n\}$. If $\dim Y = n$ and for each $m \in \{1,2,...,n\}$ there exists an m-node t_m of the basis of Y, then we shall say that $\{b_1, b_2, ..., b_n\}$ is a basis of Y with nodes and that the points $t_1, t_2, ..., t_n$ are nodes of the basis $\{b_1, b_2, ..., b_n\}$. The *support* of a function $x \in C[a,b]$ is the closure of the set $\{t \in [a,b] : x(t) > 0\}$ and shall be denoted by $suppx$.

4.2 The mathematical problem

In this section, we present the method developed in Polyrakis (1996), for the determination of the finite-dimensional lattice-subspaces of $C[a,b]$ and we shall discuss the necessary and sufficient conditions for a collection of linearly independent, positive functions, $x_1, x_2, ..., x_n$ of $C[a,b]$ to generate a lattice-subspace. Recall that the Wronski determinant of the functions x_i, $i = 1, ..., n$ is the $n \times n$ determinant which ith row is constituted of the $(i-1)$th derivatives of the functions x_i. Our first approach to the problem is given through the following Wronskian criterion:

Theorem 0.3. *Consider the closed interval $[a,b]$ of $\mathbb{R}$ and $\dim X > 2$, where $X = [x_1, x_2, ..., x_n]$. Suppose that (c,d) is an open interval of $\mathbb{R}$ which contains $[a,b]$. If the functions x_i have continuous derivatives up to the nth order in (c,d) and the Wronskian of the functions x_i is nonzero for any point of (c,d), then X is not a lattice-subspace of $C[a,b]$.*

As in the case of $\mathbb{R}^k$, let $x_1, ..., x_n$ in $C[a,b]$, we shall denote by z the sum $z = \sum_{i=1}^{n} x_i$ and by β the function $\beta : [a,b] \to \mathbb{R}^n$ such that

$$\beta(t) = \Big(\frac{x_1(t)}{z(t)}, \frac{x_2(t)}{z(t)}, ..., \frac{x_n(t)}{z(t)}\Big)$$

for each $t \in [a,b]$ with $z(t) > 0$. We shall refer to β as the *basic curve* of the functions $x_1, x_2, ..., x_n$. Also, we shall denote by $D(\beta)$ the domain and by $R(\beta)$ the range of the basic curve β of $x_1, x_2, ..., x_n$. If K is a subset of $\mathbb{R}^n$ then we shall denote by $\overline{K}$ the closure of K, by $int(K)$ the interior of K and by ∂K the boundary of K. We shall denote by $co(K)$ the convex hull of K and by $\overline{co}(K)$ the closure of $co(K)$.

The following theorem, is a criterion for lattice-subspaces and provides a full answer to the problem of whether a collection of positive functions $x_1, x_2, ..., x_n$ of $C[a,b]$ generates a lattice-subspace. In addition, if we are in the case of a lattice-subspace then the theorem determines a positive basis for $X = [x_1, x_2, ..., x_n]$.

Theorem 0.4. *The following statements are equivalent,*

(i) *X is a lattice-subspace of* $C[a,b]$.

(ii) *There exist n linearly independent* $P_1, P_2, ..., P_n$ *vectors in* $\mathbb{R}^n$, *belonging to the closure of the range of* β *such that for each* $t \in D(\beta)$ *the vector* $\beta(t)$ *is a convex combination of the vectors* $P_1, P_2, ..., P_n$, *i.e.,* $R(\beta) \subseteq co(\{P_1, P_2, ..., P_n\})$.

If (ii) is true, $P_i = \lim_{\nu\to\infty} \beta(\omega_{i\nu})$ *for each i, A is the* $n \times n$ *matrix whose ith column is the vector* P_i *and* $b_1, b_2, ..., b_n$ *are the functions defined by the formula*

$$(b_1(t), b_2(t), ..., b_n(t)) = A^{-1}(x_1(t), x_2(t), ..., x_n(t))^T,$$

then X has the following properties:

(a) *The set* $\{b_1, b_2, ..., b_n\}$ *is a positive basis of X. In addition, if* t_i *is a limit point of the sequence* $\{\omega_{i\nu} : \nu = 1, 2, ...\}$, *then* $t_i \in supp b_i$ *and* $b_k(t_i) = 0$, *for each* $k \neq i$.

(b) *The closed convex hull of* $R(\beta)$ *and the convex polygon with vertices the points* $P_1, P_2, ..., P_n$ *coincide.*

(c) *If* $P_k = \beta(t_k)$, *then* t_k *is a k-node of the basis* $\{b_1, b_2, ..., b_n\}$.

(d) *If* $P_k = \beta(t_k)$ *for some interior point* t_k *of* $[a,b]$ *and* x_i *are* C^2- *functions in a neighborhood of* t_k, *then*

$$\beta'(t_k) = \mathbf{0}.$$

The set $E(\beta)$ is the *extreme subset* of the basic curve β if there exists a subset G of $\overline{R(\beta)}$ consisting of n linearly independent vectors such that $R(\beta) \subseteq co(G)$, then we put $E(\beta) = G$, otherwise we put $E(\beta) = \varnothing$.

From Theorem 0.4 and the preceding definition the following proposition should be immediate.

Proposition 0.1. *The subspace X satisfies the properties*

(i) *X is a lattice-subspace if and only if* $E(\beta) \neq \varnothing$.

(ii) *If* $\beta(t) \in E(\beta)$, *then t is a node of the positive basis of X.*

(iii) *X has a positive basis with nodes if and only if* $E(\beta)$ *is a nonempty subset of* $R(\beta)$.

From Theorem 0.4 it is evident that if $P \in E(\beta)$ and $P \notin R(\beta)$, then we have that $P = \lim_{\nu\to\infty} \beta(t_\nu)$, where t_ν is a sequence of $D(\beta)$ having all limit points in the boundary $\partial D(\beta)$ of $D(\beta)$.

So, the *limit set* $L(\beta)$ of the curve β is defined as follows:

$$L(\beta) = \{P \in \mathbb{R}^n : \exists\{t_\nu\} \subseteq D(\beta) \text{ with its limit points in } \partial D(\beta), P = \lim_{\nu\to\infty} \beta(t_\nu)\}.$$

Also, if $a, b \in D(\beta)$ then we shall denote by $\beta(\partial[a,b])$ the set

$$\beta(\partial[a,b]) = \{\beta(a), \beta(b)\}.$$

If t is an interior point of $[a, b]$ and $\beta(t) \in E(\beta)$, then t is a root of the equation

$$\beta'(t) = \mathbf{0}, \tag{2}$$

and we shall denote by $I(\beta)$ the images of the roots of equation (2), i.e.,

$$I(\beta) = \{\beta(t) : t \in Int([a, b]) \cap D(\beta) \text{ and } t \text{ is root of the equation } (2)\}.$$

Any subset of $L(\beta) \cup I(\beta) \cup \beta(\partial[a, b])$ consisting of n linearly independent vectors will be called a *possible extreme subset* of β.

Proposition 0.2. *If the functions $x_1, x_2, ..., x_n$ are C^2−functions in the set $Int([a, b]) \cap D(\beta)$, then $E(\beta) \subseteq L(\beta) \cup I(\beta) \cup \beta(\partial[a, b])$.*

The set $\beta(\partial[a, b])$ is known because $\partial[a, b] = \{a, b\}$ and if $D(\beta) = [a, b]$ then $L(\beta) = \varnothing$. In addition, if we assume that the domain of β has the form

$$D(\beta) = [a, t_1) \cup (t_1, t_2) \cup ... \cup (t_{n-1}, t_n) \cup (t_n, b]$$

and the limits

$$P_i = \lim_{t \to t_i} \beta(t)$$

exist for each i, then

$$L(\beta) = \{P_1, P_2, ..., P_n\}.$$

In view of Proposition 0.2 one has to determine the set $L(\beta) \cup I(\beta) \cup \beta(\partial[a, b])$ and then must investigate when one of the possible extreme subsets of β is indeed an extreme subset of β. The details are included in the next algorithm.

4.3 The algorithm

Based upon Theorem 0.3, Theorem 0.4 and the discussion in Subsection 4.2, next, we illustrate the steps of an algorithm in order to decide whether the collection $\{x_1, x_2, ..., x_n\}$ generates a lattice-subspace.

(1) Does the Wronskian of the functions $x_1, x_2, ..., x_n$ have at least one root in the interval $[a, b]$?

(2) Determine the sets $L(\beta), I(\beta), \beta(\partial[a, b])$ and the possible extreme subsets of β.

(3) Is one of the possible extreme subsets an extreme subset of β ?

(4) If step (3) holds, determine a positive basis of X.

5. The computational method

5.1 Method presentation

In this section, we present a procedure that will accurately implement the ideas of algorithm 4.3 while the main concern is to further calculate the positive basis (if one exists) in order to provide an exact description of the lattice-subspace. So, the first step of our approach consists of describing the functionality of the functions **wr**, **V**, **L**, **I**, **sisets** and **xitest** from Katsikis (2008).

According to Theorem 0.3, function **wr** checks if the Wronskian of the given collection $\{x_1, x_2, ..., x_n\}$ of $C[a, b]$ has at least one root in the interval $[a, b]$. In addition, the **wr** function provides the roots (if there exist any) of the Wronskian. So, in this case the program responds with the output:

```
The Wronskian has at least one root in [a,b]
```

and it yields the roots of the Wronskian. If, instead, the Wronskian does not have any roots in the interval $[a, b]$, then the program provides only the roots outside the interval $[a, b]$ (if there exist any).
Suppose that the given collection passes the Wronskian test, then we try to determine the possible extreme subsets of the basic curve β starting with the computation of the set $\beta(\partial[a, b])$. So, in our next step we call the function **V**. Function **V** first checks whether there are any real roots of the function $z(t) = \sum_{i=1}^{n} x_i$. If that is the case it displays the message

```
Possible non empty limit set
```

so that we can continue in order to determine the limit set of the curve β. Function **V** responds with a matrix whose columns are the elements of the set $\beta(\partial[a, b])$.
In the case of a non empty limit set, we use the function **L** in order to determine the limit set of the curve β. The output of the function **L** is a matrix whose columns are the elements of the set $L(\beta)$.
In order to determine the set

$$I(\beta) = \{\beta(t) : t \in Int([a, b]) \cap D(\beta) \textit{ and t is root of the equation } (2)\},$$

we use the function **I**. The function **I** provides a matrix whose columns are the elements of the set $I(\beta)$.
Suppose that $\{P_1, ..., P_n\}$ is a possible extreme subset of β and

$$\beta(t) = \xi_1(t)P_1 + ... + \xi_n(t)P_n.$$

In order to prove that $\{P_1, ..., P_n\}$ is an extreme subset of β we must show that $\xi_i(t) \geq 0$, for each i and each $t \in [a, b]$. So, for the next step in our approach, we need to construct all the possible extreme subsets of β and check whether there exists an extreme subset of β. To this end, we make use of the function **sisets** in order to generate all the possible extreme subsets of the curve β. Note that, **sisets** calls automatically the function **xitest** in order to determine the domain where each one of the $\xi_i(t)$ are negative. Let us denote by Δ_i the domain of negativity that corresponds to the function $\xi_i(t)$, for $i = 1, ..., n$ then, if for at least one of the $\xi_i(t)$, Δ_i has non empty intersection with the interval $[a, b]$, the set $\{P_1, ..., P_n\}$ is not an extreme subset of β. In the case where an extreme subset exists we determine the positive basis by using the formula

$$(b_1(t), b_2(t), ..., b_n(t)) = A^{-1}(x_1(t), x_2(t), ..., x_n(t))^T,$$

from Theorem 0.4.

5.2 Numerical examples

For the purpose of monitoring the performance, in the following we present some examples in $C[a, b]$ for various collections of functions together with the time responses we obtained when running these examples (Table 3).

Example 0.6. Let $x_1(t) = t^2 - 2t + 2$, $x_2(t) = -t^3 + 2t^2 - t + 2$ and $x_3(t) = t^3 - 3t^2 + 3t$ and X be the subspace of $C[0, 2]$ generated by the functions x_1, x_2, x_3.
Our first step consists of loading the data of the problem by using the following commands:

```
>> syms t
>> f=t^2-2*t+2;
>> g=-t^3+2*t^2-t+2;
>> h=t^3-3*t^2+3*t;
>> K=[f g h];
```

For the above set we start our analysis by using the Wroskian criterion (Theorem 0.3) through the **wr** function as follows:

```
>> wr(K,0,2);
```

The results, then, are as follows:

```
The Wronskian has at least one root in [a,b]
ans =
     1
```

Since, the Wroskian has at least one root in the interval [0,2], then we determine the set $\beta(\partial[a,b])$ by using the **V** function as the following code suggests:

```
>> betathetaomega=V(K,0,2);
```

As a result we get

```
limit set is empty
betathetaomega=
                    1/2  1/2
                    1/2  0
                    0    1/2
```

Let us denote $P_1(\frac{1}{2},\frac{1}{2},0), P_2(\frac{1}{2},0,\frac{1}{2})$. Note that, if there is a possibility of a non empty limit set then the **V** function displays the message

```
Possible non empty limit set
```

Our next step is to determine the set $I(\beta)$ by using the **I** function which it provides a matrix whose columns are the elements of the set $I(\beta)$. Therefore,

```
>> I(K,0,2);
```

In this case the program yields

```
iotabeta =
           1/4
           1/2
           1/4
```

Let us denote $P_3(\frac{1}{4},\frac{1}{2},\frac{1}{4})$. Then, the set

$$\{P_1(\frac{1}{2},\frac{1}{2},0), P_2(\frac{1}{2},0,\frac{1}{2}), P_3(\frac{1}{4},\frac{1}{2},\frac{1}{4})\}$$

is the only possible extreme subset of β.

Suppose that

$$\beta(t) = \xi_1(t)P_1 + \xi_2(t)P_2 + \xi_3(t)P_3.$$

In order to prove that $\{P_1, P_2, P_3\}$ is an extreme subset of β we must show that $\xi_i(t) \geq 0$, for each i and each $t \in [0,2]$ and that $\sum_{i=1}^{3} \xi_i(t) = 1$. Since, in the present example, there is only one possible extreme subset of the curve β we can use the **xitest** function directly as the following code suggests:

```
>> b=[1/2 1/2 1/4;1/2 0 1/2;0 1/2 1/4];
>> xitest(K,b);
```

The results, then, are as follows:

```
sumofxi =
        1
ans =
     RealRange(Open(2), infinity)
ans =
     RealRange(-infinity,Open(0)),RealRange(Open(2),infinity)
ans =
     RealRange(-infinity, Open(0))
```

Thus, we have that $\sum_{i=1}^{3} \xi_i(t) = 1$. Also, $\Delta_1 = (2, +\infty), \Delta_2 = (-\infty, 0) \cup (2, +\infty)$ and $\Delta_3 = (-\infty, 0)$, therefore $\Delta_i \cap [0,2] = \varnothing$ for each i. As a result we have that $\{P_1, P_2, P_3\}$ is an extreme subset of β. Note that in the above code we denote by b the matrix whose columns are the elements of the set $\{P_1, P_2, P_3\}$. According to Theorem 0.4(ii), a positive basis $\{b_1, b_2, b_3\}$ of $X = [x_1, x_2, x_3]$ is given by the following code:

```
>> positivebasis=factor(inv(b)*K)
```

The results, then, are as follows:

```
positivebasis =
               [                  2]
               [-2(t  - 2)(t  - 1)  ]
               [   -4t(t  - 2)      ]
               [              2     ]
               [   2t(t  - 1)       ]
```

hence $b_1(t) = -2(t-2)(t-1)^2$, $b_2(t) = -4t(t-2)$, $b_3(t) = 2t(t-1)^2$.

Example 0.7. Let $x_1(t) = t^2(t-1)^2$, $x_2(t) = t^4(t-1)^2$ and $x_3(t) = t^4(t-1)^4$ and X be the subspace of $C[-1,2]$ generated by the functions x_1, x_2, x_3. Working as before, we load the data of the problem by using the following commands:

```
>> syms t
>> f=t^2*(t-1)^2;
>> g=t^4*(t-1)^2;
>> h=t^4*(t-1)^4;
>> K=[f g h];
```

and for the above set we start our analysis by using the Wroskian criterion as follows:

```
>> wr(K,-1,2);
```

The results, then, are as follows:

```
The Wronskian has at least one root in [a,b]
ans =
         0
         3/4
         1
```

Thus, $0, 3/4$ and 1 are the roots of the Wroskian in the interval $[-1,2]$. In this case, we determine the set $\beta(\partial[-1,2])$ with the following code:

```
>> betathetaomega=V(K,-1,2);
```

As a result we get

```
>> Possible non empty limit set
betathetaomega =
                    1/6   1/9
                    1/6   4/9
                    2/3   4/9
```

Let us denote $P_1(\frac{1}{6}, \frac{1}{6}, \frac{2}{3}), P_2(\frac{1}{9}, \frac{4}{9}, \frac{4}{9})$, then, from the above results, the possibility of a non empty limit set is further investigated. We can determine the limit set $L(\beta)$ of the curve β with the **L** function as the following code suggests:

```
>> limitset=L(K,-1,2);
```

In this case the program yields

```
limitset =
           1   1/2
           0   1/2
           0     0
```

Let us denote $P_3(1,0,0), P_4(\frac{1}{2}, \frac{1}{2}, 0)$. Our next step is to determine the set $I(\beta)$. So,

```
>> iotabeta=I(K,-1,2);
```

The results, then, are as follows:

```
iotabeta is empty
iotabeta =
           []
```

Thus, we have

$$I(\beta) \cup L(\beta) \cup \beta(\partial\Omega) = \{P_1(\frac{1}{6}, \frac{1}{6}, \frac{2}{3}), P_2(\frac{1}{9}, \frac{4}{9}, \frac{4}{9}), P_3(1,0,0), P_4(\frac{1}{2}, \frac{1}{2}, 0)\}.$$

In order to determine all the possible extreme subsets of the curve β we shall use the **sisets** function under the following code:

```
>> V=[1/6 1/9 1 1/2;1/6 4/9 0 1/2;2/3 4/9 0 0];
>> sisets(K,V);
```

where by V we denote the matrix whose columns are the elements of the set $I(\beta) \cup L(\beta) \cup \beta(\partial\Omega)$. Note that the **sisets** function not only calculates all the possible extreme subsets of the curve β but it also calls, automatically, the function **xitest** in order to determine the domain where each one of the $\xi_i(t)$ are negative. The results, then, are as follows:

```
S =
    1/6    1/9    1
    1/6    4/9    0
    2/3    4/9    0
ans =
      RealRange(Open(0.),Open(2.))
ans =
      RealRange(-infinity,Open(-1.)), RealRange(Open(3.),infinity)
ans =
      RealRange(-infinity,Open(-1.)), RealRange(Open(2.),infinity)
S =
    1/6    1/9    1/2
    1/6    4/9    1/2
    2/3    4/9    0
ans =
      RealRange(Open(1.),Open(2.))
ans =
      RealRange(Open(-1.),Open(1.))
ans =
      RealRange(-infinity,Open(-1.)), RealRange(Open(2.),infinity)
S =
    1/6    1    1/2
    1/6    0    1/2
    2/3    0    0
ans =
      NULL
ans =
      RealRange(-infinity,Open(-1.)), RealRange(Open(1.),infinity)
ans =
      RealRange(-infinity,Open(-1.)), RealRange(Open(3.),infinity)
S =
    1/9    1    1/2
    4/9    0    1/2
    4/9    0    0
ans =
      NULL
ans =
      RealRange(Open(1.),Open(2.))
ans =
      RealRange(-infinity,Open(0.)), RealRange(Open(2.),infinity)
```

In the previous results, S denotes each one of the possible extreme subsets of the curve β followed by the intervals of negativity of the corresponding $\xi_i(t)$. The conclusion here is that $X = [x_1, x_2, x_3]$ is not a lattice subspace of $C[-1,2]$ since, from the above results, no set from the above candidates is an extreme subset.

We close this section with the time responses we obtained when running Example 0.6 and Example 0.7. Note that despite the relatively small collections of functions featured in these two examples the programs needed to perform a large number of elaborate checks in order to produce an answer. It easily follows that the **wr, V, L, I sisets** and **xitest** functions provide a practical numerical way to check whether the subspace X is a lattice-subspace, and thus allows us to simplify an extremely challenging task if it were to be done manually.

Matlab Function	Total time (in seconds)	Matlab Function	Total time (in seconds)
wr	0.035	**wr**	0.047
V	0.084	**V**	0.213
I	0.053	**I**	0.166
xitest	0.036	**sisets**	0.404
		L	0.108

Table 3. Time responses for Example 0.6 Time responses for Example 0.7

6. Applications in portfolio insurance

The theory of vector sublattices and lattice-subspaces has been extensively used in the last years in Mathematical Economics, especially in the areas of incomplete markets and portfolio insurance. In this section, we shall discuss this interconnection and we shall present computational methods in order to calculate the minimum-cost insured portfolio both in $\mathbb{R}^k$ and $C[a,b]$.

6.1 Portfolio insurance in $\mathbb{R}^k$

Let us assume that in the beginning of a time period there are N securities traded in a market. Let $\mathcal{S} = \{1, ..., S\}$ denote a finite set of states and $x_n \in \mathbb{R}^S_+$ be the payoff vector of security n in S states. The payoffs $x_1, x_2, ..., x_N$ are assumed linearly independent so that there are no redundant securities. By y_s we denote the N-dimensional vector of payoffs of all securities in state s. If $\theta = (\theta_1, \theta_2, ..., \theta_N) \in \mathbb{R}^N$ is a non-zero portfolio then its payoff is the vector

$$P(\theta) = \sum_{n=1}^{N} \theta_n x_n$$

and the set of payoffs of all portfolios is the linear span of the payoffs vectors $x_1, x_2, ..., x_N$ in $\mathbb{R}^S$ which we shall denote it by X, i.e.,

$$X = [x_1, x_2, ... x_N].$$

Let us also assume that $p = (p_1, p_2, ..., p_N) \in \mathbb{R}^N$ is a vector of security prices and $\mathbf{k} = \{k, k, ..., k\}, k \in \mathbb{R}$ denotes a vector with S coordinates. Then, the insured payoff on a portfolio $\theta = (\theta_1, \theta_2, ..., \theta_N)$ at a *floor* k is the contingent claim $P(\theta) \vee \mathbf{k}$ where

$$(P(\theta) \vee \mathbf{k})(s) = \max\{P(\theta)(s), \mathbf{k}(s)\} = \max\{P(\theta)(s), k\}, \textit{ for } s = 1, ..., S.$$

The solution of the following cost minimization problem is referred to as the *minimum-cost insured portfolio*,

$$\min_{\eta \in \mathbb{R}^N} p \cdot \eta$$

subject to

$$P(\eta) \geq P(\theta) \vee \mathbf{k}.$$

It is evident from the previous analysis that in order to calculate the minimum-cost insured portfolio we have to solve a linear programming problem. In Aliprantis et al. (2000), it is proved that if the supremum $P(\theta) \vee \mathbf{k}$ exists relative to X, i.e., if $P(\theta) \vee_X \mathbf{k}$ exists, then a portfolio that generates this payoff is the minimum-cost insured portfolio. The details are presented in the next theorem,

Theorem 0.5. *The minimum-cost portfolio exists and it is price-independent for every portfolio* $\theta = (\theta_1, \theta_2, ..., \theta_N)$ *and at every floor* $\mathbf{k}$ *if and only if* X *is a lattice-subspace of* $\mathbb{R}^S$*, then the minimum-cost insured portfolio* θ^k *is given by the formula*

$$P(\theta^k) = P(\theta) \vee_X \mathbf{k}.$$

Therefore, it is evident that in the special case where the subspace X is a lattice subspace we can find the minimum-cost insured portfolio by expressing the payoff vector and the floor vector in terms of the positive basis. Under these conditions, we can calculate the minimum-cost insured portfolio without making use of a linear programming method.
To this end, one can follow the following methodology:

- Calculate, by using the `SUBlatSUB` function, a positive basis $\{b_1, b_2, ..., b_N\}$ for the subspace X.
- If we denote by x and $\mathbf{k}$ the payoff and the floor vector, respectively, then express x, $\mathbf{k}$ in terms of the positive basis i.e., determine $\lambda_i, \mu_i,\ i = 1, 2, ..., N$ such that $x = \sum_{i=1}^{N} \lambda_i b_i$ and $\mathbf{k} = \sum_{i=1}^{N} \mu_i b_i$.
- Determine the supremum of the expressed payoff and floor vector i.e, determine the following supremum

$$x \vee_X \mathbf{k} = \sum_{i=1}^{N} \max\{\lambda_i, \mu_i\} b_i.$$

- If we denote by $\theta^k = (\theta_1, \theta_2, ..., \theta_N)$ the minimum-cost insured portfolio then θ^k is the solution of the following linear system

$$\sum_{n=1}^{N} \theta_n x_n = \sum_{i=1}^{N} \max\{\lambda_i, \mu_i\} b_i.$$

The above algorithmic procedure can be implemented through the following Matlab function, namely `mcpinsurance`:

```
function [theta_k]=mcpinsurance(a,floorvector,portfolio)
%a denotes a matrix whose columns are the given
%vectors x_1,x_2,...,x_N
%floorvector denotes the vector (k,k,...,k)
%portfolio denotes the theta vector
```

```
%Note that mcpinsurance requires the presence of the
%SUBlatSUB function
payoffvector=sum(a*diag(portfolio),2);
positivebasis=SUBlatSUB(a)';
r=(positivebasis\payoffvector);
k=(positivebasis\floorvector');
w=max(r,k)';
sup=w*positivebasis';
theta_k=a\sup';
```

We illustrate the above with the following example:

Example 0.8. We consider seven securities with payoffs in ten states given by

$$x_1 = (2,2,4,3,0,0,0,0,1,1),\ x_2 = (0,0,1,1,2,3,1,3,4,4),$$
$$x_3 = (3,3,0,0,0,0,4,0,0,0),\ x_4 = (1,1,0,1,0,1,0,1,0,0),$$
$$x_5 = (0,0,1,0,1,0,1,0,1,1),\ x_6 = (0,0,0,0,0,0,6,0,0,0)$$
$$x_7 = (0,0,0,0,0,0,0,0,6,6).$$

Their linear span $X = [x_1, x_2, x_3, x_4, x_5, x_6, x_7]$ is a seven-dimensional subspace of $\mathbb{R}^{10}$. Consider the portfolio $\theta = (0,3,0,0,0,0,0)$ of three shares of security 2 at floor
$\mathbf{1} = (1,1,1,1,1,1,1,1,1,1)$. It follows that one can calculate the minimum-cost insured portfolio, i.e., the portfolio that generates the payoff $x_2 \vee_X \mathbf{1}$, by using the following code,

```
>> theta_k=mcpinsurance(a,floorvector,portfolio)
```

Here the result is $\theta^k = (0,3,0.3333,0,0,-0.2222,0)$.

It is clear that the `mcpinsurance` function is an important tool in order to calculate the minimum-cost insured portfolio.

6.2 Portfolio insurance in $C[a,b]$

In this section, we shall discuss the investment strategy called minimum-cost portfolio insurance in the case where the initial space is $C[a,b]$, the space of all continuous real functions defined on the interval $[a,b]$. In our model we use a method of comparing portfolios called portfolio dominance ordering from Aliprantis et al. (1998). This method compares portfolios by means of the ordering of their payoffs and under this consideration we are able to use the order structure of the payoff space together with the theory of lattice-subspaces. As in the case of $\mathbb{R}^k$, we calculate the minimum-cost insured portfolio under the general assumption that the asset span X is a lattice-subspace of the initial space $C[a,b]$. Also, in what follows we shall use the notation from Katsikis (2008).

The model of security markets we study here is extended over two periods, the period 0 and the period 1. We assume n securities labeled by the natural numbers $1,2,...,n$, acquired the period 0 and that these n securities are described by their payoffs at date 1. The payoff of the *ith* security is in general a positive element x_i of an ordered space E which is called *payoff space*. In addition, we assume that the payoffs $x_1, x_2, ..., x_n$ are linearly independent so that there are no redundant securities and that the securities have limited liability which ensures the positivity of $x_1, x_2, ..., x_n$.

In our model we consider E to be the space of real valued continuous functions $C[a,b]$ defined in an interval $[a,b]$. A portfolio is a vector $\theta = (\theta_1, \theta_2, ..., \theta_n)$ of $\mathbb{R}^n$ where θ_i is the number of shares of the *ith* security. The space $\mathbb{R}^n$ is then known as *portfolio space*. If $\theta = (\theta_1, \theta_2, ..., \theta_n) \in \mathbb{R}^n$ is a non-zero portfolio then its payoff is the vector

$$P(\theta) = \sum_{i=1}^{n} \theta_i x_i \in C[a,b].$$

The operator P is called the *payoff operator*. The pointwise ordering in $C[a,b]$, induces the partial ordering $\geq_P$ in the portfolio space $\mathbb{R}^n$ and is defined as follows: For each $\theta, \phi \in \mathbb{R}^n$ we have

$$\theta \geq_P \phi, \text{ if and only if } P(\theta) \geq P(\phi).$$

This ordering is known as the *portfolio dominance ordering*. The set of payoffs of all portfolios, or the range space of the payoff operator, is the linear span of the payoffs vectors $x_1, x_2, ..., x_n$ in $C[a,b]$ which we shall denote it by X, i.e.,

$$X = [x_1, x_2, ..., x_n].$$

The subspace X of $C[a,b]$ is called the *asset span* of securities or the *space of marketed securities*. Let us assume that $p = (p_1, p_2, ..., p_n) \in \mathbb{R}^n$ is a vector of security prices and θ, ϕ are two portfolios. Then, the insured payoff on the portfolio $\theta = (\theta_1, \theta_2, ..., \theta_n)$ at the *floor* ϕ and in the price p is the contingent claim $P(\theta) \vee P(\phi)$.
As in the case of $\mathbb{R}^k$, the solution of the following cost minimization problem is referred to as the *minimum-cost insured portfolio*, or a *minimum-cost insurance of the portfolio* θ *at the floor* ϕ *and in the price* p,

$$\min_{\eta \in \mathbb{R}^n} p \cdot \eta$$

subject to

$$P(\eta) \geq P(\theta) \vee P(\phi).$$

In Aliprantis et al. (2000) it is proved that if the supremum $P(\theta) \vee P(\phi)$ exists relative to X, i.e., if $P(\theta) \vee_X P(\phi)$ exists and X contains the order unit (risk-free payoff **1**) then a portfolio that generates this payoff is the minimum-cost insured portfolio. The details are presented in the next theorem,

Theorem 0.6. *The minimum-cost insured portfolio exists and it is price-independent for every portfolio* $\theta = (\theta_1, \theta_2, ..., \theta_n)$ *and at every floor* ϕ *if and only if the asset span* X*, which contains the risk-free payoff, is a lattice-subspace of* $C[a,b]$*. In this case, the minimum-cost insured portfolio* θ^{ϕ} *is given by the formula*

$$P(\theta^{\phi}) = P(\theta) \vee_X P(\phi).$$

Therefore, if X is a lattice-subspace and $\{b_1, b_2, ..., b_n\}$ is a positive basis of the asset span X, then the minimum-cost insured portfolio θ^{ϕ} can be calculated with the following methodology:

- Expand $P(\theta)$ and $P(\phi)$ in terms of the positive basis $\{b_1, b_2, ..., b_n\}$.
- Suppose that $P(\theta) = \sum_{i=1}^{n} \lambda_i b_i$, $P(\phi) = \sum_{i=1}^{n} \mu_i b_i$. Then

$$P(\theta^{\phi}) = \sum_{i=1}^{n} (\lambda_i \vee \mu_i) b_i.$$

We shall illustrate the above with a simple example.

Example 0.9. Let $C[0,2]$ be the payoff space. Suppose that our model has three securities with payoff vectors $x_1(t) = t^2 - 2t + 2$, $x_2(t) = -t^3 + 2t^2 - t + 2$ and $x_3(t) = t^3 - 3t^2 + 3t$. The asset span X is the subspace of $C[0,2]$ generated by the functions x_1, x_2, x_3.
We will investigate whether X is a lattice-subspace and in the case of a lattice-subspace we shall determine a positive basis for X. Also, we shall calculate the minimum-cost insured portfolio θ^ϕ of the portfolio $\theta = (1,3,0)$ at the floor $\phi = (2,1,1)$.
From Example 0.6, we have that X is a lattice-subspace of $C[0,2]$ and the positive basis is defined by the functions

$$b_1(t) = -2(t-2)(t-1)^2, b_2(t) = -4t(t-2), b_3(t) = 2t(t-1)^2.$$

Let us denote by S, the matrix whose columns are the numeric coefficients of the symbolic polynomials of the positive basis, then $S = \begin{bmatrix} -2 & 0 & 2 \\ 8 & -4 & -4 \\ -10 & 8 & 2 \\ 4 & 0 & 0 \end{bmatrix}$
It follows that one can calculate the minimum-cost insured portfolio, i.e., the portfolio that generates the payoff $P(\theta) \vee_X P(\phi)$, with the following code:

```
>> syms t
>> x1=t^2-2*t+2;
>> x2=-t^3+2*t^2-t+2;
>> x3=t^3-3*t^2+3*t;
>> a=[x1;x2;x3];
>> theta=[1 3 0];
>> phi=[2 1 1];
>> Ptheta=sym2poly(theta*a);
>> Pphi=[0 sym2poly(phi*a)];
>> Rthetanew=S\Rtheta';
>> Pphinew=S\Pphi';
>> theta_phi=max(Pthetanew,Pphinew)
```

As a result we get $\theta^\phi = (2, 1.75, 1.5)$ which is the minimum-cost insured portfolio at every arbitrage price.

The procedure we followed in Example 0.9 allowed us to solve the minimization problem, without making use of any linear programming method and can be used in conjunction with the **wr**, **V**, **L**, **I**, **sisets** and **xitest** functions, in order to calculate minimum-cost insured portfolios.

7. Applications in the theory of efficient funds

In this section, we shall apply the `SUBlatSUB` function in order to determine the completion of security markets and the efficient funds of the market.
Let us assume that in the beginning of a time period there are n securities traded in a market. Let $\mathcal{S} = \{1, ..., m\}$ denote a finite set of states and $x_j \in \mathbb{R}^m_+$ be the payoff vector of security j in m states. The payoffs $x_1, x_2, ..., x_n$ are assumed linearly independent so that there are no redundant securities. If $\theta = (\theta_1, \theta_2, ..., \theta_n) \in \mathbb{R}^m$ is a non-zero portfolio then its payoff is the

vector $P(\theta) = \sum_{i=1}^{n} \theta_i x_i$. The set of payoffs of all portfolios is referred as the space of *marketed securities* and it is the linear span of the payoffs vectors $x_1, x_2, ..., x_n$ in $\mathbb{R}^m$ which we shall denote it by X, i.e., $X = [x_1, x_2, ...x_n]$.
For any $x, u \in \mathbb{R}^m$ and any real number a the vector

$$c_u(x, a) = (x - au)^+$$

is the *call option* and

$$p_u(x, a) = (au - x)^+$$

is the *put option* of x with respect to the *strike vector* u and *exercise price* a.
In what follows we shall use the theoretical background introduced in Kountzakis & Polyrakis (2006). Let U be a fixed subspace of $\mathbb{R}^m$ which is called *strike subspace* and the elements of U are the *strike vectors*. Then, the *completion by options* of the subspace X with respect to U is the space $F_U(X)$ which is defined inductively as follows:

- X_1 is the subspace of $\mathbb{R}^m$ generated by $\mathcal{O}_1$, where $\mathcal{O}_1 = \{c_u(x, a) | x \in X, u \in U, a \in \mathbb{R}\}$, denotes the set of call options written on the elements of X,
- X_n is the subspace of $\mathbb{R}^m$ generated by $\mathcal{O}_n$, where $\mathcal{O}_n = \{c_u(x, a) | x \in X_{n-1}, u \in U, a \in \mathbb{R}\}$, denotes the set of call options written on the elements of X_{n-1},
- $F_U(X) = \cup_{n=1}^{\infty} X_n$.

The completion by options $F_U(X)$ of X with respect to U is the vector sublattice of $\mathbb{R}^m$ generated by the subspace $Y = X \cup U$. The details are presented in the next theorem,

Theorem 0.7. *In the above notation, we have*

(*i*) $Y \subseteq X_1$,

(*ii*) $F_U(X)$ *is the sublattice* $S(Y)$ *of* $\mathbb{R}^m$ *generated by* Y, *and*

(*iii*) *if* $U \subseteq X$, *then* $F_U(X)$ *is the sublattice of* $\mathbb{R}^m$ *generated by* X.

Any set $\{y_1, y_2, \ldots, y_r\}$ of linearly independent positive vectors of $\mathbb{R}^m$ such that $F_U(X)$ is the sublattice of $\mathbb{R}^m$ generated by $\{y_1, y_2, \ldots, y_r\}$ is a *basic set* of the market.

Theorem 0.8. *Any maximal subset* $\{y_1, y_2, \ldots, y_r\}$ *of linearly independent vectors of* $\mathcal{A}$ *is a basic set of the market, where* $\mathcal{A} = \{x_1^+, x_1^-, \ldots, x_n^+, x_n^-\}$, *if* $U \subseteq X$ *and*
$\mathcal{A} = \{x_1^+, x_1^-, \ldots, x_n^+, x_n^-, u_1^+, u_1^-, \ldots, u_d^+, u_d^-\}$, *if* $U \subsetneq X$.

The space of marketed securities X is *complete by options* with respect to U if $X = F_U(X)$.

Theorem 0.9. *The space* X *of marketed securities is complete by options with respect to* U *if and only if* $U \subseteq X$ *and* $cardR(\beta) = n$.

Theorem 0.10. *The dimension of* $F_U(X)$ *is equal to the cardinal number of* $R(\beta)$. *Therefore,* $F_U(X) = \mathbb{R}^m$ *if and only if* $cardR(\beta) = m$.

It is clear, from the previous discussion that we can use the `SUBlatSUB` function to the problem of calculating the completion of security markets. Let us describe, in detail, the procedure with an example:

Example 0.10. Suppose that in a security market, the payoff space is $\mathbb{R}^{12}$ and the primitive securities are:

$$x_1 = (1,2,2,-1,1,-2,-1,-3,0,0,0,0),$$
$$x_2 = (0,2,0,0,1,2,0,3,-1,-1,-1,-2),$$
$$x_3 = (1,2,2,0,1,0,0,0,-1,-1,-1,-2).$$

and that the strike subspace is the vector subspace U generated by the vector $u = (1,2,2,1,1,2,1,3,-1,-1,-1,-2)$. Then, a maximal subset of linearly independent vectors of $\{x_1^+, x_1^-, x_2^+, x_2^-, x_3^+, x_3^-, u_1^+, u_1^-\}$ can be calculated by using the following code:

```
>> XX = [max(X,zeros(size(X)));max(-X,zeros(size(X)))];
>> S = rref(XX');
>> [I,J] = find(S);
>> Linearindep = accumarray(I,J,[rank(XX),1],@min)';
>> W = XX(Linearindep,:)
```

where X denotes a matrix whose rows are the vectors x_1, x_2, x_3, u. The results, then, are as follows:

```
W =
  1    2    2    0    1    0    0    0    0    0    0    0
  0    2    0    0    1    2    0    3    0    0    0    0
 20   36   40    3   18   16    3   24    2    2    2    4
  0    0    0    1    0    2    1    3    0    0    0    0
  0    0    0    0    0    0    0    0    1    1    1    2
```

We can determine the completion by options of X i.e., the space $F_U(X)$, with the SUBlatSUB function by using the following code:

```
>> [VectorSublattice,Positivebasis]=SUBlatSUB(W')
```

The results then are as follows

```
vector sublattice
positivebasis =
  0    0    0    0    0    0    0    0    3    3    3    6
  0    0    0    4    0    0    4    0    0    0    0    0
  0    0    0    0    0   20    0   30    0    0    0    0
 21    0   42    0    0    0    0    0    0    0    0    0
  0   40    0    0   20    0    0    0    0    0    0    0
```

Since we know a positive basis for $F_U(X)$, then we know the completion by options of X.

In the following we assume that U is the one-dimensional subspace of $\mathbb{R}^m$ generated by a vector $u \neq 0$ of $\mathbb{R}^m$. The notion of efficient funds have been studied in many economic articles (cf. John (1981); Ross (1976)). In Kountzakis & Polyrakis (2006) the authors introduced a definition that generalizes the notion of efficient funds. In particular, a vector $e \in F_u(X)$ is an $F_u(X)$ *-efficient fund* if $F_u(X)$ is the linear subspace of $\mathbb{R}^m$ which is generated by the set of nontrivial call options and the set of nontrivial put options of e.

It is clear that in order to calculate the efficient funds of the market we must determine , by using the SUBlatSUB function, a positive basis for $F_u(X)$. Then, in order to decide when an element e is an efficient fund of the market one has to apply the following theorem.

Theorem 0.11. *Suppose that* $\{b_1, b_2, \dots, b_\mu\}$ *is a positive basis of* $F_u(X)$, $u = \sum_{i=1}^{\mu} \lambda_i b_i$, *and* $\lambda_i > 0$ *for each* i. *Then the vector* $e = \sum_{i=1}^{\mu} k_i b_i$ *of* $F_u(X)$ *is an* $F_u(X)$*-efficient fund if and only if* $\frac{k_i}{\lambda_i} \neq \frac{k_j}{\lambda_j}$ *for each* $i \neq j$.

We shall describe the computation procedure with an example:

Example 0.11. Suppose that in a security market, the payoff space is $\mathbb{R}^{12}$ and the primitive securities are as in Example 0.10 and $U = [u]$, where $u = (20, 36, 40, 3, 18, 16, 3, 24, 2, 2, 2, 4)$. Then the vector $e = (84, 16, 168, 4, 8, 20, 4, 30, 15, 15, 15, 30)$ is an $F_u(X)$-efficient fund of the market. Indeed, working as in Example 0.10 we have that a positive basis $\{b_1, b_2, b_3, b_4, b_5\}$ for $F_u(X)$ has the following form:

```
Positivebasis =
  0    0    0    0    0    0    0    0    3    3    3    6
  0    0    0    4    0    0    4    0    0    0    0    0
  0    0    0    0    0   20    0   30    0    0    0    0
 21    0    2    0    0    0    0    0    0    0    0    0
  0   40    0    0   20    0    0    0    0    0    0    0
```

Then, it easy to see that,

$$e = \sum_{i=1}^{\mu} k_i b_i = 5b_1 + b_2 + b_3 + 4b_4 + \frac{2}{5} b_5$$

and

$$u = \sum_{i=1}^{\mu} \lambda_i b_i = \frac{2}{3} b_1 + \frac{3}{4} b_2 + \frac{4}{5} b_3 + \frac{20}{21} b_4 + \frac{9}{10} b_5.$$

Therefore, $\frac{k_i}{\lambda_i} \neq \frac{k_j}{\lambda_j}$ for each $i \neq j$, and by Theorem 0.11 we have that e is an $F_u(X)$-efficient fund of the market.

8. Conclusions

This chapter describes new computational methods in order to determine vector sublattices and lattice-subspaces of $\mathbb{R}^k$ and $C[a, b]$. In order to reach our goal the study of a vector-valued function β is further involved by introducing new Matlab functions, namely `SUBlatSUB`, **wr, V, L, I, sisets** and **xitest**. The results of this work (cf. `mcpinsurance` function) can give us important tools in order to study the interesting problems of finding the minimum-cost insured portfolio and calculating the completion by options of a two-period security market as well as the efficient funds of the market.
The material of this chapter provides the opportunity for several research directions. In particular, we are convinced that, from the mathematical point of view, the proposed algorithms and methods can be further analyzed independently, in terms of formal numerical analysis. Also, the construction of a computational method that can solve the problem of whether a collection of linearly independent, positive functions, $x_1, x_2, ..., x_n$ of $C(\Omega)$ generates a lattice-subspace, where Ω denotes a compact Hausdorff topological space remains open. Finally, applications of the theory of lattice-subspaces and positive bases must be further investigated.

9. References

Abramovich, Y.A.; Aliprantis, C.D. & Polyrakis, I.A. (1994). Lattice-Subspaces and positive projections, *Proccedings of the Royal Irish Academy*, 94A, pp.237-253.

Aliprantis, C.D.; Brown, D.J. & Werner, J. (1997). Incomplete derivative markets and portfolio insurance, *Cowles Foundation Discussion Paper*, 1126R, pp.1-13.

Aliprantis, C.D.; Brown, D.J. & Polyrakis, I.A. (1998). Portfolio dominance and optimality in infinite security markets, *Journal of Mathematical Economics*, 30, pp.347-366.

Aliprantis, C.D.; Brown, D.J. & Werner, J. (2000). Minimum-cost portfolio insurance, *Journal of Economic Dynamics & Control*, 24, pp.1703-1719.

Aliprantis, C.D.; Polyrakis, I.A. & Tourky, R. (2002). The cheapest hedge, *Journal of Mathematical Economics*, 37, pp.269-295.

Barber, C.B; Dobkin, D.P. & Huhdanpaa, H.T. (1996). The Quickhull Algorithm for Convex *ACM Transactions on Mathematical Software*, 22, No. 4, pp.469-483.

Brown, D.J. & Ross, S.A. (1991). Spanning, valuation and options, *Economic Theory*, 1, pp.3-12.

Edmonds, J.; Lovász, L. & Pulleybank, W.R. (1982). Brick decompositions and the matching bank of graphs, *Combinatorica*, 2, pp.247-274.

Green, R. & Jarrow, R.A. (1987). Spanning and completness in markets with contigent claims, *Journal of Economic Theory*, 41, pp.202-210.

Henrotte, P. (1992). Existence and optimality of equilibria in markets with tradable derivative securities, *Technical report No.48 Stanford Institute for Theoretical Economics* , pp.1-39.

John, K. (1981). Efficient funds in a financial market with options: a new irrelevance proposition,*The Journal of Finance*, 36, pp.685-695.

Katsikis, V.N. (2007). Computational methods in portfolio insurance, *Applied Mathematics and Computation*, 189, pp.9-22.

Katsikis, V.N. (2008). Computational methods in lattice-subspaces of $C[a,b]$ with applications in portfolio insurance, *Applied Mathematics and Computation*, 200, pp.204-219.

Katsikis, V.N. (2009). A Matlab-based rapid method for computing lattice-subspaces and vector sublattices of $\mathbb{R}^n$: Applications in portfolio insurance, *Applied Mathematics and Computation*, 215, pp.961-972.

Kountzakis, C. & Polyrakis, I.A. (2006). The completion of security markets, *Decisions in Economics and Finance*, 29, pp.1-21.

Polyrakis, I.A. (1996). Finite-dimensional lattice-subspaces of $C(\Omega)$ and curves of $\mathbb{R}^n$, *Transactions of the American Mathematical Society*, 348, pp.2793-2810.

Polyrakis, I.A. (1999). Minimal lattice-subspaces, *Transactions of the American Mathematical Society*, 351, pp.4183-4203. *del Seminario Matematico e Fisico dell' Universita di Modena*, L, pp.327-348.

Polyrakis, I.A. (2003). Linear Optimization in $C(\Omega)$ and Portfolio Insurance, *Optimization*, 52,221-239.

Ross, S.A. (1976). Options and efficiency, *Quaterly Journal of Economics*, 90, pp.75-89.